D0192359

Read
to Write

"Exposure to the writing process, through Don Murray's work . . . has been the single most important element of my education as a writer. By teaching the lesson that writing is not magic, but a rational process that can be identified and repeated successfully, no matter what the writing task, Murray has made better writers out of me and many of my colleagues. . . . Writers are hungry for real-life examples. In our writing seminars conducted by Murray, the most successful sessions have often revolved around actual pieces of writing. *Read to Write,* I believe, will satisfy the writing student's passion for vivid illustrations of the writer at work and, thanks to Murray's incisive comments, will also reveal to them the process that can help them achieve personal writing success."

Christopher Scanlan
Providence Journal-Bulletin

Donald M. Murray

Read to Write

A Writing Process Reader

Holt, Rinehart and Winston
New York Chicago San Francisco Philadelphia Montreal
Toronto London Sydney Tokyo Mexico City
Rio de Janeiro Madrid

Library of Congress Cataloging-in-Publication Data

Murray, Donald Morison, 1924-
  Read to write.

  Includes Index
  1. College readers.   2. English language—Rhetoric.
I. Title
PE1417.M87   1986   808'.0427   85-14831

ISBN 0-03-069776-X

Copyright © 1986 by CBS College Publishing
Address correspondence to:
383 Madison Avenue
New York, N.Y. 10017
All rights reserved
Printed in the United States of America
Published simultaneously in Canada
6 7 8 9   016   9 8 7 6 5 4 3 2

CBS COLLEGE PUBLISHING
Holt, Rinehart and Winston
The Dryden Press
Saunders College Publishing

A. R. Ammons, "Cascadilla Falls" is reprinted from *Collected Poems: 1951–1971*.
    Reprinted by permission of W. W. Norton and Company, Inc. © 1972 by A.
    R. Ammons.
Maya Angelou, from *I Know Why the Caged Bird Sings*. Copyright © 1969 by Maya
    Angelou. Reprinted by permission of Random House, Inc.
James Baldwin, from *Notes of a Native Son*. Reprinted by permission of the author.
Amiri Baraki, from *The Autobiography of Leroi Jones/Amiri Baraka*. Copyright © 1984
    by Amiri Baraka. Used with permission of Freundlich Books, a division of
    Lawrence Freundlich Publications, Inc.
Jacques Barzun and Henry F. Graff, from *The Modern Researcher,* third edition. Copy-
    right © 1977 by Jacques Barzun and Henry F. Graff. Annotated and reprinted
    by permission of Harcourt Brace Jovanovich, Inc.
Robert Caro, from *The Years of Lyndon Johnson: The Path to Power*. Copyright © 1982
    by Robert A. Caro. Reprinted by permission of Alfred A. Knopf, Inc.
Raymond Carver, from *Cathedral*. Copyright © 1981, 1982, 1983 by Raymond
    Carver. From *What We Talk About When We Talk About Love*. Copyright ©
    1981 by Raymond Carver. Reprinted by permission of Alfred A. Knopf, Inc.
From *DECpage User's Guide*. Copyright © 1986 Digital Equipment Corporation. All
    rights reserved. Reprinted with permission.

(continued on page 595)

for
Minnie Mae
who shares both reading
and writing with me

To the Student

Take this book seriously, but not too seriously. None of the writing in this book—no matter how famous the author—is as important as your own evolving drafts. Read this book as a writer who is playing the same game as publishing writers play, because you are. They face a similar terror of the blank page: Will I have anything to say? How will I say it? Will anyone understand? Will anyone care? I started this paragraph asking myself those morning questions, and so do all the other authors in this book.

We begin in emptiness, fear, and need. You may not have felt the need yet, but if you become a writer it will be because you have to write. It will be your way of hanging on, of trying to figure out, of making. But even if you do not become a "writer" you will write memos to the boss, reports for the commanding officer, lab notes, grant requests, political statements, legal briefs, case histories. You do not know what you'll be called upon to write, but if you do you'll face the problems of discovering, ordering and sharing meaning solved by the writers printed here.

Watch Writers Writing and Reading

Writing is a private activity and few of us ever see the writer practicing, the writer trying to get ready to write, the writer doing the writing that doesn't work, which is so often necessary to produce writing that does work. In my text, *Write To Learn,* I took the student backstage and showed all the false starts and ineffective drafts that led to a piece of my own writing. In this book you will meet other writers at work, see some of their early drafts, and hear what they have to say about how they discover what they have to say and how to say it.

These case histories reveal a technical writer at work on a manual for a computer company, a journalist searching for the grave of a World War II casualty in France, a literary scholar examining our culture, a science writer explaining the process (and some of the hazards) of having test tube babies, and a poet finding a poem. These men and women are candid and professional. By reading what they have to say about their work—and by seeing the work itself—you will be able to understand that you and a published writer are indeed playing in the same game.

In selections from Flannery O'Connor, George Orwell, Joan Didion, Jacques Barzun and Henry Graff you will hear writers talking directly about the writing process and you will be able to see if they practice what they preach. The introductions to selections by such authors as John McPhee, James Baldwin, Richard Selzer, William Zinsser, Toni Morrison, Raymond Carver, Theodore Roethke, John Updike, E. B. White, and others include statements they have made about the writing process. The introductions to each of the principal chapters also include the voices of writers sharing their craft with you.

Read with a Writer

In those case histories you will discover how some published writers read their own work to make their drafts more effective. Throughout the book you will read comments that reveal how this writer reads other writers. The fan in the stands often sees a different game than the player on the field. Neither view is right or wrong, but if you want to play the game the player's vision will be especially instructive. My comments will show you what one writer sees in the text. I go through one article—"Up in the Old Hotel" by Joseph Mitchell—in detail, and then comment on all the other articles when I read something I find significant as a writer.

Do not copy my way of reading, but find your own. What you need to read as a writer will change as you grow in experience and as you face new writing tasks. The lesson to learn is that you can receive instruction from published writers who have faced the problems you face—and solved them in their own way.

The Writing Process at Work

The book is organized according to the model of the writing process developed in *Write To Learn:* Collect, Focus, Order, Draft, and Clarify. Many of us believe that writing can best be learned if we look at the process that begins before the blank page and ends with a final, edited draft. Of course, the process is not absolute. It changes according to the personality of the writer, the writer's experience, and the writing task, but it is still a helpful way to look at the logical, not magical, craft of making meaning with language. The selections in the book, as you will see, cannot really be contained in a single category; in fact, most demonstrate solutions to the problems encountered at each stage of the writing process, but they do show you the way in which a variety of writers move through a single step in the process of writing.

The Writers and Their Writing

The writers have been chosen from different backgrounds so that you may find writers who have experience both similar to and different from yours. We all need writers who help us see and understand our own world and other writers who help us see and understand worlds beyond our experience.

Most of the selections are nonfiction, writing built from information that can be documented in the real world, because that is the kind of writing most of you will do in school and beyond. There are examples of autobiography because most of us start by writing about ourselves and then may move on to achieve a greater distance from experience. Fiction and poetry are included because poets and fiction writers are the writers who usually move far ahead of the pack, teaching other writers what can be done that has not been done before. They are the explorers of form and language and inspire our own explorations.

The selections in this book come off my own bookshelves. Whenever I pull them down and open their pages they remind me of the possibilities of writing. They teach me how to write, and I want to share them with you as you learn to write. Those of us who are writers never stop learning. And if you become a writer you'll be blessed with a life of learning.

Help with YOUR Writing Problems

As a writer, you will share the experience of these authors as they solve the problems that you face on your own page. These are effective writers because they have solved those problems well and created texts which speak individually and clearly to readers.

To help you as you write, there is a special index at the back of the book: "Writing Problems Solved." When you are stuck, you can diagnose your problem—perhaps with the help of classmates or your teacher—and then use the index to see how other writers have dealt with a similar difficulty. Don't just imitate their solutions. Figure out what they are doing and why, so that you can create your own solutions, the ones that will fit the demands of your text, your meaning, your audience, and your own voice.

After each selection there are questions to consider that may help you appreciate the text and build a bridge to your own writing. There are also activities that you can do as a class or on your own. I hope that both questions and activities will spark your own questions and activities. They will usually be better than mine because they will grow out of your own experience and your own needs at that moment in your development as a writer.

Reading with Writing

These examples of effective writing should not be seen as examples of good or bad writing. There is no clear line between good and bad in writing. There is not correct writing as opposed to incorrect writing, right writing as opposed to wrong writing. There is little in writing that is right or wrong. I have paired the selections to demonstrate that there are different ways to approach similar writing tasks. Read E. B. White and Jean Shepherd, for example, to see the different ways two writers approach a similar subject. We should delight in the diversity possible in our craft.

Writers are grateful that there are so few absolutes. Writing is always an exploration, an adventure. Everything is possible, though everything is not achieved. Writers talk of writing that works and writing that doesn't work. Writing that works fulfills the writer's purpose and communicates to readers. The examples in this book work for me. I appreciate them as a writer and as a reader. They may not work for you. That is fine. Read them, listen to them, listen to what others—myself, your teacher, your classmates—have to say about them, and make up your own mind based on your own writing and reading experience.

Listen to the writers in this book as they talk to you about how they wrote their pieces. They have special knowledge of the history of their text as you do about the history of your text. This is not final knowledge. Take them seriously too, but not too seriously. They should not be heard as authorities, but as fellow writers, and you should compare their writing histories to the histories of your own drafts.

These examples are not machine-shop models that you can use to stamp out precise imitations. I have purposely paired selections to give you an idea of the differences there can be between writers who face similar subjects or similar technical challenges. I hope that you will compare these published writings to your own drafts and those of your classmates. This text is written by a practicing writer for practicing writers. It is designed to help you write and to help you read with a maker's point of view. I hope that you will be surprised by what some of us say as we write and read but I hope you will be surprised most of all by the reading appearing on your own page.

Write as you read and you will discover that you have joined a community of men and women who have found that they can play with language in such a way that it makes meaning of their world, and that the meaning can be shared by readers of their place and beyond, of their time and afterward. By writing and reading we learn and share, and through that sharing we escape ignorance and isolation so that we can continue a lifetime of learning.

To the Instructor

With this text, you will be able to take your students into the writer's workroom and make the connection between the problems your students face in their own drafts and the problems that accomplished, published writers have solved in their drafts. When I first taught Freshman English I had to follow a syllabus that forced the students to read prose models that the students—and I—could not relate to the problems they faced in their own writing. This reader attempts to make that connection.

Reading as a Writer

The first two chapters introduce the students to the reading skills they can use to learn from the writing of others and the skills they can apply to the reading of their own drafts in process. The writer has to be able to perform a sophisticated form of reading, which teaches the writer not only what is on the page but also what needs to be on the page. The reading role in writing is rarely discussed, but it is an essential part of the writing process and this text will document many of the ways reading relates to writing and writing relates to reading.

Documenting the Writing Process

Selections are organized according to the model of the writing process—collect, focus, order, draft, clarify—used in my companion composition text, *Write To Learn.* This reader, however, is designed to be used independently as well as with *Write To Learn.* The text is built on the belief that the writer passes through a logical, teachable process as a vague idea evolves into a finished, readable text.

Case Studies of Published Writers

Each section begins with the case study of a writer—a science writer, a literary scholar, a journalist, a technical writer, a poet—at work reading and writing. These case studies show professionals facing a diversity of writing tasks. Notes and early drafts can be examined by the student and compared to the final, publishable version. The writers also speak directly to the student in essays on writing that reveal their own methods of making meaning with language. For those who use *Write To Learn,* the case studies in this text extend and reinforce the extensive case study of my own writing as I developed a piece about my grandmother. Students who have my example in front of them can compare my methods to those of writers producing in a variety of genres.

There is also a detailed case history of one writer reading as a writer. I analyze one of my favorite pieces of writing—Joseph Mitchell's "Up in the Old Hotel"—to show students how one writer reads to write. Students and instructors should be able to compare my reading to theirs, not to see what is right or wrong but to see how different writers read so that they will receive the learning they need to reinforce and improve what they are doing in their own work.

Each selection introduces the student to the writer in a way that will allow the student to identify with the author. The introduction to William Zinsser's piece, for example, includes a letter he wrote me years ago—writer to writer—saying what he learned in writing that article for *The New Yorker.*

Reading While Writing; Writing While Reading

In each of the selections I point out places where the writer has done something that can teach a beginning writer a strategy, an attitude, a technique that the student may apply on the student's own page. This connection between texts that have been written by a writer and texts that are being written by a student is reinforced by a special index at the back of the book, entitled "Writing Problems Solved." When the student faces a particular problem—how to write an effective beginning, how to give the reader documentation, how to write a definition, how to put a narrative in context and reveal its significance, how to structure an argument—the student can turn to this index and be referred to pages in the text.

Rhetoric in Context

I have chosen to demonstrate the rhetorical strategies students need to know within an effective text. Too often the models of rhetorical techniques are isolated from any context. But good writing is always in context, and the student can better understand the rhetorical example if the student is able to see how it works within a piece of effective writing.

The selections are personal. These are not all my masters by a long shot, but they are writers to whom I have been apprenticed for an hour, a year, or a professional lifetime. Other writers and teachers will have their own masters, but this is a reader constructed from the books on one writer's shelf. In this way I can demonstrate how one writer reads and I may be able to show, therefore, the importance of reading to a writer.

The selections emphasize nonfiction forms because most students will work in that genre. There are nine poems and four short stories in the book and a special introduction to both poetry and narrative to stimulate a discussion of how those genres relate to nonfiction. Thirteen of the selections are autobiographical because students are not yet experts on academic or professional disciplines; they can attempt to understand their own experiences through writing. The discussion of these texts will help the students make connections to their own lives and also show them how to apply the lessons learned through personal narrative to other writing tasks.

The nonfiction selections have been chosen to interest students who come to composition from other disciplines across the curriculum. They include examples of science, history, technical, nature, medical, journalistic, and biographical writing as well as literary criticism.

Making the Reading Connection to Writing

The selections have been paired so that the students can see two writers attacking a similar subject or facing similar writing problems. I hope that the pairings will be combined with examples of the students' own writing and will provoke instructive class discussions. I also hope the pairings will document the fact that there is no one way to write, that each writer brings individual experiences, personal points of view, particular skills, and an identifiable human voice to the task.

Every selection is followed by discussion questions and activities designed to spark profitable class sessions, to relate the selections to each other as well as to the writing process and to the student's own writing.

As I mentioned in the preface to the student, the reader will be most valuable to those who are writing their own texts while reading these texts. The selections, and all the other material in this book, is designed to be useful to the reader who is writing. The writers in the classroom should discover, through this text, that they are part of the larger writing community beyond the classroom.

The text can be used in many ways. It can be a supplement to my own process-oriented composition text—*Write To Learn*—or other composition texts. The introductions to the stages in the writing process allow it to be used as a writing text. In any case, it can—and should—be read contrapuntally to the student's own writing. They should, at their writing desks and in class, compare their solutions to their writing problems to the solutions demonstrated in the text.

Above all, the writers collected here reveal the importance of writing and the satisfactions this profound form of play brings to both writer and reader.

Acknowledgments

I am indebted to a family which encouraged reading and to the Wollaston Public Library in Quincy, Massachusetts, which provided the books in those teen-age years when I became a reading addict.

In this project I am grateful for the help of many colleagues who inspire, prod, support, suggest, and listen. Donald H. Graves of the University of New Hampshire is always a phone call away as is Christopher Scanlan of the *Providence Journal-Bulletin.* Jane Hansen and Ruth Hubbard of the University of New Hampshire and Allan Nielsen of Mount Saint Vincent Unversity in Halifax, Nova Scotia, Canada, helped me put my views of how the writer reads in the context of reading research. Thomas Newkirk is that special colleague who constantly stimulates my learning.

I have also enjoyed unusual support from the administration of the University of New Hampshire, especially Carl Dawson, English Department Chair; Stuart Palmer, Dean of the College of Liberal Arts; Raymond Erickson, Interim Vice-President for Academic Affairs, and Gordon Haaland, President.

This book is greatly enriched by the contributions of Joseph Freda, Denise Grady, Gary Lindberg, Mekeel McBride, and Christopher Scanlan, who have shared their writing and reading with the students who will use this book.

I also appreciate the careful, critical responses I received from my reviewers: Victoria Aarons, Trinity University; Linda Dyer Doran, Volunteer State Community College; Patricia Y. Murray, De Paul University; Jack O'Keefe, Malcom X College; Christopher Scanlan, *Providence Journal-Bulletin;* Judith Stanford, Merrimack College; Christopher J. Thaiss, George Mason University. They, and all my other colleagues and editors, should get credit for what you like in the book and not be blamed for what you do not like.

This book was the suggestion of Charlyce Jones Owen, English Editor of Holt, Rinehart and Winston. She has been both editor and friend. Her suggestions have consistently improved my text. Jeanette Ninas Johnson has done an expert job of guiding my manuscript through production. I am fortunate in having the full support of Holt, Rinehart and Winston and CBS Publishing management in attempting to write texts that others would see as unconventional. Everyone has always encouraged and never interfered. All my failures are my own.

My wife, as always, has contributed to my work in so many ways that I cannot list them. Without her, I would not be published.

Contents

7   A Meaning Made Clear   515

8   Watch Out: After School May Come Reading and Writing   592

Contents by Genre and Theme

Each selection is paired with another, so that the student can study two different writers dealing with a similar subject, and in some cases writing in the same genre.

The Past

A Sense of Place

The Extraordinary in the Ordinary

Childhood and School

Literary Criticism

Parents and Children

Prejudice

Sickness and Death

Technical and Medical Writing

Music and Film

Fiction

Poetry

School

Politics

Rites of Passage

Science and Medicine

The Atomic Age

Alienation

Writing

Journalism

Humor

Biography

Autobiography

War

Argument

1

Reading as a Reader

A nightmare. You are shoved into a huge room that has dozens of doors and windows along every wall. You go to an open door and see a party you want to join. The door slams shut. You can't open it. You run to a window across the room and see a street in a city you've never visited. There are stores, restaurants, a jazz band playing, and a crowd of shoppers laughing and talking with each other in a strange language. Suddenly shutters slam shut and you can't see anything but darkness.

You step to a door where a man and a woman sit in comfortable chairs by a fireplace. They are talking to each other, but most of all you notice the way they listen. It would be wonderful to be listened to that way. They spot you, smile, and invite you to join them. The door shuts. Out another door is space and a spacewalker tumbles down, twists around, and starts to point. That door shuts. You start moving from window to door, catching a glimpse of surf rippling along an endless beach, a large book that seems to have important instructions, what looks like a movie but is far more real than that, and a formula that lies upon a laboratory table. Each door, each window slams shut. You move faster from door to window to door. You can see through each, but you can't escape the empty room. In a window, you see a newspaper with large headlines you can't understand; through a door someone beckons you to join a committee examining an accounting balance sheet; two couples dance a poem and wave as if they'd like to know you; a computer screen fills with green marks that don't make sense to you. Each window and every door shuts and you are left alone in the empty room.

That is the world of the person who can't read. Messages are delivered that can't be understood, opportunities are available that can't be taken, and, worst of all, there is a terrible loneliness, for the nonreader is isolated from the past, from what happens out of sight or off camera, from joining—and influencing—the members of those groups interested in business, the environment, religion, politics, sports, engineering, theatre, travel, art, music, and science, who communicate with each other by writing and reading.

The student in any field—medicine, public safety, language study, computer technology, environmental studies, sociology, biochemistry, political science, engineering, history, hotel management, law, business—finds it is essential to be an effective reader. Reading is increasingly important in a complex, global, technical society. We depend on the communication of an enormous amount of information and, in such a world, information, even more than money, means power. We may read books, memos, newspapers, or we may read a computer screen or printout, but read we must if we are to understand and participate in our world, to know and to influence what is going on. We also read to write, to learn the craft that not only allows us to receive information but also to discover what we know and share it.

If You Have Trouble Reading

Everybody has trouble reading. We all face texts that are incomprehensible to us. In some cases the material is extremely difficult; in some cases the author's style is difficult, and in many cases the writing is bad—we can't make the meaning come clear because there is no clear meaning. We cannot, of course, know whether the writer has anything of importance to say to us until we figure out what the writer has said. If we are reading just for recreation, then we can toss aside a book that is too difficult or has a style we don't enjoy. But on the job, as citizens, and in following our hobbies we have to read a lot of difficult writing and a lot of bad writing. Some of the worst writing unfortunately occurs in textbooks that students have to read to learn a subject or pass a course, or both. We all need to know what to do when we have trouble reading.

The Reader's Attitude

Our attitude about reading usually controls how we read as much as our attitude about writing, doing math, playing a sport, or having friends controls our effectiveness in those areas. If we approach a text believing that we are not readers, or that we can't read, that attitude may make it more difficult for us to understand the challenging text.

In some cases the attitude we have simply may not be appropriate. Most students who get to college can read moderately well, regardless of what teachers and newspapers say. What we have to do is to build on the skills we already have. Our attitude should be that we are in college to learn, and learning means being able to read a broad variety of texts more effectively. You are taking this course to learn how to read with greater skill and to learn how reading can help improve your writing.

Don't worry too much about television and film making your generation nonreaders. The myths about the past only make us guilty and they are often just myths. In the good old days when I was growing up, you were a wimp if you read, and I was a secret reader. Most people I knew did very little reading. But if you are to be educated— to make use of information from many fields and times and authorities—then you will have to improve your reading.

The best way is simply to read more. You learn to ride a bicycle by hopping aboard and pedaling until you get up enough speed. Reading is, at the beginning, a skill that takes frequent practice.

Also remember that the writer has some responsibility to go halfway or more to the reader. Writing that is hard to read is occasionally the product of a complicated and important mind; however, it is more likely the product of an arrogant and pretentious mind. Do not blame yourself for a writer's irresponsibility.

It is not helpful to feel inadequate, stupid, whipped by a text before you begin. It *is* helpful to have command of a variety of strategies which may help you decipher a text.

Reading for Experience

Humans are the animals that can live more lives than a cat, and many of them are lived through reading. As we read we go back and forth in time, pass across oceans and barriers of language, religion, and culture.

Yes, for many readers, writing is an escape. I used to hide the fact that I read to escape or, if discovered, apologize for fleeing to the make-believe world of adventure stories or mysteries as other people escape by reading science fiction, westerns, or romance novels— even though President Kennedy never apologized for using spy stories to escape the realities of international affairs, nor did President Eisenhower hide his affection for westerns. And, after my daughter Lee died suddenly when she was only twenty, I learned an important lesson—one of many. Although I had been a lifetime compulsive reader, for weeks I could not read and, when I began to read again, it was only mystery and spy stories with a strong story line that could hold my interest. I escaped and I had good reason to escape, no apologies needed. Since then I keep a piece of escape reading nearby all the time, and when I travel or can't sleep or start thinking too compulsively about what can't be thought about, I escape into a story.

We should not, however, forget that reading for escape from our world may also mean that we escape into other worlds. Reading is the enemy of ignorance, provincialism, and parochialism.

It is important that we read our way out of our own world, our own times, our own skin and live the lives of other people to find out how they feel and think. The ability to distance ourselves from ourselves and become someone else is a significant way to learn.

We may read biography or autobiography and escape into another person's life. We can, through reading, escape into the mind of a philosopher, observe with a scientist, study with a scholar, analyze with a critic, and live through a novel or a play. In this book you will go into the operating room with Richard Selzer, be taken by John Hersey to Hiroshima when the first atomic bomb went off, travel a back road with William Least Heat Moon. Reading powerful texts provides us with experience that rivals real experience in our memory, and may, in fact, influence us more than what we learn from our actual living.

Learning To Be Uncritical

To read for experience we have to learn to suppress our critical faculties for the moment and enter into the story, allowing the author to carry us along so that we absorb the world the writer has created for us. It usually helps to read fast and let the language, the flow, the energy of the text carry us along. Don't try to analyze Toni Morrison's selection the first time you read it. Go with the flow. Experience her story first; think about it later.

Reading for experience is usually an emotional as well as an intellectual activity, and in many cases all our senses are involved. We see the world of the writer, smell it, taste it, touch it. Few readers will leave the worlds of James Baldwin or William Gibson untouched. In some cases it becomes more real to us than ordinary living, the way a dream has its own special intensity. We have to learn how not to fight the text, but to give ourselves up to it, and not worry too much if we miss something here or there. We shouldn't stop to argue with the text, but to listen to the text in this first reading. Later we may want to read the text again differently, critically, more slowly. And certainly we will want to stand back from the experience we have had, the way we stand back from a party, a game, or a job, and put the experience into context, evaluate it, judge it, try to figure out what we learned from it. But first we have to have the experience.

Reading for Information

When we read for information we experience the text in a different way. Depending on the information we seek, we may not want to enter into the story, and we do not much care how the writing is written, as long as the writing does not get in the way of the information we need. Our newspapers know we want information on stocks and football standings, and so they give us this information in the form of tables and listings. That writing is hardly "written" at all. Other times we need information that is hidden in a normal text of sentences and paragraphs. In that case we have to mine the text and extract the information we need. Peter Drucker gives us information about time and John McPhee informs us about oranges. In this kind of reading we may choose to stand apart from the text, not to be involved in but simply to make use of what is said.

Scanning

To extract information from a text we need to scan, swooping over the text, looking for any clues that may help us find where the information is. We may turn first to an index or table of contents to see if it will tell us where the information we need is placed. In the case of an academic article we may read the abstract, a summary paragraph usually printed in small type at the beginning of the article to serve information gatherers and save them time.

Watching for Road Signs

If we think the text has the information we need, we should run through it, paying attention to chapter headings, crossheads (such as the one above, "Watching for Road Signs"), illustrations, diagrams, or other signals designed to help us get to the information we need. When we confront the text itself we should look for key words that will tell us that the information may be nearby. For example, if we are looking for information on the low salaries of women office workers, we may look for such words as "secretaries," "file clerks," "typists," "receptionists," "salaries," "wages," "compensation," "sexism," "prejudice," "women," "girls," "office workers," and so on. We can run through many pages of type easily, stopping only when we see something that tells us the information may be nearby.

Making Notes

In reading for information we usually have a notebook or note cards handy so that we can put down the information we find. If the information is to be quoted directly, we should put quotation marks around it so that we know when we come to use it that the note is precisely as the author presented it. If we are to put the information in our own words it's helpful to do that immediately. It's also important to note the context in which the information was presented. The context for the information on office workers might be a feminist political statement, a report by a male scholar, a study by a union that wants to organize office workers, a statement by a corporation, or a survey by a government agency. It is most important that the note include the precise reference so that it can be included in the text and so that you and your reader can go back and find the information. This means the title of the publication, the author, and all of the details about the publication itself.

Reading for Understanding

Our most important reading occurs when we read to comprehend everything that a text has to teach us. We read for the experience of the text and we read for the information we can mine from it—and more. Reading stocks our mind with information and connections between pieces of information—theories, ideas, concepts, principles—that grow and change as we grow and change, experiencing, integrating all that we take in from living and thinking. Note how Gary Lindberg and Ralph Ellison challenge us to think. We read to learn, to stimulate our minds, and so we have to learn to read well enough to make intellectual use of a great variety of texts, including many which are not easy to read. Some of them are difficult because the subject matter is difficult and the author has not been able to— or is writing for a specialized audience and feels no need to—simplify it for a general reader. Other books are difficult because the author does not write well but still has brought together information and ideas that are significant.

All our lives we will be reading texts that are difficult for us to read. We will learn about a subject, read intensely in that area, get to know significant but difficult authors, and find it relatively easy to read what was once difficult; but, at the same time, we will continue to be learners, reading in new areas, and meeting new and challenging authors.

This process of lifelong education has become true for many people who have not considered themselves intellectuals or who did not imagine they would continue to learn—or have to continue to learn—after graduation. We live, however, in a society in which change seems to be the only constant. People advised me, for example, not to leave jobs with companies that no longer exist. Some security. The best security is an education that teaches you how to learn so you can adapt to the inevitable changes life will bring. Guess who laughed at writing on a word processor and found himself using one a few weeks later?

We all have difficult friends who are worth the effort, and you will have difficult authors to read whose articles, stories, poems, manuals, monographs, plays, and books—fiction and nonfiction— are worth the effort. We have to learn strategies for dealing with these texts. We do not need to use these strategies all the time, but we do need to have them on hand when we cannot understand what we are reading and so cannot even tell if the text is worth reading.

Who Are You?

The first step toward understanding is to know what you bring to the text as a reader. If a police officer, black or white, is assigned to a neighborhood, he or she must first know what prejudices, what stereotypes, what beliefs, what fears he or she wears with the badge.

Each of us looks at the same neighborhood with significant differences, depending on our experience and our background. The same thing is true of a reader.

The effective readers know the baggage they bring with them when they approach a text. When I was in the Army I dealt with prisoners, and I bring that background to my reading of George Orwell's "A Hanging." I was in the paratroops in Germany, scheduled to go fight in Japan. I didn't know what an atomic bomb was but I cheered when I heard it was dropped. I had surprised myself by surviving combat in Europe and I did not want to go to fight in Asia. I bring my own history—and guilt—to that text.

Expert readers know what they don't know and what they know as they approach a text. They know that their prejudices, preconceptions, personal background, and experiences affect the way they read the text. We all come to a book with a complicated inventory of information, ideas, and opinions that combine to make the text our own. We have begun to realize it is important to understand this. Every text is different for every reader. That doesn't mean that we can't agree on what the text says, because we can, in discussion, usually work out a common understanding. It does mean that we often get to that understanding in very different ways. And it certainly can include the fact that we may disagree about what the text says.

The text is not separate from the reader. As the reader reads the text becomes what is read. If you see, for example, a group of teenagers with different colored skins fighting, what each observer sees is powerfully colored, pun intended, by the observer's own background. Often there is not just one truth, but many truths. And we see through our own eyes, our own experiences, our own knowledge.

Who's the Author?

Once you know who you are—at least who you are in relation to this subject—then it may help to know who the writer is. Usually there are short biographies or an identifying sentence that tells who the writer is and what is the writer's authority to write this piece: "Norbert Morrison, now a Congressman from Iowa, has been practicing cannibalism since his Freshman year in college." If you think that the background of the author is vital to your understanding of the piece, then you can use the standard reference books, such as *Who's*

Who and *Current Biography*, in the library to discover what you need
to know about the writer.

What's the Form?

It may help to understand the piece we are writing if we know the
genre or form in which it is written. This sounds obvious, but notice
how many people use the term "novel," which means a fictional
story, a work of the imagination, to describe nonfiction books of history or biography which are supposed to be based on documentable
facts. Flannery O'Connor has an essay *and* a short story in this collection. One expresses a documented opinion, the other reveals an
imaginary world that shows us truths in our less real worlds. It may
help you understand the piece you are reading if you know it is a
profile, a short biography written by someone other than the subject,
or an autobiographical essay in which the person is writing about
himself or herself. Part of form is purpose. In an argument the author
wants to persuade us, but in a personal essay about the same subject
the author may simply want to entertain. In a news story about the
same subject, the writer may simply want to deliver objective fact.
You may enjoy seeing E. B. White and Jean Shepherd deal with similar subjects in different ways and speculate about the way they have
stretched and used the personal essay.

What's the Context?

It helps to know the context or the nature of the world in which the
piece was written. Pieces that were written during the Vietnam War,
when there was both strong opposition to the war and powerful support for the war, may be confusing to a young reader who did not
experience the pressure from both sides. Maxine Hong Kingston
writes in the context of one who comes to a new world. Lewis
Thomas writes from the context of a person who has spent a lifetime
studying medical science.

  The reader should know the point of view of the publication in
which an article is published. Some political magazines, for example,
have a conservative point of view. Others are liberal. The reader
needs to know that context. It may help, for example, to know that

the discussion of a nuclear plant is written in a context of concern for human safety, for the environment, or for the economy.

Reading the Front Matter

Clues to questions of the writer's authority and the context of the book or article may be found by reading the notes about authors in a magazine or the material published on the dust jacket of a book or on a title page. It is often a good idea, for example, to see where the book was published. It may be significant to know that a book about Vietnam was published first in France, a nation that suffered their Vietnam ahead of ours. It also may be important to know if the book was written in 1958, before we got deeply involved, in 1968, when we were heavily involved, or in 1978, when the war was over. The Table of Contents, the Preface, bibliographical notes at the end, and the index are all clues that may help us unlock the meaning of the book.

Reading Uncritically

The more difficult the text, the more important it is that we read it *un*critically first. This doesn't seem to make sense until you realize that if the subject matter, the form of the writing, and the author's style are all strange to the reader, then the reader may bog down in paying too close attention to each specific piece of information, each sentence, each word. If we pay too close attention the first time around, we have no idea of the whole, no feeling for the meaning or the purpose of the piece of writing. If we read it fast, uncritically, we will miss a lot, and at times even feel as if we were in a foreign country where we can't understand what anyone is saying. But we do pick up more than we know and get a feeling for the piece of writing. Once we have an overall view of the territory we can go back and, working within that overall vision, pay close attention to the details that will give us a true understanding of the text. Remember the first time you went to a big game; you had to try to absorb the crowd, the teams, the whole atmosphere of what was going on. You probably didn't pay too much attention to the details of the game. But when you become a fan you understand the larger context and can focus your attention on a revealing detail, such as how a player moves away from the main action of the game. Reading uncritically is the first step toward reading critically.

Reading Carefully

When a text deserves close attention, then we keep repeating the pattern of looking from larger context to smaller and back. We need to know what each word means in context, and that cannot be known simply by knowing the meaning of each word. Most words have many meanings. Those meanings change, depending on all the other meanings into which they are built.

This diagram may help:

BOOK
    CHAPTER
        SECTION
            PARAGRAPH
                SENTENCE
                    PHRASE
                        WORD

It looks complicated, and it is. Reading is one of the most sophisticated, intellectual acts we perform. But remember that you bring an enormous background of experience to this task. Even if you are not a person who considers yourself a reader, you are reading other people all the time. You read your parents and your roommate, your teachers and your friends, and the strangers you meet on the street or in a bar. You read the place in which they exist—who sits behind the desk or comes around and sits beside you in a chair during an interview. You read dress—formal or casual—and whether it is appropriate to the situation and the person. We are often amused at the Freshman who tries to look middle-aged, and at the middle-aged professor who tries to look like a Freshman. You read what the person says and how he or she says it: "You look as if you're new around here, can I help you?" You read body language: the hands on hips or the arms folded across the chest, or the hand extended palm out for a shake. You come to a text bringing all these intellectual skills with you so you can apply them to written language.

The diagram shows what you already do, reading the detail (the hesitant step, the avoiding eye, the move that brings the person too close to you) and fitting it into a generalization (this guy doesn't trust people like me) that, in turn, causes you to read meaning into what seemed like insignificant details a moment before. The reader moves back and forth from concept to word and word to concept, with increasing understanding.

Some of the tricks of the careful reader's trade are:

Underline.   It may help to understand the text if you underline key words, facts, phrases, sentences, and, on occasion, paragraphs. The purpose of underlining, however, is to help you identify the points of greatest significance and make them clear by pulling them out of the text. We have all seen inexperienced students highlighting or under-lining almost every word of the text, a sure clue that they do not understand the text and are learning little from it.

Marginal comments.   Reading is a private encounter between writer and reader. Writing in the margins allows the reader to talk back—or write back—to the writer. It is a helpful way for the reader to make the text his or her own. These comments can be abrupt, quick, or extensive, sometimes even extending to a card or a piece of paper that is taped to the page. In the margin the reader agrees and disagrees, extends the text and connects it with the reader's own experience, questions the text on the basis of the reader's experience, makes connections with other experiences, other evidence, other pieces of writing. Throughout this text I will be making marginal comments to show you what one writer sees in the text. You will see an active reader, one who is participating with the written text. You should train yourself to become more than a passive reader, to enter into the act of making meaning with the writer.

Connecting.   It's often helpful to use arrows or circles or squares or lines or numbers to connect significant facts, words, or lines in a text. Sometimes you can see the importance of a word that is repeated in a text in this way, or actually draw the map of the piece right over the text, revealing how a meaning has been woven through the text.

Outlining.   The skill of outlining may be even more important to a reader than a writer. If you outline—in whatever form is comfortable to you—what is being said in the text, you will strip the text down to its essentials, and you may be able to see the meaning that lies under the text and then be able to understand what the writer was doing in the text.

Precis.   This is an old-fashioned device that is extremely helpful in understanding a text. I grumped at Miss Leavitt—no Ms. in those days—who made us precis, precis, precis our way through the eleventh grade, and groaned again when I saw my English teacher for the twelfth grade—you guesssed it: Miss Leavitt. I precised my way through the twelfth grade. But it taught me to read with a piercing eye, tracking down meaning and helping to teach me to write concise, disciplined prose.

To write a precis, say in a few paragraphs—preferably one paragraph—what is said in an entire article, chapter, or book, using your own words. The effort of compression squeezes out the nonessentials and forces you to discover the central meaning of the text.

Some of the key elements in the text that reveal meaning include:

1. *Title.* The title attempts to tell the reader what follows in a way that will attract the reader. Often it gives away the point of view or the tone of the piece of writing. I find titles extremely helpful as a way of planning writing. They often tell me how I feel as well as how I think about the subject, establish a point of view, and even set up limits for the piece of writing. The title of this book, for example, helped me focus on the fact that this text is designed to help the student read to improve the student's own writing.

2. *The lead.* The lead is a journalistic term for the introduction or beginning of a piece of writing. A formal introduction too often announces what will be in the writing, so that the piece of writing itself becomes repetitive, an expansion of what has already been said. The lead—the first sentence, the first paragraph, the first page of the text—attempts to lead the reader into the text. It is quick and direct, but it establishes the subject, the limits of the subject, and the tone of the piece. Good writers usually will not proceed until they have the lead right. I may write 50 or 60 leads to an article before I get one that is right. You will be wise to pay attention to leads, both as a reader and as a writer.

3. *The ending.* The ending is the reverse of the lead. It is the last line, the last paragraph, the last page, and it is vital, for the ending is what the reader remembers best about a piece of writing. In the formal conclusion there is usually too much repetition. It has been said, and is said again in the same way with the same evidence. Skillful writers conclude by implication, not so much summarizing as giving the reader a quotation, an anecdote, a piece of evidence that draws the piece to a close in the reader's mind. Again, a young writer should pay close attention to how effective endings are written, and the reader should pay close attention, because in the ending the author gives away what he or she thinks has been said. The end is

the writer's destination, the point toward which the writer has been writing.

4. *Turning points.* The reader should look for turning points in the text. They are like marks blazed on a tree on a mountain trail, and more. They not only point the reader to where the reader should go, but they also quickly summarize where they think the reader has been. If you spot the turning points and understand what the writer believes has been said and intends to say next, you will begin to see how the piece is working.

5. *Documentation.* One of the most revealing elements in the text is the evidence the writer uses to persuade the reader to believe what is being said. Notice how Denise Grady and Thomas Whiteside document what they have to say. The evidence is crucial, and it should be questioned by the reader. Remember that evidence is not only formal, footnoted, scholarly documentation, but the anecdotes, analogies, and metaphors the writer uses to connect the text to the reader's own experience.

6. *Voice.* The element more than any other that makes us read on, makes us believe—or disbelieve—the text, makes us think and care, is the writer's voice. When we read we listen to the text, and what we hear influences us. Read James Baldwin, Theodore Roethke, Raymond Carver, Joan Didion aloud to hear how their voices underline their meaning and carry it forward to the reader. We should look closely at how the writer uses language to understand what the writer is saying. We should be aware of the denotation of words, the precise meaning; and the connotation, what they mean in context. We can, for example, use the word bread to mean food, and by changing the context have it mean money. To hear the voice—and the meaning—it is often essential to read aloud.

7. *Key words.* Every piece of writing has key words. We must try to see what they are and to make sure we understand them. Those words often carry a huge weight of meaning, and we must attempt to understand what meanings they have in the text. A journalist writing about freedom of the press in this country uses freedom to mean protection *from* government interference, but a Russian may use the word freedom to argue for freedom *by* government interference, a concept we find very hard to understand.

When we understand what the text says, then we can stand back and judge the entire text, evaluating what was said and how it was said.

Reading for Appreciation

Another way to approach a text is for appreciation. Of course, to appreciate a text it must be experienced and understood but then the reader, knowing what is said, can consider *how* it is said.

You all have experience as critics in many fields. For example, think how you relate to "your" music. You listen to the latest in a particular tradition, usually understanding how that tradition has evolved and how it relates to other musical traditions. You notice how the songs that are popular today are different from yesterday. You notice what they say and how they say it. You study, often unconsciously, how the music itself is changing, and you not only evaluate a particular piece of music, but performers as well. You see them in a tradition and you see how they relate to each other. And you know that the more familiar you become with a kind of music, a particular song, a type of performer, or a particular performer, the better you understand and appreciate what is going on.

This is what readers do, and it is so much a part of what writers do that we will discuss much of this in greater detail before the end of the chapter. Experienced readers heighten the quality of their experience by an interest in esthetics, the "how" in writing.

Listening for the How

Readers who want to appreciate reading are good listeners. They listen for the music in the writing, the rise and fall of the voice of the writer, the rhythm, the pace, and the change in pace, the intensity. To hear the music it is a good idea to read aloud, and read with some feeling, letting yourself enter into the text, act out the text so you can hear the writer speaking. Expert readers hear what they are reading as much or more than they see it.

Sometimes a difficult text will come clear if it is read aloud. And, of course, the opposite can be true. Reading a text aloud can make the text self-destruct. The out loud reading can reveal just how badly the writer writes.

Knowing the Tradition

As in music, each tradition of writing—poetry, fiction, nonfiction, drama—has its own historical flow. And so do the subgroups under each tradition. Nonfiction prose, for example, has divisions such as argument, whose roots pass back through the Romans to the ancient Greeks; and modern reportage isn't really so modern, it goes back at least to Addison, Steele, Thomas Paine, and others in the eighteenth century. The personal new journalism of the recent past was really a cyclical movement in which writers and editors relearned the lessons of earlier periods, when personalized journalism was popular. English professors spend a lifetime studying literary traditions, how they evolved, and how they are changing. You don't have to do that to appreciate writing. But the more you know about the history of a form in which you are interested, the deeper your appreciation will be.

Knowing What You Like and Knowing What There Is To Like

The great defense of ignorance is, "I don't know anything about painting (literature, plays, movies, music), but I know what I like." You should know what you like and don't like, but you should also grow in your appreciation of what you are hearing, reading, and seeing. You should start with the assumption that what is in front of you has been done on purpose. That doesn't mean that you will like it. The cook may have very carefully prepared liver. You may not appreciate the craft and art of the chef, but you should at least taste it.

Tasting it in the arts means more than looking. It means making an attempt to understand what the artist or writer or composer was doing, and why. Don't have unrealistic expectations for a piece of writing. Joseph Freda's writing for computer users is not a poem like Mekeel McBride's. And McBride's poem doesn't make its points in the same logical way as Freda's. Both are good in their own way, doing their own job with skill. Each piece of work should be seen in its own tradition, for reading and the other arts are not just emotional experiences. They are esthetic experiences in which the emotion and the intellect combine. They are not accidental; they are purposeful. If you make a lifetime habit of trying to understand, you will find many more things that will give you appreciation—satisfaction, fulfillment, and joy. And, of course, you will find many things that you do not like, no matter what effort you make. I like liver, no reason you should.

You should know what you like, but that knowing should keep

growing, building on what you already appreciate. I like classical chamber music today. I came to it through an appreciation of small jazz combos. My understanding of what small jazz groups were trying to do allowed me to appreciate quintets, quartets, and trios, and the pleasing combat between the players. The more we know and appreciate, the more we see to know and appreciate. It keeps us forever young. Reading opens doors and windows so that we can decide what we want to learn and explore.

2

Reading as a Writer

When you play basketball you watch a game with a different understanding than those who do not play. You see the players move when they do not have the ball, appreciate the fake and the pass as much as the basket, scorn the flashy shot that looks difficult but is really easy, and appreciate the shot that looks easy but is really difficult. You see the choices made as well as the ones rejected: the pass that was not made; the player who passed up the good shot; the player who didn't get back fast enough; the play that might have worked. You are a fan, screaming, groaning, part of the crowd; and you are an imaginary player, moving down the court, cutting, getting the pass, making the basket. You watch two games simultaneously: one from the stands and another from the floor.

The same thing is true if you work at a checkout counter at a supermarket, wait on tables, pump gas. When you shop yourself, go out to dinner, pull in at a service station, you see things other people who have not worked those jobs do not see.

That's the writer's advantage. The writer reads with an insider's eyes. The reader who is writing sees a text behind the text. The person who is also writing understands how Robert Caro's abundant specifics could collapse into a jumble instead of creating a well-constructed meaning; how Christopher Scanlan could have gotten between the reader and the story instead of skillfully standing aside and allowing the reader to feel the story; how E. B. White could have fallen into sentimentality and didn't. The writer sees the choices that another writer made, sees the problems and how they were solved, sees the connection between the written text and the writer's own evolving text. This backstage view of public writing does not detract from the satisfactions of reading, but multiplies the satisfactions of the reading experience.

You Can't Write without Reading

A man who was working on my car the other day asked me what I did for a living. When he found out I was a writer, he confessed he couldn't read, but later told me that he had published several articles on trailers. What he meant was that he didn't read for recreation. And it came out that he had chosen careers in which he wouldn't have to read as part of the job. He thought he "couldn't" read, and he thought he was a poor reader, yet he wrote and published, put down words, reading them in his mind before they landed on the page, reading them as they related to the words before them and the words yet to arrive on the page. He wrote, as we all write, running ahead, backing up, changing, adding, cutting, reordering, messing around with language, making his meaning clear.

To write he had to perform a number of sophisticated reading tasks. He had to read a text that was unwritten, then being written, then written but being revised, then revised but being edited. He had to make sure that the words he chose were the right words, that they were attached to a meaning. He had to make sure that the order made his meaning clear. He had to make sure they could be understood by a reader, and he had to make sure that each part of the text and the entire text fitted the needs or tradition of the publication to which he was submitting the piece. The writer is a reader.

Writers read many different texts and to do that they need many reading skills. They read their own evolving drafts as they write. They read their fellow writers' evolving drafts in classroom writing workshops, or in editorial offices, by sharing with their writer friends. And they read the published texts of writers of their own time and time past, entering into the community of living and dead writers, learning what can be done with language on the page and how it can be done, receiving instruction and inspiration from their reading.

Write To Read

You will understand and appreciate the writing of others best if you are writing yourself. There is more similarity than difference between the writing problems of the Nobel prizewinner and the beginning writer. Each starts a new draft far more a beginner than the beginner can realize. Of course one has much more experience, but that experience is not all a help. As Eudora Welty says, "The writer himself studies intensely how to do it while he is in the thick of doing it; then when the particular novel or story is done, he is likely to forget how; he does well to. Each work is new. Mercifully, the question of *how* abides less in the abstract and less in the past, than in the specific, in the work at hand. . ."

If you write, your appreciation and understanding of what the writer is doing will multiply, and you will read both good and bad writing in a new way. It will build on what you have learned about reading as a reader. You don't lose that, but you extend it and develop it.

Seeing the Possibilities

When I read a really good piece of writing, I am inspired to write. My hand itches for a pen. When I read Mekeel McBride or George Orwell or Joseph Mitchell or Toni Morrison, I want to join them playing the game of writing. It's a dumb response, for I can't write that well, but a good response for writing should be infectious and contagious. It looks like so much fun to write well. I have the same reaction as when I see Larry Bird make a couple of impossible baskets. I want to feel the ball in my hands, get out on the court, and clumsily attempt the same moves.

Writers read to be inspired, to see the possibilities of language. They learn most about writing by writing, but they learn a great deal by reading.

Much of this reading is not studied formally, but it is absorbed. You may be involved in a story, turning pages quickly to see if the heroine can rescue the hero. But part of your mind, if you are a writer, is also recording how the magician writer is getting the rabbit into the hat.

Seeing What Works

The literary critic is almost always dealing with a completed work, and it is a great danger for critics, as the good critics are well aware, that they will become too critical, developing a surgical eye that only sees what does not work. It becomes an easy game to play, particularly if you do not write yourself, always questioning, always doubting. But as Peter Elbow teaches us, we must also believe and have faith if we are to learn.

The writer must protect himself or herself from the paralyzing distrust of every text, including his or her own. Read what Mekeel McBride says about her lack of confidence in her excellent essay— an essay she didn't know was excellent. The writer must find a way to have faith in what is written, to see what the text, no matter how strange it may appear at first, has to offer.

The writer usually uses the general term, "works," to express this attitude. What works in this text; what works in this part of the text; what works in the lead, the end, the middle, the paragraph, the line?

We learn best by seeing what is possible, but too often school emphasizes what doesn't work, what is impossible. In my lifetime I was told there would never be a four-minute mile, but once Roger Bannister broke that barrier all sorts of people ran under four-minute miles. I was told that you couldn't fly faster than the speed of sound, but once Chuck Yeager did it, it seemed to become commonplace overnight. The history of science is full of cases where people do the impossible, and immediately other people imitate and extend what has been done, even without knowing how it was done.

The writer who wants to improve his or her own writing will be reading all the time to see what works, to see the techniques another writer can use to get inside a person's head, to lay bare an event, to explore a series of actions and reactions, to explain a complex issue, to persuade people to join an unpopular cause, to simply point out the extraordinary in the ordinary.

Keep reading, first to see what works in the writing of others and in your own writing.

Seeing What Needs Work

Once you have seen what works, you can examine what needs work. Again, watch out for saying what doesn't work, what can't work, what is impossible, what is bad. It is too easy to do that. It is far harder, but more constructive and more fun, to look for what needs work in the writing of others and in your own drafts. What part of the writing could improve if the writer knew more about the subject, or chose a different point of view, or moved in closer, or stood back, or reorganized the piece of writing, or chose a different genre, or made the writing more specific, or let the music of the writing carry the meaning?

All the possibilities of good writing are there, and we should look at what isn't working in terms of what might work, trying to put ourselves into the skin of the writer to see the game from the field, so that we see the choices as the quarterback saw them, not as the howling fan imagined they were seen.

We need, as reading writers, to read empathetically, to put ourselves within the situation of the writer writing, to experience as best we can the reality of the evolving text. As readers we see what is already written in the context of what others have already written. That is a valid, significant, and interesting viewpoint. The writer, however, can take an additional viewpoint and imagine the published text unfinished: what needs to be done, what could be done, what might work. This viewpoint illuminates the text; it gives the reader a fresh understanding of the text and of the writer's work. It also helps the writer see what might be done on the writer's own text.

Reading the Text That Was Not Written

What we are talking about is an arrogant act of criticism. We are trying to imagine from our own writing and our own reading a text that does not exist. We have to realize that this text does not exist; it is a product of our imagination, no matter how educated that imagination may be.

Literary scholars, of course, can sometimes help us with this imagining. We can go back to the journals, notebooks, letters, interviews, diaries, autobiographies of some writers and see what they wrote, and hear their accounts of why they wrote what they wrote. We are including in this book some documentation of how a variety of working writers write, what texts they have produced that will not be seen by the readers of their published works. You will have a chance to compare their texts and yours to begin to get a feeling of how you can read to become a more effective writer.

To do this you will have to read the texts of writers that might have been written, and to read texts that you might write. For while we are writing we often squint down the road to see where we may go, and in doing that choose to go another way. The painter, for example, may paint a thousand pictures in his or her mind while developing one picture on the canvas.

Seeing the Problems Unsolved

A written text can be seen as a series of solutions to invisible writing problems. When the writer reads the writer attempts to make those problems visible. As you read one author's page the characters may seem to walk right off that page into your life. You can hear them, see them, touch them. Put yourself in the author's shoes when those historical characters were dry and disconnected library notes. What were the problems faced by Martin Luther King, Jr., as he spoke to a nation at a time of crisis, of James Stevenson showing a cinematographer at work, of Raymond Carver revising his own story? Once you see the problem you may be able to understand how the author presented documentary descriptions, written quotations, diary and witness accounts to reproduce a living person or event.

The better the writing the more helpful it may be to stand back and ask what the problem was that faced the writer before the first draft. Then you can understand the success of the text from a useful perspective.

As you do this, you will, of course, relate the problems that you are having in your writing and that your classmates are having in their writing to the text you're reading, and the texts you are reading become not just finished models, distant and unobtainable, but working models of solutions you may attempt to solve the problems in your own drafts.

Tuning in to the Writer Muttering

Listen to yourself as you write. You probably talk to yourself, sometimes obscenely, as you try to work out a text, urging yourself on, criticizing yourself, congratulating yourself, muttering about this possibility or that, this possible solution or that one. I didn't hear myself talking to myself while I wrote until I was the subject of a writing research project which used "protocols" to study my writing habits. A protocol is an account of the writing, during the writing, that is taperecorded by a writer. To make the tapes I had to talk about what I was doing while I was doing it. I expected this talk to be unnatural, to interfere with my concentration. It wasn't. After a day or so I became used to it, and I realized that I had silently been talking to myself as I wrote all along. Now I often hear myself as I write, and I even, sometimes, make notes recording what I am saying or thinking as I work. It seems now a natural awareness of the process I'm going through. While I read these days I often imagine I hear Leo Tolstoy or Toni Morrison, William Least Heat Moon or Joan Didion muttering away at their writing. Of course I don't know what they are saying, or even if they are saying, but I see their texts differently, more alive, more a matter of choice, what Elizabeth Bowen called, "The whittling away of alternatives." It gives me a writer's insight into the text to reconstruct what the writer may have said to make the awkward, clumsy writing into the published text which flows so easily before my eyes.

Rewriting the Masters

Hemingway said that he rewrote the end of *A Farewell to Arms* 39 times before he could get the words right. If he can mess around with that so can you. Get right into the text—rewrite the beginning, or the end, a scene, a page, a chapter, an argument, a definition, a conclusion, an introduction—to understand what is going on.

We can't come down out of the stands and play in a rerun of the short pass to the 10-yard-line that was dropped, but we can do a rerun of the written text. We can see if we can make a section that works work even better, and we can attempt to make pages that don't work, work.

We may improve on what the author has done, or we may not come close to the success the writer achieved. No matter, we have gotten inside the text, we have begun to understand the writer's problems and solutions, the writer's challenge, and the writer's craft.

Master texts should not be something distant, apart from us, something that is worshipped from afar. If we really want to understand why a good writer is effective, we need to attempt what the writer has attempted. We will understand what we are reading in a new way, and we will also begin to take the lessons of the masters and apply them to our own pages.

Editing the Masters

I was once part of a workshop in which a page from William Zinsser's fine book on writing, *On Writing Well*, was distributed to a number of professional editors—and William Zinsser. It was a page which is reproduced in the book as he edited it. Roy Peter Clark invited us to edit this page, and we went to work on the text. We all edited it differently, including William Zinsser. There are few absolutes in writing, and how we improve the text one day may be different from how we improve it another day. And, of course, our changes may not be improvements. But it is instructive to edit a text yourself. Mark this text up, editing our edited copy, or second-guess other published writers. You can xerox any text and attack the page, seeing how adding, cutting, reordering, changing a word, changing the rhythm or pace, developing or not developing, shaping, or forming a text makes a difference. Adding a comma or leaving one out can change the whole meaning of a text, and you need to participate in the editing process to fully understand and appreciate how a published text works.

Imitating the Masters

Imitation used to be the principal method of artistic and literary education, but the pendulum swung too far, and the imitators became only that. They had to have the thought, the voice, everything that the model had. Imitation is simply one way of learning, and you can imitate loosely by taking the same subject, form, or point of view as the author, using the same limitations, speaking to the same audience, and learn a great deal by comparing your product to the product of a fine writer.

You can also imitate closely by taking your own subject, one similar to the master's, and then trying to produce what the master produced. This will work best if you imitate someone you admire, not someone a teacher says you should admire. This is an instructive exercise for the writer, and it, of course, makes the writer a better reader of the author or the genre imitated. It is easy to scorn a writer or a kind of writing when you have not done it yourself.

Researching Writers' Writing

To understand what lies behind the text you see on the page you may find it helpful to research how that text was produced. There are many ways to do this. They include:

- writers' biographies
- writers' autobiographies
- writers' diaries
- writers' letters
- scholarly accounts
- critical accounts
- interviews
- essays

This is obviously not necessary with everything you write, but it is valuable for a writer to do this once in a while to remind himself or herself of all the elements that are combined and distilled on the final page—the education, the experience, the thoughts, the feelings, the research, the thinking that produces a fine piece of writing.

Reading To Write

This book is designed to help you as you write in many different ways. Examples of effective writing are printed in the book so that the apprentice writer can see masters at work and then those models are analyzed from the writer's point of view. It is important that the book be read by students who are in the act of writing while they are reading. There should be as little separation as possible between the acts of reading and writing. Over my desk is the instruction, *nulla dies sine linea*, never a day without a line—a principle of the ancient Romans which is followed by most modern, productive writers. It would be just as true to say, "Never a day without reading a line," as to say, "Never a day without writing a line." Writers read while writing and write while reading.

The Writing Process

One of the ways writing is studied and taught these days is called the process approach to writing. Those who use this approach try to understand how writing evolves from the time when there is no page, not a single word written down, until there is final published copy. This is only one way to look at how writing is made and to help students learn to write more effectively. This reader can be used with any approach, but it is organized to match one model of the writing process, the model I have used in my book, *Write To Learn*.

That is only one model of the writing process. There is not one way to study writing or teach it, and there is not one precise, single, authoritative process accepted by all of us who use the process approach. I, myself, have constructed other models, and I hope that there never will be just one model.

The process of writing changes with the writing task, the writer's experience with that writing task, and the thinking style of the writer. Still, many of us find it helpful to organize the writing process into a sequential system, to see how that works, to see how it changes with writing tasks, with experience, and with the individual variations of writers.

The model of the writing process that is used to organize this book is:

COLLECT
FOCUS
ORDER
DRAFT
CLARIFY

The selections are grouped arbitrarily to show how they demonstrate some of the skills that may be helpful to a writer in that part of the writing process. No reader, however, can contain good writing in any rigid category. Good writing demonstrates many problems solved, many qualities, many tactics and strategies reading writers may adapt to their own writing.

The Reading Process

You will notice that there is similarity between the writing process and the reading process. Although both work through an interaction between the *global* (the experience of the writer, a huge inventory of information on the topic) and the *particular* (the word, the phrase, the sentence), there is a narrowing down in both cases. The reader usually reads fast or scans the text at first, and later works with the precise connotation and denotation of significant individual words.

The writer at first collects much more information than will be used in the final draft, where the writer works line by line to get each precise detail correct.

The techniques of reading we present in this text should apply to the reading of your own drafts. You should build up an inventory of reading skills that can be used to make your drafts increasingly effective. The text is designed to help you do just that. It includes:

1. *Case histories of writers reading as they write.* The first selection in each section will show a publishing writer reading his or her own copy. A journalist, a literary scholar, a science writer, a poet, and a technical writer show how they read what they have written. You hear these writers talking about how they write, how they read, and the relationship of reading and writing in their own work, and you see the final result of their reading and writing so that you can read it through your eyes as well as theirs.

The book also includes essays by Joan Didion, George Orwell, and Flannery O'Connor who talk about what they try to do and then you will read them as they try to do it.

2. *Effective writing demonstrated.* The selections in the book are, above all, subjective. They come from books on my shelves. They are pieces of writing that interest and instruct me as a writer. The majority are nonfiction, because that is what most of you will write. But there are examples of fiction and poetry, because these forms often reveal writing at its best. They extend our minds and our craft. Not all of the selections, by any means, are "literary" in the sense of their subject matter. They extend into fields outside of English and the humanities, not only because many of you are interested in those fields, but also because we all are, and should be. Our world cannot be contained in any single discipline.

3. *A writer reading.* I will read Joseph Mitchell's wonderful article, "Up in the Old Hotel" carefully, commenting on the writing so that you can observe and second-guess a writer reading to learn from a master. My comments in the margin will show how I look at the text, what I admire and why, what I see working, what techniques are revealed to me. In all the other pieces in the book I will comment here and there on what I am learning from the text that may help my own writing. I hope you will enter in and note what you are learning as well so the book will become a personal reference book as you write in school and beyond.

I hope that my readings will not be the only model for you as you read. Note how your instructor reads, how your classmates read, and how your own reading is changing as you read to write.

4. *Questions and activities.* After each text there will be a number of questions and activities that are designed to help you read the text as a writer, to connect the text with other texts in the book and outside of the book, and above all to extend what you are learning through reading into your own writing.

Do not glamorize the writers in this text. They are talented, and they have worked hard to hone their talent. But when they go each morning to their writing desks they are more like you than you can believe. Because their careers are on the line they may, in fact, have faced greater terror than you do when you sit before the empty page. The writer starts each day anew. No matter how old you are and how much you have written, each day is fresh. That is the curse and the blessing of the experienced writer.

Question what these writers are saying and how they say it. Put yourself in their situation at the writing desk when there was no text or a hesitant, scribbled-over draft evolving before their eyes. Second-guess their solutions to their writing problems. Read these pages, and your own, to be surprised, to learn, to share the challenge and achievement of practicing the writer's craft.

Writing about Writing

A particular form of writing that you have to do in literature classes and will probably have to do while using this book is to write about writing. It is an excellent way to learn how to think critically and test that critical thinking with your instructor and classmates. It is a form of writing that will help you think and share your thinking. You may, in business, review proposals for changes in company policy; you may write a brief as a lawyer, arguing your case; you may write as an engineer reviewing plans on a project. All of those forms of writing are directly related to writing about reading. In whatever field you enter, you are likely to have to read and report to others on what you have read. We use literature to teach critical thinking because it is reading we can all understand. Literature study, for literary scholars, becomes very specialized. But in the beginning, and in a book such as this, we are reading writing that is intended for, and important to, the general public.

By using such writing, often itself a demonstration of critical thinking, the class and the teacher can share a common intellectual experience. They can discuss and write about that common text, and in this way sharpen their ability to understand, evaluate, and present their own documented opinions.

All writing is thinking. It is not thinking completed and then written down; writing is thinking itself, and it is important that all writers have the experience of thinking critically, of using written thought to perform tasks of the intellect.

Which Audience?

Those who are inexperienced in writing about writing are often confused because they do not understand that there are two different audiences for such writing, and it is important for the writer to know the difference between these two audiences *before* the writer reads what is to be written about.

The general audience does not know the text and does not consist of authorities on the subject. The writer has to tell the reader what the book says, then place what is being said by that author in a context, and finally evaluate it. In the case of a book, movie, or TV review for a general audience, for example, something of the story has to be told. The reader wants to know what to expect if the reader buys the book, goes to the movie, or turns on the television set.

Sometimes the general audience is rather specialized. The text being reviewed may be a chemistry experiment, and it may be reviewed in a journal for biochemists. The reviewer, the writer, and the readers all share a common field of expertise. But the readers do not know what the experiment has attempted and how well it has succeeded. The reviewer has to tell what is going on in the text that the readers have not yet read.

The literary audience is significantly different. Everyone in this audience—it may be a one-person audience of the instructor—have all experienced the text. There is no reason to retell the story or in any other way to say what the author has said. The important thing is to take a critical position, placing the text in a context and evaluating its success.

Academic writing is very different from the writing outside the academic world, and it is largely this matter of audience and the writer's relationship to that audience. When writing in school, the student writes for teachers and colleagues who are equal or greater authorities on the subject. For most writing out of school, the writer is the authority; the author knows more about the subject than the reader. The student should recognize this significant difference, and most composition classes give students an opportunity to perform both kinds of writing. They are allowed to write about personal experiences on which they alone can be the authority. And they are also given the challenge of writing about a common intellectual experience—the reading of a text—on which they are writing for other authorities.

The Critical Eye: Reading for Writing about Reading

When you are going to write about a text, you have to read it both to find out *what* is being said and to consider *how* it is being said. The experienced critic may be able to read a text once and perform these multiple tasks. But most writers have to read the text many times.

Usually they read it fast to get the flavor and feel of the text. In this reading they will, of course, learn something of what the text has to say to them, and they will also begin to form opinions on how effectively it is being said. It is helpful to make notes or to mark up the text, noting sentences or paragraphs that contain a distillation of meaning or demonstrate an effective or ineffective style. The reader may also see connections, turning points, and may also note false assumptions, effective or ineffective documentation, conclusions.

The writer then has to read the text again to make sure that the reviewer understands what the writer intended to say and to make sure the reviewer knows what is said. The reader may have to read the text from the perspective of the author to understand what the writer was trying to do. Then the reviewer may have to stand back and ask if the author has fulfilled that purpose.

When the reader understands the content of the piece, then the reader can examine how well that content is presented. The reviewer can consider such matters as clarity, simplicity, flow, grace, and voice. It is impossible to evaluate the writing in a text fairly until the reviewer knows the purpose of the author, what the author has to say, and to whom the author intends to say it.

In these readings the writer will note words that are just right or just wrong, phrases that ring clear or clink, sentences that flow or become choked in their own syntax, paragraphs that carry a convincing load of meaning or break down.

During all of these readings the reviewer is interacting with the text. The text causes the reader to think, and as the reader thinks the reader sees the text more clearly. The reviewer is reading, and thinking, and beginning to write the review, rehearsing it in the writer's head and on paper while the readings are going on.

The Critical Opinion

The purpose of writing about reading is to sharpen the student's intellectual tools. The student is expected to have an opinion about the text, to evaluate what has been said and how it has been said. The reader usually has an opinion of what is good about the text, and those elements should be mentioned. The reader also has an opinion of what does not work in the text, and that should be included in the review.

The opinion, of course, can also be limited. This book could be reviewed from the point of view of all who will use it, or it could be limited to the teacher's point of view, or the student's. There could even be a further limitation, and it could be reviewed from the point of view of an experienced teacher or an inexperienced one, of a class of advanced students or remedial ones.

The important thing is that the reader know the opinion of the text, what works, what doesn't work, and what the overall result is in the reviewer's mind.

Documentation

Each point that is made about the text should be documented by evidence from the text or outside the text when it is appropriate. The first evidence comes from the text itself. If the reader is told that there is bad thinking in the text or bad writing, an example should follow immediately. The reader, when reading the review, should be persuaded by specific evidence from the text itself.

Sometimes the reviewer has to go outside the text and quote other authorities or compare the writing in the text with evidence of more or less effective writing by specific examples from other texts.

The effective writer writes with information, and the information the reader wants is not only the opinion of the writer, but the documentation upon which that opinion is based. The evidence needs to be specific, accurate, in context, and made available to the reader when the reader needs it. Each opinion in a review should be anchored to evidence.

Tricks of the Critic's Trade

The experienced critic develops techniques which help the writer make the opinion of the text clear and convincing to the reader. Some of these techniques are:

1. *Anticipate the reader's questions or arguments* and answer them early in the review. It is always a good tactic to pull the fangs of a person who may have strong, opposite opinions to the ones you intend to express in the piece.
2. *Establish your authority* to do the review early in the text. Try to work it in gracefully so that the reader knows, without thinking you're an egomaniac, that you have a special qualification or special training or experience that gives you the right to examine the text critically.
3. *Establish your own territory* so that you deal with the text from a position of strength. This is often related to limiting the subject. You may be writing about a piece that discusses ethics, for example, and it may be helpful for you in the review to discuss how the issues raised in the text relate to football and to such questions as: Is it ethical to make a late hit? To fake an injury? To push the limits of the law?
4. *Try to say one thing* about the text, making one opinion dominant. Every other opinion in the text and every piece of evidence should aim toward the single dominant opinion.
5. *Try to put the text into context* so that the reader understands the relationship of what is being said to the field in which it belongs, and also compare that text to other texts so that the text you are writing about doesn't float in isolation, but is seen in perspective by the reader. It may be helpful to you to know what other authorities have said about the text, and it may also be helpful to the reader to know what they have said.

Writing about Writing Is Writing

Never forget that good writing is the same, no matter the form. It's easy to get caught up in the special demands of a particular kind of writing and forget that the differences between writing are always minor, and that the similarities—the standards of effective writing—are always major. In other words, do all those things that you have learned to do to make your writing clear, lively, believable, and effective whenever you are writing about a text or anything else.

Reading To Write and Writing To Read

Think of what you do as you read. It is an interesting and complex act. You look at the symbols on the page—the letters, the words—and take in what the writer has written. You experience the text, but that experience is mixed at the same time with all the other experiences you have had. The author's experience, and your experience, mix together as hot and cold water mix as they come out of the shower head. The text you are "reading" is no longer the author's text but a new text that has been composed by you as you read it.

Look around the class and listen to the texts that come from the same piece of writing. Jim and Mable and Beth and Les and Jorge and Amy all bring their own experiences to what they have read. In this book, for example, there is a piece by Amiri Baraka telling about his experiences as a black in an urban school. The student who has a similar background will read that far differently from the person who comes from a white suburb. And when that student from the black neighborhood reads John Updike talking about his school in Pennsylvania, the text will be different than for a white student. All through this book there are pieces of writing that will cause people to combine their experience with the author's. The black urban student, for example, will create a different text in reading Maya Angelou's piece about a rural black school, and the rural black may be alien to Baraka's text. A student from Texas will approach the Caro article with a special understanding. A student who has lost someone to cancer will read Alice Trillin's piece differently from someone who has no experience with that disease.

We write as we read, and this experience of composing a text from our reading obviously helps us learn to write. We see the material that is around us. We see how each person shapes that material. Some of you may read in this book a text you have read a few years ago, or in high school, and find that you are a different reader now. Of course. We change and grow with our experiences in living, in writing, and in reading. And we learn not passively from a text that is given to us, but actively, interacting with the text, studying it as some people study the Bible, the Torah, or the Koran, putting into the text what we can and getting out of the text what we are able to receive.

We also read as we write. The text we expect to write is not the text we write. We pour our experience with life and language through that tap, and it is mixed with the evolving text. The words we choose limit and shape our meaning. The phrases and sentences with which we hook our words together carry us in directions we did not expect to go. The denotation—the precise meaning of the words—and the connotation—the meanings that hover around the words—teach us as we write.

The text on our page moves us forward toward meaning in the same way that speech does. We all need to talk things out with a friend, a counselor, a member of the clergy, sometimes a stranger. We need to talk, not so much to get advice, but to hear what we have to say about a crisis in our life, or a decision we have to make. What we say gives discipline and form and meaning to those thoughts and feelings that are vague until we speak. We write a text through speaking, and we read it through hearing.

What appears on the page has to be read quickly as it is written, the way a football player has to read the defense while attempting to run through it. The text is in motion; it is changing as we do it. And that's something that the writer finds exciting. Too many of us have the idea that you are supposed to know what you have to say before you say it. If that were true few writers would write. We write to find what we have to say, to read a text that is changing as we read it. We read what we have just written, and that influences what is being written and continually changes what may be written. Eventually we rewrite and revise and edit to clarify the meaning that we are reading.

Readers are writers whether they know it or not. And writers are always readers. There is no reasonable separation between the acts of reading and writing. Each activity is twin to the other, providing us with information and a disciplined way of finding meaning in that information, with the special bonus of being able to share that meaning with others who, like you in reading my text, will compose your own text from it. I can no more control what you will find in your head in reading my words than I can control who my daughters may marry.

Read the articles, stories, and poems in this collection, realizing that you will be writing your own texts as you read and as you write. Write to learn how to read, and read to learn how to write.

3

Information Collected

To read to write, you have to understand that writing is an act of exploration. Writers do not so much write what they know as they write to learn what they may know. John McPhee really didn't know about oranges before he wrote the book from which an excerpt is reprinted in this chapter. He was familiar with oranges. He could find one in a supermarket; he had peeled, chomped, drunk oranges. But by writing about the orange, he got to know the orange and could share his knowledge with us. Thomas Whiteside got to know the tomato by writing about the tomato. Both of these writers found subjects that were so ordinary that many other writers might have passed them by but both knew that they shared familiarity with oranges and tomatoes with their readers—and they shared an essential ignorance as well. There was a mystery to be investigated.

Beginning writers—and not so beginning writers—share the terror of emptiness, that there is nothing to write about and when there is something to write about, there is nothing to say. I felt it this morning and performed all sorts of virtuous evasions—answering mail, making phone calls, neatening up—to avoid the emptiness. But the emptiness is the starting point of writing and I have to remind myself of that. After all, I don't want to write what I've written before—and write it in the same way. I have to remember that in despair, in terror, in hopelessness I have come to the beginning of my writing. Now I can find a new country to explore or a new way to explore a familiar land.

In this chapter, we will read writers who have found and developed a subject but never forget that they started with the same emptiness you feel, that there was writing before the final draft, and before the first draft fragments and notes and plans that were used and many more that were not used. You will see some of this process in Christopher Scanlan's piece, but only a sample. Most articles, if they were published with all their notes and drafts, would be as long as a book.

Finding the Subject To Explore

There are some subjects, of course, that are assigned to you and then the problem is how to collect the information that will allow you to develop the subject. There are also subjects that attach themselves to you; they seek you out and arrive as insistent and uncalled for as an itch. Pay attention to those subjects. They have an intensity and immediacy that other subjects do not have. You have a need to explore such a subject and good writing is often the product of such a demanding subject, "Write me, write me!"

Still there are times when you need to seek out a subject. You have to look at the world beyond yourself and within yourself to find material that may be developed and become worthy of being shared with a reader.

The Outward Search

We begin to examine the world from the point at which we are standing, connecting what we observe with our own experience first of all. We often start with questions that make a connection between ourselves and our world. These questions include:

- What would I like to know more about?
- Who would I like to know better? (This question may have led Robert Caro to begin his biography of President Lyndon Johnson. An excerpt, "The Sad Irons" is published in this chapter.)
- What process interests me?
- How is my world changing?

- What needs to be changed?
- What is happening that should—and why?
- What is *not* happening that should—and why?
- What process should I know more about?
- What do I need to know?
- What do I want to know?
- What don't I want to know?
- What event is affecting my world?
- What caused the event?
- What will result because of the event?
- What surprises me?

The questions can go on and on as we study our world, asking who, what, where, and especially why and how. The more we see the more we will see, and we will begin to look carefully at what is taking place—has taken place and will take place—in our world. Soon we begin to look at the interactions in the world around us.

- What forces are attracted to each other?
- What forces are resisted by each other?
- What forces are in conflict?
- What forces will be in conflict?
- What problems need solutions?
- What solutions will lead to new problems?
- What are those new problems?
- How may they be solved?

The writer is constantly scanning the world the way radar rotates across the horizon, and the writer keeps seeing new blips, new points of potential subject. Most of them begin with a necessary self-interest. The writer is open to the world, concerned with what the writer is seeing, hearing, smelling, tasting, touching. Every sense is in contact with the world outside the writer. Note the way in which many of the selections in this chapter—Scanlan, Caro, Mitchell, Moon, McPhee, and Whiteside—show the writer observing and recording the world, building a significant piece of writing from the specific information the writer has collected.

The Inward Search

Writers looks inward as well as outward, for writers are not only observers of society, but members of society. They know their feelings and thoughts are an integral part of the subject-seeking process.

The writers' own lives and own histories often provide important material. Writers know that what they feel and think will be felt and thought by other individuals.

In some cases—autobiography (for example, Baraka's selection in this chapter), the personal narrative (note Dryden's selection in this chapter), the familiar essay, the opinion—the writer will speak directly of the writer's inner world. In other cases the inner feelings or reactions of the writer will be the starting point for a writer's explorations of the world outside.

Some of the questions that will help the writer discover subjects within himself or herself are:

- What makes me worry?
- What makes me angry?
- Why am I reacting so strongly to this incident?
- Why am I *not* reacting strongly?
- What is making me nostalgic?
- What is making me laugh?
- What is making me sad?
- Why am I making these connections?
- Why do I think the result will be good?
- Why do I think the result will be bad?

Combining the Two

It should be obvious that it is hard, in fact impossible, to make a clear separation between the personal and the impersonal. The writer may respond to an outside stimulus, as Christopher Scanlan did, and end up revealing the personal impact of what he discovered. Or the writer may feel something in a very personal way and write about it in an objective manner, as Robert Caro has in "The Sad Irons."

In many cases, the writer combines both the outside and the inside world in a single piece of writing, moving back and forth between external observation and inward reflection as both William Least Heat Moon and Ken Dryden do in their books and in the excerpts reprinted here.

Finding the Information through Exploration

Once writers have a subject or territory to explore, they move across the countryside like a monster vacuum cleaner, gobbling up everything that may help them understand the subject. Writers know that they need far more information than they will be able to use. You can see evidence of this in Christopher Scanlan's notes, and you should realize that, as detailed as Robert Caro's piece may seem to be, the published details are selected from a necessary inventory of many more details.

Written Sources

Librarians are often the writer's best friends. They collect, organize, and can recover huge amounts of written information. Writers, such as McPhee, Whiteside, and Caro, will draw on books, newspaper clippings, magazine articles, monographs, reports, statistical collections, an enormous resource of information about the subject. Reporters, such as Whiteside and McPhee, also will use corporate reports, government reports, the publications of professional organizations, scientific papers, speeches—a vast smorgasbord of material that may reveal significant specifics that can be connected and woven into a meaning.

Librarians, public information offices, public relations officers, professional associations, government agencies, and legislative committees are but a few of the sources writers use to get information. And these are all sources that are available to the inquisitive student, who can contact them by mail, telephone, or in person.

Live Sources

In school we forget that the best source of information is often a live authority. The policeman, the judge, the social worker, the victim, the defense attorney, the prosecuting attorney, the accused, the doctor, the neighbor, the parent are all sources from which the writer can get important information. Robert Caro and his wife traveled through the Texas hill country, interviewing live sources. William Least Heat Moon, Christopher Scanlan, John McPhee, and Thomas Whiteside all use information from live sources in their selections. Joseph Mitchell, obviously, depended primarily on one live source for the information in his story.

All these people used the interview to collect information. The effective interviewer prepares for the interview by finding out as much as possible about the interviewee ahead of time and tries, whenever possible, to make appointments at the subject's convenience. Interviewers take careful notes or taperecord the interviews.

The key to an information-producing interview is good questions. I like to prepare for the interview by writing down the four to six questions that the reader has to have answered if I am to produce a good story. I work on these questions and, of course, change them as the story evolves. The best questions cannot be answered by yes or no. I try not to ask, "Did you win the game?" but, "Why did you win the game?" "How did you win the game?" "What was the key play and why did it work?" I want questions that will force the interviewee to think and respond with concrete details.

The interviewer tries to make the interview a relaxed experience. He or she tries to create an environment that is as casual as a conversation. But it is an intense experience. Behind the relaxed manner of the person asking questions is an intense listener who is trying to put each answer into context, trying to see what question needs to be asked next, trying to notice how the answers are being answered, and paying close attention to what isn't being said as well as what is said. And all the time the writer remains prepared to be surprised, to discover meaning, as Christopher Scanlan did when he interviewed the French farmer and found the real significance of the story when he did not expect to find it.

Observation

Firsthand observation is another skill that is essential to the writer. Robert Caro drove through the hill country, William Least Heat Moon was in Nameless. Joseph Mitchell went up in the old hotel. All of the writers in this section have seen the story with their own eyes. The careful observation of the world will produce much of the raw material we use in writing. I find it helpful to observe even if I do not use the material directly. If I am writing about teaching I need to sit in a class as a student, and I need to teach my own classes. I may not use any of that material, but the firsthand experience helps me put the material I have in context.

While observing, the writer is always looking for revealing details—the specific anonymity of the way the graves were numbered in Scanlan's story, for example. The writer wants the detail that gives off extra meaning. The writer wants to hear the quotation, such as when the old farmer told Scanlan, "That the young who died delivered us." Such a quotation brings another voice and a special authority to the story. The writer needs to see the place in which the story is taking place. Scanlan describes a U.S. military cemetery in France as "4,313 white crosses and Stars of David lined up on a manicured field like a marching band at half time." The mention of the marching band, of course, gives the reader a double vision of the high school Saturday game in the world of expectation and possibility that these young men had left, and the vision of the cemetery in which they were buried only months later. And seeing does not only mean seeing the physical world, but seeing the meaning in what is visualized. Scanlan and the other writers in this chapter make you see.

Memory

A writer's memory is a special contraption. In fact, the writer's memory is so special that it would be worth it to be a writer just to enjoy the product of this memory. Few writers have TV game show recall. I am typical, I think, in having a rather poor memory in that I cannot recall many names or facts or details out of context. But the act of writing stimulates my memory, and I find that information appears on the page that I didn't know I knew. I remember little about being in combat 40 years ago, but as I write about combat, I am once more in combat and my pages flood with an excess of detail that has been imprisoned in my skull for decades.

Most of us, I believe, have this writer's memory. When I collect a group of strangers in a room, in a class, or writing workshop who do not believe they are writers, and get them writing, either just free-writing or writing freely and fast about something they care about, information that they had forgotten or were not aware of remembering, tumbles out of their brains onto the page. When someone, such as Amiri Baraka, writes autobiography their history is recreated in enormous detail on the page. That history has not been remembered before writing, but it is remembered by writing, in the way that details come out of your mouth when you are describing an experience to a good listener, details that you "discover" by the act of sharing the experience.

The student writer should be impressed by the abundance of remembered detail, especially in the autobiographical pieces by such writers as James Baldwin, William Gibson, Alice Trillin, Theodore Roethke, Maya Angelou, John Updike, George Orwell, E. B. White, Jean Shepherd, Enrique Hank Lopez, and Maxine Hong Kingston in this book. To share their experience and learn from them how to make use of it, you should write at least a scene from your own biography—taking a few minutes when you first witnessed a death, or were especially scared by a place, or felt hatred, love, pity, or resentment for a person—and describe that event, place, or person in detail, giving yourself 10 pages, or 20, and writing as fast as possible to see what tumbles out of your own brain onto the page. You will discover that you also have a writer's memory, and that the act of writing stimulates your brain to reveal what you didn't know you knew.

In all these ways, and many others, of examining your outer and inner worlds and the connections between them, you will see how many subjects you have to write about and to see how many ways there are to discover the material that will develop those subjects. You will understand, through your own writing, the problems of the writers we have reprinted here and discover, through your reading, how your fellow writers have solved their problems.

Case Study: A Journalist Writes and Reads

Christopher Scanlan

Every writer builds a small writing community on which the writer depends for support, stimulation, criticism, and encouragement during the writing process. Christopher Scanlan is one of the most important members of my personal writing community. Every week we are in touch with each other by mail and phone, sharing drafts that work and don't work, listening, counseling, discussing the craft of writing that forever fascinates us.

I first met Scanlan when I was brought to the Providence, Rhode Island, *Journal/Bulletin* as a writing coach. At the first workshop I noticed his skepticism and his tough-minded interest in how writing was made. I read what he wrote and was impressed, and as I got to know him I learned with him and from him. He is one of the best writers on a newspaper known for its good writing and good editing. He also serves as liaison in our program at the *Journal/Bulletin* to improve writing, and in that role he has edited a book on newswriting, *How I Wrote the Story*, published by the Providence Journal Book Club.

Scanlan is above all a pro. He takes his turn at rewrite and covering hard news, although he is both an investigative reporter digging out material authorities do not want to divulge and a feature writer known for his sensitive stories. He is a graduate of the Columbia University School of Journalism, has worked on newspapers in Delaware and Connecticut, as well as Rhode Island, and has been a contributing editor of *Connecticut Magazine*. His nonfiction has been published in more than a dozen other publications and he has won awards for investigative reporting, spot news, business, and feature writing. Scanlan has been honored for the best series and the best feature story by The New England Associated Press News Executives Association.

In this case study he shares some of his notes and drafts with us as well as a draft revised after publication for reprinting. It is fascinating to see how many writers can't let go but keep improving their work even after it has been published. He has also written an account of how he collected, selected, and wove the information into a story that has been reprinted in five publications.

You may want to follow the history of this article as we have printed it, seeing the work evolve, or jump ahead and read the article or the account of its writing and then work through the material from which the article evolved.

❡ Most writers keep journals, daybooks or logs in which they talk to themselves about what they may write and store up material for that writing. One page from Scanlan's "Traveler's Log" follows. ❡

~~pilgrimage a journey, especially a long one, undertaken in quest of something for a particular purpose, as to pay homage.~~

From a Traveler's Log.

June 23. 8:50 a.m.

We are on the train at Gare St. Lazaee bound for Lison-
Marigny to find Pat Caḷlahan's half-brother's grave. It
is first class- like an American commuter- except that most
of the seats are reserved. We found two "non reserve" next
to two "mutile." I notice the French don't take the "mutile"
which are by the windows so we moved out of them . If no
mutile shows perhaps we can reclaim them.
It'sx a nice day- light sky with mild breezes and a promise
of a warm sunny day. We ḡave a bag with camera. This is the
train to Cherbourg from which we would leave for Ireland but
we really don't have the time. As of midnight last night
we have just 7 full daYS OF Eurail travelling left and we want
to spend at least one more day in Paris which means at the
soonest we wont leave Paris until Thursday and xitk that
just doesn't give us enough time so we'll proably head west
again to Germany and Austria...Leaving Paris now on this
Turbotrain to Cherbourg, fiix filled mostly with businessmen
one of whom seems to have a gimp;y gimpy leg from the way it's
sticking out and the way he almost lost his balance when he
changed seats. This train is comfortable and quick. I hope
we can find the grave. I'd hate for this to be a wild gxxxh
goosechase...
11:03 a.m. Arrive in Lison in 23 minutes. I'm nervous, anxious
about switching trains - whether we have to buy a ticket or
what- and hungry. We passed villages and cities, orchards and
green fields and fields of baled hay. A beautiful Cathedral
in Lisieux. It is a beautiful day.
1:13 p.m. Took bus from Lison to St. Lo and then a taxi to
Marigny (100 francs) but the American cemetery is no longer
there - only a German one. A long time ago, the taxi driver
said, they moved the graves we go no to St. Laurent to find
it.
Interview with Pedro Rivere (sp) superintendent of Normandy
cemetery:
He's from Albugurque, NM, a radio operatsor and tail gunner
in a B-26 who flew 40 missions over North African and Italy
who has been working for cemetery commission for 26 years,
with service at cemeteries in Luxembourgh and North Carthage,
Txnixkxix Tunikia.
He pulled out the book of the dead from a shelf in his office
and looked down the columns of tiny print.
"Here it is. Juba, John Jr. from Pa. He's in Brittany Cemetery
at St James." He gave us the information. Section D, Row 10
Grave 8. Killed Aug. 4, 1944. Rank Private First Class.
Serial Number 33673674. Outfit: 12 Inf. 4 Division. Winner
of Purple Heart.

❡ The lead is a journalistic term for the first sentence, paragraph, or
paragraphs that lead the reader into the story. Few journalists will
proceed with a draft until they have a working lead which
establishes the voice or tone of the article, its focus, and direction.
What follows is Scanlan's first attempt at a lead. The professional
writer knows how important it is to get something down, to write
badly—not wanting to write badly—to write well. ❡

IT was to be our firSt trip to Europe.- *together* After almost six
years of dreaming and hoping and wishing we had enough
money, we had enough. What if it was the downpayment for
a house or enough for the IBM typewriter we wanted to buy?
~~Europe~~ Some day we would have that house, ~~and that writing~~
someday that typewriter, but when would we ever have that
first trip to Eruopet together if we didn't take it now.
That's what we told each other as Kathy and I planned
our itinerary. *not going* Germany, ~~where there~~ to the Rhine Balley
where her mother was born and grew up, where she lived
until an American airmen married her and brought her
to the United States. Ireland, ~~Where my great grandparents~~
in search of my roots. France, because it was in the middle
~~of those two countries,~~ and whatever side trips we could
manage ~~in~~ on our 15 day Eurail Pass. It was all fiarly
vague which was how we wanted it. It was a vacation after
all, not a pilgrimage. Or so we thought.

~~Like every one we it old about our trip, Pat Callahan~~
~~was worker in the newsroom was enthusiastic~~

A couple of weeks before we left, Pat Callahan came
up to me at my desk in the newsroom. ~~Like other friend~~
~~and coworkers,~~ I had told him about the trip and like
other friends and co-workers, he'd been enthusiastic.
You said "You're going to France, right?" he asked now.

~~"Yes," "Yes," I said." Paris and then west to~~
~~Cherbourg." When I nodded, he continued.~~

I nodded and he said, "You know, I have a half-brother *he was only* 18.
whose buried in France. He died in *the* Normandy invasion.~~I~~
The ~~No kidding~~ thing is, nobody in family has ever been
able to visit his grave and I was wondering since you're
going to be in France, that maybe you could visit the
grave. If it's on your way, of course."

~~Why not, I thought. If it's nearby~~

Why not, I thought. ~~If we could It might make an~~
~~interesting side trip~~ I imagined Kathy and I getting off
a train with a bouquet of flowers and walking down a
dusty country road ~~lined with~~ shaded by tall leafy trees
I saw us
to the cemetery, standing before the soldier's grave, sayin

--49A

☞ The writer has been reading notes, reading drafts imagined in the writer's head and reads what has been written to see what may be written, then reads it again and again, not so much to see what doesn't work and has to be crossed out or tossed away but to see what may work on future drafts. The writer reads with surprise while writing and after writing, not thinking before writing as much as thinking by writing. Here are the first and fourth pages of a discovery draft which reveal a writer thinking by writing. ✒

```
SLUG: JUBA      ER:           DATE: 25-SEP 81  TIME: 13:42
PAP:  DAY:       ED            PG:         ORIG: SCAN  ;12/09,09-1MSG
FMT: NEWS&HJ:                  HD:        QU  SCAN   FR: SCAN  ;12/SD:
```

[ART-4]

Wait's such a drag
you get the day off
for it.

        It was to be our first trip to Europe. After almost six years of dreaming
and hoping -- and working -- we had enough money to go. ~~What if it -- as the~~
~~downpayment for a house up enough for the IBM typewriter we wanted to buy. Some~~
~~day we could have a house~~ someday ~~that typewriter~~ ~~But when would we have ever~~
~~that first trip to Europe if we didn't take it now? That's What Kathy and I~~
~~told each other~~ last spring ~~as~~ we planned our itinerary. Germany, where her
mother was born. Ireland, in search of my roots. France, because it was in the
middle, plus whatever other side trips we could manage on a 15-day Eurail Pass.
Our plans were vague, but that's how we wanted it. It was a vacation, after
all, not a pilgrimage. ~~a~~

        <BO>[Upstairs]

        <RO>   A couple of weeks before we left, I mentioned the trip to a ~~worker~~
Pat
Callahan, a co-worker ~~in the newsroom at the paper~~.

        "You're not going to France are you?" ~~he said~~ *he said.*

        "The reason I ask, *he said* is I've got a half brother buried there.
He was in the Normandy invasion *get one there so upsetting?* *Think* never made it home. Nobody in my family has
ever been able to visit his grave. ~~And I was wondering if maybe~~ you could
visit the cemetery, if it *'s not* wasn't out of your way."

        "Sure," I said. "I'd be glad to try. I'm not really sure where we're
going in France, but if we're close enough, it shouldn't be too much trouble to
stop."

        "Great," Pat said. "We've got the location where he's buried. I'll get
it from my mother." A few days later, he handed me a slip of paper ~~with this~~
message:

                            (MORE)   50A

If we're close, I'd be glad to try."

47

It was lunchtime when we got off in Lison ~~textransfer~~ to change for
the ~~xtexxxxxredxjellyxsnxx~~ spread butter and jelly
~~x~~ bus to St. Lo. We ~~finishedxourxbreakfast~~ cro~~i~~ssants ~~andx inx~~

~~theftherkrx~~ left over from breakfast ~~andxchesxex~~ as we bumped along

on the back seat of the bus as it rolled up and down narrow ~~roadsxx~~

country roads and squeezed through ~~texnexxxx~~ Main Streets hedged by

~~builstxpecked~~ stone houses. It was a hot summer day.~~andxfliexxbuxxedx~~

~~aroundxourxhandex~~ Flies buzzed around our heads. ~~I Sixkexxx~~
                                                          lay
~~layxinxaxxxilexxxx~~ The city of St Lo ~~lay~~ in a valley~~yxxx~~

~~industrialxxxxixxxhrexdedxinxdextx~~
                 miles of
After riding past ~~hedgego~~ fields latticed with hedgerows ~~xx~~

we came upon St Lo spread out on the floor of a ~~dextryx~~

valley and ended the bus ride at the train station. Marigny
                      but wasnt on a train or bus line,
was about 20 kilomters away, the ticket agent told us. There
                      either but the agent got on the phone
were no cabs in sight so he called us one and within a minute

a cream Mercedes pulled up ~~andxwexxpedxawxyxxx~~ at the door.

     The driver was in his fifties, ~~xxgrxyxx~~ gray-haired,
                    He hit 120 Kms.   passed lorries + cars
and taciturn, ~~butxhexdrexexthexteaxixlikexxxlengxx~~ but he raced

the ~~Itxwexxxxxshertxxidex~~ taxi as if it were Le MaNS instead of
                 uk r   Show
this rural highway. ~~A~~ What sounded like the Salty Brine of

St Lo chattered on the radio.

     ~~XWetrexgeingxtex~~

     ~~"NowxxeherehenexxlexeintierexAmericenexXxIxteldxhimxxxx~~

     ~~"xWetrexgeingxtexthexAmericenxremetery,XxIxteldxhimxxxxxxxxxx~~

     ~~X~~ After we had ridden in silence for a few minutes, I leaned

fotward and in my rusty French told him our destination. For the

first time he turned around.

     ~~XWhxtx~~ "There's no American cemetery in Marigny," he said.

     Just then we turned off the highway and he pointed at

a sign in a grassy graffic island. "Cimtiere allemands," it

said. There's a German cemetery there," he said. "But no

Americans."

     ~~Nex look you gerlic breethed Freg face communist chewfart,~~
     ~~we xe teme set this way to look at this dumb Poalck's grave cause~~
     ~~if we de we get a pound of American gold.~~

                    SO D

❡Scanlan read the last draft and wrote a number of handwritten attempts before starting the new second draft. We have reprinted the first page of the "final" second draft.❥

```
SLUG: JUBA                                              PAGE:  2

[ART-5]

      ``U.S. Military Cemetery.

      Marigny, France.

      Plot K, Row 9, Grave 17?.
      9 miles west of St. Lo, France.

      PFC John Juba Jr. 12 Inf. Reg.

      Died Aug. 12, 1944 (18 years old)''

      <RO>[UFstars]

<RO>    On the Michelin map the French Tourist Office <NO>check name<RO> sent u
s, Marigny

was a pinhead circle that looked to be about a 50-mile detour off the train

route from Paris to the port of Cherbourg where we planned to sail to Ireland.

We could get off the train, we figured, catch a bus or a taxi to the cemetery,

maybe have lunch in the country and still make an evening boat to Rosslare.

When we flew out of Logan Airport on June 6, our Lufthansa 727 <NO>check<RO> lea
ving

thunderstorms behind, the map was in one of our bags, an X inked beside

Marigny.
```

503

☞ We have reprinted the first, seventh, and eighth pages of the third draft.☜

cream Mercedes [handwritten] *hurtled through the Normandy countryside,*

The taxi ~~sped~~ along the country highway and for the 10th time since we left Paris that morning, I looked at the piece of paper in my hand.

"U.S. Military Cemetery.

Marigny, France.
9 miles west of St Lo [handwritten]
Row 2, Grave 10.
9 mil [handwritten]
PFc John Juba Jr. 12 Inf. 4 Reg.

Killed Aug 12, 1944. 18 years old."

~~XexxxxexxexxxxeaxidnxinxxXxanexxxxqxxxxifexXaxbxxxxxdxixx
xnax~~ [crossed out line]

is a favor to a friend [handwritten margin]
back home, my only [handwritten margin]
and I were on [handwritten margin]
a way to visit [handwritten margin]
the grave of a [handwritten margin]

~~Were~~ my wife ~~(uitil)~~ and I ~~were~~ were taking a day from our vacation in Europe to do ~~at a~~ a favor for a friend back home▪ by visiting the grave of a *half brother* [handwritten] relative killed two months after D-Day and buried in the Normandy countryside.

knew — an young [handwritten margin]
american soldier [handwritten margin]
killed in ~~these~~ [handwritten margin]
named 2 months [handwritten margin]
after D-Day. [handwritten margin]

~~"Wait a minute," our cabbie said, "there's no American cemetery in Marigny," I read him the directions. He was unim~~ ~~pressedxxxxxxxxexxurxnxxxffxthxxxxxinxhighxxxxxxxxxxxx
xindixxx~~ and when we turned off the highway at Marigny, he

'I didn't know any [handwritten margin]
one buried any [handwritten margin]
americans [handwritten margin]
~~were~~ *buried* [handwritten margin]
in Marigny," [handwritten margin]
my cousin [handwritten margin]

pointed to a sign in the grassy ~~traffic island.~~ "German soldier's cemetery" a sign said in French and German.● When we reached the town, he stopped on the sleepy Main Street and ~~exiiexixexxxxxxmanxinxxxhousexdrexxxearryingxxxxxxxppingxxaxxx~~

said our cabbie [handwritten margin]
who picked us up [handwritten margin]
at the train [handwritten margin]
station in [handwritten margin]
St Lo. [handwritten margin]

called to a woman ~~walking~~ ~~putxafxxxxxxx~~ on the sidewalk *and I asked if* [handwritten] *there was an American cemetery in town.* [handwritten]

"There's no Americans cemetery," ~~she~~ ~~m~~ ~~said too.~~ "There used to be one, but it's not there anymore. There's only Germans there now."

He slowed up to turn + pointed to a white sign planted in a grassy [handwritten]
traffic island, and pointing in the direction of Marigny [handwritten]

51A

7

The graves at Brittany Cemetery lie beyond the
Wall of the Missing - 4,313 marble crosses and ▮▮▮▮
Stars of David ▮▮▮▮▮▮▮▮▮▮▮▮▮▮▮▮▮▮ lined
up like a ▮▮▮▮ marching band at half-time. ▮▮▮▮
Section D was on the right.

"Kathy, over here," ▮▮▮▮▮▮I called, ▮▮▮▮▮▮
▮▮▮▮▮▮ breaking the stillness of the afternoon. A man
appeared in the window of a house ▮▮ beside the cemetery and
within moments ₍ₗ₎emerged wearing a tan raincoat▮ and introduced
himself as Donald Davis, the superintendent.

"D-10-8," he said, "That's right down here▮▮▮▮▮▮▮ He led
ₓₛ down nine rows of graves, turned off down the tenth and
▮▮▮▮▮▮▮▮▮▮▮▮▮▮▮▮▮ began counting off crosses.
At the eighth ₍ₗ₎we stopped and found John Juba Jr's name
cut into the marble.
                        blossoms up
I laid the flowers ₍ᴧ₎in front of the ▮ cross to take
a ▮ picture ▮ for the boy's mother.

"Wait," Mr. Davis ▮▮▮▮▮▮▮▮▮ said. He bent down
and rearranged the bouquet so the ▮▮ flowers ▮▮▮▮would face
the camera. "Otherwise, all you'll get is a ▮ picture of the
stems." Every trade has its secrets▮ ▮▮▮▮▮▮▮▮▮▮

The old ▮▮▮▮▮▮▮▮▮▮ Frenchman was outside
trimming his rose bushes when we returned.▮▮▮▮▮. He
invited us into his kitchen, ▮▮▮▮▮▮▮▮ where the
air was tangy with the smell of woodsmoke and ▮▮ poured
wine into three china cups.

His name was Pierre Letrachant,▮▮▮▮▮▮▮▮▮ he was
72 years old and he had lived most of his life in ▮▮ ₜₕₑ farm
country outside the village of St. James.
                        526

~~Finally,~~ <u>his</u> wife's family had owned the 27 acres of land where John Juba was buried until the Americans bought it after the war. In those days, it was a dairy farm. Now his wife was dead and, except for his chickens and his garden, he was retired from farming.

"The cemetery is very ~~very~~ beautiful, isn't it," he said. It was quiet most of the time, except on the last day of May ~~and in November when everyone comes~~ ~~to the cemetery with flowers.~~ "That's one of your holidays, isn't it."

But young people like you, he said, they never come to visit. "The young have forgotten all this."

What have they forgotten, we asked him.

"That the young who died delivered us," he said.."The ~~~~ young, they should come here."

We rode back to Paris on the train later that afternoon. ~~It was the first trip we had made with~~ I thought of the flowers from the old man's garden, lying at the foot of John Juba's grave, and I knew I ~~~~ would never forget.

52H

52

❡ Writers, as we have said, are members of a writing community. Scanlan showed his piece to Barbara Carton, a fellow writer on the *Providence Journal/Bulletin* who is now on the staff of the *Washington Post*. Here is her comment above the beginning of this late draft.❡

```
SLUG· JUBA2     VER·           DATE  29-SEP-01  TIME  16:47
PAP:  DAY:        ED:        PG:          ORIG: SCAN  ;25/29.16:4MSG:
FMT· NEWS6HJ:              ED              QU  SCA   FR· SCA   ;29/SD




       <NO>I think this is a really neat story. Because it's so neat   and  ecaus
   it
   was such a wonderful, unusual thing to take time out f your two  eek a year
   vacation. i want to know  more about  hy you did it and no  you felt,  ithout
   being sappy. Just the way you told it to me when you got  ack  Other ise,
   great.  <30>


       The Mercedes taxi sped along the  country highway. For the tenth time sin
   we left Paris that morning, I looked at the piece of paper in my hand.
       ``U.S. Military Cemetery.
   Marigny, France.
   9 miles west of St Lo.
   Row D Grave 12
   Pfc. John Juba Jr. 12 Inf. 4 Reg.
   Killed Aug. 1944. 19 years old.''
       That was all I knew about the man whose grave my wife and I were on our
   way to visit. Kathy and I were on a delayed honeymoon in Europe last June, a
```

53 A

❧ Now Scanlan has read his draft with Carton's comments in mind and then he writes the draft from which we have reprinted the first and last pages.❧

```
SLUG: GRA E      "ER:        DATE: 29-SEP-81  TIME: 12:15
PAP:  DAY:        E":        PG:           ORIG: SCA"  ;29/29.12:3"SG.
FMT: NEWS64J:    0052.2/0HD              ON  SCA"  FR: SCA"  ;29/SD.


<BO>By Christopher Scanlan<RC>

    The Mercedes taxi sped along the  ountry highway. For the tenth
time since we left Paris that morning, I looked at the pie e o° paper
in my hand.

    ``U.S. Military Cemetery.

    Marigny, Fra ce.

    9 miles west of St Lo.

    Ro. D Grave 12

    Pfc. John Juba Jr. 12 I f. 4 Reg.

    Killed Aug. 1944. 18 years old.''

    That was all I kne  about the ma  whose grave my wife a d I  ere
on our  ay to visit. Kathy a d I  ere o  a delayed ho eymo"  i
Europe last June, a month-lon  trip that had already ta en us to
Germa y, Holla d a d Paris. No , with a  eek left  ef re  e headed
home,  e  ere maki g g od o  a promise t  a frie d  ack i  Rhode
Island.

    Pat Callaha , a co- orker i  the <IT>Jour al<RC>  e sroo , did "t k c
much about John Juba either; his half- rother had  ee  killed  ef re
he was born. Pat didn't  now how he died, only that he was  uried i
Fra ce i  a grave  o re i  the family had ever see . He asked if  y
wife a d I  ould  i d visiti g the cemetery o  our vacatio . may e
take a picture of the  ravestone for his mother.. ``If it's o  your
way, of course,'' Pat said  ne  he ha ded  e the directio s a d that
was how we left it.

    It wasn't on our way, as it turned out, but all through our
vacation, the X  e'd marked  eside Marig y o  our map  f Fra ce
                          (MORE.)54A
```

SLUG: GRAVE   PAGE   5

woodsmoke and poured port wine into three china cups.

His name was Pierre Letrachart. He was 72 years old and for most
of his life he had lived in this farm country outside St. James. His
wife's family, in fact, had once owned the 27 acres of land where
John Juba was buried. It had been a dairy farm in those days, until
the Americans bought it after the war.

The cemetery was quiet most of the time, he said, except on the
last day of May when crowds came. ``That's one of your holidays,
isn't it.''

``But young people like you,'' he said, shaking his head, ``they
never come to visit. The young have forgotten all this.'' He didn't
sound angry, just a little sad.

What have they forgotten, we asked.

``That the young who died delivered us.'' he said. ``The young,
they should come here.''

We rode back to Paris on the train later that afternoon. I
thought of the flowers from the old man's garden lying at the foot of
John Juba's grave and I knew that I would never forget.

                              (END)

The article appeared in the *Sunday Journal Magazine,* but when it was reprinted, Scanlan touched it up some more and here is that final draft.

The Young Who Died Delivered Us

1   The Mercedes taxi sped along the country highway. For the tenth time since we left Paris that morning, I looked at the piece of paper in my hand.

2   "U.S. Military Cemetery
Marigny, France.
9 miles west of St. Lô.
Row D Grave 10.
Pfc. John Juba Jr. Inf. 4 Div.
Killed Aug. 4, 1944, 20 years old."

3   That was all I knew about the man whose grave my wife and I were on our way to visit. Kathy and I were on a delayed honeymoon in Europe, a month-long trip that had already taken us to Germany, Holland and Paris. Now, with a week left before we headed home, we were making good on a promise to a friend back home.

> ❧ Notice how quickly Scanlan gets you into the story. You are in the taxi and you know where you are and where you are going and why in just 21 lines. Also note how Scanlan uses narrative—the ancient skill of story telling—to carry the reader through the article. Finally, you should study how Scanlan has gotten out of the way. You are there. You are discovering the story with Scanlan. George Orwell, master to all journalists, tells us that "Good writing is like a window pane." Scanlan has the craft to construct a pane of glass so clear the reader does not even know it is there. ❧

4   Pat Callahan didn't know much about John Juba either; his half-brother had been killed before he was born. Pat didn't know how he died, only that he was buried in France in a grave no one in the family had ever seen. He asked if my wife and I would mind visiting the cemetery on our vacation, maybe take a picture of the gravestone for his mother. "If it's on your way, of course," Pat said when he handed me the directions, and that was how we left it.

5   It wasn't on our way, as it turned out, but all through our vacation the "X" we'd marked beside Marigny on our map of France nagged at us. I'd never met Pat's mother. Was she wondering if we'd

found the cemetery? Did she wait to hear what the place where her son was buried looked like? In the end, we didn't want to disappoint a woman who'd lost her first son in a war and never had the chance to pray at his grave. The day after we arrived in Paris we set out by train for Marigny, about 200 miles to the west.

Four hours later, the taxi we hired at the St. Lô station raced 6 through the rolling Normandy countryside, quickly eating up the nine miles left of our journey. For the first time that day I began to relax. We'd find the grave, take some pictures and make it back to Paris for a boat ride on the Seine without any problem.

"I didn't know there were any Americans buried in Marigny 7 anymore," the taxi driver said over his shoulder.

I was still trying to explain, in my rusty French, about the direc- 8 tions in my hand and how there had to be an American cemetery there because that's where this soldier was buried, when the cabbie turned off the highway towards Marigny and pointed to a sign planted in a grassy traffic island.

"German military cemetery," it said in French and German. 9 Kathy and I were staring at each other now, beginning to panic. They just don't pick up cemeteries and move them, I said. It's got to be there.

We came to a sleepy Main Street of stone shops, and the cabbie 10 stopped to consult a woman on the sidewalk.

"American cemetery?" she said. "Yes, there used to be one out- 11 side of town, but it's not there anymore. There are only Germans there now."

I wasn't ready to give up yet. "Maybe the Americans are buried 12 *with* the Germans," I suggested to the driver. He shook his head, but drove on. A few miles out of town, on a narrow road that wound its way through apple orchards and pastures, he turned onto a dirt driveway and pulled up in front of a tall, stone fence.

Behind it, we found a tree-shaded meadow lined with neat rows 13 of yellow rosebushes, like Normandy's hedgerows, stretching to the horizon. This was a curious cemetery.

There weren't many gravestones visible, just groups of brown 14 crosses set in a row and staggered among the rosebushes. The graves—11,169 of them, we learned from a brochure in the chapel—were marked by stone rectangles set into the earth. We only needed to read a few of the names inscribed on them—Heinz, Fried-rich, Gunther —to realize that our search for John Juba's grave hadn't ended. It had just begun.

❧ Note how neatly he works in the transition. ❧

15   "I think it was about 15 years ago they moved all the American graves," the cabbie told us on the way back to St. Lô. "As far as I know, there's only one American cemetery in Normandy now. It's a big one up north at Colleville sur Mer, on the shore. You could take a train to Bayeux and get a taxi out there. It's only about 30 kilometers."

16   We were hot, tired and hungry, but neither of us wanted to stop yet. We got on another train, and in less than an hour, a taxi deposited us in front of the visitors' building at the Normandy American Cemetery and Memorial.

17   In the office we found Pedro Rivera, a New Mexico native who was the cemetery's superintendent, and asked for his help. Yes, he told us, there had been an American cemetery at Marigny once, but it was a temporary one. After the war, the graves were moved to permanent cemeteries like this one perched on a cliff overlooking Omaha Beach and the English Channel.

18   He reached up to a wall shelf lined with half a dozen thick, black books, pulled one down and began flipping pages lined with columns of tiny print. If John Juba were buried overseas, Rivera said, his name would be in here. The books contained the names of American war dead buried overseas or commemorated as unknown or missing—35,000 names from World War I and more than 182,000 from World War II.

❧ Now he works in exposition, information that puts this particular veteran in context of other American war dead. ❧

19   American war dead lie in cemeteries around the world, Rivera told us, but a Normandy casualty could be found in only two places. Here, on the site of the largest amphibious assault in the history of the world, or in another cemetery about 60 miles south, in the province of Brittany.

20   "Here he is," the superintendent said, his finger stopping at the bottom of a page. "John Juba Jr. He was a Pfc." He paused and then looked up at us.

21   "Oh, I'm sorry," he said. "He's in Brittany."

22   "At least we'll be able to tell his mother where he is buried," I told Kathy outside the visitors' building. She nodded, but we were

both disappointed. We had a few hours to catch our train back to Paris, so we strolled in the cemetery, mixing with the crowds of schoolchildren, families of tourists and a contingent of French soldiers. The cemetery draws more than a million people a year, Rivera told us.

We passed by a 22-foot bronze statue of a young man, "The 23 Spirit of American Youth Rising from the Waves." The dead at Normandy lie under a carpet of grass kept green by lawn sprinklers waving back and forth over the white-marble headstones, 9,386 of them, set in single-file rows that reach to infinity. Beyond them, we came to the cliffs of Normandy and gazed down at the beach hundreds of yards below.

From books and movies, I knew something about the history 24 made on this spot, but it was hard to imagine it then.

It was raining on D-Day. Today the sun was warm, the sky as 25 blue as the water and dotted with puffy white clouds. Not an armada of ships, just a single sailboat; no dead, just a lone family sunbathing on the beach.

❡ Scanlan uses this peaceful scene to highlight the horror of war. He doesn't write with flowery language—especially adjectives and adverbs, but with specific detail. ❡

"You know, if we stop now," Kathy said, "all we can bring back 26 is what they gave us in the first place—an address."

I was surprised she wanted to go on. By now, we knew that 27 visiting John Juba's grave was going to mean spending another vacation day doing it. We'd have to return to Paris first and then set out again—this time for Brittany. "I wouldn't blame you if you wanted to quit," I said. "We tried."

"I know," she said, "but we can't stop now." She smiled. "It's 28 become a pilgrimage, like going to Lourdes."

The train back to Paris was crowded, and we had to take seats 29 apart. Kathy sat opposite two American college kids who, it turned out, had been at Normandy that day too. Omaha Beach attracted them for a reason different from ours though.

"We went," said the taller of the pair, otherwise identical in 30 shorts and nylon backpacks, "to lie on the beach, you know, catch some rays."

John Juba was 18 years old—about the same age as these two 31 college kids—when he was drafted out of trade school in 1942. Everyone called him Johnny. He loved to play football and baseball. He was engaged to a girl named Dorothy.

32   We didn't know any of this when we were searching for his grave last summer. It wasn't until we returned home that I learned more about him from his mother, Mrs. Ann Callahan, 76, who lives in the Hartford Park Housing Project in Providence.

33   Johnny grew up in New Kensington, Pa., where the family lived at the time. He wasn't happy to be drafted, his mother said. But she recalled a letter he once wrote from overseas. "I'd rather be here," he wrote, "than see a man that has a family."

34   "He stepped on a mine and it blew his legs off," his mother said. "He was still alive in the hospital, but when he found he lost his legs, the shock killed him."

35   It was raining two days later when we stepped out of a taxi at the gate to the Brittany American Cemetery and Memorial. There was no one in sight and the visitors' building was locked. We were headed for the graves when I realized that I had forgotten to bring flowers.

36   It had taken 17 years for someone to visit John Juba's grave and I wanted it to be a special occasion. Kathy was right. This was a pilgrimage, a journey to the grave of a soldier who could have been anyone's son, brother, father, husband. In some unspoken way, I felt that we had become his family, at least for this one day, and I knew that his family would have brought flowers.

37   "Wait here," I told Kathy and set off the rural highway in search of wildflowers. I was about to settle for a flowering carrot weed when I heard a radio through the open window of a stone farmhouse and saw beside it a garden bursting with white roses and snapdragons.

38   The old man who answered the back door wore scuffed black clogs, gardening clothes and a cap. His apple cheeks were whiskery with white stubble. I had interrupted his lunch; behind him, in the spartan stone kitchen, a bowl of bread, cheese and cherries sat on a table covered with an oilcloth.

❧ How quickly that man—who will be vital to the story—is made to come alive.❧

39   In my clumsy French, I told him about our search for the American soldier's grave and asked for permission to pick a few flowers from his garden. He turned away without a word.

I was about to leave myself—ready to believe that the French 40
do hate all Americans—when he reappeared with a pair of pruning
shears. He waved away my suggestion of payment. Bring your wife
back with you after you've seen the grave, he said. We'll visit and
drink some wine.

The graves at Brittany lie beyond the Wall of the Missing — 41
4,313 white crosses and Stars of David lined up on a manicured field
like a marching band at half time. Five varieties of grass keep it green
all year round. The cemetery was empty and so quiet we could hear
the rain falling on the flower beds bordering the graves.

Granite stones in the grass marked each section. I saw one 42
labelled "D" on the right side and ran over, excited and nervous at
the same time. What if he wasn't here either?

"Over here," I yelled to Kathy, a hundred yards behind me. I 43
cringed as my shout broke the stillness, and a man appeared in the
window of a house next door. Within moments he emerged, a middle-aged man in a tan raincoat who introduced himself as Donald
Davis, the superintendent of the cemetery.

"D-10-8," he said. "That's right down here." He led us down 44
nine rows of graves, turned down the tenth and began to count off
crosses. At the eighth, we stopped and found John Juba's name cut
into the white marble.

I laid the flowers in front of the cross and knelt to take a picture 45
for his mother.

"Wait." Davis bent down and turned the bouquet around so the 46
flowers faced the camera. "Otherwise, all you'll get is a picture of the
stems." Every trade has its secrets.

❡ That nice touch in the last sentence is a good example of voice. It
relieves the tension and gives the writer and the reader a chance to
express anger at what has happened to all these young men. ❦

"Rest in peace, John," I said under my breath. 47

The old Frenchman was outside trimming his rosebushes when 48
we returned. He invited us into the kitchen, where the air was tangy
with wood smoke, and poured port wine into three china cups.

His name was Piere Letranchant. He was 72 years old and for 49
most of his life he had lived in this farm country outside St. James.
His wife's family, in fact, had once owned the 27 acres of land where
John Juba was buried. It had been a dairy farm until the Americans
bought it after the war.

50   The cemetery was quiet most of the time, he said, except on the last day of May when crowds come. "That's one of your holidays, isn't it?"

51   "But young people like you," he said, shaking his head, "they never come to visit. The young have forgotten all this." He didn't sound angry, just a little sad.

52   "What have they forgotten?" we asked.

53   "That the young who died delivered us," he said. "The young, they should come here."

❡ Scanlan has found the title and the meaning of the piece. And he avoids sentimentality by getting out of the way—Orwell's counsel again—and allowing the quotation to do the job.❡

Here is Scanlan's account of how he read and wrote to produce that article.

Learning To Read Writing

1   "The Young Who Had Died Delivered Us" went through six drafts before it was published. That in itself makes it an unusual piece of writing for a working journalist like myself.

2   Journalism has been called "history in a hurry," and it is a discipline that teaches a writer to write fast and concentrate more on accuracy and clarity than style. Depending on the deadline, a reporter may only have time to try out a few leads and then forge ahead, making small changes as the writing is completed with an eye on the ticking clock.

3   While this nonfiction magazine story—a personal account of a search for a soldier's grave in Europe—gave me a luxury of time usually absent in most newsrooms, it taught me that time is not the secret in good writing: The real key to writing success is learning how to read a manuscript with a discriminating eye—and ear.

4   Studying how I wrote the story suggests the following rules to remember for the writer struggling to develop the necessary skills of "reading writing."

5   • Much of what you write will be discarded. Only a phrase on some draft pages will remain in the published version.
       • In the beginning, lower your critical standards and accept whatever pap flows from your pen or typewriter.

- The writing you think is fantastic will later prove to be dreck. The stuff you know is dreck will point you in the direction of better writing.
- The only way to improve a piece of writing is to rewrite and rewrite and rewrite and. . . .

I wish I could say that I knew all this when I began writing this 6
story, but that would be a lie. The importance of "reading writing" only became evident after I examined all of my drafts and the writing journal I keep.

The first draft of "The Young Who Died Delivered Us" was 7
2300 words long. The published version was slightly longer, about 2600 words. But a comparison of the two versions reveals that less than half of what I wrote in the first draft made it to the final version. A study of the writing process shows how crucial the reading of the text was to the changes between the beginning and end of the making of this story.

As a professional writer, my process generally begins with an 8
assignment, either from an editor or one I generate.

The story at hand began with a promise to a co-worker to look 9
up the grave of a relative killed in World War II and buried in France. Before we left, I had a vague idea that it might make a good freelance story for my paper's Sunday Magazine.

Armed with an idea, I always begin by collecting voluminous 10
amounts of information, much more than I will ever use. Much of it never appears in the final version, but I have a compulsion to learn as much about a subject as possible. I believe saturating myself gives me a confidence to write about subjects I know very little about. Journalists are expected to become instant experts, which is why a check with the newspaper's library is always one of my first, and most important, stops on any story.

During the trip chronicled in "The Young Who Had Died Deliv- 11
ered Us," I took careful notes in a travel diary, jotting down impressions and quotes from interviews. I collected brochures and other printed material at the military cemeteries we visited. After we returned home, I supplemented the field reporting with trips to the library where I consulted histories of D-Day and World War II and travel books about the regions of France we visited.

Two months passed before I sat down for my first writing ses- 12
sion one evening at the end of August. By then, I had told the story to friends so many times I was bored with it.

13   I can remember staring at the blank page for a while until I seized on an idea; transcribe your notes. That's always a good time-waster. I did that for about 45 minutes until I got bored again. I turned to my journal:

14   *One of the themes I'd like to explore is pacifism. War and Peace. What's it all about? Destroyed lives and lost chances. The cost of war. Was it worth it?*

15   Noble aims, but they didn't get me any closer to my story. Now I started talking to myself. "Can I tell you a story," I wrote.

16   "Thanks," I replied. But after a couple more exchanges like that, that bored me too.

17   Write a title. That's always a good beginning.

18   "In Search of John Juba."

19   "Searching for Juba."

20   Searching but getting nowhere. I stopped. Next morning, I tried titles again.

21   "Visiting a Soldier's Grave." Nope.

22   The only thing to do would be start at the beginning.

23   I wrote:

24   *One day in late May, I mentioned to Pat Callahan, a co-worker at the newspaper where I work, that my wife and I were going to Europe in June.*

25   After about two pages of longhand I reached the point where "Pat handed me a slip of paper with the address: U.S. Military Cemetery, Marigny, France, Plot K. Row 9, Grave 170. Pfc. John Juba Jr. Died Aug. 12, 1944 (20 years old)"

26   "The quest," I wrote now, "had begun."

27   I was amazed to find this passage staring out from my journal. The slip of paper with the address of John Juba's grave would eventually become my lead but at the time I didn't even recognize it.

28   During the writing I was experiencing the usual hair-pulling crises of confidence, mood swings and depression that accompany most of the writing I do, convinced almost until the end that I was incapable of writing anything worthwhile.

29   I know now that I was in the middle of the "rehearsal period," which follows the reporting. Like an actor practicing different deliveries, I was trying out leads and endings, hoping to discover my story and develop it by writing. I tell myself frequently to leave the judging until later (I used to keep that line taped to my typewriter. Now I use

a word processor and the line that stares at me from my VDT is one attributed to a Spanish poet: "Traveler, there is no path. Paths are made by walking.") I need to keep reminding myself that at this stage of any story, I must follow poet William Stafford's advice and lower my standards. I have to remember that to write well I must discover what a story is by writing it and rewriting it and not spend so much time hating the early drafts because they contain the promise of the final one.

At this point in the process, reading other writers is important. 30 I read for knowledge and inspiration, trying to prime the writing engine.

For instance, here is the first lead I wrote: 31

> It was to be our first trip to Europe. After almost six years of 32
> dreaming and hoping—and working—we had enough money to go.
> What if it was the downpayment for a house or enough for the IBM
> typewriter we wanted to buy. Someday we would have a house,
> someday that typewriter. But when would we ever have that first trip
> to Europe if we didn't take it now? That's what Kathy and I told each
> other last spring as we planned our itinerary. Germany, where her
> mother was born. Ireland, in search of my roots. France, because it
> was in the middle, plus whatever other sidetrips we could manage on
> a 15-day Eurail Pass. Our plans were vague, but that's how we
> wanted it. It was a vacation after all, not a pilgrimage.

My journal tells me that this lead was "inspired by Don Mur- 33 ray's essay on his daughter's rubber tree." Inspired by the voice, the emotion and his phrase "drunk on the possibility," a line came to me: "It was to be our first trip to Europe." I raced to the typewriter and in about 15 minutes wrote a lead which I like though I worry a bit about its apparent violation of some writing canons. But at least it gives me a beginning that persuades me to go on and that's all that counts.

Eventually I expanded that lead to eight legal-size pages that 34 became my first full-length draft. This was my "discovery draft." Reading this shapeless mass of prose, I discovered several things. I saw the skeleton of a story, which I used as the basis of an outline for my next draft. This draft also showed me what I wanted to say, often by the fact that I had not said it, and what I didn't want to say because I had said it and found it lacking.

For instance, by the time the next draft was finished, the open- 35 ing paragraph about our first trip to Europe was discarded. Only one element remains in the final version, the notion of a pilgrimage. All the other background—the house we wanted, the typewriter, our ethnic origins, I realized on rereading, was superfluous since this story was not about our vacation, but about the search that took it over for a few days in France.

36   A pilgrimage, that was the focus, the point, of the story I was struggling to write. Focus may be the most important *point* of all when you're reading your writing because in it lies the answers to those crucial questions a writer has about a draft: Does this line work? Is my organization sound? How do I begin my story? How do I end it?

37   As a journalist, my first responsibility is to the news, the information I am trying to convey. But in this complicated age of ours, information without context is meaningless. If the Public Utility Commission approves a rate increase for the electric company, that is the news, but the context, the focus, the point of my story, must take the news one step further in an effort to make it meaningful. Rather than write a lead that says "The PUC approved a $13 million rate hike yesterday," I would write it this way: "The electric bill for an average residential customer will go up $45 a month in January as a result of a rate increase approved yesterday by the PUC."

38   Two questions help me keep track of the focus of my stories as I write and read and rewrite. I write them at the top of my video display screen, even before the dateline. They are: What's the news? What's the point? Answering the first is usually easy. The second is often more difficult, probably because it is more crucial. The rewards are greater too, though, because forcing yourself to state the single dominant meaning may not only give you the focus. You may also hear the voice of your story.

39   A third question is essential when I know, the way a piano tuner recognizes discord, that a line just doesn't sound right. "What am I trying to say?" I ask myself. Often I type my answer and lo and behold, the problem is solved.

40   Every step along the way is critical, but for me, revision seems the most crucial. I am rarely satisfied with my writing, as this passage from my writing journal demonstrates.

41   *Session 9. 9 a.m. "Outlined a new draft (the 2nd) which I'll type today. Time is running out but the piece is getting more concise . . .:*

42   *11 a.m. Second draft completed. Now six pages, double-spaced about 1200 words, a far cry from the 2300 words of the first draft. It's closer now, but God it takes time.*

3 p.m. Second draft edited. Ready to type. Still not happy with the 43
lead, worried I'm leaving too much out. Why can't I just hand in
what I've got?"

4 p.m. "My central fear right now is that the editors at the magazine 44
will not like the piece, will have criticism of it and decide I'm no
good and never will want my stuff again."

By now I had typed the piece several times and was getting sick 45
of it.

But I still wasn't satisfied. 46

7:23 p.m. "Copy-edited. It stinks." 47

8:12 p.m. Retold the story in a tape recorder. It's better now." 48

For a long time, I thought my self-flagellation during the writing 49
process was a weakness, the sign of a hopeless neurotic. Now I see
it as a strength because it forces me to keep working on a story until
the meaning is clear. The effort has its rewards.

At one point, I had to push myself to type another draft and for 50
my pains I discovered a line that is one of my favorites. After the
cemetery superintendent told me to turn the flowers around for the
picture of the grave, the line "Every trade has its secrets" popped
into my head. So besides a clean draft, I got a good line from the
drudgery of typing.

Rewriting is like rubbing a dusty window with a cloth. The more 51
you rub the clearer the vision on the other side becomes.

Comparing an early draft with the published version of "The 52
Young Who Died Delivered Us" inspired a list of rules I try to
remember every time I write:

- Read your story with an eye out for what is missing. You may 53
  need to do more reporting.

When we went to Europe, we knew next to nothing about the 54
man whose grave we hunted. This is how I handled that paucity of
information in the early draft.

But that was about all we knew—or to this day—know about John 55
Juba. We don't know how he died or what he wanted to be if he had
made it back home. We don't know and in the end, we don't think it
really matters. What we learned standing in those cemeteries was the
price a nation pays when it goes to war.

56   That was a copout for not having the goods. A week before the final deadline I called John Juba's mother and after our conversation I knew I had the perfect juxtaposition for those two college kids we met at Normandy who went "to catch some rays."

57   *John Juba was 18 years old—about the same age as the two college kids on the train—when he was drafted out of trade school in 1942. Everyone called him Johnny. He loved to play football and baseball. He was engaged to a girl named Dorothy.*

58   It was one thing to say "What we learned standing in those cemeteries was the price a nation pays when it goes to war." It was quite another to use the details—trade school, a sports fan, a girl back home, and the awful details of death in wartime ("He stepped on a mine and it blew his legs off," his mother said. "He was still alive in the hospital, but when he found he lost his legs, the shock killed him.")

59   In three paragraphs, Juba became Everyman.

60   • Find co-readers of your work who can help you improve it.

61   While I wrote "The Young Who Died Delivered Us" credit for several important changes must be shared with people I think of as "co-readers." A co-reader is someone who has the unique capability of being able to read a piece of writing critically, and communicate their criticism in a way that does not make the writer want to push the typewriter out the window.

62   Here for example is how Barbara Carton, my newspaper colleague, encouraged me to write what is for me the most poignant passage in the story.

63   In the draft version I explained how I went off in search of flowers outside the Brittany cemetery and came across the old Frenchman who gave me my title.

64   Barbara could have said simply, "This passage doesn't work. It's too superficial and I just can't believe it. Needs work."

65   Instead she wrote, "This was such a nice thing to do." ..."I think you should explain more about how you felt too. Why you wanted to bring flowers for somebody you had never met. Without getting too maudlin, which is tough and I've never learned how to do this right."

66   And instead of ripping up the page, I found myself trying very hard to understand why I had felt it was so important to bring flowers.

It had taken 37 years for someone to visit John Juba's grave and I   67
wanted it to be a special occasion. Kathy was right. This was a
pilgrimage, a journey to the grave of a soldier who could have been
anyone's son, brother, father, husband. In some unspoken way, I felt
that we had become his family, at least for this one day, and I knew
that his family would have brought flowers.

- Read with your ears as well as your eyes.   68

The most important changes between drafts occurred after I   69
read the story aloud, either to my wife and once, even to a taperecorder. For instance, in the draft version, I wrote:

I was just about to leave, ready to finally accept the tourist truism   70
that the French hate Americans—when he reappeared with a pair of
pruning shears and added an invitation to return with my wife for a
visit and some wine.

Now there was a run-on sentence with definitely fatal syntac-   71
tical symptoms. Don Murray suggests three different types of reading
of drafts. First, a fast reading for context, at a distance, like a reader.
Have I left any questions unanswered? Have I supported my points?
Is the focus clear? (Could I say it in a single sentence?) The second
reading is slower and aimed at questions of form. Have I caught the
reader with a vivid lead that keeps its promise? Does my ending carry
the reader back through the story? Does the story have a logical basis,
answering questions and raising new ones to answer?

The third reading is line by line. The writer is a mechanic now,   72
reading to fine-tune. It is at this stage that I am looking for passive
verbs to replace with active ones, for run-on sentences to break up.

Here is how I rewrote that offending paragraph.   73

I was about to leave myself—ready to believe that the French do hate   74
all Americans—when he reappeared with a pair of pruning shears.
He waved away my suggestion of payment. Bring your wife back with
you after you've seen the grave. We'll have a visit and some wine.

By now, "The Young Who Died Delivered Us" has been pub-   75
lished five times, in *The Providence Journal, Catholic Digest, The Mil-
waukee Journal, The Pittsburgh Press* and *The Sacramento Bee.* What
has given me the most satisfaction, however, are the letters I have
received from readers who were touched by the story. "You seem to
have caught the feelings experienced by us who were there," wrote
one man who served with an Army Graves Registration unit and who

helped lay out the cemetery where John Juba is buried. A letter like that makes all the effort worthwhile.

76   But writers never stop "reading writing."

77   An editor at a writing seminar I attended a couple of years ago read the story and liked it too. But one passage needed work, he thought.

78   *I'd never met Pat's mother, but I kept wondering if we'd found the cemetery, waiting to hear what the place where her son was buried looked like.*

79   He was right. It was clumsy, which is why in the version I am sending out to editors this spring hoping they will publish it to mark the 40th anniversary of D-Day, that passage now reads:

80   *I'd never met Pat's mother. Was she wondering if we'd found the cemetery? Did she wait to hear what the place where her son was buried looked like?*

81   Is that an improvement? Well, at least it reads better.

Discussion

• What surprised you about this case study and Scanlan's writing methods? What is similar to the way you write? What is different?

• What do you think was Scanlan's most difficult problem in writing the piece? Did he solve it? How?

• What are the advantages of a taut, disciplined news style? The disadvantages? Compare his style to Caro's. What are the advantages and disadvantages of each style?

• Scanlan wrote a personal narrative of his search. What are the advantages of that approach? The disadvantages? What other ways could it have been written?

• How can you apply what Scanlan was teaching himself—according to his account—during the writing of this piece to the last piece you have written or the piece you are writing?

• Compare Scanlan's use of specific detail with Caro's in the following piece. (You may want to read ahead and compare Scanlan's use of detail to McPhee and Whiteside. You may also wish to compare Scanlan to other writers in the book who build on journalistic training. These include Mitchell, Zinsser, Orwell, Didion, Laurence and Hersey.)

Activities

- Write a different lead for the article by using something else in the piece or by changing the "I" into the third person, "he" or "she." You may even imagine some research that might have been in your notes had you been Scanlan.
- Apply one of Scanlan's "rules" to a draft of your own, and write a paragraph saying how it has affected your draft.
- Search for a person or a place that is important to the history of where you are living, and write an account of that search. Do not imitate Scanlan, but find your own way, and then compare your version to his.
- Interview a veteran of World War II, Korea or Vietnam to discover what people of your age need to know about the price of war.
- Take a draft of your own and imagine you are a journalist like Scanlan. See what happens if you use the discipline of the journalist as you rewrite your draft.
- Take a draft of your own and use specific details, as Scanlan does and as Caro does in the piece that follows. Write a paragraph describing what that does for your article.
- Ask a classmate to be a "co-reader" for a draft of your own. If someone asks you to be a co-reader, try to achieve the tone of Barbara Carton in your response.

Robert A. Caro

Writers are constantly sharing the news of other writers who have done an especially good job at our craft. John Monahan of the Worcester, Massachusetts, *Telegram/Gazette* shared his excitement at reading the chapter, "The Sad Irons" in Robert A. Caro's biography, *The Path to Power—The Years of Lyndon Johnson*. I went out the next day, bought the book, and read the chapter. Monahan had raved about the reporting that lay behind the chapter. He was right. It is a magnificent job of reporting and writing. Caro and his wife, Ina Joan Caro, who works with him, dig out details that reveal significance. This volume, the first of three, is one of the best political biographies I have read. When it was published it received the National Book Critics Circle award as the best nonfiction work of 1982.

Caro, who received the Pulitzer Prize for his biography of Robert Moses, *The Power Broker*, uses an enormous amount of detail, yet always remains the master of it, and writes with such grace that the reader is never lost in the density with which he explores the political world.

The Sad Irons

1   The source of water could be either a stream or a well. If the source was a stream, water had to be carried from it to the house, and since, in a country subject to constant flooding, houses were built well away from the streams, it had to be carried a long way. If the source was a well, it had to be lifted to the surface—a bucket at a time. It had to be lifted quite a long way; while the average depth of a well was about fifty feet in the valleys of the Hill Country, in the hills it was a hundred feet or more.

2   And so much water was needed! A federal study of nearly half a million farm families even then being conducted would show that, on the average, a person living on a farm used 40 gallons of water every day. Since the average farm family was five persons, the family used 200 gallons, or four-fifths of a ton, of water each day—73,000 gallons, or almost 300 tons, in a year. The study showed that, on the average, the well was located 253 feet from the house—and that to pump by hand and carry to the house 73,000 gallons of water a year would require someone to put in during that year 63 eight-hour days, and walk 1,750 miles.

❧ First he uses statistics, then he connects them with people below.❧

3   A farmer would do as much of this pumping and hauling as possible himself, and try to have his sons do as much of the rest as possible (it was Lyndon Johnson's adamant refusal to help his mother with the pumping and hauling that touched off the most bitter of the flareups with his father during his youth). As soon as a Hill Country youth got big enough to carry the water buckets (which held about four gallons, or thirty-two pounds, of water apiece), he was assigned the job of filling his mother's wash pots before he left for school or the field. Curtis Cox still recalls today that from the age of nine or ten, he would, every morning throughout the rest of his boyhood, make about seven trips between his house and the well, which were

about 300 feet.apart, on each of these trips carrying two large buckets, or more than 60 pounds, of water. "I felt tired," he says. "It was a lot of water." But the water the children carried would be used up long before noon, and the children would be away—at school or in the fields—and most of the hauling of water was, therefore, done by women. "I would," recalls Curtis' mother, Mary Cox, "have to get it, too—more than once a day, more than twice; oh, I don't know how many times. I needed water to wash my floors, water to wash my clothes, water to cook. . . . It was hard work. I was always packing (carrying) water." Carrying it—after she had wrestled off the heavy wooden lid which kept the rats and squirrels out of the well; after she had cranked the bucket up to the surface (and cranking—lifting thirty pounds fifty feet or more—was very hard for most women even with a pulley; most would pull the rope hand over hand, as if they were climbing it, to get their body weight into the effort; they couldn't do it with their arms alone). Some Hill Country women make wry jokes about getting water. Says Mrs. Brian Smith of Blanco: "Yes, we had running water. I always said we had running water because I grabbed those two buckets up and ran the two hundred yards to the house with them." But the joking fades away as the memories sharpen. An interviewer from the city is struck by the fact that Hill Country women of the older generation are noticeably stooped, much more so than city women of the same age. Without his asking for an explanation, it is given to him. More than once, and more than twice, a stooped and bent Hill Country farm wife says, "You see how round-shouldered I am? Well, that's from hauling the water." And, she will often add, "I was round-shouldered like this well before my time, when I was still a young woman. My back got bent from hauling the water, and it got bent when I was still young."

❡ The bent shoulders of these hill wives and their quotations make an historical situation contemporary. ❧

   The Hill Country farm wife had to haul water, and she had to   4
haul wood.
   Because there was no electricity, Hill Country stoves were wood   5
stoves. The spread of the cedar brakes had given the area a plentiful supply of wood, but cedar seared bone-dry by the Hill Country sun burned so fast that the stoves seemed to devour it. A farmer would try to keep a supply of wood in the house, or, if he had sons old enough, would assign the task to them. (Lyndon Johnson's refusal to

chop wood for his mother was another source of the tension between him and Sam.) They would cut down the trees and chop them into four-foot lengths that could be stacked in cords. When wood was needed in the house, they would cut it into shorter lengths and split the pieces so they could fit into the stoves. But as with the water, these chores often fell to the women.

6   The necessity of hauling the wood was not, however, the principal reason so many farm wives hated their wood stoves. In part, they hated these stoves because they were so hard to "start up." The damper that opened into the firebox created only a small draft even on a breezy day, and on a windless day, there was no draft—because there was no electricity, of course, there was no fan to move the air in the kitchen—and a fire would flicker out time after time. "With an electric stove, you just turn on a switch and you have heat," says Lucille O'Donnell, but with a wood stove, a woman might have to stuff kindling and wood into the firebox over and over again. And even after the fire was lit, the stove "didn't heat up in a minute you know," Lucille O'Donnell says—it might in fact take an hour. In part, farm wives hated wood stoves because they were so dirty, because the smoke from the wood blackened walls and ceilings, and ashes were always escaping through the grating, and the ash box had to be emptied twice a day—a dirty job and dirtier if, while the ashes were being carried outside, a gust of wind scattered them around inside the house. They hated the stoves because they could not be left unattended. Without devices to regulate the heat and keep the temperature steady, when the stove was being used for baking or some other cooking in which an even temperature was important, a woman would have to keep a constant watch on the fire, thrusting logs—or corncobs, which ignited quickly—into the firebox every time the heat slackened.

7   Most of all, they hated them because they were so hot.

> ❡ Caro varies the lengths of his paragraphs, using the the short ones for emphasis and the longer to carry a packed load of information to the reader. ❡

8   When the big iron stove was lit, logs blazing in its firebox, flames licking at the gratings that held the pots, the whole huge mass of metal so hot that it was almost glowing, the air in the kitchen shimmered with the heat pouring out of it. In the Winter the heat

was welcome, and in Spring and Fall it was bearable, but in the Hill Country, Summer would often last five months. Some time in June the temperature might climb to near ninety degrees, and would stay there, day after day, week after week, through the end of September. Day after day, week after week, the sky would be mostly empty, without a cloud as a shield from the blazing sun that beat down on the Hill Country, and on the sheet-iron or corrugated tin roofs of the box-like kitchens in the little dog-run homes that dotted its hills and valleys. No matter how hot the day, the stove had to be lit much of the time, because it had to be lit not only for meals but for baking; Hill Country wives, unable to afford store-bought bread, baked their own, an all-day task. (As Mrs. O'Donnell points out, "We didn't have refrigerators, you know, and without refrigerators, you just about have to start every meal from scratch.") In the Hill Country, moreover, Summer was harvest time, when a farm wife would have to cook not just for her family but for a harvesting crew—twenty or thirty men, who, working from sun to sun, expected three meals a day.

Harvest time, and canning time.   9

❡Again and again, Caro uses the natural process of what he is discussing, to carry his prose forward—getting water, washing, canning, ironing. He also uses process and process analysis to reveal political strategies and tactics and and you can use it in writing about business, sports, engineering, science.❡

In the Hill Country, canning was required for a family's very 10 survival. Too poor to buy food, most Hill Country families lived through the Winter largely on the vegetables and fruit picked in the Summer and preserved in jars.

Since—because there was no electricity—there were no refrig- 11 erators in the Hill Country, vegetables or fruit had to be canned the very day they came ripe. And, from June through September, something was coming ripe almost every day, it seemed; on a single peach tree, the fruit on different branches would come ripe on different days. In a single orchard, the peaches might be reaching ripeness over a span as long as two weeks; "You'd be in the kitchen with the peaches for two weeks," Hill Country wives recall. And after the peaches, the strawberries would begin coming ripe, and then the gooseberries, and then the blueberries. The tomatoes would become ripe before the okra, the okra before the zucchini, the zucchini before the corn. So the canning would go on with only brief intervals—all Summer.

12   Canning required constant attendance on the stove. Since boiling water was essential, the fire in the stove had to be kept roaring hot, so logs had to be continually put into the firebox. At least twice during a day's canning, moreover—probably three or four times—a woman would have to empty the ash container, which meant wrestling the heavy, unwieldy device out from under the firebox. And when the housewife wasn't bending down to the flames, she was standing over them. In canning fruit, for example, first sugar was dropped into the huge iron canning pot, and watched carefully and stirred constantly, so that it would not become lumpy, until it was completely dissolved. Then the fruit—perhaps peaches, which would have been peeled earlier—was put in the pot, and boiled until it turned into a soft and mushy jam that would be packed into jars (which would have been boiling—to sterilize them—in another pot) and sealed with wax. Boiling the peaches would take more than an hour, and during that time they had to be stirred constantly so that they would not stick to the pot. And when one load of peaches was finished, another load would be put in, and another. Canning was an all-day job. So when a woman was canning, she would have to spend all day in a little room with a tin or sheet-iron roof on which a blazing sun was beating down without mercy, standing in front of the iron stove and the wood fire within it. And every time the heat in that stove died down even a bit, she would have to make it hotter again.

13   "You'd have to can in the Summer when it was hot," says Kitty Clyde Ross Leonard, who had been Johnson's first girlfriend. "You'd have to cook for hours. Oh, that was a terrible thing. You wore as little as you could. I wore loose clothing so that it wouldn't stick to me. But the perspiration would just pour down my face. I remember the perspiration pouring down my mother's face, and when I grew up and had my own family, it poured down mine. That stove was so hot. But you had to stir, especially when you were making jelly. So you had to stand over that stove." Says Bernice Snodgrass of Wimberley: "You got so hot that you couldn't stay in the house. You ran out and sat under the trees. I couldn't stand it to stay in the house. Terrible. Really terrible. But you couldn't stay out of the house long. You had to stir. You had to watch the fire. So you had to go back into the house."

❧ Note how Caro uses quotation for authority and to bring in the voices of the hill country women as a variation on his own voice.❧

And there was no respite. If a bunch of peaches came ripe a 14 certain day, that was the day they had to be canned—no matter how the housewife might feel that day. Because in that fierce Hill Country heat, fruit and vegetables spoiled very quickly. And once the canning process was begun, it could not stop. "If you peeled six dozen peaches, and then, later that day, you felt sick, you couldn't stop," says Gay Harris. "Because you can't can something if it's rotten. The job has to be done the same day, no matter what." Sick or not, in the Hill Country, when it was time to can, a woman canned, standing hour after hour, trapped between a blazing sun and a blazing wood fire. "We had no choice, you see," Mrs. Harris says.

Every week, every week all year long—every week without 15 fail—there was washday.

The wash was done outside. A huge vat of boiling water would 16 be suspended over a larger, roaring fire and near it three large "Number Three" zinc washtubs and a dishpan would be placed on a bench.

The clothes would be scrubbed in the first of the zinc tubs, 17 scrubbed on a washboard by a woman bending over the tub. The soap, since she couldn't afford store-bought soap, was soap she had made from lye, soap that was not very effective, and the water was hard. Getting farm dirt out of clothes required hard scrubbing.

Then the farm wife would wring out each piece of clothing to 18 remove from it as much as possible of the dirty water, and put it in the big vat of boiling water. Since the scrubbing would not have removed all of the dirt, she would try to get the rest out by "punching" the clothes in the vat—standing over the boiling water and using a wooden paddle or, more often, a broomstick, to stir the clothes and swish them through the water and press them against the bottom or sides, moving the broom handle up and down and around as hard as she could for ten or fifteen minutes in a human imitation of the agitator of an automatic—electric—washing machine.

The next step was to transfer the clothes from the boiling water 19 to the second of the three zinc washtubs: the "rinse tub." The clothes were lifted out of the big vat on the end of the broomstick, and held up on the end of the stick for a few minutes while the dirty water dripped out.

20   When the clothes were in the rinse tub, the woman bent over the tub and rinsed them, by swishing each individual item through the water. Then she wrung out the clothes, to get as much of the dirty water out as possible, and placed the clothes in the third tub, which contained bluing, and swished them around in it—this time to get the bluing all through the garment and make it white—and then repeated the same movements in the dishpan, which was filled with starch.

21   At this point, one load of wash would be done. A week's wash took at least four loads: one of sheets, one of shirts and other white clothing, one of colored clothes and one of dish towels. But for the typical, large, Hill Country farm family, two loads of each of these categories would be required, so the procedure would have to be repeated eight times.

22   For each load, moreover, the water in each of the three washtubs would have to be changed. A washtub held about eight gallons. Since the water had to be warm, the woman would fill each tub half with boiling water from the big pot and half with cold water. She did the filling with a bucket which held three or four gallons—twenty-five or thirty pounds. For the first load or two of wash, the water would have been provided by her husband walking—over and over—that long walk to the spring or well, hauling up the water, hand over laborious hand, and carrying those heavy buckets back.*

23   Another part of washday was also a physical effort: the "punching" of the clothes in the big vat. "You had to do it as hard as you could—swish those clothes around and around and around. They never seemed to get clean. And those clothes were heavy in the water, and it was hot outside, and you'd be standing over that boiling water and that big fire—you felt like you were being roasted alive." Lifting the clothes out of the vat was an effort, too. A dripping mass of soggy clothes was heavy, and it felt heavier when it had to be lifted out of that vat and held up for minutes at a time so that the dirty water could drip out, and then swung over to the rinsing tub. Soon, if her children weren't around to hear her, a woman would be grunting with the effort. Even the wringing was, after a few hours, an effort. "I mean, wringing clothes might not seem hard," Mrs. Harris

---

*Because so much water was required in washing, the introduction of a gas-operated washing machine by the Maytag Company in 1935 did not help the farm wife much, even if she could afford to buy it, which most Hill Country wives could not: she still had to fill and refill the machine with water.

says, "But you have to wring every piece so many times—you wring it after you take it out of the scrub tub, and you wring it after you take it out of the rinse tub, and after you take it out of the bluing. Your arms got tired." And her hands—from scrubbing with lye soap and wringing—were raw and swollen. Of course, there was also the bending—hours of bending—over the rub boards. "By the time you got done washing, your back was broke," Ava Cox says. "I'll tell you—of the things of my life that I will never forget, I will never forget how much my back hurt on washdays." Hauling the water, scrubbing, punching, rinsing: a Hill Country farm wife did this for hours on end—while a city wife did it by pressing the button on her electric washing machine.

Washday was Monday, Tuesday was for ironing.   24

Says Mary Cox, in words echoed by all elderly Hill Country 25 farm wives; "Washing was hard work, but ironing was the worst. Nothing could ever be as hard as ironing."

The Department of Agriculture finds that "Young women today 26 are not aware of the origin of the word 'iron,' as they press clothes with lightweight appliances of aluminum or hollow stainless steel." In the Hill Country, in the 1930's an iron was IRON—a six- or seven-pound wedge of iron. The irons used in the Hill Country had to be heated on the wood stove, and they would retain their heat for only a few minutes—a man's shirt generally required two irons; a farm wife would own three or four of them, so that several could be heating while one was working. An iron with a wooden handle cost two dollars more than one without the handle, so Hill Country wives did their weekly loads of ironing—huge loads because, as Mary Cox puts it, "in those days you were expected to starch and iron almost everything"—with irons without handles. They would either transfer a separate wooden handle from one iron to another, or they would protect their hands with a thick potholder.

Since burning wood generates soot, the irons became dirty as 27 they sat heating on the stove. Or, if any moisture was left on an iron from the sprinkled clothes on which it had just been used, even the thinnest smoke from the stove created a muddy film on the bottom. The irons had to be cleaned frequently, therefore, by scrubbing them with a rag that had been dipped in salt, and if the soot was too thick, they had to be sanded and scraped. And no matter how carefully you checked the bottom of the irons, and sanded and scraped them, there would often remain some little spot of soot—as you would discover when you rubbed it over a clean white shirt or dress. Then you had to wash that item of clothing over again.

28   Nevertheless, the irons would burn a woman's hand. The wooden handle or the potholder would slip, and she would have searing metal against her flesh; by noon, she might have blister atop blister—on hands that had to handle the rag that had been dipped in salt. Ironing always took a full day—often it went on into Tuesday evening—and a full day of lifting and carrying six- or seven-pound loads was hard on even these hardy Hill Country women. "It would hurt so bad between the shoulders," Elsie Beck remembers. But again the worst aspect of ironing was the heat. On ironing day, a fire would have to be blazing in the wood stove all day, filling the kitchen, hour after hour, with heat and smoke. Ironing had to be done not only in the Winter but in the Summer—when the temperature outside the kitchen might be ninety or ninety-five or one hundred, and inside the kitchen would be considerably higher, and because there was no electricity, there was no fan to so much as stir the air. In a speech in Congress some years later, Representative John E. Rankin described the "drudgery" a typical farm wife endured, "burning up in a hot kitchen and bowing down over the washtub or boiling the clothes over a flaming fire in the summer heat." He himself remembered, he said, "seeing his mother lean over that hot iron hour after hour until it seemed she was tired enough to drop." Rankin was from Mississippi, but his description would have been familiar to the mothers of the Edwards Plateau. The women of the Hill Country never called the instruments they used every Tuesday "irons," they called them "sad irons."

29   Washing, ironing—those were chores that were performed every week. Then, of course, there were special occasions—harvest time and threshing time, when a woman had to cook not just for her family but for a crew of twenty or thirty men; the shearing, when, because there was no electricity and her husband had to work the shears, she had to crank the shearing machine, pedaling as if she were pumping a bicycle up a steep hill, pedaling, with only brief pauses, hour after hour; "He was always yelling 'Faster, faster,' " Mrs. Walter Yett of Blanco recalls. "I could hardly get up the next morning, I was so tired after that." Washing, ironing, cooking, canning, shearing, helping with the plowing and the picking and the sowing, and every day, carrying the water and the wood, and because there was no electricity, having to do everything by hand by the same

methods that had been employed by her mother and grandmother and great-great-great-grandmother before her—"They wear these farm women out pretty fast," wrote one observer. In the Hill Country, as many outside observers noted, the one almost universal characteristic of the women was that they were worn out before their time, that they were old beyond their years, old at forty, old at thirty-five, bent and stooped and tired.

> ❧Caro repeats the description of stooped women, reminding you of the reasons for it. Effective writers are always weaving such threads through their drafts.❧

A Hill Country farm wife had to do her chores even if she was 30 ill—no matter how ill. Because Hill Country women were too poor to afford proper medical care, they often suffered perineal tears in childbirth. During the 1930's, the federal government sent physicians to examine a sampling of Hill Country women. The doctors found that, out of 275 women, 158 had perineal tears. Many of them, the team of gynecologists reported, were third-degree tears, "tears so bad that it is difficult to see how they stand on their feet." But they WERE standing on their feet, and doing all the chores that Hill Country wives had always done—hauling the water, hauling the wood, canning, washing, ironing, helping with the shearing, the plowing and the picking.

Because there was no electricity.   31

Discussion

- List the techniques Caro has used to make statistics come alive. Discuss how these techniques might be used in something you are writing.
- Take a paragraph which has been packed with detail by another writer in the book—for example, McPhee, Whiteside, Baldwin, Didion—and discuss the similarities and differences in their technique.
- Discuss what techniques Caro uses to keep the reader interested. How does he use them? How could you use them on a draft you are writing?
- Make a list of the different types of details you would need to write a persuasive government report, business proposal, scientific paper, or another form of writing. If you do not know the kind of writing you will have to do after school, interview someone in the field or a professor in the area in which you may work after school.

• Outline a page of Caro, to see how he has made his case. Discuss how a similar pattern of development could be used on a page of a class-mate's draft.

Activities

• Take a page of Caro that is filled with detail and write it with gen-eralizations, then compare the two versions to see the difference that makes to the reader. Which would make you care?

• Take a paragraph from a draft you are working on and develop it with detail as Caro would.

• Interview people in your family, neighbors, and other survivors you can find to discover the kind of details Caro uses so you can recreate a moment in The Depression, the Civil Rights Movement, the Holocaust, World War II, the Korean or the Vietnam War, the Internment of Japanese Americans during World War II or some other historic moment.

• Use library sources to recreate a time far enough in the past so that there are no living survivors. Limit your subject. For example, an hour in the trek when people pulled wagons on a Mormon trek to Utah, an hour at a witch trial in colonial Massachusetts, an hour fighting the great Chicago fire.

• Imagine that you are a Caro 50 years from now who is trying to recreate the present time. Choose an activity or process or place in your life and describe it in as much detail as Caro uses.

Joseph Mitchell

In Japan, a few highly respected craftspersons are declared national treasures and the government makes sure they receive support and respect. Many nonfiction writers would vote for Joseph Mitchell as a national treasure if we had such a program. A native of North Carolina, Mitchell went to New York City in 1929, shortly after he was graduated from the University of North Carolina. He was a reporter for the *Herald Tribune* and the *World-Telegram* when those papers established a new standard for grace and wit in their writing. In 1939 he joined the staff of *New Yorker* magazine. His books include *My Ears Are Bent, McSorley's Wonderful Saloon, Old Mr.*

Flood, and *The Bottom of the Harbor.* He has published little in recent years but his books are treasured by writers who care about craft and style. I have chosen to go through this selection carefully with you because I keep going back to Mitchell to learn how to write and my comments will show an old writer studying one of his masters.

Up in the Old Hotel

Every now and then, seeking to rid my mind of thoughts of 1 death and doom, I get up early and go down to Fulton Fish Market. I usually arrive around five-thirty, and take a walk through the two huge open-fronted market sheds, the Old Market and the New Market, whose fronts rest on South Street and whose backs rest on piles in the East River. At that time, a little while before the trading begins, the stands in the sheds are heaped high and spilling over with forty to sixty kinds of finfish and shellfish from the East Coast, the West Coast, the Gulf Coast, and half a dozen foreign countries. The smoky riverbank dawn, the racket the fishmongers make, the seaweedy smell, and the sight of this plentifulness always give me a feeling of well-being, and sometimes they elate me. I wander among the stands for an hour or so. Then I go into a cheerful market restaurant named Sloppy Louie's and eat a big, inexpensive, invigorating breakfast—a kippered herring and scrambled eggs, or a shad-roe omelet, or split sea scallops and bacon, or some other breakfast specialty of the place.

❧ Notice the first two clauses, the first half of the first sentence. Mitchell immediately establishes a conversational tone, the voice of a relaxed companion telling a single human being a story. When you finish the article you will realize that there is foreshadowing— preparing the reader for what is to come—and there is also irony— the events in the piece will cause him to think of death and doom. There is also surprise in the sentence. We are immediately surprised by the fact that he is going to the Fulton Fish Market to rid his mind of thoughts of death and doom. Mitchell gives us a satisfying order of information about the fish market, working in the senses of sight, hearing, and smell. Then taste, and surprise again as he introduces us to Sloppy Louie's and their breakfast specialties. I often read this paragraph aloud for the delight I receive from its voice and its music. It is one of my favorite leads, for I cannot help but read on. ❧

2   Sloppy Louie's occupies the ground floor of an old building at 92 South Street, diagonally across the street from the sheds. This building faces the river and looks out on the slip between the Fulton Street fish pier and the old Porto Rico Line dock. It is six floors high, and it has two windows to the floor. Like the majority of the older buildings in the market district, it is made of hand-molded Hudson River brick, a rosy-pink and relatively narrow kind that used to be turned out in Haverstraw and other kiln towns on the Hudson and sent down to the city in barges. It has an ornamented tin cornice and a slate-covered mansard roof. It is one of those handsome, symmetrical old East River waterfront buildings that have been allowed to dilapidate. The windows of its four upper floors have been boarded over for many years, a rain pipe that runs down the front of it is riddled with rust holes, and there are gaps here and there on its mansard where slates have slipped off. In the afternoons, after two or three, when the trading is over and the stands begin to close, the slimy, overfed gulls that scavenge in the market roost by the hundreds along its cornice, hunched up and gazing downward.

❧ This is a beautiful example of description, written with such precise detail that it seems effortless. He brings in some history and decorates the building with the seagulls. We learn from this paragraph not only what Sloppy Louie's building looks like, but also its past and present context. ❧

3   I have been going to Sloppy Louie's for nine or ten years, and the proprietor and I are old friends. His name is Louis Morino, and he is a contemplative and generous and worldly-wise man in his middle sixties. Louie is a North Italian. He was born in Recco, a fishing and bathing-beach village thirteen miles southeast of Genoa, on the Eastern Riviera. Recco is ancient; it dates back to the third century. Families in Genoa and Milan and Turin own villas in and around it, and go there in the summer. Some seasons, a few English and Americans show up. According to a row of colored-postcard views of it Scotch-taped to a mirror on the wall in back of Louie's cash register, it is a village of steep streets and tall, square, whitewashed stone houses. The fronts of the houses are decorated with stenciled designs—madonnas, angels, flowers, fruit, and fish. The fish design is believed to protect against the evil eye and appears most often over doors and windows. Big, lush fig bushes grow in almost every yard. In the center of the village is an open-air market where fishermen

and farmers sell their produce off plank-and-sawhorse counters. Louie's father was a fisherman. His name was Giuseppe Morino, and he was called, in Genoese dialect, Beppe du Russu, or Joe the Redhead. "My family was one of the old fishing families in Recco that the priest used to tell us had been fishing along that coast since Roman times," Louis says. "We lived on a street named the Vico Saporito that was paved with broken-up sea shells and wound in and out and led down to the water. My father did a kind of fishing that's called haul-seining over here, and he set lobster traps and jigged for squid and bobbed for octopuses. When the weather was right, he used to row out to an underwater cave he knew about and anchor over it and take a bob consisting of a long line with scraps of raw meat hung from it every foot or so and a stone on the end of it and drop it in the mouth of the cave, and the octopuses would shoot up out of the dark down there and swallow the meat scraps and that would hold them, and then my father would draw the bob up slow and steady and pull the octopuses loose from the meat scraps one by one and toss them in a tub in the boat. He'd bob up enough octopuses in a couple of hours to glut the market in Recco. This cave was full of octopuses; it was choked with them. He had found it, and he had the rights to it. The other fishermen didn't go near it; they called it Beppe du Russu's cave. In addition to fishing, he kept a rickety old bathhouse on the beach for the summer people. It stood on stilts, and I judge it had fifty to sixty rooms. We called it the Bagni Margherita. My mother ran a little buffet in connection with it."

> ❦ Now Mitchell introduces Louie. Too many human beings are seen as "characters" in newspaper and magazine stories. Louie is treated with respect, and having been given the history of the building, we are now given the heritage of Louie. Note how Mitchell has made use of the postcards on the wall behind the cash register, a detail a lesser reporter would not have seen. He also allows the reader to meet Louie and hear him telling his own story. Mitchell gets out of the way whenever he can, as Scanlan did in his story, although both writers were participants in their own stories. ❧

Louie left Recco in 1905, when he was close to eighteen. "I   4
loved my family," he says, "and it tore me in two to leave, but I had five brothers and two sisters, and all my brothers were younger than me, and there were already too many fishermen in Recco, and the bathhouse brought in just so much, and I had a fear kept persisting there might not be enough at home to go around in time to come, so

I got passage from Genoa to New York scrubbing pots in the galley of a steamship and went straight from the dock to a chophouse on East 138th Street in the Bronx that was operated by a man named Capurro who came from Recco. Capurro knew my father when they both were boys." Capurro gave Louie a job washing dishes and taught him how to wait on tables. He stayed there two years. For the next twenty-three years, he worked as a waiter in restaurants all over Manhattan and Brooklyn. He has forgotten how many he worked in; he can recall the names of thirteen. Most of them were medium-size restaurants of the Steak-&-Chops, We-Specialize-in-Seafood type. In the winter of 1930, he decided to risk his savings and become his own boss. "At that time," he says, "the stockmarket crash had shook everything up and the depression was setting in, and I knew of several restaurants in midtown that could be bought at a bargain—lease, furnishings, and good will. All were up-to-date places. Then I ran into a waiter I used to work with and he told me about this old run-down restaurant in an old run-down building in the fish market that was for sale, and I went and saw it, and I took it. The reason I did, Fulton Fish Market reminds me of Recco. There's a world of difference between them. At the same time, they're very much alike—the fish smell, the general gone-to-pot look, the trading that goes on in the streets, the roofs over the sidewalks, the cats in corners gnawing on fish heads. the gulls in the gutters, the way everybody's on to everybody else, the quarreling and the arguing. There's a boss fishmonger down here, a spry old hardheaded Italian man who's got a million dollars in the bank and dresses like he's on relief and walks up and down the fish pier snatching fish out of barrels by their tails and weighing them in his hands and figuring out in his mind to a fraction of a fraction how much they're worth and shouting and singing and enjoying life, and the face on him, the way he conducts himself, he reminds me so much of my father that sometimes, when I see him, it puts me in a good humor, and sometimes it breaks my heart."

> ❡ When you read this piece for the first time you may delight in all the historical detail, the memories of the past revealed through Louie, but you may wonder why you are being given this. In effective writing every word should count, every line should move the reader forward. These details are not tossed on the page; they are all purposeful. They all lead the reader toward the meaning of the piece. They help the reader develop a respect and an interest for the

times that are past. They may make the reader stop, daydream, think about the pasts in their own lives and in the lives of their families. And Mitchell will be delighted, for the writer wants to make the reader think. All of these accounts of the past make us realize what we have lost—and that we will lose what we have. The present will become the past.❼

Louie is five feet six, and stocky. He has an owl-like face—his nose is hooked, his eyebrows are tufted, and his eyes are large and brown and observant. He is white-haired. His complexion is reddish, and his face and the backs of his hands are speckled with freckles and liver spots. He wears glasses with flesh-colored frames. He is bandy-legged, and he carries his left shoulder lower than his right and walks with a shuffling, hipshot, head-up, old-waiter's walk. He dresses neatly. He has his suits made by a high-priced tailor in the insurance district, which adjoins the fish-market district. Starting work in the morning, he always puts on a fresh apron and a fresh brown linen jacket. He keeps a napkin folded over his left arm even when he is standing behind the cash register. He is a proud man, and somewhat stiff and formal by nature, but he unbends easily and he has great curiosity and he knows how to get along with people. During rush hours, he jokes and laughs with his customers and recommends his daily specials in extravagant terms and listens to fish-market gossip and passes it on; afterward, in repose, having a cup of coffee by himself at a table in the rear, he is grave.

❧Now we have a classic example of the description of a person. Louie is made to come alive on the page. We are given details that we know from our own living and can use to draw the picture in our minds Mitchell wants us to have. Mitchell knows his readers in *The New Yorker,* where this was first published, and he knows, for example, that they will be familiar with restaurants that have staffs with "old-waiter's walk." Note how the last word, a foreshadowing and a weaving back to death and doom, sets up the transition to the next paragraph. ❼

Louie is a widower. His wife, Mrs. Victoria Piazza Morino, came from a village named Ruta that is only two and a half miles from Recco, but he first became acquainted with her in Brooklyn. They were married in 1928, and he was deeply devoted to her. She died in 1949. He has two daughters—Jacqueline, who is twenty-two and was recently graduated from the Mills College of Education, a school for nursery, kindergarten, and primary teachers on lower Fifth Avenue, and Lois, who is seventeen and was recently graduated from Fontbonne Hall, a high school on Shore Road in Brooklyn that is operated by the Sisters of St. Joseph. They are smart, bright, slim, vivid, dark-eyed girls. Louie has to be on hand in his restaurant in the early morning, and he usually gets up between four and five, but before leaving home he always squeezes orange juice and puts coffee on the stove for his daughters. Most days, he gets home before they do and cooks dinner.

> ❧ Mitchell avoids sentimentality. He doesn't write about these sad things in Louie's life with adjectives and adverbs, but primarily with details. He never talks in generalities of how Louie is both father and mother to his daughters; he tells you the anecdotal details of how he fixed breakfast for them, and ends on the flat but poignant note that he cooks dinner for them.❧

7   Louie owns his home, a two-story brick house on a maple-bordered street in the predominantly Norwegian part of the Bay Ridge neighborhood in Brooklyn. There is a saying in Recco that people and fig bushes do best close to salt water; Louie's home is only a few blocks from the Narrows, and fifteen years ago he ordered three tiny fig bushes from a nursery in Virginia and set them out in his back yard, and they have flourished. In the late fall, he wraps an accumulation of worn-out suits and dresses and sweaters and sheets and blankets around their trunks and limbs. "All winter," he says, "when I look out the back window, it looks like I got three mummies stood up out there." At the first sign of spring, he takes the wrappings off. The bushes begin to bear the middle of July and bear abundantly during August. One bush bears small white figs, and the others bear plump black figs that split their skins down one side as they ripen and gape open and show their pink and violet flesh. Louie likes to gather the figs around dusk, when they are still warm from the heat of the day. Sometimes, bending beside a bush, he plunges his face into the leaves and breathes in the musky smell of the ripening figs, a smell that fills his mind with memories of Recco in midsummer.

> ❧ Mitchell satisfies the curiosity that readers didn't know they had. He tells them about the fig trees they have seen wrapped with cloth in Italian yards. Again we are reminded of what is lost. Louie has

moved from a warm climate to a cold one, from an old world to a new one, but he saves a little bit of it. This is all told in precise, specific detail. ❧

Louie doesn't think much of the name of his restaurant. It is an 8 old restaurant with old furnishings that has had a succession of proprietors and a succession of names. Under the proprietor preceding Louie, John Barbagelata, it was named the Fulton Restaurant, and was sometimes called Sloppy John's. When Louie took it over, he changed the name to Louie's Restaurant. One of the fishmongers promptly started calling it Sloppy Louie's, and Louie made a mistake and remonstrated with him. He remonstrated with him on several occasions. As soon as the people in the market caught on to the fact that the name offended Louie, naturally most of them began using it. They got in the habit of using it. Louie brooded about the matter off and on for over three years, and then had a new swinging signboard erected above his door with SLOPPY LOUIE'S RESTAURANT on it in big red letters. He even changed his listing in the telephone book, "I couldn't beat them," he says, "so I joined them."

❧A change of pace—that is one reason that there is an extra space before the beginning of the previous paragraph. It's a signal the reader should pay attention to. A new section of the piece is beginning, and it starts with a surprise. He doesn't like the name of his restaurant. We have been having a pretty heavy dose of death and doom; now we get some humor. ❧

Sloppy Louie's is small and busy. It can seat eighty, and it 9 crowds up and thins out six or seven times a day. It opens at five in the morning and closes at eight-thirty in the evening. It has a double door in front with a show window on each side. In one window are three sailing-ship models in whiskey bottles, a giant lobster claw with eyes and a mouth painted on it, a bulky oyster shell, and a small skull. Beside the shell is a card on which Louie has neatly written, "Shell of an Oyster dredged from the bottom of Great South Bay. Weighed two and a quarter pounds. Estimated to be fifteen years old. Said to be largest ever dredged in G.S.B." Beside the skull is a similar card, which says, "This is the skull of a Porpoise taken by a dragger off Long Beach, Long Island." In the other window is an old pie cupboard with glass sides. To the left, as you enter, is a combined cigar showcase and cashier's desk, and an iron safe with a cash register on top of it. There are mirrors all around the walls. Four lamps and three electric fans with wooden blades that resemble propellers hang from the stamped-tin ceiling. The tables in Louie's are communal, and there are exactly one dozen; six jut out from the wall on one side of the room and six jut out from the wall on the other side, and a broad aisle divides them. They are long tables, and solid and old and plain and built to last. They are made of black walnut; Louie once repaired a leg on one, and said it was like driving a nail in iron. Their tops have been seasoned by drippings and spillings from thousands upon thousands of platters of broiled fish, and their edges have been scratched and scarred by the hatchets and bale hooks that hang from frogs on fishmongers' belts. They are identical in size; some seat six, and some have a chair on the aisle end and seat seven. At the back of the room, hiding the door to the kitchen, is a huge floor mirror on which, each morning, using a piece of moistened chalk, Louie writes the menu for the day. It is sometimes a lengthy menu. A good many dishes are served in Louie's that are rarely served in other restaurants. One day, interspersed among the staple seafood-restaurant dishes, Louie listed cod cheeks, salmon cheeks, cod tongues, sturgeon liver, blue-shark steak, tuna steak, squid stew, and five kinds of roe—shad roe, cod roe, mackerel roe, herring roe, and yellow-pike roe. Cheeks are delectable morsels of flesh that are found in the heads of some species of fish, one on each side, inset in bone and cartilage. The men who dress fish in the fillet houses in the market cut out a few quarts of cheeks whenever they have the time to spare and sell them to Louie. Small shipments of them come down occasionally from the Boston Fish Pier, and the fishmongers, thinking of their own gullets, let Louie buy most of them. The fishmongers use Louie's as a testing kitchen. When anything unusual is shipped to the market, it is taken to Louie's and tried out. In the course of a year, Louie's undoubtedly serves a wider variety of seafood than any other restaurant in the country.

❡Everything in this piece works in a natural order. The reader is carried along with the flow of the writing. The narrator explains why he goes to Sloppy Louie's, we see the building from the outside, we meet Louie, and now we get into the restaurant. There is an almost inexpressible amount of delight for a writer reading Mitchell, and that delight comes both from the ease of the writing (which isn't so easy to do) and the lovely little demonstrations of craft. He could have said, "The restaurant is jammed six or seven times a day."

Instead he said, "it crowds up and thins out six or seven times a day." You feel the tidal wave of customers flowing in and out. Mitchell knows, and the reader senses, that this restaurant will disappear, but it will remain in the memories of those who have eaten there and those who read this piece after they have gone. A writer has to love and read aloud the lists as Mitchell uses them. "Cod cheeks, salmon cheeks, cod tongues, sturgeon liver, blue-shark steak, tuna steak, squid stew, and five kinds of roe—shad roe, cod roe, mackerel roe, herring roe, and yellow-pike roe." Arrange that list properly and you have a poem. And notice how Mitchell works in exposition and definition, gracefully allowing the uneducated reader to discover what "cheeks" are. ❼

When I go to Sloppy Louie's for breakfast, I always try to get a   10
chair at one of the tables up front, and Louie generally comes out from behind the cash register and tells me what is best to order. Some mornings, if there is a lull in the breakfast rush, he draws him-self a cup of coffee and sits down with me. One morning a while back, he sat down, and I asked him how things were going, and he said he couldn't complain, he had about as much business as he could handle. "My breakfast trade still consists almost entirely of fishmongers and fish buyers," he said, "but my lunch trade has undergone a change. The last few years, a good many people in the districts up above the market have taken to walking down here occa-sionally for lunch—people from the insurance district, the financial district, and the coffee-roasting district. Some days, from noon to three, they outnumber the fishmongers. I hadn't realized myself how great a change had taken place until just the other day I happened to notice the mixed-up nature of a group of people sitting around one table. They were talking back and forth, the way people do in here that never even saw each other before, and passing the ketchup, and I'll tell you who they were. Sitting on one side was an insurance bro-ker from Maiden Lane, and next to him was a fishmonger named Mr. Frank Wilkisson who's a member of a family that's had a stand in the Old Market three generations, and next to him was a young Southerner that you're doing good if you understand half what he says who drives one of those tremendous big refrigerator trucks that they call reefers and hits the market every four or five days with a load of shrimp from little shrimp ports in Florida and Georgia. Sitting on the other side was a lady who holds a responsible position in Con-tinental Casualty up on William Street and comes in here for bouil-labaisse, only we call it *ciuppin di pesce* and cook it the way it's

cooked fishing-family style back in Recco, and next to her was an old gentleman who works in J. P. Morgan & Company's banking house and you'd think he'd order something expensive like pompano but he always orders cod cheeks and if we're out of that he orders cod roe and if we're out of that he orders broiled cod and God knows we're never out of that, and next to him was one of the bosses in Mooney's coffee-roasting plant at Fulton and Front. And sitting at the aisle end of the table was a man known all over as Cowhide Charlie who goes to slaughterhouses and buys green cowhides and sells them to fishing-boat captains to rig to the undersides of their drag nets to keep them from getting bottom-chafed and rock-cut and he's always bragging that right this very minute his hides are rubbing the bottom of every fishing bank from Nantucket Shoals to the Virginia Capes."

℘ Read this paragraph aloud and you'll hear the voice of the restaurant owner and see the restaurant's customers from his point of view. The quote rolls along, and it purposefully runs on. Its flow demonstrates how much Louie knows about his customers. He could talk for hours about his customers, and probably did to Mitchell.

In the paragraphs ahead Mitchell uses dialogue to break up the text and to set up the main point of the piece—remember the title: "Up in the Old Hotel." Now we are going to be introduced to the hotel. Dialogue is also good to bring in a little dramatic tension. One person knows something and the other is trying to find it out. And then you're set up for the surprise. Louie is an intelligent man, a man of sensitivity who has been tested by loss and discovery, birth and death, and yet he has never explored this museum of history above his head. The reader feels tension and suspense. Will he— we—explore? What will he—we—find? Again notice the details. "The cage is all furry with dust, and there's mold and mildew on the walls of the shaft, and the air is dead." ❦

11   Louie said that some days, particularly Fridays, the place is jammed around one o'clock and latecomers crowd together just inside the door and stand and wait and stare, and he said that this gets on his nerves. He said he had come to the conclusion that he would have to go ahead and put in some tables on the second floor.

12   "I would've done it long ago," he said, "except I need the second floor for other things. This building doesn't have a cellar. South Street is old filled-in river swamp, and the cellars along here, what

few there are, the East River leaks into them every high tide. The second floor is my cellar. I store supplies up there, and I keep my Deepfreeze up there, and the waiters change their clothes up there. I don't know what I'll do without it, only I got to make room someway."

"That ought to be easy," I said. "You've got four empty floors 13 up above."

"You mean those boarded-up floors," Louie said. He hesitated 14 a moment. "Didn't I ever tell you about the upstairs in here?" he asked. "Didn't I ever tell you about those boarded-up floors?"

"No," I said. 15

"They aren't empty," he said. 16

"What's in them?" I asked. 17

"I don't know," he said. "I've heard this and I've heard that, 18 but I don't know. I wish to God I did know. I've wondered about it enough. I've rented this building twenty-two years, and I've never been above the second floor. The reason being, that's as far as the stairs go. After that, you have to get in a queer old elevator and pull yourself up. It's an old-fashioned hand-power elevator, what they used to call a rope-pull. I wouldn't be surprised it's the last of its kind in the city. I don't understand the machinery of it, the balancing weights and the cables and all that, but the way it's operated, there's a big iron wheel up at the top of the shaft and the wheel's got a groove in it, and there's a rope that rides in this groove, and you pull on the part of the rope that hangs down one side of the cage to go up, and you pull on the part that hangs down the other side to go down. Like a dumb-waiter. It used to run from the ground floor to the top, but a long time ago some tenant must've decided he didn't have any further use for it and wanted it out of the way, so he had the shaft removed from the ground floor and the second floor. He had it cut off at the second-floor ceiling. In other words, the way it is now, the bottom of the shaft is level with the second-floor ceiling—the floor of the elevator cage acts as part of the ceiling. To get in the elevator you have to climb a ladder that leads to a trap door that's cut in the floor of the cage. It's a big, roomy cage, bigger than the ones nowadays, but it doesn't have a roof on it—just this wooden floor and some iron-framework sides. I go up the ladder sometimes and push up the trap door and put my head and shoulders inside the cage and shine a flashlight up the shaft, but that's as far as I go. Oh, Jesus, it's dark and dusty in there. The cage is all furry with dust and there's mold and mildew on the walls of the shaft and the air is dead.

"The first day I came here, I wanted to get right in the elevator 19
and go up to the upper floors and rummage around up there, see
what I could see, but the man who rented the building ahead of me
was with me, showing me over the place, and he warned me not to.
He didn't trust the elevator. He said you couldn't pay him to get in
it. 'Don't meddle with that thing,' he said. 'It's a rattlesnake. The
rope might break, or that big iron wheel up at the top of the shaft
that's eaten up with rust and hasn't been oiled for a generation might
work loose and drop on your head.' Consequently, I've never even
given the rope a pull. To pull the rope you got to get inside the cage
and stand up. You can't reach it otherwise. I've been tempted to
many a time. It's a thick hemp rope. It's as thick as a hawser. It might
be rotten, but it certainly looks strong. The way the cage is sitting
now, I figure it'd only take a couple of pulls, a couple of turns of the
wheel, and you'd be far enough up to where you could swing the cage
door open and step out on the third floor. You can't open the cage
door now; you got to draw the cage up just a little. A matter of inches.
I reached into the cage once and tried to poke the door open with a
boat hook I borrowed off one of the fishing boats, but it wouldn't
budge. It's a highly irritating situation to me. I'd just like to know for
certain what's up there. A year goes by sometimes and I hardly think
about it, and then I get to wondering, and it has a tendency to prey
on my mind. An old-timer in the market once told me that many
years ago a fishmonger down here got a bug in his head and invented
a patented returnable zinc-lined fish box for shipping fish on ice and
had hundreds of them built, sunk everything he had in them, and
they didn't catch on, and finally he got permission to store them up
on the third and fourth floors of this building until he could come to
some conclusion what to do with them. This was back before they
tinkered with the elevator. Only he never came to any conclusion,
and by and by he died. The old-timer said it was his belief the fish
boxes are still up there. The man who rented the building ahead of
me, he had a different story. He was never above the second floor
either, but he told me that one of the men who rented it ahead of
him told him it was *his* understanding there was a lot of miscella-
neous old hotel junk stored up there—beds and bureaus, pitchers
and bowls, chamber pots, mirrors, brass spittoons, odds and ends,
old hotel registers that the rats chew on to get paper to line their
nests with. God knows what all. That's what he said. I don't know.
I've made quite a study of this building for one reason and another,
and I've took all kinds of pains tracking things down, but there's a

lot about it I still don't know. I do know there was a hotel in here years back. I know that beyond all doubt. It was one of those old steamship hotels that used to face the docks all along South Street."

❧ Mitchell establishes, through Louie, the physical danger and the potential psychological danger of exploration. There's good reason, perhaps, that Louie and the owner before Louie, have not explored the past. The suspense is increased and the apprehension that we may find out what we do not want to know. ❧

"Why don't you get a mechanic to inspect the elevator?" I 20 asked. "It might be perfectly safe."

"That would cost money," Louie said. "I'm curious, but I'm not 21 that curious. To tell you the truth, I just don't want to get in that cage by myself. I got a feeling about it, and that's the fact of the matter. It makes me uneasy—all closed in, and all that furry dust. It makes me think of a coffin, the inside of a coffin. Either that or a cave, the mouth of a cave. If I could get somebody to go along with me, somebody to talk to, just so I wouldn't be all alone in there, I'd go; I'd crawl right in. A couple of times, it almost happened I did. The first time was back in 1938. The hurricane we had that fall damaged the roofs on a good many of the old South Street buildings, and the real-estate management company I rented this building from sent a man down here to see if my roof was all right. I asked the man why didn't he take the elevator up to the attic floor, there might be a door leading out on the roof. I told him I'd go along. He took one look inside the cage and said it would be more trouble than it was worth. What he did, he went up on the roof of the building next door and crossed over. Didn't find anything wrong. Six or seven months ago, I had another disappointment. I was talking with a customer of mine eats a fish lunch in here Fridays who's a contractor, and it happened I got on the subject of the upper floors, and he remarked he understood how I felt, my curiosity. He said he seldom passes an old boarded-up building without he wonders about it, wonders what it's like in there—all empty and hollow and dark and still, not a sound, only some rats maybe, racing around in the dark, or maybe some English sparrows flying around in there in the empty rooms that always get in if there's a crack in one of the boards over a broken windowpane, a crack or a knothole, and sometimes they can't find their way out and they keep on hopping and flying and hopping and flying until they starve to death. He said he had been in many such buildings in the course of his work, and had seen some peculiar things. The next time he came in for lunch, he brought along a couple of those helmets that they wear around construction work, those orange-colored helmets, and he said to me, 'Come on, Louie. Put on one of these, and let's go up and try out that elevator. If the rope breaks, which I don't think it will—what the hell, a little shaking up is good for the liver. If the wheel drops, maybe these helmets will save us.' But he's a big heavy man, and he's not as active as he used to be. He went up the ladder first, and when he got to the top he backed right down. He put it on the basis he had a business appointment that afternoon and didn't want to get all dusty and dirty. I kept the helmets. He wanted them back, but I held on to them. I don't intend to let that elevator stand in my way much longer. One of these days, I'm going to sit down awhile with a bottle of Strega, and then I'm going to stick one of those helmets on my head and climb in that cage and put that damned elevator back in commission. The very least, I'll pull the rope and see what happens. I do wish I could find somebody had enough curiosity to go along with me. I've asked my waiters, and I've tried to interest some of the people in the market, but they all had the same answer, 'Hell, no,' they said."

22   Louie suddenly leaned forward. "What about you?" he asked. "Maybe I could persuade you."

> ❨A touch of humor and believability—Louie doesn't want to spend the money to get the elevator tested, and he's afraid to go up there alone. Okay, we'll go up there with him. Notice the way Mitchell repeats "furry dust." All through a good piece of writing there are tiny repetitions, lines of thought that are woven in the text. And notice the imagery, the "coffin, the inside of a coffin." We are given caves, and people who are afraid to go up with him, and rats and birds flying in and out, and then we are brought to the invitation. Eve offers the apple.❩

23   I thought it over a few moments, and was about to suggest that we go upstairs at any rate and climb in the cage and look at the elevator, but just then a fishmonger who had finished his breakfast and wanted to pay his check rapped a dictatorial rat-a-tat on the glass top of the cigar showcase with a coin. Louie frowned and clenched his teeth. "I wish they wouldn't do that," he said getting up. "It goes right through me."

❧A writer has to love this paragraph. He never answers. That has the ring of authority. I did voluntary duty during World War II, but I don't remember volunteering; I've been married twice, but I don't remember proposing or accepting either time. Again, the reader is given a nice little surprise, one that will connect subconsciously with the reader's experience. Will the reader be conscious of all this? Of course not, but it will be there. I'm revealing one writer's reading of this text, to show what I like about it, what I can learn and relearn from it, but it is only my reading. Yours will be different and so will your teacher's and your classmates'. We all read what we need to read.❧

Louie went over and took the man's money and gave him his change. Two waiters were standing at a service table in the rear, filling salt shakers, and Louie gestured to one of them to come up front and take charge of the cash register. Then he got himself another cup of coffee and sat back down and started talking again. "When I bought this restaurant," he said, "I wasn't too enthusiastic about the building. I had it in mind to build up the restaurant and find me a location somewhere else in the market and move, the trade would follow. Instead of which, after a while I got very closely attached to the building. Why I did is one of those matters, it really doesn't make much sense. It's all mixed up with the name of a street in Brooklyn, and it goes back to the last place I worked in before I came here. That was Joe's in Brooklyn, the old Nevins Street Joe's, Nevins just off Flatbush Avenue Extension. I was a waiter there seven years, and it was the best place I ever worked in. Joe's is part of a chain now, the Brass Rail chain. In my time, it was run by a very high-type Italian restaurant man named Joe Sartori, and it was the biggest chophouse in Brooklyn—fifty waiters, a main floor, a balcony, a ladies' dining room, and a Roman Garden. Joe's was a hangout for Brooklyn political bosses and officeholders, and it got a class of trade we called the old Brooklyn family trade, the rich old intermarried families that made their money out of Brooklyn real estate and Brooklyn docks and Brooklyn streetcar lines and Brooklyn gasworks. They had their money sunk way down deep in Brooklyn. I don't know how it is now, they've probably all moved into apartment houses, but in those days a good many of them lived in steep-stoop, stain-glass mansions sitting up as solid as banks on Brooklyn Heights and Park Slope and over around Fort Greene Park. They were a big-eating class of people, and they believed in patronizing the good old Brooklyn restaurants. You'd see them in Joe's, and you'd see them in Gage & Tollner's and Lundy's and Tappen's and Villepigue's. There was a high percentage of rich old independent women among them, widows and divorced ladies and maiden ladies. They were a class within a class. They wore clothes that hadn't been the style for years, and they wore the biggest hats I ever saw, and the ugliest. They all seemed to know each other since their childhood days, and they all had some peculiarity, and they all had one foot in the grave, and they all had big appetites. They had traveled widely, and they were good judges of food, and they knew how to order a meal. Some were poison, to say the least, and some were just as nice as they could be. On the whole I liked them; they broke the monotony. Some always came to my station; if my tables were full, they'd sit in some leather chairs Mr. Sartori had up front and wait. One was a widow named Mrs. Frelinghuysen. She was very old and tiny and delicate, and she ate like a horse. She ate like she thought any meal might be her last meal. She was a little lame from rheumatism, and she used a walking stick that had a snake's head for a knob, a snake's head carved out of ivory. She had a pleasant voice, a beautiful voice, and she made the most surprising funny remarks. They were coarse remarks, the humor in them. She made some remarks on occasion that had me wondering did I hear right. Everybody liked her, the way she hung on to life, and everybody tried to do things for her. I remember Mr. Sartori one night went out in the rain and got her a cab. 'She's such a thin little thing,' he said when he came back in. 'There's nothing to her,' he said, 'but six bones and one gut and a set of teeth and a big hat with a bird on it.' Her peculiarity was she always brought her own silver. It was old family silver. She'd have it wrapped up in a linen napkin in her handbag, and she'd get it out and set her own place. After she finished eating, I'd take it to the kitchen and wash it, and she'd stuff it back in her handbag. She'd always start off with one dozen oysters in winter or one dozen clams in summer, and she'd gobble them down and go on from there. She could get more out of a lobster than anybody I ever saw. You'd think she'd got everything she possibly could, and then she'd pull the little legs off that most people don't even bother with, and suck the juice out of them. Sometimes, if it was a slow night and I was just standing around, she'd call me over and talk to me while she ate. She'd talk about people and past times, and she knew a lot; she had kept her eyes open while she was going through life.

❦ Again, a space at the beginning. A new section is starting. We want to move forward and get upstairs, but Louie sits down, and we get more background. The expert writer is constantly using narrative—storytelling—even in pieces that seem not to be narrative, to make us keep going forward, wondering what will happen next. When the narrative provides energy and makes us want to move forward, then the writer can sneak in the background we need to have. We are receiving the history that is necessary for us to have a full understanding of what is to come. ❦

"My hours in Joe's were ten in the morning to nine at night. In   25
the afternoons, I'd take a break from three to four-thirty. I saw so
much rich food I usually didn't want any lunch, the way old waiters
get—just a crust of bread, or some fruit. If it was a nice day, I'd step
over to Albee Square and go into an old fancy-fruit store named Eck-
lebe & Guyer's and pick me out a piece of fruit—an orange or two,
or a bunch of grapes, or one of those big red pomegranates that split
open when they're ripe the same as figs and their juice is so strong
and red it purifies the blood. Then I'd go over to Schermerhorn
Street. Schermerhorn was a block and a half west of Joe's. There
were some trees along Schermerhorn, and some benches under the
trees. Young women would sit along there with their babies, and old
men would sit along there the whole day through and read papers
and play checkers and discuss matters. And I'd sit there the little
time I had and rest my feet and eat my fruit and read the *New York
Times*—my purpose reading the *New York Times*, I was trying to
improve my English. Schermerhorn Street was a peaceful old back-
water street, so nice and quiet, and I liked it. It did me good to sit
down there and rest. One afternoon the thought occurred to me,
'Who the hell was Schermerhorn?' So that night it happened Mrs.
Frelinghuysen was in, and I asked her who was Schermerhorn that
the street's named for. She knew, all right. Oh, Jesus, she more than
knew. She saw I was interested, and from then on that was one of
the main subjects she talked to me about—Old New York street
names and neighborhood names; Old New York this, Old New York
that. She knew a great many facts and figures and skeletons in the
closet that her mother and her grandmother and her aunts had
passed on down to her relating to the old New York Dutch families
that they call the Knickerbockers—those that dissipated too much
and dissipated all their property away and died out and disappeared,
and those that are still around. Holland Dutch, not German Dutch,

the way I used to think it meant. The Schermerhorns are one of the oldest of the old Dutch families, according to her, and one of the best. They were big landowners in Dutch days, and they still are, and they go back so deep in Old New York that if you went any deeper you wouldn't find anything but Indians and bones and bears. Mrs. Frelinghuysen was well acquainted with the Schermerhorn family. She had been to Schermerhorn weddings and Schermerhorn funerals. I remember she told about a Schermerhorn girl she went to school with who belonged to the eighth generation, I think it was, in direct descent from old Jacob Schermerhorn who came here from Schermerhorn, Holland, in the sixteen-thirties, and this girl died and was buried in the Schermerhorn plot in Trinity Church cemetery up in Washington Heights, and one day many years later driving down from Connecticut Mrs. Frelinghuysen got to thinking about her and stopped off at the cemetery and looked around in there and located her grave and put some jonquils on it."

      ❡Another huge chunk of exposition. Mitchell may be losing his reader, but look ahead. He brings the text back to earth, breaks up the grayness of text with dialogue, and shows something more about Louie—the way he serves as a communications center for the people in the Fulton Fish Market. ❡

26   At this moment a fishmonger opened the door of the restaurant and put his head in and interrupted Louie. "Hey, Louie," he called out, "has Little Joe been in?"

27   "Little Joe that's a lumper on the pier," asked Louie, "or Little Joe that works for Chesbro, Robbins?"

28   "The lumper," said the fishmonger.

29   "He was in and out an hour ago," said Louie. "He snook in and got a cup of coffee and was out and gone the moment he finished it."

30   "If you see him," the fishmonger said, "tell him they want him on the pier. A couple of draggers just came in—the *Felicia* from New Bedford and the *Positive* from Gloucester—and the *Ann Elizabeth Kristin* from Stonington is out in the river, on her way in."

31   Louie nodded, and the fishmonger went away. "To continue about Mrs. Frelinghuysen," Louie said, "she died in 1927. The next year, I got married. The next year was the year the stock market crashed. The next year, I quit Joe's and came over here and bought this restaurant and rented this building. I rented it from a real-estate company, the Charles F. Noyes Company, and I paid my rent to

them, and I took it for granted they owned it. One afternoon four years later, the early part of 1934, around in March, I was standing at the cash register in here and a long black limousine drove up out front and parked, and a uniform chauffeur got out and came in and said Mrs. Schermerhorn wanted to speak to me, and I looked at him and said, 'What do you mean—Mrs. Schermerhorn?' And he said, 'Mrs. Schermerhorn that owns this building.' So I went out on the sidewalk, and there was a lady sitting in the limousine, her appearance was quite beautiful, and she said she was Mrs. Arthur F. Schermerhorn and her husband had died in September the year before and she was taking a look at some of the buildings the estate owned and the Noyes company was the agent for. So she asked me some questions concerning what shape the building was in, and the like of that. Which I answered to the best of my ability. Then I told her I was certainly surprised for various reasons to hear this was Schermerhorn property. I told her, 'Frankly,' I said, 'I'm amazed to hear it.' I asked her did she know anything about the history of the building, how old it was, and she said she didn't, she hadn't ever even seen it before, it was just one of a number of properties that had come down to her husband from his father. Even her husband, she said, she doubted if he had known much about the building. I had a lot of questions I wanted to ask, and I asked her to get out and come in and have some coffee and take a look around, but I guess she figured the signboard *Sloppy Louie's Restaurant* meant what it said. She thanked me and said she had to be getting on, and she gave the chauffeur an address, and they drove off and I never saw her again.

> ❧ Now we understand why that information was given to us. The writer keeps making us hunger for information, then gives us a bit more than we want, but doesn't let us get away. The writer tells us why that information is important. We are in this piece getting the history of a city, and in a sense all cities. And now we're going to get more. And we want it. We want to have this experience of exploring the past in context. ❧

"I went back inside and stood there and thought it over, and 32 the effect it had on me, the simple fact my building was an old Schermerhorn building, it may sound foolish, but it pleased me very much. The feeling I had, it connected me with the past. It connected me with Old New York. It connected Sloppy Louie's Restaurant with Old New York. It made the building look much better to me. Instead of just an old run-down building in the fish market, the way it looked to me before, it had a history to it, connections going back, and I liked that. It stirred up my curiosity to know more. A day or so later, I went over and asked the people at the Noyes company would they mind telling me something about the history of the building, but they didn't know anything about it. They had only took over the management of it in 1929, the year before I rented it, and the company that had been the previous agent had gone out of business. They said to go to the City Department of Buildings in the Municipal Building. Which I did, but the man in there, he looked up my building and couldn't find any file on it, and he said it's hard to date a good many old buildings down in my part of town because a fire in the Building Department around 1890 destroyed some cases of papers relating to them—permits and specifications and all that. He advised me to go to the Hall of Records on Chambers Street, where deeds are recorded. I went over there, and they showed me the deed, but it wasn't any help. It described the lot, but all it said about the building, it said 'the building thereon,' and didn't give any date on it. So I gave up. Well, there's a nice old gentleman eats in here sometimes who works for the Title Guarantee & Trust Company, an old Yankee fish-eater, and we were talking one day, and it happened he told me that Title Guarantee has tons and tons of records on New York City property stored away in their vaults that they refer to when they're deciding whether or not the title to a piece of property is clear. 'Do me a favor,' I said, 'and look up the records on 92 South Street—nothing private or financial; just the history—and I'll treat you to the best broiled lobster you ever had. I'll treat you to broiled lobster six Fridays in a row,' I said, 'and I'll broil the lobsters myself.'

> ❧ It helps the writer to have someone else tell the story so that we—writer and reader—can listen to this interesting guy in this interesting place talk to us. But did Louie talk this way, all in a chunk, as if he were giving a lecture at some New York Historical Association? Of course not. It is a recreated conversation, created out of many interviews and conversations over days, even perhaps years. But it shouldn't be made up. Louie should have said all these things in this way, if not at the same time and in this order. ❧

33   "The next time he came in, he said he had took a look in the Title Guarantee vaults for me, and had talked to a title searcher over there who's an expert on South Street property, and he read me off

some notes he had made. It seems all this end of South Street used to be under water. The East River flowed over it. Then the city filled it in and divided it into lots. In February, 1804, a merchant by the name of Peter Schermerhorn, a descendent of Jacob Schermerhorn, was given grants to the lot my building now stands on—92 South— and the lot next to it—91 South, a corner lot, the corner of South and Fulton. Schermerhorn put up a four-story brick-and-frame building on each of these lots—stores on the street floors and flats above. In 1872, 1873, or 1874—my friend from Title Guarantee wasn't able to determine the exact year—the heirs and assigns of Peter Schermerhorn ripped these buildings down and put up two six-story brick buildings exactly alike side by side on 92 and 93. Those buildings are this one here and the one next door. The Schermerhorns put them up for hotel purposes, and they were designed so they could be used as one building—there's a party wall between them, and in those days there were sets of doors on each floor leading from one building to the other. This building had that old hand-pull elevator in it from bottom to top, and the other building had a wide staircase in it from bottom to top. The Schermerhorns didn't skimp on materials; they used heart pine for beams and they used hand-molded, air-dried, kiln-burned Hudson River brick. The Schermerhorns leased the buildings to two hotel men named Frederick and Henry Lemmermann, and the first lease on record is 1874. The name of the hotel was the Fulton Ferry Hotel. The hotel saloon occupied the whole bottom floor of the building next door, and the hotel restaurant was right in here, and they had a combined lobby and billiard room that occupied the second floor of both buildings, and they had a reading room in the front half of the third floor of this building and rooms in the rear half, and all the rest of the space in both buildings was single rooms and double rooms and suites. At that time, there were passenger-line steamship docks all along South Street, lines that went to every part of the world, and out-of-town people waiting for passage on the various steamers would stay at the Fulton Ferry Hotel. Also, the Brooklyn Bridge hadn't yet been built, and the Fulton Ferry was the principal ferry to Brooklyn, and the ferryhouse stood directly in front of the hotel. On account of the ferry, Fulton Street was like a funnel, damned near everything headed for Brooklyn went through it. It was full of foot traffic and horse-drawn traffic day and night, and South and Fulton was one of the most ideal saloon corners in the city.

❡ We've seen the building as it looks today; now we are beginning to see it the way it had been when it was a new building, part of the growth of a bustling city, as bright and shining in its way as a new mall is today. What will happen to the new mall? We will find out.❡

34   "The Fulton Ferry Hotel lasted forty-five years, but it only had about twenty good years; the rest was downhill. The first bad blow was the bridges over the East River, beginning with the Brooklyn Bridge, that gradually drained off the heavy traffic on the Fulton Ferry that the hotel saloon got most of its trade from. And then, the worst blow of all, the passenger lines began leaving South Street and moving around to bigger, longer docks on the Hudson. Little by little, the Fulton Ferry Hotel got to be one of those waterfront hotels that rummies hole up in, and old men on pensions, and old nuts, and sailors on the beach. Steps going down. Around 1910, somewhere in there, the Lemmermanns gave up the part of the hotel that was in this building, and the Schermerhorn interests boarded up the windows on the four upper floors and bricked up the doors in the party wall connecting the two buildings. And the hotel restaurant, what they did with that, they rented it to a man named MacDonald who turned it into a quick lunch for the people in the fish market. MacDonald ran it awhile. Then a son of his took it over, according to some lease notations in the Title Guarantee records. Then a man named Jimmy Something-or-Other took it over. It was called Jimmy's while he had it. Then two Greek fellows took it over. Then a German fellow and his wife and sister and brother-in-law had it awhile. Then two brothers named Fortunato and Louie Barbagelata took it over. Then John Barbagelata took it over, a nephew of the other Barbagelatas, and eventually I came along and bought the lease and furnishings off of him. After the party wall was bricked up, the Lemmermanns held on to the building next door a few years more, and kept on calling it the Fulton Ferry Hotel, but all it amounted to, it was just a waterfront saloon with rooms for rent up above. They operated it until 1919, when the final blow hit them—prohibition. Those are the bare bones of the matter. If I could get upstairs just once in that damned old elevator and scratch around in those hotel registers up there and whatever to hell else is stored up there, it might be possible I'd find out a whole lot more."

35   "Look, Louie," I said, "I'll go up in the elevator with you."

36   "You think you would," Louie said, "but you'd just take a look at it, and then you'd back out."

"I'd like to see inside the cage, at least," I said.   37

Louie looked at me inquisitively. "You really want to go up   38
there?" he asked.

"Yes," I said.   39

"The next time you come down here, put on the oldest clothes   40
you got, so the dust don't make any difference," Louie said, "and
we'll go up and try out the elevator."

"Oh, no," I said. "Now or never. If I think it over, I'll change   41
my mind."

"It's your own risk," he said.   42

"Of course," I said.   43

❡Another space, the end of another section. He has made his
decision. We were ahead of him; we knew what he was going to do.
Louie is not so sure, and so we have more suspense. Too often
exposition is taught as if it could just be larded on the page. It can't;
it must be woven in. There must be energy that's carrying the reader
forward, and then we must create situations where the reader wants
to know the information the writer is going to provide. It may be
helpful to think of a piece of writing as a dialogue with the reader,
or a pattern of questions and answers. The reader says, "How come
this was a hotel?" And the writer tells about the ferry.❦

Louie abruptly stood up. "Let me speak to the waiter at the cash   44
register," he said, "and I'll be with you."

He went over and spoke to the waiter. Then he opened the door   45
of a cupboard in back of the cash register and took out two flashlights
and the two construction-work helmets that his customer, the contractor, had brought in. He handed me one of the flashlights and one
of the helmets. I put the helmet on and started over to a mirror to
see how I looked. "Come on," Louie said, somewhat impatiently. We
went up the stairs to the second floor. Along one wall, on this floor,
were shelves stacked with restaurant supplies—canned goods and
nests of bowls and plates and boxes of soap powder and boxes of
paper napkins. Headed up against the wainscoting were half a dozen
burlap bags of potatoes. A narrow, round-runged, wooden ladder
stood at a slant in a corner up front, and Louie went directly to it.
One end of the ladder was fixed to the floor, and the other end was
fixed to the ceiling. At the top of the ladder, flush with the ceiling,
was the bottom of the elevator cage with the trap door cut in it. The
trap door was shut. Louie unbuttoned a shirt button and stuck his

flashlight in the front of his shirt, and immediately started up the ladder. At the top, he paused and looked down at me for an instant. His face was set. Then he gave the trap door a shove, and it fell back, and a cloud of black dust burst out. Louie ducked his head and shook it and blew the dust out of his nose. He stood at the top of the ladder for about a minute, waiting for the dust to settle. Then, all of a sudden, he scrambled into the cage. "Oh, God in Heaven," he called out, "the dust in here! It's like somebody emptied a vacuum-cleaner bag in here." I climbed the ladder and entered the cage and closed the trap door. Louie pointed his flashlight up the shaft. "I thought there was only one wheel up there," he said, peering upward. "I see two." The dust had risen to the top of the shaft, and we couldn't see the wheels clearly. There was an iron strut over the top of the cage, and a cable extended from it to one of the wheels. Two thick hemp ropes hung down into the cage from the other wheel. "I'm going to risk it," Louie said. "I'm going to pull the rope. Take both flashlights, and shine one on me and shine the other up the shaft. If I can get the cage up about a foot, it'll be level with the third floor, and we can open the door."

> ❡ Now you can begin to appreciate all the foreshadowing, and also all the information we have. We are prepared for the helmets, for the restaurant supplies on the second floor, the ladder (note the hesitation as Louie started up the ladder, the nice pacing that Mitchell uses), and the dust. ❡

46   Louie grasped one of the ropes and pulled on it, and dust sprang off it all the way to the top. The wheel screeched as the rope turned it, but the cage didn't move. "The rope feels loose," Louie said. "I don't think it has any grip on the wheel." He pulled again, and nothing happened.

47   "Maybe you've got the wrong rope," I said.

48   He disregarded me and pulled again, and the cage shook from side to side. Louie let go of the rope, and looked up the shaft. "That wheel acts all right," he said. He pulled the rope again, and this time the cage rose an inch or two. He pulled five or six times, and the cage rose an inch or two each time. Then we looked down and saw that the floor of the cage was almost even with the third floor. Louie pulled the rope once more. Then he stepped over and pushed on the grilled door of the cage and shook it, trying to swing it open; it rattled, and long, lacy flakes of rust fell off it, but it wouldn't open. I

gave Louie the lights of both flashlights, and he examined the door. There were sets of hinges down it in two places. "I see," Louie said. "You're supposed to fold it back in." The hinges were stiff, and he got in a frenzy struggling with the door before he succeeded in folding it back far enough for us to get through. On the landing there was a kind of storm-door-like affair, a three-sided cubbyhole with a plain wooden door in the center side. "I guess they had that there to keep people from falling in the shaft," Louie said. "It'll be just our luck the door's locked on the other side. If it is, I'm not going to monkey around; I'm going to kick it in." He tried the knob, and it turned, and he opened the door, and we walked out and entered the front half of the third floor, the old reading room of the Fulton Ferry Hotel.

❡ Mitchell is a master of pacing. Now there's pressure to get into the hotel. The text speeds up, it drives forward. We've got to get into the hotel now. Neither the writer's impatience nor the text gets ahead or behind the reader's. It is right in step with the reader. ❡

It was pitch-dark in the room. We stood still and played the 49 lights of our flashlights across the floor and up and down the walls. Everything we saw was covered with dust. There was a thick, black mat of fleecy dust on the floor—dust and soot and grit and lint and slut's wool. Louie scuffed his shoes in it. "A-a-ah!" he said, and spat. His light fell on a roll-top desk, and he hurried over to it and rolled the top up. I stayed where I was, and continued to look around. The room was rectangular, and it had a stamped tin ceiling, and tongue-and-groove wainscoting, and plaster walls the color of putty. The plaster had crumbled down to the laths in many places. There was a gas fixture on each wall. High up on one wall was a round hole that had once held a stove-pipe. Screwed to the door leading to the rear half of the floor were two framed signs. One said, "THIS READING ROOM WILL BE CLOSED AT 1 A.M. FULTON FERRY HOTEL." The other said, "ALL GAMBLING IN THIS READING ROOM STRICTLY PROHIBITED, BY ORDER OF THE PROPRIETORS, FULTON FERRY HOTEL. F. & H. LEMMERMANN, PROPRIETORS." Some bedsprings and some ugly white knobby iron bedsteads were stacked crisscross in one corner. The stack was breast-high. Between the boarded-up windows, against the front wall, stood a marble-top table. On it were three selzer bottles with corroded spouts, a tin water cooler painted to resemble brown marble, a cracked glass bell of the kind used to cover clocks and stuffed birds, and four sugar bowls whose metal flap lids had been eaten away from their hinges by rust. On the floor, beside the table, were an umbrella stand, two brass spittoons, and a wire basket filled to the brim with whiskey bottles of the flask type. I took the bottles out one by one. Dampness had destroyed the labels; pulpy scraps of paper with nothing legible on them were sticking to a few on the bottom. Lined up back to back in the middle of the room were six bureaus with mirrors on their tops. Still curious to see how I looked in the construction-work helmet, I went and peered in one of the mirrors.

> ❦ Ashes to ashes and dust to dust, lots of dust. The writer who wanted to escape death and doom is now visiting a world that was once alive with people and excitement. There was gambling and drinking, parties and dreams, and hope, and Mitchell gives us a moment of relief by peering at himself in the mirror in his construction worker's helmet. ❧

50   Louie, who had been yanking drawers out of the roll-top desk, suddenly said, "God damn it! I thought I'd find those hotel registers in here. There's nothing in here, only rusty paper clips." He went over to the whiskey bottles I had strewn about and examined a few, and then he walked up behind me and looked in the mirror. His face was strained. He had rubbed one cheek with his dusty fingers, and it was streaked with dust. "We're the first faces to look in that mirror in years and years," he said. He held his flashlight with one hand and jerked open the top drawer of the bureau with the other. There were a few hairpins in the drawer, and some buttons, and a comb with several teeth missing, and a needle with a bit of black thread in its eye, and a scattering of worn playing cards; the design on the backs of the cards was a stag at bay. He opened the middle drawer, and it was empty. He started in on the next bureau. In the top drawer, he found a square, clear-glass medicine bottle that contained two inches of colorless liquid and half an inch of black sediment. He wrenched the stopper out, and put the bottle to his nose and smelled the liquid. "It's gone dead," he said. "It doesn't smell like anything at all." He poured the liquid on the floor, and handed the bottle to me. Blown in one side of it was "Perry's Pharmacy, Open All Night. Popular Prices. World Building, New York." All at once, while looking at the old bottle, I became conscious of the noises of the market seemingly far below, and I stepped over to one of the boarded up windows and

tried to peep down at South Street through a split in a board, but it wasn't possible. Louie continued to go through the bureau drawers. "Here's something," he said. "look at this." He handed me a foxed and yellowed photograph of a dark young woman with upswept hair who wore a lace shirtwaist and a long black skirt and sat in a fanciful fan-backed wicker chair. After a while, Louie reached the last drawer in the last bureau, and looked in it and snorted and slammed it shut. "Let's go in the rear part of the floor," he said.

❦ Now we are really deep into the exploration. Mitchell avoids making generalizations himself. It is better to let the details speak for him, and he also has Louie to speak for, going from the spookyness of looking into the mirror that hasn't been looked into for years to almost an anger at the triviality of what is being found. Mitchell doesn't say that what was important to these people is now trivial. He gives the reader room to have the thoughts themselves. The effective writer allows the reader into the text. He avoids using summary statements and general statements that tell the reader how to feel or think. He gives the reader the experience that will cause the reader to feel and think.

Note how the text speeds up as we get toward the end. The prose matches the kind of terror that we feel confronting what our world will look at if it is explored long after we are dead. The text is almost rushing forward, and it is deepening as we get to the religious placards that confront the meaning of life.❧

Louie opened the door, and we entered a hall, along which was 51 a row of single rooms. There were six rooms, and on their doors were little oval enameled number plates running from 12 to 17. We looked in Room 12. Two wooden coat hangers were lying on the floor. Room 13 was absolutely empty. Room 14 had evidently last been occupied by someone with a religious turn of mind. There was an old iron bedstead still standing in it, but without springs, and tacked on the wall above the head of the bed was a placard of the kind distributed by some evangelistic religious groups. It said, "The Wages of Sin is Death; but the Gifts of God is Eternal Life through Jesus Christ our Lord." Tacked on the wall beside the bed was another religious placard: "Christ is the Head of this House, the Unseen Host at Every Meal, the Silent Listener to Every Conversation." We stared at the placards a few moments, and then Louie turned and started back up the hall.

52   "Louie," I called, following him, "where are you going?"

53   "Let's go on back downstairs," he said.

54   "I thought we were going on up to the floors above," I said. "Let's go up to the fourth floor, at least. We'll take turns pulling the rope."

55   "There's nothing up here," he said. "I don't want to stay up here another minute. Come on, let's go."

56   I followed him into the elevator cage. "I'll pull the rope going down," I said.

57   Louie said nothing, and I glanced at him. He was leaning against the side of the cage, and his shoulders were slumped and his eyes were tired. "I didn't learn much I didn't know before," he said.

58   "You learned that the wages of sin is death," I said, trying to say something cheerful.

59   "I knew that before," Louie said. A look of revulsion came on his face. "The wages of sin!" he said. "Sin, death, dust, old empty rooms, old empty whiskey bottles, old empty bureau drawers. Come on, pull the rope faster! Pull it faster! Let's get out of this."

❧ Now this rather slow text races to its end with dialogue. The writer has to bring it all together to have the meaning made and to get out of the way as fast as possible. The inexperienced writer tries to write a conclusion, something effective writers hardly ever do. You can't tell the reader what it means at the end. The reader has to know what it means, and feel what it means. The reader has to be there experiencing the text. Mitchell does this by his wanting to go on, and Louie does not. We know Louie; he is an old man and a wise one, a man who has lost one world, who has lost a wife, who knows hope and love and death and loss, and says, "I didn't learn much I didn't know before." Mitchell has fun with him. He releases the pressure on the reader a bit with his remark about "the wages of sin is death," ironically adding that he wanted "to say something cheerful." And then we end on a note of action. There is no need for a little sermon about the past and the present and the future. Mitchell has given us an experience and provided us with enough information so that we come to that experience prepared to feel it fully and to know its significance. He has never intruded; he has told us a story, given us specific information, and allowed us to share in discovering what it means. Every time I read this piece I am moved as a reader, and I'm inspired as a writer.❧

Discussion

• What did this piece make you think of as you read it? What pictures were occurring in your mind? What were you thinking about? It's interesting to see how a good piece of writing will spark different texts in each reader's mind.

• Discuss how your readings—your own, your teacher's, your classmates'—differ from mine. Remember that no one reading is right and another wrong. Each person brings their own experience and their own needs to the text.

• Have someone read a portion of the text aloud. See if you can identify what the writer's voice brings to the text and what the reader's voice adds to it. Pick an example where Mitchell has been effective in creating music with language that underscores the meaning of the text, the way background music underscores a movie scene.

• What are the common and different elements between Scanlan's use of narrative and Mitchell's? Between the way Scanlan and Mitchell come in and out as characters in their own text?

• Discuss other ways that this idea could have been developed—other subject matter, other genres, other organizations, other use of language.

• Take a page from Caro and another page from Mitchell that is packed with details, and discuss what techniques they use to make use of information. Try to decide what is similar, what is different; what works, what doesn't work.

Activities

• Go through the text and write your own comments to the left of mine, so that you have a reading that brings your own experience and your own writer's needs to the text, then compare your reading to mine. Neither is right or wrong, but it is helpful for us to share our readings to see what we can each learn from a text.

• Of course you cannot write as long and detailed an account as Mitchell. You don't have the time to do that. But you can find abandoned storefronts, deserted early shopping malls, cellar holes, old theaters, boarded-up tenements, abandoned farms that you can visit and write your own account of the visit.

• I'm not too fond of using models; they can get overused, and we can think it is better to imitate than to develop our own voices, our own way of looking at the world. Still, it could be helpful to take the paragraph on page 87 describing Louie, or the one on page 89 describing the busy restaurant and use a similar technique or length to describe a person or a place. It may be fun for the whole class to describe the same person or place, someone or some place that is familiar to all in the class, so that you can share the exciting diversity of vision and language that is at the heart of the excitement of writing.

- Outline this piece or draw a design of it to see how it is constructed. It can be interesting to see the architects drawings that lie behind a well-made piece of writing.

William Least Heat Moon

When William Least Heat Moon's marriage fell apart and he lost his teaching job, he hit the road in his van. But he didn't use the superhighways, he traveled the back roads that are colored blue on highway maps. His marvelous book, *Blue Highways*, is an account of his wanderings on the back roads of America. It is a wise, loving book that discovers an America that is rarely seen on television or reported in writing, and the writing is spectacular. The writing reveals; it doesn't call attention to itself, but to the subject.

Nameless

1   Had it not been raining hard that morning on the Livingston square, I never would have learned of Nameless, Tennessee. Waiting for the rain to ease, I lay on my bunk and read the atlas to pass time rather than to see where I might go. In Kentucky were towns with fine names like Boreing, Bear Wallow, Decoy, Subtle, Mud Lick, Mummie, Neon; Belcher was just down the road from Mouthcard, and Minnie only ten miles from Mousie.

2   I looked at Tennessee, Turtletown eight miles from Ducktown. And also: Peavine, Wheel, Milky Way, Love Joy, Dull, Weakly, Fly, Spot, Miser Station, Only, McBurg, Peeled Chestnut, Clouds, Topsy, Isoline. And the best of all, Nameless. The logic! I was heading east, and Nameless lay forty-five miles west. I decided to go anyway.

The rain stopped, but things looked saturated, even bricks. In 3
Gainesboro, a hill town with a square of businesses around the Jackson County Courthouse, I stopped for directions and breakfast. There is one almost infallible way to find honest food at just prices in blue-highway America: count the wall calendars in a cafe.

No calendar: Same as an interstate pit stop. 4
One calendar: Preprocessed food assembled in New Jersey.
Two calendars: Only if fish trophies present.
Three calendars: Can't miss on the farm-boy breakfasts.
Four calendars: Try the ho-made pie too.
Five calendars: Keep it under your hat, or they'll franchise.

One time I found a six-calendar cafe in the Ozarks, which 5
served fried chicken, peach pie, and chocolate malts, that left me searching for another ever since. I've never seen a seven-calendar place. But old-time travelers—road men in a day when cars had running boards and lunchroom windows said AIR COOLED in blue letters with icicles dripping from the tops—those travelers have told me the golden legends of seven-calendar cafes.

> ❡Mitchell established his voice—his way of speaking, the point of view from which he views the world and the way he views it, right away. So does Least Heat Moon. Notice how he develops his system for evaluating restaurants. He doesn't need to mention all the rating systems that are established. The reader knows those. He just presents his own and it is counterpoint to all the others.❡

To the rider of back roads, nothing shows the tone, the voice of 6
a small town more quickly than the breakfast grill or the five-thirty tavern. Much of what the people do and believe and share is evident then. The City Cafe in Gainesboro had three calendars that I could see from the walk. Inside were no interstate refugees with full bladders and empty tanks, no wild-eyed children just released from the glassy cell of a stationwagon backseat, no long-haul truckers talking in CB numbers. There were only townspeople wearing overalls, or catalog order suits with five-and-dime ties, or uniforms. That is, here were farmers and mill hands, bank clerks, the dry goods merchant, a policeman, and chiropractor's receptionist. Because it was Saturday, there were also mothers and children.

❡Most of us hit the reader over the head with our opinions. The author has an opinion about superhighway travelers but he expresses it through the use of specific detail. Notice in what follows how the writer uses the waitress as a way of allowing him to explain his search to the reader without giving the reader a pompous essay on harmony.❡

7   I ordered my standard on-the-road breakfast: two eggs up, hashbrowns, tomato juice. The waitress, whose pale, almost transluscent skin shifted hue in the gray light like a thin slice of mother of pearl, brought the food. Next to the eggs was a biscuit with a little yellow Smiley button stuck in it. She said, "You from the North?"

8   "I guess I am." A Missourian gets used to Southerners thinking him a Yankee, a Northerner considering him a cracker, a Westerner sneering at his effete Easterness, and the Easterner taking him for a cowhand.

9   "So whata you doin' in the mountains?"

10   "Talking to people. Taking some pictures. Looking mostly."

11   "Lookin' for what?"

12   "A three-calendar cafe that serves Smiley buttons on the biscuits."

13   "You needed a smile. Tell me really."

14   "I don't know. Actually, I'm looking for some jam to put on this biscuit now that you've brought one."

15   She came back with grape jelly. In a land of quince jelly, apple butter, apricot jam, blueberry preserves, pear conserves, and lemon marmalade, you always get grape jelly.

16   "Whata you lookin' for?"

17   Like anyone else, I'm embarrassed to eat in front of a watcher, particularly if I'm getting interviewed. "Why don't you have a cup of coffee?"

18   "Cain't right now. You gonna tell me?"

19   "I don't know how to describe it to you. Call it harmony."

20   She waited for something more. "Is that it?" Someone called her to the kitchen. I had managed almost to finish by the time she came back. She sat on the edge of the booth. "I started out in life not likin' anything, but then it grew on me. Maybe that'll happen to you." She watched me spread the jelly. "Saw your van." She watched me eat the biscuit. "You sleep in there?" I told her I did. "I'd love to do that, but I'd be scared spitless."

"I don't mind being scared spitless. Sometimes." 21

"I'd love to take off cross country. I like to look at different 22 license plates. But I'd take a dog. You carry a dog?"

"No dogs, no cats, no budgie birds. It's a one-man campaign to 23 show Americans a person can travel alone without a pet."

"Cain't travel without a dog!" 24

"I like to do things the hard way." 25

"Shoot! I'd take me a dog to talk to. And for protection." 26

"It isn't traveling to cross the country and talk to your pug 27 instead of people along the way. Besides, being alone on the road makes you ready to meet someone when you stop. You get sociable traveling alone."

She looked out toward the van again. "Time I get the nerve to 28 take a trip, gas'll cost five dollars a gallon."

"Could be. My rig might go the way of the steamboat." I 29 remembered why I'd come to Gainesboro. "You know the way to Nameless?"

"Nameless? I've heard of Nameless. Better ask the amlance 30 driver in the corner booth." She pinned the Smiley on my jacket. "Maybe I'll see you on the road somewhere. His name's Bob, by the way."

"The ambulance driver?" 31

"The Smiley. I always name my Smileys—otherwise they all 32 look alike. I'd talk to him before you go."

"The Smiley?" 33

"The amlance driver." 34

And so I went looking for Namelsss, Tennessee, with a Smiley 35 button named Bob.

"I don't know if I got directions for where you're goin'," the 36 ambulance driver said. "I *think* there's a Nameless down the Shepardsville Road."

"When I get to Shepardsville, will I have gone too far?" 37

"Ain't no Shepardsville." 38

"How will I know when I'm there?" 39

"Cain't say for certain." 40

"What's Nameless look like?" 41

"Don't recollect." 42

"Is the road paved?" 43

"It's possible." 44

45   Those were the directions. I was looking for an unnumbered road named after a nonexistent town that would take me to a place called Nameless that nobody was sure existed.

46   Clumps of wild garlic lined the county highway that I hoped was the Shepardsville Road. It scrimmaged with the mountain as it tried to stay on top of the ridges; the hillsides were so steep and thick with oak, I felt as if I were following a trail through the misty treetops. Chickens, doing more work with their necks than legs, ran across the road, and, with a battering of wings, half leapt and half flew into the lower branches of oaks. A vicious pair of mixed breed German shepherds raced along trying to eat the tires. After miles, I decided I'd missed the town—assuming there truly *was* a Nameless, Tennessee. It wouldn't be the first time I'd qualified for the Ponce de Leon Believe Anything Award.

> ❲ Least Heat Moon doesn't tell you to appreciate life, he holds up details of places and people in such a way that you appreciate them. He celebrates life.❳

47   I stopped beside a big man loading tools in a pickup. "I may be lost."

48   "Where'd you lose the right road?"

49   "I don't know. Somewhere around nineteen sixty-five."

> ❲ A writer delights in touches like this where the author drops a philosophical statement into a conversation. It isn't even picked up by the other person in the book. But it's there for the reader. Too often we teach exposition—the explanation the reader needs to understand the text—as a separate device that stands alone. If you wrote that way the reader would leap over or stop reading. Good writers are tricky; they sneak exposition into the text so you get it without knowing you're getting it. Look for other examples of exposition woven into the texts in this book.❳

50   "Highway fifty-six, you mean?"

51   "I came down fifty-six. I think I should've turned at the last junction."

52   "Only thing down that road's stumps and huckleberries, and the berries ain't there in March. Where you tryin' to get to?"

53   "Nameless. If there is such a place."

54   "You might not know Thurmond Watts, but he's got him a store

down the road. That's Nameless at his store. Still there all right, but I might not vouch you that tomorrow." He came up to the van. "In my Army days, I wrote Nameless, Tennessee, for my place of birth on all the papers, even though I lived on this end of the ridge. All these ridges and hollers got names of their own. That's Steam Mill Holler over yonder. Named after the steam engine in the gristmill. Miller had him just one arm but done a good business."

"What business you in?" 55

"I've always farmed, but I work in Cookeville now in a heatin' 56
element factory. Bad back made me go to town to work." He pointed to a wooden building not much bigger than his truck. By the slanting porch, a faded Double Cola sign said J M WHEELER STORE. "That used to be my business. That's me—Madison Wheeler. Feller came by one day. From Detroit. He wanted to buy the sign because he carried my name too. But I didn't sell. Want to keep my name up." He gave a cigarette a good slow smoking. "Had a decent business for five years, but too much of it was in credit. Then them supermarkets down in Cookeville opened, and I was buyin' higher than they was sellin'. With these hard roads now, everybody gets out of the hollers to shop or work. Don't stay up in here anymore. This tar road under my shoes done my business in, and it's likely to do Nameless in."

"Do you wish it was still the old way?" 57

"I got no debts now. I got two boys raised, and they never been 58
in trouble. I got a brick house and some corn and tobacco and a few Hampshire hogs and Herefords. A good bull. Bull's pumpin' better blood than I do. Real generous man in town let me put my cow in with his stud. I couldna paid the fee on that specimen otherwise." He took another long, meditative pull on his filtertip. "If you're satisfied, that's all they are to it. I'll tell you, people from all over the nation—Florida, Mississippi—are comin' in here to retire because it's good country. But our young ones don't stay on. Not much way to make a livin' in here anymore. Take me. I been beatin' on these stumps all my life, tryin' to farm these hills. They don't give much up to you. Fightin' rocks and briars all the time. One of the first things I recollect is swingin' a briar blade—filed out of an old saw it was. Now they come in with them crawlers and push out a pasture in a day. Still, it's a grudgin' land—like the gourd. Got to hard cuss gourd seed, they say, to get it up out of the ground."

The whole time, my rig sat in the middle of the right lane while 59
we stood talking next to it and wiped at the mist. No one else came

or went. Wheeler said, "Factory work's easier on the back, and I don't mind it, understand, but a man becomes what he does. Got to watch that. That's why I keep at farmin', although the crops haven't ever throve. It's the doin' that's important." He looked up suddenly. "My apologies. I didn't ask what you do that gets you into these hollers."

60   I told him. I'd been gone only six days, but my account of the trip already had taken on some polish.

61   He nodded. "Satisfaction is doin' what's important to yourself. A man ought to honor other people, but he's got to honor what he believes in too."

62   As I started the engine, Wheeler said, "If you get back this way, stop in and see me. Always got beans and taters and a little piece of meat."

63   Down along the ridge, I wondered why it's always those who live on little who are the ones to ask you to dinner.

64   Nameless, Tennessee, was a town of maybe ninety people if you pushed it, a dozen houses along the road, a couple of barns, same number of churches, a general merchandise store selling Fire Chief gasoline, and a community center with a lighted volleyball court. Behind the center was an open-roof, rusting metal privy with PAINT ME on the door; in the hollow of a nearby oak lay a full pint of Jack Daniel's Black Label. From the houses, the odor of coal smoke.

> ❡One paragraph and he's caught the town. Expert description created by an artful selection from the hundreds of details he must have had in his notebook and his memory.❷

65   Next to a red tobacco barn stood the general merchandise with a poster of Senator Albert Gore, Jr., smiling from the window. I knocked. The door opened partway. A tall, thin man said, "Closed up. For good," and started to shut the door.

66   "Don't want to buy anything. Just a question for Mr. Thurmond Watts."

67   The man peered through the slight opening. He looked me over. "What question would that be?"

68   "If this is Nameless, Tennessee, could he tell me how it got that name?"

69   The man turned back into the store and called out, "Miss

Ginny! Somebody here wants to know how Nameless come to be Nameless."

Miss Ginny edged to the door and looked me and my truck 70 over. Clearly, she didn't approve. She said, "You know as well as I do, Thurmond. Don't keep him on the stoop in the damp to tell him." Miss Ginny, I found out, was Mrs. Virginia Watts, Thurmond's wife.

I stepped in and they both began telling the story, adding a 71 detail here, the other correcting a fact there, both smiling at the foolishness of it all. It seems the hilltop settlement went for years without a name. Then one day the Post Office Department told the people if they wanted mail up on the mountain they would have to give the place a name you could properly address a letter to. The community met; there were only a handful, but they commenced debating. Some wanted patriotic names, some names from nature, one man recommended in all seriousness his own name. They couldn't agree, and they ran out of names to argue about. Finally, a fellow tired of the talk; he didn't like the mail he received anyway. "Forget the durn Post Office," he said. "This here's a nameless place if I ever seen one, so leave it be." And that's just what they did.

Watts pointed out the window. "We used to have signs on the 72 road, but the Halloween boys keep tearin' them down."

"You think Nameless is a funny name," Miss Ginny said. "I see 73 it plain in your eyes. Well, you take yourself up north a piece to Difficult or Defeated or Shake Rag. Now them are silly names."

The old store, lighted only by three fifty-watt bulbs, smelled of 74 coal oil and baking bread. In the middle of the rectangular room, where the oak floor sagged a little, stood an iron stove. To the right was a wooden table with an unfinished game of checkers and a stool made from an apple-tree stump. On shelves around the walls sat earthen jugs with corncob stoppers, a few canned goods, and some of the two thousand old clocks and clockworks Thurmond Watts owned. Only one was ticking; the others he just looked at. I asked how long he'd been in the store.

"Thirty-five years, but we closed the first day of the year. We're 75 hopin' to sell it to a churchly couple. Upright people. No athians."

"Did you build this store?" 76

"I built this one, but it's the third general store on the ground. 77 I fear it'll be the last. I take no pleasure in that. Once you could come in here for a gallon of paint, a pickle, a pair of shoes, and a can of corn."

❝ I think the author does a good job of capturing local dialects without overdoing it—that's not as easy as it looks—and without patronizing or making fun of the people he's quoting. What do you think? ❞

78   "Or horehound candy," Miss Ginny said. "Or corsets and salves. We had cough syrups and all that for the body. In season, we'd buy and sell blackberries and walnuts and chestnuts, before the blight got them. And outside, Thurmond milled corn and sharpened plows. Even shoed a horse sometimes."

79   "We could fix up a horse or a man or a baby," Watts said.

80   "Thurmond, tell him we had a doctor on the ridge in them days."

81   "We had a doctor on the ridge in them days. As good as any doctor alivin'. He'd cut a crooked toenail or deliver a woman. Dead these last years.

82   "I got some bad ham meat one day," Miss Ginny said, "and took to vomitin'. All day, all night. Hangin' on the drop edge of yonder. I said to Thurmond, 'Thurmond, unless you want shut of me, call the doctor.'

83   "I studied on it," Watts said.

84   "You never did. You got him right now. He come over and put three drops of iodeen in half a glass of well water. I drank it down and the vomitin' stopped with the last swallow. Would you think iodeen could do that?"

85   "He put Miss Ginny on one teaspoon of spirits of ammonia in well water for her nerves. Ain't nothin' works better for her to this day."

86   "Calms me like the hand of the Lord."

87   Hilda, the Wattses' daughter, came out of the backroom. "I remember him," she said. "I was just a baby. Y'all were talkin' to him, and he lifted me up on the counter and gave me a stick of Juicy Fruit and a piece of cheese."

88   "Knew the old medicines," Watts said. "Only drugstore he needed was a good kitchen cabinet. None of them antee-beeotics that hit you worsen your ailment. Forgotten lore now, the old medicines, because they ain't profit in iodeen."

89   Miss Ginny started back to the side room where she and her sister Marilyn were taking apart a duck-down mattress to make bols-

ters. She stopped at the window for another look at Ghost Dancing. "How do you sleep in that thing? Ain't you all cramped and cold?"

"How does the clam sleep in his shell?" Watts said in my 90 defense.

"Thurmond, get the boy a piece of buttermilk pie afore he goes 91 on."

"Hilda, get him some buttermilk pie." He looked at me. "You 92 like good music?" I said I did. He cranked up an old Edison phonograph, the kind with the big morning-glory blossom for a speaker, and put on a wax cylinder. "This will be 'My Mother's Prayer,'" he said.

While I ate buttermilk pie, Watts served as disc jockey of 93 Nameless, Tennessee. "Here's 'Mountain Rose,'" It was one of those moments that you know at the time will stay with you to the grave: the sweet pie, the gaunt man playing the old music, the coals in the stove glowing orange, the scent of kerosene and hot bread. "Here's 'Evening Rhapsody.'" The music was so heavily romantic we both laughed. I thought: It is for this I have come.

Feathered over and giggling, Miss Ginny stepped from the side 94 room. She knew she was a sight. "Thurmond, give him some lunch. Still looks hungry."

Hilda pulled food off the woodstove in the backroom: home- 95 butchered and canned whole-hog sausage, home-canned June apples, turnip greens, cole slaw, potatoes, stuffing, hot cornbread. All delicious.

Watts and Hilda sat and talked while I ate. "Wish you would 96 join me."

"We've ate," Watts said. "Cain't beat a woodstove for flavorful 97 cookin'."

He told me he was raised in a one-hundred-fifty-year-old cabin 98 still standing in one of the hollows. "How many's left," he said, "that grew up in a log cabin? I ain't the last surely, but I must be climbin' on the list."

Hilda cleared the table. "You Watts ladies know how to cook." 99

"She's in nursin' school at Tennessee Tech. I went over for one 100 of them football games last year there at Coevul." To say *Cookeville*, you let the word collapse in upon itself so that it comes out "Coevul."

"Do you like football?" I asked. 101

"Don't know. I was so high up in that stadium, I never opened 102 my eyes."

103   Watts went to the back and returned with a fat spiral notebook that he set on the table. His expression had changed. "Miss Ginny's *Deathbook*."

104   The thing startled me. Was it something I was supposed to sign? He opened it but said nothing. There were scads of names written in a tidy hand over pages incised to crinkliness by a ballpoint. Chronologically, the names had piled up: wives, grandparents, a stillborn infant, relatives, friends close and distant. Names, Names. After each, the date of *the* unknown finally known and transcribed. The last entry bore yesterday's date.

105   "She's wrote out twenty year's worth. Ever day she listens to the hospital report on the radio and puts the names in. Folks come by to check a date. Or they just turn through the books. Read them like a scrapbook."

106   Hilda said, "Like Saint Peter at the gates inscribin' the names."

107   Watts took my arm. "Come along." He led me to the fruit cellar under the store. As we went down, he said, "Always take a newborn baby upstairs afore you take him downstairs, otherwise you'll incline him downwards."

108   The cellar was dry and full of cobwebs and jar after jar of home-canned food, the bottles organized as a shopkeeper would: sausage, pumpkin, sweet pickles, tomatoes, corn, relish, blackberries, peppers, squash, jellies. He held a hand out toward the dusty bottles. "Our tomorrows."

109   Upstairs again, he said, "Hope to sell the store to the right folk. I see now, though, it'll be somebody offen the ridge. I've studied on it, and maybe it's the end of our place." He stirred the coals. "This store could give a comfortable livin', but not likely get you rich. But just gettin' by is dice rollin' to people nowadays. I never did see my day guaranteed."

110   When it was time to go, Watts said, "If you find anyone along your way wants a good store—on the road to Cordell Hull Lake—tell them about us."

111   I said I would. Miss Ginny and Hilda and Marilyn came out to say goodbye. It was cold and drizzling again. "Weather to give a man the weary dismals," Watts grumbled. "Where you headed from here?"

112   "I don't know."

113   "Cain't get lost then."

114   Miss Ginny looked again at my rig. It had worried her from the

first as it had my mother. "I hope you don't get yourself kilt in that
durn thing gallivantin' around the country."

"Come back when the hills dry off," Watts said. "We'll go 115
lookin' for some of them round rocks all sparkly inside."

I thought a moment. "Geodes?" 116

"Them's the ones. The county's properly full of them." 117

Discussion

• Joseph Mitchell in his old hotel and William Least Heat Moon in
his old store are, in a sense, dealing with the same subject. What do they
do that is similar and what that is different? What works and what doesn't
work?

• When many writers quote people, they all sound like the writer.
Does Moon fall into this trap? If not, what does he do to keep his voice
separate from his characters' voices?

• At what points in the text do you know what the writer is thinking
about? How does he make his views known?

• What qualities do the specifics he selects share? What kind of
details was he looking for when he was collecting information?

Activities

• Interview someone and write a brief account of part of the interview—a page or two—allowing the subject to speak directly to the reader.

• Set up standards for something on which you are an authority in
your world and then reveal those standards to your reader the way the
author sets standards for on-the-road restaurants.

• Visit someone from a world that has changed or is changing and use
that visit to write a piece recording and celebrating that lost world.

• Rewrite one of the scenes in Least Heat Moon's piece as a different
form of writing—perhaps a government report on the need for establishing
historic sites, a proposal for such a site, a section in a history text, a movie
scene, a nostalgic essay such as E. B. White's starting on page 494, an
account of the store being opened when the owner was younger and the
area more heavily populated, the store as it was seen by the doctor or is
seen by the daughter. Try your own form, your own angle of vision.

• To see how effective the dialogue is, rewrite a page from the piece
without dialogue.

John McPhee

John McPhee would win the title of best nonfiction writer practicing today from all the colleagues I have in nonfiction magazine and book writing. I don't like to meet my heroes but John McPhee came to the University of New Hampshire, where he read to more than a thousand people, and I found him as natural and easy as I had hoped. He told us, for example, that he wouldn't attend any functions unless the majority of the guests were students. He was patient and open and, above all, he listened to everyone with the same attention and respect.

His writing about people and the natural world is marked by a similar respect—and wonder—at the pieces and the places he is reporting. He is learning as he reports and he allows the reader to participate in that learning. One of the marks of a great reporter is the ability to be astonished at the obvious. Oranges are obvious to most of us, yet McPhee found in the ordinary orange a *New Yorker* article that later became one of his seventeen books. Do you have to go to New York City or Hollywood to get experience to write? No, the best subjects may be on your breakfast table. In *Write To Learn*, I quote McPhee telling how a daily glass of orange juice he'd purchase in Pennsylvania Station in New York sparked the book from which this selection is chosen.

Oranges

1   The enormous factories that the frozen people have built . . .more closely resemble oil refineries than auto plants. The evaporators are tall assemblages of looping pipes, quite similar to the cat-cracking towers that turn crude oil into gasoline. When oranges arrive, in semitrailers, they are poured into giant bins, so that a plant can have a kind of reservoir to draw upon. At Minute Maid's plant in Auburndale, for example, forty bins hold four million oranges, or enough to keep the plant going for half a day. From samples analyzed by technicians who are employed by the State of Florida, the plant manager knows what the juice, sugar, and acid content is of the fruit in each bin, and blends the oranges into the assembly line accordingly, always attempting to achieve as uniform a product as possible.

An individual orange obviously means nothing in this process, and the rise of concentrate has brought about a basic change in the system by which oranges are sold.

Growers used to sell oranges as oranges. They now sell "pounds-solids," and modern citrus men seem to use the term in every other sentence they utter. The rise of concentrate has not only changed the landscape and the language; it has, in a sense, turned the orange inside out. Because the concentrate plants are making a product of which the preponderant ingredient is sugar, it is sugar that they buy as raw material. They pay for the number of pounds of solids that come dissolved in the juice in each truckload of oranges, and these solids are almost wholly sugars. Growers now worry more about the number of pounds of sugar they are producing per acre than the quality of the individual oranges on their trees. If the concentrate plants bought oranges by weight alone, growers could plant, say, Hamlins on Rough Lemon in light sand—a scion, rootstock, and soil combination that will produce extremely heavy yields of insipid and watery oranges.

As the fruit starts to move along a concentrate plant's assembly line, it is first culled. In what some citrus people remember as "the old fresh-fruit days," before the Second World War, about forty per cent of all oranges grown in Florida were eliminated at packinghouses and dumped in fields. Florida milk tasted like orangeade. Now, with the exception of the split and rotten fruit, all of Florida's orange crop is used. Moving up a conveyor belt, oranges are scrubbed with detergent before they roll on into juicing machines. There are several kinds of juicing machines, and they are something to see. One is called the Brown Seven Hundred. Seven hundred oranges a minute go into it and are split and reamed on the same kind of rosettes that are in the centers of ordinary kitchen reamers. The rinds that come pelting out the bottom are integral halves, just like the rinds of oranges squeezed in a kitchen. Another machine is the Food Machinery Corporation's FMC In-line Extractor. It has a shining row of aluminum jaws, upper and lower, with shining aluminum teeth. When an orange tumbles in, the upper jaw comes crunching down on it while at the same time the orange is penetrated from below by a perforated steel tube. As the jaws crush the outside, the juice goes through the perforations in the tube and down into the plumbing of the concentrate plant. All in a second, the juice has been removed and the rind has been crushed and shredded beyond recognition.

❡ You should be aware of the analogies that McPhee uses to compare complicated machines and other matters to images, devices and techniques to things with which we are familiar. ❡

4   From either machine, the juice flows on into a thing called the finisher, where seeds, rag, and pulp are removed. The finisher has a big stainless steel screw that steadily drives the juice through a fine-mesh screen. From the finisher, it flows on into holding tanks. Orange juice squeezed at home should be consumed fairly soon after it is expressed, because air reacts with it and before long produces a bitter taste, and the juice has fatty constituents that can become rancid. In the extractors, the finishers, and the troughs of concentrate plants, a good bit of air gets into the juice. Bacilli and other organisms may have started growing in it. So the juice has to be pasteurized. In some plants, this occurs before it is concentrated. In others, pasteurization is part of the vacuum-evaporating process—for example, in the Minute Maid plant in Auburndale, which uses the Thermal Accelerated Short Time Evaporator (T.A.S.T.E.). A great, airy network of bright-red, looping tubes, the Short Time stands about fifty feet high. Old-style evaporators keep one load of juice within them for about an hour, gradually boiling the water out. In the Short Time, juice flows in at one end in a continuous stream and comes out the other end eight minutes later.

5   Specific gravity, figured according to a special scale for sugar solutions, is the measurement of concentrate. The special scale, worked out by a nineteenth-century German scientist named Adolf F. W. Brix, is read in "degrees Brix." Orange juice as it comes out of oranges is usually about twelve degrees Brix—that is, for every hundred pounds of water there are twelve pounds of sugar. In the Short Time, orange juice passes through seven stages. At each stage, there are sampling valves. The juice at the start is plain, straightforward orange juice but with a notable absence of pulp or juice vesicles. By the third stage, the juice is up to nineteen degrees Brix and has the viscosity and heat of fairly thick hot chocolate. The flavor is rich and the aftertaste is clean. At the fifth stage, the juice is up to forty-six degrees Brix—already thicker than the ultimate product that goes into the six-ounce can—and it has the consistency of cough syrup, with a biting aftertaste. After the seventh stage, the orange juice can be as high as seventy degrees Brix. It is a deep apricot-orange in color. It is thick enough to chew, and its taste actually suggests apri-

cot-flavored gum. Stirred into enough water to take it back to twelve degrees Brix, it tastes like nothing much but sweetened water.

❡ When you can use sense other than sight in a description—in this case taste—you make a lively and helpful contact with the reader. Inexperienced writers forget to tell the reader how something smells, sounds, feels, tastes as well as how it looks. Some even forget to tell how it looks. McPhee doesn't.❡

As a season progresses, the sugar-acid ratio of oranges improves. Pineapple oranges, at their peak, are better in this respect than Hamlins at theirs; and Valencias are the best of all. So the concentrators keep big drums of out-of-season concentrate in cold-storage rooms and blend them with in-season concentrates in order to achieve even more uniformity. Advertisements can be misleading, however, when they show four or five kinds of oranges and imply that each can of the advertiser's concentrate contains an exact blend of all of them. It would be all but impossible to achieve that. The blending phase of the process is at best only an educated stab at long-term uniformity, using whatever happens to be on hand in the cold rooms and the fresh-fruit bins. The blending is, moreover, merely a mixing of old and new concentrates, still at sixty degrees Brix and still all but tasteless if reconstituted with water.

The most important moment comes when the cutback is poured in, taking the super-concentrated juice down to forty-five degrees Brix, which MacDowell and his colleagues worked out as a suitable level, because three cans of tap water seemed to be enough to thaw the juice fairly quickly but not so much that the cooling effect of the cold concentrate would be lost in the reconstituted juice. Cutback is mainly fresh orange juice, but it contains additional flavor essences, peel oil, and pulp. Among the components that get boiled away in the evaporator are at least eight hydrocarbons, four esters, fifteen carbonyls, and sixteen kinds of alcohol. The chemistry of orange juice is so subtle and complicated that most identifications are tentative, and no one can guess which components form its taste, let alone in what proportion. Some of these essences are recovered in condensation chambers in the evaporators, and they are put back into the juice. The chief flavoring element in cutback is d-limonene, which is the main ingredient of peel oil. The oil cells in the skins of all citrus fruit are ninety per cent d-limonene. It is d-limonene that burns the lips of children sucking oranges. D-limonene reddened the lips of the ladies of the seventeenth-century French court, who bit into limes for the purpose. D-limonene is what makes the leaves of all orange and grapefruit trees smell like lemons when crushed in the hand. D-limonene is what the Martini drinker rubs on the rim of his glass and then drops into his drink in a twist of lemon. The modern Martini drinker has stouter taste buds than his predecessors of the seventeenth century, when people in Europe used to spray a little peel oil on the outside of their wineglasses, in the belief that it was so strong that it would penetrate the glass and impart a restrained flavor to the wine. In the same century, peel oil was widely used in Germany in the manufacture of "preservative plague-lozenges." In the fourteenth century in Ceylon, men who dived into lakes to search the bottom for precious stones first rubbed their bodies with orange-peel oil in order to repel crocodiles and poisonous snakes. Peel oil is flammable. Peel oil is the principal flavoring essence that frozen people put into concentrated orange juice in order to attempt to recover the flavor of fresh orange juice. "We have always had the flavor of fresh oranges to come up against," MacDowell told me. "People who make things like tomato juice and pineapple juice have not had this problem."

8   Because of freezes and other variables, concentrate has its good and bad years. In the past decade, for example, the '55s and '59s were outstanding. The '60s and '73s were quite poor. The '58s were even worse. But the '64s were memorable. Concentrate plants lay down samples in a kind of frozen reference library—one six-ounce can from each half hour of each day's run. The relative excellence of any given concentrate year is established by taste panels of citrus scientists, who stand in black-walled booths that are lighted by red light bulbs and drink concentrate from brandy snifters. They decide, variously, whether the taste is stale, insipid, immature, or overmature; too sour, too sweet, too bitter, or too astringent; whether it seems to have been overheated or to contain too much peel oil; and whether it suggests buttermilk, cardboard, caster oil, or tallow.

9   Plants that make "chilled juice" are set up as concentrate plants are, but without the evaporators. Instead, the juice goes into bottles and cartons and is shipped to places as distant as Nome. Tropicana, by far the biggest company in the chilled-juice business, ships twelve thousand quarts of orange juice to Nome each month. People in Los Angeles, surprisingly enough, drink two hundred and forty thousand

quarts of Tropicana orange juice a month, and the company's Los Angeles sales are second only to sales in New York.

Tropicana used to ship orange juice by sea from Florida to New York in a glistening white tanker with seven hundred and thirty thousand gallons of juice slurping around in the hold. For guests of the company, the ship had four double staterooms and a gourmet chef. Among freeloaders, it was considered one of the seven wonders of commerce. To sailors of the merchant marine, it was the most attractive billet on the high seas. A typical week consisted of three nights in New York, two nights at sea, and two nights in Florida. There was almost no work to do. There were forty-two men in the crew, some with homes at each end. White as a yacht, the ship would glide impressively past Wall Street and under the bridges of the East River, put forth a stainless-steel tube, and quickly drain its cargo into tanks in Queens.

Tropicana unfortunately found that although this was a stylish way to transport orange juice, it was also uneconomical. The juice now goes by rail, already packed in bottles or cartons. The cartons are being phased out because they admit too much oxygen. Tropicana people are frank in appraisal of their product. "It's the closest thing to freshly squeezed orange juice you can get and not have to do the work yourself," one of the company's executives told me. To maintain the cloud in the juice and keep it from settling, enzymes have to be killed by raising the temperature of the juice to nearly two hundred degrees. Even so, there is some loss of Vitamin C if the juice remains unconsumed too long, just as there is a loss of Vitamin C if concentrate is mixed in advance and allowed to stand for some time.

During the winter, Tropicana freezes surplus orange juice in huge floes and stores it until summer, when it is cracked up, fed into an ice crusher, melted down, and shipped. In this way, the company avoids the more usual practice of chilled-juice shippers, who sell reconstituted concentrate in the summertime, adding dry juice-sacs in order to create the illusion of freshness. The juice-sacs come from California as "barreled washed pulp."

Leftover rinds, rag, pulp, and seeds at chilled-juice and concentrate plants have considerable value of their own. In most years, about fourteen million dollars are returned to the citrus industry through its by-products. Orange wine tastes like a one-for-one mixture of dry vermouth and sauterne. It varies from estate-bottled types like Pool's and Vino del Sol to Florida Fruit Bowl Orange Wine, the *vin ordinaire* of Florida shopping centers, made by National Grape

Products of Jacksonville, and sold for ninety-nine cents. Florida winos are said to like the price. Florida Life cordials are made from citrus fruit, as are Consul gin, Surf Side gin, Five Flag gin, Fleet Street gin, and Consul vodka.

14   Peel oil has been used to make not only paint but varnish as well. It hardens rubber, too, but is more commonly used in perfumes and as a flavor essence for anything that is supposed to taste of orange, from candy to cake-mixes and soft drinks. Carvone, a synthetic spearmint oil which is used to flavor spearmint gum, is made from citrus peel oil. The Coca-Cola Company is one of the world's largest users of peel oil, as anyone knows who happens to have noticed the lemony smell of the d-limonene that clings to the inside of an empty Coke bottle.

15   A million and a half pounds of polyunsaturated citrus-seed oil is processed and sold each year, for cooking. Hydrogenated orange-seed oil is more like butter, by-products researchers told me, than oleomargine. Noticing a refrigerator in their laboratory, I asked if they had some on hand. They said they were sorry, but all they had was real butter. Would I care for an English muffin?

16   Looking out a window over an orange grove, one researcher remarked, "We are growing chemicals now, not oranges." Dried juice vesicles, powdered and mixed with water, produce a thick and foamy solution which is used to fight forest fires. Albedecone, a pharmaceutical which stops leaks in blood vessels, is made from hesperidin, a substance in the peels of oranges. But the main use of the leftover rinds is cattle feed, either as molasses made from the peel sugars or as dried shredded meal. Citrus pulp and chopped rinds are dried for dairy feed much in the same way that clothes are dried in a home dryer—in a drum within a drum, whirling. The exhaust vapors perfume the countryside for miles around concentrate plants with a heavy aroma of oranges. The evaporators themselves are odorless. People often assume that they are smelling the making of orange juice when they are actually smelling cattle feed. If the aroma is not as delicate as the odor of blossoms, it is nonetheless superior to the aroma of a tire and rubber plant, a Limburger cheese factory, a pea cannery, a paper mill, or an oil refinery. Actually, the orange atmospheres of the Florida concentrate towns are quite agreeable, and, in my own subjective view, the only town in the United States which outdoes them in this respect is Hershey, Pennsylvania.

17   One plant is now concentrating juice electronically—and some citrus scientists think that this may be the process of the future. Into

a tank of juice goes a large rod which gives off high-energy short-wave pulses, energizing water molecules in the juice. The energized particles leave more rapidly in the evaporator, and fewer evaporating stages are required. Electronic concentrate of seventy-two degrees Brix can be quickly produced and will keep at thirty-two degrees Fahrenheit, whereas ordinary concentrate requires temperatures around fifteen below zero.

Dr. MacDowell, and others, think that any form of concentrate may be just an intermediate phase. "This is what we're working on," he said to me when I visited him, reaching to a shelf for a laboratory display bottle which contained light yellow crystals of dry orange juice. "Ninety-nine Brix," he said. "These are the pounds-solids that everyone talks about and almost no one ever sees." Crystals are being made in several ways. MacDowell's team uses a process called foam-mat. They introduce very small amounts of methylated cellulose or modified soybean protein as foaming agents, then heat the juice until it is stiff, like egg whites. They spread this as a kind of orange-juice mat onto perforated steel trays and blow air up through the holes in the trays until the mat is dry. At Plant City, Florida, a company called Plant Industries, Inc., is already making orange-juice crystals commercially, and by a different method. They pour concentrate onto a moving steel belt in a hot vacuum chamber. The concentrate dries on the belt in eighty seconds and is scraped off. As it is packed, a bit of peel oil, locked into sugar granules, is sprinkled into each can.

Stirred into water, crystals taste like concentrate. Plant Industries sells them to hospitals and other institutions, and to the armed forces. The trouble with crystals commercially is that they are still too expensive. After all, the crystal-making process begins with finished concentrate. The general manager at Plant Industries is a Yale graduate who was raised in St. Paul, Minnesota. He says generously that crystals produced the other way, by the foam-mat process, make fine orange juice, except that it tends to get a head on it, like a glass of beer.

18

19

Discussion

• Read the remarkable account of how McPhee writes by William Howarth, editor of *The John McPhee Reader* (Vintage/Random House, 1977) and report to the class on his writing process. Suggest how his process might be used to solve student writing problems.

• This is another piece that expresses a sense of loss through progress. How does McPhee use techniques similar to or different from Scanlan, Mitchell, and Moon?

• Work with the members of your class to think of all the ways McPhee collected the information in the selection. Pick another process used by industry in your area and list the places you might find information with which to write?

• McPhee builds his text with information. What does that mean? Where can you show him doing that? How could you apply that to your own writing or the writing of a classmate?

Activities

• Pick something ordinary as frozen orange juice in your life and write a short piece to show how extraordinary it is.

• Take a complicated subject on which you are familiar and use some of McPhee's techniques to make it clear to a reader.

• Make a list of what you know—or can observe—about a subject, order it, and then write a page, trying to turn it into clear, flowing, lively prose as McPhee does.

• Take one of McPhee's long paragraphs and rearrange the sentences to see if you can make it work a different way than McPhee.

• One way to organize a paragraph is a 2-3-1 pattern with the most important information last, the next most important information at the first, the least important information in the middle. Can you find such a paragraph? Does it work?

Thomas Whiteside

Thomas Whiteside is another professional journalist who has focused his eye on a common part of our diet—the tomato. Whiteside is also a *New Yorker* writer who has the ability to scoop up information like an intellectual vacuum cleaner. You know, reading his copy, that for each fact, quotation, detail, statistic, anecdote he serves the reader there are dozens he left in his notebook and in his files. He writes with selection, ordering and reordering his information until each fact moves the reader forward toward a greater understanding of the subject.

Tomatoes

The biggest tomato-growing and packing company in the state 1
is Florida Tomato Packers, and . . . I had arranged . . . to have a talk
with Paul J. Di Mare, the general manager of the Florida Tomato
Packers plant in Florida City, and to go out with him for a glimpse
of the commercial tomato-growing process in southern Florida . . .

Di Mare picked some samples of mature-green tomatoes, which 2
were as hard as baseballs, from the field and put them in the front
seat of the pickup. We drove back to his packinghouse in Florida
City, where, in a shed, he showed me a long line of machinery,
tended by a hundred and twenty women, into which a truckload of
apple-green tomatoes from his company's fields was being fed, to be
washed, manually culled, mechanically graded according to size,
sprayed with a thin coat of wax ("to make them look sexier," one
tomato producer said of the sheen applied), and loaded into thirty-
pound cardboard shipping cartons. The cartons would then be transferred to ethylene ripening chambers in another shed. Di Mare took
me over to see the ethylene-gas rooms. There were twenty-one of
them, faced with big aluminum doors, outside which, on a long loading platform, forklift trucks were buzzing about with cartons of tomatoes in the Florida sunshine. Di Mare opened one of the aluminum
doors, revealing a chamber about fifty feet long, twelve feet wide, and
eighteen feet high. There was a slight gassy smell. Pallets of filled
tomato cartons were piled almost to the ceiling. Di Mare said that
tomatoes at the mature-green stage were left in the ripening room for
from twenty-four to thirty-six hours, in which time they turned color
to the "starbreaker" stage—the stage at which the first blush of tan-
nish pink shows at the blossom end of the fruit. The gassed tomatoes
are then loaded into refrigerated trucks for shipment.

Di Mare told me that tomatoes had been ethylene-ripened for 3
market for years but that until fairly recently the artificially induced
ripening had been done at the receiving end of the bulk-shipping
process. Then, for various reasons, it was found to be more convenient to do it at the shipping end. Was it really impossible, I kept
wondering, to skip the ripening rooms and just let the ripening take
place in the fields, right on the tomato vines? I put the question again.
Not practical, Di Mare insisted, and we were back at the economics
of the business—the cost of the number of handpickings that would
be involved.

As Di Mare and I walked on, I began to enumerate in my mind 4 some of the economic forces that seemed to have been at work in the evolution of the present mass-marketed American tomato. A primary aim of the Florida growers in the whole exercise, it appeared, was to get fresh-market tomatoes out of the field as soon as possible after the sprouting of the seeds, and with the harvesting compressed into as close to one operation as possible. Obviously, in the last fifteen years the cost of pesticides to increase crop yields had become steadily higher, and the very increase in the cost of applying pesticides had given the growers an added incentive to curtail the growing period. The same thing was true of the spiralling cost of fertilizer. Then, the rising cost of using migrant workers for picking had given the growers an incentive to save by drastically reducing the number of pickings as the tomatoes matured on the vine toward the point of breaking color. True, the migrant workers used were employed on a piecework basis, but it seemed the growers had to contend with this calculation; poor and unorganized though the pickers were, could the growers, even if they wanted to, get the workers to pick particular fields five, six, or more times—each time collecting fewer mature-green tomatoes—without the risk of some kind of field-hand rebellion against the piece-work system? As far as the growers were concerned, the clear solution was to get the picking over with at the least cost by short-circuiting the natural ripening process on the vine and substituting for it the mass ripening in the ethylene-gas chamber. And acceptance by the industry of the principle of ethylene gassing at the shipping end had led to a further step. Up to then, tomatoes had been bred for such qualities favored by growers as high yield, disease resistance, smooth skin unbroken by ridges, and thick walls to withstand the rigors of picking and shipping. Now tomatoes that ripened well in ethylene chambers were being bred. And varieties of tomato that didn't take well to reddening by ethylene chamber, no matter how tasty they might be, were headed for obsolescence. Di Mare told me that the relatively new Walter variety, in particular, reacts well to ethylene treatment—that it was designed for uniformity of ripening. Hawkins, of the Florida Tomato Committee, had gone even further. "When we came out a few years ago with the Walter tomato, the variety had its own peculiarity," he told me. "It *had* to be gassed just after picking to ripen properly."

5   The breeding of new varieties of tomato for the firmness and retail-shelf longevity desired by packers, distributors, and supermarket operators has led to the development of a variety having not only a peculiar adaptability to ethylene treatment but also a superior resis-

tance to being knocked about by machinery. For some years, the Florida tomato-industry people have looked forward to a time when fresh-market tomatoes could be harvested by machine instead of by hand. In California and certain parts of the Midwest, tomato harvesting for commercial canneries is done exclusively by machines, and a few prototype machines for harvesting fresh-market tomatoes have been operated on an experimental basis in Florida. Just behind the vanguard of machine designers, and acting in concert with them, are the plant breeders, trying to develop a variety of tomato that is designed to withstand bruising by a mechanical picker and that happens to be particularly susceptible to the ethylene treatment. One result of these efforts has been the development of a wonder called the Florida MH-1, a tomato derived from the Walter variety. The Florida MH-1 is a tomato that has been engineered to fit the machine. I had heard about the Florida MH-1 from Hawkins, at the Florida Tomato Committee headquarters, and he had sounded enthusiastic about its bruise-resistant properties. "You could take an MH-1, stand twenty paces away from another man, and play catch with that tomato without hurting it," he declared.

Di Mare didn't have any Florida MH-1 tomatoes on hand, but, as it happened, there was an experiemtal plot of the machine-oriented tomato not far from Florida Tomato Packers headquarters—at the Homestead Agricultural Research and Education Center, a division of the University of Florida Institute of Food and Agricultural Sciences. When I had taken my leave of Di Mare and was headed back North again, I drove over to the research center, where I talked with Dr. R. B. Vohn, an assistant plant pathologist, and Dr. H. H. Bryan, an associate horticulturist. The Institute of Food and Agricultural Sciences is responsible for the development of the Florida MH-1. The institute appears to be closely geared to some of the practical needs of the Florida tomato industry, such as the development of disease-resistant strains. I found Dr. Volin and Dr. Bryan to be a bit sensitive about the implications of this connection with the industry, because public-interest advocates have charged that public funds have been used for agricultural research-and-development projects aimed not at improving nutrition but at increasing corporate profits. The two scientists felt such criticism to be unjust. In any event, the talk turned to the taste of tomatoes that one buys in supermarkets. Dr. Volin said that research studies he was familiar with indicated that there had been no decline in the taste of fresh tomatoes in recent years. The taste of new varieties was not appreciably different from that of old varieties still being grown, and appearance was superior in the new varieties, he said. "Memory has a funny way of playing tricks on people; they remember the good things and forget the bad," he told me.

7   We talked about the development of the MH-1. Dr. Volin considered such a development socially desirable. "Humanity is out there in the fields suffering, doing that handpicking and carrying of fruit," he said. "Migrant workers could be riding machines that would do that work. Some of the people who were once picking for ten hours a day now are *riding* such machines to harvest tomatoes, as well as other fruits and vegetables." Dr. Volin told me that crops of the MH-1 had already been successfully picked by machine in field tests "and shipped to test markets in Washington and Atlanta with superior results." Dr. Bryan produced for me a sample of a ripe MH-1 tomato. It was somewhat dark-hued and had a very smooth skin, only slightly ridged at the shoulder. Dr. Bryan spoke of the characteristics that made the MH-1 suitable for machine harvesting—thick skin and firm flesh. To demonstrate these qualities, Dr. Bryan tossed the MH-1 to a height of a little more than six feet and let it drop on the asbestos-tiled floor of Dr. Volin's office. The tomato landed with a thud. It lay a little lopsided—a bit flushed, it seemed to me—but the skin remained unbroken. Dr. Bryan picked it up and tossed it to nearly ceiling height for another drop to the floor. This time, the sound of the impact was louder, and the tomato split open slightly on one side, but there was no splattering of its contents. I had assumed a little internal rupturing, a little flow of tomato juice from the open crack in the skin, but the thick outer walls were proof against that. Dr. Bryan and Dr. Volin then took me out into the sunshine for a visit to an experimental plot where rows of MH-1s were growing on plastic mulch. Dr. Volin picked a red-ripe MH-1, cut it open, and offered me a half. I took a bite. It tasted like a tough tomato to me.

8   During my visit to Di Mare, I had pressed the question whether the best place to ripen a tomato wasn't on the tomato vine itself. Now, talking to Dr. Volin and Dr. Bryan, I became aware of the existence of a scheme for encouraging that, but not in quite the way I had been thinking of. So far, the scene of the ethylene ripening process had moved from the receiving end of the transport operation to the packing and shipping end. Now, I learned, another development was advancing on Tomatoland—the prospect of an artificial ethylene treatment for green tomatoes right on the vine. This biological coup

would be brought about by spraying the crops with a chemical that would stimulate ethylene production in green tomatoes and cause them to change color at a far faster rate than slow nature allows and all at the same time; thus reddened on the vine at an unprecedentedly early stage and at one chemical stroke, an entire crop could be harvested in a single picking.

Some time after leaving Dr. Volin and Dr. Bryan, I obtained a 9 pamphlet from the manufacturer and promoter of this new form of tomato processing. The chemical spray is called Ethrel and is put out by Amchem Products. At the top of the first page of the pamphlet was a fine color photograph of a magnificent sunrise, and the heading under the photograph read, "Dawn of the Plant Regulator—New Path to More Crop Profits." The plant regulator in question was described as "a formulation containing (2-chloroethyl) phosphoric acid," which on application "liberates ethylene, a natural plant hormone identified for years as nature's own ripening agent," and as "a successful crop-management tool for more profit." According to the text, the use of Ethrel "lets you actually schedule your harvest—7 to 14 days ahead of usual picking." And the grower was urged, "Just spray on Ethrel . . ."

> ❧ Whiteside gets out of the way and lets the brochure he had picked up during his research make his case for him. Usually the case is better made by an authority or document than by the writer. ❧

The development of such formulations for artificially turning 10 green tomatoes into red tomatoes right on the vine has been designed primarily for use in conjunction with mechanical harvesting. According to the Amchem people, Ethrel is already being used widely on California tomato crops that are to be mechanically harvested for canneries. So far, the system has been used for fresh-market tomatoes only on a small scale, but the Amchem people, who claim that a hundred thousand acres of tomato crops for cannery and other process uses were sprayed with Ethrel last year, seem optimistic about its use on fresh-market tomato crops. So do salesmen for companies putting out similar products. So does Dr. Volin, who thinks that the combination of the Florida MH-1 and Ethrel or a similar chemical compound would constitute "a very useful tool" for the fresh-tomato industry.

In the meantime, it's the ethylene-gas chamber as usual for 11 most of the fresh tomatoes that Americans are eating now, and will be eating for quite a while. That the production of ethylene is in fact an essential element of the ripening process of tomatoes and other fruits is undeniable. But is an ethylene-gassed tomato necessarily a ripe tomato? One of the problems of picking green tomatoes for subsequent ethylene treatment is that in order to bring out of the ethylene treatment room a tomato that will have any tomato taste at all the processors must start with green fruit that has been picked at a technically mature stage. And it seems that the only sure way of telling that any on the vine has reached the mature-green stage is to cut it open with a knife and examine it, for it is the condition of the seeds and the gel in the internal chambers which shows whether it has attained the proper stage. Almost any green tomato, mature or immature, can be made to change color in an ethylene ripening room, but in terms of taste a less than mature green tomato, no matter how pink a flush it is given by ethylene treatment, can never be brought much further than from bitter to tasteless. As R. A. Seelig and Lacy P. McColloch wrote in a booklet called "Toward Better Tomatoes," issued by the United Fresh Fruit and Vegetable Association, "tomatoes picked immature green may redden but will never be good to eat." And, according to a study conducted in the growing season of 1970-71 by Dr. C. B. Hall and D. D. Gull, both of the University of Florida, significant numbers of the Florida tomatoes packed for shipment north as mature fruit were actually immature green. In fact, the study concluded, of the tomatoes examined "at least 40 per cent of the 7 x 7 size were so immature that the seeds were cut," and it noted that "in March 12 shipment 78 per cent were in that category." When this report was presented to the Florida Tomato Committee, its manager at the time, Jack Peters, commented at a growers' meeting that "it very definitely confirms the experiments you and I have been observing for many years, and that is: much of the time we are shipping these green tomatoes [that] are mature according to [industry] standards but. . .are not really as mature as would be required to supply the consumers with a quality product." And when the fruit *is* picked at the mature-green stage and subjected to ethylene, the gassing can, at best, supply to the tomato only what its own ethylene could have supplied if the tomato had been allowed to produce the gas naturally. Dr. Stanley Burg, a plant physiologist on the staff of the University of Florida, told me, "The ripening process is a scheduled part of the life of the fruit. You can fool the tomato into ripening prematurely by ethylene application. That can trigger some of the ripening process, but only the part of it that ethylene can trigger." The development of the fruit on the vine to the stage of perceptible reddening is far more complex than that, involving among other things, the transport and subtle interaction of scores of aromatic compounds in the plant, and the development and particular balance of various sugars and acids, all of which, working together, gradually impart to the fruit ripening on the vine the peculiarly rich and generous fresh-tomato flavor. According to Dr. M. Allen Stevens, a plant geneticist at the University of California at Davis, in an article on tomato flavor published in *Western Grower & Shipper*, "high sugars and a favorable sugar/acid ratio are crucial to good tomato flavor." And he noted that many traits considered favorable by commercial growers of tomatoes "are in opposition to the ones needed for high sugars."

The general use of artificial ripening, then, is by no means the 12 only major influence at work on the present quality of store-bought tomatoes. The temperature at which tomatoes are shipped needs to be kept constant, but the shipper generally has no control over what is done in transit, because it is independent truckers who carry out most of the shipping, and the quality of the fruit may suffer accordingly. Then, when the tomatoes have been repacked and, as likely as not, put in plastic sleeves for sale in supermarkets or other retail stores, the shipment is often kept in refrigerated display cases with other food at temperatures that do the tomatoes no good. "The average supermarket refrigerator is kept at thirty-eight degrees, and tomatoes should never be stored at less than forty-eight degrees," I was told by Jerry Brownstein, the executive vice-president of Embassy Produce, which is the biggest repacker and distributor of fresh-market tomatoes in the New York area.

But this is not all that has happened to tomatoes in the retail 13 markets of the Northeast. An even more noticeable change is the disappearance of the supply of ripe tomatoes that used to be available to city people here during the local tomato-growing season. Part of this disappearance is attributable to the overrunning of nearby market-garden areas by suburban housing developments. New Jersey still has extensive tracts of land that were formerly used to supply New York with vast quantities of fresh tomatoes, but tomato wholesalers in the New York area are increasingly passing up the fresh New Jersey tomatoes in favor of the ethylene-gassed kind. In 1960, New Jersey provided New York with three hundred and seventeen carlots of fresh tomatoes (a carlot being about forty thousand pounds) during the months of July and August. During the same two months in 1975, the wholesalers bought only sixty carlots of fresh, vine-ripened New Jersey tomatoes. Largely ignoring the New Jersey tomato fields an hour's trucking distance away, they have instead been buying gassed tomatoes from California, at the rate of four hundred and eleven carlots in the two biggest local growing months.

14   Why pass up fruit that is ripening on the vine almost at one's doorstep to order gassed fruit from a continent's breadth away? Brownstein, of Embassy Produce, which distributes wholesale about half a million pounds of fresh tomatoes a week to New York chain stores and other retail outlets, told me, "We used to handle a lot of tomatoes grown in upstate New York or New Jersey, but we found that the growers give us the kind of commercial product we want to handle. Most of the Jersey tomatoes now are just for local, neighborhood consumption. It's not as though New Jersey tomatoes were bad tomatoes. There *are* good Jersey tomatoes, but unless tomatoes are consistent in quality we don't want to handle them. Most of the Jersey ones don't have any carrying quality to speak of. The important thing for us in a tomato is to get it to the consumer looking good. No blemishes, no black spots, no softness. They'll accept a soft tomato in Chicago but they won't here. Fifteen or twenty years ago, repackers in the New York area would close their doors from July to the end of August while the local ripe tomatoes came into the retail stores. But now you don't get merchants—or customers, either—who know how to treat merchandise as spoilable as local fresh tomatoes. Take those ripe Jersey tomatoes whose flavor people rave about. A merchant will put up a display of two hundred pounds of them, and at the end of the day he'll have to take off seventy pounds and throw them out, because of the abuse they've had. Just the handling by customers. Self-service—that's what has brought about thicker skins in tomatoes. The New Jersey tomatoes you used to be able to buy so easily were a No. 4 color—a full ripeness. You don't get that anymore. The product has no shelf life, and has no place in a self-service economy."

15   Further, the big supermarkets prefer to have regular dealings with the big suppliers—the repackers, who, in turn, can make advantageous financial arrangements with the big packers and growers, like Di Mare's company, which in addition to its Florida operation ships tomatoes from South Carolina and, during the summer and fall months, from California. The supermarket operators are not interested in interrupting year-round supply arrangements to deal with local growers. An old-fashioned fruit-and-vegetable-store owner

knew how to handle tomatoes—how to arrange his displays so that the ripened tomatoes would be at the front and less ripe in the rear, where they would continue to ripen. But supermarkets, dealing with huge volumes of fruit, have no time for such constant rearranging; the grocery clerks putting the fruit on display are, as likely as not, high-school students who work on a part-time basis and may never have tasted a reasonably fresh, naturally ripened tomato in their lives. Thus, as time goes on there is less and less room in the stores for fresh local produce. The supermarkets, selling the impersonal self-service economy, have brought about a shift in the standards for so-called fresh fruit, in which the considerations of year-round supply, long shelf life, and uniformity of product—however mediocre its quality—are paramount.

And thus the original humble, delicate, fragile South American 16 tomato has been transformed by American agricultural science into tough stuff—genetically manipulated and crossbred for high yield, engineered to resist the inroads of soil disease and the mangling of sorting machines alike, rendered responsive to a vast variety of pesticides, fungicides, and artificial fertilizers, bred specifically for uniform maturing and destined for coloring in gas chambers, and provided with a hide to withstand the endless shocks of shipping and repacking and the vicissitudes of supermarket display racks. Pondering recently on the toughness of the MH-1, the tomato bred for the age of mechanical picking, and on how a particular MH-1 had remained intact after a six-foot fall to a hard tiled floor in Dr. Volin's office, I began to wonder whether America was making automobiles that would stand up as stolidly to that kind of impact. Out of curiosity, I telephoned Dr. William Haddon, Jr., an auto-safety expert, who is president of the Insurance Institute for Highway Safety, and asked him if one of his technical people could compute the approximate impact speed of the Florida MH-1 in the six-foot fall I had witnessed in ratio to the minimum federal requirements for impact resistance in the bumpers of cars sold in this country. Dr. Haddon obliged, and on the basis of the figures he provided I concluded that Dr. Bryan's MH-1 was able to survive its fall to the floor at an impact speed of 13.4 miles per hour, more than two and a half times the speed which federal auto-bumper safety standards provide for the minimum safety of current-model cars. This undoubtedly represents a great step forward in tomato safety. Yet such further advances cannot but leave one nagging doubt in my mind: Now that the food industry has succeeded admirably in breeding tomatoes superior in gassability and crashworthiness, where is the flavor? Where has the basic quality that is supposed to be the raison d'etre of a tomato—that delicious fresh-tomato taste—gone? It seems to have been lost somewhere in R. & D., and to have become a discounted, dispensable factor in the whole scheme of things. So the very quality for which people supposedly buy fresh tomatoes is precisely what an advanced system of research, growing, and distribution has succeeded in filtering out as economically unimportant. And, instead of the simple fragrant, tender, juicy, and glorious-tasting fruit we once knew, we see stacks of transparent sealed boxes containing sets of three or four pinkish globes, still pallid after their stay in the gas chamber, resting peacefully in their plastic tubes, each of them embalmed in a thin coat of wax for cosmetic effect, and all uniformly dry, mealy, and insipid.

Discussion

• Compare the way McPhee deals with oranges and the way Whiteside reports on tomatoes. What do they do that is the same? What do they do that is different? What works least? What works best?
• Discuss some potential topics you walk by every day—that are as ordinary as oranges and tomatoes—and how they might be reported by McPhee and Whiteside.
• Talk to local environmentalists and insecticide users to discover what conflicts there are in your area.
• Discuss how Whiteside develops and documents his point of view. Is he fair to those on the other side? Is there any reason he should be fair?
• Discuss how Whiteside and McPhee have put their subjects in context. Discuss how important it is for information to be put into context for the reader.

Activities

• An effective writer usually answers the reader's questions as they are asked. Has Whiteside answered the question he has caused the reader to ask? Go back through the piece and put the questions in the margins to which Whiteside's paragraphs are answers.
• Talk to authorities on both sides of an environmental or other issue and write an eight-paragraph objective account of the issue without express-

ing your opinion. Then write an editorial essay or an argument expressing your opinion.

- Choose a familiar topic and list what you already know about the subject. Then list what you need to know to appreciate what McPhee and Whiteside have done and to discover what you might have to do to explore a similar subject.

- Talk to people on both sides of an issue and use quotations from them to allow the reader to hear both sides fairly presented. Get out of the way. Use Whiteside's techniques to let the readers hear and see the advocates of both sides in context.

- Take an ordinary subject, such as tomatoes, and reveal, in a draft, how extraordinary it is.

Amiri Baraka

The professional writer, such as John McPhee or Thomas Whiteside, has the financial support to gather enormous quantities of information. They can write from abundance. But many of us do not know enough about a specific subject to write from abundance, and we do not have the resources or the time to gather that information. Yet, when we write later during our educational career and afterward in other careers, we have to know how to collect an abundance of information and select meaningful pertinent pieces of information from it. The answer for most of us is autobiography. We have an enormous inventory of experience recorded in our minds. Each of us has thousands of times as much information in our memory as we remember.

Amiri Baraka wrote first as LeRoi Jones, and his has been one of the strongest black voices in our literature in this century. He has written 24 plays, two works of fiction, seven of nonfiction, and eleven books of poetry. In his autobiography he shares his life and his reactions to that life with his readers. In the selection below he tells of his experiences in going to school.

School

School was classes and faces and teachers. And sometimes trouble. School was as much the playground as the classroom. For me, it was more the playground than the classroom. One grew, one had   1 major confrontations with real life, in the playground, only rarely in the classroom. Though I had some terrible confrontations. Around discipline and what not. The only black teacher in the school at that time, Mrs. Powell, a statuesque powder-brown lady with glasses, beat me damn near to death in full view of her and my 7B class because I was acting the fool and she went off on me (which apparently was sanctioned by my mother—it probably had something to do with conflicting with the *only* black teacher in the whole school and that had to be revenged full-blood-flowingly at once as an example to any other malefactors). But Mrs. Powell was one of the only teachers to take us on frequent trips to New York. And she had us publish a monthly newspaper that I was one of the cartoonists for. But apparently I did something far out and she took me out.

> ❡ The reader hears Baraka's voice immediately. It is conversational, hard-edged, contentious. Of course, he could write polished, slick prose. He is writing this way because it reinforces what he has to say. Any good writer deserves to be read aloud, but it is almost impossible not to hear Baraka aloud. ❡

2   But when I was in kindergarten I got sick (went off with the whooping cough, then the measles). And I learned to read away from school—my first text, Targeteer comics—and when I came back I was reading—and haven't stopped since.

3   I skipped 3B a few years later—I can't tell you why. But the 3A teacher was drugged for some reason or more likely I drugged her with my perpetual-motion mouth and she made me *skip* around the room. (For some reason it makes me think of my son, Amiri!)

4   I have distorted in various books and stories and plays and what not iron confrontations in the school with the various aspects recalled at different times. The seventh-grade beating by Mrs. Powell. The weird comic strip I created, semi-plagiarized, called "The Crime Wave," which consisted of a hand with a gun sticking out of strange places holding people up. For instance, as a dude dived off the diving board the ubiquitous hand would be thrust up out of the water holding a gun and in the conversation balloon the words "Your money!" A series of those all over the goddam place and only "Your money!"

5   I think I saw the concept somewhere else but I was attracted to it and borrowed it and changed it to fit my head. But why "Your money!"?

When the curious old Miss Day, the white-haired liberal of my 6
early youth, shuffled off into retirement as principal, there came Mr.
Van Ness, hair parted down the middle, sallow-faced and sometimes
seeming about to smile but sterner-seeming than Miss Day. We loved
Miss Day, we seemed to fear Mr. Van Ness, probably because he
seemed so dressed up and stiff. (The irony of this is that I just had
drinks with old man Van Ness two months ago, up at his apartment
with my wife and a lady friend of his—a black woman!—and we
went over some of these things. Because, as it turns out, Van Ness
was an open, investigating sort, actually a rather progressive person!)

Van Ness even took some interest in the fact that my mother 7
had been to Fisk and Tuskegee. And on the basis of those startling
credentials he could ask me what was proper, "Negro" or "colored."
I said, "Negro," and Van Ness told the students, "Remember, there's
a right and a wrong way of saying that," You bet!

In the eighth grade we had a race riot. And in them days race 8
riot meant that black and white "citizens" fought each other. And
that's exactly what happened in Newark. It was supposed to have
jumped off when two white boys stopped a guy in my class named
Haley (big for his age, one of the Southern blacks put back in school
when he reached "Norf") and asked him if he was one of the niggers
who'd won the races. He answered yes and they shot him. They were
sixteen, Haley about the same age even though he was only in 8B
and most of us in our earlier teens—I was about twelve.

> ❦Black rage exists in our society, and it has been expressed brilliantly
> in black art and literature. Baraka has raged, but notice his tone
> here, how quiet and ordinary he makes his language. He allows the
> facts to enrage the reader.❧

The races they'd talked about were part of the citywide elemen- 9
tary school track meet. The black majority schools had won most of
those races and this was the apparent payoff. So rumbles raged for a
couple weeks on and off. Especially in my neighborhood, which confronted the Italian section. The Black Stompers confronted The
Romans—a black girl was stripped naked and made to walk home
through Branch Brook Park (rumor had it). A white girl got the same
treatment (the same playground rumor said). But two loud stone- and
bottle-throwing groups of Americans did meet on the bridge over-
passing the railroad tracks near Orange Street. The tracks separating

the sho-nuff Italian streets from the last thrust of then black Newark. The big boys said preachers tried to break it up and got run off with stones. It was the battle of the bridge.

10   Beneath that fabric of rumor and movement. The bright lights of adventure flashing in my young eyes and the actual tension I could see, the same tensions had rose up cross this land now the war was over and blacks expected the wartime gains to be maintained and this was resisted. Probably what came up on the streets of Newark was merely a reflection of the Dixiecrats who declared that year for the separation of the races. But whatever, that year New Jersey became the first state to declare a statute against all discrimination.

11   As a child the world was mysterious, wondrous, terrible, dangerous, sweet in so many ways. I loved to run. Short bursts, medium cruises, even long stretched-out rhythm-smooth trips. I'd get it in my head to run somewhere—a few blocks, a mile or so, a few miles through the city streets. Maybe I'd be going somewhere, I wouldn't take the bus, I'd just suddenly get it in my head and take off. And I dug that, the way running made you feel. And it was a prestigious activity around my way, if you was fast you had some note. The street consensus.

12   I only knew what was in my parents' minds through their practice. And children can't ever sufficiently "sum that up," that's why or because they're children. You deal with them on a perceptual level—later you know what they'll do in given situations (but many of their constant activities you know absolutely nothing about). Later, maybe, deadhead intellectuals will try to look back and sum their parents up, sometimes pay them back for them having been that, one's parents. Now that we are old we know so much. But we never know what it was like to have ourselves to put up with.

13   My family, as I've tried to tell, was a lower-middle-class family finally. For all the bourgeois underpinnings on my mother's side, the Depression settled the hash of this one black bourgeois family. And those tensions were always with us. My mother always had one view, it seemed even to me. A forward forward upward upward view, based on being conscious and taking advantage of any opening. I cannot even begin to describe the love factor in my mother and father's relationship, what brought them together aside from their bodies and some kind of conversation.

14   My father from the widowed wing of the lower middle class, a handsome high school graduate from the South, a barber, a truck

driver, who tells the old traditional black lie that he thought Newark was New York . . . and it wasn't until much later that . . . His family was upwardly mobile, of course, that's the ideological characteristic of the class. But what if the ruined sector of the black bourgeoisie and the bottom shadow of the petty bourgeoisie come together, the feudings in that, the fumings, the I-used-to-be's and We-would've-been's and the many many If-it-wasn't-for's . . . oh boy oh boy all such as that. The damaged aristocracy of ruined dreams. The open barn door of monopoly capitalism. What a laugh. I mean, if some big-eyed dude was to step in and give a lecture, no, if suddenly there in the darkness of my bedroom I (or whoever could pull this off sleeping in my bed) could have stepped forward into the back-and-forth of sharp voices trying to deal with their lives, in our accepted confusion of what life is, and say, "Look, the bourgeoisie of the oppressed nation always faces a tenuous existence, the petty bourgeoisie of any nation is always shaky. And yeh, they can get thrown down, like in a fixed rasslin match, thrown down among that black bubbling mass. Yeh, they can get thrown down . . . and all the lit-up fantasies of Sunday School picnics in the light-skinned church of yellow dreams could get thrown down, by the short trip home, to the vacant lots and thousands of dirty Davises, and what you-all is doin is class struggle . . . of a sort, yeh, it's only that, translated as it has to be through the specifics of your life, the particular paths, cross-roads and barricades, but that's all it is . . . you know?"

I guess their, my parents', eyes would've lit up for a second and 15 then a terrible hard loss would've settled there, because they would've figured the goddam kid is crazy, he's babbling outta his wits. What? And they'd look at each other in the half-dark, and exchange looks about what to do. I'm glad I wasn't that smashed up. What I did do, with a taste of Krueger's beer in my mouth my mother had let me sip out of her glass earlier that night when they had friends over, I just opened my eyes so they glowed softly bigly in the dark and said nothing. I heard my sister's slow deep breathing in the bed under mine.

The games and sports of the playground and streets was one 16 registration carried with us as long as we live. Our conduct, strategies and tactics, our ranking and comradeship. Our wins and losses. (Like I was a terrible terrible loser and still am.) I would fight, do anything to stop losing. I would play super-hard, attacking, with endless energy, to stop a loss. I would shout and drive my team on. Stick my hands in the opponents' faces, guard them chest to chest, or slash through the line from the backfield and catch them as they got the pass back from center. Or take the passes and cut around end and streak for the goal. Or double-step, skip, stop, leap, jump back, ram, twist, hop, back up, duck, get away, hustle, and rush into the end zone. I could leap and catch passes one-handed, backwards, on my back, on the run, over someone's shoulder, and take it in. And mostly I never got hurt. I had a fearlessness in games and sports. A feeling that I could win, that I could outrun or outhustle or outscramble or rassle or whatever to pull it out. I would slide head first into home, even first. On tar and cement. I would turn bunts into home runs, by just putting my head down and raging around the bases.

17   In ring-a-leerio, I was always with the little guys and I actually liked that. There was always more of us allowed on the team, cause we were little. But our secret was that we were fast and shifty. I had one move where just as the big boy would be about to snatch me after the run, I'd stop short very suddenly and duck down, and this would send this big dude literally flying over my shoulders. Me, Johnny Boy Holmes, Skippy, and a few others patented that move. So they had to be wary and not run so hard after you and instead try to hem you in and get a couple or three of them to run us down. So we were the dangerous ringy players. And sometimes we'd even break loose and slide into the box and free the others already caught. Streaking into the box, which was marked on the ground, and against the fence of one side of the playground, "Ring-a-leerio," we'd scream, whoever got that honor of charging through the ring of big boys to free the others. Sometimes we'd form a kind of flying wedge and come barreling in. But some other times them big dudes would smash us, block us, knock us down. Or if we didn't have our thing together, some of the really fast and shifty dudes wasn't playing for instance, they'd chop us off one by one and you had a hell of a time if it was the big boys' time to run out to stop those dudes. But we could and did. If there was enough of us we'd roam in twos and threes and tackle them suckers and sit on them. But you also had to get them back to the box, and they'd be struggling and pulling and that could be worse than just catching them.

18   But ringy was the top game for my money. It involved all the senses and all the skills and might and main of little-boydom. We played everything, baseball, basketball, football, all day every day,

according to what season it was (though we'd play basketball all the time, regardless of what the big leagues was doing). But ringy was something else again. I'd like to see a big-league ringy game and league. It's just war pursuit and liberation without weapons. Imagine a ringy game in Yankee Stadium, with karate, boxing, wrestling, great speed, evasion tactics, plus the overall military strategy and tactics that would have to be used. That would really be something.

Ringy got you so you could get away from any assault and at the same time fear no one in terms of running directly against big odds trying to free your brothers in the box. And sometimes if you were the only one left, and could keep the bigs darting and running and twisting, and outspeeding them, with the whole playground watching, that was really something, really gratifying.

Another teaching experience I had was the game "Morning." It had its variations, "Afternoon," and perhaps there was also an "Evening," though I don't think so. "Morning" happened in the mornings. The first time we came in contact with each other the first one to see the other could hit him, saying, "Morning." and though the other variations probably could be played, "Morning" was most happening I guess because at that time it was the first confrontation of the day and folks just getting up could be unawares and thus bashed.

And these suckers who most liked to play "Morning" were not kidding. When they hit they was trying to tear your shoulder off. The shoulder was the place most often hit. The real killers like this dude Big Shot would sneak up on you and hit you in the small of the back and that would take most people down and rolling on the ground in pain. Sometimes actual tears.

Close friends wouldn't actually play it or they wouldn't actually hit each other and if they did it wouldn't be a crushing blow. They'd just make believe they were playing it to keep you on your toes. But killers like Shot and some other dudes, little ugly Diddy and dudes like that, would actually try to take you off the planet.

If there was a slight tension, an outdoing or competitive thing, between dudes they would use "Morning" as an excuse to get off. But then the only thing that meant is that the other guy would come creeping around looking for an opening to bash the other one. I got hit a couple times, most times not hard—these were my main men who did it, cause I'd be watching, jim. I was not going to get "Morninged" too often. And I caught a couple of them terrible snake-ass niggers a couple times and tried to tear 'em up, though they were taller and huskier, so my mashing punch was more embarrassment and aggravation than physical wipeout. I got Shot one time and jumped off my feet punching this sucker in his back and he got mad (which was supposed to be against the "rules") and he started chasing me around the playground. But then he really got embarrassed, because his ass was too heavy to catch me. I motored away from him, ducking and twisting, just like in ringy. And finally he got tired and people was laid out on the fence of the playground laughing at his sorry ass.

24   But then he runs over to my main man Love and catches him. You see, you were supposed to say, "Morning," then the other dude couldn't hit you. So Shot zooms over and catches Love right between the shoulder blades and damn near killed him. Love and Shot were always on the verge of going around anyway. Love had a close-cut haircut and a funny, bony-looking head, according to us. And we called him bonehead or saddlehead or some such. But it was the usual joke time. With Shot it was some kind of bitter rebuke, cause Love could play ball—any kind of ball—Shot couldn't do nothing but terrorize people with his ugly-ass self.

25   Love was hurt but when he come up a fight almost started, and then goddam Shot wanted to talk about the "rules." "Like how come Love wanna fight. . .he just don't know how to play the goddam game. If you a sissie you can't play."

26   "How come you can play then, Shot?" And people cracked up, knowing he could not catch me. But from then on I had to watch Shot very close.

27   The "rules." And he had just broke 'em himself. People like that I knew about early. And also I learned how to terrorize the terrorizers.

28   The Dozens. You know the African Recrimination Songs!! Yeh yeh see, I gotta anthropological tip for you as well. But Dozens always floated around every whichaway, around my way, when you was small. Or with close friends, half lit, when you got big. But that was either fun, for fun-connected folks, or the sign that soon somebody's blood would be spilt.

29   The lesson? The importance of language and invention. The place of innovation. The heaviness of "high speech" and rhythm. And their *use*. Not in abstract literary intaglios but on the sidewalk (or tar) in the playground, with everything at stake, even your ass. How to rhyme. How to reach in your head to its outermost reaches.

How to invent and create. Your mother's a man—Your father's a woman. Your mother drink her own bath water—Your mother drink other people's. Your mother wear combat boots—Your mother don't wear no shoes at all with her country ass, she just come up here last week playin a goddam harmonica. Or the rhymed variations. I fucked your mama under a tree, she told everybody she wanted to marry me—I fucked your mama in the corner saloon, people want to know was I fucking a baboon. Or: Your mother got a dick—Your mother got a dick bigger than your father's! Point and Counterpoint. Shot and Countershot. Up and One Up.

(In the late 60's I was going through some usual state harass- 30 ment—to wit, I had supposedly cussed out a policeman in a bank. The truth being that this dude had been harassing us every few evenings, riding by the house, making remarks to the women, creep gestures at us, etc. So he comes in this bank with a shotgun out on "bank patrol" and starts talking loudly about George Wallace, who was running for President. Hooking him up with some local creep, Imperiale, and saying he was voting for Wallace. I said, "You should, it's your brother!" Or something like that. There was an ensuing baiting, a scuffle, more cops summoned, and three of us who'd been in this bank talking bad to the cop, then cops, got taken away. But it was later thrown out because the prosecution said I'd baited the cop by talking about his father. My attorney and I pointed out that while that might be the mores of Irish Americans [the prosecutor] African Americans focused on de mama, so it was an obvious frame. The judge blinked, hmmm, case dismissed. Some street anthropology. And if you could've been there, Judge, in them playgrounds, and heard it, you'd see my point. But, miraculously, he did.)

I learned that you could keep people off you if you were mouth- 31 dangerous as well as physically capable. But being Ebony Streak also helped just in case you had to express some physical adroitness. Cause your mouth might get your ass into a situation it could not handle! In which case it was the best thing to rapidly change your landscape.

Fighting, avoiding fights, observing fights, knowing when and 32 when not to fight, were all part of our open-air playground-street side education. And fights were so constant, a kind of staged event of varying seriousness. Sometimes very serious. Sometimes just a diversion, for everyone. Like two dudes or girls woofing. Woof woof woof woof woof. They'd be standing somewhere, maybe the hands on the hips, the chicks especially, hands on hips. Maybe one hand gesturing. Or each with one hand on the hip and one hand gesturing. Or they'd get closer and closer. In the purely jive fights the audience would get drugged and push the would-be combatants into each other and that could either start a real fight or it would reveal the totally jive nature of the contest.

Discussion

- Consider how Baraka uses the point of view of the child, the point of view of the adult looking back at childhood, and the two. Discuss examples of where it works well and where it doesn't work.
- Discuss how Baraka uses specific information to make you think and feel.
- Discuss how Baraka uses his street voice and his educated voice. Why does he do this? Does it work?
- List the ways that Baraka makes people come alive on the page, both himself and those he describes. Consider which are the most effective.

Activities

- Read a section aloud to hear Baraka's voice in your voice. Ask classmates to read sections aloud so you can hear Baraka's voice in their voice. Notice how their own backgrounds and language affect the reading.
- Take one of the experiences that Baraka writes about and write about a similar experience of your own in your own way, and compare it with his.
- Choose something that is special in your background—a Puerto Rican christening, a Greek wedding, an Italian street festival, an hour at a country club pool, a locker-room at half-time, a sorority meeting—and take the reader who is unfamiliar with your culture inside that experience.
- Write a brief sketch of a relative showing, as Baraka does, how that person's story tells us something significant about the people that person represents.
- Take a paragraph or two from Baraka and rewrite it with the same facts in your own tone of voice, then compare the two versions to see how voice is expressed in print and how it affects the reader.

Ken Dryden

Ken Dryden was an outstanding college hockey goalie at Cornell who went on to become a professional star when few players went from college to professional hockey. He was a key player for Team Canada against the Russians and six times played goal when the Montreal Canadiens won the Stanley Cup, the championship trophy in professional hockey.

He not only played, he thought about playing. He was an intellectual who went to law school while he was playing. For three of his ten years as a professional he made notes on his teammates, on the game itself, on being a professional athlete. And then he wrote a book that has unusual depth for a sports book. He observed his world with a sharp eye, revealed his thoughts and feelings with candor, and produced a text that can be read by hockey fans and by other readers, for he comments as much on our society as on a particular sport. And at times, as in the following selection, he achieves a level of writing that approaches poetry.

From *The Game*

The Italians have a phrase, *inventa la partita*. Translated, it means to "invent the game." A phrase often used by soccer coaches and journalists, it is now, more often than not, used as a lament. For in watching modern players with polished but plastic skills, they wonder at the passing of soccer *genius*—Pele, di Stefano, Puskas—players whose minds and bodies in not so rare moments created something unfound in coaching manuals, a new and continuously changing game for others to aspire to.   1

It is a loss they explain many ways. In the name of team play, there is no time or place for individual virtuosity, they say; it is a game now taken over by coaches, by technocrats and autocrats who empty players' minds to control their bodies, reprogramming them with X's and O's, driving them to greater *efficiency* and *work rate*, to move *systems* faster, to move games faster, until achieving mindless pace. Others fix blame more on the other side: on smothering defenses played with the same technical sophistication, efficiency,   2 and work rate, but in the nature of defense, easier to play. Still others argue it is the professional sports culture itself which says that games are not won on good plays, but by others' mistakes, where the safe and sure survive, and the creative and not-so-sure may not.

3   But a few link it to a different kind of cultural change, the loss of what they call "street soccer"; the mindless hours spent with a ball near to your feet, walking with it as if with a family pet, to school, to a store, or anywhere, playing with it, learning new things about it and about yourself, in time, as with any good companion, developing an *understanding*. In a much less busy time undivided by TV, rock music, or the clutter of modern lessons, it was a child's diversion from having nothing else to do. And, appearances to the contrary, it was creative diversion. But now, with more to do, and with a sophisticated, competitive society pressing on the younger and younger the need for training and skills, its time has run out. Soccer has moved away from the streets and playgrounds to soccer fields, from impromptu games to uniforms and referees, from any time to specific, scheduled time; it has become an *activity* like anything else, organized and maximized, done right or not at all. It has become something to be taught and learned, then tested in games; the answer at the back of the book, the one and only answer. So other time, time not spent with teams in practices or games, deemed wasteful and inefficient, has become time not spent at soccer.

⟨ It is a delight to see how Dryden moves from a sports context to a social one that implies a meaning far beyond the hockey rink.⟩

4   Recently, in Hungary, a survey was conducted asking soccer players from 1910 to the present how much each practiced a day. The answer, on a gradually shrinking scale, was three hours early in the century to eight minutes a day today. Though long memories can forget, and inflate what they don't forget, if the absolute figures are doubtful, the point is none the less valid. Today, except in the barrios of Latin America, in parts of Africa and Asia, "street soccer" is dead, and many would argue that with it has gone much of soccer's creative opportunity.

⟨ Now he uses anecdotal material about a single person to support his point. ⟩

When Guy Lafleur was five years old, his father built a small rink in the backyard of their home in Thurso, Quebec. After school and on weekends, the rink was crowded with Lafleur and his friends, but on weekdays, rushing through lunch before returning to school, it was his alone for half an hour or more. A few years later, anxious for more ice time, on Saturday and Sunday mornings he would sneak in the back door of the local arena, finding his way unseen through the engine room, under the seats, and onto the ice. There, from 7:30 until just before the manager awakened about 11, he played alone; then quickly left. Though he was soon discovered, as the manager was also coach of his team, Lafleur was allowed to continue, by himself, and then a few years later with some of his friends.

❡And, in the lines that follow he puts Lafleur's story in context.❡

There is nothing unique to this story; only its details differ from many others like it. But because it's about Lafleur it is notable. At the time, there were thousands like him across Canada on other noon-hour rinks, in other local areas, doing the same. It was when he got older and nothing changed that his story became special. For as others in the whirl of more games, more practices, more off-ice diversions, more travel and everything else gave up solitary time as boring and unnecessary, Lafleur did not. When he moved to Quebec City at fourteen to play for the Remparts, the ice at the big Colisee was unavailable at other times, so he began arriving early for the team's 6 p.m. practices, going on the ice at 5, more than thirty minutes before any of his teammates joined him. Now, many years later, the story unchanged, it seems more and more remarkable to us. In clichéd observation some would say it is a case of the great and dedicated superstar who is first on the ice, last off. But he is not. When practice ends, Lafleur leaves, and ten or twelve others remain behind, skating and shooting with Ruel. But every day we're in Montreal, at 11 a.m., an hour before Bowman steps from the dressing room as signal for practice to begin, Lafleur goes onto the ice with a bucket of pucks to be alone.

Not long ago, thinking of the generations of Canadians who learned hockey on rivers and ponds, I collected my skates and with two friends drove up the Gatineau River north of Ottawa. We didn't know it at the time, but the ice conditions we found were rare, duplicated only a few times the previous decade. The combination of a sudden thaw and freezing rain in the days before had melted winter-high snow, and with temperatures dropping rapidly overnight, the river was left with miles of smooth glare ice. Growing up in the suburbs of a large city, I had played on a river only once before, and then as a goalie. On this day, I came to the Gatineau to find what a river of ice and a solitary feeling might mean to a game.

8   We spread ourselves rinks apart, breaking into river-wide openings for passes that sometimes connected, and other times sent us hundreds of feet after what we had missed. Against the wind or with it, the sun glaring in our eyes or at our backs, we skated for more than three hours, periodically tired, continuously renewed. The next day I went back again, this time alone. Before I got bored with myself an hour or two later, with no one watching and nothing to distract me, loose and daring, joyously free, I tried things I had never tried before, my hands and feet discovering new patterns and directions, and came away feeling as if something was finally clear.

❡ When inexperienced writers report on a personal experience in a narrative such as this, they usually fail to make the reader see the significance of the story. Dryden, at all times, makes sure the reader understands the importance of what he is saying.❡

9   The Canadian game of hockey was weaned on long northern winters uncluttered by things to do. It grew up on ponds and rivers, in big open spaces, unorganized, often solitary, only occasionally moved into arenas for practices or games. In recent generations, that has changed. Canadians have moved from farms and towns to cities and suburbs; they've discovered skis, snowmobiles, and southern vacations; they've civilized winter and moved it indoors. A game we once played on rivers and ponds, later on streets and driveways and in backyards, we now play in arenas, in full team uniform, with coaches and referees, or to an ever-increasing extent we don't play at all. For, once a game is organized, unorganized games seem a wasteful use of time, and once a game moves indoors, it won't move outdoors again. Hockey has become suburbanized, and as part of our suburban middle-class culture, it has changed.

❡ Dryden writes a transition by repeating, with new material, what he has said before. That sets up what follows.❡

Put in uniforms at six or seven, by the time a boy reaches the 10
NHL, he is a veteran of close to 1,000 games—30-minute games,
later 32-, then 45-, finally 60-minute games, played more than twice
a week, more than seventy times a year between late September and
late March. It is more games from a younger age, over a longer season
than ever before. But it is less hockey than ever before. For, every
time a twelve-year-old boy plays a 30-minute game, sharing the ice
with teammates, he plays only about ten minutes. And ten minutes
a game, anticipated and prepared for all day, travelled to and from,
dressed and undressed for, means ten minutes of hockey a day, more
than two days a week, more than seventy days a hockey season. And
every day that a twelve-year-old plays only ten minutes, he doesn't
play two hours on a backyard rink, or longer on school or playground
rinks during weekends and holidays.

It all has to do with the way we look at free time. Constantly 11
preoccupied with time and keeping ourselves busy (we have come to
answer the ritual question "How are you?" with what we apparently
equate with good health, "Busy"), we treat non-school, non-sleeping
or non-eating time, unbudgeted free time, with suspicion and no little fear. For, while it may offer opportunity to learn and do new
things, we worry that the time we once spent reading, kicking a ball,
or mindlessly coddling a puck might be used destructively, in front
of TV, or "getting into trouble" in endless ways. So we organize free
time, scheduling it into lessons—ballet, piano, French—into organizations, teams, and clubs, fragmenting it into impossible-to-be-
boring segments, creating in ourselves a mental metabolism geared
to moving on, making free time distinctly unfree.

It is in free time that the special player develops, not in the 12
competitive expedience of games, in hour-long practices once a
week, in mechanical devotion to packaged, processed, coaching-
manual, hockey-school skills. For while skills are necessary, setting
out as they do the limits of anything, more is needed to transform
those skills into something special. Mostly it is time—unencumbered, unhurried, time of a different quality, more time, time to find
wrong answers to find a few that are right; time to find your own
right answers; time for skills to be practiced to set higher limits, to
settle and assimilate and become fully and completely yours, to organize and combine with other skills comfortably and easily in some
uniquely personal way, then to be set loose, trusted, to find new
instinctive directions to take, to create.

13   But without such time a player is like a student cramming for exams. His skills are like answers memorized by his body, specific, limited to what is expected, random and separate, with no overviews to organize and bring them together. And for those times when more is demanded, when new unexpected circumstances come up, when answers are asked for things you've never learned, when you must intuit and piece together what you already know to find new answers, memorizing isn't enough. It's the difference between knowledge and understanding, between a super-achiever and a wise old man. And it's the difference between a modern suburban player and a player like Lafleur.

14   For a special player has spent time with his game. On backyard rinks, in local arenas, in time alone and with others, time without short-cuts, he has seen many things, he has done many things, he has *experienced* the game. He understands it. There is *scope* and *culture* in his game. He is not a born player. What he has is not a gift, random and otherworldly, and unearned. There is surely something in his genetic make-up that allows him to be great, but just as surely there are others like him who fall short. He is, instead, *a natural.*

15   "Muscle memory" is a phrase physiologists sometimes use. It means that for many movements we make, our muscles move with no message from the brain telling them to move, that stored in the muscles is a learned capacity to move a certain way, and, given stimulus from the spinal cord, they move that way. We see a note on a sheet of music, our fingers move, no thought, no direction, and because one step of the transaction is eliminated—the information-message loop through the brain—we move faster as well.

16   When first learning a game, a player thinks through every step of what he's doing, needing to direct his body the way he wants it to go. With practice, with repetition, movements get memorized, speeding up, growing surer, gradually becoming part of the muscle's memory. The great player, having seen and done more things, more different and personal things, has in his muscles the memory of more notes, more combinations and patterns of notes, played in more different ways. Faced with a situation, his body responds. Faced with something more, something new, it finds an answer he didn't know was there. He *invents the game.*

17   Listen to a great player describe what he does. Ask Lafleur or Orr, ask Reggie Jackson, O. J. Simpson, or Julius Erving what makes them special, and you will get back something frustratingly unre-

warding. They are inarticulate jocks, we decide, but in fact they can know no better than we do. For ask yourself how you walk, how your fingers move on a piano keyboard, how you do any number of things you have made routine, and you will know why. Stepping outside yourself you can think about it and decide what *must* happen, but you possess no inside story, no great insight unavailable to those who watch. Such movement comes literally from your body, bypassing your brain, leaving few subjective hints behind. Your legs, your fingers move, that's all you know. So if you want to know what makes Orr or Lafleur special, watch their bodies, fluent and articulate, let them explain. They know.

❡ Note how expertly Dryden weaves his themes through the text. ❡

When I watch a modern suburban player, I feel the same as I 18 do when I hear Donnie Osmond or Rene Simand sing a love song. I hear a skillful voice, I see closed eyes and pleading outstretched fingers, but I hear and see only fourteen-year-old boys who can't tell me anything.

Hockey has left the river and will never return. But like the 19 "street," like an "ivory tower," the river is less a physical place than an *attitude*, a metaphor for unstructured, unorganized time alone. And if the game no longer needs the place, it needs the attitude. It is the rare player like Lafleur who reminds us.

Discussion

- How do Baraka and Dryden use sports to illuminate larger issues?
- What techniques does Dryden use to put you inside his experience?
- Discuss how Dryden weaves his themes through the essay.
- Talk about how Dryden combines first-person experience with more distant writing.
- Consider the methods Dryden uses to put his experience in a larger context. Does Baraka do this? How?
- Discuss how Dryden's selection could be an essay on writing or teaching writing. What is the role of time, lonely play, and practiced skills in learning to write?

Activities

- Dryden took an activity in which he was deeply involved and did it in an entirely different environment. Do the same thing—play jazz if you're a classical musician, play classical if you play jazz; if you're on the varsity play a sandlot game; if you commute by car, do it by bus. Look at your ordinary world through the eyes of a different experience and write about it.

- Take an ordinary experience and make the social implications of it clear.

- Write a page about a game you've played as Dryden might write it and as Baraka might.

- Take a draft you've finished and try to weave the main theme through it as Dryden does.

- Take an experience and write a piece that puts it in a context. Try another quick draft, changing the context—for example, write about playing in a rock group for fun and then for money if that's your hobby—or your after-school moneymaker.

4

A Focus Found

When writers have found a territory to explore and filled that landscape with mountains, forests, rivers, valleys, and villages of information, they experience panic. They knew they needed all that information—related facts and unrelated facts, differing opinions, confusing reports, a variety of versions of the same anecdotes, debatable statistics, authoritative quotations in conflict with one another, references to be checked, charts, jumbled notes, contradictory evidence, photocopied pages, texts on seven sides of the same issue, false leads, and loose ends. But now they have the information and they are lost in it.

Writers have to find a focus, a possible meaning in all the mess that will allow them to explore the subject in a relatively orderly fashion so they can continue through the writing process to find out if they have anything worth saying—and worth a reader's hearing.

I must back off at the this stage of the exploration so I can think about what the material means. I sit, notebook or clipboard in hand, where I cannot see the mess of research and try to write a note that tells me the single most important thing I have to say. If nothing comes, I go for a walk or a drive, day dreaming, half thinking, half not thinking about the subject until a potential focus surfaces.

If neither of those techniques work, I interview myself, asking questions similar to the ones I asked to find the subject:

- What information have I discovered that surprised me the most?
- What will surprise my reader?
- What one thing does my reader need to know?
- What one thing have I learned that I didn't expect to learn?
- What can I say in one sentence that tells me the meaning of what I have explored?
- What one thing—person, place, event, detail, fact, quotation—have I found that contains the essential meaning of the subject?
- What is the pattern of meaning I have discovered?
- What can't be left out of what I have to write?
- What one thing do I need to know more about?

There are a number of different ways to focus on a subject. The writer, of course, only uses the techniques that are necessary to achieve a focus. The focus may be obvious to the writer, or the writer may need to use one, two, three, or more of these techniques. The writer does not consciously go through these every time, but the experienced writer rarely proceeds until a focus is felt or known. Some of the ways writers achieve focus are:

1. *Voice* is one of the most common ways that writers find their focus. As they make notes about what they may write—in their heads or on the page—or rehearse how they may write it, their language may reveal a special intensity or tone that points out a focus for the subject. Too often voice is thought of as a matter of style that follows the writing, icing that is put on the cake, when it may come early in the planning process and indicate the direction in which the writer may head. In all of the selections in this chapter the writer may have heard a voice, scholarly, angry, detached, nostalgic, evangelical, that could have provided a focus for the writer.

2. *Frame* is another way to achieve focus. It tells the writer what is left out. A good subject, as we have seen, usually has a rich abundance of material. It may include not only one potential subject, but many. When the writer decides to deal only, for example, with the death of a grandmother, and to exclude the death of a pet, a life threatening illness, the brother who almost died as the result of an accident, then the writer has achieved a potential focus and can write about death in terms of one death.

3. *Distance* is a vital and often overlooked element in focusing

on a subject. Barbara Tuchman in this chapter stands at an historic distance from the Black Death. Alice Trillin writes of her personal experience with cancer. In each case the distance of the author, and therefore the reader, from the subject helps the writer achieve a focus. Notice also that the distance at which Trillin wrote is a matter of subtle adjustment. If she stands too close to her subject the reader will be embarrassed and feel uncomfortable because of the intimacy with which she is revealing her experience and her feelings. If she stands at too far a distance the reader will not care, not feel with the writer. It is often helpful to consider distance in looking for focus.

4. *Question* is extremely helpful in finding a potential focus. What is *the* question the reader will ask? What is *the* reader's question that must be answered if the writing is to work? It may help for the writer to role-play a specific reader; often I stand back from my desk and physically mimic the mannerisms and voice of a reader to see my subject from the point of view of a reader. Then I can ask, of myself, a tough question that makes me realize the focus. Alice Trillin, speaking and then writing for an audience of doctors, may have asked, for her readers, "What's it like to have cancer?" or, "What should I know in treating a patient with a life threatening illness?" James Baldwin may have made himself white and said, "What's it like to grow up black in America?"

5. *Statement* is the traditional way of finding focus. It's often called a thesis statement or a statement of potential meaning. A thesis is a proposition that will be defended by the writing. The danger is that many teachers or students believe that thesis means conclusion, and that in a thesis statement the writer has to state the final meaning of the piece that has yet to be written. The thesis statement is a guess or an estimate; it is a proposition that may or *may not* be proven by the drafts that follow. There must be room for discovery. Baldwin knew a lot about being black in America before he wrote his famous *Notes of a Native Son*, but he knew more through the act of writing.

6. *Problem* is a helpful way of finding the focus. If we can identify the problem that is to be solved, or at least explored, in the piece of writing, then we may be well along the road toward a working draft. Lindberg, for example, may have seen the problem of naming—you can look in his notes to check that out—and that may have helped him focus on his subject. Each of the selections in this chapter has problems that are dealt with in the text. We do not know if a

discovery or clarification of the problem helps the writer achieve focus, but we can see how that may have taken place.

7. *Conflict* is an effective way of finding what to focus on in an argument, in an essay, in a news story, in a play, in a social worker case study, in a management memo. The point of conflict is the place at which the forces and the subject meet; it is the point at which we can see those forces most clearly; it is the point from which the causes or the implications of the conflict can be best studied. It is obvious, for example, that both Judy Syfers and Martin Luther King, Jr. found a focus for their very different pieces of writing.

8. *Tension* is related to conflict, but it is a way of looking at those forces that are related to each other but not yet in conflict. They may be drawn together or forced apart, but if we can see, for example, in Alice Trillin's piece the forces of death and life held in a fragile suspension, then we can see a way of dealing with that subject.

9. *Happening* is a term that playwright William Gibson uses in his wise book, *Shakespeare's Game,* when he writes, "A play begins when a world in some state of equipoise, always uneasy, is broken into by a happening." This event provides a focus which initiates the action of the play. I find that fine counsel when looking for a way to focus on a short story, a novel, an essay, a ghost-written corporate speech, a news story, a memo to a dean about a problem, and many other forms of writing. The happening can provide a way in which to deal with many different forms of information relating to a single subject.

10. *Organizing item* is the technique I use most often to find a productive focus for what I'm writing. I look for an event, a quotation, a statistic, an anecdote, an individual, a place, a process, a revealing detail which can be the seed from which the entire piece of writing will grow. For example, I was once in a high school classroom in which both the teacher and I were working individually with students. Neither of us was behind the teacher's desk. A messenger from the front office came in, looked at the 27 human beings in the room quickly, did not spot the "teachers," and said out loud, "There's nobody here," and left without delivering the message. That incident could, obviously, spark an essay on how students are perceived in some schools.

11. *Opinion* is an important way of achieving focus in many forms of writing. Note the example I just gave above. The incident could have led me to an opinion, or I could have had the opinion

that students are invisible to the administration of some schools, and used that to provide me with a focus for my essay. All of these techniques, of course, overlap. Many times, however, the writer's opinion of the subject will provide the focus. In each of the following selections the writer has an opinion. In some it is more clearly expressed than others, but it is there, and it may have provided the author with a way of approaching the subject.

12. *Sequence* is another way that can show the writer a focus that may lead the writer, and therefore the reader, through the forest of information. Once Syfers looked at a wife from the point of view of her world, making believe she was a husband, a sequence of information may have flicked into place. We don't know if that's the way she found the focus, but we can see from her essay that that is one way she might have found it. There is also a sequence of events leading to the deaths of Baldwin's and Gibson's fathers. That sequence of inevitability provides a focus for the mountains of information they had in their memories. Sometimes I call this a trail, or a thread that I can see leading me through information that was contradictory or jumbled up in my mind, until I found the trail or a thread.

13. *Point of view* is the place that the subject is seen by the writer and the reader. It is a good way of focusing on a subject. We may have, for example, an enormous amount of material about a sport, a season, and a particular team. We may not know how to deal with that material, and we may find out how to deal with it when we look at the subject from the point of view of the athletic director, an alumnus, the coach, a player, the trainer, an orthopedic surgeon, a fan, a pro scout, a star, a bench-warming substitute, the referee, a sports equipment manufacturer, the coach of an opposing team, last year's star, next year's high school recruit. Every subject may be seen from many different points of view, and it can be helpful to identify one as a way of achieving focus.

14. *Image* often gives a writer the focus for a piece of writing. The Vietnam images of a young girl running in terror down the street with her clothes burned off and of a South Vietnam officer holding a pistol to the head of another human being, were images that brought that war home to Americans. I was constantly surprised by the power of those images, for such powerful images had been burned into my memory from my experience in combat in World War II, but without television, the people at home saw only a romantic, heroic Hollywood war. A powerful image is often the organizing element around

which a piece of writing can be collected. It is a magnet that draws information into a pattern of meaning clear to both writer and reader.

When the writer spots a focus for the drafts which will follow, the writer has not concluded the process of exploration. Seeing the mountain does not eliminate the adventure of climbing to its peak.

Case Study: A Scholar Writes and Reads

Gary Lindberg

Many English departments, my own included, too often consider only those who publish poetry and fiction as writers, but the university is filled with historians and scientists, philosophers and educators, researchers and theorists who publish reports, journal articles, textbooks, critical and scholarly works. One of the most skillful scholarly writers I know is Gary Lindberg, Professor of English in our own department. He was graduated magna cum laude from Harvard University, and received his Masters and Doctoral degrees in English and American Literature from Stanford Unversity. He has been on the faculty at Rhode Island College and the University of Virginia, as well as the University of New Hampshire. His first book, *Edith Wharton and the Novel of Manners*, was published by the University Press of Virginia, and his next book, *The Confidence Man in American Literature*, was published by the Oxford University Press. *American Literature* said, "Gary Lindberg's book is one of the most continually illuminating analyses of American literature and culture published in recent years."

One of his credentials I find most significant is that as a full professor and a leading scholar in our department he volunteered to take a turn as chairperson of Freshman English. I was also impressed that he not only prepared himself by teaching Freshman English, but also by studying the extensive scholarship available in composition theory.

I am glad he agreed to allow us to observe the scholar at work on a section from his new book in progress, tentatively titled, *The*

Common Sense Book of Reading Literature. This excerpt is part of a chapter titled, "Why Read Literature?" Here you can see a scholar gather his notes, develop his focus, order and document his case.

Here are examples of how Dr. Lindberg harvests his journal entries, a process he describes in his *Commentary.*

Gathering of Notes from Journal and Suggestions of Examples

H   Look at Words of Power as core of naming in that they keep our experiences clear
>   Treat as both example and necessity
>> Restorative function in bad time
>> Range of words beyond blurring—what we can deal with thru them restores wholeness

E   Enabling power of lit.: open up possibility of using words to get at parts of our experience and to share it
>   Must be willing tو risk names abt a text as well

H   Words of Power also restore scale
>   Discuss fully in relation to "Cascadilla Falls"
>   Possibly mention Frost's "On Looking Up . . ."
>> "You'll wait a long, long time for anything much
>> To happen in heaven . . ."

More Draft-Notes and Followthroughs

G   Religious issue is involved here
>   Not a matter of supernatural experience but experience of holiness
>   Recognize sacred power of words—overlap with moving in enchanted realm
>   Reverence toward world, self, and word that moves between
>   Connect with stories & poems because writers so committed to acts of imagination
>> Know and use special power of naming
>> Not just deal with world but deal with our means of dealing with world

This side of reading lit. seems too obvious to talk about—
no interpretive skills necessary

B   But again issue is putting self in useful attitude
Recognize importance & pleasure of naming and also its
non-inevitability
It's not a given, names are made, not simply there

Gathering of Examples
Audre Lorde and Naming

D   "Now whether poetry has the responsibility to effect social
change . . . it doesn't really matter. As we get in touch with the
things that we feel are intolerable, in our lives, they become
more and more intolerable. If we just once dealt with how much
we hate most of what we do, there would be no holding us back
from changing it." *American Poetry Review* interview
Points to centrality of naming

Stage of Discovering Coherences
Transition between Notes and Outline

Perhaps structure of this section needs to enact
process of clearing away wastage/junk as names
and then work back to perception of magic and
power in act of naming

C   Obsession with interpreting and decoding is socially conditioned
by preponderance of lies
Teaches both skepticism and indifference

F   Name presents our experience
Makes it present
Focuses our attention—intensifies experience
Calls it into being

Outline

(all the smaller additions toward the end were
added as additional ideas while I was writing the
earlier sections)

A   Transition on Simple pleasure of producing name
B   Naming as power in itself w/out deeper
          But hard to grasp this because. . .
C   Given condition: wastage of names
          Use Momaday in this section and previous as way of leading
          between simple and muddled

❦ Here are some of the original handscript pages—the first page, the last, and two in the middle—of the first draft Lindberg wrote from the outline so that you can see how the piece developed. ❧

<u>Naming</u>

I have been describing qualities of literature that make it seem difficult. Both ~~the strange gatherings of issues in the mind and the turning of our inner selves outward to objects events~~ When writers let their minds gather images freely or when they project inner states (?) things outside, ~~qualities onto external objects~~, they require us to ~~exercise~~ use our own imaginations and curiosities in order to follow what they say. ~~But by~~ Yet by such indirections and approximations, they ^ are actually ^ lead us toward something ~~that seems~~ much simpler. They are seeking a name. And they are reminding us that naming our experiences and our feelings is not always easy. The names are not inevitable, nor ~~are they~~ Yet we have to have those names. Without them our experience seems not quite real, and ~~when we can't name what we feel~~ for things, ~~so it makes us~~ frustates us ~~not~~ ^ as much as ^ ~~to~~ being able to name what we feel. ~~Or when we first the sight~~

(when we articulate our difficulties, we put ourselves
in a position to deal with them. words are something.

Audre Lorde, who as black poet and lesbian feminist has had to think about the relation of writing literature to politics, argues that it is naming, which makes poetry instrument: "poetry is the way we help give name to the nameless so it can be thought." ('Poetry Is Not a Luxury')

Now whether poetry has the responsibility to affect social change ... it doesn't really matter. As we get in touch with the things that we feel are intolerable, in our lives, they become more and more intolerable. If we just once dealt with how much we hate most of what we do, there would be no holding us back from changing it." (Amer. Poetry Review)

From this perspective, we can perhaps better understand that burst of illicit energy we get when someone else names our own latent or avoided feelings. As if naming were saying what is not supposed to be said. And there is something irrevocable in the gesture — what is once named is hard to unname.

Words enable us. When we articulate as

8

experiences and our difficulties, we put ourselves in a position to deal with them. Even questions are a kind of naming. When we make our puzzlings explicit, we sometimes see at once the way to go about resolving them. And if they are the kinds of questions that do not have direct resolutions, the questions themselves, when adequately formulated, can open areas of discovery for us. One of the values of stories and poems is that they remind us how words can be used to get at unacknowledged parts of our experience and then to share them. Works of the imagination can restore our faith in words as names instead of lies.

What is a name? What kind of act are we performing when we name something? A name is a representation ~~in mental space~~ to our minds of our experience ~~in a variety of spaces~~. When ~~our~~ that experience ~~involves~~ takes place in the material world outside us, there is a clear difference between

26

at all because of how we ~~last~~ name them.
Pilgermann teaches us respect for the
~~raw~~ ^substance^ ~~material~~ that predates our names, and
he ~~makes~~ ^forces^ us to resume our own responsibility as makers and users of names.
¶ The world is in continual passage back and forth
from virtuality to actuality and back again.
What makes the passage is the name. If
such an awareness ^of this passing^ keeps us properly
humble about the ^giving^ names we use, it also
~~restores our minds~~ reminds us that we are accountable.
~~Since~~ ^in a world of^
The actual is what we have chosen to
name, we need to choose well. The stone
will obey, but it will also outlast our
commands.

Naming

1   I have been describing qualities of literature that make it seem difficult. When writers let their minds gather images freely or when they project inner states onto things outside, they make us use our own imaginations and curiosities to follow what they say. But by such indirections and approximations, they are actually leading us toward something much simpler. They are seeking a name. And they are reminding us that naming our experiences and our feelings is not always easy. The names are not inevitable. Yet we have to have those names. Without them our experience seems not quite real, and few things frustrate us as much as being unable to name what we feel. Finding the right name satisfies us in a peculiarly deep way. It gives substance to our experience, and it affirms our own power to deal with it. This is what the blues is all about. People do not solve their problems or change the world by singing, but they find a name for their troubles and they find a self who made that name.

2   Stories and poems spring from our naming power, and they remind us what an astonishing power it is. If we insist on looking for "deeper meanings" in what we read, we act as if the writer is working with a code or playing a game with words. But the real force of words is in saying what they mean. The things named in literature do not need a system of interpretation to be important. The naming itself makes them significant. This seems so obvious, however, that we don't attend to it. It doesn't require interpretive skills and it doesn't lead us to concealed truths. Yet one of the purest pleasures of reading literature is that moment when we find something we had felt or suspected given a name, acknowledged as real. The trick for us as readers is not to take this pleasure for granted, not to regard the names as simply there. It is easy to become so numbed by names that we forget how they are made.

3   A good reminder of how names work is in N. Scott Momaday's novel *House Made of Dawn*. The Priest of the Sun, a Kiowa Indian running a mission in Los Angeles, preaches on the text "In the beginning was the Word":

4   *Think of Genesis. Think of how it was before the world was made . . . There was nothing. But there was darkness all around, and in the darkness something happened. Something happened!* There was a single sound. *Far away in the darkness there was a single sound. Nothing made it, but it was there; and there was no one to hear it,*

> *but it was there. It was there, and there was nothing else . . . It was*
> *almost nothing in itself, the smallest seed of sound—but it took hold*
> *of the darkness and there was light; it took hold of the stillness and*
> *there was motion forever; it took hold of the silence and there was*
> *sound . . . It scarcely was; but it was, and everything began.*

It takes something like this grasp of nothingness, this beginning 5
in the void, for us to feel the creative power of words. Everything
began. But the Priest of the Sun knows how difficult it is to regain
that simple clarity in which a name is a gesture that fills us with awe.
We have too many names. Names surround us and tangle our
experience:

> *The white man takes such things as words and literature for granted,* 6
> *as indeed he must, for nothing in his world is so commonplace. On*
> *every side of him there are words by the millions, an unending*
> *succession of pamphlets and papers, letters and books, bills and*
> *bulletins, commentaries and conversations. He has diluted and*
> *multiplied the Word, and words have begun to close in on him. He is*
> *sated and insensitive; his regard for language—for the Word itself—*
> *as an instrument of creation has diminished nearly to the point of no*
> *return. It may be that he will perish by the Word.*

Like other mass products of an industrial state, names too easily 7
become garbage. And this does more to us than dull our sensitivity.
We live in such a barrage of words that we see them as only loosely
connected with real experiences. We find words so often serving as
manipulations or more simply as lies that we distrust them. This is
why we have become so obsessed with interpreting what we read,
decoding it. We can't believe anyone says what he or she means. Our
fashionable literary theories—structuralism, deconstruction, semiol-
ogy—are themselves products of this widespread skepticism about
names working as names. The prevailing philosophy studies our
speech as if it were merely a system of codes. We live, it would seem,
by lies.

❡ Note in the previous paragraph how Lindberg documents his case.
And he gives you enough of the documentation, getting out of the
way of it, so that you can absorb it and think about it. And then at
the end of the paragraph he tells you directly what he is thinking
about the subject. Every writer has to document and interpret to
give the reader enough of both the general and the particular to
convince him or her.❡

8   There is another effect of this waste-pile of names. There seem to be more than enough of them already. Our opinions are named in statistical surveys; our sentiments, in commercial greeting cards; our anxieties, in the soaps; and our desires, in pop songs. It is no longer obvious that we need to name anything for ourselves. And as long as we remain passive in this sense—taking all these verbal formulations as if they were in the very nature of things—we are the victims of other people's names. One reason to restore our sense of naming as a deliberate act is thus political: it helps us recover our own power and clarifies our possibilities of choice. What we name and how we name it determine what we see as experiences that we can and should confront. Right to Life. Freedom of Choice. Think how differently those phrases name the issue and thus shape the reality to be dealt with. And think how the very naming of a conspiracy, as done by Senator Joe McCarthy, could create a whole system of persecution and fear. Words do not have to be arranged as political analysis or advocacy in order to have political significance. Since we cannot make deliberate choices or concerted efforts without naming our purposes or our problems, the names are themselves political gestures.

❧ As a writer I am impressed by the way in which Lindberg writes the transition at the beginning of the paragraph, connects with us in the third sentence by using a different kind of documentation, a sentence that draws upon our experience to document his point. All through this paragraph his thinking is revealed. It is intellectual writing, but it is not arrogant. He merely thinks out loud and invites you to think along with him. Critical writing of the type that Lindberg does is designed to stimulate your thought by the author's thought. It is closer to ideal conversation than argument, perhaps something even higher than that, higher than either, that might be called shared thinking, as if the author had issued an invitation, "This is interesting stuff, let's think about it together."

I had to learn when I first started writing critical papers as an English major and later papers on composition theory not to hammer at the reader, not to command, not to argue. I still have a great deal to learn from Lindberg and other writers of his caliber about how to reveal thinking on the page so it does not say, "Think like me," but "Let's think together." ❧

Audre Lorde, who as black poet and lesbian feminist has had to   9
think about the relation of literature to politics, argues that "poetry
is the way we help give name to the nameless so it can be thought."

> *Now whether poetry has the responsibility to effect social change . . .*   10
> *it doesn't really matter. As we get in touch with the things that we*
> *feel are intolerable, in our lives, they become more and more*
> *intolerable. If we just once dealt with how much we hate most of*
> *what we do, there would be no holding us back from changing it.*

When we articulate our difficulties, we put ourselves in a posi-   11
tion to deal with them. Words are enabling. From this perspective,
we can perhaps better understand that burst of illicit energy we get
when someone names our own latent or covert feelings. As if naming
were saying what is not *supposed* to be said. And there is something
irrevocable in the gesture—what is once named is hard to unname.

What is a name? What kind of act are we performing when we   12
name something? A name is a representation of our experience to
our minds. When that experience takes place in the material world
outside us, there is a clear difference between the name and the
thing, between "stone" and a stone. For this reason, our Western
philosophy and science, which are grounded in the primacy of the
material world, teach us to be skeptical about names, to regard them
as mere signs. We tend to laugh off the "primitive" beliefs from so
many other cultures that names are magical, that to know the name
of something is to gain power over it. We prefer to control stones by
learning their properties and then manipulating them. But not all of
our experience takes place in the material world. A great deal happens, for instance, in our mental space. And what happens there
clearly affects our ways of seeing and dealing with the material world
as well. In fact, there is constant traffic between our mental worlds,
our actions, and our feelings. Names get deeply entangled with our
gestures and emotions. Once we acknowledge how much of our
experience occurs in mental space and how much that kind of experience conditions all other kinds, we are in a better position to appreciate the force of names.

Names *are* the beings that inhabit our mental space. What does   13
not have a name does not exist—to our conscious minds. It may
perfectly well exist in other areas of our experience, but until it has
a name, its existence is shadowy. A name presents an experience to

our minds, makes it present. It not only intensifies the experience but literally calls it into being. Invocation. Enchantment. Incantation. The old magic deals with literal truth, and only our infatuation with materiality has made us forget this. To name is to create. To rename is to transform. Consider what happens in your head as you read this meditation from Russell Hoban's recent novel *Pilgermann*:

14   *Now as I think about it I see that we don't always know what it is that we are putting a name to. We are, for example, clever enough to know that a year is a measure of passage, not permanence; we call the seasons spring, summer, autumn, and winter, knowing that they are continually passing one into the other. We are not surprised at this but when we give to seasons of another sort the names Rome, Byzantium, Islam, or Mongol Empire we are astonished to see that each one refuses to remain what it is.*

15   This discussion reminds us what we do when we assign names. Like many other parts of Hoban's novel, it shows that the "things" we name are only things because we name them. It is as if our experience were an abstract variety of patterns and our names were our ways of seeing within it certain orderings or coherences. A new name suggests the perception of another possible order. Names are in this sense arbitrary, but that does not make them indifferent. "Rome." "Right to Life." "Communist sympathizer." These are not given entities but deliberate representations. They can be useful, but they can also be misleading if we forget what they are. When we recognize names as the acts that create the beings in our minds, we free ourselves from the dominance of others' names and take charge of our own powers as the makers and users of names.

16   Since all of language involves our naming power, it may seem that this subject is too universal for a book on the reading of imaginative literature. What is so special about naming as done in stories and poems? Most simply, it is not taken for granted. Poets and storytellers draw us back to those moments when we struggle to put our intuitions into words or when we deliberately sort out from all that is happening a sequence of events that matters to us. The blank spaces around the words in a printed poem evoke the silence—the void—within which the word appears as an act of creation. It is well for us to remember that blankness, for it makes us properly awed by the words that others have found, and it presents us with the image of our own open possibilities, our own acts of naming.

❦ Lindberg, as he explains in his commentary, has taken on a huge, abstract subject, "Commonsense and the Reading of Literature." A primary challenge he faced was to find a focus for his study, and then to find a focus for each part. Notice how this section demonstrates focus. It is focused directly on naming, and you should realize how he keeps coming back to his focus, so that both he and the reader have a point of reference, a north star, a trailmark to use as they think about the subject together. ❧

When we see naming itself as an extraordinary gesture, we are 17 less likely to look for covert meanings or hidden truths behind the words we read. We recover our faith in words as names, not lies. Instead of asking what the spider and the moth and the flower stand for, we recognize that no one *had* to call them "Assorted characters of death and blight." The poet has through this phrase precisely indicated a state of mind, a way of finding in the world something that matters. Frost's way of naming here places the immediate natural scene in a much grander drama. It announces a different stage setting. That is what naming does—it makes the stage, sets it, and fills it with action. But the new drama of death and blight and designs of darkness is not the only one. Frost keeps us aware of the miniature stage too, naming and renaming the spider and the moth who are actors on it. What makes the naming special in stories and poems is that it so readily passes into renaming. The spider is a "dimpled spider," a "kindred spider," and a "character of death and blight." The immediate reality of the spider itself is enlivened for us by this shifting of the stage on which it appears. This is what I mean by saying that literature keeps us from taking names for granted.

But if we perceive that names are arbitrary acts of choice among 18 many alternatives, we also come back to the creative power of the name. We remember that the word is what moves between the world and ourselves. Poets and storytellers not only deal with the world but they deal with our *means* of dealing with the world. Naming is our means; renaming reminds us of this fact. The old names that stay good—spider, stone, fear, rain—get freshened for us by appearing with other formulations—"Characters of death and blight," "design of darkness." Through re-creation we re-experience creation. We move once again back into the world where "spider" was first called into being, a world more pristine and holy than the junkpile of names we ordinarily confront. It is because of this feeling of being present at the creation that people so often sense a religious quality in imaginative literature. It can reveal the sacred power of words and restore our grasp of this power. Denunciations of liars, and analyses of verbal manipulation cannot recover for us a sense of names as gestures that matter. Only the actual use of such names can keep us aware of their power.

19   I have given several examples of names that are obviously, even problematically, someone's formulation of what could have been called something else: Right to Life, Assorted characters of death and blight, communist sympathizer, Rome. Each of these names is clearly conceptual, a way of summing up and organizing a whole cluster of experience so as to present it to the mind. I chose such examples to make more evident the nature of naming. But when you come down to it, *all* names are concepts. They are mental representations of experience. Even "stone" is a concept. To illustrate what I have been saying about naming in stories and poems, let me refer to three literary namings of "stone."

20   The first is by Charles Simic:

Stone

21
  Go inside a stone
  That would be my way.
  Let somebody else become a dove
  Or gnash with a tiger's tooth.
  I am happy to be a stone.

22
  From the outside the stone is a riddle:
  No one knows how to answer it.
  Yet within, it must be cool and quiet
  Even though a cow steps on it full weight,
  Even though a child throws it in a river;
  The stone sinks, slow, unperturbed
  To the river bottom
  Where the fishes come to knock on it
  And listen.

23
  I have seen sparks fly out
  When two stones are rubbed,
  So perhaps it is not dark inside after all;

Perhaps there is a moon shining   24
From somewhere, as though behind a hill—
Just enough light to make out
The strange writings, the star-charts
On the inner walls.

It would be very difficult to ask what this poem *means*. There is   25
so little conceptual language ("riddle" and "strange writings" are the
closest) that we are not forced into speculation. It seems too simple
and direct to be in a literary code. Yet it would be equally difficult to
deny our sense of mystery in reading the poem. The very opening
sentence asks us to enter the unknown, and the closing image confirms our presence in an uncanny realm. What could be more commonplace than a stone? What makes it new is that Simic asks us to
go inside it, to *be* a stone. He clears the way for our perception of a
stone by rejecting other things that one could name or write a poem
about, doves and tigers' teeth. He makes us experience the stoneness
of a stone by moving it unperturbed from one stage setting to
another. It might appear with a cow, a child, a river, fishes. What we
see here is a highly active imagination coming to terms with a stone,
making us feel what it might be like to be a stone, giving the stone
being in our minds. But if the stone itself is what sinks, slow and
unperturbed, the imagination that names it cannot be thus stopped.
It finds its own properties in the stone, mysteriously recast in the
star-charts. Without making even a hint about gods or supernatural
events, this poem is deeply religious. The beings in it are simple,
beyond the blurring effects of historical changes. We come upon
them as if they had never been seen or named before. They have all
the mystery of new creation. The fishes knock on the stone and listen. But it is not only the world of beings named in this poem that
seem holy. The naming power itself—the human imagination—is
being exercised in all its pristine authority. It creates a stone in the
mind. And such a stone it is a privilege to be.

The second naming of a stone is done by A. R. Ammons: 26

Cascadilla Falls

I went down by Cascadilla   27
Falls this
evening, the
stream below the falls,

and picked up a
handsized stone
kidney-shaped, testicular, and
thought all its motions into it,
the 800 mph earth spin,
the 190-million-mile yearly
displacement around the sun,
the overriding
grand
haul

28   of the galaxy with the 30,000
mph of where

29   the sun's going:
thought all the interweaving
motions
into myself: dropped

30   the stone to dead rest;
the stream from other motions
broke
rushing over it:
shelterless,
I turned

31   to the sky and stood still:
oh
I do
not know where I am going
that I can live my life
by this single creek.

32   If Simic draws us back into an elemental world where our imaginations work freshly, Ammons seems to do exactly the opposite. He
is not stepping outside historical change but bringing all his current
scientific knowledge to bear on the simple stone. His language is
complicated, mental, abstract. Even the description of the physical
stone itself forces us to think about ourselves analytically, organ by
organ. Ammons seems painfully self-conscious. Yet this self-con-
sciousness offers a route of its own to the magic realm of fresh naming. Ammons not only knows he's playfully shifting the stage setting;

he makes us aware of this fact as well. After composing a familiar scene—the poet in the natural world below a falls—he suddenly shifts our placing in two ways. He moves the scene into his head ("thought all its motions into it") and then out to the spinning surface of the earth. And having enlarged the setting once, he does it two more times, so that the stone is moving with the grand haul of the galaxy. But this exhilarating display of his mental powers does not comfort him, it scares him, and as he drops the stone he scares himself even more by recognizing still other motions in the stream that rushes over it. He is overwhelmed by the conceptual world that he has himself built up.

> ❦ Reading as a writer I am impressed at Lindberg's mastery of pace. Notice as he comes to the end of the section how he summarizes what he has said and then moves ahead to develop his thoughts further, then summarizes and develops again. He weaves his thoughts clearly through the piece, never getting too far ahead of his reader nor boring the reader with unnecessary and patronizing repetition.
>
> Lindberg is also a master of development. Most of us underwrite. He develops each thought so that the reader can understand what he is thinking. I am an underwriter, and I can learn from him.❥

In the first chapter I described the base of literary language as words of power, words that hold their shape over time and restore our capacities to name. Simic's poem is a fine demonstration of how the words of power actually work. Ammons' poem shows us why we need them. The issue is scale. How does Ammons *know* "all its motions" when he holds the stone? How does *anyone* know the 800 mph earth-spin, the displacement around the sun, the rush of the galaxy? Our senses cannot discern such things. They are the inferences from collective observations with complicated instruments over long periods of time. We name them as if they too set a stage on which we could observe actions, but this is illusion. Or more precisely, it is mental without supporting reference to our senses, our bodies, our own gestures. The historical conditions that surround us, the burgeoning of scientific knowledge, and the mass production of words create for us a whole world of such illusions. The free play of our minds over all this knowledge can leave us shelterless and can make our very perceptions suspect. Is a stone a stone, or merely an arbitrarily designated cluster of atoms whirled in myriad kinds of motion? Are we ourselves, our inner organs, or other collections of motion? Even the old and simple words of power are threatened by such speculations. When Ammons is frightened by what his thought has led him to, he says he "dropped the stone to dead rest." Dead rest?? Here is a perfectly simple and clear action. No one who understands English could question the meaning of this phrase. *Except in this context.* Ammons has made the concept of dead rest into pure illusion. The same thing happens again when he says he "turned to the sky and stood still." It is in the presence of such threats to our words and our everyday perceptions of our own lives, that we feel the importance of Ammons's play with stage settings. His composition of a scene below Cascadilla Falls is not arbitrary but consolatory. It is in such a setting, such a scale, that we can know who we are, or perhaps not have to know that we don't know who we are. He doesn't merely look at a stone or think about it. He picks it up. It is "a handsized stone." This is a human gesture in a human scale with the mind's names fitting the body's experience. In the course of the poem we are drawn away from this scale and into the shelterless space of dissociated speculation. But there is also an odd recovery. It may be frightening not to know where one is going. But in not knowing all the outsized truths of modern science—and for certain periods in our lives all of us live without knowing them or without having to think of them—one finds it possible to live coherently in the human scale again. I can live my life by this single creek.

34   The third naming of "stone" occurs in Russell Hoban's *Pilgermann:*

35   *Stones! When the hammers are heard on the anvils of war the stones will not be found unready; they will come to hand equally for those who besiege and those who defend. Built up into strong walls they await the rumble of the siege tower, the shock of the ram, the crash of the stone that comes whistling from the mangonel. War sets one stone against another, calls this one a missile, that one a stronghold. But the freemasonry of the stones is stronger than the temporary loyalties imposed on them; they do what is required of them but in their hardness they retain their one essential fact: they know that they are all one thing. What do the stones say? 'We have no enemy.' This I have not read in a book, this I have heard them say and I know it to be true.*

36   Like Simic, Pilgermann makes us resee the stoneness of the stones, their integrity. "We have no enemy." Like Ammons, he makes us self-conscious about naming. What makes him different

from both is that he looks from within the stones at the human gesture of naming and appropriation. Naming, we have to see, is a strategic gesture, a matter of use. "War sets one stone against another, calls this one a missile, that one a stronghold." The stones themselves outlast the names, survive the particular uses to which they are put. Pilgermann acknowledges a ground reality that was there before our names and that will continue after our names have collapsed like the "impregnable" walls of Antioch. Antioch itself is a passing entity. So is wall. So is missile. So is Pilgermann. By the time he speaks to us, he has become "waves and particles." Or more precisely, he has recognized that he always was waves and particles but that for a certain period of time in certain circumstances he had a named identity as a human being.

His discussion of how stones are renamed for war seems almost 37 transcendental. It frees us from the hard realities of missiles and strongholds and enmity, lifts us outside history itself. Yet there is nothing supernatural or mystical in Pilgermann's perception. All he does is to let us see how the realities in which we seem bound are only entities or events at all because of how we have named them. Pilgermann teaches us respect for the substance that predates our names, and he forces us to resume our own responsibilities as makers and users of names. The world is in continual passage from virtuality to actuality and back again. What makes the passage is the name. If such an awareness keeps us properly humble about the passing names we use, it also reminds us that we are accountable. Since the actual consists of what we have chosen to name, we need to choose well. The stone will obey, but it will also outlast our commands.

Discussion

• Discuss the particular tasks facing the writer who is writing a critical paper, a paper of thought. Define the problems faced by the writer, and then list solutions to each problem. Note the plural. Writing problems rarely have one solution; the writer has a number of solutions from which to choose.

• List the various forms of documentation Lindberg uses. What others might he have used?

• Read the commentary and discuss what he has said about how he had thought and written in this piece of writing.

- Discuss other kinds of writing in which the writer would want to reveal his or her thinking, for example, a proposal for a chain of slow-food restaurants, emphasizing service and atmosphere.
- Discuss other forms of writing in which the writer must examine a text or texts critically, for example, a researcher for a bank who has been asked to evaluate the proposal for a slow-food restaurant chain.
- Bring in assignments from other courses which ask you to think critically, and discuss how Lindberg's techniques might be applied to those assignments.

Activities

- Write a few paragraphs on naming, using your own thinking and your own examples to experience the task facing Lindberg. If you do this you will have a better understanding of his skills.
- Take a subject you are working on and use some of the techniques Lindberg uses in his journal to help you understand the subject better. You may want to try his method of outlining.
- Take a broad subject, such as the economy or nuclear war, and then narrow the subject down as Lindberg has, find a focus for that section, and write a few paragraphs.
- Choose an essay in the book or one of the poems published in Chapter 6, and write critically about it in the way Lindberg has thought about a text in his piece and shared his thinking with the reader.
- Take a draft of a piece of personal experience you have written and write an essay about the ideas or idea in the piece. In other words, write a piece of thinking about the experience, using examples from the experience to help you develop and document your thoughts.

Commentary

Context

1   The section I've presented here is from a book in progress on common sense and the reading of literature. I am trying to recapture general readers of literature who have lost faith because of the arcane language and mystification which current critical theory has imposed on fiction and poetry. My point is that good readers don't need training in critical systems. The chapter from which the excerpt comes is called "Why Read Literature?" It shows how many of the apparently complex techniques of imaginative literature are simply exercises of mental powers that we all use but often underrate or disregard. The

particular subject of Naming is much simpler than the preceding ones, which accounts for the elaborate transition beginning the excerpt.

Stages

I have been keeping a journal for over two years, developing the book. It has no order or propriety, only whatever comes to me as possibly relevant. Questions I raise in the journal focus my thinking after I pose them, so that days or even weeks later some answers occur, which I note in the journal. It gradually appeared to me that part of what I wanted to do was talk about common-sense ways of reading poetry and fiction, and that each deserved a chapter. But there were also matters that didn't belong to either genre separately, that were more general in nature, more rooted in the very attitudes we bring with us when we pick up a piece of imaginative literature. I gathered these in the chapter "Why Read Literature?" As I was writing the first parts of this chapter, more refined and detailed ideas about the later sections kept occurring to me, and I would add them to the journal. 2

The first stage in writing this particular section was my transcribing of notes from the journal. Here I worked with no order at all, simply looking through the journal, putting things from it on large notepads, expanding entries as I made them, thinking of examples, and generally getting my mind focused on the issues of literary naming. 3

This stage overlapped with the next because I was constantly moving back and forth. I'm not sure what to call this next stage because it doesn't correspond to many descriptions of the writing process. It is a cross between notes and discovery draft. The notes are not notes in the usual sense (gatherings of information), because they actually involve ideas, tangents of ideas, ramifications of ideas, new questions. And it's not quite discovery draft either, for the syntax is usually incomplete, the parts are not necessarily related, and I make no attempt at continuity or coherence. In other words, I have no plan. I simply put things down as they occur to me in my combination of rereading, thinking about and following out certain questions, sometimes posing new ones. Often I have two or three notepads at the same time so that I can put down one idea on one while I am following through with another idea on the other page. It's like an artist's sketch in which I'm working rapidly and approximately, 4 trying to get down the two or three semirelated things that crowd into mind at once. I give no thought to explanation, qualification, precision, phrasing, clarity. I stick with a train of thought or association as long as it lasts; then if I've made some side-jottings on other pages I follow out those. When I've played out whatever impulses had set off those thoughts, I go back and reread earlier notes, always trying to follow out larger questions, always trying to consider the possible relationships among the ideas I've sketched.

5   This note/draft stage blends into the next one, which could be called organization, but which I prefer to call discovery of coherences, orders, and shapes. Gradually my notes take the form not of fragmentary insights but of comments on the relationships among other notes. And as I relate these clusters of coherence to each other, I find the order among my ideas. This I finally condense in a rough outline of order of parts. Labeling these A, B, C . . ., I then go back over all my other notes, putting red letters beside them for where they belong. Some I find possibly belonging in two categories, and I mark them B—C, knowing that they might serve as transition points.

6   Now I am ready for the true draft, in which I present, clarify, explain, relate, and explore my ideas in complete and linear prose. I don't have to worry about losing a side thought while I concentrate on the shape of a sentence, because the side thoughts are already sketched out in the note-draft. (Of course, I find myself adding to these notes—cribbing in the margins—when some other tangential matter occurs to me as I write.) My main concentration now is on clarity and precision, as I move from rough notes and hints to well-defined and determined ideas. And as the ideas take more definite shape, they generate new ideas or complications, and I try to follow out that impulse in the writing itself. For this purpose I constantly reread what I just wrote, making sure that as I continue I am carrying on the rhythm of thought and discovery that I started earlier. And I try to read aloud as I reread. I want to hear my sentences and "hear" my thinking. (This, incidentally, is why I stopped composing at the typewriter.) To some degree this is a matter of style, sound, grammar—I make many revisions of earlier sentences by this constant rereading. But what we usually analyze as prose rhythm is often actually thought rhythm, or at least the two are closely intertwined. Look at the sequence beginning with "Pilgermann acknowledges. . ." and ending with the paragraph. Some people would stylistically analyze that as effort to develop prose rhythm by varying sentence length and structure. But it's really a succession of discov-

eries. When I wrote "Antioch itself is a passing entity," I was making a firm clarifying statement. I discovered I could simplify it by adding "So is wall." Then I realized I could pull together the larger idea about naming by recalling "So is missile." But I had no intention of returning to the speaker. That occurred to me because I was rereading and hearing what I had just said, asking if it went any further. The connection back to Pilgermann himself allowed me to bring in a whole other side of the book and to link it to what I had been saying. That linkage, of course, involves a longer and more entangled thought, hence the shift of rhythm and structure in the last sentence. That, to me, is what essay writing is like. I can allow myself such digressionary discoveries and enlargements in the draft because I have my overall outline and sense of shape to recall me in the right direction and to keep me aware of proportion. I can play around without getting lost.

Since I am continually rereading as I go and making minor 7 prose revisions for emphasis, clarity, or flow, by the time I have finished the *manuscript* draft, the writing is pretty well done. Transcribing my handwriting in the typed draft is basically mechanical, although as my students know, *reading* that handwriting is a challenge of its own. This typed version (which is what you have) will be revised again in minor ways when I read the draft of the entire book, but the further changes will involve polishing, consistency, possible trimming and condensing. The exciting stage of discovery is over, and it is for that stage that I write in the first place.

Reflections on the Process

I hadn't realized until reviewing and describing my own writing 8 stages how heretical I am. For which I of course won't apologize. But let me at least clarify the heresies.

Discovery Stage

Here I'm relatively orthodox except in a few ways. I don't free 9 write in the usual sense. I prefer a kind of outlined sketching of ideas and their followups, often using more than one page at a time to allow me both to have the flow of free-writing and to have the preliminary sorting and focusing that gives the flow some force. It's a kind of controlled counterpoint free-writing.

I depend very heavily on questions as I write. I'm almost always 10 trying to answer some question or asking a new one. I try to be aware *why* what I'm saying matters (at least to me, and at least for now).

Drafts and Revisions

11   I don't recall ever following the orthodox pattern of writing a rough discovery draft, finding my purpose as I write, making a new outline or structure, and then writing a separate revision. Because of my overlapping sequence of notes and sketched associations and gradually gathered coherences, I already have found a structure by the time I start writing my main prose draft in full sentences. For my kind of writing it doesn't make sense to move paragraphs around or to cut and paste. I did that occasionally in graduate school and always hated the results because they sounded like cut-and-paste prose with more or less interchangeable parts. When I'm writing well, I am constantly doing one of two things: either I'm moving to the center of some idea cluster, or I'm relating one idea to another. That is, transitions are for me not graceful linkings for clarity—they are the substance of the writing itself. I write transitions. An essay for me is an exploring of related ideas, which is to say a sequence of transitions. If it can be readily rearranged, it must be merely an organization of information, which I don't see as an essay at all.

Audience

12   You'll notice that in my description of process, I never once mentioned audience. That must be my major heresy. I don't consider audience. Or to be more precise, I don't consider *this* audience in relation to this or that piece of writing. I of course know that someone else is going to read what I write. That awareness is simply human decency, like paying attention to the people you're with. But such decency is so steadily developed with experience that it virtually calibrates one in time. When I say to myself "this sentence is now clear to me," I mean that it meets the demands I've gradually taken in and adjusted to over years of using language with other people. So *of course* I'm writing for an audience. But not really. Not consciously. I don't deliberately adjust what I'm saying to an audience. (Please note that I'm considering only my serious writing here. My letters, recommendations, memos, business correspondence, and so forth take precise account of audience; they are self-consciously manipulative, as such writing has to be. They bear the same relation to "real" writing as selling a product bears to inventing it.) I do not consider what my prospective reader already knows and still needs to know or what that reader's interests are. All my deliberation is reserved for the subject—*that* is what I manipulate and work out. I include as much as is necessary to make something clear *in itself* and coherent

in its relations, and this frequently involves a mixture of what the reader knows with what is new. I flatter the reader by assuming he or she is enough like me to be interested in what *I* find interesting and demonstrate to be interesting. In that regard, I think my essay writing is like someone's fiction writing or poetry—what is done for oneself is also an appeal to a "best self" in someone else, not a gesture of manipulation.

When I say that my deliberation is focused on the subject 13 instead of the reader, I am being old-fashioned enough to believe that subjects of thought have structures, that they have centers and peripheries and internal relations. The shape is intrinsic to the subject, not adapted to the audience. My job as a writer is to find it, to work it out, as a sculptor works out the shape in the stone. The viewer of the sculpture is not considered in the act of making—if the making is good, the viewer will be able to *see* the shape. I have to understand my subject well enough to convey its essence to someone else, not what I might guess that reader would need but what makes the subject whole in itself. Put another way, a consideration for audience is built deeply into my sense that a subject *matters*, it is not a superficial question of how to *approach* the subject. Do you suppose that the repeated emphasis in writing texts on calculations about audience are a reflection of how deeply Madison Avenue culture has infiltrated our educational system? I don't think it's morally healthy.

The concern with audience also involves the relationship of 14 drafts to each other. I find Linda Flower's distinction of writer-based and reader-based prose a real aid in talking to my own students about what *has* worked in their writing and what still needs attention. But Flower's distinction doesn't make sense when I consider my own writing. Put simply, she sees the first draft as allowing for the writer's process of discovery, whereas the second draft rearranges the material through consideration of the needs of the reader. My own writer-based writing, as I said, is not even prose at all, and it certainly never reaches completion as a "draft" (as you'll see in my notes). By the time I start writing a version in linear prose with complete sentences, I have already found a rough structure in the material, an approximate relation of parts, and although this structure will become more determinate and refined as I write, it will not be reorganized for the reader. Instead, the full-prose draft is simultaneously an act of discovery and an act of clarification. And this kind of order—following the course of the writer's thinking—seems to me the most satisfying and revealing for the reader as well.

15   Let me illustrate what I mean by discussing structure in "Naming." When I write an essay, I am aware of working back and forth between two kinds of gesture, one exploring the edges of a topic, the other seeking the center. If I'm feeling my way along an edge, I'm thinking of differences, qualifications, relationships, demarcations, but I'm also intuitively aware that this is the edge of *something*, so I'm tentatively groping as well toward a definition of the center. When I'm determining the center, in turn, I'm establishing a basis for seeing more edges and seeing them more precisely. So it's back and forth, back and forth. How did I begin "Naming"? I was thinking of the edge between my last subject (projection of the writer's inner self outward into events and scenes and characters) and my new one. The transition was from a peculiarly complex aspect of literature to one of its simplest pleasures, and that transition made me realize the centrality of simple pleasure for my subject of naming. That realization, in turn, generated the sequence of sections A, B, and C in my outline, for I recognized that we could only *realize* simple pleasure by the mental act of clearing away complexity. Then, having worked with the edges, I would be ready to approach the center. Sections D and E move toward it by elaborating on our personal feelings as we name things. Then in F I'm ready for a virtually philosophical discussion of what naming is. But that, in turn, reveals a new edge— what's special about literary naming in contrast to all others, and that finally leads into my three analytic examples. That's the way my sense of edges and centers revealed to me the basic shape in my material.

16   But there were still constantly discoveries along the way, refinements, fresh seeings. Let me illustrate with one that I noted while I was writing. Look at the full paragraph beginning, "When we see naming itself as an extraordinary gesture,. . .". My motive here was to illustrate what I had just said about artists drawing us back to language as creation. I wanted something quick and clear, and I didn't want to have to do a long lead-in to the example because that would break the flow of my real discussion. So I went back to the immediately preceding section of the chapter where I had discussed Frost's "Design," and reexamined some phrases that I now knew the reader would recognize. The interesting thing happened when I wrote the sentence "Frost's way of naming here places the immediate natural scene in a much grander drama." The metaphor in the last phrase is almost a cliché for a literary critic—all of us draw unwittingly on such metaphors as we write. But then I stopped and thought about it

and made my thought explicit in the next sentence: "It announces a different stage setting." I liked that, thought about it some more, and redefined my central subject in a totally unplanned way: "That is what naming does—it makes the stage, sets it, and fills it with action." The rest of the paragraph plays out that discovery, not only doing what I intended—clarifying an abstract point from a preceding paragraph—but opening to me a new approach to my subject. If you now look at my commentary on Ammons's "Cascadilla Falls," you'll see how much I needed that conception of naming as stage setting, as establishing of context, a conception I didn't even have until I was writing about Frost. Such discoveries are to me the life-blood of writing, and I like to leave them for the reader as discoveries too instead of rearranging the material to announce at the beginning that one of the powers of naming is to set a stage.

Attitude as Writer

One last heresy—I love the rhythm of the old saw about writing as process: "How do I know what I think till I see what I say?" But it really doesn't correspond to the way I work. It is much too passive, too will-less, too accidental. It acknowledges a writer's own work but it leaves the backdoor open to inspiration. Thoughts *do* rise unbidden, as I just illustrated, but they usually rise where we're looking for them. I tend to generate new ideas by questioning, by shifting contexts, by exploring relations, by puzzling, all quite deliberate activities. Some of my best insights do come to me while taking a bath, driving a car, sleeping, but I'm not just sleeping, I'm "sleeping *on* it," which is almost a deliberate gesture. You have to know what you're sleeping on. My revision of the maxim wrecks the rhythm, and it's too complicated to be quotable, but I think it has the advantage of being accurate: How do I know what I think till I put it down and *work it out?*

Ralph Ellison

Ralph Ellison is one of those writers who has the satisfaction and the disadvantages of having written a work that reached so many readers that it almost instantly became part of our culture, and made him famous for that single work. Such writers are often trapped by their fame, and Ellison's novel, *Invisible Man*, which was published in 1952, made a permanent impression on many readers, both black and white. I know that I saw the world a bit differently after reading that book, and I find myself more than 30 years later seeing the world through Ellison's eyes every few minutes. Ellison, however, didn't just write that one book. He has written many stories and many essays, such as the one here, which was first an address sponsored by the Gertrude Clarke Whittall Foundation, and given at the Library of Congress on January 6, 1964. In many ways he, like Lindberg, is talking about naming. And he moves back and forth between personal experience and critical thinking in this essay.

Hidden Name and Complex Fate
A Writer's Experience in the United States

1   In *Green Hills of Africa* Ernest Hemingway reminds us that both Tolstoy and Stendhal had seen war, that Flaubert had seen a revolution and the Commune, that Dostoievsky had been sent to Siberia and that such experiences were important in shaping the art of these great masters. And he goes on to observe that "writers are forged in injustice as a sword is forged." He declined to describe the many personal forms which injustice may take in this chaotic world—who would be so mad as to try?—nor does he go into the personal wounds which each of these writers sustained. Now, however, thanks to his brother and sister, we do know something of the injustice in which he himself was forged, and this knowledge has been added to what we have long known of Hemingway's artistic temper.

2   In the end, however, it is the quality of his art which is primary. It is the art which allows the wars and revolutions which he knew, and the personal and social injustice which he suffered, to lay claims upon our attention; for it was through his art that they achieved their most enduring meaning. It is a matter of outrageous irony, perhaps, but in literature the great social clashes of history no less than the painful experience of the individual are secondary to the meaning which they take on through the skill, the talent, the imagination and personal vision of the writer who transforms them into art. Here they are reduced to more manageable proportions; here they are imbued with humane values; here, injustice and catastrophe become less important in themselves than what the writer makes of them. This is *not* true, however, of the writer's struggle with that recalcitrant angel

called Art; and it was through *this* specific struggle that Ernest Hemingway became *Hemingway* (now refined to a total body of transcendent work, after forty years of being endlessly dismembered and resurrected, as it continues to be, in the styles, the themes, the sense of life and literature of countless other writers). And it was through this struggle with form that he became the master, the culture hero, whom we have come to know and admire.

It was suggested that it might be of interest if I discussed here 3 this evening some of my notions of the writer's experience in the United States, hence I have evoked the name of Hemingway, not by way of inviting farfetched comparisons but in order to establish a perspective, a set of assumptions from which I may speak, and in an attempt to avoid boring you by emphasizing those details of racial hardship which for some forty years now have been evoked whenever writers of my own cultural background have essayed their experience in public.

I do this *not* by way of denying totally the validity of these by 4 now stylized recitals, for I have shared and still share many of their detailed injustices—what Negro can escape them?—but by way of suggesting that they are, at least in a discussion of a writer's experience, as *writer*, as artist, somewhat beside the point.

For we select neither our parents, our race nor our nation; these 5 occur to us out of the love, the hate, the circumstances, the fate, of others. But we *do* become writers out of an act of will, out of an act of choice; a dim, confused and ofttimes regrettable choice, perhaps, but choice nevertheless. And what happens thereafter causes all those experiences which occurred before we began to function as writers to take on a special quality of uniqueness. If this does not happen then as far as writing goes, the experiences have been misused. If we do not make of them a value, if we do not transform them into forms and images of meaning which they did not possess before, then we have failed as artists.

Thus for a writer to insist that this personal suffering is of spe- 6 cial interest in itself, or simply because he belongs to a particular racial or religious group, is to advance a claim for special privileges which members of his group who are not writers would be ashamed to demand. The kindest judgment one can make of this point of view is that it reveals a sad misunderstanding of the relationship between suffering and art. Thomas Mann and Andre Gide have told us much of this and there are critics, like Edmund Wilson, who have told of the connection between the wound and the bow.

7   As I see it, it is through the process of making artistic forms—plays, poems, novels—out of one's experience that one becomes a writer, and it is through this process, this struggle, that the writer helps give meaning to the experience of the group. And it is the process of mastering the discipline, the techniques, the fortitude, the culture, through which this is made possible that constitutes the writer's real experience as *writer*, as artist. If this sounds like an argument for the artist's withdrawal from social struggles, I would recall to you W. H. Auden's comment to the effect that:

8   *In our age, the mere making of a work of art is itself a political act. So long as artists exist, making what they please, and think they ought to make, even if it is not terribly good, even if it appeals to only a handful of people, they remind the Management of something managers need to be reminded of, namely, that the managed are people with faces, not anonymous members, that* Homo Laborans *is also* Homo Ludens. . . .

9   Without doubt, even the most *engagé* writer—and I refer to true artists, not to artists *manqués*—begin their careers in play and puzzlement, in dreaming over the details of the world in which they become conscious of themselves.

10   Let Tar Baby, that enigmatic figure from Negro folklore, stand for the world. He leans, black and gleaming, against the wall of life utterly noncommittal under our scrutiny, our questioning, starkly unmoving before our naive attempts at intimidation. Then we touch him playfully and before we can say *Sonny Listen!* we find ourselves stuck. Our playful investigations become a labor, a fearful struggle, an *agon*. Slowly we perceive that our task is to learn the proper way of freeing ourselves to develop, in other words, technique.

11   Sensing this, we give him our sharpest attention, we question him carefully, we struggle with more subtlety; while he, in his silent way, holds on, demanding that we perceive the necessity of calling him by his true name as the price of our freedom. It is unfortunate that he has so many, many "true names"—all spelling chaos; and in order to discover even one of these we must first come into the possession of our own names. For it is through our names that we first place ourselves in the world. Our names, being the gift of others, must be made our own.

12   Once while listening to the play of a two-year-old girl who did not know she was under observation, I heard her saying over and over again, at first with questioning and then with sounds of growing

satisfaction, "I am Mimi Livisay? . . . *I* am Mimi Livisay. I *am* Mimi Livisay . . . I am *Mimi* Li-vi-say! I am Mimi . . .—

And in deed and in fact she was—or became so soon thereafter, 13 by working playfully to establish the unit between herself and her name.

❧ I am impressed by the skill with which Ellison uses documentation from literature, folklore, observation, personal experience and weaves them all into his own thinking. I am able to see Ellison thinking, and thinking about how he is thinking. And in that way he, like Lindberg, stimulates my own thinking. I cannot read this piece without examining my own naming and what it has meant to me. ❧

For many of us this is far from easy. We must learn to wear our 14 names within all the noise and confusion of the environment in which we find ourselves; make them the center of all of our associations with the world, with man and with nature. We must charge them with all our emotions, our hopes, hates, loves, aspirations. They must become our masks and our shields and the containers of all those values and traditions which we learn and/or imagine as being the meaning of our familial past.

And when we are reminded so constantly that we bear, as 15 Negroes, names originally possessed by those who owned our enslaved grandparents, we are apt, especially if we are potential writers, to be more than ordinarily concerned with the veiled and mysterious events, the fusions of blood, the furtive couplings, the business transactions, the violations of faith and loyalty, the assaults; yes, and the unrecognized and unrecognizable loves through which our names were handed down unto us.

So charged with emotion does this concern become for some of 16 us, that we have, earlier, the example of the followers of Father Divine and, now, the Black Muslims, discarding their original names in rejection of the bloodstained, the brutal, the sinful images of the past. Thus they would declare new identities, would clarify a new program of intention and destroy the verbal evidence of a willed and ritualized discontinuity of blood and human intercourse.

Not all of us, actually only a few, seek to deal with our names 17 in this manner. We take what we have and make of them what we can. And there are even those who know where the old broken connections lie, who recognize their relatives across the chasm of historical denial and the artificial barriers of society, and who see themselves as bearers of many of the qualities which were admirable in the original sources of their common line (Faulkner has made much of this); and I speak there not of mere forgiveness, nor of obsequious insensitivity to the outrages symbolized by the denial and the division, but of the conscious acceptance of the harsh realities of the human condition, of the ambiguities and hypocrisies of human history as they have played themselves out in the United States.

18   Perhaps, taken in aggregate, these European names which (sometimes with irony, sometimes with pride, but always with personal investment) represent a certain triumph of the spirit, speaking to us of those who rallied, reassembled and transformed themselves and who under dismembering pressures refused to die. "Brothers and sisters," I once heard a Negro preacher exhort, "let us make up our faces before the world, and our names shall sound throughout the land with honor! For we ourselves are our *true* names, not their epithets! So let us, I say, Make Up Our Faces and Our Minds!"

19   Perhaps my preacher had read T. S. Eliot, although I doubt it. And in actuality, it was unnecessary that he do so, for a concern with names and naming was very much part of that special area of American culture from which I come, and it is precisely for this reason that this example should come to mind in a discussion of my own experience as a writer.

20   Undoubtedly, writers begin their *conditioning* as manipulators of words long before they become aware of literature—certain Freudians would say at the breast. Perhaps. But if so, that is far too early to be of use at this moment. Of this, though, I am certain: that despite the misconceptions of those educators who trace the reading difficulties experienced by large numbers of Negro children in Northern schools to their Southern background, these children are, in *their* familiar South, facile manipulators of words. I know, too, that the Negro community is deadly in its ability to create nicknames and to spot all that is ludicrous in an unlikely name or that which is incongruous in conduct. Names are not qualities; nor are words, in this particular sense, actions. To assume that they are could cost one his life many times a day. Language skills depend to a large extent upon a knowledge of the details, the manners, the objects, the folkways, the psychological patterns, of a given environment. Humor and wit depend upon much the same awareness, and so does the suggestive power of names.

21   "A small brown bowlegged Negro with the name 'Franklin D.

Roosevelt Jones' might sound like a clown to someone who looks at him from the outside," said my friend Albert Murray, "but on the other hand he just might turn out to be a hell of a fireside operator. He might just lie back in all of that comic juxtaposition of names and manipulate you deaf, dumb and blind—and you not even suspecting it, because you're thrown out of stance by his name! There you are, so dazzled by the F.D.R. image—which you *know* you can't see—and so delighted with your own superior position that you don't realize that it's *Jones* who must be confronted."

Well, as you must suspect, all of this speculation on the matter of names has a purpose, and now, because it is tied up so ironically with my own experience as a writer, I must turn to my own name. 22

For in the dim beginnings, before I ever thought consciously of writing, there was my own name, and there was, doubtless, a certain magic in it. From the start I was uncomfortable with it, and in my earliest years it caused me much puzzlement. Neither could I understand what a poet was, nor why, exactly, my father had chosen to name me after one. Perhaps I could have understood it perfectly well had he named me after his own father, but that name had been given to an older brother who died and thus was out of the question. But why hadn't he named me after a hero, such as Jack Johnson, or a soldier like Colonel Charles Young, or a great seaman like Admiral Dewey, or an educator like Booker T. Washington, or a great orator and abolitionist like Frederick Douglass? Or again, why hadn't he named me (as so many Negro parents had done) after President Teddy Roosevelt? 23

Instead, he named me after someone called Ralph Waldo Emerson, and then, when I was three, he died. It was too early for me to have understood his choice, although I'm sure he must have explained it many times, and it was also too soon for me to have made the connection between my name and my father's love for reading. Much later, after I began to write and work with words, I came to suspect that he was aware of the suggestive powers of names and of the magic involved in naming. 24

I recall an odd conversation with my mother during my early teens in which she mentioned their interest in, of all things, prenatal culture! But for a long time I actually knew only that my father read a lot, and that he admired this remote Mr. Emerson, who was something called a "poet and philosopher"—so much so that he named his second son after him. 25

I knew, also, that whatever his motives, the combination of 26 names he'd given me caused me no end of trouble from the moment when I could talk well enough to respond to the ritualized question which grownups put to very young children. Emerson's name was quite familiar to Negroes in Oklahoma during those days when World War I was brewing, and adults, eager to show off their knowledge of literary figures, and obviously amused by the joke implicit in such a small brown nubbin of a boy carrying around such a heavy moniker, would invariably repeat my first two names and then to my great annoyance, they'd add "Emerson."

27   And I, in my confusion, would reply, "No, *no, I'm* not Emerson, he's the little boy who lives next door." Which only made them laugh all the louder. "Oh no," they'd say, *"you're* Ralph Waldo Emerson." while I had fantasies of blue murder.

28   For a while the presence next door of my little friend, Emerson, made it unnecessary for me to puzzle too often over this peculiar adult confusion. And since there were other Negro boys named Ralph in the city, I came to suspect that there was something about the combination of names which produced their laughter. Even today I know of only one other Ralph who had as much comedy made out of his name, a campus politician and deep-voiced orator whom I knew at Tuskegee, who was called in friendly ribbing, *Ralph Waldo Emerson Edgar Allen Poe*, spelled Powe. This must have been quite a trial for him, but I had been initiated much earlier.

Discussion

- Compare the techniques of critical thinking practiced by Lindberg and Ellison. What do they do that is similar? That is different?
- Discuss the advantages of such intellectual writing. Discuss its limitations.
- Compare Ellison's piece with Baraka's and Baldwin's. How were their purposes different? How did they each use personal experience?
- Compare the voice used by Ellison, Baraka, and Baldwin. What are the advantages and disadvantages of each?
- Consider the distance at which Ellison stands from his subject. What are some other distances at which he might have chosen to stand? How would a different distance change the writing?
- Consider the focus of Ellison's piece. Discuss how that focus helps him and also helps the reader.

- Choose a different focus for the same material and discuss how that would change the writing of the essay.

Activities

- Outline Ellison's essay to see the skeleton of thought upon which the essay was grown.
- Take a paragraph of personal experience which Ellison uses to document his thoughts. Rewrite it, standing closer to the subject or using a different voice—a voice of anger, involvement, or sadness.
- Take a draft of your own and rewrite it as Ellison might have if he were to use it in an essay.
- Take a paragraph from Baraka, from Baldwin, and from Ellison which involved personal experience, and rewrite them, having, for example, Ellison write Baraka, Baraka write Baldwin, and Baldwin write Ellison. Pick your own combination.
- Write a short piece about your own naming without consciously imitating Ellison. Compare your piece with his, not to see what you have done wrong or right, but simply to discover how your experience and your voice produced a draft that is different from his.

James Baldwin

James Baldwin is a major American writer who has been able to take his particular human experience and use it to both speak of the black experience in America and also to speak of the universal experience of people of all races, sexes, and conditions. He has been an important writer since he was very young, and his voice has changed and developed, but it always has been his own. He has spoken with his own particular hurt and rage in a language that is disciplined and effective. I have never been able to read his pages untouched, first as a human being and second as a writer. He reaches my gut, and then engages me as a writer, admiring the technical skill with which he has spoken.

One of his strongest pieces is the one I have selected to include in this book, a classic essay that was written at a special moment in our history. But it is just as alive today as it was when it was written. Baldwin has said, "When you're writing, you're trying to find out something which you don't know. The whole language of writing for me is finding out what you don't want to know, what you don't want to find out." At another time he said, "You go into a book and you're in the dark, really. You go in with a certain fear and trembling. You know one thing. You know that you will not be the same person when this voyage is over." In this piece you can sense the author, hurt, angry, mourning, searching for meaning in what is happening within him and around him.

Notes of a Native Son

❦ Note the irony right away in the title. Baldwin has been alienated from his father and from his country. At the time he published this he had been living in Europe for eight years. The title establishes the focus and the tone of the essay.❧

1   On the 29th of July, in 1943, my father died. On the same day, a few hours later, his last child was born. Over a month before this, while all our energies were concentrated in waiting for these events, there had been, in Detroit, one of the bloodiest race riots of the century. A few hours after my father's funeral, while he lay in state in the undertaker's chapel, a race riot broke out in Harlem. On the morning of the 3rd of August, we drove my father to the graveyard through a wilderness of smashed plate glass.

❦ This is a superb example of a lead that puts the reader right into the story. The writer dares you not to read on. As a writer I am impressed by the fact that Baldwin has understated the terrible personal and public events that are described. The events themselves are so strong that he can write of them in an almost flat tone. I'm also impressed as a writer with the power of the specific at the end of the paragraph.❧

2   The day of my father's funeral had also been my nineteenth birthday. As we drove him to the graveyard, the spoils of injustice, anarchy, discontent, and hatred were all around us. It seemed to me that God himself had devised, to mark my father's end, the most sustained and brutally dissonant of codas. And it seemed to me, too, that the violence which rose all about us as my father left the world had been devised as a corrective for the pride of his eldest son. I had declined to believe in that apocalypse which had been central to my

father's vision; very well, life seemed to be saying, here is something that will certainly pass for an apocalypse until the real thing comes along. I had inclined to be contemptuous of my father for the conditions of his life, for the conditions of our lives. When his life had ended I began to wonder about that life and also, in a new way, to be apprehensive about my own.

I had not known my father very well. We had got on badly, partly because we shared, in our different fashions, the vice of stubborn pride. When he was dead I realized that I had hardly ever spoken to him. When he had been dead a long time I began to wish I had. It seems to be typical of life in America, where opportunities, real and fancied, are thicker than anywhere else on the globe, that the second generation has no time to talk to the first. No one, including my father, seems to have known exactly how old he was, but his mother had been born during slavery. He was of the first generation of free men. He, along with thousands of other Negroes, came North after 1919 and I was part of that generation which had never seen the landscape of what Negroes sometimes call the Old Country.

He had been born in New Orleans and had been a quite young man there during the time that Louis Armstrong, a boy, was running errands for the dives and honky-tonks of what was always presented to me as one of the most wicked of cities—to this day, whenever I think of New Orleans, I also helplessly think of Sodom and Gomorrah. My father never mentioned Louis Armstrong, except to forbid us to play his records; but there was a picture of him on our wall for a long time. One of my father's strong-willed female relatives had placed it there and forbade my father to take it down. He never did, but he eventually maneuvered her out of the house and when, some years later, she was in trouble and near death, he refused to do anything to help her.

He was, I think, very handsome. I gather this from photographs and from my own memories of him, dressed in his Sunday best and on his way to preach a sermon somewhere, when I was little. Handsome, proud, and ingrown, "like a toe-nail," somebody said. But he looked to me, as I grew older, like pictures I had seen of African tribal chieftans: he really should have been naked, with war-paint on and barbaric mementos, standing among spears. He could be chilling in the pulpit and idescribably cruel in his personal life and he was certainly the most bitter man I have ever met; yet it must be said that there was something else in him, buried in him, which lent him his tremendous power and, even, a rather crushing charm. It had something to do with his blackness, I think—he was very black—with his blackness and his beauty, and with the fact that he knew that he was black but did not know that he was beautiful. He claimed to be proud of his blackness but it had also been the cause of much humiliation and it had fixed bleak boundaries to his life. He was not a young man when we were growing up and he had already suffered many kinds of ruin; in his outrageously demanding and protective way he loved his children, who were black like him and menaced, like him; and all these things sometimes showed in his face when he tried, never to my knowledge with any success, to establish contact with any of us. When he took one of his children on his knee to play, the child always became fretful and began to cry; when he tried to help one of us with our homework the absolutely unabating tension which emanated from him caused our minds and our tongues to become paralyzed, so that he, scarcely knowing why, flew into a rage and the child, not knowing why, was punished. If it ever entered his head to bring a surprise home for his children, it was, almost unfailingly, the wrong surprise and even the big watermelons he often brought home on his back in the summertime led to the most appalling scenes. I do not remember, in all those years, that one of his children was ever glad to see him come home. From what I was able to gather of his early life, it seemed that this inability to establish contact with other people had always marked him and had been one of the things which had driven him out of New Orleans. There was something in him, therefore, groping and tentative, which was never expressed and which was buried with him. One saw it most clearly when he was facing new people and hoping to impress them. But he never did, not for long. We went from church to smaller and more improbable church, he found himself in less and less demand as a minister, and by the time he died none of his friends had come to see him for a long time. He had lived and died in an intolerable bitterness of spirit and it frightened me, as we drove him to the graveyard through those unquiet, ruined streets, to see how powerful and overflowing this bitterness could be and to realize that this bitterness now was mine.

❡As a writer I reread and reread this spectacular paragraph which covers so many complicated matters, interweaving them. Many of us have had very complicated relations with our parents, and we can identify with the difficulty the author is feeling in confronting his father after his death. ❡

When he died I had been away from home for a little over a   6
year. In that year I had had time to become aware of the meaning of
all my father's bitter warnings, had discovered the secret of his
proudly pursed lips and rigid carriage: I had discovered the weight of
white people in the world. I saw that this had been for my ancestors
and now would be for me an awful thing to live with and that the
bitterness which had helped to kill my father could also kill me.

He had been ill a long time—in the mind, as we now realized,   7
reliving instances of his fantastic intransigence in the new light of his
affliction and endeavoring to feel a sorrow for him which never,
quite, came true. We had not known that he was being eaten up by
paranoia, and the discovery that his cruelty, to our bodies and our
minds, had been one of the symptoms of his illness was not, then,
enough to enable us to forgive him. The younger children felt, quite
simply, relief that he would not be coming home anymore. My mother's observation that it was he, after all, who had kept them alive all
these years meant nothing because the problems of keeping children
alive are not real for children. The other children felt, with my father
gone, that they could invite their friends to the house without fear
that their friends would be insulted or, as had sometimes happened
with me, being told that their friends were in league with the devil
and intended to rob our family of everything we owned. (I didn't fail
to wonder, and it made me hate him, what on earth we owned that
anybody else would want.)

His illness was beyond all hope of healing before anyone real-   8
ized that he was ill. He had always been so strange and had lived,
like a prophet, in such unimaginably close communion with the Lord
that his long silences which were punctuated by moans and hallelu-
jahs and snatches of old songs while he sat at the living-room window never seemed odd to us. It was not until he refused to eat
because, he said, his family was trying to poison him that my mother
was forced to accept as a fact what had, until then, been only an
unwilling suspicion. When he was committed, it was discovered that
he had tuberculosis and, as it turned out, the disease of his mind
allowed the disease of his body to destroy him. For the doctors could
not force him to eat, either, and, though he was fed intravenously, it
was clear from the beginning that there was no hope for him.

In my mind's eye I could see him, sitting at the window, locked   9
up in his terrors; hating and fearing every living soul including his
children who had betrayed him, too, by reaching towards the world

which had despised him. There were nine of us. I began to wonder what it could have felt like for such a man to have had nine children whom he could barely feed. He used to make little jokes about our poverty, which never, of course, seemed very funny to us; they could not have seemed very funny to him, either, or else our all too feeble response to them would never have caused such rages. He spent great energy and achieved, to our chagrin, no small amount of success in keeping us away from the people who surrounded us, people who had all-night rent parties to which we listened when we should have been sleeping, people who cursed and drank and flashed razor blades on Lenox Avenue. He could not understand why, if they had so much energy to spare, they could not use it to make their lives better. He treated almost everybody on our block with a most uncharitable asperity and neither they, nor, of course, their children were slow to reciprocate.

10   The only white people who came to our house were welfare workers and bill collectors. It was almost always my mother who dealt with them, for my father's temper, which was at the mercy of his pride, was never to be trusted. It was clear that he felt their very presence in his home to be a violation; this was conveyed by his carriage, almost ludicrously stiff, and by his voice, harsh and vindictively polite. When I was around nine or ten I wrote a play which was directed by a young, white schoolteacher, a woman, who then took an interest in me, and gave me books to read and, in order to corroborate my theatrical bent, decided to take me to see what she somewhat tactlessly referred to as "real" plays. Theater-going was forbidden in our house, but, with the really cruel intuitiveness of a child, I suspected that the color of this woman's skin would carry the day for me. When, at school, she suggested taking me to the theater, I did not, as I might have done if she had been a Negro, find a way of discouraging her, but agreed that she should pick me up at my house one evening. I then, very cleverly, left all the rest to my mother, who suggested to my father, as I knew she would, that it would not be very nice to let such a kind woman make the trip for nothing. Also, since it was a schoolteacher, I imagine that my mother countered the idea of sin with the idea of "education," which word, even with my father, carried a kind of bitter weight.

11   Before the teacher came my father took me aside to ask *why* she was coming, what *interest* she could possibly have in our house, in a boy like me. I said I didn't know but I, too, suggested that it had something to do with education. And I understood that my father was

waiting for me to say something—I didn't quite know what; perhaps that I wanted his protection against this teacher and her "education." I said none of these things and the teacher came and we went out. It was clear, during the brief interview in our living room, that my father was agreeing very much against his will and that he would have refused permission if he had dared. The fact that he did not dare caused me to despise him; I had no way of knowing that he was facing in that living room a wholly unprecedented and frightening situation.

Later when my father had been laid off from his job, this woman 12 became very important to us. She was really a very sweet and generous woman and went to a great deal of trouble to be of help to us, particularly during one awful winter. My mother called her by the highest name she knew; she said she was a "christian." My father could scarcely disagree but during the four or five years of our relatively close association he never trusted her and was always trying to surprise in her open, Midwestern face the genuine, cunningly hidden, and hideous motivation. In later years, particularly when it began to be clear that this "education" of mine was going to lead me to perdition, he became more explicit and warned me that my white friends in high school were not really my friends and that I would see, when I was older, how white people would do anything to keep a Negro down. Some of them could be nice, he admitted, but none of them were to be trusted and most of them were not even nice. The best thing was to have as little to do with them as possible. I did not feel this way and I was certain, in my innocence, that I never would.

But the year which preceded my father's death had made a great 13 change in my life. I had been living in New Jersey, working in defense plants, working and living among southerners, white and black. I knew about the south, of course, and about how southerners treated Negroes and how they expected them to behave, but it had never entered my mind that anyone would look at me and expect *me* to behave that way. I learned in New Jersey that to be a Negro meant, precisely, that one was never looked at but was simply at the mercy of the reflexes the color of one's skin caused in other people. I acted in New Jersey as I had always acted, that is as though I thought a great deal of myself—I had to *act* that way—with results that were simply unbelievable. I had scarcely arrived before I had earned the enmity, which was extraordinarily ingenious, of all my superiors and nearly all my co-workers. In the beginning, to make matters worse, I simply did not know what was happening. I did not know what I had done, and I shortly began to wonder what *anyone* could possibly do, to bring about such unanimous, active, and unbearably vocal hostility. I knew about jim-crow but I had never experienced it. I went to the same self-service restaurant three times and stood with all the Princeton boys before the counter, waiting for a hamburger and coffee; it was always an extraordinarily long time before anything was set before me; but it was not until the fourth visit that I learned that, in fact, nothing had ever been set before me; I had simply picked something up. Negroes were not served there, I was told, and they had been waiting for me to realize that I was always the only Negro present. Once I was told this, I determined to go there all the time. But now they were ready for me and, though some dreadful scenes were subsequently enacted in that restaurant, I never ate there again.

14   It was the same story all over New Jersey, in bars, bowling alleys, diners, places to live. I was always being forced to leave, silently, or with mutual imprecations. I very shortly became notorious and children giggled behind me when I passed and their elders whispered or shouted—they really believed that I was mad. And it did begin to work on my mind, of course; I began to be afraid to go anywhere and to compensate for this I went places to which I really should not have gone and where, God knows, I had no desire to be. My reputation in town naturally enhanced my reputation at work and my working day became one long series of acrobatics designed to keep me out of trouble. I cannot say that these acrobatics succeeded. It began to seem that the machinery of the organization I worked for was turning over, day and night, with but one aim: to eject me. I was fired once, and contrived, with the aid of a friend from New York, to get back on the payroll; was fired again, and bounced back again. It took a while to fire me for the third time, but the third time took. There were no loopholes anywhere. There was not even any way of getting back inside the gates.

❧ Notice all through this piece how Baldwin uses point of view—the adult looking back and reflecting upon experience—to control the flood of all the material of his life and to put it in context. We can walk beside him as he tries to record, and then to understand, his life. ❧

15   That year in New Jersey lives in my mind as though it were the year during which, having an unsuspected predilection for it, I first contracted some dread, chronic disease, the unfailing symptom of

which is a kind of blind fever, a pounding in the skull and fire in the bowels. Once this disease is contracted, one can never be really carefree again, for the fever, without an instant's warning, can recur at any moment. It can wreck more important things than race relations. There is not a Negro alive who does not have this rage in his blood— one has the choice, merely, of living with it consciously or surrendering to it. As for me, this fever has recurred in me, and does, and will until the day I die.

❦ The following anecdote is a powerful form of documentation. Here Baldwin writes a one-paragraph anecdote about his experience in the diner, and then follows it with an extended anecdote of his experience in a restaurant. The anecdote is a little narrative similar to the biblical parable that tells a story and makes a point. ❧

My last night in New Jersey, a white friend from New York took 16 me to the nearest big town, Trenton, to go to the movies and have a few drinks. As it turned out, he also saved me from, at the very least, a violent whipping. Almost every detail of that night stands out very clearly in my memory. I even remember the name of the movie we saw because its title impressed me as being so patly ironical. It was a movie about the German occupation of France, starring Maureen O'Hara and Charles Laughton and called *This Land Is Mine*. I remember the name of the diner we walked into when the movie ended; it was the "American Diner." When we walked in the counterman asked what we wanted and I remember answering with the casual sharpness which had become my habit: "We want a hamburger and a cup of coffee, what do you think we want?" I do not know why, after a year of such rebuffs, I so completely failed to anticipate his answer, which was, of course, "We don't serve Negroes here." This reply failed to discompose me, at least for the moment. I made some sardonic comment about the name of the diner and we walked out into the streets.

This was the time of what was called the "brown-out," when 17 the lights in all American cities were very dim. When we re-entered the streets something happened to me which had the force of an optical illusion, or a nightmare. The streets were very crowded and I was facing north. People were moving in every direction but it seemed to me, in that instant, that all of the people I could see, and many more than that, were moving toward me, against me, and that everyone was white. I remember how their faces gleamed. And I felt, like a physical sensation, a *click* at the nape of my neck as though some interior string connecting my head to my body had been cut. I began to walk. I heard my friend call after me, but I ignored him. Heaven only knows what was going on in his mind, but he had the good sense not to touch me—I don't know what would have happened if he had—and to keep me in sight. I don't know what was going on in my mind, either; I certainly had no conscious plan. I wanted to do something to crush these white faces, which were crushing me. I walked for perhaps a block or two until I came to an enormous, glittering, and fashionable restaurant in which I knew not even the intercession of the Virgin would cause me to be served. I pushed through the doors and took the first vacant seat I saw, at a table for two, and waited.

18   I do not know how long I waited and I rather wonder, until today, what I could possibly have looked like. Whatever I looked like, I frightened the waitress who shortly appeared, and the moment she appeared all of my fury flowed towards her. I hated her for her white face, and for her great, astounded, frightened, eyes. I felt that if she found a black man so frightening I would make her fright worthwhile.

19   She did not ask me what I wanted, but repeated, as though she had learned it somewhere, "We don't serve Negroes here." She did not say it with the blunt, derisive hostility to which I had grown so accustomed, but, rather, with a note of apology in her voice, and fear. This made me colder and more murderous than ever. I felt I had to do something with my hands. I wanted her to come close enough for me to get her neck between my hands.

20   So I pretended not to have understood her, hoping to draw her closer. And she did step a very short step closer, with her pencil poised incongruously over her pad, and repeated the formula: ". . .don't serve Negroes here."

21   Somehow, with the repetition of that phrase, which was already ringing in my head like a thousand bells of a nightmare, I realized that she would never come any closer and that I would have to strike from a distance. There was nothing on the table but an ordinary watermug half full of water, and I picked this up and hurled it with all my strength at her. She ducked and it missed her and shattered against the mirror behind the bar. And, with that sound, my frozen blood abruptly thawed, I returned from wherever I had been, I saw, for the first time, the restaurant, the people with their mouths open, already, as it seemed to me, rising as one man, and I realized what I

had done, and where I was, and I was frightened. I rose and began running for the door. A round, potbellied man grabbed me by the nape of the neck just as I reached the doors and began to beat me about the face. I kicked him and got loose and ran into the streets. My friend whispered, *"Run!"* and I ran.

My friend stayed outside the restaurant long enough to misdi- 22 rect my pursuers and the police, who arrived, he told me, at once. I do not know what I said to him when he came to my room that night. I could not have said much. I felt, in the oddest, most awful way, that I had somehow betrayed him. I lived it over and over and over again, the way one relives an automobile accident after it has happened and one finds oneself alone and safe. I could not get over two facts, both equally difficult for the imagination to grasp, and one was that I could have been murdered. But the other was that I had been ready to commit murder. I saw nothing very clearly but I did see this: that my life, my *real* life, was in danger, and not from anything other people might do but from the hatred I carried in my own heart.

I had returned home around the second week in June—in great 23 haste because it seemed that my father's death and my mother's confinement were both but a matter of hours. In the case of my mother, it soon became clear that she had simply made a miscalculation. This had always been her tendency and I don't believe that a single one of us arrived in the world, or has since arrived anywhere else, on time. But none of us dawdled so intolerably about the business of being born as did my baby sister. We sometimes amused ourselves, during those endless, stifling weeks, by picturing the baby sitting within in the safe, warm dark, bitterly regretting the necessity of becoming a part of our chaos and stubbornly putting it off as long as possible. I understood her perfectly and congratulated her on showing such good sense so soon. Death, however, sat as purposefully at my father's bedside as life stirred within my mother's womb and it was harder to understand why he so lingered in that long shadow. It seemed that he had bent, and for a long time, too, all of his energies towards dying. Now death was ready for him but my father held back.

All of Harlem, indeed, seemed to be infected by waiting. I had 24 never before known it to be so violently still. Racial tensions throughout this country were exacerbated during the early years of the war, partly because the labor market brought together hundreds of thousands of ill-prepared people and partly because Negro soldiers, regardless of where they were born, received their military training

in the south. What happened in defense plants and army camps had
repercussions, naturally, in every Negro ghetto. The situation in Harlem had grown bad enough for clergymen, policemen, educators,
politicians, and social workers to assert in one breath that there was
no "crime wave" and to offer, in the very next breath, suggestions
as to how to combat it. These suggestions always seemed to involve
playgrounds, despite the fact that racial skirmishes were occurring in
the playgrounds, too. Playground or not, crime wave or not, the Harlem police force had been augmented in March, and the unrest
grew—perhaps, in fact, partly as a result of the ghetto's instinctive
hatred of policemen. Perhaps the most revealing news item, out of
the steady parade of reports of muggings, stabbings, shootings,
assaults, gang wars, and accusations of police brutality, is the item
concerning six Negro girls who set upon a white girl in the subway
because, as they all too accurately put it, she was stepping on their
toes. Indeed she was, all over the nation.

25   I had never before been so aware of policemen, on foot, on
horseback, on corners, everywhere, always two by two. Nor had I
ever been so aware of small knots of people. They were on stoops
and on corners and in doorways, and what was striking about them,
I think, was that they did not seem to be talking. Never, when I
passed these groups, did the usual sound of a curse or a laugh ring
out and neither did there seem to be any hum of gossip. There was
certainly, on the other hand, occurring between them communication extraordinarily intense. Another thing that was striking was the
unexpected diversity of the people who made up these groups. Usually, for example, one would see a group of sharpies standing on the
street corner, jiving the passing chicks; or a group of older men, usually, for some reason, in the vicinity of a barber shop, discussing
baseball scores, or the numbers, or making rather chilling observations about women they had known. Women, in a general way,
tended to be seen less often together—unless they were church
women, or very young girls, or prostitutes met together for an
unprofessional instant. But that summer I saw the strangest combinations: large, respectable, churchly matrons standing on the stoops
or the corners with their hair tied up, together with a girl in sleazy
satin whose face bore the marks of gin and the razor, or heavy-set,
abrupt, no-nonsense older men, in company with the most disrep-
utable and fanatical "race" men, or these same "race" men with the
sharpies, or these sharpies with the churchly women. Seventh Day
Adventists and Methodists and Spiritualists seemed to be hobnob-

bing with Holy Rollers and they were all, alike, entangled with the most flagrant disbelievers; something heavy in their stance seemed to indicate that they had all, incredibly, seen a common vision, and on each face there seemed to be the same strange, bitter shadow.

❡ Do you hear echoes of the boy preacher in his style? I do. I hear the preachers of my childhood as they recited lists of events or verses to work up to a moral point. I also hear parables, the anecdotes or little stories by which the Bible preaches. And I hear fragments of the music of the preacher, the pacing, rhythm, sound of churchly speech. ❡

The churchly women and the matter-of-fact, no-nonsense men 26
had children in the Army. The sleazy girls they talked to had lovers there, the sharpies and the "race" men had friends and brothers there. It would have demanded an unquestioning patriotism, happily as uncommon in this country as it is undesirable, for these people not to have been disturbed by the bitter letters they received, by the newspaper stories they read, not to have been enraged by the posters, then to be found all over New York, which described the Japanese as "yellow-bellied Japs." It was only the "race" men, to be sure, who spoke ceaselessly of being revenged—how this vengeance was to be exacted was not clear—for the indignities and dangers suffered by Negro boys in uniform; but everybody felt a directionless, hopeless bitterness, as well as that panic which can scarcely be suppressed when one knows that a human being one loves is beyond one's reach, and in danger. This helplessness and this gnawing uneasiness does something, at length, to even the toughest mind. Perhaps the best way to sum all this up is to say that the people I knew felt, mainly, a peculiar kind of relief when they knew that their boys were being shipped out of the south, to do battle overseas. It was, perhaps, like feeling that the most dangerous part of a dangerous journey had been passed and that now, even if death should come, it would come with honor and without the complicity of their countrymen. Such a death would be, in short, a fact with which one could hope to live.

It was on the 28th of July, which I believe was a Wednesday, 27
that I visited my father for the first time during his illness and for the last time in his life. The moment I saw him I knew why I had put off this visit so long. I had told my mother that I did not want to see him because I hated him. But this was not true. It was only that I *had*

hated him and I wanted to hold on to this hatred. I did not want to look on him as a ruin: it was not a ruin I had hated. I imagine that one of the reasons people cling to their hates so stubbornly is because they sense, once hate is gone, that they will be forced to deal with pain.

28   We traveled out to him, his older sister and myself, to what seemed to be the very end of a very Long Island. It was hot and dusty and we wrangled, my aunt and I, all the way out, over the fact that I had recently begun to smoke and, as she said, to give myself airs. But I knew that she wrangled with me because she could not bear to face the fact of her brother's dying. Neither could I endure the reality of her despair, her unstated bafflement as to what had happened to her brother's life, and her own. So we wrangled and I smoked and from time to time she fell into a heavy reverie. Covertly, I watched her face, which was the face of an old woman; it had fallen in, the eyes were sunken and lightless; soon she would be dying, too.

29   In my childhood—it had not been so long ago—I had thought her beautiful. She had been quick-witted and quick-moving and very generous with all the children and each of her visits had been an event. At one time one of my brothers and myself had thought of running away to live with her. Now she could no longer produce out of her handbag some unexpected and yet familiar delight. She made me feel pity and revulsion and fear. It was awful to realize that she no longer caused me to feel affection. The closer we came to the hospital the more querulous she became and at the same time, naturally, grew more dependent on me. Between pity and guilt and fear I began to feel that there was another me trapped in my skull like a jack-in-the-box who might escape my control at any moment and fill the air with screaming.

30   She began to cry the moment we entered the room and she saw him lying there, all shriveled and still, like a little black monkey. The great, gleaming apparatus which fed him and would have compelled him to be still even if he had been able to move brought to mind, not beneficence, but torture; the tubes entering his arm made me think of pictures I had seen when a child, of Gulliver, tied down by the pygmies on that island. My aunt wept and wept, there was a whistling sound in my father's throat; nothing was said; he could not speak. I wanted to take his hand, to say something. But I do not know what I could have said, even if he could have heard me. He was not really in that room with us, he had at last really embarked on his journey; and though my aunt told me that he said he was going to

meet Jesus, I did not hear anything except that whistling in his throat. The doctor came back and we left, into that unbearable train again, and home. In the morning came the telegram saying that he was dead. Then the house was suddenly full of relatives, friends, hysteria, and confusion and I quickly left my mother and the children to the care of those impressive women, who, in Negro communities at least, automatically appear at times of bereavement armed with lotions, proverbs, and patience, and an ability to cook. I went downtown. By the time I returned, later the same day, my mother had been carried to the hospital and the baby had been born.

> ❦All the way through this powerful piece of writing, Baldwin speaks of a race by speaking of individuals. He presents the particulars of private, family conflict and tragedy against the backdrop of national crisis and tragedy. This is what the writer does: the abstract is made particular and the specific is put in context so its significance may be understood. ❧

For my father's funeral I had nothing black to wear and this 31 posed a nagging problem all day long. It was one of those problems, simple, or impossible of solution, to which the mind insanely clings in order to avoid the mind's real trouble. I spent most of that day at the downtown apartment of a girl I knew, celebrating my birthday with whiskey and wondering what to wear that night. When planning a birthday celebration one naturally does not expect that it will be up against competition from a funeral and this girl had anticipated taking me out that night, for a big dinner and a night club afterwards. Sometime during the course of that long day we decided that we would go out anyway, when my father's funeral service was over. I imagine I decided it, since, as the funeral hour approached, it became clearer and clearer to me that I would not know what to do with myself when it was over. The girl, stifling her very lively concern as to the possible effects of the whiskey on one of my father's chief mourners, concentrated on being conciliatory and practically helpful. She found a black shirt for me somewhere and ironed it and, dressed in the darkest pants and jacket I owned, and slightly drunk, I made my way to my father's funeral.

The chapel was full, but not packed, and very quiet. There were, 32 mainly, my father's relatives, and his children, and here and there I saw faces I had not seen since childhood, the faces of my father's one-time friends. They were very dark and solemn now, seeming

somehow to suggest that they had known all along that something
like this would happen. Chief among the mourners was my aunt, who
had quarreled with my father all his life; by which I do not mean to
suggest that her mourning was insincere or that she had not loved
him. I suppose that she was one of the few people in the world who
had, and their incessant quarreling proved precisely the strength of
the tie that bound them. The only other person in the world, as far
as I knew, whose relationship to my father rivaled my aunt's in depth
was my mother, who was not there.

33   It seemed to me, of course, that it was a very long funeral. But
it was, if anything, a rather shorter funeral than most, nor, since there
were no overwhelming, uncontrollable expressions of grief, could it
be called—if I dare to use the word—successful. The minister who
preached my father's funeral sermon was one of the few my father
had still been seeing as he neared his end. He presented to us in his
sermon a man whom none of us had ever seen—a man thoughtful,
patient, and forbearing, a Christian inspiration to all who knew him,
and a model for his children. And no doubt the children, in their
disturbed and guilty state, were almost ready to believe this; he had
been remote enough to be anything and, anyway, the shock of the
incontrovertible, that it was really our father lying up there in that
casket, prepared the mind for anything. His sister moaned and this
grief-stricken moaning was taken as corroboration. The other faces
held a dark, non-committal thoughtfulness. This was not the man
they had known, but they had scarcely expected to be confronted
with *him*; this was, in a sense deeper than questions of fact, the man
they had not known, and the man they had not known may have
been the real one. The real man, whoever he had been, had suffered
and now he was dead; this was all that was sure and all that mattered
now. Every man in the chapel hoped that when his hour came he,
too, would be eulogized, which is to say forgiven, and that all of his
lapses, greeds, errors, and strayings from the truth would be invested
with coherence and looked upon with charity. This was perhaps the
last thing human beings could give each other and it was what they
demanded, after all, of the Lord. Only the Lord saw the midnight
tears, only He was present when one of His children, moaning and
wringing hands, paced up and down the room. When one slapped
one's child in anger the recoil in the heart reverberated through
heaven and became part of the pain of the universe. And when the
children were hungry and sullen and distrustful and one watched
them, daily, growing wilder, and further away, and running headlong

into danger, it was the Lord who knew what the charged heart endured as the strap was laid to the backside; the Lord alone who knew what one *would* have said if one had had, like the Lord, the gift of the living word. It was the Lord who knew of the impossibility every parent in that room faced; how to prepare the child for the day when the child would be despised and how to *create* in the child— by what means?—a stronger antidote to this poison than one had found for oneself. The avenues, side streets, bars, billiard halls, hospitals, police stations, and even the playgrounds of Harlem—not to mention the houses of correction, the jails, and the morgue—testified to the potency of the poison while remaining silent as to the efficacy of whatever antidote, irresistibly raising the questions of whether or not such an antidote existed; raising, which was worse, the question of whether or not an antidote was desirable; perhaps poison should be fought with poison. With these several schisms in the mind and with more terrors in the heart than could be named, it was better not to judge the man who had gone down under an impossible burden. It was better to remember: *Thou knowest this man's fall; but thou knowest not his wrassling.*

While the preacher talked and I watched the children—years 34 of changing their diapers, scrubbing them, slapping them, taking them to school, and scolding them had had the perhaps inevitable result of making me love them, though I am not sure I knew this then—my mind was busily breaking out with a rash of disconnected impressions. Snatches of popular songs, indecent jokes, bits of books I had read, movie sequences, faces, voices, political issues—I thought I was going mad; all these impressions suspended, as it were, in the solution of the faint nausea produced in me by the heat and liquor. For a moment I had the impression that my alcoholic breath, inefficiently disguised with chewing gum, filled the entire chapel. Then someone began singing one of my father's favorite songs and, abruptly, I was with him, sitting on his knee, in the hot, enormous, crowded church which was the first church we attended. It was the Abyssinia Baptist Church on 138th Street. We had not gone there long. With this image, a host of others came. I had forgotten, in the rage of my growing up, how proud my father had been of me when I was little. Apparently, I had had a voice and my father had liked to show me off before the members of the church. I had forgotten what he had looked like when he was pleased but now I remembered that he had always been grinning with pleasure when my solos ended. I even remembered certain expressions on his face when he teased my mother—had he loved her? I would never know. And when had it all begun to change? For now it seemed that he had not always been cruel. I remembered being taken for a haircut and scraping my knee on the footrest of the barber's chair and I remembered my father's face as he soothed my crying and applied the stinging iodine. Then I remembered our fights, fights which had been of the worst possible kind because my technique had been silence. . . .

35   I remembered the one time in all our life together when we had really spoken to each other.

36   It was on a Sunday and it must have been shortly before I left home. We were walking, just the two of us, in our usual silence, to or from church. I was in high school and had been doing a lot of writing and I was, at about this time, the editor of the high school magazine. But I had also been a Young Minister and had been preaching from the pulpit. Lately, I had been taking fewer engagements and preached as rarely as possible. It was said in the church, quite truthfully, that I was "cooling off."

37   My father asked me abruptly, "You'd rather write than preach, wouldn't you?"

38   I was astonished at his question—because it was a real question. I answered, "Yes."

39   That was all we said. It was awful to remember that that was all we had *ever* said.

40   The casket now was opened and the mourners were being led up the aisle to look for the last time on the deceased. The assumption was that the family was too overcome with grief to be allowed to make this journey alone and I watched while my aunt was led to the casket and, muffled in black, and shaking, led back to her seat. I disapproved of forcing the children to look on their dead father, considering that the shock of his death, or, more truthfully, the shock of death as a reality, was already a little more than a child could bear, but my judgment in this matter had been overruled and there they were, bewildered and frightened and very small, being led, one by one, to the casket. But there is also something very gallant about children at such moments. It has something to do with their silence and gravity and with the fact that one cannot help them. Their legs, somehow, seem *exposed*, so that it is at once incredible and terribly clear that their legs are all they have to hold them up.

41   I had not wanted to go to the casket myself and I certainly had not wished to be led there, but there was no way of avoiding either of these forms. One of the deacons led me up and I looked on my

father's face. I cannot say that it looked like him at all. His blackness had been equivocated by powder and there was no suggestion in that casket of what his power had or could have been. He was simply an old man dead, and it was hard to believe that he had ever given anyone either joy or pain. Yet his life filled that room. Further up the avenue his wife was holding his newborn child. Life and death so close together, and love and hatred, and right and wrong, said something to me which I did not want to hear concerning man, concerning the life of man.

After the funeral, while I was downtown desperately celebrating 42 my birthday, a Negro soldier, in the lobby of the Hotel Braddock, got into a fight with a white policeman over a Negro girl. Negro girls, white policemen, in or out of uniform, and Negro males—in or out of uniform—were part of the furniture of the lobby of the Hotel Braddock and this was certainly not the first time such an incident had occurred. It was destined, however, to receive an unprecedented publicity, for the fight between the policeman and the soldier ended with the shooting of the soldier. Rumor, flowing immediately to the streets outside, stated that the soldier had been shot in the back, an instantaneous and revealing invention, and that the soldier had died protecting a Negro woman. The facts were somewhat different—for example, the soldier had not been shot in the back, and was not dead, and the girl seems to have been as dubious a symbol of womanhood as her white counterpart in Georgia usually is, but no one was interested in the facts. They preferred the invention because this invention expressed and corroborated their hates and fears so perfectly. It is just as well to remember that people are always doing this. Perhaps many of those legends, including Christianity, to which the world clings, began their conquest of the world with just some such concerted surrender to distortion. The effect, in Harlem, of this particular legend was like the effect of a lit match in a tin of gasoline. The mob gathered before the doors of the Hotel Braddock simply began to swell and to spread in every direction, and Harlem exploded.

The mob did not cross the ghetto lines. It would have been easy, 43 for example, to have gone over Morningside Park on the west side or to have crossed the Grand Central railroad tracks at 125th Street on the east side, to wreak havoc in white neighborhoods. The mob seems to have been mainly interested in something more potent and real than the white face, that is, in white power, and the principal damage done during the riot of the summer of 1943 was to white business establishments in Harlem. It might have been a far bloodier story, of course, if, at the hour the riot began, these establishments had still been open. From the Hotel Braddock the mob fanned out, east and west along 125th, 135th, and so on—bars, stores, pawnshops, restaurants, even little luncheonettes had been smashed open and entered and looted—looted, it might be added, with more haste than efficiency. The shelves really looked as though a bomb had struck them. Cans of beans and soup and dog food, along with toilet paper, corn flakes, sardines and milk tumbled every which way, and abandoned cash registers and cases of beer leaned crazily out of the splintered windows and were strewn along the avenues. Sheets, blankets, and clothing of every description formed a kind of path, as though people had dropped them while running. I truly had not realized that Harlem *had* so many stores until I saw them all smashed open; the first time the word *wealth* ever entered my mind in relation to Harlem was when I saw it scattered in the streets. But one's first, incongruous impression of plenty was countered immediately by an impression of waste. None of this was doing anybody any good. It would have been better to have left the plate glass as it had been and the goods lying in the stores.

> ❧ Study how Baldwin brings order to the confusion he is describing so that the reader can understand the confusion. If Baldwin just records confusion, we will have a confused text and not be able to understand it. If the text is too ordered, we will not experience the riot. It seems to me that he maintains an impressive balance between both extremes—an example of the tension between freedom and discipline that is central to the creative process. Also note the expert use of details context. ❧

44   It would have been better, but it would also have been intolerable, for Harlem had needed something to smash. To smash something is the ghetto's chronic need. Most of the time it is the members of the ghetto who smash each other, and themselves. But as long as the ghetto walls are standing there will always come a moment when these outlets do not work. That summer, for example, it was not enough to get into a fight on Lenox Avenue, or curse out one's cronies in the barber shops. If ever, indeed, the violence which fills Harlem's churches, pool halls, and bars erupts outward in a more direct fashion, Harlem and its citizens are likely to vanish in an apocalyptic

flood. That this is not likely to happen is due to a great many reasons, most hidden and powerful among them the Negro's real relation to the white American. This relation prohibits, simply, anything as uncomplicated and satisfactory as pure hatred. In order really to hate white people, one has to blot so much out of the mind—and the heart—that this hatred itself becomes an exhausting and self-destructive pose. But this does not mean, on the other hand, that love comes easily: the white world is too powerful, too complacent, too ready with gratuitous humiliation, and, above all, too ignorant and too innocent for that. One is absolutely forced to make perpetual qualifications and one's own reactions are always canceling each other out. It is this, really, which has driven so many people mad, both white and black. One is always in the position of having to decide between amputation and gangrene. Amputation is swift but time may prove that the amputation was not necessary—or one may delay the amputation too long. Gangrene is slow, but it is impossible to be sure that one is reading one's symptoms right. The idea of going through life as a cripple is more than one can bear, and equally unbearable is the risk of swelling up slowly, in agony, with poison. And the trouble, finally, is that the risks are real even if the choices do not exist.

"But as for me and my house," my father had said, "we will 45
serve the Lord." I wondered, as we drove him to his resting place, what this line had meant for him. I had heard him preach it many times. I had preached it once myself, proudly giving it an interpretation different from my father's. Now the whole thing came back to me, as though my father and I were on our way to Sunday school and I were memorizing the golden text: *And if it seem evil unto you to serve the Lord, choose you this day whom you will serve; whether the gods which your fathers served that were on the other side of the flood, or the gods of the Amorites, in whose land ye dwell: but as for me and my house, we will serve the Lord.* I suspected in these familiar lines a meaning which had never been there for me before. All of my father's texts and songs, which I had decided were meaningless, were arranged before me at his death like empty bottles, waiting to hold the meaning which life would give them for me. This was his legacy: nothing is ever escaped. That bleakly memorable morning I hated the unbelievable streets and the Negroes and whites who had, equally, made them that way. But I knew that it was folly, as my father would have said, this bitterness was folly. It was necessary to hold on to the things that mattered. The dead man mattered, the new life mattered;

blackness and whiteness did not matter; to believe that they did was to acquiesce in one's own destruction. Hatred, which could destroy so much, never failed to destroy the man who hated and this was an immutable law.

❦ In the next paragraph Baldwin writes a formal conclusion in which he states directly what he believes is the meaning he has discovered in the experiences he has shared with us. Notice the care with which he balances two complicated ideas and the vigor of the language he chooses for the conclusion of the essay. ❧

It began to seem that one would have to hold in the mind for- 46 ever two ideas which seemed to be in opposition. The first idea was acceptance, the acceptance, totally without rancor, of life as it is, and men as they are: in the light of this idea, it goes without saying that injustice is a commonplace. But this did not mean that one could be complacent, for the second idea was of equal power: that one must never, in one's own life, accept these injustices as commonplace but must fight them with all one's strength. This fight begins, however, in the heart and it now had been laid to my charge to keep my own heart free of hatred and despair. This intimation made my heart heavy and, now that my father was irrecoverable, I wished that he had been beside me so that I could have searched his face for the answers which only the future would give me now.

Discussion

• Choose a page in which Baldwin's voice is especially strong. Discuss the elements in voice and compare his voice to Ellison's and to Baraka's.
• Baldwin once said, "I remember standing on a streetcorner with the black painter Beauford Delaney down in the Village, waiting for the light to change, and he pointed down and said, 'Look.' I looked and all I saw was water. And he said, 'Look again,' which I did, and I saw oil on the water and the city reflected in the puddle. It was a great revelation to me. I can't explain it. He taught me how to see, and how to trust what I saw. Painters have often taught writers how to see. And once you've had that experience, you see differently. . .I'm still learning how to write. I don't know what

technique is. All I know is that you have to make the reader *see* it." Discuss how Baldwin makes the reader see.

• Discuss other methods Baldwin could have used to describe his alienation.

• What could Baldwin have used to focus on his subject instead of his father's death? How would that focus have changed the piece?

• Baldwin has said, "Writing for me must be a very controlled exercise, formed by passions and hopes. . . .The act of writing itself is cold." Discuss what Baldwin meant. Is there evidence of control and coldness in the text? If so, is it effective?

• Baldwin has also said, "You learn how little you know. It becomes more difficult because the hardest thing in the world is simplicity. And the most fearful thing, too. It becomes more difficult because you have to strip yourself of all your disguises, some of which you didn't know you had. You want to write a sentence as clean as a bone. That is the goal." Pick a sentence or a paragraph that demonstrates what Baldwin means. Is this simplicity effective?

Activities

• Write a short draft about an emotional experience in your life, such as the death of a parent. Write another paragraph stating what you learned by writing about that experience.

• Take a description that you have written, imagine what Baldwin would add to it, and then add it.

• Go through a page of Baldwin and take out the specific details to see what happens to the prose.

• Go back to the anecdote with the waitress and write it from the point of view of the waitress or the friend outside, or someone in the restaurant to see how an incident can be viewed from different angles and how each angle of vision may provide a different meaning.

William Gibson

William Gibson is a poet, novelist, nonfiction writer, and playwright. His plays include *Two for the Seesaw, The Miracle Worker,* and *Golda.* And although he is best known for his work for the theater, he confessed to me that he shared a special feeling for his book, *A Mass for the Dead*, which was published in 1968, but has been out of print for years. I had told him that my edition is worn and battered from reading and rereading, and that I would teach it, as I once did, if it were in print again. Unfortunately it isn't, but this excerpt will give you an idea of the quality of the book.

Gibson and Baldwin are of the same generation and come from the same city. Both are writers and both here focus on the death of their father. These pairings through the book, and this one certainly, should make it clear that there is no right, no single correct way to deal with a subject in writing, and there is no wrong, no single, ineffective way to deal with a subject in writing. What we can appreciate are two sons writing of their different backgrounds and their similar problems in coming to terms with their fathers and their fathers' deaths. Both are powerful pieces of writing, and we should not try to rate one over the other, but to learn from both of them.

Sunset I Saw By

1   Downtown, in a neighborhood grimy with warehouses and bridges, the old hospital was our gathering place for fifteen days. My father was in a room with two beds, and whoever lay in the other I hardly saw; at his bedside near the window my mother and I met— my sister was away on her vacation—for idle chats, making light of his stay, until the period of tests was done. I was there when our doctor in a careful choice of words explained to my father, propped up in a bedgown, that the nature of his ulcer made surgery a wise procedure, and my father said with a twitch of fear in his downward smile, "All kinds of ulcers, I have to have the worst kind." I knew the fear was unnecessary, but my mother called my sister home from the country, and the three of us were in the hospital corridor the morning my father was wheeled out. The surgeon had informed us the chances were fifty-fifty it was an ulcer he could cut out, in which case the operation would take several hours, else my father would soon be back; we sat in a small corner room, all restive, but I with a book was counting on a long wait, and my sister talked with my mother, still on the edge of a chair. It was not an hour when my mother, now in and out of the corridor, appeared with her face stricken and said, "Daddy's back." I walked in a confusion to his doorway and saw a nurse busy at his bed, with a substance of legs beneath the white spread, but half guessed the surgery was simpler

than predicted, and after I returned to our corner room the three of us stood in uncertainty, five minutes, ten minutes, until the surgeon came to find my mother. Courteous and prompt, he said he could do nothing for her husband, it was a stomach cancer and inoperable. Yet only when she stammered, "Doctor, how long does he have?" and the surgeon said, "Six months," did I comprehend the truth: the earth that opened at my feet in that minute was never to close. In the unreal hour that followed my tremulous mother instructed us my father was not to know, and that afternoon it was she who through his fog of anesthesia delivered the good news to him, the ulcer was cured and he would soon be getting better at home.

For out of my sickly mother now came a rigor, not unpredict-   2
able, which was to cope with whatever befell. Old neighbors, rela-
tives, fellows from the bank, came to congratulate my father in the week he was recovering from the knife, and one took a snapshot of my mother in a rattan chair on the hospital roof; with her children standing beside her—a healthy blonde miss in a summerprint frock, dangling a white purse, and a lank youth in unpressed wool slacks and jacket, shirt wide open—she sits in a neat polka-dot dress, a lean lady of fifty with legs crossed, looking forty in her pearl earrings, and a white chrysanthemum at her bodice; all the feet are sporty in white shoes on the roof tiles, underneath which my father convalesces in his bed, unseen and doomed. It is the faces that baffle me, the youth's in a surly grin, the girl's prettily beaming, my mother's eager with a lipsticked smile to please the camera, all caught in the family lie from which I had fled to my suffering minorities. Only, my mother's hands are knotted against her stomach, and I was to watch how her bright denial of the underworld was armor to carry her through it; back of the brittle smile, which for half a year she wore for my father, was the durable will of an older mother who had buried a husband and fourteen sons.

I was at the hospital with the Ford the morning my father was   3
discharged, and the four of us rode home together; I drove in the slow lane of traffic, not to jar his abdominal wound. Still in some pain, but out again in the air of life, my father at a back window gazed contentedly at whatever we passed, and with her gay chatter my mother beside him shared his view of the towering city in which he had been born, of the midtown streets they had strolled in the horsecar days of their courtship, of the bridge over the islanded river and the green ballpark where Sundays in the benchstands they would not again sit with orange pop and franks, of the boulevard they had often crossed

from the prosperity in their winebrick colony to the poverty in her sister Minnie's flat, and at last the parkway, pleasant with grass and woodland and the vision they first had together from it of rooftops in a suburban multitude below, and among these, in a street still young with saplings, the little house in which he was to die. I parked at the curb, my mother hurried up the driveway to unlock the front door from within, my sister stood by with his suitcase, and I helped my father out of the back seat; with him bent on my forearm we advanced up the steps, past my mother, and through the sun porch into the comfort of the living room, where my father, welcomed home by us as he looked around at his easy chair, the sofa and twin lamptables, his piano and stool, startled us with a half-sob and, still upon my arm, cried tears. Seated with him on the sofa, my mother was all cheery banter, promising his strength back. I then supported him up the staircase, along the hallway to the front room, and onto the twin bed that waited with coverlet turned down, where I left him to be undressed by my mother and put to bed.

4   So began the six months of an old sorrow, but new to us. I took a step so natural that only now it seems a choice, I broke up my flat and came back to live in my room. My sister turned to the faith that moved mountains, was unfailingly at mass on Sunday, in the city prayed in a church before work each morning, and, making novena after novena at night with other petitioners on their knees, read from her prayerbook that "all you ask the Father in My name He will give you"; a literal believer, she asked that hers not die. I was to make the same prayer, but only in my dreams. My mother's lips, whatever the hope of holy miracle in her head, were right; she told the truth to almost nobody, not even to my father's mother and sisters in Jersey, lest someone in a slip let it out in his hearing, and month after month the air in the house was heavier with our secret.

5   For all, the first month was the easiest. My father was incapacitated most by the wound, which knitted, and aided at the outset by whosever arm was handy, but soon unhelped, he was back and forth the dozen steps to the toilet, dressed himself, shaved, and was of good cheer; a higher official from the bank, visiting, bade him not to hurry his return to work. Downstairs, my mother and the official sat on the sun porch in a low-voiced conversation, in which he told her of the bank's decision to continue my father on salary until his death. Though weekdays my sister and I left for work, neighbors and other visitors came in and my mother was not always alone, except in her thoughts; half the time the housework was shared by her "oldest and

dearest friend'' Nelie, who at night slept on the sofa in a dusting cap, and Minnie arriving by subway and bus for the day would fill the house with her "for Gawd's sake" joshing of her brother-in-law. Only these two women, the one monosyllable, the other our generous bungler, knew what my mother knew. My father grew strong enough to make his way downstairs, a gala day; now the household was almost normal, he tuned the radio to baseball, tried the piano, and in the flowering backyard sat on the springy chair my mother brought him, head back and eyes closed, renewing himself in the sun. The boys from the bank who visited in threes and fours found him there, all smiles to see them, and hale enough for a cigarette—forbidden on the ulcer diet, cigarettes were again permitted by the merciful doctor—which my father explained as a success of the surgery. For such guests my mother was blithe, and for the first time kept liquor in the house to serve, instead of pineapple juice; new to bartending, she made highballs with ginger ale in her tallest tumblers, half whiskey, and the visits were gay indeed. On the weekend I chauffeured my parents on gentle rides of a few miles out of one community into another, replicas, but a change of scene for my father. . .

Without appetite, he was growing thin, and the strength was   6
reluctant to come into his legs, but it came. It would have been less difficult to see him worse; what was grievous was to watch his gratitude in the abortive recoveries. Once again on my mother's arm, setting himself distances, he left the bedpan behind, and for a week sat at open windows in his pants, shirt, slippers, and then worked his way down the banister to the living room, to the sun porch, to the backyard, and the color of pleasure returned to his face, each day a restoral, each destination a further reach: the next shock of hemorrhage erased it all. My mother settled him in the bed, her hands quick with the ice-bag, and quick in the kitchen to boil and assemble the parts of the hypodermic, but upstairs she was timid to pierce his arm with it, and I took over the task. In bed my father lay with eyes closed, the rubber ice-bag on his belly, a blanket keeping him warm in the heat of the summer day, and slept; and I walked the five blocks to my store, where I put aside the play and undertook to write him my parting word, or loveletter, which was a poem.

I was three weeks over it; he was bedridden still, or again, the   7
morning I took the typed page in, said I had written something for him, and left it in his hands. Back now on the job, I could not linger but in any case was embarrassed to, the forty lines were too frank an avowal of how much of him I hoped was in me, named his goodness

as the homework of my knowledge of man, and, muted by what I could not mention except as the fate all must share, said neither of us was to enter the silence with my debt unspoken. Home at five-thirty, I went upstairs to his room to say hello, as always, and saw my page on the night table between the twin beds; his eyes following mine, my father said, "Bill, it's beautiful," and I said I was glad, there was a pause, and he said, "What does it mean?" So, in some despair at the isolateness even of my art, I sat upon the other bed, and with the poem in hand explained it word by word in prose.

8   Summer went under, the year was ebbing and so too the outer edge of my father's world; the last time he took to his chair in the backyard he grew uneasy, and shuffled indoors, not to emerge again. I was not in the house the evening he forewent the downstairs half, and with it the brotherly companion of his life, the Horace Waters piano. Up or down the ten steps to the bedroom, he would now sit upon them midway, for breath; on a visit to my sister the giant youth who was once her beau saw my father at the stairfoot pause, hand on newel, awaiting the will to climb, and simply carried him in his arms up the stairs.

9   At the bedside there stood henceforth an enamelled white bucket, containing a few inches of water, for the next spewing of blood. It was not yet frequent, but my father was enfeebled by loss of hunger and abdominal pain, glum that the incision was so slow to heal, and critical of the city doctor who he said was "not doing me any good"; at the doctor's advice we called in a local "consultant", and on the sun porch my mother confided the facts to his suave face. For a month my father's hopes were up as the new doctor wrote out a variety of prescriptions, my mother observed to my sister only that the pharmacist was his brother, and the bottles of expensive medicine accumulated on the night table, to no effect. Exhausted by a third and fourth vomiting my father said, "He doesn't understand my case," and my mother called in another doctor to add encouragement; this man said bluntly he "hated like hell" to have such a patient, sat at my father's bedside with his bagful of useless instruments, scribbled a prescription for sugar pills, and that autumn lent his burly comfort more to us than to my father, who, emptier of faith, said indifferently, "He's a fake."

10   Nothing in the weariness of his day upstairs could distract him from the gnawing ache in his stomach. Off for work, my sister and I were in the bedroom each morning to say goodbye—I was old enough to kiss him again, the sweet odor of his brow at my lips recall-

ing the Sunday mornings when as children we climbed into bed with him to giggle over his nonsensical stories, all forgotten, but not how we loved the odor of his pillow dent—and until evening my mother, in the midst of housecleaning, tried to lighten his pain with a diversity of moves. She would plump up two bed-pillows for the mahogany rocker so my father, sitting at the window, could have a view of the red-tinned roof of our sun porch with the bit of tranquil street beyond, and in my sister's room she plumped up pillows for another chair at the rear window to which he came to see his backyard garden, kept trim by her for his eyes; back and forth between the two chairs, in one soon restless for the other, my father travelled on her arm, and in them an hour of the long morning, an hour of the longer afternoon, would pass. The pillows were needed because the flesh was leaving him, his buttocks were bony, and more often he was at rest upon one of the twin beds. On good days, with my mother's support he would get into the old pants and shirt that now hung loose on him, and feel more optimistic for being dressed; other days he kept to his bed, in pajamas, where my mother would bathe him with alcohol, and twice daily unmake and remake the bed to freshen it for his back. Left alone, my father would read for an hour—a newspaper, a cheap novel his chick or I brought him from the drugstore library—or dial around my little radio for some daytime music, find only the soap operas, and click it off. Visitors came, to pass another hour. My mother would use it for downstairs work, but whatever chores she could bring up to the bedroom she saved for their departure, peeling vegetables then in the rocker, brightly gossiping, and misquoting the doctor in prediction of an upturn tomorrow to perk up his spirits. It was all in vain, the heel of his hand pressing was futile to ease the bellyache always under his ribs, and worsening; his one desire was for the morphine.

❡ It may be the writer's obligation to record with a terrible honesty what we do not see or what we refuse to see. Gibson goes over the same territory again and again, describing his father's dying with specific details that are awful, yet true, and somehow necessary because of their awfulness. We try to avert ourselves from life, but our artists keep holding life up to us, telling us how important life is and what it is really like, the love and the hate, the pain and the joy pressing right up against one another. E. B. White, in a day before we were educated to sexist language, said, "Don't write about Man, write about A man." The adage still stands. If you want to write about subjects such as death and fathers and sons and leaving and coming home and sickness and health, write about a specific person, as Gibson has. The more specific you are the more general your audience will become. Each reader will be forced to confront his or her own life. 🍷

11   My father disrespected himself for asking it of us, and my mother and I were uncertain when to grant it. In the kitchen the doctor had counselled us to be sparing, how insufferable the cancer might grow was not known, and if we habituated his body to morphine in the beginning we could give him no help at the end; concerned thus, my mother and I would conspire to talk him out of it. My father at first was with us, still expecting nature to mend what the surgeon had somehow botched, and to be a "hophead" when on his feet again was a worry to him. All day he bit down the words, until I was home to boil the needle; but the interludes of numbness to the pain grew briefer. It was less often we heard him say he "wouldn't want to get to depend on it", and what in August was a contest of my father with himself had by September turned into one between him and us. I was acceding to his wish for the morphine before I left in the morning, and my mother withstood his pleas throughout the afternoon as best she could, then yielded too, overcoming her finickiness about the needle. To see my father relax after it—going limp, murmuring "how good that felt", letting his eyebrows unknit at last—eased us too, but we bargained with him to put it off, for two hours, one hour, half an hour, and would agree to a time by the clock upon his night table; he would lie with eyes sidelong to it, and be unable not to plead with us again, too early. I injected his arm a few times with sterile water or a solution of half a pellet, but he was not deceived, accused me of it, and distrusted my denials; our needs had parted company, and the candor in his blue eyes was clouded with a new doubt of us. . . .

12   I had gone on a second leave from my job, and was hanging around the house. I ran errands to the avenue for my mother, like taking a suit of my father's to be cleaned and pressed, and three days later fetched it again to put in the downstairs closet, knowing it would next be worn by him in a coffin. I shovelled coal into the furnace, and fed the dog, and settled to work at my play, and wrote a letter to my teacher apologizing that I could not; I read until my head was dulled, and waited for my father to die.

13   Daily I was in the mahogany rocker in his sickroom to keep him company, but the talk was a trickle. I would ask could I get him any-

thing, he would say no; I was not in his focus, another of the liars, and I sat in a misery of silence with fifty years of him to ask into, too late, my begetter was dying with the riddle of our life untold; I would ask was he comfortable enough, he would say yes; bedridden, his head awry to the window like a plant to the thin sunlight, he lay with eyes large as a child's and blank, lost in whatever a dying man thinks, why me, and I was of the enemy who would outlive him, tonguetied with it, too craven to say a word that would confess the last of our differences and let us share it for an hour; I would ask did he want the radio on, he would say no. Dumb in that bedroom with the alarm clock ticking, the cottonlace curtains moveless, the boudoir suite of twin beds with ruffles and chifforobe and mirrored vanity-table so feminine around us, every surface with its dolly, I felt an ennui that would not let me breathe, and what was in my heart I hardly knew, so never said, that he was my true love and I could not forgive it in my mother that she was forever between us. I would fix the needle whenever he spoke for it now, lulling his organs to sleep, but not the scatter of outlaw cells in them that had shrunk his flesh to this, so close to inhuman earth again; whatever flowering had been possible to it was at an end. One such afternoon he asked what time it was and I told him, he seemed asleep, two minutes later he asked again what time it was and I told him, and after some thought he said in a murmur, "Almost the same time." Interminably in the ebb of sunlight the clock ticked on, afternoon into afternoon, and I would think, Die, let me go.

Poor as it was, my father clung to consciousness. Downstairs at lunch my mother and I were interrupted by a dreadful thud in the ceiling; with her at my heels, I was up the stairs three at a time and into the sickroom, where on the floor between the twin beds I saw my father inert on his back, and knowing the scream I heard was my own, an oddity I had read of, I ran to lift, pull, push him onto the bed, but he was dead weight and I was too rattled; my mother helped, the two of us falling upon the blankets with more than a corpse, he was breathing. My mother nursed him back to an awareness of us which was confused, and after that he was rarely without a bedside watcher. In December he lay so skeletal that his bones poked at his skin, chafing it to bedsores, and these nagged him in every which position; my mother laved him with alcohol, and cut up rolls of absorbent cotton to tape as pads onto his shoulders, elbows, hips, and with pillows under the blankets kept their burden from his shins. Morning, afternoon, night, she "took wonderful care of him", her own face a wedge of worn flesh, pale and inexhaustible. I was not loth when, the leave up, I could escape my job; and after six weeks in Mt. Vernon my grandmother was taken home by Ada for Christmas in Trenton, not to see her son again, but it was a suffering to sit with him now. Yet my mother sat with him, and supported his head in her hands when every few days he retched over the white bucket until "all his insides came out" in great bloody chunks, and death would not them part.

15   It was my sister's habit, after frost killed off the backyard garden, to bring her father home a handful of flowers she bought in the subway, but toward the end his mind was too errant for such tokens; one evening he stared at me and asked who I was. I tried not to be hurt when for two days he would not have me in the room, yet I took it as the rebuke for my life. In and out of a half-delirium my father more than once called for all the lights on, the frilly lamps and the pink ceiling fixture, and required everyone in the household to sit where he could see us; abruptly then he would banish lights and family, to lie in the dark, and we heard him muttering to himself that he was "too young to die", the spectre was out now, and my father with his fist banged on the wall, intoning, "I don't want to die, I don't want to die," banged methodically on the wall till that hammering unnerved us. My mother, putting on the lamp to dissuade him, would be pained with the sight of his knuckles bleeding.

16   In the last week he went blind. Christmas was with us again, and in the sickroom—grown brilliant with the arrival of poinsettias, other plants, bouquets, and a hundred greeting cards propped everywhere, even atop the radiators—my mother set up a diminutive fir and hung it with a few of the ornaments that had been ours for two decades; my father was unable to make any of it out. Of that joyless day I retain little, but my sister remembers how our mother described each plant in the room to him. Presents too were there, a vestige of the old spill of plenty, and become a bitterness; we put into my father's fingers such things as the soft new pajamas he would never wear, and earlier he had instructed his chick to shop with his money from the vanity drawer, so my mother unwrapped the three or four packages he could not see, stockings, a waffle iron, a slip, his last gifts to her. Or not quite, for in that week when her face was gone my father held to her fingers, said, "Oh God, how I love you," and left her that too.

17   Two days passed, and my sister and I at the bedside each morn-

ing, kissing his brow and taking with us the word or two he murmured, saw no change; that he was sleeping the third morning was
not unusual. Yet a few hours later my mother, seated in the rocker
in the quiet sickroom, heard a break in the rhythm of his breathing.
She called to her spinster schoolmate, and for some minutes the two
women kept watch at the bed with its burden of skin and bone,
which breathed, and faltered, took in a mouthful of air, exhaled, left
off; my mother said, "Is he gone?" and the emaciated head on the
pillow breathed again, and the spinster said almost but told her not
to "cry or talk to him, you'll only bring him back," and so my mother
stood over him, dumb, waiting for the next breath. It never came,
and when she knew the discoloring body was at the end of its effort
to live my mother said, "Now I can cry."

Around his unseeing corpse, the household which was his life- 18
work slowly set about its business of survival. My mother went into
the neighbor's phone, and throughout the afternoon the front and
back doors let in a traffic of doctor, undertaker and assistants,
women of the family, neighbors, a houseful simmering with the suppressed excitement of death; at work my sister was interrupted by
word her father was "very ill", knew, and travelled home, where she
found my mother red-eyed over a cup of tea in the kitchen and the
funeral arrangements in the expert hands of Will's widow, who had
buried a second husband in recent years; upstairs in the bedroom
with pails, scalpels, tubes, the embalmers were at their labors over
my father's cadaver on a table, disembowelling it, draining off its
corruptible fluids, and repacking its refuse of viscera, disinfected. My
sister escorted my mother away to buy the first of the black clothes
that she would wear for a year.

Inaccessible by phone, I knew none of this, served out my 19
workday among storage bins, and, homecoming at dusk to the
monotony of leafless hedge and stoops, saw the door to our house
was hung with a lamentation of flowers. Inside, the downstairs was
lively enough with others moving the furniture back for the wake,
and after I talked with my mother I took my way up the carpeted
steps to the hall; here all was still, and I stood in the doorway of the
bedroom. The embalmers gone, nothing in the room was different
since morning except that now on the twin bed my father, clad in
his gray suit, pallid hands clasped, lay forever dead, and his good face
which was like no other in the world was a stranger to me. I went
no nearer, and I had no tears, something in me had become stony in

those six months, and it would be weeks before I cried, but once begun, was never quite done, for of course he never let me go. After a time I rejoined the living, and when later the coffin was delivered the men carried my father downstairs in a wicker basket, to create a flowery retreat of the living room with his corpse as its centerpiece, and my mother shut the keyboard lid of the piano; upstairs she stripped the deathbed, and remade it with clean sheets. It was occupied that night by the spinster in her dusting cap, and in the adjacent bed my mother for the first time slept without the sound of her husband's breathing in the room, or perhaps did not sleep.

20   In the morning the undertaker was at our door with his discreet box of cosmetics, to touch up the unstable face of my father, and so opened the wake. For three days and nights the little house was crowded with people, all the other faces of my life, the half-forgotten neighbors of childhood, my aunts, uncles, cousins, clerks by the score from the bank, each of whom stood his silent minute at the coffin and then lingered, in muted conversation, from dining room to sun porch; the sheaves of flowers they sent so swamped the house that everywhere they were stepped upon, and were even hung on the walls. In the sickly fragrance my father's mother for three days immovably filled the easy chair opposite the body, hardly speaking, hardly caring, sat. In the kitchen, with its swingdoor closed, the talk was more cheerful. The coffee pot was always perking on the range, the tablecloth was set with platterfuls of cold cuts, salads, cakes brought in by the neighbors, my mother was in and out anxious that everyone eat, and the visitors on chairs, or squeezed into the breakfast nook, or standing with cups in hand against the refrigerator and sink, gossiped of other matters; I sat with them chatting, nodding, smiling, until a sudden widening of my inner eye saw what lay beyond the swingdoor, my father already forgotten, and I condemned us all. Only once was my mother somewhat beside herself, upstairs, when she and Ben's minx collapsed in a hysteria of laughing, excusable as "something Irv must want us to do". I had asked one friend to come, and so at the coffin my mother first received the girl who would bear two of her grandsons, and led her from the dead man to introduce her to the family and the food; the girl in wonder took in how gentiles mourned. By ten o'clock at night the house was emptied, save for a relative or two who slept over, ourselves, and the body. On the eve of the funeral the bedroom allotments put me downstairs on the sofa not far from the coffin; I awoke in the small

hours to lie with eyes open and breath held, listening, half afraid of the warm effigy that so unreasonably had befriended me, and I had somehow let die.

It was an icy day when the hearse waited at the curb and barren 21 tree, with a black limousine behind, and from our house in both directions the cars of relatives and friends waited one after the other along the street. In the living room some folding chairs had been delivered by the undertaker, but too few, and the fifty or so who had come for the minister's valediction were backed into doorways, stood against walls, sat two on each step of the staircase that led up from the dining room; on the top step, unseen of all, sat my mother. I have no recollection of anything said by the minister, a stranger to us, but when the brief ceremony died into silence I heard from above me a scream, bulletlike, abruptly sent and broken off, and knew it was my mother. I was embarrassed by it, yet now realize she chose that step because from nowhere else could she see over heads down into the coffin and take leave of my father's face as the lid was shut upon it. So he disappeared finally from our sight, and was carried in the coffin out the front door, and was placed in the elegant hearse, and the sidewalk was busy with the dispersal of people to cars, and at the limousine a gathering of women in black—his mother, sisters, wife, daughter—was helped in, I joined them, and the headlights of the many cars came on, pale and dreamlike in the day; in slow procession we followed the hearse that bore my father's body out of the dream the four of us had lived in together.

The cemetery gates were a dozen miles away, and here, at a 22 tombstone among others in a field patchy with snow, the grave was open. At the edge of this pit in the frozen earth my mother, with my sister and me at either elbow, and roundabout a silent party of watchers, saw the coffin lowered by straps until it came to rest, with something in it that was and was not her husband, and not in virgin clay; deeper were the remains of my uncle Will and his two children, in ground offered by his widow, and the women who stood in survival near that pit wept for more than my father, who was the oldest in it, having lived for fifty years, nine months, and twenty-five days; in her black half-veil my mother endured the last minute of rite and prayer, the flower tossed in, the first shovelful of dirt, and then turned away to the icy lane and the limousine. It drove us out of the gates, no headlights of procession now, a single carful of mourners going back to an empty house.

23   Yet it was late night before we were alone in it. Other carfuls
returned to the street, and people again, food, a distraction of voices,
filled the downstairs till dusk came, some of my mother's kin and her
in-laws stayed for supper, and she sent my sister with her suitor off
to the movies, common sense was the mood, but the hour was inevitable when all the dishes were washed, dried, put away, the com-
forters were gone, and my sister and I sat with our mother in a house
which had disowned us. It was the last day of the year, and in the
living room, so void of its coffin, the three of us with our tired talk
saw the old year out, the worst we had known and good riddance,
but with it came to another end; the decorum around our eyes, in
chintz drapes, sofa and coffee table, console radio, easy chair, the
upright piano and its stool, had been set to rights and was as before,
only its heartbeat was done, the house too was dead, and not one of
us but through its walls saw the reality of winter on the plot of earth
under which my father in his gray suit was laid to rot. We had come
to the end of our tale as a family, now each of us must find his own
and other place in the world.

24   So in the first hour of the new year we separated for bed,
upstairs, and hereafter lay not quite apart either, when in the dark of
different rooms, and under a dozen other roofs, in each of our dreaming heads my father lived again, and died too, over and over.

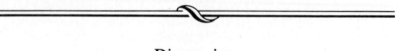

Discussion

- Describe Gibson's voice, the style with which he writes. How is it
different from or similar to Baldwin, Ellison, Trillin, Tuchman?
- Discuss the techniques Gibson uses to describe the people in his
piece and their world. How do his descriptions change at those times of the
greatest horror?
- Discuss the way in which Gibson and Baldwin each put their father's
dying in the context of a specific time and place.
- Discuss the techniques Gibson and Baldwin use to put themselves
in the piece of writing and to get out of the piece of writing. What are the
advantages and disadvantages of the writer being there or not being there?
- Can you imagine some of the changes that Gibson would have to
make to turn this chapter into a scene in a play?
- Gibson writes in fully developed paragraphs. What is similar
between his paragraphs writing about personal experience and Lindberg's
and Ellison's paragraphs writing about ideas?

Activities

- Take a paragraph of a piece of your own and try to write it as Gibson might, to see how his voice differs from yours. You should not adopt his voice, but merely do this to see another way you might write.
- Take a 1000-word chunk of Gibson and cut it to 250 words to see what is lost and what is gained.
- Write about your relationship with a parent or someone with whom you have lived. Reread it to make sure that the reader will see the general issues in your specific account. If you have to make changes, make them, but try not to tell the reader directly how to think or feel.
- Take a scene within this chapter and write it as a scene in a play or movie or television production. Make up the dialogue, of course. By doing this you may discover some important differences between drama and prose.

Judy Syfers

Sometimes when the writer has a focus—an idea—the whole piece can be seen almost instantly. I don't know if that was how it happened to the author of this piece, but it certainly could have happened this way. The title is the focus, and the writing simply has to develop that idea. Syfers does a superb job of developing the idea. It is written with humor, vigor, and economy. It isn't overdone; it's done just right. It has been one of the most popular reprints from *Ms.* magazine since it was published in 1971.

I Want A Wife

I belong to that classification of people known as wives. I am A   1
Wife. And, not altogether incidentally, I am a mother.

Not too long ago a male friend of mine appeared on the scene   2
fresh from a recent divorce. He had one child, who is, of course, with his ex-wife. He is looking for another wife. As I thought about him while I was ironing one evening, it suddenly occurred to me that I, too, would like to have a wife. Why do I want a wife?

❧ Note the neat organization of this piece. She makes five categories of
   service, develops each one of them in a paragraph, and then comes
   to an inevitable conclusion. ❧

3   I would like to go back to school so that I can become economically independent, support myself, and, if need be, support those
dependent upon me. I want a wife who will work and send me to
school. And while I am going to school I want a wife to take care of
my children. I want a wife to keep track of the children's doctor and
dentist appointments. And to keep track of mine, too. I want a wife
to make sure my children eat properly and are kept clean. I want a
wife who will wash the children's clothes and keep them mended. I
want a wife who is a good nurturant attendant to my children, who
arranges for their schooling, makes sure that they have an adequate
social life with their peers, takes them to the park, the zoo, etc. I
want a wife who takes care of the children when they are sick, a wife
who arranges to be around when the children need special care,
because, of course, I cannot miss classes at school. My wife must
arrange to lose time at work and not lose the job. It may mean a small
cut in my wife's income from time to time, but I guess I can tolerate
that. Needless to say, my wife will arrange and pay for the care of the
children while my wife is working.

4   I want a wife who will take care of *my* physical needs. I want a
wife who will keep my house clean. A wife who will pick up after my
children, a wife who will pick up after me. I want a wife who will
keep my clothes clean, ironed, mended, replaced when need be, and
who will see to it that my personal things are kept in their proper
place so that I can find what I need the minute I need it. I want a
wife who cooks the meals, a wife who is a good cook. I want a wife
who will plan the menus, do the necessary grocery shopping, prepare
the meals, serve them pleasantly, and then do the cleaning up while
I do my studying. I want a wife who will care for me when I am sick
and sympathize with my pain and loss of time from school. I want a
wife to go along when our family takes a vacation so that someone
can continue to care for me and my children when I need a rest and
change of scene.

5   I want a wife who will not bother me with rambling complaints
about a wife's duties. But I want a wife who will listen to me when I
feel the need to explain a rather difficult point I have come across in
my course of studies. And I want a wife who will type my papers for
me when I have written them.

6   I want a wife who will take care of the details of my social life.
When my wife and I are invited out by my friends, I want a wife who
will take care of the babysitting arrangements. When I meet people
at school that I like and want to entertain, I want a wife who will

have the house clean, will prepare a special meal, serve it to me and my friends, and not interrupt when I talk about things that interest me and my friends. I want a wife who will have arranged that the children are fed and ready for bed before my guests arrive so that the children do not bother us. I want a wife who takes care of the needs of my guests so that they feel comfortable, who makes sure that they have an ashtray, that they are passed the hors d'oeuvres, that they are offered a second helping of the food, that their wine glasses are replenished when necessary, that their coffee is served to them as they like it. And I want a wife who knows that sometimes I need a night out by myself.

I want a wife who is sensitive to my sexual needs, a wife who 7 makes love passionately and eagerly when I feel like it, a wife who makes sure that I am satisfied. And, of course, I want a wife who will not demand sexual attention when I am not in the mood for it. I want a wife who assumes the complete responsibility for birth control, because I do not want more children. I want a wife who will remain sexually faithful to me so that I do not have to clutter up my intellectual life with jealousies. And I want a wife who understands that my sexual needs may entail more than strict adherence to monogamy. I must, after all, be able to relate to people as fully as possible.

If, by chance, I find another person more suitable as a wife than 8 the wife I already have, I want the liberty to replace my present wife with another one. Naturally, I will expect a fresh, new life; my wife will take the children and be solely responsible for them so that I am left free.

When I am through with school and have a job, I want my wife 9 to quit working and remain at home so that my wife can more fully and completely take care of a wife's duties.

My God, who wouldn't want a wife? 10

Discussion

• Discuss other ways this focus could have been developed. Also consider other genre that could have delivered the same message—a speech, a TV situation comedy, a short story, or any other form that might work.

• Describe the author's voice, and show evidence of that voice. What other voice might she have used?

- Discuss whether the piece is fair and whether it needs to be fair. What is the purpose of the piece? Does it achieve it?
- What are the advantages of her neat organization? What are its limitations?

Activities

- She has created a formula, and it may be interesting to use the formula to write a piece on "I want a husband," "I want a boss," "I want an employee," "I want a parent," "I want a kid." But watch out, I think this piece is fresh and vigorous. Imitated it could quickly become a cliché and a stereotype.
- Take a subject you feel strongly about and try to state your opinion in as short a piece, making it vigorous, but not following the formula she has established.
- Take a long piece you have written, or a selection from the book. Give it as precise and direct a focus as Syfers has, and write a short piece from the long one.

Martin Luther King, Jr.

On August 28, 1963, the Reverend Martin Luther King, Jr., led 200,000 persons from the Washington Monument to the Lincoln Memorial in Washington, D. C. For eight years he had been a leader in the Civil Rights movement, and this march in the Capital celebrated the centennial of Lincoln's Emancipation Proclamation which freed the slaves. King, the great advocate of nonviolence, was to be assassinated five years later. But at this moment he made a speech that is a landmark in our history. Millions saw it on television, and there are millions of us, black and white, reading this speech who feel sadness and joy, frustration and rage, despair and hope at its words.

I Have a Dream

1   I am happy to join with you today in what will go down in history as the greatest demonstration for freedom in the history of our nation.

Five score years ago, a great American, in whose symbolic 2
shadow we stand today, signed the Emancipation Proclamation. This
momentous decree came as a great beacon light of hope to millions
of Negro slaves who had been seared in the flames of withering injustice. It came as a joyous daybreak to end the long night of their
captivity.

But one hundred years later, the Negro is still not free; one 3
hundred years later, the life of the Negro is still sadly crippled by the
manacles of segregation and the chains of discrimination; one
hundred years later, the Negro lives on a lonely island of poverty in
the midst of a vast ocean of material prosperity; one hundred years
later, the Negro is still languishing in the corners of American society
and finds himself in exile in his own land.

> ❧A speech is an interesting genre. It has to be paced entirely
> differently than most writing. Note how King used repetition to
> make his meaning clear to a vast audience. Read the speech aloud to
> appreciate the music and power of the language.❧

So we've come here today to dramatize a shameful condition. 4
In a sense we've come to our nation's capital to cash a check. When
the architects of our republic wrote the magnificent words of the
Constitution and the Declaration of Independence, they were signing
a promissory note to which every American was to fall heir. This note
was the promise that all men, yes black men as well as white men,
would be guaranteed the unalienable rights of life, liberty, and the
pursuit of happiness.

It is obvious today that America has defaulted on this promis- 5
sory note insofar as her citizens of color are concerned. Instead of
honoring this sacred obligation, America has given the Negro people
a bad check, a check which has come back marked "insufficient
funds." But we refuse to believe that the bank of justice is bankrupt.
We refuse to believe that there are insufficient funds in the great
vaults of opportunity of this nation. And so we've come to cash this
check—a check that will give us upon demand the riches of freedom
and the security of justice.

We have also come to this hallowed spot to remind America of 6
the fierce urgency of *now*. This is no time to engage in the luxury of
cooling off or to take the tranquilizing drug of gradualism. *Now* is the
time to make real the promises of democracy; *now* is the time to rise
from the dark and desolate valley of segregation to the sunlit path of

racial justice; *now* is the time to lift our nation from the quicksands of racial injustice to the solid rock of brotherhood; *now* is the time to make justice a reality for all of God's children. It would be fatal for the nation to overlook the urgency of the moment. This sweltering summer of the Negro's legitimate discontent will not pass until there is an invigorating autumn of freedom and equality.

❧ Look back and see how King used the analogy of a check to make his listeners understand the obligation the nation had to its black citizens. We connect with our audiences when we use experiences common to them. Analogy is a powerful device, dangerous if it is not accurate. I think it works here and is fair. Do you? ❧

7   Nineteen sixty-three is not an end, but a beginning. And those who hope that the Negro needed to blow off steam and will now be content, will have a rude awakening if the nation returns to business as usual. There will be neither rest nor tranquility in America until the Negro is granted his citizenship rights. The whirlwinds of revolt will continue to shake the foundations of our nation until the bright day of justice emerges.

❧ His problem here was to turn from speaking to the white majority and address the black minority. How do you make such a transition? One editor told me, "Just do it." Good advice. King just does it, simply and directly. ❧

8   But there is something that I must say to my people, who stand on the warm threshold which leads into the palace of justice. In the process of gaining our rightful place, we must not be guilty of wrongful deeds. Let us not seek to satisfy our thirst for freedom by drinking from the cup of bitterness and hatred. We must forever conduct our struggle on the high plain of dignity and discipline. We must not allow our creative protest to degenerate into physical violence. Again and again we must rise to the majestic heights of meeting physical force with soul force. The marvelous new militancy, which has engulfed the Negro community, must not lead us to a distrust of all white people. For many of our white brothers, as evidenced by their presence here today, have come to realize that their destiny is tied up with our destiny. And they have come to realize that their freedom is inextricably bound to our freedom. We cannot walk alone. And as

we walk, we must make the pledge that we shall always march ahead. We cannot turn back.

There are those who are asking the devotees of Civil Rights, 9 "When will you be satisfied?" We can never be satisfied as long as the Negro is the victim of the unspeakable horrors of police brutality; we can never be satisfied as long as our bodies, heavy with the fatigue of travel, cannot gain lodging in the motels of the highways and the hotels of the cities; we cannot be satisfied as long as the Negro's basic mobility is from a smaller ghetto to a larger one; we can never be satisfied as long as our children are stripped of their selfhood and robbed of their dignity by signs stating "For White Only"; we cannot be satisfied as long as the Negro in Mississippi cannot vote and a Negro in New York believes he has nothing for which to vote. No! No, we are not satisfied, and we will not be satisfied until "justice rolls down like waters and righteousness like a mighty stream."

❦ Now he speaks to Civil Rights activists black and white. ❦

I am not unmindful that some of you have come here out of 10 great trials and tribulations. Some of you have come fresh from narrow jail cells. Some of you have come from areas where your quest for freedom left you battered by the storms of persecution and staggered by the winds of police brutality. You have been the veterans of creative suffering. Continue to work with the faith that unearned suffering is redemptive. Go back to Mississippi. Go back to Alabama. Go back to South Carolina. Go back to Georgia. Go back to Louisiana. Go back to the slums and ghettos of our Northern cities, knowing that somehow this situation can and will be changed. Let us not wallow in the valley of despair.

❦ There is a terrible irony, that his dream is nothing more than the extension to all citizens of the freedom we already promise all citizens. By speaking of such a dream, over and over again, he made his point clearly and powerfully. And notice how specific he is. His dream is not vague, but made clear in terms every listener can understand. ❦

I say to you today, my friends, so even though we face the dif- 11 ficulties of today and tomorrow, I still have a dream. It is a dream deeply rooted in the American dream. I have a dream that one day this nation will rise up and live out the true meaning of its creed, "We hold these truths to be self-evident; that all men are created equal." I have a dream that one day on the red hills of Georgia, sons of former slaves and the sons of former slave owners will be able to sit down together at the table of brotherhood. I have a dream that one day even the state of Mississippi, a state sweltering with the heat of injustice, sweltering with the heat of oppression, will be transformed into an oasis of freedom and justice. I have a dream that my four little children will one day live in a nation where they will not be judged by the color of their skin, but by the content of their character.

12   I HAVE A DREAM TODAY!

13   I have a dream that one day down in Alabama—with its vicious racists, with its governor having his lips dripping with the words of interposition and nullification—one day right there in Alabama, little black boys and black girls will be able to join hands with little white boys and white girls as sisters and brothers.

14   I HAVE A DREAM TODAY!

15   I have a dream that one day every valley shall be exalted, and every hill and mountain shall be made low. The rough places will be plain, and the crooked places will be made straight, "and the glory of the Lord shall be revealed, and all flesh shall see it together."

16   This is our hope. This is the faith that I go back to the South with. With this faith we will be able to hew out of the mountain of despair a stone of hope. With this faith we will be able to transform the jangling discords of our nation into a beautiful symphony of brotherhood. With this faith we will be able to work together, to pray together, to struggle together, to go to jail together, to stand up for freedom together, knowing that we will be free one day. And this will be the day. This will be the day when all of God's children will be able to sing with new meaning, "My country 'tis of thee, sweet land of liberty, of thee I sing. Land where my fathers died, land of the pilgrim's pride, from every mountainside, let freedom ring." And if America is to be a great nation, this must become true.

17   So let freedom ring from the prodigious hilltops of New Hampshire; let freedom ring from the mighty mountains of New York; let freedom ring from the heightening Alleghenies of Pennsylvania; let freedom ring from the snow-capped Rockies of Colorado; let freedom ring from the curvaceous slopes of California. but not only that. Let freedom ring from Stone Mountain of Georgia; let freedom ring

from Lookout Mountain of Tennessee; let freedom ring from every hill and molehill of Mississippi. "From every mountainside, let freedom ring."

And when this happens, and when we allow freedom to ring, 18 when we let it ring from every village and every hamlet, from every state and every city, we will be able to speed up that day when all of God's children, black men and white men, Jews and Gentiles, Protestants and Catholics, will be able to join hands and sing in the words of the old Negro spiritual: "Free at last. Free at last. Thank God Almighty, we are free at last."

Discussion

• King was a black Baptist minister. What characteristics of this speech come from the traditions of the sermon? What elements come from the tradition of the Protestant, evangelical sermon? What elements come from the Black church?

• Discuss how a speech is different from writing that is not meant to be spoken but is meant to be read.

• Discuss how this speech would be different if it were delivered to a handful of government leaders in a living room, to fifty people at a Rotary luncheon, on a television interview show where most listeners would be alone or with one or two other people. (The television audience of the speech were observing a speech given to 200,000 people.)

• Discuss how Syfers and King have used very different voices to discuss issues of freedom and equality.

• Discuss how both King and Syfers have achieved brevity and focus in presenting large ideas.

Activities

• Take an issue you feel strongly about and write a short speech to be delivered to 200,000 people.

• Take that speech you have written and write it for a small audience or a different medium.

• Rewrite King's speech as an ironic article for a magazine, and rewrite Syfer's piece as a speech to be delivered to 200,000 feminists. (Or 200,000 husbands.)

- Take a page from Ellison and show how King might have written that page for an audience at the Library of Congress. Take a page of King's speech and rewrite it as Ellison might have written it for an audience of 200,000.

Barbara W. Tuchman

Barbara Tuchman, who has twice won the Pulitzer Prize, has published seven books of history and a collection of essays. In her writing and talking about writing she has given us all good counsel:

- "Research is endlessly seductive; writing is hard work. One has to sit down on that chair and think and transform thought into readable, conservative, interesting sentences that both make sense and make the reader turn the page. It is laborious, slow, often painful, sometimes agony. It means rearrangement, revision, adding, cutting, rewriting. But it brings a sense of excitement, almost of rapture; a moment on Olympus. In short, it is an act of creation."
- "Structure is chiefly a problem of selection, an agonizing business because there is always more material than one can use or fit into a story. The problem is how and what to select out of all that happened without, by the very process of selection, giving an over- or underemphasis which violates truth. One cannot put in everything: The result would be a shapeless mass."
- ". . . blocks (for me) generally come from difficulty of organization—that the material is resistant, or that I don't adequately understand it; it needs rethinking or additional research and a new approach."
- "I try for motion in every paragraph. I hate sentences that begin, 'There was a storm.' Instead, write, 'A storm burst.'"
- "After seven years' apprenticeship in journalism I discovered that an essential element for good writing is a good ear. One must *listen* to the sound of one's own prose."
- ". . . short words are always preferable to long ones; the fewer syllables the better, and monosyllables, beautiful and pure like 'bread' and 'sun' and 'grass' are the best of all."

And my favorite:

- ". . . nothing is more satisfying than to write a good sentence. It is no fun to write lumpishly, dully, in prose the reader must plod through like wet sand. But it is a pleasure to achieve, if one can, a clear running prose that is simple yet full of surprises. This does not just happen. It requires skill, hard work, a good ear, and continued practice . . ."

The following selection is taken from *A Distant Mirror—The Calamitous 14th Century.*

"This Is the End of the World": The Black Death

In October 1347, two months after the fall of Calais, Genoese   1
trading ships put into the harbor of Messina in Sicily with dead and dying men at the oars. The ships had come from the Black Sea port of Caffa (now Feodosiya) in the Crimea, where the Genoese maintained a trading post. The diseased sailors showed strange black swellings about the size of an egg or an apple in the armpits and groin. The swellings oozed blood and pus and were followed by spreading boils and black blotches on the skin from internal bleeding. The sick suffered severe pain and died quickly within five days of the first symptoms. As the disease spread, other symptoms of continuous fever and spitting of blood appeared instead of the swellings or buboes. These victims coughed and sweated heavily and died even more quickly, within three days or less, sometimes in 24 hours. In both types everything that issued from the body—breath, sweat, blood from the buboes and lungs, bloody urine, and blood-blackened excrement—smelled foul. Depression and despair accompanied the physical symptoms, and before the end "death is seen seated on the face."

❡ It is interesting to see how Tuchman starts with information. The reader asks, "What is this disease?" and then she gives the name. She provides the definition when the reader needs it. ❡

The disease was bubonic plague, present in two forms: one that   2
infected the bloodstream, causing the buboes and internal bleeding, and was spread by contacts; and a second, more virulent pneumonic type that infected the lungs and was spread by respiratory infection. The presence of both at once cause the high mortality and speed of contagion. So lethal was the disease that cases were known of persons going to bed well and dying before they woke, of doctors catch-

ing the illness at a bedside and dying before the patient. So rapidly did it spread from one to another that to a French physician, Simon de Covino, it seemed as if one sick person "could infect the whole world." The malignity of the pestilence appeared more terrible because its victims knew no prevention and no remedy.

3   The physical suffering of the disease and its aspect of evil mystery were expressed in a strange Welsh lament which saw "death coming into our midst like black smoke, a plague which cuts off the young, a rootless phantom which has no mercy for fair countenance. Woe is me of the shilling in the armpit! It is seething, terrible . . . a head that gives pain and causes a loud cry . . . a painful angry knob . . . Great is its seething like a burning cinder . . . a grievous thing of ashy color." Its eruption is ugly like the "seeds of black peas, broken fragments of brittle sea-coal! . . . the early ornaments of black death, cinders of the peelings of the cockle weed, a mixed multitude, a black plague like halfpence, like berries . . ."

☞ Note how she works in various forms of documentation. ☜

4   Rumors of a terrible plague supposedly arising in China and spreading through Tartary (Central Asia) to India and Persia, Mesopotamia, Syria, Egypt, and all of Asia Minor had reached Europe in 1346. They told of a death toll so devastating that all of India was said to be depopulated, whole territories covered by dead bodies, other areas with no one left alive. As added up by Pope Clement VI at Avignon, the total of reported dead reached 25,840,000. In the absence of a concept of contagion, no serious alarm was felt in Europe until the trading ships brought their black burden of pestilence into Messina while other infected ships from the Levant carried it to Genoa and Venice.

5   By January 1348 it penetrated France via Marseille, and North Africa via Tunis. Shipborne along coasts and navigable rivers, it spread westward from Marseille through the ports of Languedoc to Spain and northward up the Rhone to Avignon, where it arrived in March. It reached Narbonne, Montpelier, Carcassonne, and Toulouse between February and May, and at the same time in Italy spread to Rome and Florence and their hinterlands. Between June and August it reached Bordeaux, Lyon, and Paris, spread to Burgundy and Normandy, and crossed the Channel from Normandy into southern England. From Italy during the same summer it crossed the Alps into Switzerland and reached eastward to Hungary.

In a given area the plague accomplished its kill within four to six months and then faded, except in the larger cities, where, rooting into the close-quartered population, it abated during the winter, only to reappear in spring and rage for another six months.

In 1349 it resumed in Paris, spread to Picardy, Flanders, and the Low Countries, and from England to Scotland and Ireland as well as to Norway, where a ghost ship with a cargo of wool and a dead crew drifted offshore until it ran aground near Bergen. From there the plague passed into Sweden, Denmark, Prussia, Iceland, and as far as Greenland. Leaving a strange pocket of immunity in Bohemia, and Russia unattacked until 1351, it had passed from most of Europe by mid-1350. Although the mortality rate was erratic, ranging from one fifth in some places to nine tenths or almost total elimination in others, the overall estimate of modern demographers has settled—for the area extending from India to Iceland—around the same figure expressed in Froissart's casual words: "a third of the world died." His estimate, the common one at the time, was not an inspired guess but a borrowing of St. John's figure for mortality from plague in Revelation, the favorite guide to human affairs of the Middle Ages.

❡ Tuchman weaves statistics through these pages with great skill . . . And she writes actively. Her sentences move the reader through the text. ❜❜

A third of Europe would have meant about 20 million deaths. No one knows in truth how many died. Contemporary reports were an awed impression, not an accurate count. In crowded Avignon, it was said, 400 died daily; 7,000 houses emptied by death were shut up; a single graveyard received 11,000 corpses in six weeks; half the city's inhabitants reportedly died, including 9 cardinals or one third of the total, and 70 lesser prelates. Watching the endlessly passing death carts, chroniclers let normal exaggeration take wings and put the Avignon death toll at 62,000 and even at 120,000, although the city's total population was probably less than 50,000.

When graveyards filled up, bodies at Avignon were thrown into the Rhone until mass burial pits were dug for dumping the corpses. In London in such pits corpses piled up in layers until they overflowed. Everywhere reports speak of the sick dying too fast for the living to bury. Corpses were dragged out of homes and left in front of doorways. Morning light revealed new piles of bodies. In Florence the dead were gathered up by the Compagnia della Misericordia—

founded in 1244 to care for the sick—whose members wore red robes and hoods masking the face except for the eyes. When their efforts failed, the dead lay putrid in the streets for days at a time. When no coffins were to be had, the bodies were laid on boards, two or three at once, to be carried to graveyards or common pits. Families dumped their own relatives into the pits, or buried them so hastily and thinly "that dogs dragged them forth and devoured their bodies."

❡ The material is so powerful that Tuchman stands back at a distance and simply reports. ❡

10   Amid accumulating death and fear of contagion, people died without last rites and were buried without prayers, a prospect that terrified the last hours of the stricken. A bishop in England gave permission to laymen to make confession to each other as was done by the Apostles, "or if no man is present then even to a woman," and if no priest could be found to administer extreme unction, "then faith must suffice." Clement VI found it necessary to grant remissions of sin to all who died of the plague because so many were unattended by priests. "And no bells tolled," wrote a chronicler of Siena, "and nobody wept no matter what his loss because almost everyone expected death . . . And people said and believed, 'This is the end of the world.'"

11   In Paris, where the plague lasted through 1349, the reported death rate was 800 a day, in Pisa 500, in Vienna 500 to 600. The total dead in Paris numbered 50,000 or half the population. Florence, weakened by the famine of 1347, lost three to four fifths of its citizens, Venice two thirds, Hamburg and Bremen, though smaller in size, about the same proportion. Cities, as centers of transportation, were more likely to be affected than villages, although once a village was infected, its death rate was equally high. At Givry, a prosperous village in Burgundy of 1,200 or 1,500 people, the parish register records 615 deaths in the space of fourteen weeks, compared to an average of thirty deaths a year in the previous decade. In three villages of Cambridgeshire, manorial records show a death rate of 47 percent, 57 percent, and in one case 70 percent. When the last survivors, too few to carry on, moved away, a deserted village sank back into the wilderness and disappeared from the map altogether, leaving only a grass-covered ghostly outline to show where mortals once had lived.

In enclosed places such as monasteries and prisons, the infec- 12 tion of one person usually meant that of all, as happened in the Franciscan convents of Carcassonne and Marseille, where every inmate without exception died. Of the 140 Dominicans at Montpellier only seven survived. Petrarch's brother Gherardo, member of a Carthusian monastery, buried the prior and 34 fellow monks one by one, sometimes three a day, until he was left alone with his dog and fled to look for a place that would take him in. Watching every comrade die, men in such places could not but wonder whether the strange peril that filled the air had not been sent to exterminate the human race. In Kilkenny, Ireland, Brother John Clyn of the Friars Minor, another monk left alone among dead men, kept a record of what had happened lest "things which should be remembered perish with time and vanish from the memory of those who come after us." Sensing "the whole world, as it were, placed within the grasp of the Evil One," and waiting for death to visit him too, he wrote, "I leave parchment to continue this work, if perchance any man survive and any of the race of Adam escape this pestilence and carry on the work which I have begun." Brother John, as noted by another hand, died of the pestilence, but he foiled oblivion.

The largest cities of Europe, with populations of about 100,000, 13 were Paris and Florence, Venice and Genoa. At the next level, with more than 50,000, were Ghent and Bruges in Flanders, Milan, Bologna, Rome, Naples, and Palermo, and Cologne. London hovered below 50,000, the only city in England except York with more than 10,000. At the level of 20,000 to 50,000 were Bordeaux, Toulouse, Montpellier, Marseille, and Lyon in France, Barcelona, Seville, and Toledo in Spain, Siena, Pisa, and other secondary cities in Italy, and the Hanseatic trading cities of the Empire. The plague raged through them all, killing anywhere from one third to two thirds of their inhabitants. Italy, with a total population of 10 to 11 million, probably suffered the heaviest toll. Following the Florentine bankruptcies, the crop failures and workers' riots of 1346-47, the revolt of Cola di Rienzi that plunged Rome into anarchy, the plague came as the peak of successive calamities. As if the world were indeed in the grasp of the Evil One, its first appearance on the European mainland in January 1348 coincided with a fearsome earthquake that carved a path of wreckage from Naples up to Venice. Houses collapsed, church towers toppled, villages were crushed, and the destruction reached as far as Germany and Greece. Emotional response, dulled by horrors, underwent a kind of atrophy epitomized by the chronicler who wrote, "And in these days was burying without sorrows and wedding without friendschippe."

14   In Siena, where more than half the inhabitants died of the plague, work was abandoned on the great cathedral, planned to be the largest in the world, and never resumed, owing to loss of workers and master masons and "the melancholy and grief" of the survivors. The cathedral's truncated transept still stands in permanent witness to the sweep of death's scythe. Agnolo di Tura, a chronicler of Siena, recorded the fear of contagion that froze every other instinct. "Father abandoned child, wife husband, one brother another," he wrote, "for this plague seemed to strike through the breath and sight. And so they died. And no one could be found to bury the dead for money or friendship . . . And I, Angelo di Tura, called the Fat, buried my five children with my own hands, and so did many other likewise."

15   There were many to echo his account of inhumanity and few to balance it, for the plague was not the kind of calamity that inspired mutual help. Its loathsomeness and deadliness did not herd people together in mutual distress, but only prompted their desire to escape each other. "Magistrates and notaries refused to come and make the wills of the dying," reported a Franciscan friar of Piazza in Sicily; what was worse, "even the priests did not come to hear their confessions." A clerk of the Archbishop of Canterbury reported the same of English priests who "turned away from the care of their benefices from fear of death." Cases of parents deserting children and children their parents were reported across Europe from Scotland to Russia. The calamity chilled the hearts of men, wrote Boccaccio in his famous account of the plague in Florence that serves as introduction to the Decameron. "One man shunned another . . . kinsfolk held aloof, brother was forsaken by brother, oftentimes husband by wife; nay, what is more, and scarcely to be believed, fathers and mothers were found to abandon their own children to their fate, untended, unvisited as if they had been strangers." Exaggeration and literary pessimism were common in the 14th century, but the Pope's physician, Guy de Chauliac, was a sober, careful observer who reported the same phenomenon: "A father did not visit his son, nor the son his father. Charity was dead."

16   Yet not entirely. In Paris, according to the chronicler Jean de Venette, the nuns of the Hôtel Dieu or municipal hospital, "having no fear of death, tended the sick with all sweetness and humility." New nuns repeatedly took the places of those who died, until the

majority "many times renewed by death now rest in peace with Christ as we may piously believe."

When the plague entered northern France in July 1348, it set- 17 tled first in Normandy and, checked by winter, gave Picardy a deceptive interim until the next summer. Either in mourning or warning, black flags were flown from church towers of the worst-stricken villages of Normandy. "And in that time," wrote a monk of the abbey of Fourcarment, "the mortality was so great among the people of Normandy that those of Picardy mocked them." The same unneighborly reaction was reported of the Scots, separated by a winter's immunity from the English. Delighted to hear of the disease that was scourging the "southrons," they gathered forces for an invasion, "laughing at their enemies." Before they could move, the savage mortality fell upon them too, scattering some in death and the rest in panic to spread the infection as they fled.

In Picardy in the summer of 1349 the pestilence penetrated the 18 castle of Coucy to kill Enguerrand's mother, Catherine, and her new husband. Whether her nine-year-old son escaped by chance or was perhaps living elsewhere with one of his guardians is unrecorded. In nearby Amiens, tannery workers, responding quickly to losses in the labor force, combined to bargain for higher wages. In another place villagers were seen dancing to drums and trumpets, and on being asked the reason, answered that, seeing their neighbors die day by day while their village remained immune, they believed they could keep the plague from entering "by the jollity that is in us. That is why we dance." Further north in Tournal on the border of Flanders, Gilles li Muisis, Abbot of St. Martin's, kept one of the epidemic's most vivid accounts. The passing bells rang all day and all night, he recorded, because sextons were anxious to obtain their fees while they could. Filled with the sound of mourning, the city became oppressed by fear, so that the authorities forbade the tolling of bells and the wearing of black and restricted funeral services to two mourners. The silencing of funeral bells and of criers' announcements of deaths was ordained by most cities. Siena imposed a fine on the wearing of mourning clothes by all except widows.

Flight was the chief recourse of those who could afford it or 19 arrange it. The rich fled to their country places like Boccaccio's young patricians of Florence, who settled in a pastoral palace "removed on every side from the roads" with "wells of cool water and vaults of rare wines." The urban poor died in their burrows, "and only the stench of their bodies informed neighbors of their death." That the poor were more heavily afflicted than the rich was clearly remarked at the time, in the north as in the south. A Scottish chronicler, John of Fordun, stated flatly that the pest "attacked especially the meaner sort and common people—seldom the magnates." Simon de Covino of Montpellier made the same observation. He ascribed it to the misery and want and hard lives that made the poor more susceptible, which was half the truth. Close contact and lack of sanitation was the unrecognized other half. It was noticed too that the young died in greater proportion than the old; Simon de Covino compared the disappearance of youth to the withering of flowers in the fields.

20   In the countryside peasants dropped dead on the roads, in the fields, in their houses. Survivors in growing helplessness fell into apathy, leaving ripe wheat uncut and livestock untended. Oxen and asses, sheep and goats, pigs and chickens ran wild and they too, according to local reports, succumbed to the pest. English sheep, bearers of the precious wool, died throughout the country. The chronicler Henry Knighton, canon of Leicester Abbey, reported 5,000 dead in one field alone, "their bodies so corrupted by the plague that neither beast nor bird would touch them," and spreading an appalling stench. In the Austrian Alps wolves came down to prey upon sheep, and then, "as if alarmed by some invisible warning, turned and fled back into the wilderness." In remote Dalmatia bolder wolves descended upon a plague-stricken city and attacked human survivors. For want of herdsmen, cattle strayed from place to place and died in hedgerows and ditches. Dogs and cats fell like the rest.

21   The dearth of labor held a fearful prospect because the 14th century lived close to the annual harvest both for food and for next year's seed. "So few servants and laborers were left," wrote Knighton, "that no one knew where to turn for help." The sense of a vanishing future created a kind of dementia of despair. A Bavarian chronicler of Neuberg on the Danube recorded that "Men and women . . . wandered around as if mad" and let their cattle stray "because no one had any inclination to concern themselves about the future." Fields went uncultivated, spring seed unsown. Second growth with nature's awful energy crept back over cleared land, dikes crumbled, salt water reinvaded and soured the lowlands. With so few hands remaining to restore the work of centuries, people felt, in Walsingham's words, that "the world could never again regain its former prosperity."

22   Though the death rate was higher among the anonymous poor,

the known and the great died too. King Alfonso XI of Castile was the only reigning monarch killed by the pest, but his neighbor King Pedro of Aragon lost his wife, Queen Leonora, his daughter Marie, and a niece in the space of six months. John Cantacuzene, Emperor of Byzantium, lost his son. In France the lame Queen Jeanne and her daughter-in-law Bonne de Luxemburg, wife of the Dauphin, both died in 1349 in the same phase that took the life of Enguerrand's mother. Jeanne, Queen of Navarre, daughter of Louis X, was another victim. Edward III's second daughter, Joanna, who was on her way to marry Pedro, the heir of Castile, died in Bordeaux. Women appear to have been more vulnerable than men, perhaps because, being more housebound, they were more exposed to fleas. Boccaccio's mistress Fiammetta, illegitimate daughter of the King of Naples, died, as did Laura, the beloved—whether real or fictional—of Petrarch. Reaching out to us in the future, Petrarch cried, "Oh happy posterity who will not experience such abysmal woe and will look upon our testimony as a fable."

In Florence Giovanni Villani, the great historian of his time, died at 68 in the midst of an unfinished sentence; ". . . *e dure questo pistolenza fino a . . .* (in the midst of this pestilence there came to an end . . .)," Siena's master painters, the brothers Ambrogio and Pietro Lorenzetti, whose names never appear after 1348, presumably perished in the plague, as did Andrea Pisano, architect and sculptor of Florence. William of Ockham and the English mystic Richard Rolle of Hampole both disappear from mention after 1349. Francisco Datini, merchant of Prato, lost both his parents and two siblings. Curious sweeps of mortality afflicted certain bodies of merchants in London. All eight wardens of the Company of Cutters, all six wardens of the Hatters, and four wardens of the Goldsmiths died before July 1350. Sir John Pulteney, master draper and four times Mayor of London, was a victim, likewise Sir John Montgomery, Governor of Calais.

Among the clergy and doctors the mortailty was naturally high because of the nature of their professions. Out of 24 physicians in Venice, 20 were said to have lost their lives in the plague, although, according to another account, some were believed to have fled or to have shut themselves up in their houses. At Montpellier, site of the leading medieval medical school, the physician Simon de Covino reported that, despite the great number of doctors, "hardly one of them escaped." In Avignon, Guy de Chauliac confessed that he performed his medical visits only because he dared not stay away for fear of infamy, but "I was in continual fear." He claimed to have contracted the disease but to have cured himself by his own treatment; if so, he was one of the few who recovered.

25   Clerical mortality varied with rank. Although the one third toll of cardinals reflects the same proportion as the whole, this was probably due to their concentration in Avignon. In England, in strange and almost sinister procession, the Archbishop of Canterbury, John Stratford, died in August 1348, his appointed successor died in May 1349, and the next appointee three months later, all three within a year. Despite such weird vagaries, prelates in general managed to sustain a higher survival rate than the lesser clergy. Among bishops the deaths have been estimated at about one in twenty. The loss of priests, even if many avoided their fearful duty of attending the dying, was about the same as among the population as a whole.

26   Government officials, whose loss contributed to the general chaos, found, on the whole, no special shelter. In Siena four of the nine members of the governing oligarchy died, in France one third of the royal notaries, in Bristol 15 out of the 52 members of the Town Council or almost one third. Tax-collecting obviously suffered, with the result that Phillip VI was unable to collect more than a fraction of the subsidy granted him by the Estates in the winter of 1347–48.

27   Lawlessness and debauchery accompanied the plague as they had during the great plague of Athens of 430 B.C., when according to Thucydides, men grew bold in the indulgence of pleasure: "For seeing how the rich died in a moment and those who had nothing immediately inherited their property, they reflected that life and riches were alike transitory and they resolved to enjoy themselves while they could." Human behavior is timeless. When St. John had his vision of plague in Revelation, he knew from some experience or race memory that those who survived "repented not of the work of their hands. . . . Neither repented they of their murders, nor of their sorceries, nor of their fornication, nor of their thefts."

Discussion

• Select one of the pieces of Tuchman's advice about writing reprinted in the introduction and consider if she has followed her own advice. Cite examples where she has or has not.

• Discuss the techniques Tuchman uses to keep the text moving forward so that the reader will turn the page. How can you do the same thing with your writing?

• Do you believe Tuchman's version of the plague? Why? How has she convinced you?

• How does Tuchman make another time come alive to readers living centuries later?

• Does Tuchman underwrite, almost coldly presenting the facts. If so, why does she do this? Does it work? Where might it work in a piece of your own?

• Discuss how Tuchman achieves focus in the entire selection. In a paragraph.

Activities

• Look up a newspaper account of a catastrophe—an explosion, earthquake, famine, fire—and compare it to Tuchman's. What could the author of that piece and Tuchman teach each other?

• Write an account of an event in your world—an accident, a game, a party, an election—as if you were a historian writing 500 years from now.

• Take a piece of your own or one from a classmate and put it in historical perspective.

• Write about something that interests you that requires statistics and other documentation as if you were Barbara Tuchman. If you have such a piece in your folder, edit it as if you were her.

• You have 250 words to report on the Black Death. Choose the words from Tuchman or use her material to write your own 250-word report.

Alice Stewart Trillin

Ever since Alice Trillin gave me this article, I have reread it regularly for wisdom and for technique, but never at the same time. Read it first to hear what she has to say about living, then read it again to learn from how she said it. I have used it in many classes and we have all spent some time, time well spent, to talk about the important issues of life and death and the meaning of life that are usually not allowed in the classroom. But the power of the content should not obscure the skill with which the author writes.

The article has an interesting history. It was a talk addressed to medical students at both Cornell and Albert Einstein medical schools. It meant so much to the medical profession that it was published in the March 19, 1981, issue of the distinguished journal, *The New England Journal of Medicine.*

Of Dragons and Garden Peas

1   When I first realized that I might have cancer, I felt immediately that I had entered a special place, a place I came to call "The Land of the Sick People." The most disconcerting thing, however, was not that I found that place terrifying and unfamiliar, but that I found it so ordinary, so banal. I didn't feel different, didn't feel that my life had radically changed at the moment the word *cancer* became attached to it. The same rules still held. What had changed, however, was other people's perceptions of me. Unconsciously, even with a certain amount of kindness, everyone—with the single rather extraordinary exception of my husband—regarded me as someone who had been altered irrevocably. I don't want to exaggerate my feeling of alienation or to give the impression that it was in any way dramatic. I have no horror stories of the kind I read a few years ago in the *New York Times;* people didn't move their desks away from me at the office or refuse to let their children play with my children at school because they thought that cancer was catching. My friends are all too sophisticated and too sensitive for that kind of behavior. Their distance from me was marked most of all by their inability to understand the ordinariness, the banality of what was happening to me. They marveled at how well I was "coping with cancer." I had become special, no longer like them. Their genuine concern for what had happened to me, and their complete separateness from it, expressed exactly what I had felt all my life about anyone I had ever known who had experienced tragedy.

❡ Bang. Trillin doesn't fool around. Note how quickly we are taken inside the world that she was taken to so quickly with her diagnosis. And note how quickly she instructs us (and the doctors she was addressing) about how to behave with someone who has a serious illness or has suffered another kind of loss. One reason this piece means so much to me is because of the death of a daughter, and Trillin's experiences and her wisdom in many ways parallel what my wife, daughters, and I have felt and learned. In using this in class I have found that it instructs and touches many people. And that is, of course, what writing should do. The more honestly and directly we speak of the personal, as Trillin does, the more we reach out to a larger audience. 🦋

When asked to speak to a group of doctors and medical students about what it was like to be a cancer patient, I worried for a long time about what I should say. It was a perfect opportunity— every patient's fantasy—to complain about doctors' insensitivity, nurses who couldn't draw blood properly, and perhaps even the awful food in hospitals. Or, instead, I could present myself as the good patient, full of uplifting thoughts about how much I had learned from having cancer. But, unlike many people, I had had very good experiences with doctors and hospitals. And the role of the brave patient troubled me, because I was afraid that all the brave things I said might no longer hold if I got sick again. I had to think about this a great deal during the first two years after my operation as I watched my best friend live out my own worst nightmares. She discovered that she had cancer several months after I did. Several months after that, she discovered that it had metastasized; she underwent eight operations during the next year and a half before she died. All my brave talk was tested by her illness as it has not yet been tested by mine.

And so I decided not to talk about the things that separate those of us who have cancer from those who do not. I decided that the only relevant thing for me to talk about was the one thing that we all have most in common. We are all afraid of dying.

Our fear of death makes it essential to maintain a distance between ourselves and anyone who is threatened by death. Denying our connection to the precariousness of others' lives is a way of pretending that we are immortal. We need this deception—it is one of the ways we stay sane—but we also need to be prepared for the times when it doesn't work. For doctors, who confront death when they go to work in the morning as routinely as other people deal with balance sheets and computer printouts, and for me, to whom a chest x-ray or a blood test will never again be a simple, routine procedure, it is particularly important to face the fact of death squarely, to talk about it with one another.

Cancer connects us to one another because having cancer is an embodiment of the existential paradox that we all experience: we feel that we are immortal, yet we know that we will die. To Tolstoy's

Ivan Ilyich, the syllogism he had learned as a child, "'Caius is a man, men are mortal, therefore Caius is mortal,' had always seemed . . . correct as applied to Caius but certainly not as applied to himself." Like Ivan Ilyich, we all construct an elaborate set of defense mechanisms to separate ourselves from Caius. To anyone who has had cancer, these defense mechanisms become talismans that we invest with a kind of magic. These talismans are essential to our sanity, and yet they need to be examined.

6   First of all, we believe in the magic of doctors and medicine. The purpose of a talisman is to give us control over the things we are afraid of. Doctors and patients are accomplices in staging a kind of drama in which we pretend that doctors have the power to keep us well. The very best doctors—and I have had the very best—share their power with their patients and try to give us the information that we need to control our own treatment. Whenever I am threatened by panic, my doctor sits me down and tells me something concrete. He draws a picture of my lung, or my lymph nodes; he explains as well as he can how cancer cells work and what might be happening in my body. Together, we approach my disease intelligently and rationally, as a problem to be solved, an exercise in logic to be worked out. Of course, through knowledge, through medicine, through intelligence, we do have some control. But at best this control is limited, and there is always the danger that the disease I have won't behave rationally and respond to the intelligent argument we have constructed. Cancer cells, more than anything else in nature, are likely to behave irrationally. If we think that doctors and medicine can always protect us, we are in danger of losing faith in doctors and medicine when their magic doesn't work. The physician who fails to keep us well is like an unsuccessful witch doctor; we have to drive him out of the tribe and look for a more powerful kind of magic.

7   The reverse of this, of course, is that the patient becomes a kind of talisman for the doctor. Doctors defy death by keeping people alive. To a patient, it becomes immediately clear that the best way to please a doctor is to be healthy. If you can't manage that, the next best thing is to be well-behaved. (Sometimes the difference between being healthy and being well-behaved becomes blurred in a hospital, so that it almost seems as if being sick were being badly behaved.) If we get well, we help our doctors succeed; if we are sick, we have failed. Patients often say that their doctors seem angry with them when they don't respond to treatment. I think that this phenomenon is more than patients' paranoia or the result of overdeveloped med-

ical egos. It is the fear of death again. It is necessary for doctors to become a bit angry with patients who are dying, if only as a way of separating themselves from someone in whom they have invested a good bit of time and probably a good bit of caring. We all do this to people who are sick. I can remember being terribly angry with my mother who was prematurely senile, for a long time. Somehow I needed to think that it was her fault that she was sick, because her illness frightened me so much. I was also angry with my friend who died of cancer. I felt that she had let me down, that perhaps she hadn't fought hard enough. It was important for me to find reasons for her death, to find things that she might have done to cause it, as a way of separating myself from her and as a way of thinking that I would somehow have behaved differently, that I would somehow have been able to stay alive.

> ❡ One of the distinguishing marks of her writing is compassion. Note the understanding that she has for different patterns of behavior and how she speaks honestly of her own behavior when it was not ideal. She doesn't line up her piece with the good guys on one side and the bad ones on the other side. It isn't a matter of absolute right and absolute wrong; it's much more complicated than that. And she deals directly and skillfully with some of the most complicated feelings that human beings can have. ❡

So, once we have recognized the limitations of the magic of doctors and medicine, where are we? We have to turn to our own magic, to our ability to "control" our bodies. For people who don't have cancer, this often takes the form of jogging and exotic diets and transcendental meditation. For people who have cancer, it takes the form of conscious development of the will to live. For a long time after I found out that I had cancer, I loved hearing stories about people who had simply decided that they would not be sick. I remember one story about a man who had a lung tumor and a wife with breast cancer and several children to support; he said, "I simply can't afford to be sick." Somehow the tumor went away. I think I suspected that there was a missing part to this story when I heard it, but there was also something that sounded right to me. I knew what he meant. I also found the fact that I had cancer unacceptable; the thought that my children might grow up without me was as ridiculous as the thought that I might forget to make appointments for their dental checkups and polio shots. I simply had to be there. Of course, doctors give a lot of credence to the power of the will over illness, but I have always suspected that the stories in medical books about this power might also have missing parts. My friend who died wanted to live more than anyone I have ever known. The talisman of will didn't work for her.

9   The need to exert some kind of control over the irrational forces that we imagine are loose in our bodies also results in what I have come to recognize as the "brave act" put on by people who have cancer. We all do it. The blood-count line at Memorial Hospital can be one of the cheeriest places in New York on certain mornings. It was on this line, during my first visit to Memorial, that a young leukemia patient in remission told me, "They treat lung cancer like the common cold around here." (Believe me, that was the cheeriest thing anyone had said to me in months.) While waiting for blood counts, I have heard stories from people with lymphoma who were given up for dead in other hospitals and who are feeling terrific. The atmosphere in that line suggests a gathering of knights who have just slain a bunch of dragons. But there are always people in the line who don't say anything at all, and I always wonder if they have at other times felt the exhilaration felt by those of us who are well. We all know, at least, that the dragons are never quite dead and might at any time be around, ready for another fight. But our brave act is important. It is one of the ways we stay alive, and it is the way that we convince those who live in "The Land of the Well People" that we aren't all that different from them.

10   As much as I rely on the talisman of the will, I know that believing in it too much can lead to another kind of deception. There has been a great deal written (mostly by psychiatrists) about why people get cancer and which personality types are most likely to get it. Susan Sontag has pointed out that this explanation of cancer parallels the explanations for tuberculosis that were popular before the discovery of the tubercle bacillus. But it is reassuring to think that people get cancer because of their personalities, because that implies that we have some control over whether we get it. (On the other hand, if people won't give up smoking to avoid cancer, I don't see how they can be expected to change their personalities on the basis of far less compelling evidence.) The trouble with this explanation of cancer is the trouble with any talisman: it is only useful when its charms are working. If I get sick, does that mean that my will to live isn't strong enough? Is being sick a moral and psychological failure? If I feel suc-

cessful, as if I had slain a dragon, because I am well, should I feel guilty, as if I have failed, if I get sick?

❦ This section begins with a piece by Lindberg that deals with thinking, and it ends with a piece by Trillin that deals more with feelings. But I am impressed with the similarities. Each, it seems, is written at the appropriate distance, is filled with specifics, and evolves in a logical, natural manner. In neither piece are we lectured, although this article was first given as a lecture. Instead, we are invited to share the thinking or the feeling with the writer. ❧

One of the ways that all of us avoid thinking about death is by 11 concentrating on the details of our daily lives. The work that we do every day and the people we love—the fabric of our lives—convince us that we are alive and that we will stay alive. William Saroyan said in a recent book, "Why am I writing this book? To save my life, to keep from dying, of course. That is why we get up in the morning." Getting up in the morning seems particularly miraculous after having seriously considered the possibility that these mornings might be limited. A year after I had my lung removed, my doctors asked me what I cared about most. I was about to go to Nova Scotia, where we have a summer home, and where I had not been able to go the previous summer because I was having radiation treatments, and I told him that what was most important to me was garden peas. Not the peas themselves, of course, though they were particularly good that year. What was extraordinary to me after that year was that I could again think that peas were important, that I could concentrate on the details of when to plant them and how much mulch they would need instead of thinking about platelets and white cells. I cherished the privilege of thinking about trivia. Thinking about death can make the details of our lives seem unimportant, and so, paradoxically, they become a burden—too much trouble to think about. This is the real meaning of depression: feeling weighed down by the concrete, unable to make the effort to move objects around, overcome by ennui. It is the fear of death that causes that ennui, because the fear of death ties us too much to the physical. We think too much about our bodies, and our bodies become too concrete—machines not functioning properly.

The other difficulty with the talisman of the moment is that it 12 is often the very preciousness of these moments that makes the thought of death so painful. As my friend got closer to death she became rather removed from those she loved the most. She seemed to have gone to some place where we couldn't reach her—to have died what doctors sometimes call a "premature death." I much preferred to think of her enjoying precious moments. I remembered the almost ritualistic way she had her hair cut and tied in satin ribbons before brain surgery, the funny, somehow joyful afternoon that we spent trying wigs on her newly shaved head. Those moments made it seem as if it wasn't so bad to have cancer. But of course it was bad. It was unspeakably bad, and toward the end she couldn't bear to speak about it or to be too close to the people she didn't want to leave. The strength of my love for my children, my husband, my life, even my garden peas has probably been more important than anything else in keeping me alive. The intensity of this love is also what makes me so terrified of dying.

13   For many, of course, a response to the existential paradox is religion—Kierkegaard's irrational leap toward faith. It is no coincidence that such a high number of conversions take place in cancer hospitals; there is even a group of Catholic nurses in New York who are referred to by other members of their hospital staff as "the death squad." I don't mean to belittle such conversions or any help that religion can give to anyone. I am at this point in my life simply unqualified to talk about the power of this particular talisman.

14   In considering some of the talismans we all use to deny death, I don't mean to suggest that these talismans should be abandoned. However, their limits must be acknowledged. Ernest Becker, in *The Denial of Death,* says that "skepticism is a more radical experience, a more manly confrontation of potential meaninglessness than mysticism." The most important thing I know now that I didn't know four years ago is that this "potential meaninglessness" can in fact be confronted. As much as I rely on my talismans—my doctors, my will, my husband, my children, and my garden peas—I know that from time to time I will have to confront what Conrad described as "the horror." I know that we can—all of us—confront that horror and not be destroyed by it, even, to some extent, be enhanced by it. To quote Becker again: "I think that taking life seriously means something such as this: that whatever man does on this planet has to be done in the lived truth of the terror of creation, of the grotesque, of the rumble of panic underneath everything. Otherwise it is false."

15   It astonishes me that having faced the terror, we continue to live, even to live with a great deal of joy. It is commonplace for peo-

ple who have cancer—particularly those who feel as well as I do—
to talk about how much richer their lives are because they have confronted death. Yes, my life is very rich. I have even begun to understand that wonderful line in *King Lear*, "Ripeness is all." I suppose
that becoming ripe means finding out that none of the really important questions have answers. I wish that life had devised a less terrifying, less risky way of making me ripe. But I wasn't given any
choice about this.

> ❦ The stronger the feelings we deal with in writing the more effective
> it usually is to use common, specific, ordinary language and
> experiences. This is a rhetorical device, but it also seems to be a
> philosophical truth. Life rescues us at its most terrible moments
> from the abstract and the general and presents us with the wonder
> of the concrete and the specific, as Trillin does at the end of this
> essay. ❧

William Saroyan said recently, "I'm growing old! I'm falling   16
apart! And it's VERY INTERESTING!" I'd be willing to bet that Mr.
Saroyan, like me, would much rather be young and all in one piece.
But somehow his longing for youth and wholeness doesn't destroy
him or stop him from getting up in the morning and writing, as he
says, to save his life. We will never kill the dragon. But each morning
we confront him. Then we give our children breakfast, perhaps put
a bit more mulch on the peas, and hope that we can convince the
dragon to stay away for a while longer.

Discussion

- Discuss the ways in which Trillin gives the reader room and keeps
the reader from being unnecessarily uncomfortable in confronting this
subject.
- Note how the author mentions, but gets beyond, the bad aspects of
her treatment in the hospital early in the piece. Notice other examples of
where she does this.
- Discuss how she weaves the death of her friend and her feelings for
that friend and about that death through the piece as a counterpoint to her
own experience and feelings. What does that enable her to do as a writer?
- The paper was first given to instruct doctors in how to deal with
patients with serious illness. What does she tell the doctors to do? How well

does she get her message across? What other ways could she have done it? How effective would they have been?

• What is the focus of this piece? What role does the title, which comes from the last paragraph, play in the focus. Most times we think of focus as coming from the beginning. Can the focus come from the end? And can reader and writer work toward the focus?

• Discuss how Tuchman and Trillin use voice to carry much of the meaning of what they have to say. Is each voice appropriate to each subject? If the voice in each piece is "natural" to each author, how might Tuchman and Trillin write each other's pieces?

• Discuss the distance at which Trillin and Tuchman stand from their subject. How does the distance help the writer and the reader?

• Imagine how the piece might have been written if it were given to an audience of people who fear they might have cancer, or people who have had cancer, rather than an audience of doctors.

Activities

• Imagine the last paragraph as the lead, and outline the piece that would be written as the result.

• Imagine the first paragraph as the ending, and outline the piece that would be written as the result.

• Write a piece of your own that deals with an issue of life or death in your experience.

• Rewrite a paragraph from Trillin, using your own voice to speak of her subject.

• Draft a lead for a piece that would report on what Trillin said for a newspaper; that would use what Trillin said for a lead on a magazine article about people who have had cancer; that would use Trillin's experience for the lead of a brochure raising money for cancer research; or that would use her experience for the lead of a short story about someone similar to Trillin.

5

An Order Designed

The writer who has found the focus for a piece of writing is like a sailor who is lost in a stormy sea and then glimpses, through the clouds, the North Star. Once that point of reference is found, the sailor can navigate the ocean. And once the writer has the focus it is possible to create a design that will carry the writer through the text.

Of course that plan will have to be changed as the experience of the writing blows the writer off course, causes the draft to slow down or speed up, even makes it necessary to change the destination and head for port along the way. But a plan—altered according to changing conditions—is essential if the voyage is to be successful.

Sometimes the plan is obvious once the focus is seen. The experienced writer—drawing on familiarity with the subject, the reader, the task—knows instinctively what has to be done. Most of the time, however, the writer has to have a sketch of the voyage that may be taken in the writer's head or scribbled down on a notebook page. Sometimes these sketches are precise, detailed, and as formal as the "Harvard Outline," in which each element is a complete sentence. But I have never known a writer who needs such a detailed plan. Most designs or outlines are loose enough to allow discovery or change in midcourse. They do not eliminate exploration, but encourage it. Some of the methods writers use to design a piece of writing will be discussed in the following pages.

Titles are a favorite planning device of mine. I may draft as many as 150 titles, but that doesn't take me much time, for I can play with lists of titles when turning from a commercial during a television show, waiting for a meeting to start, sitting in a traffic jam, waiting for my wife to come out of the supermarket, doodling while waiting for a long-distance phone call to be completed. I don't want to write titles with great intensity during long periods of time; I want to play with a variety of possible titles, and then spend time refining a title that may work.

Each draft title contains the seed for the meaning that may grow in the draft. The poet, John Ashberry, who writes titles before he writes his poems, says, "I feel it's a kind of opening into a potential poem, a door that suddenly pops open and leads into an unknown space." Each title establishes the potential horizons and structure of the draft. Most of all, each title hints at the voice in which the draft may be written. In the selections for this chapter note how Richard Selzer's title, "Letters to a Young Surgeon III," not only targets the reader but helps establish the voice of an experienced surgeon speaking to an inexperienced one. After you have read Raymond Carver's stories you will see how his two titles relate to the two texts. I do not know if these titles were written first. Most writers do not write their titles first, but I can see how the title could have helped those writers plan what they might write, and I would encourage you to play with titles as a way of planning.

Leads are more helpful to me than any other single planning device. The lead is a journalistic term that refers to the first sentence, paragraph, or paragraphs of a piece of writing. The lead catches the reader's attention, and readers—even sometimes when they are assigned reading by a teacher—will not continue to read unless the lead reaches out to them. John L'Heureux says, "The first lines of the story teach us how to read it. Tone gives us the clue. It prepares us for the story we are going to read." He could also have said that the lead tells how to write the story. Read the beginnings of pieces in this book to see how the first lines or paragraphs help you decide how to read—and the writer to write—the piece. Notice how important for the writer and the reader Selzer's lead is: "All right. You fainted in the operating room, had to go sit on the floor in a corner and put your head down." Look at Zinsser's lead: "Jazz came to China for the first time on the afternoon of June 2, 1981 . . ." Note how Stevenson uses light in his lead, the ideal way to begin an article on a photographer. Read the first sentence of the Toni Morrison story: "Nuns go by as quiet as lust, and drunken men and sober eyes sing in the lobby of the Greek hotel." Stand in awe before the tiny surprises and significant contradictions that help establish the beat and music of her prose.

But the lead is just as important for the writer. The lead makes it possible for the writer to see and hear how the piece may be written. John McPhee, who is reprinted in this text, says, "Leads, like titles, are flashlights that shine down into the story." Joan Didion, who is also reprinted in this text, says, "What's so hard about that first sentence is that you're stuck with it. Everything else is going to flow out of that sentence. And by the time you've laid down the first *two* sentences your options are all gone." Some of the techniques experienced lead writers use include the anecdote or brief story, a statement of news or surprise, a quotation, a statistic, a scene, a significant fact, the introduction of a person important to the story. Study the leads in the selections in this chapter, in the other selections in the book, and my own leads to see how those crucial first sentences have helped the writer find a way of writing the piece. In my case the lead may come early, but I often do not know that that early lead is the right one until I have drafted dozens of others in my head and on my notebook page. I write these mostly in fragments of time, the way I write titles, but I do not start a draft until I have a lead written and polished that I think will work.

Endings are almost as important as leads. In talking with the best writers on the newspapers where I have served as writing coach, I find that they have a good idea of where they will end before they begin. William Gibson, playwright, poet, novelist, and nonfiction writer, who has a selection reprinted in this chapter, says, "I always know the end. The end of everything I write is somehow always implicit from the beginning. What I don't know is the middle. I don't know how I'm going to get there." And John McPhee, who is also published in this book, says, "I generally know what the last line of the story will be before I know the first. The purpose of building a structure is to try to know where you are going."

Writers may not end up where they plan to go—the Saturday afternoon trip to the beach may turn into a party at a lake along the way—but the sense of destination, at the very least, gets the trip started. There would be no party at the lake unless we were headed for the beach. Sometimes I merely have an idea of where I will end that is too vague to be written down, but clear enough for me to aim at it. Other times I will have a note reminding me of an anecdote or a statistic or a quotation, or some such ending point which allows me not so much to conclude as to give readers a piece of information that allows them to draw the conclusion I want in their own minds. Study the endings in the pieces in this book to see how the writer draws what is written to a conclusion, and note how those techniques, which are often good techniques for writing leads, can help the writer develop the text.

Sequence is a trail of information that may lead the writer and the reader from the lead to the end. In my case this is usually three to five points that have to be made, developed, and documented if I am going to arrive at a believable conclusion, and if the reader is going to travel forward with me. Identify the main points made in the selections in this chapter to see how the knowledge of those points may have helped the writer during the draft. I say may, because we cannot always recreate the process of development. Study what Joseph Freda has to say in the case history to see how he worked. But then imagine how the writers of the other pieces may have worked. Don't believe that the imaginary history of the draft is the real one. The writers may have discovered those points during the writing; they may have inserted them during a revision, or they may, indeed, have known them before they began the draft. The point is that it can be a help to know the main points in a text before beginning the draft.

Outlines come in many forms. They can be formal and informal. Sometimes I use Roman numerals and Arabic numbers, capital letters and small letters to design something I may write. Other times I simply write the crossheads and subtitles first, as I have in these chapters, and then add other ones, such as "Outlines" as I go along. Sometimes I put the items to be included in the text on separate 3x5 cards and rearrange them into a meaningful pattern, the technique used most frequently by movie scriptwriters. Often I sort the piles of materials I have on a nonfiction piece of writing into file folders and rearrange the folders themselves into an effective order. Share your outlining techniques with your classmates, and listen to the methods they used that helped them *before* the first draft or *after* a draft is completed and they are planning a revision.

The Reader's Questions is such a powerful form of outlining that I am including it as a separate item. Each piece of effective writing may be described as a conversation between reader and writer, in which the writer anticipates the reader's questions and answers them just before they are asked. To test this go through the selections of this chapter or in this book and write the questions down in the margin that the writer has answered. You will find that effective writers have known when you will need a definition; a clarifying description of a process; an answer to such questions as, what does this mean, is this a common problem, who says, why should I believe you, what can I do about it?

If you role-play your reader, you will find that you can anticipate the four, five, or six questions the reader must have answered. Then you can put those questions in the order the reader will ask them. Occasionally in writing a text or a brochure you may even want to use the questions as crossheads, but most of the time they are invisible—but very much there.

Design is an effective way of seeing the order with which a piece of writing may be developed. The visual pattern or structure of a piece of writing may be seen in the writer's head, or actually written down on the page. My daybooks, or journals, are filled with the shapes I may use to develop a piece of writing. John Updike, who is reprinted in this text, has said, "I really begin with some kind of solid, coherent image, some notion of the shape of the book and even of its texture. The *Poorhouse Fair* was meant to have a sort of Y shape. *Rabbit Run* was a kind of zig-zag. The *Centaur* was sort of a sandwich." One of my novels became clear to me when I saw it as a sort of fever chart, with the actions and emotions of the main characters rising to peaks and falling into valleys, with crucial actions taking place when the lines on the fever chart intersected.

One of my nonfiction books appeared to me as a stone thrown into a pond, with each chapter being a concentric circle.

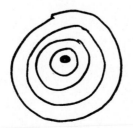

I often use a cone lying on its side to show me a pattern of development from a point or development to a point.

Sometimes I use a sequence of building blocks or stairs.

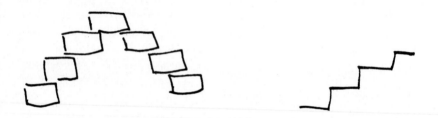

The important thing is not that anybody else understands my designs, but that I do, that they help me see how I may develop a piece of writing.

Genre is the form or type of writing that will help the writer discover meaning and share it with the reader. Some of the genre you may read and write include argument, poetry, expository essay, news story, science report, short story, research or term paper, autobiography. Each genre has its own traditions. These traditions should not be seen as absolute rules, but as lessons or counsel from explorers who have gone before. We do not have to follow their advice, but we are wise if we know when we are departing from it and aware of the hazards that entails. Each effective writer has the illusion, I think, that they are writing the first short story or the first research paper, because they need to feel that they are not just filling in the blanks in a formula, but are using the genre to help them say something new. I like to think of genre as a lens, a way of seeing how I may find out what I have to say. In this chapter we have many genre—Freda's pages from a software manual; Richard Selzer's essay; William Zinsser's and James Stevenson's profiles; Flannery O'Connor's essay on writing short stories together with short stories by Flannery O'Connor and Raymond Carver, as well as part of a novel by Toni Morrison. Look at these different genre, not as forms which restricted the writers, but as forms which helped the writers explore their subjects.

All the pieces in this book have found an order, for structure is as important to effective writing as skeletons are to human beings. Take away your bones and you'd be a messy heap of stuff. To learn how to write it is helpful to strip away the text from the structures upon which they are built. Outline some of these pieces of writing, realizing that the outline you create may not be an outline the writer needed. But you should have in your mind a number of structures that will help you design the one you need to create your text for your reader.

Case Study: A Technical Writer Writes and Reads

Joseph Freda

Joseph Freda, who was a Senior Software Writer for Digital Equipment Corporation, one of the largest computer manufacturers in the world, is now Publications Manager for Tegra Corporation in Billerica, Massachusetts.

Before going to work for Digital he worked as a carpenter, railroad trackman, canoe guide, and writing teacher at the University of New Hampshire, where he received a Masters degree in writing. He is a novelist, but he has also become an award winning technical writer. Technical writing has become an expanding career for writers in an age of high technology. These writers provide the link between our marvelous new machines and the people who use them. He has written books for Digital on typesetting and publishing software, and has also written instructional manuals and textbooks for software, such as text editors and programming languages. Freda designed and edited Digital's best-selling book, *Introduction to BASIC,* which won a regional Award of Excellence from the Society of Technical Communication. He also won an international Award of Distinction from the same organization for a set of books he designed and edited, *BASIC for Beginners* and *More BASIC for Beginners.*

Canoe Paddling and the Craft of Communicating Concepts

Writing on a Straight Course

1   I used to teach canoeing on the Delaware River. For some time, I started my training session by explaining the paddle: choosing the appropriate length, holding the paddle, stroking. Then I dispatched everybody to the canoes, where, I assumed, they would paddle down the river on a perfectly straight course. Instead, they struggled to haul their canoes over the rocks at the river's edge. They pondered which end of the canoe was which, tipped over on getting in, sat on thwarts instead of seats. Wet, frustrated, and sure of their imminent demise, they gripped the paddles much as they would rakes or snow shovels or vacuum wands and then hacked and flailed at the river. One young husband-and-wife team sat at either end of the canoe, backs toward each other, paddling furiously in opposite directions.

2   What was wrong? I had explained the parts of the paddle, had carefully demonstrated forward strokes and backwatering, had over-seen their practice on dry land. The husband and wife churning away in opposite directions gave me my clue: even though I had told them how to *move* the canoe, I hadn't told them a thing about the craft itself. I hadn't distinguished the bow from the stern, hadn't shown them how to float the canoe through the shallows or how to get into it. Of course they had forgotten my paddling instruction—they had enough trouble just confronting a canoe for the first time. They didn't know a thing about it, and *that* was my fault. In teaching how to paddle a canoe, I hadn't started at the beginning.

3   The concept of paddling a canoe, I realized, could be broken into a hierarchy of its parts: the canoe, the paddle, paddling the canoe. By starting out teaching about the paddle, I had simply started out too low in the hierarchy. So I changed my method, started with the canoe—describing its parts, showing how to get in and out,—and *then* went on to teach paddling. It worked. Although nobody ever paddled off on that perfectly straight course I pictured in my mind, subsequent students usually avoided the confusion and ineptitude that their forbears had felt while getting underway.

4   Teaching a person to paddle a canoe is not that different from teaching a person to do just about anything: make pea soup, write an essay, or use computer software, which is what I do now as a technical writer. Concepts exist in hierarchies, and to explain a concept,

you need to break it into a herarchy of its parts. Then you present each part in logical sequence, working from the top of the hierarchy toward the bottom. Think of this as *linear* writing, or writing on a straight course.

To do this, you should:⁵

1. Define the concept in simple terms.
2. Divide the concept into its parts.
3. Show how the parts work together.

If you were to follow these steps in writing a book on how to ⁶ paddle a canoe, they might look like this:

1. Define the concept of paddling a canoe. Show pictures of a person paddling a canoe. This is a simple definition; it fixes the concept in readers' minds.
2. Divide the concept into its parts—canoe and paddle.
   Canoe: show a diagram of the canoe, labeling bow, stern, thwarts, gunwales, seats, and so on. Explain how each of these parts functions toward the overall performance of the canoe.
   Paddle: show a diagram of a paddle, labeling grip, shaft, and blade. Show how to hold the paddle. Explain how each part functions toward the overall performance of the paddle.
3. Explain how the paddle and canoe work together. Show diagrams of strokes and their effects on the movement of the canoe.

By fleshing out this outline with explanations and diagrams, you ⁷ would give your readers a fair idea of how to paddle a canoe. If, however, you were to begin your explanation with a description of a paddle—as I used to do—your readers would have no *context* in which to place the explanation. This is the key to describing technical information to a nontechnical audience: by working your way down the hierarchy, you give readers a context into which they can place each new piece of information.

The hierarchies of many concepts are not so easy to spot as that ⁸ of paddling a canoe. You cannot simply look at a concept and *shazam!* determine its parts in their correct order. To discover these parts you have to do plenty of brainstorming, freewriting, rewriting, and just plain stumbling around. (I perceived the hierarchy in canoe paddling only in the midst of splashing water, banging aluminum, and shouting people—an extremely nonlinear method of discovery.)

But after you have discovered the hierarchy—and you should use any means available to do this—your *presentation* will be much clearer if you follow a logical sequence.

9   The piece of writing that follows is an introductory chapter from a manual I wrote for Digital Equipment Corporation. It describes how to use a software product called DECpage, which is a system that typesets text and prints it on a laser printer. The three drafts show how I tried to explain the concepts of DECpage in a hierarchical fashion, and how I used certain devices to do this. A discussion of these devices follows the final draft.

FIRST DRAFT

What is DECpage?

DECpage is a text-processing system that produces typeset, paginated text on the ~~velro~~ laser printer. ——— too much like B.C./A.D.

[Before DECpage,] If you wanted to typeset text, you had to go through ——— vague
a [laborious, lengthy process.] You had to type your text on a
typewriter or word processor and take it to a typesetter, who retyped
it all into his or her computerized text composition system. In this
step the typesetter also had to type in a lot of lengthy markup
commands to tell the composition system how to format the text. This ——— The steps are all here, but it's not as
step ended when the composed text came out of the phototypesetter in   clear as it could be. Make a list?
the form of typeset galley. The typesetter then sent the galley to
the printer, who ran off the necessary number of copies on a printing
press.

This process was labor-intensive, time-consuming, and hence, very ——— Weak — doesn't really convey the
expensive. With DECpage, you don't have to go through all this. You   power the text has.
simply type your text on a Digital word processor, and DECpage
handles the rest. It's easier, quicker, and cheaper.

[From your point of view,] DECpage has two main [components: text] you ——— Sounds condescending, or like I'm
type in and text DECpage prints out. There are two concepts you need   hiding something.
to learn to use DECpage: keying conventions and styles.   not really parallel — try to get across
                                                                            impact of concept without sounding technical

What are Keying Conventions?

Every document can be subdivided into its component parts. For
instance, a report is made up of chapters, a chapter is made up of
paragraphs, headings, tables, lists, and so on. We can recognize ——— gives a non-computer touch, but it's
these and other components in any piece of text, [whether it be a   not really necessary. But should I
technical manual, a novel, or a magazine article.]   give up the friendly touch to gain efficiency?

By following certain keying conventions, you enable DECpage to ——— Something feels wrong here. The info is
recognize certain text components and format your documents   there but it seems clunky. Is there a
accordingly. When DECpage recognizes the convention for a list, for   way to present it in a "snappier"?
instance, it formats the text that follows as a list. DECpage
continues to format text as a list until it encounters a different
convention. By using the conventions for paragraphs, lists, and ——— gets off the track — gets into the
other text components, you enable DECpage to format your text   next section too early.
according to a certain style. You need not be concerned with the
style of the document while you are creating it, however. With
DECpage, you can concentrate on the content of your document and let
the software worry about the style. ——— Because I got off the track with the
                                          style stuff, this sentence seems just
The following chapter explains keying conventions more fully. ———   thrown in.

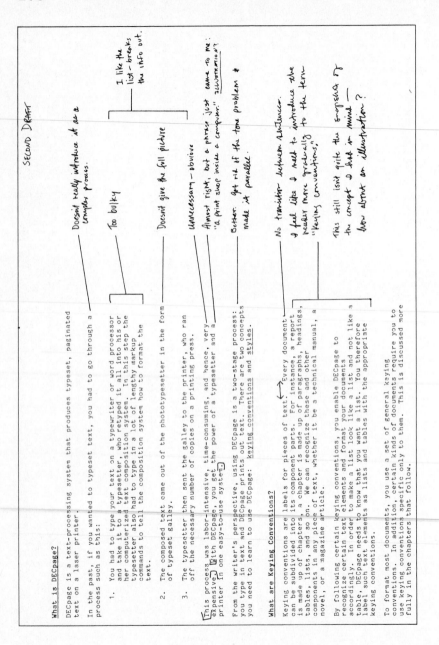

SECOND DRAFT

What is DECpage?

DECpage is a text-processing system that produces typeset, paginated text on a laser printer.

In the past, if you wanted to typeset text, you had to go through a process such as this:

1. You had to type your text on a typewriter or word processor and take it to a typesetter, who retyped it all into his or her computerized text composition system. In this step the typesetter also had to type in a lot of lengthy markup commands to tell the composition system how to format the text.

2. The composed text came out of the phototypesetter in the form of typeset galley.

3. The typesetter then sent the galley to the printer, who ran off the necessary number of copies on a printing press.

This process was labor-intensive, time-consuming, and hence, very expensive. With DECpage, you get the power of a typesetter and a printer in one easy-to-use system.

From the writer's perspective, using DECpage is a two-stage process: you type in text and DECpage prints out text. There are two concepts you need to learn to use DECpage: keying conventions and styles.

What are Keying Conventions?

Keying conventions are labels for pieces of text. Every document can be subdivided into its component parts. For instance, a report is made up of chapters, a chapter is made up of paragraphs, headings, tables, lists, and so on. We can recognize these and other components in any piece of text, whether it be a technical manual, a novel, or a magazine article.

By following certain keying conventions, you enable DECpage to recognize certain text elements and format your documents accordingly. In order to make a list look like a list and not like a table, DECpage needs to know that you want a list. You therefore label such text elements as lists and tables with the appropriate keying conventions.

To format most documents, you use a set of general keying conventions. In addition, certain kinds of documents require you to use keying conventions specific only to them. This is discussed more fully in the chapters that follow.

Handwritten annotations:

Doesn't really introduce it as a complex process.

Too bulky ⎤
⎦ I like the list — breaks the info out.

Doesn't give the full picture

Unnecessary — obvious

Almost right, but a phrase just came to me: "A print shop inside a computer." Illustration?

Better. Get rid of the tone problem & made it parallel.

No transition between sentences.

I feel like I need to introduce the reader more gradually to the term "keying conventions."

This still isn't quite the emphasis I have in mind — the concept I had in mind — how about an illustration?

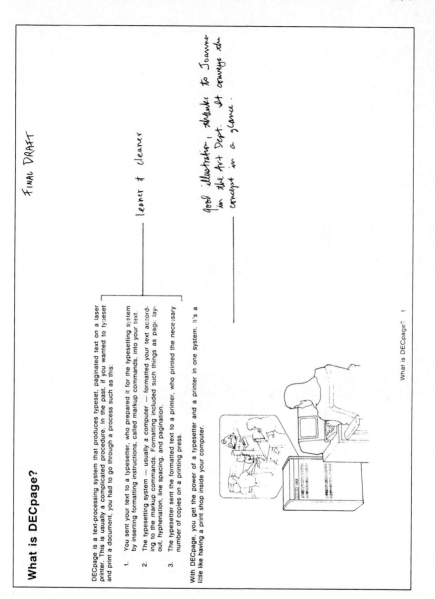

FINAL DRAFT

leaner & cleaner

Good illustration, thanks to Joanne in the Art Dept. It conveys the concept in a glance.

What is DECpage?

DECpage is a text-processing system that produces typeset, paginated text on a laser printer. This is usually a complicated procedure. In the past, if you wanted to typeset and print a document, you had to go through a process such as this:

1. You sent your text to a typesetter, who prepared it for the typesetting system by inserting formatting instructions, called markup commands, into your text.

2. The typesetting system — usually a computer — formatted your text according to the markup commands. Formatting included such things as page layout, hyphenation, line spacing, and pagination.

3. The typesetter sent the formatted text to a printer, who printed the necessary number of copies on a printing press.

With DECpage, you get the power of a typesetter and a printer in one system. It's a little like having a print shop inside your computer.

What is DECpage? 1

Using DECpage is a two-stage process:

1. Creating a document with DECpage keying conventions
2. Printing the document

The following two sections give an overview of DECpage keying conventions and styles. The next chapter, Creating DECpage Documents, gives a more detailed explanation of keying conventions. The final chapter shows how to print DECpage documents.

What are Keying Conventions?

In order to format your text correctly, DECpage needs to know how you want it to look. For instance, to make a paragraph look like a paragraph and not like a list, DECpage needs to know that you want a paragraph. You must, in effect, tag your text with labels that say "This is a paragraph" or "This is a list."

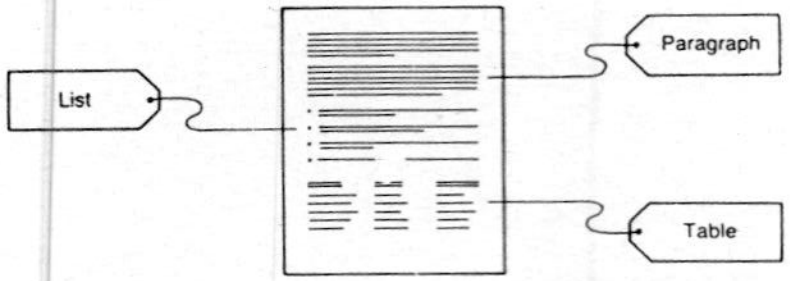

For the most part, you do this already. Think of how you start a new paragraph on a word processor. You probably type two RETURNs. That is, as you finish one paragraph and start a new one, you press RETURN twice at the end of the first paragraph and then continue typing. The second RETURN puts a blank line into your text to signal a new paragraph.

You do the same thing with DECpage. DECpage recognizes two RETURNs as the start of a new paragraph. When you use specific key sequences to "label" text, you are following certain keying conventions.

You use established keying conventions all the time to create such things as lists, tables, and headings. For instance, when you denote headings in a report by underlining them, you are following the keying conventions for headings in that particular report. In another report, you might bold the headings, or you might use a combination of underlining and bolding to denote different levels of headings. Whatever the case, you use keying conventions to achieve the effects you want.

What is DECpage?   2

Handwritten margin annotations:

This is simpler — break the unit into a list, which provides a more immediate conceptual grasp.

Illustration supplements the text to get the concept across.

A concrete example backs up the illustration.

And then ties the concept to the term "keying conventions."

What is DECpage?

DECpage is a text-processing system that produces typeset, paginated text on a laser printer. This is usually a complicated procedure. In the past, if you wanted to typeset and print a document, you had to go through a process such as this:

1. You sent your text to a typesetter, who prepared it for the typesetting system by inserting formatting instructions, called markup commands, into your text.

2. The typesetting system — usually a computer — formatted your text according to the markup commands. Formatting included such things as page layout, hyphenation, line spacing, and pagination.

3. The typesetter sent the formatted text to a printer, who printed the necessary number of copies on a printing press.

With DECpage, you get the power of a typesetter and a printer in one system. It's a little like having a print shop inside your computer.

What is DECpage?   1

Using DECpage is a two-stage process:

1.   Creating a document with DECpage keying conventions
2.   Printing the document

The following two sections give an overview of DECpage keying conventions and styles. The next chapter, Creating DECpage Documents, gives a more detailed explanation of keying conventions. The final chapter shows how to print DECpage documents.

What are Keying Conventions?

In order to format your text correctly, DECpage needs to know how you want it to look. For instance, to make a paragraph look like a paragrph and not like a list, DECpage needs to know that you want a paragraph. You must, in effect, tag your text with labels that say "This is a paragraph" or "This is a list."

For the most part, you do this already. Think of how you start a new paragraph on a word processor. You probably type two RETURNs. That is, as you finish one paragraph and start a new one, you press RETURN twice at the end of the first paragraph and then continue typing. The second RETURN puts a blank line into your text to signal a new paragraph.

You do the same thing with DECpage. DECpage recognizes two RETURNs as the start of a new paragraph. When you use specific key sequences to "label" text, you are following certain *keying conventions*.

You use established keying conventions all the time to create such things as lists, tables, and headings. For instance, when you denote headings in a report by underlining them, you are following the keying conventions for headings in that particular report. In another report, you might bold the headings, or you might use a combination of underlining and bolding to denote different levels of headings. Whatever the case, you use keying conventions to achieve the effects you want.

A Technical Writer's Toolkit

The preceding excerpt attempts to communicate a fairly tech- 10
nical computer concept to a nontechnical audience. To do this, the
technical writer usually has to present information in the hierarchical
fashion described earlier. There are several devices to help with this
job, including:

- Headings
- Analogies
- Illustrations
- Examples
- Lists
- Tables

The following sections discuss each of these. 11

Headings—One of the most obvious ways to direct readers 12
through the hierarchy of a concept is with headings. In the sample
chapter, there is one main heading and two subheadings:

What is DECpage?
What are Keying Conventions?
What are Styles?

The structure of the chapter, and hence its hierarchical orga- 13
nization, is obvious: DECpage is the overriding concept, and keying
conventions and styles are the components that constitute it. By
quickly scanning the headings, readers see that the overall concept
is explained first, and that two supporting concepts are also
explained.

In this sample, I phrased the headings as questions because I 14
figured these would be foremost in readers' minds. If readers see
their own questions laid out in headings, they assume answers will
appear in the text. They begin to trust the piece of writing. This is
always a primary concern in writing about computer software: people
have a lot of anxiety, mistrust, and insecurity about computers; it is
usually up to the written material—called *documentation*—to allay
these feelings.

Analogies—It often helps to describe a technical concept in eas- 15
ily recognizable terms. Analogies work well for this. Consider the
print shop analogy from the sample. By explaining the traditional
process of typesetting and printing a document, and then telling
readers that a similar process goes on inside their computers, I

defined the concept of DECpage. The reader then had a context into which all other information would fit.

16   *Illustrations*—Illustrations provide a "snapshot" of a concept. We are visual as well as verbal beings, so many times a simple picture can help us envision a concept that might take several paragraphs to explain. The first illustration in the sample reinforces the print shop analogy by providing a visual image of the concept. The second illustration does the same thing for the concept of keying conventions.

17   *Examples*—As in any kind of writing, specific examples are essential to give readers a concrete grasp of a concept. If, after defining a concept by analogy and/or illustration, you follow with a specific example of the concept, you marry the *idea* of the concept to the real thing. For example, look at the paragraph immediately after the illustration of keying conventions. With the illustration in front of them, readers get a concrete example of a keying convention: typing two RETURNs to begin a paragraph.

18   *Lists*—Another device that communicates concepts is the list. In most kinds of writing, when we need to list a few items, we simply list them in a sentence and separate them with commas or semicolons. In technical writing we use a vertical list, which separates the items more clearly. For example, consider the following list:

19   *DECpage allows you to typeset and print three types of letters, including block letters, the most common style in business correspondence; modified block letters, also a business style but less frequently used; and informal letters, used in personal correspondence.*

20   Compare that paragraph with the following vertical list:
DECpage allows you to typeset and print three types of letters:

- Block letters—most common style in business correspondence
- Modified block letters—also a business style, but less frequently used
- Informal letters—a style for personal correspondence

21   The information in the vertical list is clearly more accessible than that in the paragraph. Notice again that the information is broken into a hierarchy, and that the parts of the hierarchy are presented in logical sequence.

22   *Tables*—Tables also help break information into parts that are

easily grasped. In this manual on DECpage, I wanted to provide a way for readers to fix problems they might have in printing their documents. What should they do, for instance, when they pick up their letter or memo from the laser printer, and the paragraphs run into each other or are too narrow? If I could provide a guide to problem solving, readers would be less confused and frustrated when they had problems. I started doing this in conventional paragraph form:

> *If your paragraphs run into each other, it is because you didn't insert* 23
> *the paragraph convention at the beginning of a new paragraph. To fix*
> *this problem, simply insert two RETURNs between paragraphs.*

> *If your paragraph margins are too narrow, it is because the* 24
> *paragraph is preceded by a list or table with narrower paragraphs,*
> *and the convention to end the list or table is missing. To fix this*
> *problem, reset the ruler at the end of the list or table.*

The problems and their solutions were there, but they weren't 25 as obvious as they could have been. The paragraphs seemed dense, and I worried about losing readers in thickets of words—not a very good way to solve their problems. Then I remembered my Volkswagen repair manual—it contained a troubleshooting guide that had broken the information into logical blocks. I looked it up, and applied the technique to my manual. The result is a chapter called Troubleshooting, a long table that looks like this:

Symptom	Possible Cause	Suggested Solution
Paragraphs run into each other.	Paragraph convention wasn't inserted between paragraphs	Insert two RETURNs between paragraphs.
Paragraph margins are too narrow.	Paragraph is preceded by a list or table with narrower paragraphs, and the convention to end the list or table is missing.	Reset the ruler at the end of the list or table.

Thinking on a Straight Course

We've heard a lot about the coming of the "Information Age." 26 Well, it's here. But information can only have value if it is transmitted from a source to a terminus, and we as writers are often cast in the role of transmitter. We fill this role whether we are teachers, reporters, business managers, real estate agents, biological researchers, or graphic artists. And we don't do it only on the job. We must communicate information to spouses, parents, postal clerks, insurance agents, and auto mechanics. We will be more successful on our jobs and in our private lives if we not only *communicate* logically and clearly, but also *think* that way.

27   I have never seen an analysis of the kinds of thinking that go on in the human mind, so I can only hypothesize on the test subject I know best. For every ordered, structured idea I have, there are hundreds—thousands—that are scattered, fuzzy, or somehow muddled enough to keep me from using them in a productive way. I realize that sometimes, in order to be productive, thoughts should be free-ranging and unencumbered by structure—while writing fiction or poetry, for example. Or during the beginning stages of any kind of writing. And without daydream, fantasy, and imagination, we would cease to be what we consider human. But for handling many kinds of day-to-day information, I work best if I can apply the kind of logical, hierarchical analysis I've discussed here.

28   It doesn't come easy. Overcoming chaos demands work. One of the best ways I've found to think logically is to write logically. It is practice for logical thought, so when I discuss my job performance with my boss or argue about a parking ticket with the town clerk or explain paddling a canoe to a novice, I can better communicate my ideas.

Discussion

- Compare the kind of directed, practical writing that Freda does with the critical writing of Lindberg and Ellison. What do each have to teach the other?
- List the forms of writing you have to do in school and apply the lessons Freda has to teach to those tasks.
- Investigate the kind of writing you will have to do on the job after you graduate. Apply Freda's techniques to those writing tasks.
- Consider what typographical techniques you can use to make your meaning clear. Remember that writers are influenced by how they see writing on the page.

- Using Freda as a beginning point, make a class checklist to help you make a complicated subject clear. Discuss the checklist in terms of the kind of writing you and your classmates have to do in school and out.
- Discuss how the writing tasks of the technical writer are similar and different from writers in other genre.
- Discuss what we can all learn from technical writers.
- Bring a manual or a computer or a software program to class. Compare it to Freda's pages. Decide what works and what needs work.

Activities

- Take part of a technical subject you know well (how to sit in a chair if you're a nontechnical person like myself) and give clear instructions to a person who has never done it before.
- Take a page that you have written previously and see if you can apply Freda's techniques to it.
- Take a technical manual for a computer, car repair, setting of a digital watch, hi-fi assembly, whatever, and apply Freda's techniques to increase its clarity.
- Take a process from the McPhee or Whiteside article and use Freda's techniques to tell someone how to perform that process.
- Rewrite Freda's instructions in normal prose style to see which form is most effective.

Richard Selzer

Richard Selzer is a practicing surgeon and a professor at Yale Medical School, who writes of surgery from the point of view of an insider. His powerful essays and short stories are collected in *Letters to a Young Doctor*, from which the following selection is taken, and *Rituals of Surgery, Mortal Lessons: Notes on the Art of Surgery,* and *Confessions of a Knife.* If you have trouble finding time to write, consider his schedule. "I go to bed early—9 o'clock—and wake up without an alarm clock at 1 in the morning and write from 1 to 3," Selzer says. "Then I go to sleep until 6. I keep to this regimen unless there is a family commitment." It is clear that Selzer writes as a means to explore his experience, to try to discover meaning in what he sees and does in the operating room. He says, "One sits down and writes a sentence and then one writes another. I, for one, don't know where I'm going." Because of his explorations the reader has the opportunity to go into the mind of the surgeon and follow that mind as it tries to order experience into meaning.

Letter To A Young Surgeon III

1   All Right. You fainted in the operating room, had to go sit on the floor in a corner and put your head down. You are making altogether too much of it. You have merely announced your humanity. Only the gods do not faint at the sight of the MYSTERIUM TREMENDUM; they have too jaded a glance. At the same place in the novitiate I myself more than once slid ungracefully to the floor in the middle of things. It is less a sign of weakness than an expression of guilt. A flinching in the face of the forbidden.

2   The surgeon is an explorer in the tropical forest of the body. Now and then he reaches up to bring closer one of the wondrous fruits he sees there. Before he departs this place, he knows that he must pluck one of them. He knows, too, that it is forbidden to do so. But it is a trophy, no, a SPOIL that has been demanded of him by his patron, the patient, who has commissioned and outfitted him for this exploration. At last the surgeon holds the plucked organ in his hand, but he is never wholly at ease. For what man does not grow shy, fearful, before the occult uncovered?

3   Don't worry. The first red knife is the shakiest. This is as true for the assassin as it is for the surgeon. The assassin's task is easier, for he is more likely to be a fanatic. And nothing steadies the hand like zeal. The surgeon's work is madness icily reined in to a good purpose. Still I know that it is perverse to relieve pain by inflicting it. This requires that the patient give over to you his free will and his trust. It is too much to ask. Yet we do every day, and with the arrogance born of habit and custom, and grown casual, even charming.

✏ Pay attention to his voice and how he uses that voice to take you inside the experience of surgery. And then notice the ways in which he puts that experience in context. He never forgets how unnatural it is to commit surgery. This is one of the ways that the piece develops density and is much more than a superficial account of surgery.🖋

"Come, lie down on this table," you say, and smile. Your voice is soft and reasonable.   4

"Where will you cut me open?" the patient asks. And he grips   5 his belly as though he and it were orphan twins awaiting separate adoption. The patient's voice is NOT calm; it trembles and quavers.

"From here . . . to here," you reply, and you draw a fingernail   6 across his shuddering flesh. His navel leaps like a flushed bird. Oh, God! He has heard the knell of disembowelment. You really DO mean to do it! And you do, though not with the delectation that will be attributed to you by those who do not do this work.

The cadaver toward which I have again and again urged you is   7 like an abundant nest from which the birds have long since flown. It is a dry, uninhabited place—already dusty. It is a "thing" that the medical student will pull apart and examine, seeking evidence, clues from which he can reconstruct the life that once flourished there. The living patient is a nest in which a setting bird huddles. She quivers, but does not move when you press aside leaves in order to see better. Your slightest touch frightens her. You hold your breath and let the leaves spring back to conceal her. You want so much for her to trust you.

In order to do good works throughout his lifetime, a man must   8 strive ever higher to carry out his benefices; he must pray, defer pleasure and steel himself against temptation. And against fainting. The committing of surgery grows easier and easier, it seems, until the practice is second nature. Come, come! You fainted! Why don't you admit that you are imperfect, and that you strain to appeal to yourself and to others? Surgery is, in one sense, a judicious contrivance, like poetry. But . . . it is an elect life, here among the ranting machinery and brazen lamps of the operating room, where on certain days now the liquidity of the patient reminds me of the drought that is attacking my own flesh. Listen, I will tell you what you already know: There is nothing like an honest piece of surgery. Say what you will, there is nothing more satisfying to the spirit than . . . the lancing of a boil!

Behold the fierce, hot protuberance compressing the howling   9 nerves about it. You sound it with your fingers. A light tap brings back a malevolent answering wave, and a groan from the patient. Now the questing knife rides your hand. Go! And across the swelling gallops a thin red line. Again! Deeper, plowing. All at once there lifts a wave of green mud. Suddenly the patient's breathing comes more easily, his tense body relaxes, he smiles. For him it is like being touched by the hand of God. It is a simple act, requiring not a flicker of intellect nor a whisker of logic. To outwit disease it takes a peasant's cunning, not abstract brilliance. It is like the felling of a tree for firewood. Yet not poetry, nor music nor mathematics can bring such gladness, for riding out upon that wave of pus has come the black barque of pain. Just so will you come to love the boils and tumors of your patients.

10   I shall offer you two antidotes to fainting in the operating room.

11   1. Return as often as possible to the Anatomy Laboratory. As the sculptor must gain unlimited control over his marble, the surgeon must "own" the flesh. As drawing is to the painter, so is anatomy to the surgeon. You must continue to dissect for the rest of your life. To raise a flap of skin, to trace out a nerve to its place of confluence, to carry a tendon to its bony insertion, these are things of grace and beauty. They are simple, nontheoretical, workaday acts which, if done again and again, will give rise to that profound sense of structure that is the birthplace of intuition.

12   It is only at the dissecting table that you can find the models of your art. Only there that you will internalize the structure and form of the body so that any variations or anomalies or unforeseen circumstances are not later met with dismay and surprise. Unlike the face, the internal organs bear a remarkable sameness to one another. True, there are differences in the size of normal kidneys, livers and spleens, and there are occasional odd lobulations and unusual arrangements of ducts and vessels, but by and large, one liver is very like another. A kidney is a kidney. Unlike a face, it bears no distinctive mark or expression that would stamp it as the kidney of Napoleon Bonaparte, say, or Herman Melville. It is this very sameness that makes of surgery a craft that can be perfected by repetition and industry. Therefore, return to the Anatomy Laboratory. Revere and follow your prosector. The worship and awe you show the cadavers will come back to you a thousandfold. Even now, such an old knife as I goes to that place to dissect, to probe, to delve. What is an operating room but a prosectorium that has been touched into life?

13   2. Do not be impatient to wield the scalpel. To become a surgeon is a gradual, imperceptible, subtle transformation. Do not hurry from the side of the one who instructs you, but stay with your "master" until he bids you to go. It is his office to warm you with his

words, on rounds and in the operating room, to color the darkness and shade the brilliance of light until you have grown strong enough to survive. Then, yes, leave him, for no sapling can grow to fullness in the shade of a big tree.

Do these things that I have told you and you will not faint in 14 the operating room. I do not any longer faint, nor have I for thirty years. But now and then, upon leaving the hospital after a long and dangerous operation has been brought to a successful close, I stroke the walls of the building as though it were a faithful animal that has behaved itself well.

Discussion

- Discuss how Selzer, by going so deeply into his subject, establishes a universality. Consider how the piece could be written as a letter to a young soldier, teacher, salesman, lawyer, carpenter, mother, father, farmer, pilot, writer.
- Think of other ways the piece could be organized around an incident or a single operation, for example.
- Consider the language he uses and whether or not the words with which we are not familiar are clear in the context he establishes.
- Consider techniques other than personal, human experience a writer can use to make a technical subject clear to the general reader.
- Note the ways in which the author establishes his authority to speak on this subject.

Activities

- Take a job or a skill you know and write a letter of advice to someone just starting out in the same area.
- Choose a technical subject with which you are familiar and make it clear to someone who does not know the subject.
- List the ways an author can establish authority within a text, using a specific subject on which you are an authority.
- Outline three other ways Selzer could have organized his essay. Outline three other ways you could organize one of your own essays.
- Rewrite a few paragraphs of the essay from the point of view of the young doctor, the patient, or a nurse observing the doctor.

William Zinsser

William Zinsser is the author of one of the best books on writing I have ever read, and he practices what he preaches in *On Writing Well*. He has published seven books; was a newspaper columnist for the New York *Herald Tribune*, a "writer's" newspaper that set high standards for journalism; was also a columnist for *Life* and *Look*; is a successful editor, yet he is still learning. One of the reasons I am proud to be a writer is that you can be a member of a community of people who never stop learning.

When the following piece was first published in *The New Yorker*, I wrote a letter to Bill congratulating him on a job well done, and received a letter that included the following paragraph. This is no old pro speaking, tired and bitter in middle age, but a writer still young, still full of enthusiasm about writing.

> *I really value your comments about "Shanghai Blues" because it pleased me as much as anything I've ever done. Writing it taught me some interesting lessons. Though it was unusually long and complex in structure, I wrote it faster and more easily than any piece I can remember. The reason, I think, is that I was very close emotionally to the material: to both Willie and Dwike and to their music and their work as teachers and what they were doing in China. Moral: write about what you feel strongly about, or what is most personal. The other lesson is that the piece was perhaps 1,000 words longer when I wrote it. What Shawn [The New Yorker editor] took out was the stuff that was in fact most personal—it explained how I happened to know both men and what my emotional commitment to them was. In other words, he took me out of the piece as a person and left me in as a reporter, and I was afraid that the reader would need and miss this material. As it turned out, readers found the piece tremendously moving emotionally, and many found themselves crying near the end; quite a few said that it was obvious that I knew these two men very well. Moral: lay the facts in as cleanly and coherently as possible, and the emotions will take care of themselves. Or: trust your material. This discovery came as a complete and delightful surprise to me (though you undoubtedly know it well as a principle), and it has changed my thinking about writing ever since.*

Shanghai

Jazz came to China for the first time on the afternoon of June 1
2, 1981, when the American bassist and French-horn player Willie
Ruff introduced himself and his partner, the pianist Dwike Mitchell,
to several hundred students and professors who were crowded into
a large room at the Shanghai Conservatory of Music. The students
and the professors were all expectant, without knowing quite what
to expect. They only knew that they were about to hear the first
American jazz concert ever presented to the Chinese. Probably they
were not surprised to find that the two musicians were black, though
black Americans are a rarity in the People's Republic. What they
undoubtedly didn't expect was that Ruff would talk to them in
Chinese, and when he began they murmured with delight.

Ruff is a lithe, dapper man in his early fifties who takes visible 2
pleasure in sharing his enthusiasms, and it was obvious that there was
no place he would rather have been than in China's oldest conservatory, bringing the music of his people to still another country
deprived of that commodity. In 1959 he and Mitchell—who have
played together as the Mitchell-Ruff Duo for almost thirty years—
introduced jazz to the Soviet Union, and for that occasion Ruff taught
himself Russian, his seventh language. In 1979 he hit on the idea of
making a similar trip to China, and he began taking intensive courses
in Chinese at Yale, where he is a professor of music and of Afro-
American studies. By the winter of 1981 he felt that he was fluent
enough in Mandarin to make the trip.

❧ Most beginning writers write what we call the breakfast-to-bed
story, starting the account of the fishing trip with the ring of the
alarm clock. Zinsser could have started with the invitation to go to
China or Ruff packing his bags. Instead, he takes the reader right
into the heart of the China trip in the first paragraph. Then when
the reader is interested puts the first paragraph in context, bringing
in the exposition the reader needs to know to understand what is
going on. And then in the third paragraph continues the account of
this one concert. The piece will end with the end of that concert,
and Zinsser will use the device of that one concert to keep the
reader interested, filling in whatever else the reader needs to know
or what Zinsser wants the reader to know. ❧

Now Ruff stood at the front of the room surveying the Chinese 3
faces. He looked somewhat like an Oriental sage himself—or at least

like the traditional carving of one; he is the color of old ivory, with a bald head and the beginnings of a Mandarin beard. He was holding several sheets of paper on which he had written, in Chinese characters, what he wanted to tell his listeners about the origins of jazz.

4   "In the last three hundred and fifty years," he began, "black people in America have created a music that is a rich contribution to Western culture. Of course three hundred and fifty years, compared to the long and distinguished history of Chinese music, seems like only a moment. But please remember that the music of American black people is an amalgam whose roots are deep in African history and also that it has taken many characteristics from the music of Europe."

5   Ruff has an amiable voice, and as he declaimed the first sentences, relishing the swoops and cadences of his latest adopted language, he had already established contact with the men and women in the room. They were attentive but relaxed—not an audience straining to decipher a foreigner's accent.

6   "In Africa the drum is the most important musical instrument," Ruff went on. "But to me the intriguing thing is that the people also use their drums to talk. Please imagine that the drum method of speech is so exquisite that Africans can, without recourse to words, recite proverbs, record history and send long messages. The drum is to West African society what the book is to literate society."

7   I wondered what the audience would make of that. Not only was China the oldest of literate societies, we were in the one Asian city that was encrusted with Western thought as transmitted in books, in journals and in musical notation—a city whose symphony orchestra, when it was founded in 1922, consisted entirely of Europeans. Even the architecture of Shanghai was a patchwork of Western shapes—a residue of the days when the city had a huge foreign population and was divided into districts that were controlled by different European countries. At the conservatory we were in the former French concession, and its main building was in a red brick French provincial style, with a sloping red tile roof and a porte cochere. Another French-style building housed the conservatory's library of one hundred thousand books about music—definitely not the oral tradition. Newer buildings served as classrooms and practice rooms, and the music that eddied out of their windows was the dreary fare of Western academic rigor: vocal scales endlessly rising, piano arpeggios repeated until they were mastered, chamber groups starting and stopping and starting again. We could have been in Vienna of the

nineties or Paris of the twenties. In any case, we were a long way from Africa. And we were farther still from music created spontaneously.

"In the seventeenth century," Ruff continued, "when West 8 Africans were captured and brought to America as slaves, they brought their drums with them. But the slave owners were afraid of the drum because it was so potent; it could be used to incite the slaves to revolt. So they outlawed the drum. This very shrewd law had a tremendous effect on the development of black people's music. Our ancestors had to develop a variety of drum substitutes. One of them, for example, was tap dancing—I'm sure you've all heard of that. Now I'd like to show you a drum substitute that you probably don't know about, one that uses the hands and the body to make rhythm. It's called hambone."

There was no translating "hambone" into Mandarin—the odd 9 word hung in the air. But Ruff quickly had an intricate rhythm going, slapping himself with the palms of his hands and smacking his open mouth to create a series of resonating pops. Applause greeted this proof that the body could be its own drum.

"By the time jazz started to develop," Ruff went on, "all African 10 instruments in America had disappeared. So jazz borrowed the instruments of Western music, like the ones we're playing here today." He went over to his own instrument, the bass, and showed how he used it as a percussion instrument by picking the strings with his fingers instead of playing them with a bow. "Only this morning," he said, "I gave a lesson to your distinguished professor of bass, and he is already *very good.*"

Moving from rhythm to terrain that was more familiar to his 11 listeners, he pointed out that jazz took its structural elements from European harmony. "Mr. Mitchell will now give you an example of the music that American slaves found in the Christian churches— Protestant hymns that had been brought from Europe. Slaves were encouraged to embrace Christianity and to use its music. Please listen."

Mitchell played an old Protestant hymn. "The slaves adopted 12 these harmonies and transformed them into their own very emotional spirituals," Ruff said. "Mr. Mitchell and I will sing you a famous Negro spiritual from the days of slavery. It's called 'My Lord, What a Morning.'" With Mitchell playing a joyful accompaniment, the two men sang five or six choruses of the lovely old song, Mitchell carrying the melody in his deep voice, Ruff taking the higher second part. The moment, musically beautiful, had an edge of faraway sadness. I couldn't help thinking of another alien culture onto which the Protestant hymns of Europe had once been strenuously grafted. It was just beyond the conservatory gates.

13   "Mr. Mitchell will now show you how the piano can be used as a substitute for the instruments of the orchestra," Ruff said. "Please notice that he uses his left hand to play the bass and also to make his rhythm section. Later he will use his right hand to play the main melody and to fill in the harmony. This style is called ragtime." Mitchell struck up a jaunty rag. The students perked up at the playful pattern of the notes. Ruff looked out at his class and beamed. The teacher in him was beginning to slip away, the musician in him was tugging at his sleeve and telling him to start the concert.

14   I have known Willie Ruff and Dwike Mitchell since 1973, when I became master of Branford College at Yale. Ruff also lived in the college, as a resident fellow. He had recently persuaded Yale to hold a convocation at which forty of America's greatest black musicians were honored and were named Duke Ellington Fellows. They included Ellington himself, Dizzy Gillespie, Odetta, Charlie Mingus, Benny Carter, Slam Stewart, Bessie Jones, William Warfield, Marian Anderson, Roland Hayes, Paul Robeson, Honi Coles—in short, the pantheon of black composers, instrumentalists, arrangers, singers and dancers.

15   Ruff's idea had two components. One was that Yale should recognize "the conservatory without walls," as he calls the informal system whereby black musicians hand their heritage down. The other was that the Ellington Fellows would come to New Haven periodically to play for Yale students and for the pupils of the city's predominantly black public schools. Over the subsequent years Ruff shepherded these giants through our lives. First they would give a concert for New Haven schoolchildren in a Yale auditorium; then Ruff would trot them into his own classes and out to various city schools. The musicians, far from wilting, blossomed. Their life work had been almost obliterated by three social forces that coincided in the 1960s: the rise of rock, the death of nightclubs because of television, and the exclusion of black performers from network TV. Now they were old and the hour was late. Facing a generation that didn't even know they existed, they summoned ancient reserves of energy and skill.

16   While Ruff's stars came and went, the same person was always at the piano—a large black man with a shy smile, who never said

anything and didn't have to. His piano said it all. However disparate the visiting musicians might be, he was sensitive to their tradition. Dwike Mitchell was the best jazz pianist I had heard in all my years of listening to pianists I admired—especially Cy Walter, Bill Evans, Oscar Peterson, Dave Brubeck, Billy Taylor and George Shearing—and trying to find their sophisticated chords on my own piano. Micthell's harmonies were elegant and stunning, his technique was awesome, his taste was impeccable. I became a Mitchell addict. Whenever he came up from New York to play with Ruff in a concert or a class I was there, sitting where I could watch his big and miraculous hands.

But what gave me my affection for Mitchell and Ruff was that they seemed to be under some moral persuasion to pass their experience along. I wanted to know who had stamped this idea on them. What teachers had crossed their own lives when they were growing up in small Southern towns? 17

They met in 1947 when they were servicemen at Lockbourne Air Force Base, outside Columbus, Ohio. Mitchell then seventeen and a pianist in the unit band, needed an accompanist, and he gave the newly arrived Ruff, a sixteen-year-old French-horn player, a crash course in playing the bass. Thus the Mitchell-Ruff Duo was unofficially born. When they were discharged they followed separate paths and lost contact. Mitchell went to the Philadelphia Musical Academy. Ruff went to the Yale School of Music, where he studied with Paul Hindemith. Venturing out with his master's degree in 1954, he was told that no American symphony orchestra would hire a black musician, and he accepted an offer to join the Tel Aviv Symphony as first French horn. Shortly before he was to leave he happened to turn his television set on to *The Ed Sullivan Show*. Lionel Hampton's band was playing, and as the camera panned over to the piano Ruff saw a familiar figure at the keyboard. Mitchell, it turned out, had been Hampton's pianist for the past two years. Ruff telephoned him backstage at the CBS studio; Mitchell hinted at imminent vacancies in the brass section. A few days later Israel lost—and Hampton got—a superb French horn. 18

The Mitchell-Ruff Duo—"the oldest continuous group in jazz without personnel changes," Ruff says—was officially formed in 1955 when the two men left Hampton and struck out on their own. They were booked regularly by the major nightclubs as the second act with the great bands of the day: Louis Armstrong, Duke Ellington, Dizzy Gillespie, Miles Davis. "They were our mentors," Ruff recalls. 19

"They'd play a set and then we'd play a set and they'd hang around and tell us what we could be doing better. We learned everything from those men. Count Basie's band raised us. In 1956 they were the hottest band in the country—they were the most expensive band and we were the cheapest—and we sold out Birdland every night. One evening Miles Davis brought Billie Holiday in to hear us and we just about fell through the floor. We were just kids."

20   Meanwhile they caught the attention of another group of patrons—one at the opposite end of music's social scale. It was a group of older women in New York who had formed an organization called Young Audiences to introduce elementary school and high school students to chamber music. For their teachers the women chose young professionals who could communicate with words as well as with music, and Mitchell and Ruff were the first people they selected to teach jazz. "It was done," Ruff recalls, "under the supervision of the founders—Mrs. Lionello Perera, a great patron of music, and Mrs. Edgar Leventritt, who started the Leventritt Competition—and Nina Collier and several other ladies who sat on the board. They taught us definite techniques, such as how to catch the attention of children, and they also gave us lessons in grooming and enunciation and conduct. They were very stern and really quite unpleasant, but instructive. Everything they told us turned out to be true."

21   Armed with these graces, Mitchell and Ruff hit the road for Young Audiences, often giving seven or eight performances a day, going from school to school, first in New York and later in Boston, Baltimore and San Francisco. They even did a tour of Indian Schools in New Mexico. The Duo alternated these forays with its stands in Manhattan clubs. Then, in 1959, it made its famous trip to Russia. Ruff arranged the trip himself with Soviet officials after the State Department, which had been trying for two years to get Louis Armstrong into the Soviet Union, declined to help. In Russia the two Americans—playing and teaching for five weeks at conservatories in Leningrad, Moscow, Kiev, Yalta, Sochi and Riga—found a thirst for jazz that surprised even them. When they left Moscow, nine hundred people turned up at the train station to see them off and throw flowers into their compartment. Mitchell, in turn, still remembers being moved by many Russian songs that resembled spirituals he had heard in the black churches of his boyhood. Whether a scholar could find any such link doesn't matter to him; in music he operates on an emotional level that has no need for evidence. "I felt a mysterious bond

between their people and my people," he says. "I think I connected with their suffering."

Not long after that, the house of jazz began to crumble. Television was the new medium and rock the new musical message. "Nightclubs started closing in the very early sixties," Ruff recalls. "The number of jazz performers who quit, died or just disappeared was astounding. Many of them moved to Europe. Three of the greatest rhythm players—Oscar Pettiford, Bud Powell and Kenny Clarke—were living in Paris and playing for peanuts because they couldn't find any work in the United States. How devastating it was for us to play in Europe and see so many of these great men so reduced!" Mitchell and Ruff survived because of their teaching bent. They had caught the attention of two venerable booking agencies, Pryor-Menz and Alkahest, that wanted a young act to give jazz concerts for college audiences and also explain the music, and thereby they found the format—sixty or seventy concerts a year, mainly at colleges—that has been their main source of income to this day.

A new tool came their way in 1967 when CBS Television sent them to Brazil to make a one-hour film tracing the African roots of Brazilian music. Ruff saw the value of film as a teaching device and went back to college to study film. Since then he has visited Bali, Senegal and the Pygmies of the Central African Republic to make films about the drum music and drum language of those societies. He always came back to Yale elated by new rhythmical affinities that he had found among diverse cultures and among seemingly unrelated forms of life. His seminars on rhythm began to make startling connections as he brought Yale professors into them from such disciplines as neurology, geology, limnology, art, English, astronomy, physiology and physics. The professors, in fact, became almost as excited as Ruff.

Maybe I should have guessed that Ruff would want to introduce jazz to China. But his projects always took me by surprise because they reflected still another interest I hadn't known about. He is a man on the move, a listener and a learner, a hustler and a charmer, making his own luck. Mitchell, by contrast, seemed during those years at Yale to be withdrawn and laconic. But when I moved back to New York in 1979 I asked if he would take me on as a student, and he turned out to be a man of great warmth and humor. Still, he is glad to leave life's arrangements to someone who enjoys making them. He stays in his New York apartment, practicing from morning to

night, until Ruff calls and tells him where they are going next. As he
has discovered, it could be Senegal or Shanghai.

25   "If it sounds right to me," he says, "I just tell him, 'O.K., Ruff,
let's go.'"

> ❡ The organization of this piece is so useful it may be a help to
> diagram it. One way to do that would be to turn a page of paper
> longways, put a note at the left that says, "Concert starts," and
> draw a line across the paper. At the end of that say, "Concert
> ends." Then go down a line or two and put a line for the beginning
> and end of the next section, and so on, until you can see this
> pattern. It is important, because most of us want to give the
> background first so the reader will understand what is being written.
> That's logical, but it doesn't work. The reader will not be interested
> in the background unless the reader knows its significance. The
> writer has to find a way to make the reader interested, and then to
> take advantage of that interest. The writer also has to find a way to
> hold the reader's interest. And the narrative, which Zinsser uses, is a
> powerful device to hold interest. This piece deserves careful study
> for its artless appearing yet careful craftsmanship. ❡

26   We flew to Shanghai on a Chinese 747—Ruff walked up and
down the aisles trying out his Chinese on the passengers—and the
next day we called on Professor Tan Shu-chen, deputy director of the
Shanghai Conservatory of Music, who was, so far, our only contact.
Originally, Ruff had sought the sponsorship of the Center for United
States-China Arts Exchange, the group that was sending American
musicians to China, but his letter got no answer. Ruff felt that no
matter how many great American artists went to China—Isaac Stern,
the Boston Symphony Orchestra, Roberta Peters—the music that
they played and sang would be European music. The indigenous
music of America was jazz, and the Chinese had never heard it in a
live performance. (When Ruff asked a Chinese man on the plane
whether his people were familiar with jazz, he said, "Oh, yes, we
know Stephen Foster very well.") Lacking official support, Ruff
decided to go anyway. He booked himself and Mitchell on a two-
week tour to Shanghai and Peking, the two cities that had major conservatories, and then went looking for money. He got a grant from
Coca-Cola that would cover their expenses and the costs of filming
their visit.

27   To have Professor Tan as our host was all that we could have
asked. He had come to New York the previous winter in connection

with the Academy Award-winning film *From Mao to Mozart—Isaac Stern in China*, in which he describes his imprisonment during China's Cultural Revolution. Ruff invited him to visit the Yale School of Music, in the long-range hope of fostering some kind of collaboration that would help both institutions—an exchange of students or teachers or manuscripts between Yale and the Shanghai Conservatory. While Professor Tan was at Yale he attended a class in which Ruff and Mitchell were playing, and he invited them, in turn, to visit his conservatory. That was all that a born improviser needed to hear. Now we were at the conservatory, and Professor Tan was showing us around. He had arranged the jazz concert for the next afternoon.

The Shanghai Conservatory of Music, which was founded in 28 1927 and which prides itself on being part of the cultural conscience of China, has six hundred and fifty students—the youngest are eight years old—and three hundred teachers. Most of the students live on the campus. Quite a few are from Shanghai, but a large number are recruited from all over China by faculty members, who hold regional auditions.

The conservatory has five departments of instruction—piano; 29 voice; strings and winds; composing and conducting; and traditional Chinese instruments—and two of musicology. One of these is a musical research institute. The other, devoted to Chinese traditional and folk music, was recently formed to broaden the conservatory's involvement with the heritage of its own country. But the tilt is definitely Westward. Most of the conservatory's original teachers were Europeans, and many of its graduates have lived in the West and won recognition there. The curriculum, from what I could hear of it, was rooted in Europe: Bach, Scarlatti, Mozart, Beethoven, Brahms, Schubert, Chopin, Verdi. The biggest class that we saw consisted of a forty-piece student orchestra, led by a student conductor, playing Dvorak's Cello Concerto.

Professor Tan was a product of this tradition—and was one of 30 its first casualties when the Cultural Revolution struck. He was born in 1907, and as a boy he studied violin privately with Dutch and Italian teachers who were living in China. When he joined the Shanghai Municipal Orchestra, in 1927, he was its first Chinese member. He recalls the conductor, an Italian named Mario Paci, as a man of such fierce temper that he constantly broke his baton. Thus he learned at an early age that one of the liveliest currents running through Western music is high emotion among its practitioners.

In 1929 Professor Tan turned to teaching—at one point he was 31 teaching violin at six different colleges in Shanghai—and he rejoined the symphony in 1937. by that time it had four Chinese members; obviously Shanghai was still a creature of the West, its white population continuing to dream of a world that would never change. Pearl Harbor put an end to that reverie. During World War II the Japanese occupied Shanghai, foreigners were interned in concentration camps, and the colonizing grip of the West was finally pried loose.

32   It was no time or place for a musician to earn a living—"one month's salary would buy one shoe," Professor Tan recalled—and, seeking a more practical trade, he went to architecture school and earned his degree. He returned to music after the war, however, joining the Shanghai Conservatory in 1947 and becoming its deputy director in 1949, when the Communists came to power. The school thereupon began its biggest era of growth. The student body expanded and European music regained its hold. But the older students were also required to go away and work for three months every year on farms and in factories.

33   "The peasants and workers disliked the Western music because it belonged to the rich people," Professor Tan told me. "And our students couldn't practice much because they met so much criticism. Here at the conservatory we never knew where we stood. Periods of criticism would alternate with periods of relaxation. It was an uneasy time. In fact, just before the Cultural Revolution I was thinking of retiring from teaching. I had a sense of a coming storm. We are like animals—we can feel that."

34   The storm broke on June 5, 1966. The first winds of the Cultural Revolution hit the conservatory from within. "On the first day, posters were put up and meetings were held denouncing the director, Professor Ho Lu-ting," Professor Tan said. "The next day the attack was aimed at me. I was accused of poisoning the minds of the students. My crime was that I was teaching Mozart. I happen to be a blind admirer of European and American people and music and culture, so everything I had been teaching was poison. Bach and Beethoven were poison. And Brahms. And Paganini.

35   "At first it was only posters and meetings. Then the conservatory was closed and much of our music was destroyed. We were beaten every day by students and by young people who came in from outside. Boys of ten or eleven would throw stones at us. They really believed we were bad people—especially any professor who was over forty. The older you were, the worse you were. For a year, more than a hundred of us older teachers were beaten and forced to spend

every day shut up together in a closed shed. Then there was a year when we had to do hard labor. Ten professors died from the strain; one of them had a heart attack when a young guard made him run after him for a mile. He just dropped dead at the end.

"Then came the solitary confinement. Our director was kept in 36 prison, in chains, for five years. I was put in the worst room they could find here—a very small room in the basement, hardly any bigger than my bed. It had no light and no windows, and it was smelly because it was next to a septic tank, and there was nothing to do to pass the time. I was kept there for fourteen months."

In 1971 Professor Tan was allowed to go home to live with his 37 family, pending the verdict on his "crimes," but he still had to do physical labor at the conservatory during the day. Finally, in 1976, the Gang of Four was overthrown, the professors were declared innocent, and the conservatory reopened. Professor Tan told me that among the students he readmitted were many who had beaten and tormented him. I said that I could hardly imagine such forbearance. "I didn't think about that," he said. "The past is the past."

Professor Tan is a small, gentle man with white hair and a mod- 38 est manner. He dresses in the informal work clothes that everybody wears in Shanghai; nobody would take him for one of the city's cultural eminences. He moves somewhat slowly and has fairly strong glasses—marks, perhaps, of his long captivity. "The students have made astonishing progress since 1976," he told me "because now they can play wholeheartedly. I love being able to teach the violin again. It's such an enjoyment to hear people who are truly talented. Yesterday a girl played the 'Scottish Fantasy' of Max Bruch, and although I was supposed to be teaching her I only sat and listened and never said a word. It was just right."

He was equally pleased by the thought of bringing jazz to his 39 students. "I've never seen any jazz musicians in China," he said. "Nobody here knows anything about jazz. When I heard Mr. Ruff and Mr. Mitchell play at Yale I realized that it was very important music. I wanted my teachers and my students to hear it. I wanted them to know what real American jazz is like."

When Mitchell finished his ragtime tune the audience 40 clapped—apparently glad to hear some of the converging elements that Ruff had talked about earlier. "Now," Ruff said, "we're going to give you an example of blues." It was another word that didn't lend itself to Mandarin, and it sounded unusually strung out: *blooooooze*

"One of the fundamental principles of jazz is form," Ruff continued, "and blues are a perfect illustration. Blues almost always have a twelve-bar form. This twelve-bar form never changes. It wouldn't change even if we stayed here and played it all night." He paused to let this sink in. "But you don't have to worry—we aren't going to play it that long." It was his first joke in Chinese, and it went over well. Mitchell then played an easygoing blues—a classic example of what came up the river from New Orleans, with a strong left hand ornamented by graceful runs in the right hand. Ruff joined in on his bass, and they played several twelve-bar choruses.

41   After that Ruff brought up the matter of improvisation, which he called "the lifeblood of jazz." He said that when he was young he worried because his people hadn't developed from their experience in America a written tradition of opera, like Chinese opera, that chronicled great or romantic events. "But later I stopped worrying because I saw that the master performers of our musical story—Louis Armstrong, Ella Fitzgerald and so many others—have enriched our culture with the beauty of what they created spontaneously. Now please listen one more time to the blues form, and count the measures along with me." He wanted his listeners to count, he said, because the rules of jazz require the improviser, however wild his melodic journeys, to repeat the harmonic changes that went into the first statement of the theme. "After you count with me a few times through, Mr. Mitchell will begin one of his famous improvisations."

42   Mitchell played a simple blues theme, emphasizing the chord changes, and Ruff counted the twelve bars aloud in English. Mitchell then restated the theme, embroidering it slightly, and this time Ruff counted in Chinese: "*Yi, er, san, si, wu, liu, qi, ba . . .*" This so delighted the students that they forgot to join him. "I can't hear you," Ruff said, teacher fashion, but they kept quiet and enjoyed his climb up the numerical ladder. Mitchell then embarked on a series of improvisations, some constructed of Tatum-like runs, some built on strong chord progressions (he can move immense chord clusters up and down the keyboard with incredible speed). Next, Ruff took a chorus on the bass; then they alternated their improvised flights, moving in twelve-bar segments to an ending that seemed as inevitable as if they had played it a hundred times before.

43   Changing the mood, Ruff announced that Mitchell would play a song called "Yesterday," Jerome Kern's plaintive melody is hardly the stuff of traditional jazz, nor was Mitchell's rendition of it—a

treatment of classical intricacy, closer to Rachmaninoff (one of his heroes) than to any jazz pianist. The students applauded with fervor. Staying in a relatively classical vein, Ruff switched to the French horn and the two men played Billy Strayhorn's "Lush Life" in a mood which was slow and lyrical, almost like a German *lied*, and which perhaps surprised the students with its lack of an obvious rhythm.

The next number was one that I didn't recognize. It moved at 44 a bright tempo and had several engaging themes that were brought back by the piano or the French horn—the usual jazzmen's game of statement and response. Twice, Mitchell briefly introduced a contrapuntal motif that was a deliberate imitation of Bach, and each time it drew a ripple of amusement from the professors and the students. It was the first time they had heard a kind of music that they knew from their own studies.

"That number," Ruff said, "is called 'Shanghai Blues.' We just 45 made it up." The audience buzzed with amazement and pleasure.

I had been watching the professors and the students closely 46 during the concert. Their faces had the look of people watching the slow approach of some great natural force—a tornado or a tidal wave. They had been listening to music that their experience had not prepared them to understand. Two black men were playing long stretches of music without resorting to any printed notes. Yet they obviously hadn't memorized what they were playing; their music took unexpected turns, seemingly at the whim of the musicians, straying all over the keyboard and all over the landscape of Western tonality. Nevertheless there was order. Themes that had been abandoned came back in different clothes. If the key changed, as it frequently did, the two men were always in the same key. Often there was a playfulness between the two instruments, and always there was rapport. But if the two players were exchanging any signals, the message was too quick for the untrained eye.

From the quality of the listeners' attention I could tell that the 47 music was holding them in a strong grip. Their minds seemed to be fully engaged. Their bodies, however, were not. Only three pairs of feet in the whole room were tapping—Mitchell's, Ruff's and mine. Perhaps this was a Chinese characteristic, this stillness of listening. But beyond that, the music wasn't easy. It never again approached the overt syncopation of the ragtime that Mitchell had played early in the program; that was where the essential gaiety of jazz had been most accessible. Nor did it have the flat-out gusto that an earlier generation of black musicians might have brought to China—the thumping rhythms and simpler harmonies of a James P. Johnson or a Fats Waller.

48   It wasn't that Mitchell and Ruff were playing jazz that was pedantic or sedate; on the contrary, I have seldom heard Mitchell play with more exuberant shifts of energy. But the music was full of subtleties—even a Westerner accustomed to jazz would have been charmed by its subtlety and wit. I had to remind myself that the Chinese had heard no Western music of any kind from 1966 to 1976. A twenty-one-year-old student in the audience, for instance, would only have begun to listen to composers like Mozart and Brahms within the past five years. The jazz that he was hearing now was not so different as to be a whole new branch of music. Mitchell was clearly grounded in Bach and Chopin; Ruff's French horn had echoes of all the classical works—Debussy's "Reverie," Ravel's "Pavane"—in which that instrument has such uncanny power to move us.

49   After "Shanghai Blues" Ruff invoked the ancient device of teachers who know they have been presenting too much material too fast. He asked for questions. The serious faces relaxed.

50   "Where do people go to study jazz in America?" a student wanted to know. "What kind of courses do they take?"

51   Ruff explained that jazz courses, where they existed at all, would be part of a broad college curriculum that included, say, languages and history and physics. "But, really, jazz isn't learned in universities or conservatories," he said. "It's music that is passed on by older musicians to those of us who are younger."

52   It was not a helpful answer. What kind of subject doesn't have its own academy? A shyness settled over the room, though the students seemed full of curiosity. Professor Tan got up and stood next to Ruff. "I urge you to ask questions," he said. "I can assure you that jazz has many principles that apply to your studies here. In fact, I have many questions myself."

53   An old professor stood up. "When you created 'Shanghai Blues' just now," he said, "did you have a form for it, or a logical plan?"

54   "I just started tapping my foot," Ruff replied, tapping his foot to reconstruct the moment. "And then I started to play the first thought that came into my mind with the horn. And Mitchell heard it. And he answered. And after that we heard and answered, heard and answered, heard and answered."

55   "But how can you ever play it again?" the old professor said.

"We never can," Ruff replied. 56

"That is beyond our imagination," the professor said. "Our stu- 57
dents here play a piece a hundred times, or two hundred times, to
get it exactly right. You play something once—something very beautiful—and then you just throw it away."

Now the questions tumbled out. What was most on the stu- 58
dents' minds quickly became clear: it was the mystery of improvisation. (The Chinese don't even have a word for improvisation of this
kind; Ruff translated it as "something created during the process of
delivery.") All the questions poked at this central riddle—"Could a
Chinese person improvise?" and "Could two strangers improvise
together?" and "How can you compose at such speed?"—and it was
at this point that Ruff took one question and turned it into a moment
that stood us all on our ear.

❡ The writer knows it is almost always better to show rather than tell,
or at least to show, then tell. Zinsser has come to the most complex
cultural difference between the performers and the audience,
between American jazz musicians and Chinese musicians, and he
deals with it in an expertly told anecdote. ❡

Was it really possible, a student wanted to know, to improvise 59
on any tune at all—even one that the musicians had never heard
before?

Ruff's reply was casual. "I would like to invite one of the pia- 60
nists here to play a short traditional Chinese melody that I'm sure
we would not know," he said, "and we will make a new piece based
on that."

The room erupted in oohs and cheers. I caught a look on Mitch- 61
ell's face that said, "This time you've gone too far." The students
began to call the name of the young man they wanted to have play.
When they found him in the crowd he was so diffident that he got
down on the floor to keep from being dragged out. But his friends
dragged him out anyway, and, regaining his aplomb, he walked to
the piano and sat down with the formality of a concert artist. He was
about twenty-two. Mitchell stood at one side, looking grave.

The young man played his melody beautifully and with great 62
feeling. It seemed to be his own composition, unknown to the other
people. It began with four chords of distinctively Chinese structure,
moved down the scale in a stately progression, paused, turned itself
around with a transitional figure of lighter weight, and then started

back up, never repeating itself and finally resolving the theme with a suspended chord that was satisfying because it was so unexpected. It was a perfect small piece, about fourteen bars long. The student walked back to his seat and Mitchell went back to the piano. The room got very quiet.

63   Mitchell's huge hands hovered briefly over the keys, and then the young man's melody came back to him. It was in the same key; it had the same chords, slightly embellished near the end, and, best of all, it had the same mood. Having stated the theme, Mitchell broadened it the second time, giving it a certain majesty, coloring the student's chords with dissonances that were entirely apt; he gave the "Chinese" chords a jazz texture but still preserved their mood. Then Ruff joined him on his bass, and they took the melody through a number of variations. Mitchell giving it a whole series of new lives but never losing its integrity. I listened to his feat with growing excitement. For me it was the climax of years of marveling at his ear and at his sensitivity to the material at hand. The students were equally elated and astonished. For them it was the ultimate proof—because it touched their own heritage—that for a jazz improviser no point of departure is alien.

64   After that a few more questions were asked, and Mitchell and Ruff concluded with a Gershwin medley from *Porgy and Bess* and a genial rendition of "My Old Flame." Professor Tan thanked the two men and formally ended the concert. Then he went over to Mitchell and took his hands in his own. "You are an artist," he said.

65   Later I told Mitchell that I thought Ruff had given him an unduly nervous moment when he invited one of the students to supply a melody.

66   "Well, naturally I was nervous," he said, "because I didn't have any idea what to expect. But, you know, that boy phrased his piece *perfectly*. The minute he started to play I got his emotions. I understood exactly what he was feeling, and the rest was easy. The notes and the chords just fell into place."

Discussion

• Count the number of paragraphs directly about the concert and the number of paragraphs of background or exposition. Figure out the percentage of each and discuss how Zinsser has made it possible for the reader to accept that amount of exposition.

• It is very hard to write about one art, such as music, in the media of another art. Discuss how Zinsser does this and whether it works.

• Go back to Zinsser's letter to me in the introduction and discuss the issues he raises, and how the piece demonstrates that he learned the lessons, or if he did.

• Discuss other ways that Zinsser could have organized this account of the China trip.

• In his book on writing Zinsser launches an all-out attack on clutter. Discuss how Zinsser achieves the clean, lean prose with which he writes this piece. Discuss its advantages and disadvantages.

• Consider the advantages and disadvantages of being as involved as Selzer and as detached as Zinsser.

• Discuss how Zinsser moves in and out of the first person in the piece. Discuss why he does it and how effective it is.

Activities

• Cover a concert to see how well Zinsser did this one, and to discover other ways you can cover an event.

• Write the first page of an account of an event from the point of view of a distant reporter, an involved member of the audience, a personal friend of someone involved in the event, a participant in the event. Study the four pages to see the advantages and disadvantages of each one.

• Take a page of your own prose and do not imitate Zinsser's voice, but try in your own way to achieve the leanness of his prose.

• Write a paragraph describing a piece of music to see how well you can communicate how it sounds to someone who has not heard it.

James Stevenson

James Stevenson is both a successful *New Yorker* cartoonist and a *New Yorker* writer. In this piece he has the advantage of bringing an artist's eye to the subject—a profile of one of the best cinematographers in the movie business. The people who photograph the movies, like artists and writers, are the people who make us see the world as we have not seen it before. It was Conrad

who said, "My task . . . is, by the power of the written word, to
make you hear, to make you feel—it is, before all, to make you
see." And James Baldwin, who we've already met in this book, once
said, "The importance of a writer . . . is that he is here to describe
things which other people are too busy to describe." The chances
are that most of you have seen the world differently—remember
how it is to walk out of a movie theater and see what you have not
seen before, because you have seen the world through the lens of
Gordon Willis, who received an Oscar in 1984.

Cinematographer

1

so much depends
upon
a red wheel
barrow
glazed with rain
water
beside the white
    chickens

William Carlos Williams

2   It is four o'clock in the morning in New York. A hot, thick, star-
less August night is fading. In Sutton Square, where Fifty-eighth
Street terminates above the East River, yellow street lights throw
shadows of plane trees across the pavement and up the walls of the
low, elegant houses. In the square, at the end of the street, there is
an iron railing, some stone steps descending to a small terrace, and
then the river. The railing trembles steadily to the traffic in the tunnel
of the East River Drive below. The river is dark, except where reflec-
tions of street lights on Roosevelt Island glitter across its surface; the
choppy current moves swiftly north, carrying smooth pools lazily
turning, and passes under the Queensboro Bridge. From the bridge's
roadways come melancholy moaning sounds: the keening of tires on
pavement. The lower span of the bridge is lit with yellow bulbs; on
top, blue lights are set at intervals, following the carnival outlines of
the Victorian structure. They exude bluish halos. Above the horizon,
over Queens, the darkness erodes to a ghastly hue: peach ice cream
mixed with motor oil.

3   A man stands on the steps of the terrace, staring at the night

and the bridge. He is a tall, lean man in his forties—curly-haired, dressed in a T-shirt, slacks, and sneakers—and he is concentrating intently. He looks this way and that. He raises an object—it is a light meter—to his right eye and peers through it. He puts it down, stares, raises it again. He has the appearance of a mariner searching for something with a glass. He is as totally isolated as if he were alone in a boat. He lowers the light meter, and walks up the steps. As he reaches the top, a street lamp lights his face for an instant from above: a craggy cherubic face with a chunky nose; curly gray hair spinning upward and outward; eyes deep-set and lost in shadow under heavy brows. Then the light is behind him; he is a silhouette, and he is walking down the street.

Thirty yards away, a group of people are waiting for him, stand-   4
ing by trucks, watching him; what he says to these people will dictate what they do. They are a film crew, and he is the cinematographer— the director of photography. His name is Gordon Willis. He has been the director of photography on such films as "Interiors," "Annie Hall," "All the President's Men," "The Parallax View," "The Drown- ing Pool," "September 30, 1955," "Paper Chase," "The Godfather," "The Godfather, Part II," "Bad Company," "Comes a Horseman," and "Klute," and now he is engaged in shooting this one. The crew waits for him patiently, respectfully. His presence on any film is a guarantee that the finished movie—in addition to its other merits, or despite its lack of them—will have a distinctive look and feeling; visually, at least, it will be a work of high quality. In addition to this, the members of the crew—many of whom have worked with him on other films—like him as a person. Willis is under a tight deadline on this shot: it must be filmed at dawn. There is no way for him to know when the light will be exactly right, or what it will look like when it is, but for the purposes of the movie Willis needs dawn. He will be shooting without artificial light, depending entirely on the sky. At the moment it is hung with low clouds.

> ❡ Stevenson practices a variation on the same technique that Zinsser used. He starts his piece with a famous poem of an American imagist that attempts to state the importance of seeing and paying attention. William Carlos Williams said, for example, "No ideas but in things." Then the author lets us see in a particular way. We study the New York dawn, and then we see a man looking at that dawn, and finally we are introduced to him in the context paragraph that tells us who he is and what the piece is going to be about. We are made to see before we are told about how this man and his art see. ❡

5   A few minutes earlier, a large yellow Ryder truck—a lift-gate truck, open at the rear—backed into the street, its interior luridly lit by a twin-tube fluorescent lamp sitting on a rack of tripods. The truck was packed with equipment of all kinds—cameras, dollies, cans of film, batteries, cables, tools, wedges of wood, boxes of lenses—and Jimmy Hovey, a short, tattooed, tough-looking first assistant camera-man, was standing in the midst of it like a gypsy by firelight as the rest of the caravan, consisting of four more trucks, one with a trailer, pulled up behind. Hovey began cleaning a Panavision camera, spray-ing the parts with a hose attached to a cylinder of nitrogen. Behind him in the truck was a small darkroom, with a hand-lettered sign on the door saying "Hovey's Outhouse," where more film, in cans hold-ing a thousand feet, was stored. The street filled up with people, many of them carrying plastic cups of coffee. A park bench was taken from one of the trucks and set in front of the iron railing next to the street lamp. The sequence to be shot would show a couple sitting on the bench at dawn. They would be dressed in formal clothes: the end of a long evening. After talking for a while, they would get up and walk slowly up Sutton Square, away from the river.

6   Willis, the assistant director, the director (who is also acting in this film), and the chief cameraman are crouching on the shadowy sidewalk now, about a third of the way up the block from the bench. They take turns looking through a director's viewfinder; they talk, point, agree. A chalk mark is made at their feet; Hovey, with a tape measure, measures the vertical distance from the sidewalk to the viewfinder, which Willis, still crouching, is now holding to his eye; a dolly is rolled up to the chalk mark; Hovey sets a Panavision camera on the dolly, and—turning a wheel—raises the camera to the proper height. Willis instructs him to put on a 75-mm anamorphic lens; then Hovey attaches a loaded film magazine to the top of the camera. "Roll 94," says an adhesive tape label stuck to the side of the mag-azine, and "820 Out. 990 Dev. to .065 GAMMA." All four men stand up. Through the camera's viewer are now framed—in a small, black-bordered rectangle that has the same proportions as a Panavision screen (2.35 to 1)—the street leading to the bench; the bench; the street lamp next to it; a concrete tub of flowers; the railing; part of the Queensboro Bridge; and the unpredictable sky. Except for the lights and the horizon, everything is gray.

   ❡ I'm interested in the way that Stevenson uses the technical detail and the technical jargon to give us the insider's view, and I'm also

interested in the fact that the reader understands what is being said
because it is in context. The author's command of these details
helps the reader believe the piece, and increases the author's
authority. ❧

"Take out the street light, Dusty," says Willis."   7
"O.K., Gordy."   8
Dusty, the gaffer, or chief electrician, who is a tall, burly man   9
with a red bandanna tied around his forehead, walks over to the
street lamp, kneels down, and expertly opens a panel at the base.
Immediately, New York City has one less street light. Willis studies
the scene again with his light meter.
The actors rehearse. Willis lights a cigarette. "There's still not 10
enough light," he says to a visitor, watching the sky. He is not visibly
nervous or impatient—simply alert. "In exterior shooting, you're
always at the mercy of the light and the weather. It can change very
fast, so a lot of the time you work as if you were being chased by the
police. Last summer, I had bits of film strung out all over Colorado.
Every day at noon, it would rain, so you'd have to go back later for
matching shots."
The sky is showing touches of pale blue; the queasy peach color   11
over Queens is gradually shifting to a dull pink. Presently, the bridge
is cast in lavender-grays; it looks like a Monet, then a Whistler. The
pink disappears; gray, wet clouds move overhead, with patches of
dull white. The sky is mottled and uneven—a poorly stirred blueberry yogurt. Then it is dawn. The dark-gray leaves on the plane trees
suddenly acquire green; the gray flowers in the concrete tub show
pink; gray letters on a "No Parking" sign turn dull red—color leaps
out everywhere. The actors are in place; the cameraman is behind
the camera. "Roll it," says Willis to the assistant Director.
"Stand by!" shouts the assistant director.   12
"Right *now!*" says Willis, and the take begins.   13

In the United States, a director of photography, or cinematog-   14
rapher, does not operate a camera; that is the cameraman's job.
When Willis has completed his painstaking preparations for a take—
designed the picture or sequence of pictures that will occupy the
frame; planned the colors, values, contrasts, and shapes; fixed the
position of the camera or the path of its movement; selected the lens
and its openings; picked the filter; lit the scene, with a variety of
lights and light filters, and diffused them with screens called flags and

cutters; arranged the actors in certain patterns and made sure that they will be photographed in the right light at the proper angles; checked and rehecked everything with light meters; and done all these things and others in such a way that the resulting film not only will connect dramatically and aesthetically with the scenes prior to it and the scenes that are to follow but will be in keeping with the vision of the movie as a whole—then, an instant before the shot is filmed as the assistant director calls "Stand by!," Willis steps away from the camera. Suddenly, one is reminded of the torero in a corrida who, having worked the bull with his cape, executing precise and daring maneuvers one after another, abruptly turns his back on the baffled bull and walks away.

> ❡ Stevenson uses quick transitions, moving quickly from quote to quote, scene to scene. We are used to this kind of quick transition because of film, and the author may be able to get away with it because he is writing about film. ❡

15   Fred Schuler, chief cameraman: "I've often worked on films where the director of photography is really schlocky and doesn't contribute anything. Gordon has total influence and total control over the visual aspect, from A to Z. Everything is well thought out and carefully planned. It's really a pleasure working with somebody so professional. But there's not much for *me* to do."

16   Dusty, gaffer: "Gordy is way ahead of them all."

17   Bobby, electrician, who, like Dusty, has worked with Willis before: "He's a pro."

18   When Willis raises the viewfinder to his eye and squints through it, he often holds it between his thumb and his first two fingers; it is a grip of some delicacy—one that a person might use on a glass of champagne.

19   Willis's eyes are blue. They are long horizontally, like a Panavision screen, and set back under heavy lids that are like a prizefighter's. The lids descend from arching eyebrows on a high, broad forehead, and seem like special packaging for a valuable item. When the lids are low, the eyes suggest an animal peering out from under an overhanging rock. At times, the eyes seem Oriental. Full face, with his curly gray hair awry, Willis can appear leonine. When he is talk-

ing about the possibilities of a good shot, say, his eyes widen, brightening with excitement, delight, and a kind of mischief. Then, when he is preparing the shot, his eyes narrow down almost to slits. There is a rakish outdoor air to him: the look of a loner, somebody who works on a boat—a merchant seaman, or possibly a pirate. He usually wears informal clothes and blue-and-white Puma sneakers. He is unpretentious, and his disposition is generally amiable and cheerful. He smiles a lot, laughs often, makes others laugh. He seems to understand people and get along with them; he's quick to perceive and appreciate situations, sensitivities, and surroundings. He has a light touch, but he is a serious man, and he can get angry. Despite the appalling complexity of his work, and the nearly intolerable pressures under which it must be carried on a good deal of the time, he is ordinarily serene. His serenity, while it may come partly from his nature, seems to come largely from confidence in himself and what he does. When the people around him talk to him, it is implicit in the way they stand and the way they speak that they defer to his judgment. Talking once about a certain scene in one of his films—a shot that was visually sparse but very evocative—Willis remarked, "What is not there is sometimes more interesting than what is." The same seems true of him. He speaks softly; he is inclined to understatement, wryness, personal reticence. There is an absence of excessive physical movement, of agitation, of uncertainty. His energy is contained; he has the central ease and repose one sees in, for example, a fine hockey player, who never really moves much until he has to, and then, at precisely the right instant, bursts into action.

Willis: "I'm interested in space, and the positioning of people 20 in space."

"There's no better cinematographer than Gordon," says Alan 21 Pakula, who became a director in 1969, after producing seven films. As a director, Pakula has worked with Willis on four: "Klute," "Comes a Horseman," "The Parallax View," and "All the President's Men." Working with him is collaboration at its best. It's a joy, it's fun, it's camaraderie—like being kids and playing after school. They say about certain film editors that they have "gifted fingers." Gordon has that kind of eye. The thought is all in the work. He's embarrassed talking about it; he's very private about it, and I love that. He'll talk as long as you can talk specifics, but he has a gifted ear for crap. He doesn't give respect easily.

22   "I remember meeting him years ago to talk about doing 'Klute.'
We met in a West Side bar—he was doing another film at the time—
and talked about the final conception. Months later, when we were
shooting, at one point he said, 'That's not what the conception was.'
He keeps you pure. Every film we've done together has been a different visual experience. 'Klute' had a nervous, claustrophobic feeling, a disturbing sense of compression. There were great verticals,
and people lived on top of them or lived under them—underground,
as if in tunnels. 'Comes a Horseman' was the reverse. The land was
a character in the film. I wanted a sense of a haunted place, and
haunted sets. Indoors, the human conflict make the people seem like
giants; then they go outside into this enormous physical world and
they're nothing. Gordon's lighting was more like 'Wuthering Heights'
than like a Western. 'The Parallax View' had a cold, hard look, like
Pop Art—sharply defined but hollow, like the society it showed. Gordon hates overlighting—he likes faces going in and out -and he's
known for very dark films. When we started doing 'All the President's Men,' I wanted the *Washington Post* newsroom to have a tough,
hard white light, and I was concerned that Gordon wouldn't want to
do it that way, but that's the way he did it. For him there's always a
conception, and there are very few accidents in his work. He is
essentially a classicist, not a mannerist. He hates tricks. He's so easy
to work with, so easy to understand. Then, on another level, he's a
very mysterious man. He's his own creation—highly sophisticated—
and he's very much a loner. Most good creative work comes out of a
need to do it, and often it comes from pain. There are certain people
it's impossible to divorce from their work. More than most people,
Gordon is most fully alive when he's working. When he takes time
off and goes to his place in the Adirondacks, I imagine him almost
hibernating. I imagine him being very interested in his own reactions
to what he sees."

❧ Because Stevenson uses the cinematic technique we are able to see
clearly interesting juxtapositions—Willis' quote, for example,
immediately followed by somebody else's quote about Willis. ❧

23   Willis is gazing out a control-room window that overlooks a vast
television studio at WNEW-TV, on Sixty-seventh Street near Third
Avenue. The camera is set up behind him, staring past twenty-four
monitor screens toward the window. In front of him, beyond the
glass, there are dozens of spotlights pointing this way and that, form-

ing a canopy of illumination over the floor thirty feet below. Normally, the floor is used for the evening news; this morning, it has been converted into a set for a talk show that is to be part of a movie. The director is talking to three actors on the set. Willis looks through his viewer at the set, then leans against a table. There are many lulls in shooting, and this is one of them. "It's funny," he says to his visitor, "My father used to have a radio program on WNEW back in the forties. It was a show for women—a program on beauty—called 'Here's Looking at You.' He talked directly to ordinary women—not like *Vogue*, which he called 'the comic book of fashion.' He had been a makeup man at the Warner Brothers studio in Brooklyn during the Depression. I used to hang around and watch them make movies. It was a wonderful time for me, a period of taking it in. They made a lot of shorts. Sometimes my father would put me in one of these. I liked it, and I thought maybe I'd be an actor."

Willis is giving the script supervisor, Kay Chapin, a ride in his 24 car, a Honda, from one location to the next. They chat about cars, the high cost of repairs, and the unreliability of mechanics. "I service my cars myself," says Willis, driving up Madison Avenue. "It's good occupational therapy. I buy the parts. I wouldn't give a car to a garage."

A cinematographer must have an easy grasp of such things as 25 color-reversal internegatives, aspect ratios, lenses, T-stops, brutes, color temperatures, Steenbecks, mattes, pushing and flashing, film resolution, freeze frames, Arriflexes, match cuts, halation, dye transfers, fish-eyes, three-strip processes, pull-down mechanisms, glass shots, tilts, emulsions, Kenworthy snorkels, film generations, diffusers, tracking, dollies, dailies, and inserts—and also a pretty good knowledge of carpentry, electricity, sound, set design, costumes, makeup, optics, meteorology, and the history of art and architecture, and a complete, up-to-date acquaintance with major movies, foreign and domestic, extending back to the Lumieres and Melies. He needs, of course, a strong sense of color, composition, contrast, and narrative developments, and he must be able to work effectively with large groups of temperamental individuals. He should have a vivid pictorial imagination, and be able to design what is seen in every frame of a movie (which usually has from a hundred and twenty to a hundred and fifty thousand frames, stretching over a mile and a half of film) so that it contributes to the movie's general pace and feeling, and he must know how to get this done within a fixed budget and a limited time. When the film is completed, it not only should satisfy him and those connected with it but must engage the interest of several million spectators in order to be financially successful.

26   Willis: "The most important part of making a movie is the planning, and it's always very difficult. After there's a script, I spend a great deal of time with the director finding out what he ultimately wants to say in the movie. How do you project the ideas—how do you make them play on a given level? Once that's established, you start planning the nuts and bolts. A movie is not an art form; it's a commercial venture, and the art comes out of the craft.

27   "The ideal thing—although management and money may interfere with it—is to reduce the most sophisticated ideas to the simplest terms, and make them wonderful. For the people who stand in line and pay three dollars."

28   Willis, the director, the assistant director, the production manager, and a few of the staff are walking around Nyack, New York, looking for locations. It is a beautiful Saturday afternoon. They walk back and forth near a marina on the Hudson River, peering in the windows of shops. What they want is a good store window facing the marina and the river. The shot will be from inside the store, looking out. The actor will be seen through the window, framed by books; behind him will be the boats and the docks and the far side of the Hudson. But the best windows are set sidewise to the river—no good. The group ambles around, gazing this way and that, wishing for a window. Finally, everybody is standing in front of a shop that has an excellent window facing the wrong way, and Willis says, "Why don't we just build a window like this one? Then we can put it anywhere we want, and shoot through it." Everybody agrees that that is the perfect solution, and the group moves on to the next problem.

29   Willis: "When I was a teen-ager, I went to Manhasset High School. My father lived in Manhasset; my mother lived in Birmingham, Alabama. They had split, and I spent some time in both places. I was an only child, but I had a lot of aunts and uncles, so I had a sense of a pretty big family. I did acting in school, and acted for two summers in stock at Gloucester, Massachusetts. I got into stage lighting and scenery there—everybody did everything—and after a while I realized that I was really more interested in the creative end from

a distance. It was such a great time. I feel sorry for kids today, because there is no summer stock for them, where they can learn. In the same way, there are no B movies anymore, where cameramen can learn. Today, you have to fight to learn your craft.

"I was very much interested in drawing and painting when I 30 was a teen-ager, and I did a lot of it, but I never could learn to draw hands. Gradually, I got into photography. I took pictures of everything, but mostly people. I built my own darkroom and lived in it twenty-four hours a day; nobody ever saw me.

"I went to a lot of Broadway plays, and I saw a lot of movies. I 31 was very much impressed with plays like 'Streetcar' and 'Picnic.' That whole world had a lot of magic for me, but I wasn't formed. I had a lot of information about it all, but an unproductive intellect."

On location at night: Willis stands about twelve feet away from 32 a group of four actors. He is bent forward from the waist, looking at them through his viewer. Presently, he murmurs to Hovey, who in response runs the tape measure from the ground up to the lens. "Mark it," says Willis, whereupon the second assistant cameraman tears strips of tape off a roll and sticks them on the ground at Willis's feet; more tapes are stuck where the actors are standing. Willis moves away, and the camera is rolled into position at the tape where Willis was standing. Hovey watches. "Gordon's the only one I know who never moves a camera once the tape is down," he says. "Other cinematographers will move it back and forth, back and forth, all over the place. They don't know what they want. Gordon has absolute precision."

Willis: "I've never made a movie that was easy. There's some- 33 thing awful in making each one. But I love making movies, and the people you work with are the key to everything.

"I believe that a picture should be made for a certain amount 34 of money within a set period of time. That's right. Then the profit enables the producer to make more movies. Everybody on a production has different concerns, and often the producer is mostly concerned about getting it in on time. But nobody ever thanked anybody for bringing a bad picture in on time. If you don't get off on the right foot on a film—if it doesn't go right at the very beginning—it's never going to be right, and it's the better part of valor to stop, knock off for a week, and start over. Otherwise, it's like adding color after color trying to get white—and, of course, ending up with black.''

❦ In what follows Stevenson gives us a scene complete with dialogue about the making of a scene. As a writer I laugh out loud with excitement at what he is doing in writing about movie-making, in a sense, by making a written movie.❧

35   In a brown-wood-panelled corner office of the firm of Rohrer, Hibler & Replogle, on the third floor of the Maison Française, at Fifth Avenue and Forty-ninth Street, are a large sofa, several chairs, and a big executive desk, but no executive. Next to the desk is a five-foot stepladder, its bottom rungs piled with sandbags. A plank about ten feet long has been clamped to one of the top rungs and weighted down with more sandbags, and it extends horizontally from the ladder to an open window, where it rests on the ledge. The final three feet of the plank projects out over the south side of the broad promenade of Rockefeller Center, fifty feet below, which runs west from Fifth Avenue to the skating rink. At the tip of the board, its mount screwed into the wood, is a Panavision camera. It is angled downward by two wooden chocks wedged under its base; a zoom lens points toward the brown marquee of 30 Rockefeller Plaza, a hundred and fifty yards almost due west. Fred Schuler, the cameraman—lean, taciturn, and, as usual, dressed in khaki—is kneeling on a pillow on the windowsill, peering through the camera viewer, and Jimmy Hovey, holding a walkie-talkie, straddles the sill. Seven other members of the crew are in the room, collapsed on the sofa, slumped in chairs, leaning against the desk: Everybody is exhausted. It is after seven o'clock in the evening of a savagely hot and humid day, and they have all been working since early morning, when a sequence was shot in an apartment on upper Park Avenue—in a room without air-conditioning, and with the heat multiplied by hot lights. (The next day's shooting is to begin at 8 A.M.; today's must be accomplished within the hour, since union rules demand a twelve-hour break between workdays. The rule can be broken, but the subsequent cost in overtime pay would be enormous.)

36   The blue-trousered shins and blue-and-white Pumas of Gordon Willis are just visible at the doorway of 30 Rockefeller Plaza; the rest of him, because of the angle, is blocked by the brown marquee. His voice, however, is audible over several walkie-talkies in the office. At the moment, he is talking to Hovey.

Willis: That puts it a sop and a half under.   37

Hovey: Right, Gordy.   38

Hovey alters the lens opening, and then recites the exposure   39
notes back to Willis over the walkie-talkie and also to the second
assistant cameraman, who writes them down in a small notebook,
using the plank as a desk. (It is Willis's custom to keep a log of exposure notes on every shot of every movie, primarily in order to be able
to match the shot later, if need be.)

"One-hundred-and-eighty-degree shutter," Hovey reads.   40

There is a take. First, Hovey leans perilously far out the window   41
and holds the slate—the small blackboard on which are chalked the
name of the production, the name of the cinematographer, the number of the take, and other information—in front of the lens. He pulls
it away, and Schuler refocusses on three actors, who came out of 30
Rockefeller Plaza, talking, cross the street, walk around the promenade above the skating rink, and come to a stop just under the window. The dialogue has been previously recorded on a "wild track"—
a sound track without pictures—so the action must be of matching
duration. Kay Chapin, the script supervisor, standing by a window,
holds a stopwatch in her hand, and, as the take ends, she says, "It's
not timing out right. Thirty-seven seconds short." There will be
another take.

"Did you see that old man staring at them?" says Schuler.   42

In addition to the shortage of time, the changing of the light as   43
the sun goes down, the need to match the "wild track," and the weariness of the crew, there is another problem: the nonfilm people—
tourists and natives—who are wandering around Rockefeller Plaza,
in and out of the Panavision frame, inadvertently mixing with the
production extras who are posing as tourists and natives. None of
these pedestrians seem to notice the camera sticking out of the window, but sometimes during a take they will spot one of the actors—
a recognizable movie star—and gawk, follow him, or even try to
catch up and get an autograph or a snapshot. Production members
with walkie-talkies are mingling with the crowd in an effort to prevent such activity from ruining the takes.

Willis: Put Hovey on.   44

Hovey: Yes, Gordy?   45

Willis: Two lines light on eight-and-a-half . . .   46

The take is made. Kay looks at her stopwatch. "Twenty seconds   47
short," she says.

48   Willis: Did you see those paparazzi chasing after him trying to get a shot?

49   Another take. Then:

50   Hovey: Gordy, the little red light on the camera came on for a couple of seconds and then went off.

51   Willis (after a pause): Got a battery up there?

52   Hovey: Yes.

53   Willis: Change it.

54   Another take is about to begin.

55   Hovey: Wait, Gordy—we've got a problem.

56   Willis: What's the problem?

57   Hovey: A wedge slipped.

58   Willis: Hurry up . . . If that light goes on, you better get it off or I'm going to come up and push it out the window.

59   Hovey gets the wedge back where it belongs.

60   Willis: Is the camera level?

61   Hovey: Yes.

62   Willis: Thank you.

63   Hovey: I'll be standing by for a stop.

64   It is getting darker. Willis can be seen walking around looking through his light meter.

65   Willis: Three stops down.

66   Hovey: O.K., Gordy.

67   The next take is going well until, at the last moment, a tourist notices the movie star and comes trotting after him. One of the production staff grabs the tourist from behind and virtually wrestles him out of the picture; the startled tourist presumably thinks he is being mugged—just what he expected to happen to him in New York.

68   Schuler: No flicker this time, Gordy.

69   Willis: That's refreshing.

70   The crew laughs. Another take begins. Then: "Oh, my God," says one of the grips, who is standing by a window. "Look!"

71   The actors are walking across the street toward the rink. At that instant, into the plaza from Fifth Avenue comes a troop of twenty-five green-uniformed Girl Scouts, moving briskly toward the actors; they are on a collision course. "Cut!" shouts the assistant director. It is ten minutes to eight.

72   Willis: "There are a lot of cameramen but not so many photographers. And a lot of cameramen attack from a technical approach without much imagination. They look, but they don't *see*."

It is hard to generalize about where a movie director's work 73 ends and his cinematographer's work begins; the team should be invisible. A director with strong visual ability might need no more than a technician to operate the camera; a gifted cinematographer might require a director merely to tell the actors what to say. If the cinematographer is increasingly important today, it is partly because the nature of storytelling has moved in a direction that gives great weight to the way a story is told and less weight to the story itself. The look of a film becomes the author's voice, reflecting and revealing the mood, the attitude, the sensibilities. It often happens that form and content are not exactly balanced or united: where the content is familiar, meagre, or absent altogether, form may get the upper hand. A cinematographer can prevent this from showing: he can enhance a slow, shallow, artificial story to such an extent that it seems exciting, real, even profound. He must have the necessary proficiency, however, and the autonomy—granted or grabbed—to pull it off. Willis, as a rule, has both.

Willis is sitting in the sun with his visitor on a bench in a small 74 park across from the Englewood, New Jersey, railroad station. It is around noon. He is supposed to meet the director, a stunt man, and some other people here, in order to plan a sequence involving a runaway car. For the moment, glancing around the park, he is simply waiting, and he talks a little bit about himself. "By the time I finished Manhasset High School, the Korean War had started," he says. "I enlisted in the Air Force and got classified as a photographer. They sent me to film school in Burbank, California. At that time, I was still more interested in the ambience of filmmaking than I was in the execution, but I learned a tremendous amount about film, including lab work. For the next three years, I was a cameraman, making documentaries on things like jungle survival and the F-100. I shot a lot of film.

"When I was stationed in Florida in my last year, I met this 75 marvelous girl, and we got married. We've been married twenty-three years now, and we have three children—two boys and a girl. We moved to New York when I got out, and the struggle to get into the cameramen's union began. I was fortunate enough to run into some very decent cameramen, and they gave me some opportunities to work as an assistant cameraman, and I finally got into the Eastern local. In Hollywood, to get into the West Coast local you have to start as a loader, and by the time you work your way up through all the categories to cameraman you're a hundred and ten years old. It was a real fight, later on, for me to get into that local. I even had to use lawyers.

76   "In New York, I did documentaries and TV commercials. I spent a lot of time in steel mills and I.B.M. plants. It was a wonderful period to learn your craft: TV was coming of age, and making commercials was a very good school. A lot of the commercials were explorative and imaginative; people attempted a lot, and there was a level of technology that probably exceeded every Disney. They were always putting Chevrolets on mountaintops in those days. When you have to show a little guy climbing out of a peanut-butter jar, you learn about the technique of matte shots—and also how to get the job done.

77   "Finally, I got an opportunity to become director of photography on a commercial movie. It was called 'End of the Road,' and Aram Avakian directed it. We shot it in Massachusetts. Stacy Keach and James Earl Jones were in it. I went along photographing it at a level that I thought was interesting; my hands were never tied. I felt that there was some extraordinary work in it. I guess it was slightly ahead of its time. After that, I got a lot of offers."

78   A station wagon pulls up next to the railroad depot, and the people from the movie crew pile out. They wave to Willis. He gets up and goes to work.

79   A night location: Willis's temper suddenly flares. Seventy-five extras are standing ready; two cameras have been set up, and there are lights all over the place. What's missing is Willis's walkie-talkie. Whoever may be at fault, it means loss of precious time for a trivial reason, and Willis starts yelling. An alarmed young member of the production staff runs zigzagging through the crowd of extras, his own walkie-talkie sputtering and squawking at his side. The voice on the walkie-talkie is warning, "Willis is really burned!"

80   Willis: "Structure in a film is everything. The cutting. Light to dark. Big to small. Fast to slow.

81   "In a good movie, you lead the audience along. I want the audience to get caught up in the film and not be aware of what we're doing. I don't like tricks, but I like magic. I want magic."

82   "The Godfather," directed by Francis Ford Coppola, with Willis as director of photography, was released in 1972 and was a great

success at the box office. Willis says, "The film was a horrendous experience. The worst time of my life was the last month of making it. I was very tired, everybody had been under a lot of pressure, and Francis and I were not getting along well. I've always taken a strong stand from the start on what it is I'm doing, and been fortunate enough to see it through. I have to do what I feel is right. I'm happy I don't feel the same way about things as other people in this business, and I've never tried to. Throughout the making of 'The Godfather,' we were getting unfavorable feedback from people who were not used to seeing an idea mounted in the way we were doing it. They'd look at the film and say 'It's too light' or 'It's too dark— they'll never see it in the drive-ins.' Most of the bumpiness in this business comes from the inability of the system to accept anything new. Studio executives want what they feel safe with. Success is apparent only when it's a success.

"Coppola is a very gifted guy. After the experience we had on 83 'The Godfather,' it took a lot of chutzpah for him to come back and ask me to make 'The Godfather, Part II,' but I'm very glad he did. The personality things that seemed relevant to me at one time no longer seemed relevant, and we made a very good picture, with a lot of class."

"The Godfather, Part II," which was released in 1974, is a fas- 84 tidiously designed three-and-a-half-hour Mafia saga that exploits light and dark and color and composition as theme and symbol, but it is the visual beauty—frame after frame—that dominates the film, rather than the density of its implications.

"I shoot color as if it were black-and-white," Willis once 85 remarked. "The problem with color is to control it. I hate blue. I wear it, but I mean on the screen. It's vulgar; it tends to take over. Certain yellows are overwhelming, too. I like earth tones—blacks and browns."

In "The Godfather, Part II," Willis is working from the rich, 86 dark, subdued palette that he likes. With few exceptions, the primary colors are severely held down: when they appear, their appearance is calculated. Since it is a gangster movie, an inordinate number of people get killed—the film is a who's-next, not a whodunit—but the first time the blood of a victim trickles down his white shirtfront the impact on the audience is the result of more than just shock or revulsion at the gruesome sight; the audience is not conscious of having seen bright red before.

87   The film cuts back and forth between several generations and three basic settings, jumping from the brooding chiaroscuro of the young Godfather's house in Nevada to the harsh landscape of Sicily and on to the streets of New York's Little Italy in the days of the First World War. There are side trips to Miami and Cuba, too. Willis has imposed a distinctive look on each.

88   In the sequences inside the Godfather's house there is a stifled, airless, mausoleum quality; the idea of death dominates. Giant close-ups crowd the screen, the faces emerging from blackness rather than from nature, and emphasizing isolation, inhumanity. The faces are lit primarily from above, with a yellow light; half-hidden in shadow, they glow with an unnatural red-orange hue, as if scared by a steady hellish flame. The camera hardly moves.

89   The scenes in the streets of Little Italy are, by contrast, open and full of vitality; the camera tracks joyfully through crowds of moving people and vehicles—a sightseer. The sky is held down to a very pale, foggy blue, and, against a carefully orchestrated progression of muted natural colors—brick walls, brown wool, burlap, canvas, black iron, wood—suddenly light-green lettuce on a pushcart jumps to life, white eggs gleam, lemons sparkle, golden loaves of bread glow. Interior scenes are hazy and radiant; sunlight comes through windows like a solid. There is, toward the end of the movie, a particularly stunning sequence on the rooftops of the tenements; it is without dialogue, and it combines a number of elements of extraordinary filmmaking. Robert De Niro, dressed in brown, is moving across the roofs. In the street below, there is a religious parade; De Niro is about to kill somebody down there—when he gets to the stairs of the right building. De Niro moves across the black tar roofs, past black pipes and brick chimneys, against walls of low rooftop structures—a brown figure in motion against constantly changing shapes, varying textures, and subtle, harmonious colors. Behind this is a broken panorama of softly rendered tenements.

❡ Again, I am delighted by what Stevenson is trying to do. He's trying to take you inside the cinematographer's art to show you the images that they see. He's gotten everything out of the way, and he makes the comparison, without saying it, between Williams' poem and these scenes. They are quick; they are precise; they seem to me to be exactly right. This is what I want to do, I tell myself. I want to get right at the center of what I write, to get everything out of the way so that I can be right there and the reader can be right there with me. ❡

The movie is full of splendid sights: 90

A rocky, barren Sicilian landscape occupying the entire screen, 91 with the camera holding. Then, from the bottom left-hand corner of the frame, a tiny group of figures—a pathetic funeral procession— moving slowly into view.

A snow scene: a black car moving through a gate of vertical 92 black bars and down a gray road past black tree trunks; everything else white.

Under a melancholy sky, windblown autumn leaves skittering 93 across a lawn toward a dark house.

Ellis Island: massed brown figures in a huge, lofty room; light 94 from the tall windows a pale green.

An outdoor lunch in Sicily: glasses of red wine on a white 95 tablecloth.

A search at night with dark running figures; abrupt, blinding, 96 floodlights; dots of flashlights bobbing across a black screen.

A formal dance in Havana; a flowing arrangement of white 97 dresses, black tuxedos, white jackets; then, between the dancers— appearing and disappearing—the gleaming red-brown surface of the dance floor.

A statue of Christ carried in a parade through Little Italy: the 98 figure seen in fragments as the camera moves along the sidewalk, looking upward, its view intersected and interrupted by the black overhanging awnings of the vegetable stands.

A man murdered in the doorway of a penthouse at night, with 99 white curtains blowing crazily around him, concealing the murderer. A theatrical performance in Little Italy: the actors lit by wonderfully amateurish footlights.

Miami: sunlit pastel colors on a residential street; then the God- 100 father's car—a two-tone red-and-black—driving up.

An ambush in a city street, filmed from above: small black fig- 101 ures running, fanning outward in a swift ballet.

A man in a white suit and a black overcoat moving through a 102 dark crowd, carrying an orange.

An outdoor party in Nevada, late afternoon: the ordinary guests 103 in sunlight, the mobsters almost always in shadow.

A killing in Sicily: the camera pulling back, the frame becoming, 104 in effect, a proscenium arch, lending the scene the formal staging of an opera.

Sicily: a greenish-black train at a gray platform puffing off-white 105 smoke against distant pale-blue mountains.

106 Another train: The Godfather riding at night; an exterior shot of the train almost entirely black, except for a small lit portion of the screen where the Godfather is seated by the window, the curtains and the night looping around him like the drapings of a catafalque.

107 One of the few significant uses of blue in the film: a scene in which the Godfather condemns his brother to death, with the two figures indoors, silhouettes framed by windows overlooking a lake—rectangles of cold blue, with snow falling.

108 The Godfather at the end of the film: sitting alone outdoors in winter, and cast in a green light, as if he were already dead.

109 When people tell Willis they have just seen "The Godfather, Part II," Willis does not ask them, "How did you like it?" He says, "Was it a good print?"

110 Willis: "I've been accused of directing movies for directors. The truth is, I make movies *with* directors. Some of them have very special minds and may not be accomplished at the physical execution, but ultimately it's their idea that I'm executing. I find that most directors I work for are interested in making a better movie, and not particularly interested in presenting some ego projection. I admire a lot of them, and I know which directors I don't want to work with. This winter, I'm going to be directing a movie of my own.

111 "I don't make studies of movies. I don't even have particular favorites I see again and again. There's a lot of film mythology—one hundred people are making films today, and fifty thousand people are writing books about films—and a lot if it isn't true. I have very little patience with a director who remembers something from some other film and wants to do something using it as a reference point. I feel you're not on your own set of wheels.

112 "There are some of the finest technicians in the world in Hollywood, but the application of their mechanics is horrifying at times. They apply themselves badly in that town. Things that are wonderful, different, and exciting rarely come out of Hollywood. People there see things in a two-dimensional way; they reduce each other to doing the same old stuff. Mystery scares the hell out of them. Something happens to people's minds out there. They've forgotten that the rest of America is breathing or walking. Their bead on life comes from driving between the tennis court and the outskirts of Beverly Hills. It's not the way to live. When I go to Hollywood—I live in New York State—I run into people I know, and I say, 'How are you?' They

answer, 'I'm shooting this or that film,' and they go on; and finally they say, 'When are you going to move out?' I never do get an answer to the 'How are you?'

"When the actors, agents, and lawyers began to take over the 113 business, you began to see the destruction of motion pictures. Most of them are motivated by money. They're peddlers of crap. Men like Goldwyn and Selznick and Harry Cohn liked profits, too, but, whatever else you may say about them, they had great instincts for making entertainment, and they loved movies. I feel that in order to get movies back on the right track creative producers and directors will have to regain control. Right now, what makes me unhappy is there's more and more hamburger and less and less steak."

A film lab on the third floor of a building in the West Forties is 114 a smelly, bustling place where there are many small rooms, each with a pane of glass in the door through which a dark figure can be discerned peering at tiny pictures. The corridor winds this way and that, past rows of silvery film cans in six-foot stacks against the walls; rooms glitter with shelves of them, and carts piled high with them are pushed along, just missing other carts, similarly loaded, coming the opposite way. To stand in the corridor is like being in a fast-moving river with great schools of odd silver fish. Near the end of the corridor, in a dark and quiet fifty-seat projection room, Willis, the director, the assistant director, the producer, Hovey, Schuler, and several members of the production staff are watching the dailies—the bits of film that were shot the day before. It is early evening, and once again everybody is bone-tired. The crew has been shooting every day, often from early morning to late at night, and on weekends there have been locations to look at and other matters to deal with, and there are still nine weeks of production to go. "If we ever get the chance," Willis said earlier, "my wife and I drive up to a place we've got in the Adirondacks. I chop a lot of wood. We go on nature walks; watch the heavens. Just take it all in. If I ever take a picture, I go to Instamatics and Polaroids—just to record what's going on, and just for fun."

Willis sits in one of three big chairs behind a desk at the back 115 of the dim room—Hovey and Schuler sit on either side—and the stream of light from the projector comes trembling out of a small window just above his head, catching idling trails of smoke from his cigarette. "I know what I'm going to see in the dailies," Willis says. "There are no surprises. It's what the lab has done to the film that

I'm looking for. The labs today are the big problem. You can't count on them. Since television, they've become interested in yardage, not quality. There used to be good people working in labs, but they've mostly left—in disgust. If you give a lab something good, they take it out; if you give them something bad, they leave it in. Tomorrow, we've got to go back and reshoot that big crowd scene with all the extras. Lab problems. They always know which one to louse up." Willis laughs.

116   In the old days of Hollywood productions, each sequence of a film was shot in a number of ways, from several points of view, leaving the selection of the most effective shot up to the film editor and the director, at the end of production. Willis does not work like this. Whenever possible, he shoots a sequence exactly the way he wants it, offering no alternatives. To watch the dailies of a Willis film is to see the same sequence over and over again; the changes are mostly variations of pacing, dialogue, and performance. On the screen, a couple of arms reach out with the slate, the number of the take chalked in on it, and then—whack!—the slapstick is slapped, the arms and the slate disappear, and the sequence proceeds. Actors flub lines, change their timing and inflection, but it all happens within the same frame, seen by the same eye in the same way. Willis is in control.

> ❨ A good way to end is to echo the lead, and Stevenson does just that. You are shown the dawn, and now that you are educated through the piece you see the filmmaker's photographs of the dawn. This gives you a sense of completeness, something every reader likes to experience at the end of a piece of writing. ❩

117   On the screen now, it is dawn in Sutton Square. A couple are sitting on a bench by the railing. Behind them is the Queensboro Bridge. "I used a grad on the sky—a filter to darken it a little and keep the bridge strong," says Willis, watching. The couple on the screen talk, and then they rise and walk away from the bench toward the camera. The slate and arms appear; the slapstick is slapped. Another take, and then another. Each is slightly different, but one element remains the same: the soft, subtle beauty of the scene, perfectly composed and rendered, the actors cutting across the landscape in precisely the right way; the delicate suffusion of dawn. No tricks, but a lot of magic.

Discussion

- Discuss how Stevenson has used movie techniques in his writing, and then discuss how movies and television have influenced other forms of writing.
- Since Stevenson uses some of the techniques of the subject he's writing about, it might be interesting to consider other subjects that would have techniques that could be used by someone writing about them. For example, a story about what a social worker does might be told through, or at least partially through, case reports.
- Discuss how the poem at the beginning of the piece relates to the piece. It is there for a purpose. Discuss whether it helps the reader or not.
- Pick a section and show how Stevenson's artist's eye helps us to see.
- Discuss how the organization of this piece compares to Zinsser's article, or other articles in the book, such as Scanlan, Mitchell, Baldwin, and Gibson.

Activities

- Go to a place familiar to you and your classmates and write what you see as if you were a cinematographer.
- Go to a place on campus—the library, the gym, a dining hall, a lounge area, and record images. Arrange these images in such a way that they are the whole text, but give the reader the experience of being there.
- Take a scene from Scanlan, Caro, Mitchell, Moon, Baraka, Baldwin, Gibson, and write a memo on how it could be shot as a movie.
- Pick a movie or television show you have seen recently and write down how a technique used on film could improve a draft of your writing.
- Go to a familiar place and describe it, using every sense, but sight—sound, smell, taste, touch.

A Note on Narrative

I can't tell, sitting here behind the page, if you are black or white, tall or short, portly or scrawny, young or old, eat liver and onions or ginger ice-cream, but I do know that when you were young you demanded, "Tell me a story." The hunger for story seems born within us; the need for story must go far back beyond the cave paintings of the hunt.

Narrative, the grown-up word for story, retells experience so that it has the flavor of experience, but contains a meaning that is clearer than life. Story is the fundamental writing form, the most powerful genre, and yet it is often left out of the college writing course as if it were a childish form of writing, something inferior to argument, the expository essay, the research paper.

Narrative uses time to organize events in sequence. In the beginning, the structure of story is simple and children tell the breakfast to bed story in which all events—the putting on of socks, the way Uncle Herbert was gobbled up by the whale, the eating of the peanut butter sandwich—all are given equal time and importance. This pattern continues with inexperienced writers and causes many college instructors to scorn personal narratives by students. Their complaint should not be with the form but its use. The personal narrative that has no meaning, that reveals no significance, does not need to be outlawed so much as to be developed.

To reveal meaning, the narrative distorts time, giving more space to one event and compressing the time given to less important events. Eventually the student may learn how to jump ahead in time and "flashback" in time. I find students and readers are able to move more quickly through time because of the experience of viewing TV commericals which can flash through a series of events in seconds.

Once students become masters of time, they can begin to experiment with point of view and then with the significant shift from first person to third. These questions of technique all force the student to achieve distance from the subject, to become more objective, to evaluate, to think. Narrative is certainly not the only form of writing, but it's basic and sophisticated, a form worthy of study in any writing class.

This book includes many nonfiction examples of narrative— biography and autobiography, history and chronicles of events, travel narrative and poetic narrative—and it has in the selections which follow some examples of fictional narrative, story-telling that is made up but which tells the truth. One of our best novel and short story writers, the late Flannery O'Connor, talks about "Writing Short Stories." And then we have reprinted an example of one of her short stories that she talks about in that piece. It may be a good idea to jump ahead and to read Joan Didion's "Why I Write" in the next chapter, for she is both a nonfiction and a fiction writer, and that essay talks about the writing of fiction as well as nonfiction. We've also published an excerpt from Toni Morrison's first novel and two versions of the same story by Raymond Carver.

You should read and study these stories—and the poems in the next chapter—for delight first of all. These writers, the great masters of our craft, are fun to read. They create a make-believe world that is more real many times than the world in which we live. It is so real that we can enter and live in their manufactured experience. By doing this we see and understand and experience a special kind of living. We also, by hearing their voices, hear the music of our language and see how it can be pushed to the edge of meaning by Toni Morrison and made, at the other extreme, into a stark and disciplined song by Raymond Carver.

We should also read narrative as practiced by masters of narrative, because all writers of nonfiction have their roots in poetry and fiction. In one sense all forms of prose writing are a variation on narrative. In many forms of writing—the lawyer's brief, the analysis of supermarket sales, the political argument, the news story, the critical essay, even the research paper—there is a narrative imbedded in the text, and the reader follows that imbedded narrative to find out what happens.

We also use narrative when writing in other forms, such as exposition. We use little anecdotes or incidents to document or illuminate the text. We use a narrative of process in a scientific paper, or a narrative of a case history to make an argument. Each of the writers whose drafts we have printed here have written a narrative of their own writing, even though they may not seem to be narratives at first glance.

We cannot understand the nonfiction writing craft and perform it with skill unless we appreciate narrative, learn from it, and use the lessons of narrative, when appropriate, in all forms of our writing.

Flannery O'Connor

Flannery O'Connor, who died in 1964, continues to live in her fiction. She published four books during her lifetime, *Wise Blood, A Good Man Is Hard to Find, The Violent Bear It Away,* and *Everything That Rises Must Converge.* She lived a life of pain, but continued to write despite her continual battle with disseminated lupus erythematosus, and left us her individual vision of the world. Every writer needs discipline, but she had a disease in which the treatments were often as debilitating as the disease itself, and yet she kept writing. On my desk I have one of her statements, perhaps my favorite statement on writing: "Every morning between 9 and 12 I go to my room and sit before a piece of paper. Many times I just sit for three hours with no ideas coming to me. But I know one thing: If an idea does come between 9 and 12, I am there ready for it."

Writing Short Stories

1   I have heard people say that the short story was one of the most difficult literary forms, and I've always tried to decide why people feel this way about what seems to me to be one of the most natural and fundamental ways of human expression.* After all, you begin to hear and tell stories when you're a child, and there doesn't seem to be anything very complicated about it. I suspect that most of you have been telling stories all your lives, and yet here you sit—come to find out how to do it.

2   Then last week, after I had written down some of these serene thoughts to use here today, my calm was shattered when I was sent seven of your manuscripts to read.

3   After this experience, I found myself ready to admit, if not that the short story is one of the most difficult literary forms, at least that it is more difficult for some than for others.

4   I still suspect that most people start out with some kind of ability to tell a story but that it gets lost along the way. Of course, the ability to create life with words is essentially a gift. If you have it in the first place, you can develop it; if you don't have it, you might as well forget it.

5   But I have found that the people who don't have it are frequently the ones hell-bent on writing stories. I'm sure anyway that they are the ones who write the books and the magazine articles on

---

* In another mood on another occasion Flannery O'Connor began as follows: "I have very little to say about short-story writing. It's one thing to write short stories and another thing to talk about writing them, and I hope you realize that your asking me to talk about story-writing is just like asking a fish to lecture on swimming. The more stories I write, the more mysterious I find the process and the less I find myself capable of analyzing it. Before I started writing stories, I suppose I could have given you a pretty good lecture on the subject, but nothing produced silence like experience, and at this point I have very little to say about how stories are written."

how-to-write-short-stories. I have a friend who is taking a correspondence course in this subject, and she has passed a few of the chapter headings on to me—such as, "The Story Formula for Writers," "How to Create Characters," "Let's Plot!" This form of corruption is costing her twenty-seven dollars.

I feel that discussing story-writing in terms of plot, character, 6 and theme is like trying to describe the expression on a face by saying where the eyes, nose, and mouth are. I've heard students say, "I'm very good with plot, but I can't do a thing with character," or, "I have this theme but I don't have a plot for it," and once I heard one say, "I've got the story but I don't have any technique."

Technique is a word they all trot out. I talked to a writers' club 7 once, and during the question time, one good soul said, "Will you give me the technique for the frame-within-a-frame short story?" I had to admit I was so ignorant I didn't even know what that was, but she assured me there was such a thing because she had entered a contest to write one and the prize was fifty dollars.

But setting aside the people who have no talent for it, there are 8 others who do have the talent but who flounder around because they don't really know what a story is.

I suppose that obvious things are the hardest to define. Everybody thinks he knows what a story is. But if you ask a beginning 9 student to write a story, you're liable to get almost anything—a reminiscence, an episode, an opinion, an anecdote, anything under the sun but a story. A story is a complete dramatic action—and in good stories, the characters are shown through the action and the action is controlled through the characters, and the result of this is meaning that derives from the whole presented experience. I myself prefer to say that a story is a dramatic event that involves a person because he is a person, and a particular person—that is, because he shares in the general human condition and in some specific human situation. A story always involves, in a dramatic way, the mystery of personality. I lent some stories to a country lady who lives down the road from me, and when she returned them, she said, "Well, them stories just gone and shown you how some folks *would* do," and I thought to myself that that was right; when you write stories, you have to be content to start exactly there—showing how some specific folks *will* do, *will* do in spite of everything.

Now this is a very humble level to have to begin on, and most 10 people who think they want to write stories are not willing to start there. They want to write about problems, not people; or about abstract issues, not concrete situations. They have an idea, or a feeling, or an overflowing ego, or they want to Be A Writer, or they want to give their wisdom to the world in a simple-enough way for the world to be able to absorb it. In any case, they don't have a story and they wouldn't be willing to write it if they did; and in the absence of a story, they set out to find a theory or a formula or a technique.

11   Now none of this is to say that when you write a story, you are supposed to forget or give up any moral position that you hold. Your beliefs will be the light by which you see, but they will not be what you see and they will not be a substitute for seeing. For the writer of fiction, everything has its testing point in the eye, and the eye is an organ that eventually involves the whole personality, and as much of the world as can be got into it. It involves judgment. Judgment is something that begins in the act of vision, and when it does not, or when it becomes separated from vision, then a confusion exists in the mind which transfers itself to the story.

12   Fiction operates through the senses, and I think one reason that people find it so difficult to write stories is that they forget how much time and patience is required to convince through the senses. No reader who doesn't actually experience, who isn't made to feel, the story is going to believe anything the fiction writer merely tells him. The first and most obvious characteristic of fiction is that it deals with reality through what can be seen, heard, smelt, tasted, and touched.

13   Now this is something that can't be learned only in the head; it has to be learned in the habits. It has to become a way that you habitually look at things. The fiction writer has to realize that he can't create compassion with compassion, or emotion with emotion, or thought with thought. He has to provide all these things with a body; he has to create a world with weight and extension.

14   I have found that the stories of beginning writers usually bristle with emotion, but *whose* emotion is often very hard to determine. Dialogue frequently proceeds without the assistance of any characters that you can actually see, and uncontained thought leaks out of every corner of the story. The reason is usually that the student is wholly interested in his thoughts and his emotions and not in his dramatic action, and that he is too lazy or highfalutin to descend to the concrete where fiction operates. He thinks that judgment exists in one place and sense-impression in another. But for the fiction writer, judgment begins in the details he sees and how he sees them.

15   Fiction writers who are not concerned with these concrete details are guilty of what Henry James called "weak specification."

The eye will glide over their words while the attention goes to sleep. Ford Madox Ford taught that you couldn't have a man appear long enough to sell a newspaper in a story unless you put him there with enough detail to make the reader see him.

I have a friend who is taking acting classes in New York from a   16 Russian lady who is supposed to be very good at teaching actors. My friend wrote me that the first month they didn't speak a line, they only learned to see. Now learning to see is the basis for learning all the arts except music. I know a good many fiction writers who paint, not because they're any good at painting, but because it helps their writing. It forces them to look at things. Fiction writing is very seldom a matter of saying things; it is a matter of showing things.

However, to say that fiction proceeds by the use of detail does   17 not mean the simple, mechanical piling-up of detail. Detail has to be controlled by some overall purpose, and every detail has to be put to work for you. Art is selective. What is there is essential and creates movement.

❲ It is interesting to note how her discussion of detail relates to Stevenson's piece on Gordon Willis. ❳

Now all this requires time. A good short story should not have   18 less meaning than a novel, nor should its action be less complete. Nothing essential to the main experience can be left out of a short story. All the action has to be saisfactorily accounted for in terms of motivation, and there has to be a beginning, a middle, and an end, though not necessarily in that order. I think many people decide that they want to write short stories because they're short, and by short, they mean short in every way. They think that a short story is an incomplete action in which a very little is shown and a great deal suggested, and they think you suggest something by leaving it out. It's very hard to disabuse a student of this notion, because he thinks that when he leaves something out, he's being subtle; and when you tell him that he has to put something in before anything can be there, he thinks you're an insensitive idiot.

Perhaps the central question to be considered in any discussion   19 of the short story is what we do mean by short. Being short does not mean being slight. A short story should be long in depth and should give us an experience of meaning. I have an aunt who thinks that nothing happens in a story unless somebody gets married or shot at the end of it. I wrote a story about a tramp who marries an old woman's idiot daughter in order to acquire the old woman's automobile. After the marriage, he takes the daughter off on a wedding trip in the automobile and abandons her in an eating place and drives on by himself. Now that is a complete story. There is nothing more relating to the mystery of that man's personality that could be shown through that particular dramatization. But I've never been able to convince my aunt that it's a complete story. She wants to know what happened to the idiot daughter after that.

20   Not long ago that story was adapted for a television play, and the adapter, knowing his business, had the tramp have a change of heart and go back and pick up the idiot daughter and the two of them ride away, grinning madly. My aunt believes that the story is complete at last, but I have other sentiments about it—which are not suitable for public utterance. When you write a story, you only have to write one story, but there will always be people who will refuse to read the story you have written.

21   And this naturally brings up the awful question of what kind of a reader you are writing for when you write fiction. Perhaps we each think we have a personal solution for this problem. For my own part, I have a very high opinion of the art of fiction and a very low opinion of what is called the "average" reader. I tell myself that I can't escape him, that this is the personality I am supposed to keep awake, but that at the same time, I am also supposed to provide the intelligent reader with the deeper experience that he looks for in fiction. Now actually, both of these readers are just aspects of the writer's own personality, and in the last analysis, the only reader he can know anything about is himself. We all write at our own level of understanding, but it is the peculiar characteristic of fiction that its literal surface can be made to yield entertainment on an obvious physical plane to one sort of reader while the selfsame surface can be made to yield meaning to the person equipped to experience it there.

22   Meaning is what keeps the short story from being short. I prefer to talk about the meaning in a story rather than the theme of a story. People talk about the theme of a story as if the theme were like the string that a sack of chicken feed is tied with. They think that if you can pick out the theme, the way you pick the right thread in the chicken-feed sack, you can rip the story open and feed the chickens. But this is not the way meaning works in fiction.

23   When you can state the theme of a story, when you can separate it from the story itself, then you can be sure the story is not a very good one. The meaning of a story has to be embodied in it, has to be

made concrete in it. A story is a way to say something that can't be said any other way, and it takes every word in the story to say what the meaning is. You tell a story because a statement would be inadequate. When anybody asks what a story is about, the only proper thing is to tell him to read the story. The meaning of fiction is not abstract meaning but experienced meaning, and the purpose of making statements about the meaning of a story is only to help you to experience that meaning more fully.

❡ The previous paragraph is as wise and as important a statement as I can remember reading. It's also true of most good nonfiction. The meaning of it cannot really be separated from the text. ❡

Fiction is an art that calls for the strictest attention to the real— 24 whether the writer is writing a naturalistic story or a fantasy. I mean that we always begin with what is or with what has an eminent possibility of truth about it. Even when one writes a fantasy, reality is the proper basis of it. A thing is fantastic because it is so real, so real that it is fantastic. Graham Greene has said that he can't write, "I stood over a bottomless pit," because that couldn't be true, or "Running down the stairs I jumped into a taxi," because that couldn't be true either. But Elizabeth Bowen can write about one of her characters that "she snatched at her hair as if she heard something in it," because that is eminently possible.

I would even go so far as to say that the person writing a fantasy 25 has to be even more strictly attentive to the concrete detail than someone writing in a naturalistic vein—because the greater the story's strain on the credulity, the more convincing the properties in it have to be.

A good example of this is a story called "The Metamorphosis" 26 by Franz Kafka. This is a story about a man who wakes up one morning to find that he has turned into a cockroach overnight, while not discarding his human nature. The rest of the story concerns his life and feelings and eventual death as an insect with human nature, and this situation is accepted by the reader because the concrete detail of the story is absolutely convincing. The fact is that this story describes the dual nature of man in such a realistic fashion that it is almost unbearable. The truth is not distorted here, but rather, a certain distortion is used to get at the truth. If we admit, as we must, that appearance is not the same thing as reality, then we must give the artist the liberty to make certain rearrangements of nature if these will lead to greater depths of vision. The artist himself always has to remember that what he is rearranging *is* nature, and that he has to know it and be able to describe it accurately in order to have the authority to rearrange it at all.

27   The peculiar problem of the short-story writer is how to make the action he describes reveal as much of the mystery of existence as possible. He has only a short space to do it in and he can't do it by statement. He has to do it by showing, not by saying, and by showing the concrete—so that his problem is really how to make the concrete work double time for him.

28   In good fiction, certain of the details will tend to accumulate meaning from the action of the story itself, and when this happens they become symbolic in the way they work. I once wrote a story called "Good Country People," in which a lady Ph.D. has her wooden leg stolen by a Bible salesman whom she has tried to seduce. Now I'll admit that, paraphrased in this way, the situation is simply a low joke. The average reader is pleased to observe anybody's wooden leg being stolen. But without ceasing to appeal to him and without making any statements of high intention, this story does manage to operate at another level of experience, by letting the wooden leg accumulate meaning. Early in the story, we're presented with the fact that the Ph.D. is spiritually as well as physically crippled. She believes in nothing but her own belief in nothing, and we perceive that there is a wooden part of her soul that corresponds to her wooden leg. Now of course this is never stated. The fiction writer states as little as possible. The reader makes this connection from things he is shown. He may not even know that he makes the connection, but the connection is there nevertheless and it has its effect on him. As the story goes on, the wooden leg continues to accumulate meaning. The reader learns how the girl feels about her leg, how her mother feels about it, and how the country woman on the place feels about it; and finally, by the time the Bible salesman comes along, the leg has accumulated so much meaning that it is, as the saying goes, loaded. And when the Bible salesman steals it, the reader realizes that he has taken away part of the girl's personality and has revealed her deeper affliction to her for the first time.

> ❧ Students often have a misunderstanding about how writing is written that comes from the way literature is too often taught. It is understandable that students think that you harvest a crop of symbols, spread them out, and then lay a story over them. That isn't the way it's done. And Flannery O'Connor speaks to how it is done.❧

If you want to say that the wooden leg is a symbol, you can say 29
that. But it is a wooden leg first, and as a wooden leg it is absolutely
necessary to the story. It has its place on the literal level of the story,
but it operates in depth as well as on the surface. It increases the
story in every direction, and this is essentially the way a story escapes
being short.

Now a little might be said about the way in which this happens. 30
I wouldn't want you to think that in that story I sat down and said,
"I am now going to write a story about a Ph.D. with a wooden leg,
using the wooden leg as a symbol for another kind of affliction." I
doubt myself if many writers know what they are going to do when
they start out. When I started writing that story, I didn't know there
was going to be a Ph.D. with a wooden leg in it. I merely found myself
one morning writing a description of two women that I knew something about, and before I realized it, I had equipped one of them with
a daughter with a wooden leg. As the story progressed, I brought in
the Bible salesman, but I had no idea what I was going to do with
him. I didn't know he was going to steal that wooden leg until ten or
twelve lines before he did it, but when I found out that this was what
was going to happen, I realized that it was inevitable. This is a story
that produces a shock for the reader, and I think one reason for this
is that it produced a shock for the writer.

Now despite the fact that this story came about in this seem- 31
ingly mindless fashion, it is a story that almost no rewriting was done
on. It is a story that was under control throughout the writing of it,
and it might be asked how this kind of control comes about, since it
is not entirely conscious.

I think the answer to this is what Maritain calls "the habit of 32
art." It is a fact that fiction writing is something in which the whole
personality takes part—the conscious as well as the unconscious
mind. Art is the habit of the artist; and habits have to be rooted deep
in the whole personality. They have to be cultivated like any other
habit, over a long period of time, by experience; and teaching any
kind of writing is largely a matter of helping the student develop the
habit of art. I think this is more than just a discipline, although it is
that; I think it is a way of looking at the created world and of using
the senses so as to make them find as much meaning as possible in
things.

Now I am not so naive as to suppose that most people come to 33
writers' conferences in order to hear what kind of vision is necessary
to write stories that will become a permanent part of our literature.

Even if you do wish to hear this, your greatest concerns are immediately practical. You want to know how you can actually write a
good story, and further, how you can tell when you've done it; and
so you want to know what the form of a short story is, as if the form
were something that existed outside of each story and could be
applied or imposed on the material. Of course, the more you write,
the more you will realize that the form is organic, that it is something
that grows out of the material, that the form of each story is unique.
A story that is any good can't be reduced, it can only be expanded.
A story is good when you continue to see more and more in it, and
when it continues to escape you. In fiction two and two is always
more than four.

> ❡ In another place O'Connor has said, "I write because I don't know
> what I think until I read what I say." This is true of most kinds of
> writing—fiction, poetry, and nonfiction. We write to think. Writing
> is always a voyage of discovery. ❡

34   The only way, I think, to learn to write short stories is to write
them, and then to try to discover what you have done. The time to
think of technique is when you've actually got the story in front of
you. The teacher can help the student by looking at his individual
work and trying to help him decide if he has written a complete
story, one in which the action fully illuminates the meaning.

35   Perhaps the most profitable thing I can do is to tell you about
some of the general observations I made about these seven stories I
read of yours. All of these observations will not fit any one of the
stories exactly, but they are points nevertheless that it won't hurt
anyone interested in writing to think about.

36   The first thing that any professional writer is conscious of in
reading anything is, naturally, the use of language. Now the use of
language in these stories was such that, with one exception, it would
be difficult to distinguish one story from another. While I can recall
running into several clichés, I can't remember one image or one metaphor from the seven stories. I don't mean there weren't images in
them; I just mean that there weren't any that were effective enough
to take away with you.

37   In connection with this, I made another observation that startled me considerably. With the exception of one story, there was
practically no use made of the local idiom. Now this is a Southern
Writers' Conference. All the addresses on these stories were from

Georgia or Tennesse, yet there was no distinctive sense of Southern life in them. A few place-names were dropped, Savannah or Atlanta or Jacksonville, but these could just as easily have been changed to Pittsburgh or Passaic without calling for any other alteration in the story. The characters spoke as if they had never heard any kind of language except what came out of a television set. This indicates that something is way out of focus.

There are two qualities that make fiction. One is the sense of mystery and the other is the sense of manners. You get the manners from the texture of existence that surrounds you. The great advantage of being a Southern writer is that we don't have to go anywhere to look for manners; bad or good, we've got them in abundance. We in the South live in a society that is rich in contradiction, rich in irony, rich in contrast, and particularly rich in its speech. And yet here are six stories by Southerners in which almost no use is made of the gifts of the region.

Of course the reason for this may be that you have seen these gifts abused so often that you have become self-conscious about using them. There is nothing worse than the writer who doesn't *use* the gifts of the region, but wallows in them. Everything becomes so Southern that it's sickening, so local that it is unintelligible, so literally reproduced that it conveys nothing. The general gets lost in the particular instead of being shown through it.

However, when the life that actually surrounds us is totally ignored, when our patterns of speech are absolutely overlooked, then something is out of kilter. The writer should then ask himself if he is not reaching out for a kind of life that is artificial to him.

An idiom characterizes a society, and when you ignore the idiom, you are very likely ignoring the whole social fabric that could make a meaningful character. You can't cut characters off from their society and say much about them as individuals. You can't say anything meaningful about the mystery of a personality unless you put that personality in a believable and significant social context. And the best way to do this is through the character's own language. When the old lady in one of Andrew Lytle's stories says contemptuously that she has a mule that is older than Birmingham, we get in that one sentence a sense of a society and its history. A great deal of the Southern writer's work is done for him before he begins, because our history lives in our talk. In one of Eudora Welty's stories a character says, "Where I come from, we use fox for yard dogs and owls for chickens, but we sing true." Now there is a whole book in that

38

39

40

41

one sentence; and when the people of your section can talk like that, and you ignore it, you're just not taking advantage of what's yours. The sound of our talk is too definite to be discarded with impunity, and if the writer tries to get rid of it, he is liable to destroy the better part of his creative power.

42   Another thing I observed about these stories is that most of them don't go very far inside a character, don't reveal very much of the character. I don't mean that they don't enter the character's mind, but they simply don't show that he has a personality. Again this goes back partly to speech. These characters have no distinctive speech to reveal themselves with; and sometimes they have no really distinctive features. You feel in the end that no personality is revealed because no personality is there. In most good stories it is the character's personality that creates the action of the story. In most of these stories, I feel that the writer has thought of some action and then scrounged up a character to perform it. You will usually be more successful if you start the other way around. If you start with a real personality, a real character, then something is bound to happen; and you don't have to know what before you begin. In fact it may be better if you don't know what before you begin. You ought to be able to discover something from your stories. If you don't, probably nobody else will.

❦ Now you can read a story by Flannery to see if she practiced what she preached. ❧

Good Country People

1   Besides the neutral expression that she wore when she was alone, Mrs. Freeman had two others, forward and reverse, that she used for all her human dealings. Her forward expression was steady and driving like the advance of a heavy truck. Her eyes never swerved to left or right but turned as the story turned as if they followed a yellow line down the center of it. She seldom used the other expression because it was not often necessary for her to retract a statement, but when she did, her face came to a complete stop, there was an almost imperceptible movement of her black eyes, during which they seemed to be receding, and then the observer would see

that Mrs. Freeman, though she might stand there as real as several grain sacks thrown on top of each other, was no longer there in spirit. As for getting anything across to her when this was the case, Mrs. Hopewell had given it up. She might talk her head off. Mrs. Freeman could never be brought to admit herself wrong on any point. She would stand there and if she could be brought to say anything, it was something like, "Well, I wouldn't of said it was and I wouldn't of said it wasn't," or letting her gaze range over the top kitchen shelf where there was an assortment of dusty bottles, she might remark, "I see you ain't ate many of them figs you put up last summer."

❧ Notice how quickly and how well you get to know Mrs. Freeman. O'Connor connects her with my experience, I recognize the Mrs. Freemans I have known. ❧

They carried on their most important business in the kitchen at breakfast. Every morning Mrs. Hopewell got up at seven o'clock and lit her gas heater and Joy's. Joy was her daughter, a large blonde girl who had an artificial leg. Mrs. Hopewell thought of her as a child though she was thirty-two years old and highly educated. Joy would get up while her mother was eating and lumber into the bathroom and slam the door, and before long, Mrs. Freeman would arrive at the back door. Joy would hear her mother call, "Come on in," and then they would talk for a while in low voices that were indistinguishable in the bathroom. By the time Joy came in, they had usually finished the weather report and were on one or the other of Mrs. Freeman's daughters, Glynese or Carramae. Joy called them Glycerin and Caramel. Glynese, a redhead, was eighteen and had many admirers; Carramae, a blonde, was only fifteen but already married and pregnant. She could not keep anything on her stomach. Every morning Mrs. Freeman told Mrs. Hopewell how many times she had vomited since the last report.

Mrs. Hopewell liked to tell people that Glynese and Carramae were two of the finest girls she knew and that Mrs. Freeman was a *lady* and that she was never ashamed to take her anywhere or introduce her to anybody they might meet. Then she would tell how she had happened to hire the Freemans in the first place and how they were a godsend to her and how she had had them four years. The reason for her keeping them so long was that they were not trash. They were good country people. She had telephoned the man whose name they had given as a reference and he had told her that Mr. Freeman was a good farmer but that his wife was the nosiest woman ever to walk the earth. "She's got to be into everything," the man said. "If she don't get there before the dust settles, you can bet she's dead, that's all. She'll want to know all your business. I can stand him real good," he had said, "but me nor my wife neither could have stood that woman one more minute on this place." That had put Mrs. Hopewell off for a few days.

❲ It doesn't take O'Connor long to start weaving her story from the conflicts between the characters. ❳

4   She had hired them in the end because there were no other applicants but she had made up her mind beforehand exactly how she would handle the woman. Since she was the type who had to be into everything, then, Mrs. Hopewell had decided, she would not only let her be into everything, she would *see to it* that she was into everything—she would give her the responsibility of everything, she would put her in charge. Mrs. Hopewell had no bad qualities of her own but she was able to use other people's in such a constructive way that she never felt this lack. She had hired the Freemans and she had kept them four years.

5   Nothing is perfect. This was one of Mrs. Hopewell's favorite sayings. Another was: that is life! And still another, the most important, was: Well, other people have their opinions too. She would make these statements, usually at the table, in a tone of gentle insistence as if no one held them but her, and the large hulking Joy, whose constant outrage had obliterated every expression from her face, would stare just a little to the side of her, her eyes icy blue, with the look of someone who has achieved blindness by an act of will and means to keep it.

6   When Mrs. Hopewell said to Mrs. Freeman that life was like that, Mrs. Freeman would say, "I always said so myself." Nothing had been arrived at by anyone that had not first been arrived at by her. She was quicker than Mr. Freeman. When Mrs. Hopewell said to her after they had been on the place a while, "You know, you're the wheel behind the wheel," and winked, Mrs. Freeman had said, "I know it. I've always been quick. It's some that are quicker than others."

7   "Everybody is different," Mrs. Hopewell said.

"Yes, most people is," Mrs. Freeman said. 8

"It takes all kinds to make the world." 9

"I always said it did myself." 10

The girl was used to this kind of dialogue for breakfast and more 11
of it for dinner; sometimes they had it for supper too. When they had
no guest they ate in the kitchen because that was easier. Mrs. Freeman always managed to arrive at some point during the meal and to
watch them finish it. She would stand in the doorway if it were summer but in the winter she would stand with one elbow on top of the
refrigerator and look down on them, or she would stand by the gas
heater, lifting the back of her skirt slightly. Occasionally she would
stand against the wall and roll her head from side to side. At no time
was she in any hurry to leave. All this was very trying on Mrs.
Hopewell but she was a woman of great patience. She realized that
nothing is perfect and that in the Freemans she had good country
people and that if, in this day and age, you get good country people,
you had better hang onto them.

She had had plenty of experience with trash. Before the Free- 12
mans she had averaged one tenant family a year. The wives of these
farmers were not the kind you would want to be around you for very
long. Mrs. Hopewell, who had divorced her husband long ago,
needed someone to walk over the fields with her; and when Joy had
to be impressed for these services, her remarks were usually so ugly
and her face so glum that Mrs. Hopewell would say, "If you can't
come pleasantly, I don't want you at all," to which the girl standing
square and rigid-shouldered with her neck thrust slightly forward,
would reply, "If you want me, here I am—LIKE I AM."

Mrs. Hopewell excused this attitude because of the leg (which 13
had been shot off in a hunting accident when Joy was ten). It was
hard for Mrs. Hopewell to realize that her child was thirty-two now
and that for more than twenty years she had had only one leg. She
thought of her still as a child because it tore her heart to think instead
of the poor stout girl in her thirties who had never danced a step or
had any *normal* good times. Her name was really Joy but as soon as
she was twenty-one and away from home, she had had it legally
changed. Mrs. Hopewell was certain that she had thought and
thought until she had hit upon the ugliest name in any language.
Then she had gone and had the beautiful name, Joy, changed without
telling her mother until after she had done it. Her legal name was
Hulga.

❧ I'm fascinated by how O'Connor tunes her voice so that it becomes the voice of the story. In many kinds of writing we do, we should tell the story in language that is appropriate to the story. For example, reread the sentence beginning: "She thought of her still. . . ." ❧

14   When Mrs. Hopewell thought the name, Hulga, she thought of the broad blank hull of a battleship. She would not use it. She continued to call her Joy to which the girl responded but in a purely mechanical way.

15   Hulga had learned to tolerate Mrs. Freeman who saved her from taking walks with her mother. Even Glynese and Carramae were useful when they occupied attention that might otherwise have been directed at her. At first she had thought she could not stand Mrs. Freeman for she had found that it was not possible to be rude to her. Mrs. Freeman would take on strange resentments and for days together she would be sullen but the source of her displeasure was always obscure; a direct attack, a positive leer, blatant ugliness to her face—these never touched her. And without warning one day, she began calling her Hulga.

16   She did not call her that in front of Mrs. Hopewell who would have been incensed but when she and the girl happened to be out of the house together, she would say something and add the name Hulga to the end of it, and the big spectacled Joy-Hulga would scowl and redden as if her privacy had been intruded upon. She considered the name her personal affair. She had arrived at it first purely on the basis of its ugly sound and then the full genius of its fitness had struck her. She had a vision of the name working like the ugly sweating Vulcan who stayed in the furnace and to whom, presumably, the goddess had to come when called. She saw it as the name of her highest creative act. One of her major triumphs was that her mother had not been able to turn her dust into Joy, but the greater one was that she had been able to turn it herself into Hulga. However, Mrs. Freeman's relish for using the name only irritated her. It was as if Mrs. Freeman's beady steel-pointed eyes had penetrated far enough behind her face to reach some secret fact. Something about her seemed to fascinate Mrs. Freeman and then one day Hulga realized that it was the artificial leg. Mrs. Freeman had a special fondness for the details of secret infections, hidden deformities, assaults upon children. Of diseases, she preferred the lingering or incurable. Hulga had heard Mrs. Hopewell give her the details of the hunting accident, how the

leg had been literally blasted off, how she had never lost consciousness. Mrs. Freeman could listen to it any time as if it had happened an hour ago.

When Hulga stumped into the kitchen in the morning (she 17 could walk without making the awful noise but she made it—Mrs. Hopewell was certain—because it was ugly-sounding), she glanced at them and did not speak. Mrs. Hopewell would be in her red kimono with her hair tied around her head in rags. She would be sitting at the table, finishing her breakfast and Mrs. Freeman would be hanging by her elbow outward from the refrigerator, looking down at the table. Hulga always put her eggs on the stove to boil and then stood over them with her arms folded, and Mrs. Hopewell would look at her—a kind of indirect gaze divided between her and Mrs. Freeman—and would think that if she would only keep herself up a little, she wouldn't be so bad looking. There was nothing wrong with her face that a pleasant expression wouldn't help. Mrs. Hopewell said that people who looked on the bright side of things would be beautiful even if they were not.

Whenever she looked at Joy this way, she could not help but 18 feel that it would have been better if the child had not taken the Ph.D. It had certainly not brought her out any and now that she had it, there was no more excuse for her to go to school again. Mrs. Hopewell thought it was nice for girls to go to school to have a good time but Joy had "gone through." Anyhow, she would not have been strong enough to go again. The doctors had told Mrs. Hopewell that with the best of care, Joy might see forty-five. She had a weak heart. Joy had made it plain that if it had not been for this condition, she would be far from these red hills and good country people. She would be in a university lecturing to people who knew what she was talking about. And Mrs. Hopewell could very well picture her there, looking like a scarecrow and lecturing to more of the same. Here she went about all day in a six-year-old skirt and a yellow sweat shirt with a faded cowboy on a horse embossed on it. She thought this was funny; Mrs. Hopewell thought it was idiotic and showed simply that she was still a child. She was brilliant but she didn't have a grain of sense. It seemed to Mrs. Hopewell that every year she grew less like other people and more like herself—bloated, rude, and squint-eyed. And she said such strange things! To her own mother she had said—without warning, without excuse, standing up in the middle of a meal with her face purple and her mouth half full—"Woman! do you ever look inside? Do you ever look inside and see what you are *now*? God!"

she had cried sinking down again and staring at her plate, "Malebranche was right: we are not our own light. We are not our own light!" Mrs. Hopewell had no idea to this day what brought that on. She had only made the remark, hoping Joy would take in it, that a smile never hurt anyone.

19 The girl had taken the Ph.D. in philosophy and this left Mrs. Hopewell at a complete loss. You could say, "My daughter is a nurse," or "My daughter is a school teacher," or even, "My daughter is a chemical engineer." You could not say, "My daughter is a philosopher." That was something that had ended with the Greeks and Romans. All day Joy sat on her neck in a deep chair, reading. Sometimes she went for walks but she didn't like dogs or cats or birds or flowers or nature or nice young men. She looked at nice young men as if she could smell their stupidity.

> ❧ Think of point of view and what it does for the reader—and the writer. O'Connor is a master of point of view. This is Joy's story and the author's sympathy is with Joy, but she tells the story from the point of view of those who do not understand her and who are her affliction. This makes the reader see, hear, and experience Joy's world.❧

20 One day Mrs. Hopewell had picked up one of the books the girl had just put down and opening it at random, she read, "Science, on the other hand, has to assert its soberness and seriousness afresh and declare that it is concerned solely with what-is. Nothing—how can it be for science anything but a horror and a phantasm? If science is right, then one thing stands firm: science wishes to know nothing of nothing. Such is after all the strictly scientific approach to Nothing. We know it by wishing to know nothing of Nothing." These words had been underlined with a blue pencil and they worked on Mrs. Hopewell like some evil incantation in gibberish. She shut the book quickly and went out of the room as if she were having a chill.

21 This morning when the girl came in, Mrs. Freeman was on Carramae. "She thrown up four times after supper," she said, "and was up twice in the night after three o'clock. Yesterday she didn't do nothing but ramble in the bureau drawer. All she did. Stand up there and see what she could run up on."

22 "She's got to eat," Mrs. Hopewell muttered, sipping her coffee, while she watched Joy's back at the stove. She was wondering what the child had said to the Bible salesman. She could not imagine what kind of a conversation she could possibly have had with him.

He was a tall gaunt hatless youth who had called yesterday to 23 sell them a Bible. He had appeared at the door, carrying a large black suitcase that weighted him so heavily on one side that he had to brace himself against the door facing. He seemed on the point of collapse but he said in a cheerful voice, "Good morning, Mrs. Cedars!" and set the suitcase down on the mat. He was not a bad-looking young man though he had on a bright blue suit and yellow socks that were not pulled up far enough. He had prominent face bones and a streak of sticky-looking brown hair falling across his forehead.

"I'm Mrs. Hopewell," she said. 24

"Oh!" he said, pretending to look puzzled but with his eyes 25 sparkling, "I saw it said 'The Cedars,' on the mailbox so I thought you was Mrs. Cedars!" and he burst out in a pleasant laugh. He picked up the satchel and under cover of a pant, he fell forward into her hall. It was rather as if the suitcase had moved first, jerking him after it. "Mrs. Hopewell!" he said and grabbed her hand. "I hope you are well!" and he laughed again and then all at once his face sobered completely. He paused and gave her a straight earnest look and said, "Lady, I've come to speak of serious things."

"Well, come in," she muttered, none too pleased because her 26 dinner was almost ready. He came into the parlor and sat down on the edge of a straight chair and put the suitcase between his feet and glanced around the room as if he were sizing her up by it. Her silver gleamed on the two sideboards; she decided he had never been in a room as elegant as this.

"Mrs. Hopewell," he began, using her name in a way that 27 sounded almost intimate, "I know you believe in Christian service."

"Well yes," she murmured. 28

"I know," he said and paused, looking very wise with his head 29 cocked on one side, "that you're a good woman. Friends have told me."

Mrs. Hopewell never liked to be taken for a fool. "What are you 30 selling?" she asked.

"Bibles," the young man said and his eye raced around the 31 room before he added, "I see you have no family Bible in your parlor, I see that is the one lack you got!"

Mrs. Hopewell could not say, "My daughter is an atheist and 32 won't let me keep the Bible in the parlor." She said, stiffening slightly, "I keep my Bible by my bedside." This was not the truth. It was in the attic somewhere.

"Lady," he said, "the word of God ought to be in the parlor." 33

34   "Well, I think that's a matter of taste," she began, "I think . . ."

35   "Lady," he said, "for a Christian, the word of God ought to be in every room in the house besides in his heart. I know you're a Christian because I can see it in every line of your face."

36   She stood up and said, "Well, young man, I don't want to buy a Bible and I smell my dinner burning."

37   He didn't get up. He began to twist his hands and looking down at them, he said softly, "Well lady, I'll tell you the truth—not many people want to buy one nowadays and besides, I know I'm real simple. I don't know how to say a thing but to say it. I'm just a country boy." He glanced up into her unfriendly face. "People like you don't like to fool with country people like me!"

38   "Why!" she cried, "good country people are the salt of the earth! Beside, we all have different ways of doing, it takes all kinds to make the world go 'round. That's life!"

    ☛ See how she weaves the phrase that is the title through the story. ☚

39   "You said a mouthful," he said.

40   "Why, I think there aren't enough good country people in the world!" she said, stirred. "I think that's what's wrong with it!"

41   His face had brightened. "I didn't introduce myself," he said. "I'm Manley Pointer from out in the country around Willohobie, not even from a place, just from near a place."

42   "You wait a minute," she said. "I have to see about my dinner." She went out to the kitchen and found Joy standing near the door where she had been listening.

43   "Get rid of the salt of the earth," she said, "and let's eat."

44   Mrs. Hopewell gave her a pained look and turned the heat down under the vegetables. "*I* can't be rude to anybody," she murmured and went back into the parlor.

45   He had opened the suitcase and was sitting with a Bible on each knee.

46   "You might as well put those up," she told him. "I don't want one."

47   "I appreciate your honesty," he said. "You don't see any more real honest people unless you go way out to the country."

48   "I know," she said. "real genuine folks!" Through the crack in the door she heard a groan.

49   "I guess a lot of boys come telling you they're working their way through college," he said, "but I'm not going to tell you that. Some-

how," he said, "I don't want to go to college. I want to devote my life to Christian service. See," he said, lowering his voice, "I got this heart condition. I may not live long. When you know it's something wrong with you and you may not live long, well then, lady . . ." He paused, with his mouth open, and stared at her.

He and Joy had the same conditon! She knew that her eyes were 50 filling with tears but she collected herself quickly and murmured, "Won't you stay for dinner? We'd love to have you!" and was sorry the instant she heard herself say it.

"Yes mam," he said in an abashed voice, "I would sher love to 51 do that!"

Joy had given him one look on being introduced to him and 52 then throughout the meal had not glanced at him again. He had addressed several remarks to her, which she had pretended not to hear. Mrs. Hopewell could not understand deliberate rudeness, although she lived with it, and she felt she had always to overflow with hospitality to make up for Joy's lack of courtesy. She urged him to talk about himself and he did. He said he was the seventh child of twelve and that his father had been crushed under a tree when he himself was eight years old. He had been crushed very badly, in fact, almost cut in two and was practically not recognizable. His mother had got along the best she could by hard working and she had always seen that her children went to Sunday School and that they read the Bible every evening. He was now nineteen years old and he had been selling Bibles for four months. In that time he had sold seventy-seven Bibles and had the promise of two more sales. He wanted to become a missionary because he thought that was the way you could do most for people. "He who losest his life shall find it," he said simply and he was so sincere, so genuine and earnest that Mrs. Hopewell would not for the world have smiled. He prevented his peas from sliding onto the table by blocking them with a piece of bread which he later cleaned his plate with. She could see Joy observing sidewise how he handled his knife and fork and she saw too that every few minutes, the boy would dart a keen appraising glance at the girl as if he were trying to attract her attention.

After dinner Joy cleared the dishes off the table and disappeared 53 and Mrs. Hopewell was left to talk with him. He told her again about his childhood and his father's accident and about various things that had happened to him. Every five minutes or so she would stifle a yawn. He sat for two hours until finally she told him she must go because she had an appointment in town. He packed his Bibles and thanked her and prepared to leave, but in the doorway he stopped and wrung her hand and said that not on any of his trips had he met a lady as nice as her and he asked if he could come again. She had said she would always be happy to see him.

54   Joy had been standing in the road, apparently looking at something in the distance, when he came down the steps toward her, bent to the side with his heavy valise. He stopped where she was standing and confronted her directly. Mrs. Hopewell could not hear what he said but she trembled to think what Joy would say to him. She could see that after a minute Joy said something and that then the boy began to speak again, making an excited gesture with his free hand. After a minute Joy said something else at which the boy began to speak once more. Then to her amazement, Mrs. Hopewell saw the two of them walk off together, toward the gate. Joy had walked all the way to the gate with him and Mrs. Hopewell could not imagine what they had said to each other, and she had not yet dared to ask.

55   Mrs. Freeman was insisting upon her attention. She had moved from the refrigerator to the heater so that Mrs. Hopewell had to turn and face her in order to seem to be listening. "Glynese gone out with Harvey Hill again last night," she said. "She had this sty."

56   "Hill," Mrs. Hopewell said absently, "is that the one who works in the garage?"

57   "Nome, he's the one that goes to chiropracter school," Mrs. Freeman said. "She had this sty. Been had it two days. So she says when he brought her in the other night he says, 'Lemme get rid of that sty for you,' and she says, 'How?' and he says, 'You just lay yourself down acrost the seat of that car and I'll show you.' So she done it and he popped her neck. Kept on a-popping it several times until she made him quit. This morning," Mrs. Freeman said, "she ain't got no sty. She ain't got no traces of a sty."

58   "I never heard of that before," Mrs. Hopewell said.

59   "He ast her to marry him before the Ordinary," Mrs. Freeman went on, "and she told him she wasn't going to be married in no *office.*"

60   "Well, Glynese is a fine girl," Mrs. Hopewell said. "Glynese and Carramae are both fine girls."

61   "Carramae said when her and Lyman was married Lyman said it sure felt sacred to him. She said he said he wouldn't take five hundred dollars for being married by a preacher."

62   "How much would he take?" the girl asked from the stove.

"He said he wouldn't take five hundred dollars," Mrs. Freeman 63
repeated.

"Well, we all have work to do," Mrs. Hopewell said. 64

"Lyman said it just felt more sacred to him," Mrs. Freeman 65
said. "The doctor wants Carramae to eat prunes. Says instead of
medicine. Says them cramps is coming from pressure. You know
where I think it is?"

"She'll be better in a few weeks," Mrs. Hopewell said. 66

"In the tube," Mrs. Freeman said. "Else she wouldn't be as sick 67
as she is."

Hulga had cracked her two eggs into a saucer and was bringing 68
them to the table along with a cup of coffee that she had filled too
full. She sat down carefully and began to eat, meaning to keep Mrs.
Freeman there by questions if for any reason she showed an inclination to leave. She could perceive her mother's eye on her. The first
round-about question would be about the Bible salesman and she did
not wish to bring it on. "How did he pop her neck?" she asked.

Mrs. Freeman went into a description of how he had popped 69
her neck. She said he owned a '55 Mercury but that Glynese said she
would rather marry a man with only a '36 Plymouth who would be
married by a preacher. The girl asked what if he had a '32 Plymouth
and Mrs. Freeman said what Glynese had said was a '36 Plymouth.

Mrs. Hopewell said there were not many girls with Glynese's 70
common sense. She said what she admired in those girls was their
common sense. She said that reminded her that they had had a nice
visitor yesterday, a young man selling Bibles. "Lord," she said, "he
bored me to death but he was so sincere and genuine I couldn't be
rude to him. He was just good country people, you know," she said,
"—just the salt of the earth."

"I seen him walk up," Mrs. Freeman said, "and then later—I 71
seen him walk off," and Hulga could feel the slight shift in her voice,
the slight insinuation, that he had not walked off alone, had he? Her
face remained expressionless but the color rose into her neck and
she seemed to swallow it down with the next spoonful of egg. Mrs.
Freeman was looking at her as if they had a secret together.

"Well, it takes all kinds of people to make the world go 72
'round," Mrs. Hopewell said. "It's very good we aren't all alike."

"Some people are more alike than others," Mrs. Freeman said. 73

Hulga got up and stumped, with about twice the noise that was 74
necessary, into her room and locked the door. She was to meet the

Bible salesman at ten o'clock at the gate. She had thought about it half the night. She had started thinking of it as a great joke and then she had begun to see profound implications in it. She had lain in bed imagining dialogues for them that were insane on the surface but that reached below to depths that no Bible salesman would be aware of. Their conversation yesterday had been of this kind.

75   He had stopped in front of her and had simply stood there. His face was bony and sweaty and bright, with a little pointed nose in the center of it, and his look was different from what it had been at the dinner table. He was gazing at her with open curiosity, with fascination, like a child watching a new fantastic animal at the zoo, and he was breathing as if he had run a great distance to reach her. His gaze seemed somehow familiar but she could not think where she had been regarded with it before. For almost a minute he didn't say anything. Then on what seemed an insuck of breath, he whispered, "You ever ate a chicken that was two days old?"

76   The girl looked at him stonily. He might have just put this question up for consideration at the meeting of a philosophical association. "Yes," she presently replied as if she had considered it from all angles.

77   "It must have been mighty small!" he said triumphantly and shook all over with little nervous giggles, getting very red in the face, and subsiding finally into his gaze of complete admiration, while the girl's expression remained exactly the same.

78   "How old are you?" he asked softly.

79   She waited some time before she answered. Then in a flat voice she said, "Seventeen."

80   His smiles came in succession like waves breaking on the surface of a little lake. "I see you got a wooden leg," he said. "I think you're real brave. I think you're real sweet."

81   The girl stood blank and solid and silent.

82   "Walk to the gate with me," he said. "You're a brave sweet little thing and I liked you the minute I seen you walk in the door."

83   Hulga began to move forward.

84   "What's your name?" he asked, smiling down on the top of her head.

85   "Hulga," she said.

86   "Hulga," he murmured, "Hulga. Hulga. I never heard of anybody name Hulga before. You're shy, aren't you, Hulga?" he asked.

87   She nodded, watching his large red hand on the handle of the giant valise.

"I like girls that wear glasses," he said. "I think a lot. I'm not like these people that a serious thought don't ever enter their heads. It's because I may die."

"I may die too," she said suddenly and looked up at him. His eyes were very small and brown, glittering feverishly.

"Listen," he said, "don't you think some people was meant to meet on account of what all they got in common and all? Like they both think serious thoughts and all?" He shifted the valise to his other hand so that the hand nearest her was free. He caught hold of her elbow and shook it a little. "I don't work on Saturday," he said. "I like to walk in the woods and see what Mother Nature is wearing. O'er the hills and far away. Pic-nics and things. Couldn't we go on a pic-nic tomorrow? Say yes, Hulga," he said and gave her a dying look as if he felt his insides about to drop out of him. He had even seemed to sway slightly toward her.

During the night she had imagined that she seduced him. She imagined that the two of them walked on the place until they came to the storage barn beyond the two back fields and there, she imagined, that things came to such a pass that she very easily seduced him and that then, of course, she had to reckon with his remorse. True genius can get an idea across even to an inferior mind. She imagined that she took his remorse in hand and changed it into a deeper understanding of life. She took all his shame away and turned it into something useful.

She set off for the gate at exactly ten o'clock, escaping without drawing Mrs. Hopewell's attention. She didn't take anything to eat, forgetting that food is usually taken on a picnic. She wore a pair of slacks and a dirty white shirt, and as an afterthought, she had put some Vapex on the collar of it since she did not own any perfume. When she reached the gate no one was there.

She looked up and down the empty highway and had the furious feeling that she had been tricked, that he had only meant to make her walk to the gate after the idea of him. Then suddenly he stood up, very tall, from behind a bush on the opposite embankment. Smiling, he lifted his hat which was new and wide-brimmed. He had not worn it yesterday and she wondered if he had bought it for the occasion. It was toast-colored with a red and white band around it and was slightly too large for him. He stepped from behind the bush still carrying the black valise. He had on the same suit and the same yellow socks sucked down in his shoes from walking. He crossed the highway and said, "I knew you'd come!"

94   The girl wondered acidly how he had known this. She pointed to the valise and asked, "Why did you bring your Bibles?"

95   He took her elbow, smiling down on her as if he could not stop. "You can never tell when you'll need the word of God, Hulga," he said. She had a moment in which she doubted that this was actually happening and then they began to climb the embankment. They went down into the pasture toward the woods. The boy walked lightly by her side, bouncing on his toes. The valise did not seem to be heavy today; he even swung it. They crossed half the pasture without saying anything and then, putting his hand easily on the small of her back, he asked softly, "Where does your wooden leg join on?"

96   She turned an ugly red and glared at him and for an instant the boy looked abashed. "I didn't mean you no harm," he said. "I only meant you're so brave and all. I guess God takes care of you."

97   "No," she said, looking forward and walking fast. "I don't even believe in God."

98   At this he stopped and whistled. "No!" he exclaimed as if he were too astonished to say anything else.

99   She walked on and in a second he was bouncing at her side, fanning with his hat. "That's very unusual for a girl," he remarked, watching her out of the corner of his eye. When they reached the edge of the wood, he put his hand on her back again and drew her against him without a word and kissed her heavily.

100   The kiss, which had more pressure than feeling behind it, produced that extra surge of adrenalin in the girl that enables one to carry a packed trunk out of a burning house, but in her, the power went at once to the brain. Even before he released her, her mind, clear and detached and ironic anyway, was regarding him from a great distance, with amusement but with pity. She had never been kissed before and she was pleased to discover that it was an unexceptional experience and all a matter of the mind's control. Some people might enjoy drain water if they were told it was vodka. When the boy, looking expectant but uncertain, pushed her gently away, she turned and walked on, saying nothing as if such business, for her, were common enough.

101   He came along panting at her side, trying to help her when he saw a root that she might trip over. He caught and held back the long swaying blades of thorn vine until she had passed beyond them. She led the way and he came breathing heavily behind her. Then they came out on a sunlit hillside, sloping softly into another one a little

smaller. Beyond, they could see the rusted top of the old barn where the extra hay was stored.

The hill was sprinkled with small pink weeds. "Then you ain't saved?" he asked suddenly, stopping. 102

The girl smiled. It was the first time she had smiled at him at all. "In my economy," she said, "I'm saved and you are damned but I told you I didn't believe in God." 103

Nothing seemed to destroy the boy's look of admiration. He gazed at her now as if the fantastic animal at the zoo had put its paw through the bars and given him a loving poke. She thought he looked as if he wanted to kiss her again and she walked on before he had the chance. 104

"Ain't there somewheres we can sit down sometime?" he murmured, his voice softening toward the end of the sentence. 105

"In that barn," she said. 106

They made for it rapidly as if it might slide away like a train. It was a large two-story barn, cool and dark inside. The boy pointed up the ladder that led into the loft and said, "It's too bad we can't go up there." 107

"Why can't we?" she asked. 108

"Yer leg," he said reverently. 109

The girl gave him a contemptuous look and putting both hands on the ladder, she climbed it while he stood below, apparently awestruck. She pulled herself expertly through the opening and then looked down at him and said, "Well, come on if you're coming," and he began to climb the ladder, awkwardly bringing the suitcase with him. 110

"We won't need the Bible," she observed. 111

"You never can tell," he said, panting. After he had got into the loft, he was a few seconds catching his breath. She had sat down in a pile of straw. A wide sheath of sunlight, filled with dust particles, slanted over her. She lay back against a bale, her face turned away, looking out the front opening of the barn where hay was thrown from a wagon into the loft. The two pink-speckled hillsides lay back against a dark ridge of woods. The sky was cloudless and cold blue. The boy dropped down by her side and put one arm under her and the other over her and began methodically kissing her face, making little noises like a fish. He did not remove his hat but it was pushed far enough back not to interfere. When her glasses got in his way, he took them off of her and slipped them into his pocket. 112

113   The girl at first did not return any of the kisses but presently she began to and after she had put several on his cheek, she reached his lips and remained there, kissing him again and again as if she were trying to draw all the breath out of him. His breath was clear and sweet like a child's and the kisses were sticky like a child's. He mumbled about loving her and about knowing when he first seen her that he loved her, but the mumbling was like the sleepy fretting of a child being put to sleep by his mother. Her mind, throughout this, never stopped or lost itself for a second to her feelings. "You ain't said you loved me none," he whispered finally, pulling back from her. "You got to say that."

114   She looked away from him off into the hollow sky and then down at a black ridge and then down farther into what appeared to be two green swelling lakes. She didn't realize he had taken her glasses but this landscape could not seem exceptional to her for she seldom paid any close attention to her surroundings.

115   "You got to say it," he repeated. "You got to say you love me."

116   She was always careful how she committed herself. "In a sense," she began, "if you use the word loosely, you might say that. But it's not a word I use. I don't have illusions. I'm one of those people who see *through* to nothing."

117   The boy was frowning. "You got to say it. I said it and you got to say it," he said.

118   The girl looked at him almost tenderly. "You poor baby," she murmured. "It's just as well you don't understand," and she pulled him by the neck, face-down, against her. "We are all damned," she said, "but some of us have taken off our blindfolds and see that there's nothing to see. It's a kind of salvation."

119   The boy's astonished eyes looked blankly through the ends of her hair. "Okay," he almost whined, "but do you love me or don'tcher?"

120   "Yes," she said and added, "in a sense. But I must tell you something. There mustn't be anything dishonest between us." She lifted his head and looked him in the eye. "I am thirty years old," she said. "I have a number of degrees."

121   The boy's look was irritated but dogged. "I don't care," he said. "I don't care a thing about what all you done. I just want to know if you love me or don'tcher?" and he caught her to him and wildly planted her face with kisses until she said, "Yes, yes."

122   "Okay then," he said, letting her go. "Prove it."

123   She smiled, looking dreamily out on the shifty landscape. She

had seduced him without even making up her mind to try. "How?" she asked, feeling that he should be delayed a little.

He leaned over and put his lips to her ear. "Show me where 124 your wooden leg joins on," he whispered.

The girl uttered a sharp little cry and her face instantly drained 125 of color. The obscenity of the suggestion was not what shocked her. As a child she had sometimes been subject to feelings of shame but education had removed the last traces of that as a good surgeon scrapes for cancer; she would no more have felt it over what he was asking than she would have believed in his Bible. But she was as sensitive about the artificial leg as a peacock about his tail. No one ever touched it but her. She took care of it as someone else would his soul, in private and almost with her own eyes turned away. "No," she said.

"I known it," he muttered, sitting up. "You're just playing me 126 for a sucker."

"Oh no no!" she cried. "It joins on at the knee. Only at the 127 knee. Why do you want to see it?"

The boy gave her a long penetrating look. "Because," he said, 128 "it's what makes you different. You ain't like anybody else."

She sat staring at him. There was nothing about her face or her 129 round freezing-blue eyes to indicate that this had moved her; but she felt as if her heart had stopped and left her mind to pump her blood. She decided that for the first time in her life she was face to face with real innocence. This boy, with an instinct that came from beyond wisdom, had touched the truth about her. When after a minute, she said in a hoarse high voice, "All right," it was like surrendering to him completely. It was like losing her own life and finding it again, miraculously, in his.

Very gently he began to roll the slack leg up. The artificial limb, 130 in a white sock and brown flat shoe, was bound in a heavy material like canvas and ended in an ugly jointure where it was attached to the stump. The boy's face and his voice were entirely reverent as he uncovered it and said, "Now show me how to take it off and on."

She took it off for him and put it back on again and then he 131 took it off himself, handling it as tenderly as if it were a real one. "See! he said with a delighted child's face. "Now I can do it myself!"

"Put it back on," she said. She was thinking that she would run 132 away with him and that every night he would take the leg off and every morning put it back on again. "Put it back on," she said.

"Not yet," he murmured, setting it on its foot out of her reach. 133 "leave it off for a while. You got me instead."

134   She gave a little cry of alarm but he pushed her down and began to kiss her again. Without the leg she felt entirely dependent on him. Her brain seemed to have stopped thinking altogether and to be about some other function that it was not very good at. Different expressions raced back and forth over her face. Every now and then the boy, his eyes like two steel spikes, would glance behind him where the leg stood. Finally she pushed him off and said, "Put it back on me now."

135   "Wait," he said. He leaned the other way and pulled the valise toward him and opened it. It had a pale blue spotted lining and there were only two Bibles in it. He took one of these out and opened the cover of it. It was hollow and contained a pocket flask of whiskey, a pack of cards, and a small blue box with printing on it. He laid these out in front of her one at a time in an evenly spaced row, like one presenting offerings at the shrine of a goddess. He put the blue box in her hand. THIS PRODUCT TO BE USED ONLY FOR THE PRE-VENTION OF DISEASE, she read, and dropped it. The boy was unscrewing the top of the flask. He stopped and pointed, with a smile, to the deck of cards. It was not an ordinary deck but one with an obscene picture on the back of each card. "Take a swig," he said, offering her the bottle first. He held it in front of her but like one mesmerized, she did not move.

136   Her voice when she spoke had an almost pleading sound. "Aren't you," she murmured, "aren't you just good country people?"

137   The boy cocked his head. He looked as if he were just beginning to understand that she might be trying to insult him. "Yeah," he said, curling his lip slightly, "but it ain't held me back none. I'm as good as you any day in the week."

138   "Give me my leg," she said."

139   He pushed it farther away with his foot. "Come on now, let's begin to have us a good time," he said coaxingly. "We ain't got to know one another good yet."

140   "Give me my leg!" she screamed and tried to lunge for it but he pushed her down easily.

141   "What's the matter with you all of a sudden?" he asked, frowning as he screwed the top on the flask and put it quickly back inside the Bible. "You just a while ago said you didn't believe in nothing. I thought you was some girl!"

142   Her face was almost purple. "You're a Christian!" she hissed. "You're a fine Christian! You're just like them all—say one thing and do another. You're a perfect Christian, you're . . ."

The boy's mouth was set angrily. "I hope you don't think," he   143
said in a lofty indignant tone, "that I believe in that crap! I may sell
Bibles but I know which end is up and I wasn't born yesterday and
I know where I'm going!"

"Give me my leg!" she screeched. He jumped up so quickly that   144
she barely saw him sweep the cards and the blue box back into the
Bible and throw the Bible into the valise. She saw him grab the leg
and then she saw it for an instant slanted forlornly across the inside
of the suitcase with a Bible at either side of its opposite ends. He
slammed the lid shut and snatched up the valise and swung it down
the hole and then stepped through himself.

When all of him had passed but his head, he turned and   145
regarded her with a look that no longer had any admiration in it.
"I've gotten a lot of interesting things," he said. "One time I got a
woman's glass eye this way. And you needn't to think you'll catch
me because Pointer ain't really my name. I use a different name at
every house I call at and don't stay nowhere long. And I'll tell you
another thing, Hulga," he said, using the name as if he didn't think
much of it, "you ain't so smart. I been believing in nothing ever since
I was born!" and then the toast-colored hat disappeared down the
hole and the girl was left, sitting on the straw in the dusty sunlight.
When she turned her churning face toward the opening, she saw his
blue figure struggling successfully over the green speckled lake.

Mrs. Hopewell and Mrs. Freeman, who were in the back pas-   146
ture, digging up onions, saw him emerge a little later from the woods
and head across the meadow toward the highway. "Why, that looks
like that nice dull young man that tried to sell me a Bible yesterday,"
Mrs. Hopewell said, squinting. "He must have been selling them to
the Negroes back in there. He was so simple," she said, "but I guess
the world would be better off if we were all that simple."

Mrs. Freeman's gaze drove forward and just touched him before   147
he disappeared under the hill. Then she returned her attention to the
evil-smelling onion shoot she was lifting from the ground. "Some
can't be that simple," she said. "I know I never could."

Discussion

• Discuss how O'Connor's description of the process of writing fiction
relates to the writing of nonfiction.

- Consider how "Good Country People" documents what she says about writing short stories. How does she practice what she preaches? How does she fail to practice what she preaches?
- Consider how O'Connor's statements about detail relate to pieces you have read in this book, and to your own drafts.
- How is the wooden leg real—and symbolic?
- What surprised you in what O'Connor said about writing and in her short story?
- Talk about the way O'Connor uses her voice to reveal the voices of her characters and the voice of the story. What is the role of voice in fiction and nonfiction?

Activities

- Take a draft that you have written and triple or triple-triple the number of specific details that you have on the page to see what you discover.
- Write for an hour as hard and as fast as you can, without worrying about how well it is written. Just try to write honestly about something of importance to you, and don't censor what you're saying. Let the writing come and see if you can spot the organic form growing out of what you have to say. See if the writing is shaping itself into a particular story, or essay, or argument, or poem, or article.
- Take a draft you have written and imagine you are Flannery O'Connor. What would she say about it? What would you do to respond to what she says?
- Take a page you have written and turn it into fiction if it is nonfiction or vice-versa. Write a page discussing the difference the change in genre made.
- Write a short piece using the voice of people you know in the way that O'Connor wrote in the voice of her neighbors in Georgia.

Toni Morrison

I can still remember the excitement when I read the first pages of Toni Morrison's first novel. You are going to read some of these pages. They took off like a jet plane, and I felt that I was standing at the edge of the runway feeling the power and the force of her prose. For a while this first novel was out of print, and I went to the library and xeroxed the whole novel and kept it in a notebook, until it came back into print. Now Toni Morrison is recognized as one of our major novelists. She has published *Sula, Song of Solomon,* and *Tar Baby,* but I have a particularly warm spot for this first novel.

"After my first novel, *The Bluest Eye,*" Morrison has said, "writing became a way to be coherent in the world. It became necessary and possible for me to sort the past, and the selection process, being disciplined and guided, was genuine thinking as opposed to simple response or problem-solving. Writing was the only work I did that was for myself and by myself. In the process, one exercises sovereignty in a special way. All sensibilities are engaged, sometimes simultaneously, sometimes sequentially. While I am writing, all of my experience is vital and useful and possibly important. It may not appear in the work, but it is valuable. Writing gives me what I think dancers have on stage in their relation to gravity and space and time. It is energetic and balanced, fluid and in repose. And there is always the possibility of growth; I could never hit the highest note so I'd never have to stop. Writing has for me everything that good work ought to have, all the criteria. I love even the drudgery, the revision, the proofreading."

The Bluest Eye

Nuns go by as quiet as lust, and drunken men and sober eyes   1
sing in the lobby of the Greek hotel. Rosemary Villanucci, our next-door friend who lives above her father's cafe, sits in a 1939 Buick eating bread and butter. She rolls down the window to tell my sister Frieda and me that we can't come in. We stare at her, wanting her bread, but more than that wanting to poke the arrogance out of her eyes and smash the pride of ownership that curls her chewing mouth. When she comes out of the car we will beat her up, make red marks on her white skin, and she will cry and ask us do we want her to pull

her pants down. We will say no. We don't know what we should feel or do if she does, but whenever she asks us, we know she is offering us something precious and that our own pride must be asserted by refusing to accept.

2   School has started, and Frieda and I get new brown stockings and cod-liver oil. Grown-ups talk in tired, edgy voices about Zick's Coal Company and take us along in the evening to the railroad tracks where we fill burlap sacks with the tiny pieces of coal lying about. Later we walk home, glancing back to see the great carloads of slag being dumped, red hot and smoking, into the ravine that skirts the steel mill. The dying fire lights the sky with a dull orange glow. Frieda and I lag behind, staring at the patch of color surrounded by black. It is impossible not to feel a shiver when our feet leave the gravel path and sink into the dead grass in the field.

3   Our house is old, cold, and green. At night a kerosene lamp lights one large room. The others are braced in darkness, peopled by roaches and mice. Adults do not talk to us—they give us directions. They issue orders without providing information. When we trip and fall down they glance at us; if we cut or bruise ourselves, they ask us are we crazy. When we catch colds, they shake their heads in disgust at our lack of consideration. How, they ask us, do you expect anybody to get anything done if you all are sick? We cannot answer them. Our illness is treated with contempt, foul Black Draught, and castor oil that blunts our minds.

❡ Notice how quickly you are involved in the piece. Notice the voice. Notice the music in the language. Notice the word choice. Notice the point of view. Notice the energy. Notice, notice, notice—a writer is at work. ❡

4   When, on a day after a trip to collect coal, I cough once, loudly, through bronchial tubes already packed tight with phlegm, my mother frowns. "Great Jesus. Get on in that bed. How many times do I have to tell you to wear something on your head? You must be the biggest fool in this town. Frieda? Get some rags and stuff that window."

5   Frieda restuffs the window. I trudge off to bed, full of guilt and self-pity. I lie down in my underwear, the metal in my black garters hurts my legs, but I do not take them off, for it is too cold to lie stockingless. It takes a long time for my body to heat its place in the bed. Once I have generated a silhouette of warmth, I dare not move,

for there is a cold place one-half inch in any direction. No one speaks to me or asks how I feel. In an hour or two my mother comes. Her hands are large and rough, and when she rubs the Vicks salve on my chest, I am rigid with pain. She takes two fingers' full of it at a time, and massages my chest until I am faint. Just when I think I will tip over into a scream, she scoops out a little of the salve on her forefinger and puts it in my mouth, telling me to swallow. A hot flannel is wrapped about my neck and chest. I am covered up with heavy quilts and ordered to sweat, which I do—promptly.

Later I throw up, and my mother says, "What did you puke on   6
the bed clothes for? Don't you have sense enough to hold your head out the bed? Now, look what you did. You think I got time for nothing but washing up your puke?"

The puke swaddles down the pillow onto the sheet—green-   7
gray, with flecks of orange. It moves like the insides of an uncooked egg. Stubbornly clinging to its own mass, refusing to break up and be removed. How, I wonder, can it be so neat and nasty at the same time?

My mother's voice drones on. She is not talking to me. She is   8
talking to the puke, but she is calling it my name: Claudia. She wipes it up as best she can and puts a scratchy towel over the large wet place. I lie down again. The rags have fallen from the window crack, and the air is cold. I dare not call her back and am reluctant to leave my warmth. My mother's anger humiliates me; her words chafe my cheeks, and I am crying. I do not know that she is not angry at me, but at my sickness. I believe she despises my weakness for letting the sickness "take holt." By and by I will not get sick; I will refuse to. But for now I am crying. I know I am making more snot, but I can't stop.

My sister comes in. Her eyes are full of sorrow. She sings to me: 9
"When the deep purple falls over sleepy garden walls, someone thinks of me. . ." I doze, thinking of plums, walls, and "someone."

But was it really like that? As painful as I remember? Only   10
mildly. Or rather, it was a productive and fructifying pain. Love, thick and dark as Alaga syrup, eased up into that cracked window. I could smell it—taste it—sweet, musty, with an edge of wintergreen in its base—everywhere in that house. It stuck, along with my tongue, to the frosted windowpanes. It coated my chest, along with the salve, and when the flannel came undone in my sleep, the clear, sharp curves of air outlined its presence on my throat. And in the night, when my coughing was dry and tough, feet padded into the room,

hands repinned the flannel, readjusted the quilt, and rested a moment on my forehead. So when I think of autumn, I think of somebody with hands who does not want me to die.

11   It was autumn too when Mr. Henry came. Our roomer. Our roomer. The words ballooned from the lips and hovered about our heads—silent, separate, and pleasantly mysterious. My mother was all ease and satisfaction in discussing his coming.

12   "You know him," she said to her friends. "Henry Washington. He's been living over there with Miss Della Jones on Thirteenth Street. But she's too addled now to keep up. So he's looking for another place."

13   "Oh, yes." Her friends do not hide their curiosity. "I been wondering how long he was going to stay up there with her. They say she's real bad off. Don't know who he is half the time, and nobody else."

14   "Well, that old crazy nigger she married up with didn't help her head none."

15   "Did you hear what he told folks when he left her?"

16   "Uh-uh. What?"

17   "Well, he run off with that trifling Peggy—from Elyria. You know."

18   "One of Old Slack Bessie's girls?"

19   "That's the one. Well, somebody asked him why he left a nice good church woman like Della for that heifer. You know Della always did keep a good house. And he said the honest-to-God real reason was he couldn't take no more of that violet water Della Jones used. Said he wanted a woman to smell like a woman. Said Della was just too clean for him."

20   "Old dog. Ain't that nasty!"

21   "You telling me. What kind of reasoning is that?"

22   "No kind. Some men just dogs."

23   "Is that what give her them strokes?"

24   "Must have helped. But you know, none of them girls wasn't too bright. Remember that grinning Hattie? She wasn't never right. And their Auntie Julia is still trotting up and down Sixteenth Street talking to herself."

25   "Didn't she get put away?"

26   "Naw. County wouldn't take her. Said she wasn't harming anybody."

27   "Well, she's harming me. You want something to scare the liv-

ing shit out of you, you get up at five-thirty in the morning like I do and see that old hag floating by in that bonnet. Have mercy!"

They laugh. 28

Freida and I are washing Mason jars. We do not hear their 29 words, but with grown-ups we listen to and watch out for their voices.

"Well, I hope don't nobody let me roam around like that when 30 I get senile. It's a shame."

"What they going to do about Della? Don't she have no 31 people?"

"A sister's coming up from North Carolina to look after her. I 32 expect she wants to get aholt of Della's house."

"Oh, come on. That's a evil thought, if ever I heard one." 33

"What you want to bet? Henry Washington said that sister ain't 34 seen Della in fifteen years."

"I kind of thought Henry would marry her one of these days." 35

"That old woman?" 36

"No, but he ain't no buzzard, either." 37

"He ever been married to anybody?" 38

"No." 39

"How come? Somebody cut it off?" 40

"He's just picky." 41

"He ain't picky. You see anything around here you'd marry?" 42

"Well. . .no." 43

"He's just sensible. A steady worker with quiet ways. I hope it 44 works out all right."

"It will. How much you charging?" 45

"Five dollars every two weeks." 46

"That'll be a big help to you." 47

"I'll say." 48

Their conversation is like a gently wicked dance: sound meets 49 sound, curtsies, shimmies, and retires. Another sound enters but is upstaged by still another: the two circle each other and stop. Sometimes their words move in lofty spirals; other times they take strident leaps, and all of it is punctuated with warm-pulsed laughter—like the throb of a heart made of jelly. The edge, the curl, the thrust of their emotions is always clear to Freida and me. We do not, cannot, know the meanings of all their words, for we are nine and ten years old. So we watch their faces, their hands, their feet, and listen for truth in timbre.

☞ Read this paragraph aloud. What have you read before that is like it, and different? Look back at the paragraph in italics at the beginning of the Welty piece. Delight in the similarity and the difference.☜

50   So when Mr. Henry arrived on a Saturday night, we smelled him. He smelled wonderful. Like trees and lemon vanishing cream, and Nu Nile Hair Oil and flecks of Sen-Sen.

51   He smiled a lot, showing small even teeth with a friendly gap in the middle. Frieda and I were not introduced to him—merely pointed out. Like, here is the bathroom; the clothes closet is here; and these are my kids, Frieda and Claudia; watch out for this window; it don't open all the way.

52   We looked sideways at him, saying nothing and expecting him to say nothing. Just to nod, as he had done at the clothes closet, acknowledging our existence. To our surprise, he spoke to us.

53   "Hello there. You must be Greta Garbo, and you must be Ginger Rogers."

54   We giggled. Even my father was startled into a smile.

55   "Want a penny?" He held out a shiny coin to us. Frieda lowered her head, too pleased to answer. I reached for it. He snapped his thumb and forefinger, and the penny disappeared. Our shock was laced with delight. We searched all over him, poking our fingers into his socks, looking up the inside back of his coat. If happiness is anticipation with certainty, we were happy. And while we waited for the coin to reappear, we knew we were amusing Mama and Daddy. Daddy was smiling, and Mama's eyes went soft as they followed our hands wandering over Mr. Henry's body.

56   We loved him. Even after what came later, there was no bitterness in our memory of him.

57   She slept in bed with us. Frieda on the outside because she is brave—it never occurs to her that if in her sleep her hand hangs over the edge of the bed "something" will crawl out from under it and bite her fingers off. I sleep near the wall because that thought *has* occurred to me. Pecola, therefore, had to sleep in the middle.

58   Mama had told us two days earlier that a "case" was coming— a girl who had no place to go. The county had placed her in our house for a few days until they could decide what to do, or, more precisely, until the family was reunited. We were to be nice to her and not fight. Mama didn't know "what got into people," but that old Dog Breed-

love had burned up his house, gone upside his wife's head, and everybody, as a result, was outdoors.

Outdoors, we knew, was the real terror of life. The threat of being outdoors surfaced frequently in those days. Every possibility of excess was curtailed with it. If somebody ate too much, he could end up outdoors. If somebody used too much coal, he could end up outdoors. People could gamble themselves outdoors, drink themselves outdoors. Sometimes mothers put their sons outdoors, and when that happened, regardless of what the son had done, all sympathy was with him. He was outdoors, and his own flesh had done it. To be put outdoors by a landlord was one thing—unfortunate, but an aspect of life over which you had no control, since you could not control your income. But to be slack enough to put oneself outdoors, or heartless enough to put one's own kin outdoors—that was criminal.

There is a difference between being put *out* and being put out *doors*. If you are put out, you go somewhere else; if you are outdoors, there is no place to go. The distinction was subtle but final. Outdoors was the end of something, an irrevocable, physical fact, defining and complementing our metaphysical condition. Being a minority in both caste and class, we moved about anyway on the hem of life, struggling to consolidate our weaknesses and hang on, or to creep singly up into the major folds of the garment. Our peripheral existence, however, was something we had learned to deal with—probably because it was abstract. But the concreteness of being outdoors was another matter—like the difference between the concept of death and being, in fact, dead. Dead doesn't change, and outdoors is here to stay.

Knowing that there was such a thing as outdoors bred in us a hunger for property, for ownership. The firm possession of a yard, a porch, a grape arbor. Propertied black people spent all their energies, all their love, on their nests. Like frenzied, desperate birds, they overdecorated everything; fussed and fidgeted over their hard-won homes; canned, jellied, and preserved all summer to fill the cupboards and shelves; they painted, picked, and poked at every corner of their houses. And these houses loomed like hothouse sunflowers among the rows of weeds that were the rented houses. Renting blacks cast furtive glances at these owned yards and "some nice little old place." In the meantime, they saved, and scratched, and piled away what they could in the rented hovels, looking forward to the day of property.

Cholly Breedlove, then, a renting black, having put his family outdoors, had catapulted himself beyond the reaches of human consideration. He had joined the animals; was, indeed, an old dog, a snake, a ratty nigger. Mrs. Breedlove was staying with the woman she worked for; the boy, Sammy, was with some other family; and Pecola was to stay with us. Cholly was in jail.

63   She came with nothing. No little paper bag with the other dress, or a nightgown, or two pair of whitish cotton bloomers. She just appeared with a white woman and sat down.

64   We had fun in those few days Pecola was with us. Frieda and I stopped fighting each other and concentrated on our guest, trying hard to keep her from feeling outdoors.

65   When we discovered that she clearly did not want to dominate us, we liked her. She laughed when I clowned for her, and smiled and accepted gracefully the food gifts my sister gave her.

66   "Would you like some graham crackers?"

67   "I don't care."

68   Frieda brought her four graham crackers on a saucer and some milk in a blue-and-white Shirley Temple cup. She was a long time with the milk, and gazed fondly at the silhouette of Shirley Temple's dimpled face. Frieda and she had a loving conversation about how cu-ute Shirley Temple was. I couldn't join them in their adoration because I hated Shirley. Not because she was cute, but because she danced with Bojangles, who was *my* friend, *my* uncle, *my* daddy, and who ought to have been soft-shoeing it and chuckling with me. Instead he was enjoying, sharing, giving a lovely dance thing with one of those little white girls whose socks never slid down under their heels. So I said, "I like Jane Withers."

69   They gave me a puzzled look, decided I was incomprehensible, and continued their reminiscing about old squint-eyed Shirley.

70   Younger than both Frieda and Pecola, I had not yet arrived at the turning point in the development of my psyche which would allow me to love her. What I felt at that time was unsullied hatred. But before that I had felt a stranger, more frightening thing than hatred for all the Shirley Temples of the world.

71   It had begun with Christmas and the gift of dolls. The big, the special, the loving gift was always a big, blue-eyed Baby Doll. From the clucking sounds of adults I knew that the doll represented what they thought was my fondest wish. I was bemused with the thing itself, and the way it looked. What was I supposed to do with it? Pretend I was its mother? I had no interest in babies or the concept of motherhood. I was interested only in humans my own age and

size, and could not generate any enthusiasm at the prospect of being a mother. Motherhood was old age, and other remote possibilities. I learned quickly, however, what I was expected to do with the doll: rock it, fabricate storied situations around it, even sleep with it. Picture books were full of little girls sleeping with their dolls. Raggedy Ann dolls usually, but they were out of the question. I was physically revolted by and secretly frightened of those round moronic eyes, the pancake face, and orangeworms hair.

The other dolls, which were supposed to bring me great plea- 72 sure, succeeded in doing quite the opposite. When I took it to bed, its hard unyielding limbs resisted my flesh—the tapered fingertips on those dimpled hands scratched. If, in sleep, I turned, the bone-cold head collided with my own. It was a most uncomfortable, patently aggressive sleeping companion. To hold it was no more rewarding. The starched gauze or lace on the cotton dress irritated any embrace. I had only one desire: to dismember it. To see of what it was made, to discover the dearness, to find the beauty, the desirability that had escaped me, but apparently only me. Adults, older girls, shops, magazines, newspapers, window signs—all the world had agreed that a blue-eyed, yellow-haired, pink-skinned doll was what every girl child treasured. "Here," they said, "this is beautiful, and if you are on this day 'worthy' you may have it." I fingered the face, wondering at the single-stroke eyebrows; picked at the pearly teeth stuck like two piano keys between red bowline lips. Traced the turned-up nose, poked the glassy blue eyeballs, twisted the yellow hair. I could not love it. But I could examine it to see what it was that all the world said was lovable. Break off the tiny fingers, bend the flat feet, loosen the hair, twist the head around, and the thing made one sound—a sound they said was the sweet and plaintive cry, "Mama," but which sounded to me like the bleat of a dying lamb, or, more precisely, our icebox door opening on rusty hinges in July. Remove the cold and stupid eyeball, it would bleat still, "Ahhhhh," take off the head, shake out the sawdust, crack the back against the brass bed rail, it would bleat still. The gauze back would split, and I could see the disk with six holes, the secret of the sound. A mere metal roundness.

Grown people frowned and fussed: "You-don't-know-how-to- 73 take-care-of-nothing. I-never-had-a-baby-doll-in-my-whole-life-and-used-to-cry-my-eyes-out-for-them. Now-you-got-one-a-beautiful-one-and-you-tear-it-up-what's-the-matter-with-you?"

How strong was their outrage. Tears threatened to erase the 74 aloofness of their authority. The emotion of years of unfulfilled long-ing preened in their voices. I did not know why I destroyed those dolls. But I did know that nobody ever asked me what I wanted for Christmas. Had any adult with the power to fulfill my desires taken me seriously and asked me what I wanted, they would have known that I did not want to have anything to own, or to possess any object. I wanted rather to feel something on Christmas day. The real ques-tion would have been, "Dear Claudia, what experience would you like on Christmas?" I could have spoken up, "I want to sit on the low stool in Big Mama's kitchen with my lap full of lilacs and listen to Big Papa play his violin for me alone." The lowness of the stool made for my body, the security and warmth of Big Mama's kitchen, the smell of the lilacs, the sound of the music, and, since it would be good to have all of my senses engaged, the taste of a peach, perhaps, afterward.

75   Instead I tasted and smelled the acridness of tin plates and cups designed for tea parties that bored me. Instead I looked with loathing on new dresses that required a hateful bath in a galvanized zinc tub before wearing. Slipping around on the zinc, no time to play or soak, for the water chilled too fast, no time to enjoy one's nakedness, only time to make curtains of soapy water careen down between the legs. Then the scratchy towels and the dreadful and humiliating absence of dirt. The irritable, unimaginative cleanliness. Gone the ink marks from legs and face, all my creations and accumulations of the day gone, and replaced by goose pimples.

76   I destroyed white baby dolls.

77   But the dismembering of dolls was not the true horror. The truly horrifying thing was the transference of the same impulses to little white girls. The indifference with which I could have axed them was shaken only by my desire to do so. To discover what eluded me: the secret of the magic they weaved on others. What made people look at them and say, "Awwwww," but not for me? The eye slide of black women as they approached them on the street, and the possessive gentleness of their touch as they handled them.

78   If I pinched them, their eyes—unlike the crazed glint of the baby doll's eyes—would fold in pain, and their cry would not be the sound of an icebox door, but a fascinating cry of pain. When I learned how repulsive this disinterested violence was, that it was repulsive because it was disinterested, my shame floundered about for refuge. The best hiding place was love. Thus the conversion from pristine sadism to fabricated hatred, to fraudulent love. It was a small

step to Shirley Temple. I learned much later to worship her, just as I learned to delight in cleanliness, knowing, even as I learned, that the change was adjustment without improvement.

"Three quarts of milk. That's wha was *in* that icebox yesterday. Three whole quarts. Now they ain't none. Not a drop. I don't mind folks coming in and getting what they want, but three quarts of milk! What the devil does *anybody* need with three quarts of milk?"

The "folks" my mother was referring to was Pecola. The three of us, Pecola, Frieda, and I, listened to her downstairs in the kitchen fussing about the amount of milk Pecola had drunk. We knew she was fond of the Shirley Temple cup and took every opportunity to drink milk out of it just to handle and see sweet Shirley's face. My mother knew that Frieda and I hated milk and assumed Pecola drank it out of greediness. It was certainly not for us to "dispute" her. We didn't initiate talk with grown-ups; we answered their questions.

Ashamed of the insults that were being heaped on our friend, we just sat there: I picked toe jam, Frieda cleaned her fingernails with her teeth, and Pecola finger-traced some scars on her knee—her head cocked to one side. My mother's fussing soliloquies always irritated and depressed us. They were interminable, insulting, and although indirect (Mama never named anybody—just talked about folks and *some* people), extremely painful in their thrust. She would go on like that for hours, connecting one offense to another until all of the things that chagrined her were spewed out. Then, having told everybody and everything off, she would burst into song and sing the rest of the day. But it was such a long time before the singing part came. In the meantime, our stomachs jellying and our necks burning, we listened, avoided each other's eyes, and picked toe jam or whatever.

". . .I don't know what I'm suppose to be running here, a charity ward, I guess. Time for me to get out of the *giving* line and get in the *getting* line. I guess I ain't sup *posed* to have nothing. I'm sup *posed* to end up in the poorhouse. Look like nothing I do is going to keep me out of there. Folks just spend all their time trying to figure out ways to send *me* to the poorhouse. I got about as much business with another mouth to feed as a cat has with side pockets. As if I don't have trouble enough trying to feed my own and keep out the poorhouse, now I got something else in here that's just going to *drink* me on in there. Well, naw, she ain't. Not long as I got strength in my body and a tongue in my head. There's a limit to everything. I ain't got nothing to just throw *away*. Don't *no* body need *three* quarts of milk. Henry *Ford* don't need three quarts of milk. That's just downright *sin* ful. I'm willing to do what I can for folks. Can't nobody say I ain't. But this has got to stop, and I'm just the one to stop it. Bible say watch as *well* as pray. Folks just dump they children off on you and go on 'bout they business. Ain't nobody even *peeped* in here to see whether that child has a loaf of bread. Look like they would just *peep* in to see whether I had a loaf of bread to give her. But naw. That thought don't cross they mind. That old trifling Cholly been out of jail *two* whole days and ain't been here *yet* to see if his own child was 'live or dead. She could be *dead* for all he know. And that *mama* neither. What kind of something is that?"

83 When Mama got around to Henry Ford and all those people who didn't care whether she had a loaf of bread, it was time to go. We wanted to miss the part about Roosevelt and the CCC camps.

84 Frieda got up and started down the stairs. Pecola and I followed, making a wide arc to avoid the kitchen doorway. We sat on the steps of the porch, where my mother's words could reach us only in spurts.

85 It was a lonesome Saturday. The house smelled of Fels Naptha and the sharp odor of mustard greens cooking. Saturdays were lonesome, fussy, soapy days. Second in misery only to those tight, starchy, cough-drop Sundays, so full of "don'ts" and "set'cha self downs."

86 If my mother was in a singing mood, it wasn't so bad. She would sing about hard times, bad times, and somebody-done-gone-and-left-me times. But her voice was so sweet and her singing-eyes so melty I found myself longing for those hard times, yearning to be grown without "a thin di-i-ime to my name." I looked forward to the delicious time when "my man" would leave me, when I would "hate to see that evening sun go down. . .'"cause then I would know "my man has left this town." Misery colored by the greens and blues in my mother's voice took all of the grief out of the words and left me with a conviction that pain was not only endurable, it was sweet.

87 But without song, those Saturdays sat on my head like a coal scuttle, and if Mama was fussing, as she was now, it was like somebody throwing stones at it.

88 ". . .and here I am poor as a bowl of yak-me. What do they think I am? Some kind of Sandy Claus? Well, they can just take they stocking down 'cause it *ain't* Christmas. . ."

89 We fidgeted.

"Let's do something," Frieda said. 90

"What do you want to do?" I asked. 91

"I don't know. Nothing." Frieda stared at the tops of the trees. 92
Pecola looked at her feet.

"You want to go up to Mr. Henry's room and look at his girlie 93
magazines?"

Frieda made an ugly face. She didn't like to look at dirty pic- 94
tures. "Well," I continued, "we could look at his Bible. *That's*
pretty." Frieda sucked her teeth and made a *phttt* sound with her
lips. "O.K., then. We could go thread needles for the half-blind lady.
She'll give us a penny."

Frieda snorted. "Her eyes look like snot. I don't feel like look- 95
ing at them. What *you* want to do, Pecola?"

"I don't care," she said. "Anything you want." 96

I had another idea. "We could go up the alley and see what's 97
in the trash cans."

"Too cold," said Frieda. She was bored and irritable. 98

"I know. We could make some fudge." 99

"You kidding? With Mama in there fussing? When she starts 100
fussing at the walls, you know she's gonna be at it all day. She
wouldn't even let us."

"Well, let's go over to the Greek hotel and listen to them cuss." 101

"Oh, who wants to do *that*? Besides, they say the same old 102
words all the time."

My supply of ideas exhausted, I began to concentrate on the 103
white spots on my fingernails. The total signified the number of boy-
friends I would have. Seven.

Mama's soliloquy slid into the silence ". . .Bible say feed the 104
hungry. That's fine. That's all right. But I ain't feeding no elephants. . .Anybody need three quarts of milk to *live* need to get out
of here. They in the wrong place. What is this? Some kind of *dairy*
farm?"

Suddenly Pecola bolted straight up, her eyes wide with terror. 105
A whinnying sound came from her mouth.

"What's the matter with *you*? Frieda stood up too. 106

Then we both looked where Pecola was staring. Blood was run- 107
ning down her legs. Some drops were on the steps. I leaped up.
"Hey. You cut yourself? Look. It's all over your dress."

A brownish-red stain discolored the back of her dress. She kept 108
whinnying, standing with her legs far apart.

Frieda said, "Oh. Lordy! I know. I know what that is!" 109

110   "What?" Pecola's fingers went to her mouth.

111   "That's ministratin'."

112   "What's that?"

113   "You know."

114   "Am I going to die?" she asked.

115   "Noooo. You won't die. It just means you can have a baby!"

116   "What?"

117   "How do *you* know?" I was sick and tired of Frieda knowing everything.

118   "Mildred told me, and Mama too."

119   "I don't believe it."

120   "You don't have to, dummy. Look. Wait here. Sit down, Pecola. Right here." Frieda was all authority and zest. "And you," she said to me, "you go get some water."

121   "Water?"

122   "Yes, stupid. Water. And be quiet, or Mama will hear you."

123   Pecola sat down again, a little less fear in her eyes. I went into the kitchen.

124   "What you want, girl?" Mama was rinsing curtains in the sink.

125   "Some water, ma'am."

126   "Right where I'm working, naturally. Well, get a glass. Not no clean one neither. Use that jar."

127   I got a Mason jar and filled it with water from the faucet. It seemed a long time filling.

128   "Don't nobody never want nothing till they see me at the sink. Then everybody got to drink water. . . ."

129   When the jar was full, I moved to leave the room.

130   "Where you going?"

131   "Outside."

132   "Drink that water right here!"

133   "I ain't gonna break nothing."

134   "You don't know what you gonna do."

135   "Yes, ma'am. I do. Lemme take it out. I won't spill none."

136   "You bed' not."

137   I got to the porch and stood there with the Mason jar of water. Pecola was crying.

138   "What you crying for? Does it hurt?"

139   She shook her head.

140   "Then stop slinging snot."

141   Frieda opened the back door. She had something tucked in her

blouse. She looked at me in amazement and pointed to the jar. "What's that supposed to do?"

"You told me. You *said* get some water." 142

"Not a little old jar full. Lots of water. To scrub the steps with, 143 dumbbell!"

"How was I supposed to know?" 144

"Yeah. How was you. Come on." She pulled Pecola up by the 145 arm. "Let's go back here." They headed for the side of the house where the bushes were thick.

"Hey. What about me? I want to go." 146

"Shut uuuup," Frieda stage-whispered. "Mama will hear you. 147 You wash the steps."

They disappeared around the corner of the house. 148

I was going to miss something. Again. Here was something 149 important, and I had to stay behind and not see any of it. I poured the water on the steps, sloshed it with my shoe, and ran to join them.

Frieda was on her knees; a white rectangle of cotton was near 150 her on the ground. She was pulling Pecola's pants off. "Come on. Step out of them." She managed to get the soiled pants down and flung them at me. "Here."

"What am I supposed to do with these?" 151

"Bury them, moron." 152

Frieda told Pecola to hold the cotton thing between her legs. 153

"How she gonna walk like that?" I asked. 154

Frieda didn't answer. Instead she took two safety pins from the 155 hem of her skirt and began to pin the ends of the napkin to Pecola's dress.

I picked up the pants with two fingers and looked about for 156 something to dig a hole with. A rustling noise in the bushes startled me, and turning towards it, I saw a pair of fascinated eyes in a dough-white face. Rosemary was watching us. I grabbed for her face and succeeded in scratching her nose. She screamed and jumped back.

"Mrs. MacTeer! Mrs. MacTeer!" Rosemary hollered. "Frieda 157 and Claudia are out here playing nasty! Mrs. MacTeer!"

Mama opened the window and looked down at us. 158

"What?" 159

"They're playing nasty, Mrs. MacTeer. Look. And Claudia hit 160 me 'cause I seen them!"

Mama slammed the window shut and came running out the 161 back door.

162   "What you all doing? Oh. Uh-huh. Uh-huh. Playing nasty, huh?" She reached into the bushes and pulled off a switch. "I'd rather raise pigs than some nasty girls. Least I can slaughter *them*!"

163   We began to shriek. "No, Mama. No, ma'am. We wasn't! She's a liar! No, ma'am, Mama! No, ma'am, Mama!"

164   Mama grabbed Frieda by the shoulder, turned her around, and gave her three or four stinging cuts on her legs. "Gonna be nasty, huh? Naw you ain't!"

165   Frieda was destroyed. Whippings wounded and insulted her.

166   Mama looked at Pecola. "You too!" she said. "Child of mine or not!" She grabbed Pecola and spun her around. The safety pin snapped open on one end of the napkin, and Mama saw it fall from under her dress. The switch hovered in the air while Mama blinked. "What the devil is going on here?"

167   Frieda was sobbing. I, next in line, began to explain. "She was bleeding. We was just trying to stop the blood!"

168   Mama looked at Frieda for verification. Frieda nodded. "She's ministratin'. We was just helping."

169   Mama released Pecola and stood looking at her. Then she pulled both of them toward her, their heads against her stomach. Her eyes were sorry. "All right, all right. Now, stop crying. I didn't know. Come on, now. Get on in the house. Go on home, Rosemary. The show is over."

170   We trooped in, Frieda sobbing quietly, Pecola carrying a white tail, me carrying the little-girl-gone-to-woman pants.

171   Mama led us to the bathroom. She prodded Pecola inside, and taking the underwear from me, told us to stay out.

172   We could hear water running into the bathtub.

173   "You think she's going to drown her?"

174   "Oh, Claudia. You so dumb. She's just going to wash her clothes and all."

175   "Should we beat up Rosemary?"

176   "No. Leave her alone."

177   The water gushed, and over its gushing we could hear the music of my mother's laughter.

178   That night, in bed, the three of us lay still. We were full of awe and respect for Pecola. Lying next to a real person who was really ministratin' was somehow sacred. She was different from us now— grown-up-like. She, herself, felt the distance, but refused to lord it over us.

After a long while she spoke very softly, "Is it true that I can 179
have a baby now?"

"Sure," said Frieda drowsily. "Sure you can." 180

"But. . .how?" Her voice was hollow with wonder. 181

"Oh," said Frieda, "somebody has to love you." 182

"Oh." 183

There was a long pause in which Pecola and I thought this over. 184
It would involve, I supposed, "my man," who, before leaving me,
would love me. But there weren't any babies in the songs my mother
sang. Maybe that's why the women were sad: the men left before they
could make a baby.

Then Pecola asked a question that had never entered my mind. 185
"How do you do that? I mean, how do you get somebody to love
you?" But Frieda was asleep. And I didn't know.

Discussion

- Discuss how what Toni Morrison does relates to what Flannery
O'Connor says a writer should do.
- As nonfiction writers we continue to learn our craft from our poets
and our fiction writers. What can you learn from this selection and apply
to your nonfiction?
- Compare this novel about growing up to the autobiographical writings of Baraka, Dryden, Gibson. In what ways are they similar and in what
ways do they differ?
- What surprised you about Morrison's writing? How is it different
from what you expected? How does it involve you? How does it make you
feel? How does it make you think?
- How does Morrison use detail? Where does it work for you? Where
doesn't it?
- How does Morrison use point of view?
- What gives her writing such force and energy?

Activities

- Rewrite a page of your prose as Morrison might.
- "I write out of ignorance," Morrison has said. "I write about the
things I don't have any resolutions for, and when I'm finished, I think I
know a little bit more about it. I don't write out of what I know. It's what I

don't know that stimulates me. I merely know enough to get started." Grace Paley has said something that seems to clarify what Morrison means. Paley said, "We write about what we don't know about what we know." Write a draft about something in your life which you don't fully understand and need to understand.

• Morrison should liberate you. Don't write the way she writes, but write with the courage she displays to reveal herself, to hear herself, to use her language to explore her world. Create a free-writing draft to hear the voice you do not yet know that you have.

• Take a page from O'Connor and write it as Morrison might. Then let O'Connor go to work on a page of Morrison.

Raymond Carver

Raymond Carver is one of the best short-story writers publishing today. He writes in a spare style that is radically different from the way Morrison writes. Neither is right or wrong. Their diversity is what delights; their diversity and their accomplishment. Carver reveals, by artful understatement, the tragedies and joys in ordinary lives which, of course, become extraordinary under his pen.

We have reprinted two versions of the same story which show a writer growing and developing after publication. He is, like most writers, a great rewriter. "Much of this work time, understand," Carver says, speaking of his writing habits, "is given over to revising and rewriting. There's not much that I like better than to take a story that I've had around the house a while and work it over again." Another time he explained, "It doesn't take that long to do the first draft of a story, that usually happens in one sitting, but it does take a while to do the various versions of the story. I've done as many as twenty or thirty drafts of a story. Never less than ten or twelve drafts." Carver has also said, "I like to mess around with my stories. I'd rather tinker with a story after writing it, and then tinker some more, changing this, changing that, than have to write the story in the first place. . . .Maybe I revise because it gradually takes me into the heart of what the story is about. I have to keep trying to see if I can find that out. It's a process more than a fixed position."

The Bath

Saturday afternoon the mother drove to the bakery in the shopping center. After looking through a loose-leaf binder with photographs of cakes taped onto the pages, she ordered chocolate, the child's favorite. The cake she chose was decorated with a spaceship and a launching pad under a sprinkling of white stars. The name SCOTTY would be iced on in green as if it were the name of the spaceship.

> ❧ One paragraph and you hear another writer's voice, a writer who is able to make his own music, using ordinary details of a very ordinary situation.❧

The baker listened thoughtfully when the mother told him Scotty would be eight years old. He was an older man, this baker, and he wore a curious apron, a heavy thing with loops that went under his arms and around his back and then crossed in front again where they were tied in a very thick knot. He kept wiping his hands on the front of the apron as he listened to the woman, his wet eyes examining her lips as she studied the samples and talked.

He let her take her time. He was in no hurry.

The mother decided on the spaceship cake, and then she gave the baker her name and her telephone number. The cake would be ready Monday morning, in plenty of time for the party Monday afternoon. This was all the baker was willing to say. No pleasantries, just this small exchange, the barest information, nothing that was not necessary.

Monday morning, the boy was walking to school. He was in the company of another boy, the two boys passing a bag of potato chips back and forth between them. The birthday boy was trying to trick the other boy into telling what he was going to give in the way of a present.

At an intersection, without looking, the birthday boy stepped off the curb, and was promptly knocked down by a car. He fell on his side, his head in the gutter, his legs in the road moving as if he were climbing a wall.

The other boy stood holding the potato chips. He was wondering if he should finish the rest or continue on to school.

The birthday boy did not cry. But neither did he wish to talk anymore. He would not answer when the other boy asked what it felt like to be hit by a car. The birthday boy got up and turned back for home, at which time the other boy waved good-bye and headed off for school.

9   The birthday boy told his mother what had happened. They sat together on the sofa. She held his hands in her lap. This is what she was doing when the boy pulled his hands away and lay down on his back.

10   Of course, the birthday party never happened. The birthday boy was in the hospital instead. The mother sat by the bed. She was waiting for the boy to wake up. The father hurried over from his office. He sat next to the mother. So now the both of them waited for the boy to wake up. They waited for hours, and then the father went home to take a bath.

11   The man drove home from the hospital. He drove the streets faster than he should. It had been a good life till now. There had been work, fatherhood, family. The man had been lucky and happy. But fear made him want a bath.

12   He pulled into the driveway. He sat in the car trying to make his legs work. The child had been hit by a car and he was in the hospital, but he was going to be all right. The man got out of the car and went up to the door. The dog was barking and the telephone was ringing. It kept ringing while the man unlocked the door and felt the wall for the light switch.

13   He picked up the receiver. He said, "I just got in the door!"

14   "There's a cake that wasn't picked up."

15   This is what the voice on the other end said.

16   "What are you saying?" the father said.

17   "The cake," the voice said. "Sixteen dollars."

18   The husband held the receiver against his ear, trying to understand. He said, "I don't know anything about it."

19   "Don't hand me that," the voice said.

20   The husband hung up the telephone. He went into the kitchen and poured himself some whiskey. He called the hospital.

21   The child's condition remained the same.

22   While the water ran into the tub, the man lathered his face and shaved. He was in the tub when he heard the telephone again. He got himself out and hurried through the house, saying, "Stupid, stupid," because he wouldn't be doing this if he'd stayed where he was in the hospital. He picked up the receiver and shouted, "Hello!:

The voice said, "It's ready . . ."   23

🐚 The momentum in Morrison's writing seemed to come in large part from the flood of language, but notice how you are being swept along in this story. Where does this momentum come from? 🐚

The father got back to the hospital after midnight. The wife was   24
sitting in the chair by the bed. She looked up at the husband and then she looked back at the child. From an apparatus over the bed hung a bottle with a tube running from the bottle to the child.

"What's this?" the father said.   25
"Glucose," the mother said.   26
The husband put his hand to the back of the woman's head.   27
"He's going to wake up," the man said.   28
"I know," the woman said.   29
In a little while the man said, "Go home and let me take over."   30
She shook her head. "No," she said.   31
"Really," he said. "Go home for a while. You don't have to   32
worry. He's sleeping, is all."
A nurse pushed open the door. She nodded to them as she went   33
to the bed. She took the left arm out from under the covers and put her fingers on the wrist. She put the arm back under the covers and wrote on the clipboard attached to the bed.

"How is he?" the mother said.   34
"Stable," the nurse said. Then she said, "Doctor will be in again   35
shortly."
"I was saying maybe she'd want to go home and get a little   36
rest," the man said. "After the doctor comes."
"She could do that," the nurse said.   37
The woman said, "We'll see what the doctor says." She brought   38
her hand up to her eyes and leaned her head forward.
The nurse said, "Of course."   39

The father gazed at his son, the small chest inflating and deflat-   40
ing under the covers. He felt more fear now. He began shaking his head. He talked to himself like this. The child is fine. Instead of sleeping at home, he's doing it here. Sleep is the same wherever you do it.

The doctor came in. He shook hands with the man. The woman   41
got up from the chair.

42   "Ann," the doctor said and nodded. The doctor said, "Let's just see how he's doing." He moved to the bed and touched the boy's wrist. He peeled back an eyelid and then the other. He turned back the covers and listened to the heart. He pressed his fingers here and there on the body. He went to the end of the bed and studied the chart. He noted the time, scribbled on the chart, and then he considered the mother and the father.

43   This doctor was a handsome man. His skin was moist and tan. He wore a three-piece suit, a vivid tie, and on his shirt were cufflinks.

44   The mother was talking to herself like this. He has just come from somewhere with an audience. They gave him a special medal.

45   The doctor said, "Nothing to shout about, but nothing to worry about. He should wake up pretty soon." The doctor looked at the boy again. "We'll know more after the tests are in."

46   "Oh, no," the mother said.

47   The doctor said, "Sometimes you see this."

48   The father said, "You wouldn't call this a coma, then?"

49   The father waited and looked at the doctor.

50   "No, I don't want to call it that," the doctor said. "He's sleeping. It's restorative. The body is doing what it has to do."

51   "It's a coma," the mother said. "A kind of coma."

52   The doctor said, "I wouldn't call it that."

53   He took the woman's hands and patted them. He shook hands with the husband.

54   The woman put her fingers on the child's forehead and kept them there for a while. "At least he doesn't have a fever," she said. Then she said, "I don't know. Feel his head."

55   The man put his fingers on the boy's forehead. The man said, "I think he's supposed to feel this way."

56   The woman stood there a while longer, working her lip with her teeth. Then she moved to her chair and sat down.

57   The husband sat in the chair beside her. He wanted to say something else. But there was no saying what it should be. He took her hand and put it in his lap. This made him feel better. It made him feel he was saying something. They sat like that for a while, watching the boy, not talking. From time to time he squeezed her hand until she took it away.

58   "I've been praying," she said.

59   "Me too," the father said. "I've been praying too."

A nurse came back in and checked the flow from the bottle. 60

A doctor came in and said what his name was. This doctor was 61 wearing loafers.

"We're going to take him downstairs for more pictures," he 62 said. "And we want to do a scan."

"A scan?" the mother said. She stood between this new doctor 63 and the bed.

"It's nothing," he said. 64

"My God," she said. 65

Two orderlies came in. They wheeled a thing like a bed. They 66 unhooked the boy from the tube and slid him over onto the thing with wheels.

It was after sunup when they brought the birthday boy back out. 67 The mother and father followed the orderlies into the elevator and up to the room. Once more the parents took up their places next to the bed.

They waited all day. The boy did not wake up. The doctor came 68 again and examined the boy again and left after saying the same things again. Nurses came in. Doctors came in. A technician came in and took blood.

"I don't understand this," the mother said to the technician. 69

"Doctor's orders," the technician said. 70

The mother went to the window and looked out at the parking 71 lot. Cars with their lights on were driving in and out. She stood at the window with her hands on the sill. She was talking to herself like this. We're into something now, something bad.

She was afraid. 72

She saw a car stop and a woman in a long coat get into it. She 73 made believe she was that woman. She made believe she was driving away from here to someplace else.

The doctor came in. He looked tanned and healthier than ever. 74 He went to the bed and examined the boy. He said, "His signs are fine. Everything's good."

The mother said, "But he's sleeping." 75

"Yes," the doctor said. 76

The husband said, "She's tired. She's starved." 77

The doctor said, "She should rest. She should eat. Ann," the 78 doctor said.

79   "Thank you," the husband said.

80   He shook hands with the doctor and the doctor patted their shoulders and left.

❡ Remember that Morrison said that everything you've experienced is in the story, even if it isn't written. I am fascinated by how much is in this story that isn't written, how much that comes from Carver's experience, how much that comes from the reader's experience. How much that isn't on the page, and yet is. And you'll find out how true that is when you come to the end of this version of the story.❡

81   "I suppose one of us should go home and check on things," the man said, "The dog needs to be fed."

82   "Call the neighbors," the wife said. "Someone will feed him if you ask them to."

83   She tried to think who. She closed her eyes and tried to think anything at all. After a time she said, "Maybe I'll do it. Maybe if I'm not here watching, he'll wake up. Maybe it's because I'm watching that he won't."

84   "That could be it," the husband said.

85   "I'll go home and take a bath and put on something clean," the woman said.

86   "I think you should do that," the man said.

87   She picked up her purse. He helped her into her coat. She moved to the door, and looked back. She looked at the child, and then she looked at the father. The husband nodded and smiled.

88   She went past the nurses' station and down to the end of the corridor, where she turned and saw a little waiting room, a family in there, all sitting in wicker chairs, a man in a khaki shirt, a base ball cap pushed back on his head, a large woman wearing a housedress, slippers, a girl in jeans, hair in dozens of kinky braids, the table littered with flimsy wrappers and styrofoam and coffee sticks and packets of salt and pepper.

89   "Nelson," the woman said. "Is it about Nelson?"

90   The woman's eyes widened.

91   "Tell me now, lady," the woman said, "Is it about Nelson?"

92   The woman was trying to get up from her chair. But the man had his hand closed over her arm.

93   "Here, here," the man said.

"I'm sorry," the mother said. "I'm looking for the elevator. My   94
son is in the hospital. I can't find the elevator."

"Elevator is down that way," the man said, and he aimed a   95
finger in the right direction.

"My son was hit by a car," the mother said. "But he's going to   96
be all right. He's in shock now, but it might be some kind of coma
too. That's what worries us, the coma part. I'm going out for a little
while. Maybe I'll take a bath. But my husband is with him. He's
watching. There's a chance everything will change when I'm gone.
My name is Ann Weiss."

The man shifted in his chair. He shook his head.   97

He said, "Our Nelson."   98

She pulled into the driveway. The dog ran out from behind the   99
house. He ran in circles on the grass. She closed her eyes and leaned
her head against the wheel. She listened to the ticking of the engine.

She got out of the car and went to the door. She turned on lights   100
and put on water for tea. She opened a can and fed the dog. She sat
down on the sofa with her tea.

The telephone rang.   101

"Yes!" she said. "Hello!" she said.   102

"Mrs. Weiss," a man's voice said.   103

"Yes," she said. "This is Mrs. Weiss. Is it about Scotty?" she   104
said.

"Scotty," the voice said. "It is about Scotty," the voice said. "It   105
has to do with Scotty, yes."

❧ Now read the second version of the story, and then go back and
compare the first with the second, discovering how the author has
developed what he wrote the first time. ❧

A Small, Good Thing

Saturday afternoon she drove to the bakery in the shopping   1
center. After looking through a loose-leaf binder with photographs of
cakes taped onto the pages, she ordered chocolate, the child's favorite. The cake she chose was decorated with a space ship and launching pad under a sprinkling of white stars, and a planet made of red
frosting at the other end. His name, SCOTTY, would be in green let-

ters beneath the planet. The baker, who was an older man with a thick neck, listened without saying anything when she told him the child would be eight years old next Monday. The baker wore a white apron that looked like a smock. Straps cut under his arms, went around in back and then to the front again, where they were secured under his heavy waist. He wiped his hands on his apron as he listened to her. He kept his eyes down on the photographs and let her talk. He let her take her time. He'd just come to work and he'd be there all night, baking, and he was in no real hurry.

2   She gave the baker her name, Ann Weiss, and her telephone number. The cake would be ready on Monday morning, just out of the oven, in plenty of time for the child's party that afternoon. The baker was not jolly. There were no pleasantries between them, just the minimum exchange of words. the necessary information. He made her feel uncomfortable, and she didn't like that. While he was bent over the counter with the pencil in his hand, she studied his coarse features and wondered if he'd ever done anything else with his life besides be a baker. She was a mother and thirty-three years old, and it seemed to her that everyone, especially someone the baker's age—a man old enough to be her father—must have children who'd gone through this special time of cakes and birthday parties. There must be that between them, she thought. But he was abrupt with her—not rude, just abrupt. She gave up trying to make friends with him. She looked into the back of the bakery and could see a long, heavy wooden table with aluminum pie pans stacked at one end, and beside the table a metal container filled with empty racks. There was an enormous oven. A radio was playing country-Western music.

3   The baker finished printing the information on the special order card and closed up the binder. He looked at her and said, "Monday morning." She thanked him and drove home.

4   On Monday morning, the birthday boy was walking to school with another boy. They were passing a bag of potato chips back and forth and the birthday boy was trying to find out what his friend intended to give him for his birthday that afternoon. Without looking, the birthday boy stepped off the curb at an intersection and was immediately knocked down by a car. He fell on his side with his head in the gutter and his legs out in the road. His eyes were closed, but his legs moved back and forth as if he were trying to climb over something. His friend dropped the potato chips and started to cry.

The car had gone a hundred feet or so and stopped in the middle of the road. The man in the driver's seat looked back over his shoulder. He waited until the boy got unsteadily to his feet. The boy wobbled a little. He looked dazed, but okay. The driver put the car into gear and drove away.

The birthday boy didn't cry, but he didn't have anything to say   5
about anything either. He wouldn't answer when his friend asked him what it felt like to be hit by a car. He walked home, and his friend went on to school. But after the birthday boy was inside his house and was telling his mother about it—she sitting beside him on the sofa, holding his hands in her lap, saying, "Scotty, honey, are you sure you feel all right, baby?" thinking she would call the doctor anyway—he suddenly lay back on the sofa, closed his eyes, and went limp. When she couldn't wake him up, she hurried to the telephone and called her husband at work. Howard told her to remain calm, remain calm, and then he called an ambulance for the child and left for the hospital himself.

Of course, the birthday party was canceled. The child was in   6
the hospital with a mild concussion and suffering from shock. There'd been vomiting, and his lungs had taken in fluid which needed pumping out that afternoon. Now he simply seemed to be in a very deep sleep—but no coma, Dr. Francis had emphasized, no coma, when he saw the alarm in the parents' eyes. At eleven o'clock that night, when the boy seemed to be resting comfortably enough after the many X-rays and the lab work, and it was just a matter of his waking up and coming around, Howard left the hospital. He and Ann had been at the hospital with the child since that afternoon, and he was going home for a short while to bathe and change clothes. "I'll be back in an hour," he said. She nodded. "It's fine," she said. "I'll be right here." He kissed her on the forehead, and they touched hands. She sat in the chair beside the bed and looked at the child. She was waiting for him to wake up and be all right. Then she could begin to relax.

Howard drove home from the hospital. He took the wet, dark   7
streets very fast, then caught himself and slowed down. Until now, his life had gone smoothly and to his satisfaction—college, marriage, another year of college for the advanced degree in business, a junior partnership in an investment firm. Fatherhood. He was happy and, so far, lucky—he knew that. His parents were still living, his brothers and his sister were established, his friends from college had gone out to take their places in the world. So far, he had kept away from any

real harm, from those forces he knew existed and that could cripple or bring down a man if the luck went bad, if things suddenly turned. He pulled into the driveway and parked. His left leg began to tremble. He sat in the car for a minute and tried to deal with the present situation in a rational manner. Scotty had been hit by a car and was in the hospital, but he was going to be all right. Howard closed his eyes and ran his hand over his face. He got out of the car and went up to the front door. The dog was barking inside the house. The telephone rang and rang while he unlocked the door and fumbled for the light switch. He shouldn't have left the hospital, he shouldn't have. "Goddamn it!" he said. He picked up the receiver and said, "I just walked in the door!"

8   "There's a cake here that wasn't picked up," the voice on the other end of the line said.

9   "What are you saying?" Howard said.

10   "A cake," the voice said. "A sixteen-dollar cake."

11   Howard held the receiver against his ear, trying to understand. "I don't know anything about a cake," he said. "Jesus, what are you talking about?"

12   "Don't hand me that," the voice said

13   Howard hung up the telephone. He went into the kitchen and poured himself some whiskey. He called the hospital. But the child's condition remained the same; he was still sleeping and nothing had changed there. While water poured into the tub, Howard lathered his face and shaved. He'd just stretched out in the tub and closed his eyes when the telephone rang again. He hauled himself out, grabbed a towel, and hurried through the house, saying, "Stupid, stupid," for having left the hospital. But when he picked up the receiver and shouted, "Hello!" there was no sound at the other end of the line. Then the caller hung up.

14   He arrived back at the hospital a little after midnight. Ann still sat in the chair beside the bed. She looked up at Howard, and then she looked back at the child. The child's eyes stayed closed, the head was still wrapped in bandages. His breathing was quiet and regular. From an apparatus over the bed hung a bottle of glucose with a tube running from the bottle to the boy's arm.

15   "How is he?" Howard said. "What's all this?" waving at the glucose and the tube.

16   "Dr. Francis's orders," she said. "He needs nourishment. He

needs to keep up his strength. Why doesn't he wake up, Howard? I don't understand, if he's all right."

Howard put his hand against the back of her head. He ran his 17 fingers through her hair. "He's going to be all right. He'll wake up in a little while. Dr. Francis knows what's what."

After a time, he said, "Maybe you should go home and get some 18 rest. I'll stay here. Just don't put up with this creep who keeps calling. Hang up right away."

"Who's calling?: she asked. 19

"I don't know who, just somebody with nothing better to do 20 than call up people. You go on now."

She shook her head. "No," she said, "I'm fine." 21

"Really," he said. "Go home for a while, and then come back 22 and spell me in the morning. It'll be all right. What did Dr. Francis say? He said Scotty's going to be all right. We don't have to worry. He's just sleeping now, that's all."

A nurse pushed the door open. She nodded at them as she went 23 to the bedside. She took the left arm out from under the covers and put her fingers on the wrist, found the pulse, then consulted her watch. In a little while, she put the arm back under the covers and moved to the foot of the bed, where she wrote something on a clipboard attached to the bed.

"How is he?" Ann said. Howard's hand was a weight on her 24 shoulder. She was aware of the pressure from his fingers.

"He's stable," the nurse. Then she said, "Doctor will be in 25 again shortly. Doctor's back in the hospital. He's making rounds right now."

"I was saying maybe she'd want to go home and get a little 26 rest," Howard said. "After the doctor comes," he said.

"She could do that," the nurse said. "I think you should both 27 feel free to do that, if you wish." The nurse was a big Scandinavian woman with blond hair. There was the trace of an accent in her speech.

"We'll see what the doctor says," Ann said. "I want to talk to 28 the doctor. I don't think he should keep sleeping like this. I don't think that's a good sign." She brought her hand up to her eyes and let her head come forward a little, Howard's grip tightened on her shoulder, and then his hand moved up to her neck, where his fingers began to knead the muscles there.

"Dr. Francis will be here in a few minutes," the nurse said. 29 Then she left the room.

30   Howard gazed at his son for a time, the small chest quietly rising and falling under the covers. For the first time since the terrible minutes after Ann's telephone call to him at his office, he felt a genuine fear starting in his limbs. He began shaking his head. Scotty was fine, but instead of sleeping at home in his own bed, he was in a hospital bed with bandages around his head and a tube in his arm. But this help was what he needed right now.

31   Dr. Francis came in and shook hands with Howard, though they'd just seen each other a few hours before. Ann got up from the chair. "Doctor?"

32   "Ann," he said and nodded. "Let's just first see how he's doing," the doctor said. He moved to the side of the bed and took the boy's pulse. He peeled back one eyelid and then the other. Howard and Ann stood beside the doctor and watched. Then the doctor turned back the covers and listened to the boy's heart and lungs with his stethoscope. He pressed his fingers here and there on the abdomen. When he was finished, he went to the end of the bed and studied the chart. He noted the time, scribbled something on the chart, and then looked at Howard and Ann.

33   "Doctor, how is he?" Howard said. "What's the matter with him exactly?"

34   "Why doesn't he wake up?" Ann said.

35   The doctor was a handsome, big-shouldered man with a tanned face. He wore a three-piece blue suit, a striped tie, and ivory cufflinks. His gray hair was combed along the sides of his head, and he looked as if he had just come from a concert. "He's all right," the doctor said. "Nothing to shout about, he could be better, I think. But he's all right. Still, I wish he'd wake up. He should wake up pretty soon." The doctor looked at the boy again. "We'll know some more in a couple of hours, after the results of a few more tests are in. But he's all right, believe me, except for the hairline fracture of the skull. He does have that.

36   "Oh, no," Ann said.

37   "And a bit of a concussion, as I said before. Of course, you know he's in shock," the doctor said. "Sometimes you see this in shock cases. This sleeping."

38   "But he's out of any real danger?" Howard said. "You said before he's not in a coma. You wouldn't call this a coma, then—would you, doctor?" Howard waited. He looked at the doctor.

39   "No, I don't want to call it a coma," the doctor said and glanced

over at the boy once more. "He's just in a very deep sleep. It's a restorative measure the body is taking on its own. He's out of any real danger, I'd say that for certain, yet. But we'll know more when he wakes up and the other tests are in," the doctor said.

"It's a coma," Ann said. "Of sorts." 40

"It's not a coma yet, not exactly," the doctor said. "I wouldn't 41 want to call it a coma. Not yet, anyway. He's suffered shock. In shock cases, this kind of reaction is common enough; it's a temporary reaction to bodily trauma. Coma. Well, coma is a deep, prolonged unconsciousness, something that could go on for days, or weeks even. Scotty's not in that area, not as far as we can tell. I'm certain his condition will show improvement by morning. I'm betting that it will. We'll know more when he wakes up, which shouldn't be long now. Of course, you may do as you like, stay here or go home for a time. But by all means feel free to leave the hospital for a while if you want. This is not easy, I know." The doctor gazed at the boy again, watching him, and then he turned to Ann and said, "You try not to worry, little mother. Believe me, we're doing all that can be done. It's just a question of a little more time now." He nodded at her, shook hands with Howard again, and then he left the room.

Ann put her hand over the child's forehead. "At least he doesn't 42 have a fever," she said. Then she said, "My God, he feels so cold, though. Howard? Is he supposed to feel like this? Feel his head."

Howard touched the child's temples. His own breathing had 43 slowed. "I think he's supposed to feel this way right now," he said. "He's in shock, remember? That's what the doctor said. The doctor was just in here. He would have said something if Scotty wasn't okay."

Ann stood there a while longer, working her lip with her teeth. 44 Then she moved over to her chair and sat down.

Howard sat in the chair next to her chair. They looked at each 45 other. He wanted to say something else and reassure her, but he was afraid, too. He took her hand and put it in his lap, and this made him feel better, her hand being there. He picked up her hand and squeezed it. Then he just held her hand. They sat like that for a while, watching the boy and not talking. From time to time, he squeezed her hand. Finally, she took her hand away.

"I've been praying," she said. 46

He nodded. 47

She said, "I almost thought I'd forgotten how, but it came back 48 to me. All I had to do was close my eyes and say, 'Please God, help us—help Scotty,' and then the rest was easy. The words were right there. Maybe if you prayed, too," she said to him.

49   "I've already prayed," he said. "I prayed this afternoon—yesterday afternoon, I mean—after you called, while I was driving to the hospital. I've been praying," he said.

50   "That's good," she said. For the first time, she felt they were together in it, this trouble. She realized with a start that, until now, it had only been happening to her and to Scotty. She hadn't let Howard into it, though he was there and needed all along. She felt glad to be his wife.

51   The same nurse came in and took the boy's pulse again and checked the flow from the bottle hanging above the bed.

52   In an hour, another doctor came in. He said his name was Parsons, from Radiology. He had a bushy mustache. He was wearing loafers, a Western shirt, and a pair of jeans.

53   "We're going to take him downstairs for more pictures," he told them. "We need to do some more pictures, and we want to do a scan."

54   "What's that?" Ann said. "A scan?" She stood between this new doctor and the bed. "I thought you'd already taken all your X-rays."

55   "I'm afraid we need some more," he said. "Nothing to be alarmed about. We just need some more pictures, and we want to do a brain scan on him."

56   "My God," Ann said.

57   "It's perfectly normal procedure in cases like this," this new doctor said. "We just need to find out for sure why he isn't back awake yet. It's normal medical procedure, and nothing to be alarmed about. We'll be taking him down in a few minutes," this doctor said.

58   In a little while, two orderlies came into the room with a gurney. They were black-haired, dark-complexioned men in white uniforms, and they said a few words to each other in a foreign tongue as they unhooked the boy from the tube and moved him from his bed to the gurney. Then they wheeled him from the room. Howard and Ann got on the same elevator. Ann gazed at the child. She closed her eyes as the elevator began its descent. The orderlies stood at either end of the gurney without saying anything, though once one of the men made a comment to the other in their own language, and the other man nodded slowly in response.

Later that morning, just as the sun was beginning to lighten the 59 windows in the waiting room outside the X-ray department, they brought the boy out and moved him back up to his room. Howard and Ann rode up on the elevator with him once more, and once more they took up their places beside the bed.

They waited all day, but still the boy did not wake up. Occa- 60 sionally, one of them would leave the room to go downstairs to the cafeteria to drink coffee and then, as if suddenly remembering and feeling guilty, get up from the table and hurry back to the room. Dr. Francis came again that afternoon and examined the boy once more and then left after telling them he was coming along and could wake up at any minute now. Nurses, different nurses from the night before, came in from time to time. Then a young woman from the lab knocked and entered the room. She wore white slacks and a white blouse and carried a little tray of things which she put on the stand beside the bed. Without a word to them, she took blood from the boy's arm. Howard closed his eyes as the woman found the right place on the boy's arm and pushed the needle in.

"I don't understand this," Ann said to the woman. 61

"Doctor's orders," the young woman said. "I do what I'm told. 62 They say draw that one, I draw. What's wrong with him, anyway?" she said. "He's a sweetie."

"He was hit by a car," Howard said. "A hit-and-run." 63

The young woman shook her head and looked again at the boy. 64 Then she took her tray and left the room.

"Why won't he wake up?" Ann said. "Howard? I want some 65 answers from these people."

Howard didn't say anything. He sat down again in the chair and 66 crossed one leg over the other. He rubbed his face. He looked at his son and then he settled back in the chair, closed his eyes, and went to sleep.

Ann walked to the window and looked out at the parking lot. It 67 was night, and cars were driving into and out of the parking lot with their lights on. She stood at the window with her hands gripping the sill, and knew in her heart that they were into something now, something hard. She was afraid, and her teeth began to chatter until she tightened her jaws. She saw a big car stop in front of the hospital and someone, a woman in a long coat, get into the car. She wished she were that woman and somebody, anybody, was driving her away from here to somewhere else, a place where she would find Scotty waiting for her when she stepped out of the car, ready to say MOM and let her gather him in her arms.

68   In a little while, Howard woke up. He looked at the boy again. Then he got up from the chair, stretched, and went over to stand beside her at the window. They both stared out at the parking lot. They didn't say anything. But they seemed to feel each other's insides now, as though the worry had made them transparent in a perfectly natural way.

69   The door opened and Dr. Francis came in. He was wearing a different suit and tie this time. His gray hair was combed along the sides of his head, and he looked as if he had just shaved. He went straight to the bed and examined the boy. "He ought to have come around by now. There's just no good reason for this," he said. "But I can tell you we're all convinced he's out of any danger. We'll just feel better when he wakes up. There's no reason, absolutely none, why he shouldn't come around. Very soon. Oh, he'll have himself a dilly of a headache when he does, you can count on that. But all of his signs are fine. They're as normal as can be."

70   "Is it a coma, then?" Ann said.

71   The doctor rubbed his smooth cheek. "We'll call it that for the time being, until he wakes up. But you must be worn out. This is hard. I know this is hard. Feel free to go out for a bite," he said. "It would do you good. I'll put a nurse in here while you're gone if you'll feel better about going. Go and have yourselves something to eat."

72   "I couldn't eat anything," Ann said.

73   "Do what you need to do, of course," the doctor said. "Anyway, I wanted to tell you that all the signs are good, the tests are negative, nothing showed up at all, and just as soon as he wakes up he'll be over the hill."

74   "Thank you, doctor," Howard said. He shook hands with the doctor again. The doctor patted Howard's shoulder and went out.

75   "I suppose one of us should go home and check on things," Howard said. "Slug needs to be fed, for one thing."

76   "Call one of the neighbors," Ann said. "Call the Morgans. Anyone will feed a dog if you ask them to."

77   "All right," Howard said. After a while, he said, "Honey, why don't YOU do it? Why don't you go home and check on things, and then come back? It'll do you good. I'll be right here with him. Seriously," he said. "We need to keep up our strength on this. We'll want to be here for a while even after he wakes up."

"Why don't YOU go?" she said. "Feed Slug. Feed yourself."   78

"I already went," he said. " I was gone for exactly an hour and   79
fifteen minutes. You go home for an hour and freshen up. Then come
back."

She tried to think about it, but she was too tired. She closed her   80
eyes and tried to think about it again. After a time, she said, "Maybe
I WILL go home for a few minutes. Maybe if I'm not just sitting right
here watching him every second, he'll wake up and be all right. You
know? Maybe he'll wake up if I'm not here. I'll go home and take a
bath and put on clean clothes. I'll feed Slug. Then I'll come back."

"I'll be right here," he said. "You go on home, honey. I'll keep   81
an eye on things here." His eyes were bloodshot and small, as if he'd
been drinking for a long time. His clothes were rumpled. His beard
had come out again. She touched his face, and then she took her
hand back. She understood he wanted to be by himself for a while,
not have to talk or share his worry for a time. She picked her purse
up from the nightstand, and he helped her into her coat.

"I won't be gone long," she said.   82

"Just sit and rest for a little while when you get home," he said.   83
"Eat something. Take a bath. After you get out of the bath, just sit
for a while and rest. It'll do you a world of good, you'll see. Then
come back," he said. "Let's try not to worry. You heard what Dr.
Francis said."

She stood in her coat for a minute trying to recall the doctor's   84
exact words, looking for any nuances, any hint of something behind
his words other than what he had said. She tried to remember if his
expression had changed any when he bent over to examine the child.
She remembered the way his features had composed themselves as
he rolled back the child's eyelids and then listened to his breathing.

She went to the door, where she turned and looked back. She   85
looked at the child, and then she looked at the father. Howard nodded. She stepped out of the room and pulled the door closed behind
her.

She went past the nurses' station and down to the end of the   86
corridor, looking for the elevator. At the end of the corridor, she
turned to her right and entered a little waiting room where a Negro
family sat in wicker chairs. There was a middle-aged man in a khaki
shirt and pants, a baseball cap pushed back on his head. A large
woman wearing a housedress and slippers was slumped in one of the
chairs. A teenaged girl in jeans, hair done in dozens of little braids,
lay stretched out in one of the chairs smoking a cigarette, her legs

crossed at the ankles. The family swung their eyes to Ann as she entered the room. The little table was littered with hamburger wrappers and Styrofoam cups.

87   "Franklin," the large woman said as she roused herself. "Is it about Franklin?" Her eyes widened, "Tell me now, lady," the woman said. "Is it about Franklin?" She was trying to rise from her chair, but the man had closed his hand over her arm.

88   "Here, here," he said. "Evelyn."

89   "I'm sorry," Ann said. "I'm looking for the elevator. My son is in the hospital, and now I can't find the elevator."

90   "Elevator is down that way, turn left," the man said as he aimed a finger.

91   The girl drew on her cigarette and stared at Ann. Her eyes were narrowed to slits, and her broad lips parted slowly as she let the smoke escape. The Negro woman let her head fall on her shoulder and looked away from Ann, no longer interested.

92   "My son was hit by a car," Ann said to the man. She seemed to need to explain herself. "He has a concussion and a little skull fracture, but he's going to be all right. He's in shock now, but it might be some kind of coma, too. That's what really worries us, the coma part. I'm going out for a little while, but my husband is with him. Maybe he'll wake up while I'm gone."

93   "That's too bad," the man said and shifted in the chair. He shook his head. He looked down at the table, and then he looked back at Ann. She was still standing there. He said, "Our Franklin, he's on the operating table. Somebody cut him. Tried to kill him. There was a fight where he was at. At this party. They say he was just standing and watching. Not bothering nobody. But that don't mean nothing these days. Now he's on the operating table. We're just hoping and praying, that's all we can do now." He gazed at her steadily.

94   Ann looked at the girl again, who was still watching her, and at the older woman, who kept her head down, but whose eyes were now closed. Ann saw the lips moving silently, making words. She had an urge to ask what those words were. She wanted to talk more with these people who were in the same kind of waiting she was in. She was afraid, and they were afraid. They had that in common. She would have liked to have said something else about the accident, told them more about Scotty, that it had happened on the day of his birthday, Monday, and that he was still unconscious. Yet she didn't know how to begin. She stood looking at them without saying anything more.

She went down the corridor the man had indicated and found 95
the elevator. She waited a minute in front of the closed doors, still
wondering if she was doing the right thing. Then she put out her
finger and touched the button.

She pulled into the driveway and cut the engine. She closed her 96
eyes and leaned her head against the wheel for a minute. She listened
to the ticking sounds the engine made as it began to cool. Then she
got out of the car. She could hear the dog barking inside the house.
She went to the front door, which was unlocked. She went inside and
turned on lights and put on a kettle of water for tea. She opened some
dogfood and fed Slug on the back porch. The dog ate in hungry little
smacks. It kept running into the kitchen to see that she was going to
stay. As she sat down on the sofa with her tea, the telephone rang.

"Yes!" she said as she answered, "Hello!" 97

"Mrs. Weiss," a man's voice said. It was five o'clock in the 98
morning, and she thought she could hear machinery or equipment
of some kind in the background.

"Yes, yes! What is it?" she said. "This is Mrs. Weiss. This is she. 99
What is it, please?" She listened to whatever it was in the background. "Is it Scotty, for Christ's sake?"

"Scotty," the man's voice said. "It's about Scotty, yes. It has to 100
do with Scotty, that problem. Have you forgotten about Scotty?" the
man said. Then he hung up.

She dialed the hospital's number and asked for the third floor. 101
She demanded information about her son from the nurse who
answered the telephone. Then she asked to speak to her husband. It
was, she said, an emergency.

She waited, turning the telephone cord in her fingers. She 102
closed her eyes and felt sick at her stomach. She would have to make
herself eat. Slug came in from the back porch and lay down near her
feet. He wagged his tail. She pulled at his ear while he licked her
fingers. Howard was on the line.

"Somebody just called here," she said. She twisted the tele- 103
phone cord. "He said it was about Scotty," she cried.

"Scotty's fine," Howard told her. "I mean, he's still sleeping. 104
There's been no change. The nurse has been in twice since you've
been gone. A nurse or else a doctor. He's all right."

"This man called. He said it was about Scotty," she told him. 105

"Honey, you rest for a little while, you need the rest. It must be 106 that same caller I had. Just forget it. Come back down here after you've rested. Then we'll have breakfast or something."

107   "Breakfast," she said. "I don't want any breakfast."

108   "You know what I mean," he said. "Juice, something. I don't know. I don't know anything. Ann. Jesus, I'm not hungry, either, Ann, it's hard to talk now, I'm standing here at the desk. Dr. Francis is coming again at eight o'clock this morning. He's going to have something to tell us then, something more definite. That's what one of the nurses said. She didn't know any more than that. Ann? Honey, maybe we'll know something more then. At eight o'clock. Come back here before eight. Meanwhile, I'm right here and Scotty's all right. He's still the same," he added.

109   "I was drinking a cup of tea," she said, "when the telephone rang. They said it was about Scotty. There was a noise in the background. Was there a noise in the background on that call you had, Howard?"

110   "I don't remember," he said. "Maybe the driver of the car, maybe he's a psychopath and found out about Scotty somehow. But I'm here with him. Just rest like you were going to do. Take a bath and come back by seven or so, and we'll talk to the doctor together when he gets here. It's going to be all right, honey, I'm here, and there are doctors and nurses around. They say his condition is stable."

111   "I'm scared to death," she said.

112   She ran water, undressed, and got into the tub. She washed and dried quickly, not taking the time to wash her hair. She put on clean underwear, wool slacks, and a sweater. She went into the living room, where the dog looked up at her and let its tail thump once against the floor. It was just starting to get light outside when she went out to the car.

113   She drove into the parking lot of the hospital and found a space close to the front door. She felt she was in some obscure way responsible for what had happened to the child. She let her thoughts move to the Negro family. She remembered the name Franklin and the table that was covered with hamburger papers, and the teenaged girl staring at her as she drew on her cigarette. "Don't have children," she told the girl's image as she entered the front door of the hospital. "For God's sake, don't."

114   She took the elevator up to the third floor with two nurses who were just going on duty. It was Wednesday morning, a few minutes

before seven. There was a page for a Dr. Madison as the elevator doors slid open on the third floor. She got off behind the nurses, who turned in the other direction and continued the conversation she had interrupted when she'd gotten into the elevator. She walked down the corridor to the little alcove where the Negro family had been waiting. They were gone now, but the chairs were scattered in such a way that it looked as if people had just jumped up from them the minute before. The tabletop was cluttered with the same cups and papers, the ashtray was filled with cigarette butts.

She stopped at the nurses' station. A nurse was standing behind the counter, brushing her hair and yawning. 115

"There was a Negro boy in surgery last night," Ann said. "Franklin was his name. His family was in the waiting room. I'd like to inquire about his condition." 116

"He passed away," said the nurse at the counter. The nurse held the hairbrush and kept looking at her. "Are you a friend of the family or what?" 117

"I met the family last night," Ann said. "My own son is in the hospital. I guess he's in shock. We don't know for sure what's wrong. I just wondered about Franklin, that's all. Thank you." She moved down the corridor. Elevator doors the same color as the walls slid open and a gaunt, bald man in white pants and white canvas shoes pulled a heavy cart off the elevator. She hadn't noticed these doors last night. The man wheeled the cart out into the corridor and stopped in front of the room nearest the elevator and consulted a clipboard. Then he reached down and slid a tray out of the cart. He rapped lightly on the door and entered the room. She could smell the unpleasant odors of warm food as she passed the cart. She hurried on without looking at any of the nurses and pushed open the door to the child's room. 118

Howard was standing at the window with his hands behind his back. He turned around as she came in. 119

"How is he?" she said. She went over to the bed. She dropped her purse on the floor beside the nightstand. It seemed to her she had been gone a long time. She touched the child's face. "Howard?" 120

"Dr. Francis was here a little while ago," Howard said. She looked at him closely and thought his shoulders were bunched a little. 121

"I thought he wasn't coming until eight o'clock this morning," she said quickly. 122

"There was another doctor with him. A neurologist." 123

124   "A neurologist," she said.

125   Howard nodded. His shoulders were bunching, she could see that. "What'd they say, Howard? For Christ's sake, what'd they say? What is it?"

126   "They said they're going to take him down and run more tests on him, Ann. They think they're going to operate, honey. Honey, they ARE going to operate. They can't figure out why he won't wake up. It's more than just shock or concussion, they know that much now. It's in his skull, the fracture, it has something, something to do with that, they think. So they're going to operate. I tried to call you, but I guess you'd already left the house."

127   "Oh, God," she said. "Oh, please, Howard, please," she said, taking his arms.

128   "Look!" Howard said. "Scotty! Look, Ann!" He turned her toward the bed.

129   The boy had opened his eyes, then closed them. He opened them again now. The eyes stared straight ahead for a minute, then moved slowly in his head until they rested on Howard and Ann, then traveled away again.

130   "Scotty," his mother said, moving to the bed.

131   "Hey, Scott," his father said. "Hey, son."

132   They leaned over the bed. Howard took the child's hand in his hands and began to pat and squeeze the hand. Ann bent over the boy and kissed his forehead again and again. She put her hands on either side of his face. "Scotty, honey, it's Mommy and Daddy," she said. "Scotty?"

133   The boy looked at them, but without any sign of recognition. Then his mouth opened, his eyes scrunched closed, and he howled until he had no more air in his lungs. His face seemed to relax and soften then. His lips parted as his last breath was puffed through his throat and exhaled gently through the clenched teeth.

134   The doctors called it a hidden occlusion and said it was a one-in-a-million circumstance. Maybe if it could have been detected somehow and surgery undertaken immediately, they could have saved him. But more than likely not. In any case, what would they have been looking for? Nothing had shown up in the tests or in the X-rays.

135   Dr. Francis was shaken. "I can't tell you how badly I feel. I'm so very sorry, I can't tell you," he said as he led them into the doctors' lounge. There was a doctor sitting in a chair with his legs

hooked over the back of another chair, watching an early-morning TV show. He was wearing a green delivery-room outfit, loose green pants and green blouse, and a green cap that covered his hair. He looked at Howard and Ann and then looked at Dr. Francis. He got to his feet and turned off the set and went out of the room. Dr. Francis guided Ann to the sofa, sat down beside her, and began to talk in a low, consoling voice. At one point, he leaned over and embraced her. She could feel his chest rising and falling evenly against her shoulder. She kept her eyes open and let him hold her. Howard went into the bathroom, but he left the door open. After a violent fit of weeping, he ran water and washed his face. Then he came out and sat down at the little table that held a telephone. He looked at the telephone as though deciding what to do first. He made some calls. After a time, Dr. Francis used the telephone.

"Is there anything else I can do for the moment?" he asked 136 them.

Howard shook his head. Ann stared at Dr. Francis as if unable 137 to comprehend his words.

The doctor walked them to the hospital's front door. People 138 were entering and leaving the hospital. It was eleven o'clock in the morning. Ann was aware of how slowly, almost reluctantly, she moved her feet. It seemed to her that Dr. Francis was making them leave when she felt they should stay, when it would be more the right thing to do to stay. She gazed out into the parking lot and then turned around and looked back at the front of the hospital. She began shaking her head, "No, no," she said. "I can't leave him here, no." She heard herself say that and thought how unfair it was that the only words that came out were the sort of words used on TV shows where people were stunned by violent or sudden deaths. She wanted her words to be her own. "No," she said, and for some reason the memory of the Negro woman's head lolling on the woman's shoulder came to her. "No," she said again.

"I'll be talking to you later in the day," the doctor was saying 139 to Howard. "There are still some things that have to be done, things that have to be cleared up to our satisfaction. Some things that need explaining."

"An autopsy," Howard said. 140

Dr. Francis nodded. 141

"I understand," Howard said. Then he said, "Oh, Jesus. No, I 142 don't understand, doctor, I can't, I can't, I just can't,"

Dr. Francis put his arm around Howard's shoulders. "I'm sorry, 143

God, how I'm sorry." He let go of Howard's shoulders and held out his hand. Howard looked at the hand, and then he took it. Dr. Francis put his arms around Ann once more. He seemed full of some goodness she didn't understand. She let her head rest on his shoulder, but her eyes stayed open. She kept looking at the hospital. As they drove out of the parking lot, she looked back at the hospital.

144   At home, she sat on the sofa with her hands in her coat pockets. Howard closed the door to the child's room. He got the coffee-maker going and then he found an empty box. He had thought to pick up some of the child's things that were scattered around the living room. But instead he sat down beside her on the sofa, pushed the box to one side, and leaned forward, arms between his knees. He began to weep. She pulled his head over into her lap and patted his shoulder. "He's gone," she said. She kept patting his shoulder. Over his sobs, she could hear the coffee-maker hissing in the kitchen. "There, there," she said tenderly. "Howard, he's gone. He's gone and now we'll have to get used to that. To being alone."

145   In a little while, Howard got up and began moving aimlessly around the room with the box, not putting anything into it, but collecting some things together on the floor at one end of the sofa. She continued to sit with her hands in her coat pockets. Howard put the box down and brought coffee into the living room. Later, Ann made calls to relatives. After each call had been placed and the party had answered, Ann would blurt out a few words and cry for a minute. Then she would quietly explain in a measured voice, what had happened and tell them about arrangements. Howard took the box out to the garage, where he saw the child's bicycle. He dropped the box and sat down on the pavement beside the bicycle. He took hold of the bicycle awkwardly so that it leaned against his chest. He held it, the rubber pedal sticking into his chest. He gave the wheel a turn.

146   Ann hung up the telephone after talking to her sister. She was looking up another number when the telephone rang. She picked it up on the first ring.

147   "Hello," she said, and she heard something in the background, a humming noise. "Hello!" she said. "For God's sake," she said. "Who is this? What is it you want?"

148   "Your Scotty, I got him ready for you," the man's voice said. "Did you forget him?"

149   "You evil bastard!" she shouted into the receiver. "How can you do this, you evil son of a bitch?"

"Scotty," the man said. "Have you forgotten about Scotty?" 150
Then the man hung up on her.

Howard heard the shouting and came in to find her with her 151
head on her arms over the table, weeping. He picked up the receiver
and listened to the dial tone.

Much later, just before midnight, after they had dealt with many 152
things, the telephone rang again.

"You answer it," she said. "Howard, it's him, I know." They 153
were sitting at the kitchen table with coffee in front of them. Howard
had a small glass of whiskey beside his cup. He answered on the third
ring.

"Hello," he said. "Who is this? Hello! Hello!" The line went 154
dead. "He hung up," Howard said. "Whoever it was."

"It was him," she said. "That bastard. I'd like to kill him," she 155
said. "I'd like to shoot him and watch him kick," she said.

"Ann, my God," he said. 156

"Could you hear anything?" she said. "In the background? A 157
noise, machinery, something humming?"

"Nothing, really. Nothing like that," he said. "There wasn't 158
much time. I think there was some radio music. Yes, there was a
radio going, that's all I could tell. I don't know what in God's name
is going on," he said.

She shook her head. "If I could, could get my hands on him." 159
It came to her then. She knew who it was. Scotty, the cake, the tele-
phone number. She pushed the chair away from the table and got up.
"Drive me down to the shopping center," she said. "Howard."

"What are you saying?" 160

"The shopping center. I know who it is who's calling, I know 161
who it is. It's the baker, the son-of-a-bitching baker, Howard. I had
him bake a cake for Scotty's birthday. That's who's calling. That's
who has the number and keeps calling us to harass us about that
cake. The baker, that bastard."

❧ The following scene, the new ending of the story, is one of the most
  moving scenes I have ever read. Perhaps I bring my own
  autobiography to the story. I lost a child; I felt the rage—and still
  feel it—and I came to the first reading of this scene full of anger.
  What happened was a surprise to me, a healing surprise. And it has
  been a comfort to me. This story, like so many fine pieces of
  writing, has become a part of my life. Reading, for a writer, is an

experience equal to the experience of living. The living illuminates the writing, and the writing illuminates the living, and both blend in an instructive memory. 🍂

162   They drove down to the shopping center. The sky was clear and stars were out. It was cold, and they ran the heater in the car. They parked in front of the bakery. All of the shops and stores were closed, but there were cars at the far end of the lot in front of the movie theater. The bakery windows were dark, but when they looked through the glass they could see a light in the back room and, now and then, a big man in an apron moving in and out of the white, even light. Through the glass, she could see the display cases and some little tables with chairs. She tried the door. She rapped on the glass. But if the baker heard them, he gave no sign. He didn't look in their direction.

163   They drove around behind the bakery and parked. They got out of the car. There was a lighted window too high up for them to see inside. A sign near the back door said THE PANTRY BAKERY, SPECIAL ORDERS. She could hear faintly a radio playing inside and something creak—an oven door as it was pulled down? She knocked on the door and waited. Then she knocked again, louder. The radio was turned down and there was a scraping sound now, the distinct sound of some thing, a drawer, being pulled open and then closed.

164   Someone unlocked the door and opened it. The baker stood in the light and peered out at them. "I'm closed for business," he said. "What do you want at this hour? It's midnight. Are you drunk or something?"

165   She stepped into the light that fell through the open door. He blinked his heavy eyelids as he recognized her. "It's you," he said.

166   "It's me," she said. "Scotty's mother. This is Scotty's father. We'd like to come in."

167   The baker said, "I'm busy now. I have work to do."

168   She had stepped inside the doorway anyway. Howard came in behind her. The baker moved back. "It smells like a bakery in here. doesn't it smell like a bakery in here, Howard?"

169   "What do you want?" the baker said. "Maybe you want your cake? That's it, you decided you want your cake. You ordered a cake, didn't you?"

170   "You're pretty smart for a baker," she said. "Howard, this is the man who's been calling us." She clenched her fists. She stared at him

fiercely. There was a deep burning inside her, an anger that made her feel larger than herself, larger than either of these men.

"Just a minute here," the baker said. "You want to pick up your 171 three-day-old cake? That it? I don't want to argue with you, lady. There it sits over there, getting stale. I'll give it to you for half of what I quoted you. No. You want it? You can have it. It's no good to me no good to anyone now. It cost me time and money to make that cake. If you want it, okay, if you don't that's okay too. I have to get back to work." He looked at them and rolled his tongue behind his teeth.

"More cakes," she said. She knew she was in control of it, of 172 what was increasing in her. She was calm.

"Lady, I work sixteen hours a day in this place to earn a living," 173 the baker said. He wiped his hands on his apron. "I work night and day in here, trying to make ends meet." A look crossed Ann's face that made the baker move back and say, "No trouble, now." He reached to the counter and picked up a rolling pin with his right hand and began to tap it against the palm of his other hand. "You want the cake or not? I have to get back to work. Bakers work at night," he said again. His eyes were small, mean-looking, she thought, nearly lost in the bristly flesh around his cheeks. His neck was thick with fat.

"I know bakers work at night," Ann said. "They make phone 174 calls at night, too. You bastard," she said.

The baker continued to tap the rolling pin against his hand. He 175 glanced at Howard. "Careful, careful," he said to Howard.

"My son's dead," she said with a cold, even finality. "He was 176 hit by a car Monday morning. We've been waiting with him until he died. But, of course, you couldn't be expected to know that, could you? Bakers can't know everything—can they, Mr. Baker? But he's dead. He's dead, you bastard!" Just as suddenly as it had welled in her, the anger dwindled, gave way to something else, a dizzy feeling of nausea. She leaned against the wooden table that was sprinkled with flour, put her hands over her face, and began to cry, her shoulders rocking back and forth. "It isn't fair," she said. "It isn't, isn't fair."

Howard put his hand at the small of her back and looked at the 177 baker. "Shame on you," Howard said to him. "Shame."

The baker put the rolling pin back on the counter. He undid his 178 apron and threw it on the counter. He looked at them, and then he shook his head slowly. He pulled a chair out from under the card table that held papers and receipts, an adding machine, and a telephone directory. "Please sit down," he said. "Let me get you a chair," he said to Howard. "Sit down now, please." The baker went into the front of the shop and returned with two little wrought-iron chairs. "Please sit down, you people."

179   Ann wiped her eyes and looked at the baker. "I wanted to kill you," she said. "I wanted you dead."

180   The baker had cleared a space for them at the table. He shoved the adding machine to one side, along with the stacks of notepaper and receipts. He pushed the telephone directory onto the floor, where it landed with a thud. Howard and Ann sat down and pulled their chairs up to the table. The baker sat down, too.

181   "Let me say how sorry I am," the baker said, putting his elbows on the table. "God alone knows how sorry. Listen to me. I'm just a baker. I don't claim to be anything else. Maybe once, maybe years ago, I was a different kind of human being. I've forgotten, I don't know for sure. But I'm not any longer, if I ever was. Now I'm just a baker. That don't excuse my doing what I did, I know. But I'm deeply sorry. I'm sorry for your son, and sorry for my part in this," the baker said. He spread his hands out on the table and turned them over to reveal his palms. "I don't have any children myself, so I can only imagine what you must be feeling. All I can say to you now is that I'm sorry. Forgive me, if you can," the baker said. "I'm not an evil man, I don't think. Not evil, like you said on the phone. You got to understand what it comes down to is I don't know how to act anymore, it would seem. Please," the man said, "let me ask you if you can find it in your hearts to forgive me?"

182   It was warm inside the bakery. Howard stood up from the table and took off his coat. He helped Ann from her coat. The baker looked at them for a minute and then nodded and got up from the table. He went to the oven and turned off some switches. He found cups and poured coffee from an electric coffee-maker. He put a carton of cream on the table, and a bowl of sugar.

183   "You probably need to eat something," the baker said. "I hope you'll eat some of my hot rolls. You have to eat and keep going. Eating is a small, good thing in a time like this," he said.

184   He served them warm cinnamon rolls just out of the oven, the icing still runny. He put butter on the table and knives to spread the butter. Then the baker sat down at the table with them. He waited. He waited until they each took a roll from the platter and began to eat. "It's good to eat something," he said, watching them. "There's

more. Eat up. Eat all you want. There'a all the rolls in the world in here."

They ate rolls and drank coffee. Ann was suddenly hungry, and 185 the rolls were warm and sweet. She ate three of them, which pleased the baker. Then he began to talk. They listened carefully. Although they were tired and in anguish, they listened to what the baker had to say. They nodded when the baker began to speak of loneliness, and of the sense of doubt and limitation that had come to him in his middle years. He told them what it was like to be childless all these years. To repeat the days with the ovens endlessly full and endlessly empty. The party food, the celebrations he'd worked over. Icing knuckle-deep. The tiny wedding couples stuck into cakes. Hundreds of them, no, thousands by now. Birthdays. Just imagine all those candles burning. He had a necessary trade. He was a baker. He was glad he wasn't a florist. It was better to be feeding people. This was a better smell anytime than flowers.

"Smell this," the baker said, breaking open a dark loaf. "It's a 186 heavy bread, but rich." They smelled it, then he had them taste it. It had the taste of molasses and coarse grains. They listened to him. They ate what they could. They swallowed the dark bread. It was like daylight under the fluorescent trays of light. They talked on into the early morning, the high, pale cast of light in the windows, and they did not think of leaving.

Discussion

• Which story do you like best? Why? What are the differences? What works and fails to work in each story?

• Why do you think Carver rewrote the story?

• What are the strengths and weaknesses of the way in which Morrison writes and the way in which Carver writes?

• What other ways could Carver have rewritten the story?

• Compare the way in which Trillin and Carver deal with the issues of life and death. Compare Baldwin, Gibson, and Carver.

• How would this story be written as a piece of nonfiction—a first-person account by one of the parents, a detached essay by an observer, a news story?

• How would you describe the distance from the subject at which Morrison and Carver write? What are the advantages of each distance? What other distances might they have written from?

Activities

• Take the pages you wrote after reading Morrison and rewrite them after reading Carver.

• Take an incident from your own experience and write it in your own voice, but trying to achieve the spareness of Carver's first version. Then develop it as Carver developed incidents in the first story.

• Take an experience from your childhood and write a page from your point of view as a child. Use, in other words, the point of view that Morrison used in her novel. Then rewrite the incident in the third person from the point of view of an observer, as Carver does.

• Describe how Carver and four other authors from the book or in your classroom might write about the same incident, giving a short paragraph to each author.

• Take a draft you have written earlier and read it from Carver's point of view, putting down what Carver might say, and then follow his advice to see if it works.

6

A Draft Developed

Now the writer stands at the edge of the high diving platform—and steps back. No matter how experienced the writer, there is always the terror of the blank page, the first line from which there seems no recovery. Writing is fearful public commitment, a revelation to others—and, worse still, to ourselves—of all we know and all we are.

The writer has to remember all that went before, the experience of writing other successful drafts, the subject that has been identified and the information that has been collected about that subject, the focus that has been found, the order that has been designed. At least 60 percent of the work of writing is done and it is time to attempt a draft.

The writer also has to remember that a draft is just that, a draft. It is an experiment in meaning and form. In writing a first draft, the writer discovers what may be said and how it may be said. There will be time to read the draft and toss it away or call it a final draft, time to eliminate part of the text and to insert new text, time for more research or more drafts, time to rearrange the order and to replace one word with another, time for revision and time for editing.

Remembering all that the writer steps to the edge of the platform again, carefully trying not to look down, takes a deep breath and takes off into the draft.

With experience, the writer learns a ritual that works to get a draft down, the critical stage of writing that turns possibility into real-

413

ity. Writers write by hand or word processor, type or dictate, use yellow paper or green, write early in the morning or late at night, play the radio or work in silence. There are a thousand ways to write, and all of them are right if the writer has a first draft at the end.

There are some tricks of the trade that may help:

1. *Write Fast* is the advice followed by many writers to achieve a first draft. The very act of writing fast gives the writing energy, an energy that gains momentum as it goes along. This energy creates a vital flow that brings together many bits of information into meanings that surprise the writer and may surprise the reader.

Of course, fast is a relative term, and writers do write at different paces. But the majority of writers produce the first draft at their top speed. You may be one of the minority of writers who write slowly, correcting each sentence, paragraph, or page until it is right. And obviously that is the right way for you to write if you, your editor or teacher, your readers are satisfied with what you are producing. But you should play around with increasing the speed of your writing. Slow writing can clog the pipes and block them completely. There are times when I write slowly, but my best writing always seems to come at top speed, after there has been time for conscious and unconscious immersion in the material and rehearsal about how the material will be used. Try it yourself. Write so fast that it is uncomfortable. Choose the form of writing—typing, handwriting, dictating—that is easiest for you to perform and then charge through a draft. When you go back to this top speed draft you may be surprised at what you have accomplished, at the meanings the speed has produced, and at the twists and turns of language it has also produced.

2. *Write without Notes* is almost always good advice. Plodding writing is often turned out by a writer who plods through the notes conscientiously moving from one card file to another. The text becomes clogged with indiscriminate facts and references.

You have been absorbed in the subject. It is time to put the notes away and write what you remember—what the process of writing makes you remember. What you forget is probably what should be forgotten, and what you remember is probably that which is significant. When you come to a quotation or a statistic, don't go back to your notes; put a marker in the text so you'll know to look it up later. At *Time* magazine we would use the letters TK, for to come. For example, we might write, "President's qte. TK" Work out your own system. Sometimes I put such a note to myself in parentheses, or I leave a big space and put a key word in the middle to trigger my memory at revision time, or make a note in the margin. It doesn't matter what you do as long as you do not stop the essential flow of the draft.

But no matter, after the crucial first draft is done you will be able to return to your notes, check the quotation, make sure the reference is right, double-check the statistic. The job now is to get a draft done, to think through writing. The producing of a draft, after all, is not a matter of reporting thinking that has been done; but it is an act of thinking, an act of intellectual exploration and discovery.

3. *Suspend Critical Judgment* while writing the draft. There are times in producing every draft when my stomach cramps up or a pair of great tongs start crushing my skull. I lose faith in what I am writing, and I lose faith in myself as a writer. I feel despair, hopelessness, failure. I know that I cannot write this piece; I know that the draft is a mistake, that it will not work, that I cannot write it, that I cannot write. And sometimes I'm right. But I cannot know whether I am right or wrong until the draft is completed, and so I must force myself to keep the draft going until the end at any cost. And I must admit nine times out of ten, perhaps 19 times out of 20 I have a first draft that works. Of course, it needs revision and editing, sometimes a little, sometimes a great deal; but it is a working first draft. I no longer have an unachieveable dream of what I may write, I have a text.

4. *When Interrupted* stop in the middle of a sentence so that you will be able to write the rest of the sentence when you get back to the text. There is an enormous inertia to overcome each time we sit down to write. The trick of stopping in the middle of a sentence that we know how to finish vaults us right into the act of writing, and we do not have to overcome the inertia of starting another draft.

5. *Develop with Information* not inflated language, words that float off over the treetops like untethered hot-air balloons. Even the reader of poetry wants information. Notice how Mekeel McBride and Theodore Roethke write their poems with specific information, details, images, the down-to-earth and solid, practical materials of our world. Readers need a fullness and a completeness that comes from documentation, evidence, description, reference, quotation, statistics, revealing details—all the many forms by which we can take information from our brain and our world and place it within the brain of a reader.

6. *Write with Your Ear* is the most important advice of all. *Writ-*

ing that is broadly read has the illusion of speech. The reader hears an individual writer speaking to an individual reader. The reader hears a writer's voice.

Voice is the element that makes writing most effective. Voice is the way that language sounds from the page. It carries meaning to the reader, but also it carries the context, the concern, the emotion, the power of the text. When we write we should hear the evolving text. Listen to how Didion and Orwell, White and Shepherd, McBride and Roethke, Angelou and Updike sound. Each voice is different, distinctive; each voice is appropriate and strong.

I have picked out the best writers in a strange city room by observing those whose lips move while they write. They are not all the good writers, for some good writers have learned to speak the text as they write it without moving their lips. But it is a signal that the writer is hearing what is being said as it is being said.

We all have much more experience speaking and listening than we have writing and reading. We draw on this experience to achieve emphasis and grace, flow and feeling, pace and rhythm as we produce a draft—and later as we revise and edit that draft.

We should not in this society be producing a text that cannot be read aloud, because our readers are hearing the text. If we write sentences that are so long we cannot breathe, or so pompous we cannot read them aloud without laughing at ourselves, then we must revise the text.

Voice, of course, is not a simple matter. We begin with our own natural voice. The way we speak, depends, in part, on our psychology. The timid do not speak with confidence, and the confident with anxiety. The way we speak reflects the way we respond to the world. Voice is also a matter of ethics. We may be honest or dishonest in our speech, authoritarian or passive, aggressive or receptive.

We also speak the way we do because of the way we have learned language—at home, on the street, in school. Our speech will be influenced by the language we speak at home—English, Spanish, French-Canadian, Japanese. Whatever language we learned at birth may affect our writing. It may cause some errors, but it can also cause a particular flavor and a wonderful effectiveness in how we speak. We are also influenced by the dialect of our family and our neighborhoods. We have regional dialects and racial dialects that can also produce problems, at times, in formal speech, but can give our language a special energy, music, and force. Out of all that we are we evolve a personal voice that is ours as much as a thumbprint is ours.

We can identify the speaker in the next room or out of doors even without understanding the words if that person is a family member or a close friend. Each of us has a way of speaking.

We also have the ability to adapt that voice to the situation. Children, for example, have to learn to speak softly in public places. We all learn to adapt our voice to the playground, to the church, to the conversation with the best friend, to the visit to grandmother. We speak one way in a street argument, another way at a funeral. As we learn to write we have to adapt our voice, being formal when it is appropriate to be formal, and informal when it is appropriate. We have to learn to speak strongly and softly, smoothly or with a blunt edge, being patient or impatient, humorous or serious, angry or soothing, adapting the whole range of human interaction into our text. We do not lose our individuality, but adapt it to the task at hand.

As we produce a text we use what we have learned from our reading, not copying directly the way other people write, but learning from the voices we hear and read the ways in which we may speak, adapting what others have done to our own voices, our own readers, our own purposes. As writers we should constantly read, listening carefully to hear how others develop their texts with information and communicate that information in a voice that is their own.

Case Study: A Poet Writes and Reads

Mekeel McBride

Every teacher has those moments in class when a question comes off the wall. One question that startled me was, "Who would you like to be?" I heard myself answer, without hesitation, "Mekeel McBride" and I knew I had answered right. Yes, I'd like to be my colleague Mekeel McBride for her talent, her craft, and, most of all, for her attitude. Too many of my writer friends, and myself, wallow in despair, rise for a few moments on wings of self-adulation, then fall to self-pity, taking everything, especially ourselves, very, very seriously.

Mekeel McBride is a serious poet who has been published in the most competitive journals; has produced three books; won a

Radcliffe Institute Fellowship and received an NEH grant; has taught at Harvard, Wheaton, Princeton and is on the faculty at the University of New Hampshire. Yet she always seems to keep her work in perspective.

"I know so many writers who think that life is tragic and that only tragic life can produce great art," she says. "I think that's bullshit. I think that some people use writing as an excuse to live painful, complicated lives. I'm happy when I'm writing. That's why I do it. Some people feel good *only* when they're writing. When they're not writing, their lives are misery. That's not true for me."

She writes in great bound ledgers that she carries with her and she makes writing a natural part of every day. "Writing a poem is a process of discovery," she says as she continues to make discoveries, "and you don't know what you're going to learn about yourself or what you're going to learn about the world until you're through with that poem." We are fortunate that she agreed to share a poem with us. Mekeel agreed to contribute before the poem began so we have her journal entries and the twelve drafts from which we've published the ones reproduced on the following pages. We are also fortunate to have her account of how she read and wrote to produce that poem.

Lackawanna car swollen with helpful ~~too~~ wheat
& faulty thunder.   1/11/84   19

Feet are invisible anyway & the newspaper reporter's feet
are never in one place long enough. The tight rope walker & the
avalanche expert wear different shoes but still experience
a spiritual horror at the notion of duplication. Amputee,
cripple & computer expert really don't care. Oh, there's a lover
somewhere, bare footed & careless, romancing simple grass
with earth stained toes. And that person knows, yes, knows
when to leave well enough alone.

I don't suppose, in this case, that there will be any
new ground to stand on. Only the courage to walk away
although the earth under one's feet is always the same.
HE FEELS RELIEF. And you've got a full life and
you've got a sense that in zero degree weather (& that is
the weather) you can still romp in the snow -- not duty --
but choice and that this all mattered, helped put the
tiger back together.

Train whistle. Believe I will always
remember Anton Joseph with the sound of a train
passing. And then, the train gone. How to live with
the silence. The huge beautiful shatter of immense
presence & passage. The absence of past or future
just freight train after freight train spilling
across faulty but durable rails, sailing away full of
Idaho potatoes coffins, licorice & helpful wheat, chamois
shirts & swollen cream -- yes, let's repeat that -- oranges
Each click & spin of the train almost off the rail
something like my heart trying to keep track of
what is passing, what I'm in the presence of —

20

I am witness to every possible imagined loss-- cargo
hot· spit·and· damn flashing past with lightning's
blessing. The bridge I stend on shakes, almost
shatters with the passing. Gone. And then its gone.
And I could mourn. And I could play statue.(The)
orphan of silence. orphan of the storm. But it was there! the train
Rumbling, plummeting out of pure summer air. Honest in
its passage. Ominous & luminous. Shook my bones Blamed
my hair(?) --only for a moment·· into a place dawn
birds might bless & bombast with open song, shook me, stood
me up held me hopeless in one long whistle blast gave
me ripe oranges , promised nothing was itself in every
failing, made its way, was gone. But it was there.
      never faltered!
+··

⌜adored the tame lawns
⌞shuttered houses, tainted dreams⌟
shamelessly trespassing through
the small dreams of the unhappily married

hidden suitcases full of gladiolas & apples
tape measures & Mexican jumping beans
French porcelain ⌜coffee from Peru

⟨2⟩

Enough

[The] Train

(And then the huge beautiful ~~shatter~~ *just* ~~of~~ *hope* ~~immense presence~~
~~and passage~~. Absence of ~~past~~ or ~~future~~. Just freight
(A)~~train~~ after [freight car, spilling across faulty,
but durable rails, sailing away/full

of coffins and potatoes, (licorace and ~~camisoles~~)
[~~Irish~~ linens and tangerines. Lackawana cars
swollen with helpful wheat and favorite thunder. [Yes,
and coal that will never be diamonds. ~~Let's repeat that~~].

[Never ~~be~~ diamonds.] Each click and spill (of the train/
almost off the rail, ~~some~~ *an* immense tattered heart
that keeps beating long after the date of its predicted
death, my heart trying to keep track of what

(s passing, what I'm [n the presence of.] witness
to every possible loss -- cargo *n* not-spit-and-damn *of uncharitable*
flashing past with lightnings blessing. Bridge *cargo*
I stand on shakes almost shatters with the passing.

Gone and then, it's gone. [I could mourn, play statue,
orphan of silence, orphan of the storm. But
it was here.] Train, train, rumbling, plummeting
out of pure summer air. Honest in (its) passage,

luminous and ominous. Shook my bones. Bloomed
my hair -- only for a moment -- into a place
dawn birds might bless and bombast with open song,
Shook me, Stood me up, held me hopeless in one blast

of whistle, getting *me* there and *made* getting, getting.
Gave me ripe oranges, a lust for the long, worthless
wheat fields of America.✗ Sealed baggage cars
singing out the contents of locked suiteases:

(gladiola,s, apples, tape measures, the atom bomb,
gladiola, apple, Aunt So-andSo's life insurance,
the last letter from death row, the whole
secret of winter sealed into the Idaho potatoe.
history   '*under the calm skin of an Idaho p.*
Shamelessly trespassing through the ~~small~~ sleep
~~dreams~~ of the unhappily married, violating their
small violent dreams of parole. Prudence
absent even in the in-need-of-paint blue caboose.
               ↗ afraid of almost everything (some anyway)
Getting and getting there, itself in every
failing,/taking nothing with it that it can't
discard, mad parent to every steadfast oak it passes
wont' come back and always there. Sheep dozing

in the tiny meaodow of each box car alongside ~~the~~ *xxx* cars *containing*
[that carry] the red letters of separated lovers.
Keeps to ~~some kind of~~ schedule. Bridge sinks (into silence,
tracks, an utterly still lesson in the failure
               Static *no*   /*stiffens*

future   love the
seperate or parallel

of trying to stay parallel. Still you saw
how in perspective that train spit its way into
the horizon, dragged tracks and distance, and even in
sunset into one small dot on your visable map   topography
                                    the
married in blaze, disappeared entirely, except
        it

    ? Even perspective < but not without

a struggle, not without the paid for
                            unexpected surprise

of letting you know

            erased.....into a marriage of black vanishing

made of itself the small black dot where
all things married in blaze, scarcely lamplont
by the gentle indigo haze that may have
born future or simple dusk (a million disappointment
                    ordinary

    simple portent of the   or the odd somber restront

in admitting that it was enough.. Enough.

            shapeless
    simple residue of memory

II

MM

Jan 29. 84

        Princeton

③

Train

~~I'm trying to keep track of what~~ I witness passing --
~~the~~ Hot-spit-and-damn of unchartable cargo flashing past
with lightning's blessing. Bridge I stand on shakes,

almost shatters with the passing. Gone, and then it's
gone. Train, train rumbling, plummeting out of pure summer air.
Honest in its passage, luminous and ominous.

Shook my bones, bloomed my hair -- only for a moment --
into a place dawn birds might bless and bombast with open
song. Shook me, stood me up, held me hopeless in one long

whistle blast, getting me there and getting, getting.
Lackawana cars swollen with helpful ~~wheat~~ and favorite
thunder, coffins and ~~potatoes~~, camisoles and tangerines.

Gave me ripe ~~oranges~~ plums, a lust for the long worthless
wheatfields of America. Made sealed baggage cars sing out
the contents ~~of locked suitcases~~: gladiola, appale,

aunt so-and-so's ~~life insurance~~, last letters from death row,
the whole secret of snow sealed under ~~the~~ calm skins
of ~~an~~ Idaho potato. Shamelessly tresspassing through the sleep

of the unhappily married, ~~violating~~ their small violent dreams
of parole. Prudance absent even in the ~~in-need-of-pain~~ blue caboose. Getting and getting there, itself in every

failing, afraid of almost everything, going anyway, taking
nothing with it that ~~it couldn't~~ discard, mad parent
to each steadfast ~~oak~~ it passed. Won't come back and always

here. Sheep ~~dozing~~ ~~in~~ the tiny meadow of a box car next
~~to cars containing~~ the red letters of separated lovers. Keeps
~~to~~ no schedule, keeps nothing and keeps going.

Now the bridge I stand on stiffens into silence; tracks,
an utterly static lesson in the failure of trying to love
the parallel. Still, I saw that train spits its way

into the future, dragging tracks ~~and distance~~, sunset, ~~even~~
perspective , marries them all in a blaze of horizon
scarely hampered by the indigo haze that may have been

simple portent of the future, or ordinary dusk
or the odd embarrassment of having to admit
that having been there in the passing was enough. enough.

Red Letters

(handwritten: Seduces & then stands you up) *(circled: 4)*

Hot-spit-and-damn of uncharable cargo flashes past
~~with~~ lightning ~~a~~ blessing. Bridge (~~I stand on~~ shakes, almost
shatters with the passing. Gone, and then it's

gone. Train, ~~(train,~~ rumbling, plummeting out of pure ~~summer~~ *almost*
air. Honest in its passage, luminous, ~~and~~ ominous, Shookes
~~my~~ bones, bloomed ~~my~~ hair ~~into a place dawn birds might~~

~~bless and bombast with open song.~~ Shook me, ~~stood~~ me up, *akes you syk you*
~~held~~ ~~me~~ hopeless in one long whistle blast, getting ~~me~~ there *bed worms*
~~and~~ getting, getting. Lackawana cars swollen with helpful

wheat and favorite thunder, coffins, ~~and~~ tomatoes, camisoles
and tangerines. Gave me ripe plums, a lust for the long,
worthless farmlands of America. Made sealed baggage cars *K'*

sing out their locked contents: gladiola, apple, Aunt So-
and-So's black lace-up shoes, last letter from death row,
complete lack of ~~quite~~ packed under ~~calm~~ ~~sikskins~~ *the silk skins*
of Maine potatoes. Shamelessly trespassing ~~through the sleep~~ *quile* *invading*
of the unhappily married, inventing their small, violent *(tropical?)*
dreams of parole, Prudence absent even in the once-was-blue

~~b~~caboose. Getting and getting ~~there,~~ itself in every
failing, afraid of almost everything, going anyway, taking
nothing that it can't discard; mad parent to each steadfast *tree*

~~tree/~~it passes. Wond't be back with its bereaved sheep, *grazing*
~~grazing~~ in the tiny meadow of a box car next to ~~the red letters~~ *the red letters*
~~the red letters/~~ of separated lovers. ~~Always here.~~ Keeps *no schedule, keeps*

~~no schedule,~~ keeps nothing and keeps going. Spits its way *into the future*
~~into the future,~~ dragging with it tracks and vantage point,
sunset and/perspective, marries them all in a black blze *of closed*

~~of~~ horizon, leaves only a ~~gentle~~ haze that is not birth *slight sigh*
of storm, just ordinary dusk and the odd embarassment
~~of~~ having to ~~dmit~~ ~~a~~that ~~to~~ ~~witness~~ thepassing was enough. (It was) enough.
witnessing passage

4|MM Princeton
January 31, 1984

(handwritten: admitting that to witness passage was enough. Enough.)

(handwritten: in the shaken trees, no)

(handwritten: in of having to admit that being witness was enough.)

EDITOR:
Copy by Mekeel of Jane's Comments

Mekeel McBride

6

Red Letters

Hot-spit-and-damn of unchartable cargo flashes past,
lightning blessed. Bridge shakes, almost
shatters with the passing. Gone, and then it's

you're telling too much

gone. Train, rumbling and plummeting out of ~~pure~~ summer
air. ~~Honest in its passage, luminous and ominous,~~ shakes
bones, blooms hair. Seduces and then stands you up,

Why honest? In this list it seems to raise more questions than it answers.

helpful & favorite cute thunder just seem cute to me. I like the juxtaposition of wheat & coffins better. They seem like true & more surprising opposites — Then I like the list

~~holds you~~ hopeless in one long whistle blast, almost
gets you there, getting and getting. Lackawana cars
swollen with ~~helpful~~ wheat and ~~favorite thunder~~;

coffins, tomatoes, ~~camisoles~~ and tangerines. Gives you
~~ripe plums~~, a lust for the long ~~earthless~~
farmlands of America. Makes sealed baggage cars sing out

Here this might go out because it is more surprising to change the thought with "lust" not just continue the list.

seems wrong—maybe a physical image

their locked contents: gladiola, apple, Aunt So-and-So's
black lace-up shoes, last letter from death row,
nothing but snow sealed under the silk skins

This list is great. The order seems right.

seems strange in this particular list because it's mostly food & death

of Maine potatoes. Shamelessly invading bedrooms
of the unhappily married, inventing their semi-tropical
dreams of parole. Prudence, absent even in the once-was-blue

beautiful

nice!

caboose. ~~Getting and getting, itself in every failing,~~
~~afraid of almost everything, going anyway, taking only~~
~~what it can discard,~~ mad sweetheart to each steadfast tree

The language here seems flat to me. Also the effort seems too dramatic here, too hyped

I'm not sure you need this...

I like the image of steadfast trees, etc. Maybe this can be worked in

it passes, won't be back, with its bereaved sheep,
grazing in the tiny meadow of a box car next to the red
letters of separated lovers. Keeps no schedule, keeps

can you tie up "prudence won't be back."

nice

nothing and keeps going. Spits its way into the future,
dragging with it tracks and vantage point, sunset
and perspective, marries them all in a black daze of closed

great

horizon, leaves only a slight sigh in the shaken trees;
no birth of storm, just ordinary dusk and the ~~odd embarrassment~~
of having to admit that being witness was enough.

nice ending !!!

I'm not sure I like this — definitely take out the word "odd" — each noun here is modified by an adjective so I'd have a noun free by itself. Is embarrassment really the word you want... How about the idea of burden? or something more complex? In other words human in its pain... not just embarrassment

I love this!

I like the idea of beginning in the poem of imagining the contents
of the closed cars... imagining what is inside that is somehow
hidden, inaccessible, flashing past.

This poem could stand losing one stanza. since it's about speed... +
things flashing past... I think the changes would speed it up +
also that way you won't get stuck in your lists — or being overly
explanatory with other short passages.

Red Letters

Hot-spit-and-damn of unchartable cargo flashes past
lightning blessed. Bridge shakes, almost shatters
with the passing. Gone, and then its gone. Train

rumbling and plummeting out of summer air. Honest
in its passage, shakes bones, blooms hair. Seduces
and then stands you up, hopeless, in one long whistle blast,

almost gets you there, getting and getting. Lackawana/cars
swollen with foreign thunder, tangerines xxxx
camisoles and coffins. Gives you soot-stained wind,

a lust for the worthless gold wheatfields of America.
Makes sealed baggage cars sing out their locked contents:
gladiola, apple, Aunt So-and-So's black lace up shoes,

a last letter from death row, nothing but snow
sealed under the silk skins of Maine potatoes. Shamelessly
invades the bedrooms of the unhappily married, inventing

their semi-tropical dreams of parole. Prudence, absent
even in the once-was-blue caboose. Won't be back
with its bereaved sheep grazing in the tiny meadow

of a box car next to the red letters of separated lovers.
Keeps no schedule, keeps nothing, and keeps going,
mad sweetheart to each steadfast tree it passes,

spits its way into the future, dragging with it
tracks and vantage point, sunset and perspective,
marries them all in a black daze of closed horison

leaving only a slight sigh in the shaken trees, no birth
of storm, just ordinary dusk and the old burden
of having to admit that being witness was enough.

Draft 10
MM/Prince
MAR 21, 1984

Many people think that poets write with flowery general language. But poets are masters of precision. They are the writers who use exactly the right word and exactly the right space between words. They teach all of us who write how to write with accuracy and with discipline. Note how specific McBride is, and note that she doesn't tell you how to feel or think. She causes you to feel and think. This is another thing that we can learn from the poet. The bad poet may use words like beautiful or sad, words that conclude and command the reader to a feeling or a thought. The good poet—and the good writer in any form—does not command a reaction to the writing; the writer creates a reaction by giving the reader information that causes the reader to think or feel. Poets remind us not to preach, but merely to reveal.

Red Letters

Hot-spit-and-damn of unchartable cargo flashes past   1
lightning blessed. Bridge shakes, almost shatters
with the passing. Gone, and then it's gone. Train

rumbling and plummeting out of summer air. Honest   2
in its passage, shakes bones, blooms hair. Seduces
and then stands you up, hopeless, in one long whistle blast,

almost gets you there, getting and getting. Lackawanna   3
cars swollen with omniscient thunder, coffins, cheap
wine from Hungary. Gives you soot-stained wind,

a lust for the long worthless wheatfields of America.   4
Makes sealed baggage cars sing out their locked contents;
gladiola, apple, Aunt So-and-So's black lace-up shoes,

a last letter from death row, nothing but snow   5
sealed under the silk skins of Maine potatoes. Shamelessly
invades the bedrooms of the unhappily married, inventing

their semi-tropical dreams of parole. Prudence, absent   6
even in the once-was-blue caboose. Won't be back
with its bereaved sheep grazing in the tiny meadow

of a boxcar next to the red letters of separated lovers.   7
Keeps no schedule, keeping nothing, and keeps going,
mad sweetheart to each steadfast tree it passes,

8   spits its way into the future, dragging with it
tracks and vantage point, sunset and perspective,
marries them all in a black daze of closed horizon

9   leaving only a slight sigh in the shaken trees, no birth
of storm, just ordinary dusk and the common burden
of having to admit that being witness was enough.

Discussion

• Discuss how poetry compresses and distills experience. Consider
how McBride's subject would be expressed in an essay or in a short story.
What would be lost by its expansion?

• Discuss the relationship between the sentence in prose and the line
in poetry. How are they different? What do they each do well?

• Discuss how the poet uses specifics, a basic building block of much
of the prose in this text. Is there a close relationship between the poet and
the prose writer's use of specifics? What is it?

• What can the nonfiction writer learn from the poet?

• Have someone read the poem aloud and then discuss its music.
Have several people read the poem aloud and discuss how the responses
vary to each reading.

• Compare McBride to other writers in the book, such as Carver, Morrison, Gibson, Baldwin, O'Connor, Baraka. Discuss how their voices and
their visions of the world are similar and different.

Activities

• Write a poem of your own. Especially write a poem of your own if
you have never written a poem. Do not worry about rhyme or meter. Create
a list poem from specifics, or write with the line. Simply try to distill experience and write according to the music the poem provides for your dance.

• Mess around with McBride's poem. See how it would work if the
line breaks came in different places, if the lines were shorter and the stanzas
longer. Rearrange it to see how it was constructed.

• Rewrite the poem as prose. Then take a paragraph of writing from
someone else in the book or from one of your own drafts and rewrite it as
a poem.

• Read some other contemporary poets and write a page, telling yourself—and other prose writers—specific things they can learn to do because
of what McBride and other poets show them.

• Write a page about an important experience in your life, then turn it into a poem by making it more concrete and more specific. (Nonpoets write poems with adjectives and adverbs, with flatulent language; most contemporary poets write with precise images.)

❡ Now we have the poet's own account of the poem's making: ❡

The countess in Giraudoux's *The Madwoman of Chaillot* explains   1
to a potential suicide:

> *To be alive is to be fortunate. . . . all you need to feel the call of life*   2
> *once more is a letter in your mail giving you your schedule for the*
> *day—your mending, your shopping, that letter to your grandmother*
> *that you never seem to get around to . . . then you're armed, you're*
> *strong, you're ready, you can begin again . . .*

Her grandmother is long dead and she writes these letters con-   3
taining schedules to herself, mails them, reads them, recreates herself
daily. Like the Countess, whose rather eccentric life depends somewhat on her ability to read her own writing, I keep a journal and read
it regularly. There I find I have invented myself.

And there, too, I find my own Countess who leaves me all sorts   4
of odd messages. This, for instance, from some rainy evening late in
December: "If you dare to romance the moon, then you have insin-
uated in a practical sort of way that you will spend your fair share of
time waltzing with the dust-lovely, frayed and lonely broom." Here
is evidence that I am concerned with planetary matters as well as
solid earth. Here is evidence I am concerned.

Reading teaches me the present tense of things.   5

Zero degrees, January, midnight. I sit up late at the kitchen   6
table writing in the journal. In a few weeks I have to move from
Dover, New Hampshire, to Princeton, New Jersey. No wonder I write
about various kinds of feet: the feet of dancers, tigers, newspaper
reporters, avalanche experts. Frightened with movement, I'd like to
disguise the magnitude of that fear and so speculate on exotic creatures walking about in imagined places. But then I hear the whistle
from some freight train in the distance. Clear, cold air carries the
sound close. Immediately I'm transported back to summer, late ripe
summer and a train that I came upon and watched with a great deal
of wonder.

In the journal, I forget feet and lapse into train-reverie, trying   7
in any way possible to capture the exact memory. There's no critical

part of me reading over my shoulder, saying, "But you're writing in sentence fragments. You've used the word *orange* three times. You have neglected sensible transitions." My only concern is to be back in the experience, back in summer, watching the train. I have no notion that I've begun a poem.

8   My handwriting disintegrates visibly as I become absorbed in the happiness of recording images, keys, and clues to the experience. But bad handwriting is a certain sign that I'll go back and try to write a poem. I never recognize that until later.

9   In this rush to get things down, I find that words seem to group by themselves and cause me a great deal of delight. "Luminous and ominous," for instance, rattle about in my head—summoning up miles of tumbling, purposeful boxcars somehow as shy as elephants, that unwieldy, that unexpected. And as they passed me then, and pass me now (in imagination), splendid in their uncompromising speed, their secret contents are almost a kind of taunt. So it is satisfying to read that the dark Lackawanna cars contain "potatoes, coffins, licorice, wheat, and camisoles."

10   Perhaps the biggest surprise is that I have associated the train, its whistle, its vibrant passage, and the summer day itself with a person who is, now, just as absent as the train. William Dickey asks, "Is the point of being a poet to clean your plate, use up things, make every loss valuable?" Not always, but in this case, yes. This draft, as rough and clunky and fast as the train, celebrates more than the mechanics of passage. I write until I've caught the memory and then, comforted, go to bed. Subsequent journal entries include detailed reports of trainless dreams, mention of a haircut, lists of things to take to New Jersey. I do not even reread what I've written about the summer train.

11   Less than a month later I'm in New Jersey, feeling homesick and displaced, up late again, writing in my journal, when I hear a train whistle. The sound of Dover, the sound from summer. It's a shock to me how easily, sometimes, the most disparate landscapes and weathers can unite. The simple sound of a passing train in the distance places me at home in a suddenly mild climate and makes me aware that since I wrote the initial journal entry, there has been the gentlest tugging going on, a tugging that I've not been paying attention to. Simple—go back and write the poem.

12   An aside. As a poor speller, I grew up with an enormous hatred of the dictionary. How, after all, do you look up pterodactyl when you're convinced it starts with a *t*? As a writer, I've come to see the

dictionary as a book of miracles. There, a word's origins may be discovered and words, like people, have histories and patterns of growth. Although a word's original meaning may not be relevant in contemporary usage, still, that initial meaning breeds and dreams in the word as surely as any vivid experience from childhood informs the adult.

Since I am concerned here with how I read an experience, and how, then, I read various drafts of the poem that translates that experience into words, I look up *read* in the *Oxford English Dictionary*. And I find that *read* originally meant "to deliberate, to consider, to attend to." 13

Good news. A correspondence right away. I attended the passage of that train with such concentration that if an eight-foot giant, covered in sequins, had approached me with news that I'd just won the New Hampshire lottery, I would not have noticed. Perhaps I exaggerate but as Gaston Bachelard says, "Exaggeration is the surest sign of wonder," and wonder is surely what I felt in watching the train and later, in writing about it. 14

It is, as I had guessed and hoped, that *to read* is a verb that pertains to more than the act of a student scanning fifty pages on the mating habits of woodchucks. Another original meaning for *read*: "to make out or discover the significance of . . ." So I read the train by attending fully to my experience of it and I make out, or discover the significance of it by writing a poem, reading draft after draft, rewriting until the discovery is complete. The happiest coincidence of all (I prefer to call it correspondence): just as a train stitches together and connects the most unlikely destinations, so the act of reading concerns and connects physical experience, active memory, writing and revision, and the finished poem. 15

I pull out my journal, read the train entry and begin to work on the second draft. I want the lines to be long in order to imitate the railroad tracks. I need a fast, snappy rhythm to catch the train's movement. Once, standing on an Amtrack platform in Princeton, I witnessed an Amtrack commuter train shoot through so quickly that the wind from it blew off my hat and pushed me back on the platform. I asked a conductor how fast the train was going. "You don't want to know," he said. I asked again. "One hundred and twenty-five miles." *That's* how fast I want this poem to be. 16

Since this train represents marriage to the present moment, whatever that moment may be, everyone and everything has to be on it; lovers, criminals, relatives, sheep, tangerines, even the atom 17 bomb. Well, it is a second draft, after all. When I read this draft, it becomes clear to me that there's a fairly large "atom bomb" category, that is, images and emotions and words I've tossed in during the exuberant process of trying to *get it all down*, strange little tresspassers who slipped in past my notice.

18   Reading reveals them to be duds, imposters, uninvited, out of place. Why after all, should this particular train carry "coal that will never be diamonds," "tape measures," or "the atom bomb"? No good reason. I toss them all out and also begin to remove my irrelevant personal asides—"I could mourn, play statue/orphan of silence, orphan of the storm." Sentimental and forced. True, I like the sound of "mourn" with "storm" but as for the melodrama involved, I'm perfectly comfortable leaving that to the heroines of silent movies.

19   This first typed draft is as it should be, large enough to allow me a lot of cutting room. I need to be able to see the exaggerated poem so that I can read and reread it, discover what's bad, what needs to be taken out. I scarcely ever begin with a skinny poem and then fatten it up.

20   Titles, right from the start, are a tricky, difficult business. Usually I make myself write a minimum of twenty, then cross them off, starting with the corniest, worst ones and whatever gets left becomes the title—a process that I imagine beauty pageant judges use. Out go Miss Nebraska, Miss Idaho, and Miss Alaska, leaving Miss California as the winner. This poem's title changes little. There are three weak initial attempts, "Train," "The Train," and "Enough" before I discover "Red Letters." It places appropriate emphasis on the letters of the separated lovers and only vaguely suggests "red letter" day—the habit of marking church holidays on the calendar in red ink. The vision of the train *was* a kind of spiritual holiday occurring with determined speed right in the middle of a perfectly normal summer afternoon when everything else was far too hot to move at all. Of course I'm making this up. The title simply announced itself. I liked it and kept it.

21   In early drafts, and all too frequently in later ones as well, I have an unerring ability to fall in love with my worst lines. Now, for draft three, I retrieve the line "my heart trying to keep track of what/ is passing" from the fourth stanza and make it the first line with only a vague attempt to remove it from the maudlin. It reads, in the revised version, "I'm trying to keep track of what I witness passing." I won't realize until later that I've told the reader what to think,

rather than evoking for him the feeling of being a witness. No matter. This is an early draft. Priority now is to place images in the best possible order. I read draft two over and over to hear what sounds silly. Quite a bit. The "immense tattered heart" sounds like it crept right out of a bad science-fiction movie and it is discarded. I love bad science-fiction movies the way I love bad lines in my poems. They are low-budget bridges, but fairly reliable and the imagination uses them to move to higher regions.

22   In the meantime, I toss out the tattered heart, licorice, Irish linens, and change the aunt's life insurance to black, lace-up shoes. I want the lines to be longer, the entire poem to happen more quickly, to have more whoosh, one-hundred-twenty-five miles worth of whoosh.

23   How do I read a draft of a poem? I type it up, then read it over lunch, during dinner, while I'm waiting for a bus. Working on this essay, I discover I've typed *bud* instead of bus. Typographical errors are usually quiet, accurate little messengers from the mysterious part of the brain that harbors insight and inspiration. Bus is okay but bud is wonderful. I keep reading the poem in order to find out *what will blossom*. That means a lot of waiting around and daydreaming.

24   I pencil in a word and remove the word three hours later. For instance, the word camisole (as part of the train's cargo) appears in the original draft and nine more times in subsequent drafts. It's removed three times and does not appear in the final version. Originally it was included because I liked the idea that a huge, loud train might carry, as cargo, women's fragile dressing gowns. Ultimately I omitted it because I lost interest in the contrast. No bud.

25   In draft three I decide that "Bloomed/my hair only for a moment—into a place dawn birds might bless and bombast with open/song" are some of the best lines I've ever written and congratulate myself on them at some length. In draft four I toss them out. Sentimental. Suggests that birds or at least their songs are all tangled up in my hair which is funny, very messy, and bad writing.

26   I read the draft before I have coffee in the morning. I cross out and add. I scarcely know what I'm doing. This whole process involves the wedding of whimsy and intuition. It's the same way I buy a dress. Whimsy, or what seems like whimsy, says—That blue one, there, that looks like silk. Intuition has already secretly confirmed that the dress will fit and that I own matching shoes. And so, in the poem, whimsy invents sheep grazing in a boxcar and intuition places them next to the car containing letters of separated lovers. It's

right, although I'm not sure why. Later, when the poem's finished, I can tell you that the unfortunate sheep are on their way to be slaughtered. The lovers, too, are in trouble, forced to maintain their connection through easily lost, necessarily fragmented letters. Somehow, sheep and lovers modify each other correctly. But when I discover the sheep and lovers while writing about them I know only that they belong where they are. That's all.

27   Constant rereading of a draft allows me to see what the poem really wants to say and helps me to remove what I'm trying to force it to say. I have written that the train trespasses through the sleep of the unhappily married, *violating* their small, *violent* dreams of parole. Reading it for the 10th or 20th time I realize that train-sound invents, in the sleep of the unhappily married, dreams of parole. Now I can leave them alone for awhile and search out other areas that need to be clarified.

28   Does this train pass mile after mile of nothing but oak trees? Of course not. Initially I wanted the trees to be oaks because the oak is a symbol of wisdom. A sure sign of trouble—trying to use symbols. So the oaks vanish in favor of the generic word *tree*. Now more work needs to be done with those sheep. They have been, up to this point, dozing, but doze is a lazy, rather gentle word. A so-what word. These sheep, stationed as they are, next to the cars containing the letters of separated lovers, are actively upset sheep. I add "bereaved" to modify them correctly. I make them graze.

29   And it's clear that if I want this poem to have more movement than it does, I had best drop the turgid first line and begin with "Hot-spit-and-damn of unchartable cargo flashes past." I may fall deeply in love with rotten lines but, just as quickly, fall out of love and file rejects in folders titled "Failed." That's where "I'm trying to keep track of what I witness passing" goes. Into the "Failed" folder. Sometimes when I'm stuck, unable to work on a particular poem, I'll browse through the failed folders and find phrases, words, even whole stanzas that I can recycle and use in the new poem. These files are much like the Salvation Army, filled, for the most part with gawdy junk, but housing a few genuine treasures.

30   By draft six I've gotten rid of most of the offensive and/or sentimental garbage. The poem has attractive three-line stanzas; line breaks seem about right; rhythm's quick, smooth, trainlike; images are sharp and effective. Or so I think. I've worked on this poem so hard that I've become trapped *in it*. It's like being an architect caught ladderless in the attic of a half-built building of her own design. She

can't stand on the lawn where she'd have the proper perspective to see that the builders have forgotten the back porch, that the southern wall needs another window, etc. From the inside, everything looks fine.

Being trapped *in* the poem results from taking myself and the 31 poem too seriously; from working hard without allowing proper intervals so that I can "forget" the poem in order to see it correctly. Finally, there's only so much that I can do alone. This poem (any poem) is written with an audience in mind and so at some point in the reading/revision process I have to work up the courage to show the poem to an unbiased, honest friend.

I usually send work to my poet friend, Jane Shore. I send this 32 particular poem when I'm almost certain it's quite likely to receive only the highest praise. I say "almost certain" because there's some small part of me that knows how much I need Jane's intelligent objectivity, need her to stand on the lawn and say, "Oh come on. Take that heart-shaped swimming pool out of the baby's bedroom. Let's have a screened-in front porch facing the mountains. I love the skylights over the kitchen working area." Etc.

Jane's a healthy balance to my own internal critic who thinks 33 the poem is perfect, awful, finished, unfinishable, so busy sending me contradictory messages that if I listened with any seriousness, I wouldn't write at all. Even writing this essay causes me a great deal of anxiety. My own voice seems squeaky and simple-minded. Here's part of a journal entry (July 15, 1984) that talks about it:

> *Worked all day on the "Red Letters" essay. Finished at quarter to* 34
> *eight. But still am not finished. Yes, I tortured myself the whole way*
> *through with the usual stuff: This is stupid. No one would ever want*
> *to read it. Etc. Nevertheless, the prism in the window threw rainbows*
> *all over the pages and I loved being in the clean writing room. And*
> *no matter what the voice of insecurity might say, also feels good to*
> *dream and invent my way through a draft.*

> *Disquieting to work so closely with "Red Letters" (essay) but* 35
> *comforting, too, because the whole point seems to be that you love*
> *people, places, things, and then, when it's time, let go. The man on*
> *the burning roof drifts away on his ladder of smoke. The white-haired*
> *man, Mr. King of the Moon, continues his jangly dance long past the*
> *brief span of road my eyes cover and I'll never know where he goes.*
> *W. shows up every six months or so to tell me I'm "heaven" and then*
> *he, too, vanishes. Strange life. In the meantime I eat salad for dinner,*
> *quilt, write and wonder. Yes, wonder.*

36   Well, let the critical voice babble on. Finally what always pulls me through (no matter how small or insignificant it may seem) is the pleasure of dreaming and inventing my way through a draft, the wonder. From that, I garden (and I mean *garden*, the difficult work of watering and weeding and tending) the courage that allows me to show imperfect drafts of this essay to my editor, Don Murray, and poem-in-process to Jane Shore.

37   The internal critic isn't really interested in discovery or creation of any sort. She wants me to buy a bag of potato chips and eat them while watching reruns of "I Dream of Jeannie" on a twenty-inch color TV for the rest of my life. Jane Shore and Don Murray, as objective critics and good writers, offer me many valid suggestions that mean I have to change my prejudices and work hard in order for the writing to succeed. They also offer necessary support and encouragement.

38   To put it another way, Jane and Don are the tough but honest umpires in a baseball game that I win, no matter what, as long as I keep playing. My internal critic's the thunderstorm that tries to disrupt the entire event.

39   Finally, Giraudoux's Countess has some good advice on this matter: "Everyone knows that little by little, as one wears pearls, they become real." It means, trust yourself. And trust the world.

40   Back to the train poem. Jane returns it with responses written in all the margins. She has, with faultless precision, crossed out most of what I like best. About "Honest in its passage, luminous and ominous" she says "Why *honest*? in this list . . . it seems to raise more questions than it answers." Black lines through my favorite stanza: "Getting and getting, itself in every failing,/afraid of almost everything, going anyway, taking only/what it can discard . . ." Jane's comments here, "The language seems flat to me. Also . . . the effort seems too dramatic, too hyped. I'm not sure you need this."

41   At this point I am only able to see what I might mistakenly call negative criticism. But there are many things in the poem that she likes and she says so. For instance, she writes "beautiful" next to "nothing but snow sealed under the silk skins/ of Maine potatoes." She thinks the 5th stanza is "great," writes and underlines "nice ending" and at the end, writes "I love this."

42   I'm confused. I decide the poem stinks and put it in a drawer. Most of this is sulking. I'm still trapped *in* the poem, only able to see it one way, *my* way. I leave the poem in a drawer (and any drawer will do, cosmetics drawer in the bathroom, cutlery drawer in the

kitchen, pet-food cabinet, etc.—just to get the poem out of my sight) until I've regained some sense of perspective and playfulness about the entire revision process. That means being able to re-see the poem as a movable, changeable thing: a river, rather than a stone.

Of "helpful wheat and favorite thunder" Jane says, "just seems 43 too cute to me." Helpful wheat and favorite thunder sustained me through all of the beginning drafts but the more I think about it, I realize that, literally speaking, I'm suggesting that a stalk of wheat is capable of helping me into a chair and that I might, on some stormy evening wander out into a field and exclaim "Oh, why there's my favorite thunder!" Jane's right. Too cute. Something Shirley Temple might have dreamed up when she was six. I save thunder, make it "omniscient" and wheat works its way into an ordinary field.

Jane helps me the most with the last stanza. I had written "the 44 odd embarrassment/of having to admit that being witness was enough." She writes:

> I'm not sure I like this. Definitely take out the word odd. Each noun 45
> here is modified by an adjective. So I'd have a noun free by itself. Is
> embarrassment the word you really want . . . how about the idea of
> burden? Or something more complex?

Suddenly I'm embarrassed by the word embarrassment. Bur- 46 den's what I want but it must be modified, because alone, it's too somber, too full of sympathy for its solitary unmodified self. Finally I discover "common burden" and that's it. Not just one light bulb switches on, but the entire chandelier.

In typing final versions there's a sense I'm moving almost 47 effortlessly to some imaginary but real finish line. I've got the euphoria a runner feels in the last surge past ache, past doubt, past lack of breath. I've found what I need: this train's simply the meta-phor for anything beautiful and transitory—love affair, movie with Fred Astaire, a sunset, a life, the process of writing a poem; therefore, witnessing it, loving it and letting it pass is both shared gift and com-mon burden. Roethke says it better:

> I cherish what I have 48
> Had of the temporal:
> I am no longer young
> But the winds and waters are;
> What falls away will fall.
> All things bring me to love.

Theodore Roethke

I first observed Theodore Roethke, the man, when I was a student at the University of New Hampshire and worked at the summer writing conference unfolding chairs and lining them up, folding chairs and stacking them back up, as good an apprenticeship for a young poet as any. I heard poets read and I saw poets backstage, before and after the readings being very human, as ordinary as plumbers and short-order cooks.

Roethke could have worked behind the counter in a diner near a Navy Yard. He was burly, brawling, competitive, and argumentative. He had to win at tennis, and at conversation. He was loud and overbearing. And then I read his poetry, and met the sensitive poet that lived inside that bulk. I didn't particularly like the man, but I loved the poet. And so did others. He became one of our major poets. He won the Pulitzer Prize, the National Book Award, the Bollingen Prize, but most of all he has won a life in poetry that has survived his death. He worked hard at his craft, once saying, "Eternal apprenticeship is the life of the true poet." He worked to make his poems appear easy. He said, ". . . you will come to know how, by working slowly, to be spontaneous" and "I'm a terribly spontaneous writer: it takes me months, often, to get some of these tiny effects." His poems continue to stimulate me, to make me hear, to make me see, to make me feel. They give me moments of quiet, and they sustain me.

Do not read these poems silently and do not read them once. Read them aloud, and read them many times. Notice the difference in the two versions of "Cuttings." Don't worry too much about understanding the poem. Be receptive, let the poem come to you through its music, through its feeling. You don't have to "understand" it necessarily any more than you have to "understand" a song. And your understanding will not be mine. It will change with your living. "Elegy for Jane" meant a great deal to me when I first read it. It meant more to me when I read it after I became a teacher and one of my students died. It means even more to me after it was read at my daughter's burial. Read "Frau Bauman, Frau Schmidt, and Frau Schwartze" and "My Papa's Waltz" the way you read such autobiographical prose as Baraka, Baldwin, and Gibson. Read, "The Waking" to enjoy its music and to let its meaning—your meaning—grow inside of you. Don't be afraid of poetry or be skittish about it; it's nothing more than play with words, play that illuminates, play that stimulates, play that produces the highest form of writing.

Six Poems

My Papa's Waltz

> The whiskey on your breath   1
> Could make a small boy
>   dizzy;
> But I hung on like death;
> Such waltzing was not easy.
>
> We romped until the pans   2
> Slid from the kitchen shelf;
> My mother's countenance
> Could not unfrown itself.
>
> The hand that held my wrist   3
> Was battered on one knuckle;
> At every step you missed
> My right ear scraped a buckle.
>
> You beat time on my head   4
> With a palm caked hard by
>   dirt,
> Then waltzed me off to bed
> Still clinging to your shirt.

Elegy for Jane

My Student, Thrown by a Horse

I remember the neckcurls, limp and damp as tendrils;   1
And her quick look, a sidelong pickerel smile;
And how, once startled into talk, the light syllables leaped for
      her,
And she balanced in the delight of her thought,
A wren, happy, tail into the wind,
Her song trembling the twigs and small branches.
The shade sang with her;
The leaves, their whispers turned to kissing;
And the mold sang in the bleached valleys under the rose.

2   Oh, when she was sad, she cast herself down into such a pure
         depth,
     Even a father could not find her;
     Scraping her cheek against straw;
     Stirring the clearest water.

3   My sparrow, you are not here,
     Waiting like a fern, making a spiny shadow.
     The sides of wet stones cannot console me,
     Nor the moss, wound with the last light.

4   If only I could nudge you from this sleep,
     My maimed darling, my skittery pigeon.
     Over this damp grave I speak the words of my love:
     I, with no rights in this matter,
     Neither father nor lover.

Frau Bauman, Frau Schmidt, and Frau Schwartze

Gone the three ancient ladies
Who creaked on the greenhouse ladders,
Reaching up white strings
To wind, to wind
The sweet-pea tendrils, the smilax,
Nasturtiums, the climbing
Roses, to straighten
Carnations, red
Chrysanthemums; the stiff
Stems, jointed like corn,
They tied and tucked,—
These nurses of nobody else.
Quicker than birds, they dipped
Up and sifted the dirt;
They sprinkled and shook;
They stood astride pipes,
Their skirts billowing out wide into tents,
Their hands twinkling with wet;
Like witches they flew along rows
Keeping creation at ease;
With a tendril for needle
They sewed up the air with a stem;
They teased out the seed that the cold kept asleep,—

All the coils, loops, and whorls.
They trellised the sun; they plotted for more than themselves.
I remember how they picked me up, a spindly kid,
Pinching and poking my thin ribs
Till I lay in their laps, laughing,
Weak as a whiffet;
Now, when I'm alone and cold in my bed,
They still hover over me,
These ancient leathery crones,
With their bandannas stiffened with sweat,
And their thorn-bitten wrists,
And their snuff-laden breath blowing lightly over me in my first
sleep.

Cuttings

Sticks-in-a-drowse droop over sugary loam, 1
Their intricate stem-fur dries;
But still the delicate slips keep coaxing up water;
The small cells bulge;

One nub of growth 2
Nudges a sand-crumb loose
Pokes through a musty sheath
Its pale tendrilous horn.

Cuttings

(later) 1
This urge, wrestle, resurrection of dry sticks,
Cut stems struggling to put down feet,
What saint strained so much,
Rose on such lopped limbs to a new life?

I can hear, underground, that sucking and sobbing, 2
In my veins, in my bones I feel it,—
The small waters seeping upward,
The tight grains parting at last,
When sprouts break out,
Slippery as fish,
I quail, lean to beginnings, sheath-wet.

The Waking

1   I wake to sleep, and take my waking slow.
           I feel my fate in what I cannot fear.
           I learn by going where I have to go.

2   We think by feeling. What is there to know?
           I hear my being dance from ear to ear.
           I wake to sleep, and take my waking slow.

3   Of those so close beside me, which are you?
           God bless the Ground! I shall walk softly there,
           And learn by going where I have to go.

4   Light takes the Tree; but who can tell us how?
           The lowly worm climbs up a winding stair;
           I wake to sleep, and take my waking slow.

5   Great Nature has another thing to do
           To you and me; so take the lively air,
           And, lovely, learn by going where to go.

6   This shaking keeps me steady, I should know.
           What falls away is always. And is near.
           I wake to sleep, and take my waking slow.
           I learn by going where I have to go.

Discussion

- Discuss the similarities and the differences between McBride and Roethke.
- Discuss how Roethke's voice is the same through all the poems, and how it is different in the individual poems.
- Compare the two autobiographical poems of his childhood to the autobiographical pieces you have read in the book and from your classmates. What are the advantages of poetry, and the disadvantages? What can we learn from the poet?
- Calculate how McBride's and Roethke's poems are organized. Poems give us an entire piece in a short space, and we can study the whole piece of writing easily. Look to the poem's construction to see ways we can construct not only poems but prose.

- Discuss how these subjects of Roethke might have been written in prose—a botanical report for cuttings, a letter of sympathy to the student's parents, for example.
- Have one of the poems read aloud by several people and discuss the role of voice and music in poetry and in other forms of writing.
- Compare the Roethke and McBride poems with the poem by William Carlos Williams at the beginning of the Stevenson piece. How are they similar and different? Do you think they may have been influenced by Williams? If so, how?

Activities

- Mess around with a poem by Roethke, rearranging the line breaks and the lines to see what other patterns might have been used.
- Look up another poem by Roethke or McBride and put each line on a separate piece of paper, and then have your classmates arrange these lines to see if they come up with the same pattern as the poet—or a better one.
- Look back at an autobiographical experience similar to the moment caught in "My Papa's Waltz" and capture it yourself in your own words in a page of prose or a poem, or both.
- Take a page from an autobiographical piece you have written and make it a poem.
- Observe nature as Roethke did and make a poem out of the observation, remembering to be specific. Roethke once said, "Nothing seen, nothing said." And Wallace Stevens, another great American poet, said, "The tongue is an eye." Our poets are instructive see-ers.
- Take an account from your experience or from a newspaper about an accident and turn it into a poem that captures the moment and your feelings about it.

Maya Angelou

Maya Angelou is a dancer, a theater producer and director, an actor, a political activist, a journalist, a TV producer and writer, and a poet, but she is best known for the first of her autobiographical volumes, *I Know Why the Caged Bird Sings.* The selection here is Chapter 23 of that book, which I have called "Graduation."

Graduation

1   The children in Stamps trembled visibly with anticipation. Some adults were excited too, but to be certain the whole young population had come down with graduation epidemic. Large classes were graduating from both the grammar school and the high school. Even those who were years removed from their own day of glorious release were anxious to help with preparations as a kind of dry run. The junior students who were moving into the vacating classes' chairs were tradition-bound to show their talents for leadership and management. They strutted through the school and around the campus exerting pressure on the lower grades. Their authority was so new that occasionally if they pressed a little too hard it had to be overlooked. After all, next term was coming, and it never hurt a sixth grader to have a play sister in the eighth grade, or a tenth-year student to be able to call a twelfth grader Bubba. So all was endured in a spirit of shared understanding. But the graduating classes themselves were the nobility. Like travelers with exotic destinations on their minds, the graduates were remarkably forgetful. They came to school without their books, or tablets or even pencils. Volunteers fell over themselves to secure replacements for the missing equipment. When accepted, the willing workers might or might not be thanked, and it was of no importance to the pregraduation rites. Even teachers were respectful of the now quiet and aging seniors, and tended to speak to them, if not as equals, as being only slightly lower than themselves. After tests were returned and grades given, the student body, which acted like an extended family, knew who did well, who excelled, and what piteous ones had failed.

2   Unlike the white high school, Lafayette County Training School distinguished itself by having neither lawn, nor hedges, nor tennis court, nor climbing ivy. Its two buildings (main classrooms, the grade school and home economics) were set on a dirt hill with no fence to limit either its boundaries or those of bordering farms. There was a large expanse to the left of the school which was used alternately as a baseball diamond or a basketball court. Rusty hoops on the swaying poles represented the permanent recreational equipment, although bats and balls could be borrowed from the P. E. teacher if the borrower was qualified and if the diamond wasn't occupied.

3   Over this rocky area relieved by a few shady tall persimmon trees the graduating class walked. The girls often held hands and no longer bothered to speak to the lower students. There was a sadness

about them, as if this old world was not half home and they were bound for higher ground. The boys, on the other hand, had become more friendly, more outgoing. A decided change from the closed attitude they projected while studying for finals. Now they seemed not ready to give up the old school, the familiar paths and classrooms. Only a small percentage would be continuing on to college—one of the South's A & M (agricultural and mechanical) schools, which trained Negro youths to be carpenters, farmers, handymen, masons, maids, cooks and baby nurses. Their future rode heavily on their shoulders, and blinded them to the collective joy that had pervaded the lives of the boys and girls in the grammar school graduating class.

Parents who could afford it had ordered new shoes and ready-made clothes for themselves from Sears and Roebuck or Montgomery Ward. They also engaged the best seamstresses to make the floating graduating dresses and to cut down secondhand pants which would be pressed to a military slickness for the important event.   4

Oh, it was important, all right. Whitefolks would attend the ceremony, and two or three would speak of God and home, and the Southern way of life, and Mrs. Parsons, the principal's wife, would play the graduation march, while the lower-grade graduates paraded down the aisles and took their seats below the platform. The high school seniors would wait in empty classrooms to make their dramatic entrance.   5

In the Store I was the person of the moment. The birthday girl. The center. Bailey had graduated the year before, although to do so he had had to forfeit all pleasures to make up for his time lost in Baton Rouge.   6

My class was wearing butter-yellow pique dresses, and Momma launched out on mine. She smocked the yoke into tiny crisscrossing puckers, then shirred the rest of the bodice. Her dark fingers ducked in and out of the lemony cloth as she embroidered raised daisies around the hem. Before she considered herself finished she had added a crocheted cuff on the puff sleeves, and a pointy crocheted collar.   7

I was going to be lovely. A walking model of all the various styles of fine hand sewing and it didn't worry me that I was only twelve years old and merely graduating from the eighth grade. Besides, many teachers in Arkansas Negro schools had only that diploma and were licensed to impart wisdom.   8

The days had become longer and more noticeable. The faded   9 beige of former times had been replaced with strong and sure colors. I began to see my classmates' clothes, their skin tones, and the dust that waved off pussy willows. Clouds that lazed across the sky were objects of great concern to me. Their shiftier shapes might have held a message that in my new happiness and with a little bit of time I'd soon decipher. During that period I looked at the arch of heaven so religiously my neck kept a steady ache. I had taken to smiling more often, and my jaws hurt from the unaccustomed activity. Between the two physical sore spots, I suppose I could have been uncomfortable, but that was not the case. As a member of the winning team (the graduating class of 1940) I had outdistanced unpleasant sensations by miles. I was headed for the freedom of open fields.

10   Youth and social approval allied themselves with me and we trammeled memories of slights and insults. The wind of our swift passage remodeled my features. Lost tears were pounded to mud and then to dust. Years of withdrawal were brushed aside and left behind, as hanging ropes of parasitic moss.

11   My work alone had awarded me a top place and I was going to be one of the first called in the graduating ceremonies. On the classroom black board, as well as on the bulletin board in the autitorium, there were blue stars and white stars and red stars. No absences, no tardinesses, and my academic work was among the best of the year. I could say the preamble to the Constitution even faster than Bailey. We timed ourselves often: "WethepeopleoftheUnitedStatesinorderto-formamoreperfectunion . . ." I had memorized the Presidents of the United States from Washington to Roosevelt in chronological as well as alphabetical order.

12   My hair pleased me too. Gradually the black mass had lengthened and thickened, so that it kept at last to its braided pattern, and I didn't have to yank my scalp off when I tried to comb it.

13   Louise and I had rehearsed the exercises until we tired out ourselves. Henry Reed was class valedictorian. He was a small, very black boy with hooded eyes, a long, broad nose and an oddly shaped head. I had admired him for years because each term he and I vied for the best grades in our class. Most often he bested me, but instead of being disappointed I was pleased that we shared top places between us. Like many Southern Black children, he lived with his grandmother, who was as strict as Momma and as kind as she knew how to be. He was courteous, respectful and soft-spoken to elders, but on the playground he chose to play the roughest games. I

admired him. Anyone, I reckoned, sufficiently afraid or sufficiently dull could be polite. But to be able to operate at a top level with both adults and children was admirable.

His valedictory speech was entitled "To Be or Not to Be." The 14 rigid tenth-grade teacher had helped him write it. He'd been working on the dramatic stresses for months.

The weeks until graduation were filled with heady activities. A 15 group of small children were to be presented in a play about butter-cups and daisies and bunny rabbits. They could be heard throughout the building practicing their hops and their little songs that sounded like silver bells. The older girls (non-graduates, of course) were assigned the task of making refreshments for the night's festivities. A tangy scent of ginger, cinnamon, nutmeg and chocolate wafted around the home economics building as the budding cooks made samples for themselves and their teachers.

In every corner of the workshop, axes and saws split fresh tim- 16 ber as the woodshop boys made sets and stage scenery. Only the graduates were left out of the general bustle. We were free to sit in the library at the back of the building or look in quite detachedly, naturally, on the measures being taken for our event.

Even the minister preached on graduation the Sunday before. 17 His subject was, "Let your light so shine that men will see your good works and praise your Father, Who is in Heaven." Although the ser-mon was purported to be addressed to us, he used the occasion to speak to backsliders, gamblers and general ne'er-do-wells. But since he had called our names at the beginning of the service we were mollified.

Among Negroes the tradition was to give presents to children 18 going only from one grade to another. How much more important this was when the person was graduating at the top of the class. Uncle Willie and Momma had sent away for a Mickey Mouse watch like Bailey's. Louise gave me four embroidered handkerchiefs. (I gave her three crocheted doilies.) Mrs. Sneed, the minister's wife, made me an underskirt to wear for graduation, and nearly every customer gave me a nickel or maybe even a dime with the instruction "Keep on moving to higher ground," or some such encouragement.

Amazingly the great day finally dawned and I was out of bed 19 before I knew it. I threw open the back door to see it more clearly, but Momma said, "Sister, come away from that door and put your robe on."

20   I hoped the memory of that morning would never leave me. Sunlight was itself still young, and the day had none of the insistence maturity would bring it in a few hours. In my robe and barefoot in the backyard, under cover of going to see about my new beans, I gave myself up to the gentle warmth and thanked God that no matter what evil I had done in my life He had allowed me to live to see this day. Somewhere in my fatalism I had expected to die, accidentally, and never have the chance to walk up the stairs in the auditorium and gracefully receive my heard-earned diploma. Out of God's merciful bosom I had won reprieve.

21   Bailey came out in his robe and gave me a box wrapped in Christmas paper. He said he had saved his money for months to pay for it. It felt like a box of chocolates, but I knew Bailey wouldn't save money to buy candy when we had all we could want under our noses.

22   He was as proud of the gift as I. It was a soft-leather-bound copy of a collection of poems by Edgar Allan Poe, or, as Bailey and I called him, "Eap." I turned to "Annabel Lee" and we walked up and down the garden rows, the cool dirt between our toes, reciting the beautifully sad lines.

23   Momma made a Sunday breakfast although it was only Friday. After we finished the blessing, I opened my eyes to find the watch on my plate. It was a dream of a day. Everything went smoothly and to my credit, I didn't have to be reminded or scolded for anything. Near evening I was too jittery to attend to chores, so Bailey volunteered to do all before his bath.

24   Days before, we had made a sign for the Store, and as we turned out the lights Momma hung the cardboard over the doorknob. It read clearly: CLOSED, GRADUATION.

25   My dress fitted perfectly and everyone said that I looked like a sunbeam in it. On the hill, going toward the school, Bailey walked behind with Uncle Willie, who muttered, "Go on Ju." He wanted him to walk ahead with us because it embarrassed him to have to walk so slowly. Bailey said he'd let the ladies walk together, and the men would bring up the rear. We all laughed, nicely.

26   Little children dashed by out of the dark like fireflies. Their crepe-paper dresses and butterfly wings were not made for running and we heard more than one rip, dryly, and the regretful "uh uh" that followed.

⚑ Angelou has taken almost 40 percent of the piece and spent it on the anticipation of graduation. That seems to me appropriate the way she has written about it, because the anticipation of such events is often more than the events themselves. This extensive foreshadowing makes us worry that the event won't live up to the promise. Writers have to be concerned with the proportions between the parts of the writing. How much buildup and how much delivery, how much description and how much dialogue, how much problem and how much solution? Writers have to make sure they can get away with a chunk that is sizable. The foreshadowing in this case is a large chunk, but the author knows that most readers (even those who flunked out of high school the way I did and were not allowed to attend graduation) can identify with Angelou's experience. Her specifics spark the specifics of our own memories and keep the text lively and moving forward. ❼

The school blazed without gaiety. The windows seemed cold 27 and unfriendly from the lower hill. A sense of ill-fated timing crept over me, and if Momma hadn't reached for my hand I would have drifted back to Bailey and Uncle Willie, and possibly beyond. She made a few slow jokes about my feet getting cold, and tugged me along to the now-strange building.

Around the front steps, assurance came back. There were my 28 fellow "greats," the graduating class. Hair brushed back, legs oiled, new dresses and pressed pleats, fresh pocket handkerchiefs and little handbags, all homesewn. Oh, we were up to snuff, all right. I joined my comrades and didn't even see my family go in to find seats in the crowded auditorium.

The school band struck up a march and all classes filed in as 29 had been rehearsed. We stood in front of our seats, as assigned, and on a signal from the choir director, we sat. No sooner had this been accomplished than the band started to play the national anthem. We rose again and sang the song, after which we recited the pledge of allegiance. We remained standing for a brief minute before the choir director and the principal signaled to us, rather desperately I thought, to take our seats. The command was so unusual that our carefully rehearsed and smooth-running machine was thrown off. For a full minute we fumbled for our chairs and bumped into each other awkwardly. Habits change or solidify under pressure, so in our state of nervous tension we had been ready to follow our usual assembly pattern: the American national anthem, then the pledge of allegiance, then the song every Black person I knew called the Negro National Anthem. All done in the same key, with the same passion and most often standing on the same foot.

❦ In the next paragraph Angelou tips her hand. I wish she had been able to do this by implication. In fact, I think she already has prepared us for "worse things to come" and she doesn't need to tell us directly. ❧

30   Finding my seat at last, I was overcome with a presentiment of worse things to come. Something unrehearsed, unplanned, was going to happen, and we were going to be made to look bad. I distinctly remember being explicit in the choice of pronoun. It was "we," the graduating class, the unit, that concerned me then.

31   The principal welcomed "parents and friends" and asked the Baptist minister to lead us in prayer. His invocation was brief and punchy, and for a second I thought we were getting back on the high road to right action. When the principal came back to the dais, however, his voice had changed. Sounds always affected me profoundly and the principal's voice was one of my favorites. During assembly it melted and lowed weakly into the audience. It had not been in my plan to listen to him, but my curiosity was piqued and I straightened up to give him my attention.

32   He was talking about Booker T. Washington, our "late great leader," who said we can be as close as the fingers on the hand, etc. . . . Then he said a few vague things about friendship and the friendship of kindly people to those less fortunate than themselves. With that his voice nearly faded, thin, away. Like a river diminishing to a stream and then to a trickle. But he cleared his throat and said, "Our speaker tonight, who is also our friend, came from Texarkana to deliver the commencement address, but due to the irregularity of the train schedule, he's going to, as they say, 'speak and run.'" He said that we understood and wanted the man to know that we were most grateful for the time he was able to give us and then something about how we were willing always to adjust to another's program, and without more ado—"I give you Mr. Edward Donleavy."

33   Not one but two white men came through the door offstage. The shorter one walked to the speaker's platform, and the tall one moved over to the center seat and sat down. But that was our principal's seat, and already occupied. The dislodged gentleman bounced around for a long breath or two before the Baptist minister gave him his chair, then with more dignity than the situation deserved, the minister walked off the stage.

Donleavy looked at the audience once (on reflection, I'm sure 34
that he wanted only to reassure himself that we were really there),
adjusted his glasses and began to read from a sheaf of papers.

He was glad "to be here and to see the work going on just as it 35
was in the other schools."

At the first "Amen" from the audience I willed the offender to 36
immediate death by choking on the word. But Amens and Yes, sir's
began to fall around the room like rain through a ragged umbrella.

He told us of the wonderful changes we children in Stamps had 37
in store. The Central School (naturally, the white school was Central)
had already been granted improvements that would be in use in the
fall. A well-known artist was coming from Little Rock to teach art to
them. They were going to have the newest microscopes and chemistry equipment for their laboratory. Mr. Donleavy didn't leave us
long in the dark over who made these improvements available to
Central High. Nor were we to be ignored in the general betterment
scheme he had in mind.

He said that he had pointed out to people at a very high level 38
that one of the first-line football tacklers at Arkansas Agricultural and
Mechanical College had graduated from good old Lafayette County
Training School. Here fewer Amen's were heard. Those few that did
break through lay dully in the air with the heaviness of habit.

He went on to praise us. He went on to say how he had bragged 39
that "one of the best basketball players of Fisk sank his first ball right
here at Lafayette County Training School."

The white kids were going to have a chance to become Galileos 40
and Madame Curies and Edisons and Gauguins, and our boys (the
girls weren't even in on it) would try to be Jesse Owenses and Joe
Louises.

❦ I feel her anger, and I am moved by it, but there's an interesting
question here: By making so much of her own anger, I wonder if she
doesn't cheat me a bit of the chance to feel the anger myself. I think
that's what she wants me to feel. She can't give me the black
experience, but she wants to give me just a little taste of it, and by
allowing the anger to settle so much on her head it's like lightning
that has run off from the lightning rod on the barn and doesn't
affect me as directly as it might had it hit the barn. This is the issue
that was brought up in the discussion of poetry. Do you tell the
reader how to feel, or do you make the reader feel? ❧

41   Owens and the Brown Bomber were great heroes in our world, but what school official in the white-goddom of Little Rock had the right to decide that those two men must be our only heroes? Who decided that for Henry Reed to become a scientist he had to work like George Washington Carver, as a bootblack, to buy a lousy microscope? Bailey was obviously always going to be too small to be an athlete, so which concrete angel glued to what county seat had decided that if my brother wanted to become a lawyer he had to first pay penance for his skin by picking cotton and hoeing corn and studying correspondence books at night for twenty years?

42   The man's dead words fell like bricks around the auditorium and too many settled in my belly. Constrained by hard-learned manners I couldn't look behind me, but to my left and right the proud graduating class of 1940 had dropped their heads. Every girl in my row had found something new to do with her handkerchief. Some folded the tiny squares into love knots, some into triangles, but most were wadding them, then pressing them flat on their yellow laps.

43   On the dais, the ancient tragedy was being replayed. Professor Parsons sat, a sculptor's reject, rigid. His large, heavy body seemed devoid of will or willingness, and his eyes said he was no longer with us. The other teachers examined the flag (which was draped stage right) or their notes, or the windows which opened on our now famous playing diamond.

44   Graduation, the hush-hush magic time of frills and gifts and congratulations and diplomas, was finished for me before my name was called. The accomplishment was nothing. The meticulous maps, drawn in three colors of ink, learning and spelling decasyllabic words, memorizing the whole of *The Rape of Lucrece*—it was for nothing. Donleavy had exposed us.

45   We were maids and farmers, handymen and washerwomen, and anything higher that we aspired to was farcical and presumptuous.

46   Then I wished that Gabriel Prosser and Nat Turner had killed all whitefolks in their beds and that Abraham Lincoln had been assassinated before the signing of the Emancipation Proclamation, and that Harriet Tubman had been killed by that blow on her head and Christopher Columbus had drowned in the *Santa Maria*.

    ❧ On the other hand, if she had kept herself out of it, would she have been allowed to communicate this rage that does move me as she speaks directly to me? Writing is always a matter of choice; gain one thing here and you lose something else there. The writing reader is always making these second-guesses, trying out the kinds of choices he or she has to make on the daily page.🍂

It was awful to be Negro and have no control over my life. It was brutal to be young and already trained to sit quietly and listen to charges brought against my color with no chance of defense. We should all be dead. I thought I should like to see us all dead, one on top of the other. A pyramid of flesh with the whitefolks on the bottom, as the broad base, then the Indians with their silly tomahawks and teepees and wigwams and treaties, the Negroes with their mops and recipes and cotton sacks and spirituals sticking out of their mouths. The Dutch children should all stumble in their wooden shoes and break their necks. The French should choke to death on the Louisiana Purchase (1803) while silkworms ate all the Chinese with their stupid pigtails. As a species, we were an abomination. All of us. 47

Donleavy was running for election, and assured our parents that if he won we could count on having the only colored paved playing field in that part of Arkansas. Also—he never looked up to acknowledge the grunts of acceptance—also, we were bound to get some new equipment for the home economics building and the workshop. 48

He finished, and since there was no need to give any more than the most perfunctory thank-you's, he nodded to the men on the stage, and the tall white man who was never introduced joined him at the door. They left with the attitude that now they were off to something really important. (The graduation ceremonies at Lafayette County Training School had been a mere preliminary.) 49

The ugliness they left was palpable. An uninvited guest who wouldn't leave. The choir was summoned and sang a modern arrangement of "Onward, Christian Soldiers," with new words pertaining to graduates seeking their place in the world. But it didn't work. Elouise, the daughter of the Baptist minister, recited "Invictus," and I could have cried at the impertinence of "I am the master of my fate, I am the captain of my soul." 50

My name had lost its ring of familiarity and I had to be nudged to go and receive my diploma. All my preparations had fled. I neither marched up to the stage like a conquering Amazon, nor did I look in the audience for Bailey's nod of approval. Marguerite Johnson, I 51 heard the name again, my honors were read, there were noises in the audience of appreciation, and I took my place on the stage as rehearsed.

52   I thought about colors I hated: ecru, puce, lavender, beige and black.

53   There was shuffling and rustling around me, then Henry Reed was giving his valedictory address, "To Be or Not to Be." Hadn't he heard the whitefolks? We couldn't *be*, so the question was a waste of time. Henry's voice came out clear and strong. I feared to look at him. Hadn't he got the message? There was no "nobler in the mind" for Negroes because the world didn't think we had minds, and they let us know it. "Outrageous fortune"? Now, that was a joke. When the ceremony was over I had to tell Henry Reed some things. That is, if I still cared. Not "rub," Henry, "erase," "Ah, there's the erase." Us.

54   Henry had been a good student in elocution. His voice rose on tides of promise and fell on waves of warnings. The English teacher had helped him to create a sermon winging through Hamlet's soliloquy. To be a man, a doer, a builder, a leader, or to be a tool, an unfunny joke, a crusher of funky toadstools. I marveled that Henry could go through with the speech as if we had a choice.

55   I had been listening and silently rebutting each sentence with my eyes closed; then there was a hush, which in an audience warns that something unplanned is happening. I looked up and saw Henry Reed, the conservative, the proper, the A student, turn his back to the audience and turn to us (the proud graduating class of 1940) and sing, nearly speaking,

56   *"Lift ev'ry voice and sing*
        Till earth and heaven ring
        Ring with the harmonies of Liberty. . ."

57   It was the poem written by James Weldon Johnson.
58   It was the music composed by J. Rosamond Johnson.
59   It was the Negro national anthem. Out of habit we were singing it.
60   Our mothers and fathers stood in the dark hall and joined the hymn of encouragement. A kindergarten teacher led the small children onto the stage and the buttercups and daisies and bunny rabbits marked time and tried to follow:

> *Stony the road we trod* 61
> *Bitter the chastening rod*
> *Felt in the days when hope, unborn, had died*
> *Yet with a steady beat*
> *Have not our weary feet*
> *Come to the place for which our fathers sighed?*

Every child I knew had learned that song with his ABC's and 62
along with "Jesus Loves Me This I Know." But I personally had never
heard it before. Never heard the words, despite the thousands of
times I had sung them. Never thought they had anything to do with
me.

On the other hand, the words of Patrick Henry had made such 63
an impression on me that I had been able to stretch myself tall and
trembling and say, "I know not what course others may take, but as
for me, give me liberty or give me death . . ."

And now I heard, really for the first time: 64

> *We have come over a way that with tears* 65
> *has been watered,*
> *We have come, treading our path through*
> *the blood of the slaughtered.*

While echoes of the song shivered in the air, Henry Reed bowed 66
his head, said "Thank you," and returned to his place in the line.
The tears that slipped down many faces were not wiped away in
shame.

We were on top again. As always, again. We survived. The 67
depths had been icy and dark, but now a bright sun spoke to our
souls. I was no longer simply a member of the proud graduating class
of 1940; I was a proud member of the wonderful, beautiful Negro
race.

Oh, Black known and unknown poets, how often have your 68
auctioned pains sustained us? Who will compute the lonely nights
made less lonely by your songs, or by the empty pots made less tragic
by your tales?

If we were a people much given to revealing secrets, we might 69
raise monuments and sacrifice to the memories of our poets, but slavery cured us of that weakness. It may be enough, however, to have it
said that we survive in exact relationship to the dedication of our
poets (include preachers, musicians and blues singers).

Discussion

- Discuss the proportions of the sections in Angelou's piece and compare them to the proportions in the major parts of other pieces in the book.
- Discuss the advantages and disadvantages of Angelou's speaking directly to the reader.
- In what ways is her autobiographical piece similar to other such pieces in the book? How is she different?
- Consider her point of view. Is she writing from the point of view of a child, or from an adult looking back at childhood? What is the range of options she has? What are the advantages and disadvantages of each option?
- Compare Roethke's autobiographical poem to this piece of autobiographical prose. What are the advantages and disadvantages of these genre?

Activities

- Write an account of your own graduation.
- Take a page of Angelou and edit it, cutting, adding, rearranging, to make her message clearer or stronger.
- Outline the piece as it would have to be written if it were going to be part of a play, a TV show, or a movie.
- Write the beginning of other forms about the subject—an editorial criticizing the position of the speaker or supporting that racial attitude. Write a news account of the graduation for a white newspaper and a black newspaper.
- Edit part of her account from the point of view of a white observer who is aware of what is happening and sympathetic to Angelou's feelings.

John Updike

John Updike is one the master stylists and most productive writers of our time. Year in and year out he produces novels, short stories, book reviews, critical articles, and poetry. "Creativity is merely a plus name for regular activity" Updike has said. "The ditchdigger, dentist, and artist go about their tasks in much the same way, and any activity becomes creative when the doer cares about doing it right, or better. Out of my own slim experience, I would venture the opinion that the artistic impulse is a mix, in varying proportions, of childhood habits of fantasizing brought on by not necessarily unhappy periods of solitude; a certain hard wish to perpetuate and propagate the self; a craftsmanly affection for the materials and process; a perhaps superstitious receptivity to moods of wonder; and a not-often-enough mentioned ability, within the microcosm of the art, to organize, predict, and persevere."

The following excerpt from "The Dogwood Tree" deals with some of the same experiences of childhood that other writers in this text have written about. I have included a number of such excerpts, because they demonstrate that the raw material of fine writing exists in the lives you have lived and are living, in the experiences, thoughts, feelings, facts of your own existence. We all have our own individual histories, and it should interest you to see the different ways such writers as Baraka, Baldwin, Gibson, Angelou, and Updike—with others to come later in the book—see the common events and anxieties of childhood through their own eyes and how they report it with their own language.

Schools

The elementary school was a big brick cube set in a square of 1 black surfacing chalked and painted with the diagrams and runes of children's games. Wire fences guarded the neighboring homes from the playground. Whoever, at soccer, kicked the ball over the fence into Snitzy's yard had to bring it back. It was very terrible to have to go into Snitzy's yard, but there was only one ball for each grade. Snitzy was a large dark old German who might give you the ball or lock you up in his garage, depending upon his mood. He did not move like other men; suddenly the air near your head condensed, and his heavy hands were on you.

On the way to school, walking down Lancaster Avenue, we 2 passed Henry's, a variety store where we bought punch-out licorice belts and tablets with Edward G. Robinson and Hedy Lamarr smiling on the cover. In October, Halloween masks appeared, hung on wire clotheslines. Hanging limp, these faces of Chinamen and pirates and witches were distorted, and, thickly clustered and rustling against each other, they seemed more frightening masking empty air than they did mounted on the heads of my friends—which was frightening enough. It is strange how fear resists the attacks of reason, how you can know with absolute certainty that it is only Mark Wenrich or Jimmy Trexler whose eyes are moving so weirdly in those almond-shaped holes, and yet still be frightened. I abhorred that effect of double eyes a mask gives; it was as bad as seeing a person's mouth move upside down.

3   I was a Crow. That is my chief memory of what went on inside the elementary school. In music class the singers were divided into three groups. Nightingales, Robins, and Crows. From year to year the names changed. Sometimes the Crows were Parrots. When visitors from the high school, or elsewhere "outside," came to hear us sing, the Crows were taken out of the room and sent upstairs to watch with the fifth grade an educational film about salmon fishing in the Columbia River. Usually there were only two of us, me and a girl from Philadelphia Avenue whose voice was in truth very husky. I never understood why I was a Crow, though it gave me a certain derisive distinction. As I heard it, I sang rather well.

4   The other Crow was the first girl I kissed. I just did it, one day, walking back from school along the gutter where the water from the ice plant ran down, because somebody dared me to. And I continued to do it every day, when we reached that spot on the pavement, until a neighbor told my mother, and she, with a solemn weight that seemed unrelated to the airy act, forbade it.

> ❦ As a writer I delight in the simplistic yet powerful lines in the paragraph beginning, "I was a Crow." We are all Crows, and Updike knows it. And in the next paragraph Updike creates the naivete and innocence, and then destroys it with the deft touch of the master stylist. What skill goes into these words, "With a solemn weight that seemed unrelated to the airy act, forbade it." ❧

I walked to school mostly with girls. It happened that the mothers of Philadelphia Avenue and, a block up, of Second Street had borne female babies in 1932. These babies now teased me, the lone boy in their pack, by singing the new song, "Oh, Johnny, oh, Johnny, how you can love!" and stealing my precious rubber-lined bookbag. The queen of these girls later became the May Queen of our senior class. She had freckles and thick pigtails and green eyes and her mother made her wear high-top shoes long after the rest of us had switched to low ones. She had so much vitality that on the way back from school her nose would start bleeding for no reason. We would be walking along over the wings of the maple seeds and suddenly she would tip her head back and rest it on a wall while someone ran and soaked a handkerchief in the ice-plant water and applied it to her streaming, narrow, crimson-shining nostrils. She was a Nightingale. I loved her deeply, and ineffectually.

My love for that girl carries through all those elementary-school 6 cloakrooms; they always smelled of wet raincoats and rubbers. That tangy, thinly resonant, lonely smell: can love have a better envelope? Everything I did in grammar school was meant to catch her attention. I had a daydream wherein the stars of the music class were asked to pick partners and she, a Nightingale, picked me, a Crow. The teacher was shocked; the class buzzed. To their amazement I sang superbly; my voice, thought to be so ugly, in duet with hers was beautiful. Still singing, we led some sort of parade.

In the world of reality, my triumph was getting her to slap me 7 once, in the third grade. She was always slapping boys in those years; I could not quite figure out what they did. Pull her pigtails, untie her shoes, snatch at her dress, tease her (they called her "Pug")—this much I could see. But somehow there seemed to be under these offensive acts a current running the opposite way; for it was precisely the boys who behaved worst to her that she talked to solemnly at recess, and walked with after school, and whose names she wrote on the sides of her books. Without seeing this current, but deducing its presence, I tried to jump in; I entered a tussle she was having with a boy in homeroom before the bell. I pulled the bow at the back of her dress, and was slapped so hard that children at the other end of the hall heard the crack. I was overjoyed; the stain and pain on my face seemed a badge of initiation. But it was not. The distance between us remained as it was. I did not really want to tease her, I wanted to rescue her, and to be rescued by her. I lacked—and perhaps here the only child suffers a certain deprivation—that kink in the instincts on which childish courtship turns. He lacks a certain easy roughness with other children.

All the years I was at the elementary school the high school 8 loomed large in my mind. Its students—tall, hairy, smoke-breathing—paced the streets seemingly equal with adults. I could see part of its immensity from our rear windows. It was there that my father performed his mysteries every day, striding off from breakfast, down through the grape arbor, his coat pocket bristling with defective pens. He now and then took me over there; the incorruptible smell of varnish and red sweeping wax, the size of the desks, the height of the drinking fountains, the fantastic dimensions of the combination gymnasium-auditorium made me feel that these were halls in which a race of giants had ages ago labored through lives of colossal bliss. At the end of each summer, usually on Labor Day Monday, he and I went into his classroom, Room 201, and unpacked the books and arranged the tablets and the pencils on the desks of his homeroom pupils. Sharpening forty pencils was a chore, sharing it with him a solemn pleasure. To this day I look up at my father through the cedar smell of pencil shavings. To see his key open the front portals of oak, to share alone with him for an hour the pirate hoard of uncracked books and golden pencils, to switch off the lights and leave the room and walk down the darkly lustrous perspective of the forbidden. The very silence of the pavilion, after the daylong click of checkers and *pokabok* of ping-pong, was like a love-choked hush.

    ☞ Go back and read this paragraph. Note how the high school "loomed large in my mind," how the students were "tall, hairy, smoke-breathing," that his father "performed his mysteries" every day, "his pocket bristling with defective pens," how he still sees his father "through the cedar smell of pencil shavings." A writer delights in this skill the way a professional baseball player admires the ease with which an all-star scoops an impossible grounder and with practiced ease flips it to second to start the double play.☜

9   Reality seemed more intense at the playground. There was a dust, a daring. It was a children's world; nowhere else did we gather in such numbers with so few adults over us. The playground occupied a platform of earth; we were exposed, it seems now, to the sun and sky. Looking up, one might see a buzzard or witness a portent.

Three Boys

1   A, B, and C, I'll say, in case they care. A lived next door; he *loomed* next door, rather. He seemed immense—a great wallowing fatso stuffed with possessions; he was the son of a full-fashioned knitter. He seemed to have a beer-belly; after several generations beer-bellies may become congenital. Also his face had no features. It was just a blank ball on his shoulders. He used to call me "Ostrich," after Disney's Ollie Ostrich. My neck was not very long; the name seemed horribly unfair; it was its injustice that made me cry. But nothing I could say, or scream, would make him stop, and I still, now and then—in reading, say, a book review by one of the apple-cheeked savants of the quarterlies or one of the pious gremlins who manufacture puns for *Time*—get the old sensations: my ears close up, my eyes

go warm, my chest feels thin as an eggshell, my voice churns silently in my stomach. From A I received my first impression of the smug, chinkless, irresistible *power* of stupidity; it is the most powerful force on earth. It says "Ostrich" often enough, and the universe crumbles.

A was more than a boy, he was a force-field that could manifest itself in many forms, that could take the wiry, disconsolate shape of wide-mouthed, tiny-eared boys who would now and then beat me up on the way back from school. I did not greatly mind being beaten up, though I resisted it. For one thing, it firmly involved me, at least during the beating, with the circumambient humanity that so often seemed evasive. Also, the boys who applied the beating were misfits, periodic flunkers, who wore corduroy knickers with threadbare knees and men's shirts with the top button buttoned—this last an infallible sign of deep poverty. So that I felt there was some justice, some condonable revenge, being applied with their fists to this little teacher's son. And then there was the delicious alarm of my mother and grandmother when I returned home bloody, bruised, and torn. My father took the attitude that it was making a boy of me, an attitude I dimly shared. He and I both were afraid of me becoming a sissy— he perhaps more afraid than I.

When I was eleven or so I met B. It was summer and I was down at the playground. He was pushing a little tank with moving rubber treads up and down the hills in the sandbox. It was a fine little toy, mottled with camouflage green; patriotic manufacturers produced throughout the war millions of such authentic miniatures which we maneuvered with authentic, if miniature, militance. Attracted by the toy, I spoke to him; though taller and a little older than I, he had my dull straight brown hair and a look of being also alone. We became fast friends. He lived just up the street—toward the poorhouse, the east part of the street, from which the little winds of tragedy blew. He had just moved from the Midwest, and his mother was a widow. Beside wage war, we did many things together. We played marbles for days at a time, until one of us had won the other's entire coffee-canful. With jigsaws we cut out of plywood animals copied from comic books. We made movies by tearing the pages from Big Little Books and coloring the drawings and pasting them in a strip, and winding them on toilet-paper spools, and making a cardboard carton a theatre. We rigged up telephones, and racing wagons, and cities of the future, using orange crates and cigar boxes and peanut-butter jars and such potent debris. We loved Smokey Stover and were always saying "Foo." We had an intense spell of Monopoly. He called me "Uppy"—the only person who ever did. I remember once, knowing he was coming down that afternoon to my house to play Monopoly, in order to show my joy I set up the board elaborately, with the Chance and Community Chest cards fanned painstakingly, like spiral staircases. He came into the room, groaned, "Uppy, what are you doing?" and impatiently scrabbled the cards together in a sensible pile. The older we got, the more the year between us told, and the more my friendship embarrassed him. We fought. Once, to my horror, I heard myself taunting him with the fact that he had no father. The unmentionable, the unforgivable. I suppose we patched things up, children do, but the fabric had been torn. He had a long, pale, serious face, with buckteeth, and is probably an electronics engineer somewhere now, doing secret government work.

4   So through B I first experienced the pattern of friendship. There are three stages. First, acquaintance: we are new to each other, make each other laugh in surprise, and demand nothing beyond politeness. The death of the one would startle the other, no more. It is a pleasant stage, a stable stage; on austere rations of exposure it can live a lifetime, and the two parties to it always feel a slight gratification upon meeting, will feel vaguely confirmed in their human state. Then comes intimacy: now we laugh before two words of the joke are out of the other's mouth, because we know what he will say. Our two beings seem marvelously joined, from our toes to our heads, along tingling points of agreement; everything we venture is right, everything we put forth lodges in a corresponding socket in the frame of the other. The death of one would grieve the other. To be together is to enjoy a mounting excitement, a constant echo and amplification. It is an ecstatic and unstable stage, bound of its own agitation to tip into the third: revulsion. One or the other makes a misjudgment; presumes; puts forth that which does not meet agreement. Sometimes there is an explosion; more often the moment is swallowed in silence, and months pass before its nature dawns. Instead of dissolving, it grows. The mind, the throat, are clogged; forgiveness, forgetfulness, that have arrived so often, fail. Now everything jars and is distasteful. The betrayal, perhaps a tiny fraction in itself, has inverted the tingling column of agreement, made all pluses minuses. Everything about the other is hateful, despicable; yet he cannot be dismissed. We have confided in him too many minutes, too many words; he has those minutes and words as hostages, and his confidences are embedded in us where they cannot be scraped away, and

even rivers of time cannot erode them completely, for there are indelible stains. Now—though the friends may continue to meet, and smile, as if they had never trespassed beyond acquaintance—the death of the one would please the other.

An unhappy pattern to which C is an exception. He was my friend before kindergarten, he is my friend still. I go to his home now, and he and his wife serve me and my wife with alcoholic drinks and slices of excellent cheese on crisp crackers, just as twenty years ago he served me with treats from his mother's refrigerator. He was a born host, and I a born guest. Also he was intelligent. If my childhood's brain, when I look back at it, seems a primitive mammal, a lemur or shrew, his brain was an angel whose visitation was widely hailed as wonderful. When in school he stood to recite, his cool rectangular forehead glowed. He tucked his right hand into his left armpit and with his left hand mechanically tapped a pencil against his thigh. His answers were always correct. He beat me at spelling bees and, in another sort of competition, when we both collected Big Little Books, he outbid me for my supreme find (in the attic of a third boy), the first Mickey Mouse. I can still see that book, I wanted it so badly, its paper tan with age and its drawings done in Disney's primitive style, when Mickey's black chest is naked like a child's and his eyes are two nicked oblongs. Losing it was perhaps a lucky blow; it helped wean me away from hope of ever having possessions.

C was fearless. He deliberately set fields on fire. He engaged in rock-throwing duels with tough boys. One afternoon he persisted in playing quoits with me although—as the hospital discovered that night—his appendix was nearly bursting. He was enterprising. He peddled magazine subscriptions door-to-door; he mowed neighbors' lawns; he struck financial bargains with his father. He collected stamps so well his collection blossomed into a stamp company that filled his room with steel cabinets and mimeograph machinery. He collected money—every time I went over to his house he would get out a little tin box and count the money in it for me: $27.50 one week, $29.95 the next, $30.90 the next—all changed into new bills nicely folded together. It was a strange ritual, whose meaning for me was: since he was doing it, I didn't have to. His money made me richer. We read Ellery Queen and played chess and invented board games and discussed infinity together. In later adolescence, he collected records. He liked the Goodman quintets but loved Fats Waller. Sitting there in that room so familiar to me, where the machinery of the Shilco Stamp Company still crowded the walls and for that matter the tin box of money might still be stashed, while my thin friend grunted softly along with that dead dark angel on "You're Not the Only Oyster in the Stew," I felt, in the best sense, patronized: the perfect guest of the perfect host. What made it perfect was that we had both spent our entire lives in Shillington.

Discussion

- Compare how Angelou and Updike deal with similar content.
- Choose a paragraph from Updike and a similar paragraph from other autobiographical writers in this book and discuss how these paragraphs were made, what they intended to say, and how they said it.
- Describe Updike's voice and discuss how much his white, middle-class, Pennsylvania background influenced his voice, as the racial, economic, and regional backgrounds of other writers have influenced their voices.
- Discuss the phrase, those groups of words that are less than a sentence that rub together and give off a particularly appropriate meaning. What are some of the ways to make a phrase work, weight playing against airy, hairy bumping against smoke-breathing, bristling fighting with defective, the smell of cedar and the sight of shavings. Select phrases from other writers in the book and see how they make a few words do more than those words alone could ever do.
- Discuss how Updike connects with his readers, involving their experiences in his text.
- Discuss how the autobiographical writers, such as Updike, use point of view to control the abundance of material their memories hold about their childhood.

Activities

- List as many specifics as you can about a schoolyard, a school, a classmate, a classroom, a teacher, and then write about that subject using some of the specifics and using some of the new ones that occur to you during the writing.
- Write an account of part of your schooldays, not imitating Updike or the other writers in the book, but being stimulated by their vision.

- Rearrange the phrases in an Updike paragraph—or a paragraph from another author, to see if you can carve a poem out of the prose.
- Make an outline of one of Updike's paragraphs to see how it is constructed. That could be very helpful, but don't think that that's the way he wrote it. The process of writing is much less rigid and more exciting than that. "Writing and rewriting are a constant search for what one is saying," Updike has said. At another time he said, "I don't make an outline or anything. I figure that I can hold the events in my head and then hope that things will happen which will surprise me, that the characters will take on life and talk." So go ahead and outline to see what he has constructed. That will teach you something about how effective writing works. Your own writing, however, will teach you how it is made.
- If you find outlining one of Updike's paragraphs helpful, try the same thing on paragraphs of other writers in the book that you have liked.
- Rewrite a paragraph of Updike as it might have been written by Baraka, Welty, Baldwin, Gibson, or Angelou. And then be Updike and rewrite one of their paragraphs.

George Orwell

Although George Orwell is known for his novels, such as *1984,* he will be best remembered for the power and style of his political reporting and his essays. Anyone who is a serious nonfiction writer in our time has learned from Orwell.

In one of his best known essays, "Politics and the English Language," he gives a famous list of rules for writing:

(i) Never use a metaphor, simile or other figure of speech which you are used to seeing in print.
(ii) Never use a long word where a short one will do.
(iii) If it is possible to cut the word out, always cut it out.
(iv) Never use the passive where you can use the active.
(v) Never use a foreign phrase, a scientific word, or a jargon word if you can think of an everyday English equivalent.
(vi) Break any of these rules sooner than say anything outright barbarous.

Why I Write

1   From a very early age, perhaps the age of five or six, I knew that when I grew up I should be a writer. Between the ages of about seventeen and twenty-four I tried to abandon this idea, but I did so with the consciousness that I was outraging my true nature and that sooner or later I should have to settle down and write books.

2   I was the middle child of three. but there was a gap of five years on either side, and I barely saw my father before I was eight. For this and other reasons I was somewhat lonely, and I soon developed disagreeable mannerisms which made me unpopular throughout my schooldays. I had the lonely child's habit of making up stories and holding conversations with imaginary persons, and I think from the very start my literary ambitions were mixed up with the feeling of being isolated and undervalued. I knew that I had a facility with words and a power of facing unpleasant facts, and I felt that this created a sort of private world in which I could get my own back for my failure in everyday life. Nevertheless the volume of serious—*i.e.,* seriously intended—writing which I produced all through my childhood and boyhood would not amount to half a dozen pages. I wrote my first poem at the age of four or five, my mother taking it down to dictation. I cannot remember anything about it except that it was about a tiger and the tiger had "chair-like teeth"—a good enough phrase, but I fancy the poem was a plagiarism of Blake's "Tiger, Tiger." At eleven, when the war of 1914-18 broke out, I wrote a patriotic poem which was printed in the local newspaper, as was another, two years later, on the death of Kitchener. From time to time, when I was a bit older, I wrote bad and usually unfinished "nature poems" in the Georgian style. I also, about twice, attempted a short story which was a ghastly failure. That was the total of the would-be serious work that I actually set down on paper during all those years.

3   However, throughout this time I did in a sense engage in literary activities. To begin with there was the made-to-order stuff which I produced quickly, easily and without much pleasure to myself. Apart from school work I wrote *vers d'occasion*, semi-comic poems which I could turn out at what now seems to me astonishing speed—at fourteen I wrote a whole rhyming play, in imitation of Aristophanes, in about a week—and helped to edit school magazines, both printed and in manuscript. These magazines were the most pitiful burlesque stuff that you could imagine, and I took far less trouble with them

than I now would with the cheapest journalism. But side by side with all this, for fifteen years or more, I was carrying out a literary exercise of a quite different kind: this was the making up of a continuous "story" about myself, a sort of diary existing only in the mind. I believe this is a common habit of children and adolescents. As a very small child I used to imagine that I was, say, Robin Hood, and picture myself as the hero of thrilling adventures, but quite soon my "story" ceased to be narcissistic in a crude way and became more and more a mere description of what I was doing and the things I saw. For minutes at a time this kind of thing would be running through my head: "He pushed the door open and entered the room. A yellow beam of sunlight, filtering through the muslin curtains, slanted on to the table, where a matchbox, half open, lay beside the inkpot. With his right hand in his pocket he moved across to the window. Down in the street a tortoiseshell cat was chasing a dead leaf," etc., etc. This habit continued till I was about twenty-five, right through my non-literary years. Although I had to search, and did search, for the right words, I seemed to be making this descriptive effort almost against my will, under a kind of compulsion from outside. The "story" must, I suppose, have reflected the styles of the various writers I admired at different ages, but so far as I remember it always had the same meticulous descriptive quality.

When I was about sixteen I suddenly discovered the joy of mere   4
words, *i.e.* the sounds and associations of words. The lines from *Paradise Lost*—

> So hee with difficulty and labour hard   5
> Moved on: with difficulty and labour hee,

which do not now seem to me so very wonderful, sent shivers down   6
my backbone; and the spelling "hee" for "he" was an added pleasure. As for the need to describe things, I knew all about it already. So it is clear what kind of books I wanted to write, in so far as I could be said to want to write books at that time. I wanted to write enormous naturalistic novels with unhappy endings, full of detailed descriptions and arresting similes, and also full of purple passages in which words were used partly for the sake of their sound. And in fact my first completed novel, *Burmese Days*, which I wrote when I was thirty but projected much earlier, is rather that kind of book.

I give all this background information because I do not think   7
one can assess a writer's motives without knowing something of his early development. His subject matter will be determined by the age

he lives in—at least this is true in tumultuous, revolutionary ages like our own—but before he ever begins to write he will have acquired an emotional attitude from which he will never completely escape. It is his job, no doubt, to discipline his temperament and avoid getting stuck at some immature stage, or in some perverse mood: but if he escapes from his early influences altogether, he will have killed his impulse to write. Putting aside the need to earn a living, I think there are four great motives for writing, at any rate for writing prose. They exist in different degrees in every writer, and in any one writer the proportions will vary from time to time, according to the atmosphere in which he is living. They are:

8   (1) Sheer egoism. Desire to seem clever, to be talked about, to be remembered after death, to get your own back on grownups who snubbed you in childhood, etc., etc. It is humbug to pretend that this is not a motive, and a strong one. Writers share this characteristic with scientists, artists, politicians, lawyers, soldiers, successful businessmen—in short, with the whole top crust of humanity. The great mass of human beings are not acutely selfish. After the age of about thirty they abandon individual ambition—in many cases, indeed, they almost abandon the sense of being individuals at all—and live chiefly for others, or are simply smothered under drudgery. But there is also the minority of gifted, wilful people who are determined to live their own lives to the end, and writers belong in this class. Serious writers, I should say, are on the whole more vain and self-centered than journalists, though less interested in money.

9   (2) Esthetic enthusiasm. Perception of beauty in the external world, or, on the other hand, in words and their right arrangement. Pleasure in the impact of one sound on another, in the firmness of good prose or the rhythm of a good story. Desire to share an experience which one feels is valuable and ought not to be missed. The esthetic motive is very feeble in a lot of writers, but even a pamphleteer or a writer of textbooks will have pet words and phrases which appeal to him for non-utilitarian reasons; or he may feel strongly about typography, width of margins, etc. Above the level of a railway guide, no book is quite free from esthetic considerations.

10   (3) Historical impulse. Desire to see things as they are, to find out true facts and store them up for the use of posterity.

11   (4) Political purpose—using the word "political" in the widest possible sense. Desire to push the world in a certain direction, to alter other people's idea of the kind of society that they should strive after. Once again, no book is genuinely free from political bias. The

opinion that art should have nothing to do with politics is itself a political attitude.

It can be seen how these various impulses must war against one another, and how they must fluctuate from person to person and from time to time. By nature—taking your "nature" to be the state you have attained when you are first adult—I am a person in whom the first three motives would outweigh the fourth. In a peaceful age I might have written ornate or merely descriptive books, and might have remained almost unaware of my political loyalties. As it is I have been forced into becoming a sort of pamphleteer. First I spent five years in an unsuitable profession (the Indian Imperial Police, in Burma), and then I underwent poverty and the sense of failure. This increased my natural hatred of authority and made me for the first time fully aware of the existence of the working classes, and the job in Burma had given me some understanding of the nature of imperialism: but these experiences were not enough to give me an accurate political orientation. Then came Hitler, the Spanish civil war, etc. By the end of 1935 I had still failed to reach a firm decision. I remember a little poem that I wrote at that date, expressing my dilemma:

> A happy vicar I might have been
> Two hundred years ago,
> To preach upon eternal doom
> And watch my walnuts grow;
>
> But born, alas, in an evil time,
> I missed that pleasant haven,
> For the hair has grown on my upper lip
> And the clergy are all clean-shaven.
>
> And later still the times were good,
> We were so easy to please,
> We rocked our troubled thoughts to sleep
> On the bosoms of the trees.
>
> All ignorant we dared to own
> The joys we now dissemble;
> The greenfinch on the apple bough
> Could make my enemies tremble.
> But girls' bellies and apricots,
> Roach in a shaded stream,
> Horses, ducks in flight at dawn,
> All these are a dream.

17   *It is forbidden to dream again;*
We maim our joys or hide them;
Horses are made of chromium steel
And little fat men shall ride them.

18   *I am the worm who never turned,*
The eunuch without a harem;
Between the priest and the commissar
I walk like Eugene Aram;

19   *And the commissar is telling my fortune*
While the radio plays,
But the priest has promised an Austin Seven,
For Duggie always pays.

20   *I dreamed I dwelt in marble halls,*
And woke to find it true;
I wasn't born for an age like this;
Was Smith? Was Jones? Were you?

21   The Spanish war and other events in 1936-7 turned the scale and thereafter I knew where I stood. Every line of serious work that I have written since 1936 has been written, directly or indirectly, *against* totalitarianism and *for* democratic socialism, as I understand it. It seems to me nonsense, in a period like our own, to think that one can avoid writing of such subjects. Everyone writes of them in one guise or another. It is simply a question of which side one takes and what approach one follows. And the more one is conscious of one's political bias, the more chance one has of acting politically without sacrificing one's esthetic and intellectual integrity.

22   What I have most wanted to do throughout the past ten years is to make political writing into an art. My starting point is always a feeling of partisanship, a sense of injustice. When I sit down to write a book, I do not say to myself, "I am going to produce a work of art." I write it because there is some lie that I want to expose, some fact to which I want to draw attention, and my initial concern is to get a hearing. But I could not do the work of writing a book, or even a long magazine article, if it were not also an esthetic experience. Anyone who cares to examine my work will see that even when it is downright propaganda it contains much that a full-time politician would consider irrelevant. I am not able, and I do not want, completely to abandon the world-view that I acquired in childhood. So long as I remain alive and well I shall continue to feel strongly about prose style, to love the surface of the earth, and to take a pleasure in solid

objects and scraps of useless information. It is no use trying to suppress that side of myself. The job is to reconcile my ingrained likes and dislikes with the essentially public, non-individual activities that this age forces on all of us.

It is not easy. It raises problems of construction and of language, 23 and it raises in a new way the problem of truthfulness. Let me give just one example of the cruder kind of difficulty that arises. My book about the Spanish civil war, *Homage to Catalonia*, is, of course, a frankly political book, but in the main it is written with a certain detachment and regard for form. I did try very hard in it to tell the whole truth without violating my literary instincts. But among other things it contains a long chapter, full of newspaper quotations and the like, defending the Trotskyists who were accused of plotting with Franco. Clearly such a chapter, which after a year or two would lose its interest for any ordinary reader, must ruin the book. A critic whom I respect read me a lecture about it. "Why did you put in all that stuff?" he said. "You've turned what might have been a good book into journalism." What he said was true, but I could not have done otherwise. I happened to know, what very few people in England had been allowed to know, that innocent men were being falsely accused. If I had not been angry about that I should never have written the book.

In one form or another this problem comes up again. The prob- 24 lem of language is subtler and would take too long to discuss. I will only say that of late years I have tried to write less picturesquely and more exactly. In any case I find that by the time you have perfected any style of writing, you have always outgrown it. *Animal Farm* was the first book in which I tried, with full consciousness of what I was doing, to fuse political purpose and artistic purpose into one whole. I have not written a novel for seven years, but I hope to write another fairly soon. It is bound to be a failure, every book is a failure, but I do know with some clarity what kind of book I want to write.

Looking back through the last page or two, I see that I have 25 made it appear as though my motives in writing were wholly public-spirited. I don't want to leave that as the final impression. All writers are vain, selfish and lazy, and at the very bottom of their motives there lies a mystery. Writing a book is a horrible, exhausting struggle, like a long bout of some painful illness. One would never undertake such a thing if one were not driven on by some demon whom one can neither resist nor understand. For all one knows that demon is simply the same instinct that makes a baby squall for attention. And yet it is also true that one can write nothing readable unless one constantly struggles to efface one's own personality. Good prose is like a window pane. I cannot say with certainty which of my motives are the strongest, but I know which of them deserve to be followed. And looking back through my work, I see that it is invariably where I lacked a *political* purpose that I wrote lifeless books and was betrayed into purple passages, sentences without meaning, decorative adjectives and humbug generally.

A Hanging

❧ The very first sentence of this piece gives me a goosebump or two every time I read it. With these simple words he so quickly establishes the place, the time, the climate, the mood. ❧

1   It was in Burma, a sodden morning of the rains. A sickly light, like yellow tinfoil, was slanting over the high walls into the jail yard. We were waiting outside the condemned cells, a row of sheds fronted with double bars, like small animal cages. Each cell measured about ten feet by ten and was quite bare within except for a plank bed and a pot for drinking water. In some of them brown, silent men were squatting at the inner bars, with their blankets draped round them. These were the condemned men, due to be hanged within the next week or two.

2   One prisoner had been brought out of his cell. He was a Hindu, a puny wisp of a man, with a shaven head and vague liquid eyes. He had a thick, sprouting moustache, absurdly too big for his body, rather like the moustache of a comic man on the films. Six tall Indian warders were guarding him and getting him ready for the gallows. Two of them stood by with rifles and fixed bayonets, while the others handcuffed him, passed a chain through his handcuffs and fixed it to their belts, and lashed his arms tight to his sides. They crowded very close about him, with their hands always on him in a careful, caressing grip, as though all the while feeling him to make sure he was there. It was like men handling a fish which is still alive and may jump back into the water. But he stood quite unresisting, yielding his arms limply to the ropes, as though he hardly noticed what was happening.

❦ Pay attention to the way this paragraph is written. Notice the phrase, "careful, caressing grip," which is so like some of the phrases that delight us in Updike. These phrases are not tricky, however; remember that. They are effective only if they clarify meaning, if they make us see, feel, and comprehend. Note also the simile, "like men handling a fish." Also notice the distance at which the writer stands from the subject. Orwell is an observer, but a close, concerned observer. Part of him is a participant, for he served five years with the Indian Imperial Police in Burma, but part of him was the writer watching the scene in which he was acting. ❧

Eight o'clock struck and a bugle call, desolately thin in the wet 3 air, floated from the distant barracks. The superintendent of the jail, who was standing apart from the rest of us, moodily prodding the gravel with his stick, raised his head at the sound. He was an army doctor, with a grey toothbrush moustache and a gruff voice. "For God's sake hurry up, Francis," he said irritably. "The man ought to have been dead by this time. Aren't you ready yet?"

Francis, the head jailer, a fat Dravidian in a white drill suit and 4 gold spectacles, waved his black hand. "Yes sir, yes sir," he bubbled. "All iss satisfactorily prepared. The hangman iss waiting. We shall proceed."

"Well, quick march, then. The prisoners can't get their break- 5 fast till this job's over."

We set out for the gallows. Two warders marched on either side 6 of the prisoner, with their rifles at the slope; two others marched close against him, gripping him by arm and shoulder, as though at once pushing and supporting him. The rest of us, magistrates and the like, followed behind. Suddenly, when we had gone ten yards, the procession stopped short without any order or warning. A dreadful thing had happened—a dog, come goodness knows whence, had appeared in the yard. It came bounding among us with a loud volley of barks and leapt round us wagging its whole body, wild with glee at finding so many human beings together. It was a large woolly dog, half Airedale, half pariah. For a moment it pranced round us, and then, before anyone could stop it, it had made a dash for the pris- oner, and jumping up tried to lick his face. Everybody stood aghast, too taken aback even to grab the dog.

"Who let that bloody brute in here?" said the superintendent 7 angrily. "Catch it, someone!"

A warder detached from the escort, charged clumsily after the 8 dog, but it danced and gambolled just out of his reach, taking everything as part of the game. A young Eurasian jailer picked up a handful of gravel and tried to stone the dog away, but it dodged the stones and came after us again. Its yaps echoed from the jail walls. The prisoner, in the grasp of the two warders, looked on incuriously, as though this was another formality of the hanging. It was several minutes before someone managed to catch the dog. Then we put my handkerchief through its collar and moved off once more, with the dog still straining and whimpering.

9   It was about forty yards to the gallows. I watched the bare brown back of the prisoner marching in front of me. He walked clumsily with his bound arms, but quite steadily, with that bobbing gait of the Indian who never straightens his knees. At each step his muscles slid neatly into place, the lock of hair on his scalp danced up and down, his feet printed themselves on the wet gravel. And once, in spite of the men who gripped him by each shoulder, he stepped lightly aside to avoid a puddle on the path.

10   It is curious; but till that moment I had never realized what it means to destroy a healthy, conscious man. When I saw the prisoner step aside to avoid the puddle I saw the mystery, the unspeakable wrongness of cutting a life short when it is in full tide. This man was not dying, he was alive just as we are alive. All the organs of his body were working—bowels digesting food, skin renewing itself, nails growing, tissues forming—all toiling away in solemn foolery. His nails would still be growing when he stood on the drop, when he was falling through the air with a tenth-of-a-second to live. His eyes saw the yellow gravel and the grey walls, and his brain still remembered, foresaw, reasoned—even about puddles. He and we were a party of men walking together, seeing, hearing, feeling, understanding the same world; and in two minutes, with a sudden snap, one of us would be gone—one mind less, one world less.

❧ Pay attention to that puddle. If you want to know what a specific can do, reread the previous two paragraphs. We see through the specific, through the revealing detail, the small significant act. The artist makes us see the importance of what seems trivial and is not.❧

11   The gallows stood in a small yard, separate from the main grounds of the prison, and overgrown with tall prickly weeds. It was a brick erection like three sides of a shed, with planking on top, and above that two beams and a crossbar with the rope dangling. The

hangman, a greyhaired convict in the white uniform of the prison, was waiting beside his machine. He greeted us with a servile crouch as we entered. At a word from Francis the two warders, gripping the prisoner more closely than ever, half led, half pushed him to the gallows and helped him clumsily up the ladder. Then the hangman climbed up and fixed the rope round the prisoner's neck.

We stood waiting, five yards away. The warders had formed in 12 a rough circle round the gallows. And then, when the noose was fixed, the prisoner began crying out to his god. It was a high, reiterated cry of "Ram! Ram! Ram! Ram!" not urgent and fearful like a prayer or cry for help, but steady, rhythmical, almost like the tolling of a bell. The dog answered the sound with a whine. The hangman, still standing on the gallows, produced a small cotton bag like a flour bag and drew it down over the prisoner's face. But the sound, muffled by the cloth, still persisted, over and over again: "Ram! Ram! Ram! Ram! Ram!"

The hangman climbed down and stood ready, holding the lever. 13 Minutes seemed to pass. The steady, muffled crying from the prisoner went on and on, "Ram! Ram! Ram!" never faltering for an instant. The superintendent, his head on his chest, was slowly poking the ground with his stick; perhaps he was counting the cries, allowing the prisoner a fixed number—fifty, perhaps, or a hundred. Everyone had changed colour. The Indians had gone grey like bad coffee, and one or two of the bayonets were wavering. We looked at the lashed hooded man on the drop, and listened to his cries—each cry another second of life; the same thought was in all our minds; oh, kill him quickly, get it over, stop that abominable noise!

Suddenly the superintendent made up his mind. Throwing up 14 his head he made a swift motion with his stick. "Chalo!" he shouted almost fiercely.

There was a clanking noise, and then dead silence. The prisoner 15 had vanished, and the rope was twisting on itself. I let go of the dog, and it galloped immediately to the back of the gallows; but when it got there it stopped short, barked, and then retreated into a corner of the yard, where it stood among the weeds looking timorously out at us. We went round the gallows to inspect the prisoner's body. He was dangling with his toes pointed straight downwards, very slowly revolving, as dead as a stone.

❡ Here's that issue of proportion or pacing again. In the Angelou piece we had a great deal of text before the graduation. Here we come to the hanging, but it doesn't stop. Orwell goes on, and we experience the real horror that comes after the act is done. 🞂

16   The superintendent reached out with his stick and poked the bare brown body; it oscillated slightly. *"He's* all right," said the superintendent. He backed out from under the gallows, and blew out a deep breath. The moody look had gone out of his face quite suddenly. He glanced at his wrist-watch. "Eight minutes past eight. Well, that's all for this morning, thank God."

17   The warders unfixed bayonets and marched away. The dog, sobered and conscious of having misbehaved itself, slipped after them. We walked out of the gallows yard, past the condemned cells with their waiting prisoners, into the big central yard of the prison. The convicts, under the command of warders armed with lathis, were already receiving their breakfast. They squatted in long rows, each man holding a tin pannikin, while two warders with buckets marched round ladling out rice; it seemed quite a homely, jolly scene, after the hanging. An enormous relief had come upon us now that the job was done. One felt an impulse to sing, to break into a run, to snigger. All at once everyone began chattering gaily.

18   The Eurasian boy walking beside me nodded towards the way we had come, with a knowing smile: "Do you know, sir, our friend (he meant the dead man) when he heard his appeal had been dismissed, he pissed on the floor of his cell. From fright. Kindly take one of my cigarettes, sir. Do you not admire my new silver case, sir? From the boxwallah, two rupees eight annas. Classy European style."

19   Several people laughed—at what, nobody seemed certain.

20   Francis was walking by the superintendent, talking garrulously: "Well, sir, all has passed off with the utmost satisfactoriness. It was all finished—flick! Like that. It iss not always so—oah, no! I have known cases where the doctor wass obliged to go beneath the gallows and pull the prisoner's legs to ensure decease. Most disagreeable!"

21   "Wriggling about, eh? That's bad," said the superintendent.

22   "Arch, sir, it iss worse when they become refractory! One man, I recall, clung to the bars of hiss cage when we went to take him out. You will scarcely credit, sir, that it took six warders to dislodge him, three pulling at each leg. We reasoned with him, 'My dear fellow,' we said 'think of all the pain and trouble you are causing to us!' But no, he would not listen! Ach, he wass very troublesome!"

23   I found that I was laughing quite loudly. Everyone was laughing.

Even the superintendent grinned in a tolerant way. "You'd better all come out and have a drink," he said quite genially. "I've got a bottle of whiskey in the car. We could do with it."

We went through the big double gates of the prison into the 24 road. "Pulling at his legs!" exclaimed a Burmese magistrate suddenly, and burst into a loud chuckling. We all began laughing again. At that moment Francis' anecdote seemed extraordinarily funny. We all had a drink together, native and European alike, quite amicably. The dead man was a hundred yards away.

Discussion

• Discuss what Orwell has said about why he is a writer. Relate it to your own experience with writing, relate it to the other writers in the text, relate it to what Updike said about creativity in the quotation cited in the introduction to his selection.

• Consider the standards of good writing Orwell has established in his six rules and in "Why I Write." Does he live up to them in "A Hanging"?

• Consider if other writers in the text have lived up to his standards.

• Discuss how Orwell implicates himself. He doesn't stand apart from the human race but criticizes himself as he criticizes others. How does he manage to be both participant and critical observer at the same time? Does it work?

• Relate what Orwell has said to current poltical speeches and statements as well as politcal reporting.

• Consider how other writers in the text might have covered the hanging.

• Discuss how the hanging might have been covered on television. What would be the advantages of film? The limitations?

Activities

• Apply Orwell's rules and his suggestion that "good prose is like a windowpane" to several pages of another writer in this text, editing those pages to fulfill Orwell's counsel. Do the same thing to one of your own drafts.

• Write a short essay on "Why I Write," "Why I Don't Write," "Why I Should Write," "What Happens When I Write."

• Write the lead and then outline a piece that might be similar to "A

Hanging." For example, a funeral where people walk away laughing and joking. Consider the proportions in the piece.

- Edit "A Hanging" to make it an essay by an uninvolved observer or an insensitive participant.
- Revise a piece of your own using Orwell's technique of particpant-observer.
- Create your own list of six rules for clear, vigorous writing.

Joan Didion

Joan Didion, like Orwell, writes both fiction and nonfiction, and both forms are marked with the precision of vision and her language. Her caring and concern are honed by the discipline of her prose. "My writing is a process of rewriting," she has said, "of going back and changing and filling in. In the rewriting process you discover what's going on, and you go back and bring it up to that point." Since she is so skilled at her trade the rewriting never shows to the ordinary reader, but the writer knows that such clear, well-organized prose could only be the result of expert polishing.

Why I Write

1   Of course I stole the title for this talk from George Orwell. One reason I stole it was that I like the sound of the words: *Why I Write.* There you have three short unambiguous words that share a sound, and the sound they share is this:

2   *I*
        I
        I

3   In many ways writing is the act of saying I, of imposing oneself upon other people, of saying *listen to me, see it my way, change your mind.* It's an aggressive, even a hostile act. You can disguise its aggressiveness all you want with veils of subordinate clauses and qualifiers and tentative subjunctives, with ellipses and evasions—with the whole manner of intimating rather than claiming, of alluding rather than stating—but there's no getting around the fact that setting words on paper is the tactic of a secret bully, an invasion, an

imposition of the writer's sensibility on the reader's most private space.

I stole the title not only because the words sounded right but because they seemed to sum up, in a no-nonsense way, all I have to tell you. Like many writers I have only this one "subject," this one "area"; the act of writing. I can bring you no reports from any other front. I may have other interests: I am "interested," for example, in marine biology, but I don't flatter myself that you would come out to hear me talk about it. I am not a scholar. I am not in the least an intellectual, which is not to say that when I hear the word "intellectual" I reach for my gun, but only to say that I do not think in abstracts. During the years when I was an undergraduate at Berkeley I tried, with a kind of hopeless late-adolescent energy, to buy some temporary visa into the world of ideas, to forge for myself a mind that could deal with the abstract.

In short I tried to think. I failed. My attention veered inexorably back to the specific, to the tangible, to what was generally considered, by everyone I knew then and for that matter have known since, the peripheral. I would try to contemplate the Hegelian dialectic and would find myself concentrating instead on a flowering pear tree outside my window and the particular way the petals fell on my floor. I would try to read linguistic theory and would find myself wondering instead if the lights were on in the bevatron up the hill. When I say that I was wondering if the lights were on in the bevatron you might immediately suspect, if you deal in ideas at all, that I was registering the bevatron as a political symbol, thinking in shorthand about the military-industrial complex and its role in the university community, but you would be wrong. I was only wondering if the lights were on in the bevatron and how they looked. A physical fact.

4

5

❡ Didion echoes a theme that has been running throughout the book—the importance of the specific. Notice how Orwell never entered into the great debate on capital punishment; he simply noticed how a man on the way to a hanging avoided stepping in a puddle. ❡

I had trouble graduating from Berkeley, not because of this inability to deal with ideas—I was majoring in English, and I could locate the house-and-garden imagery in *The Portrait of a Lady* as well as the next person, "imagery" being by definition the kind of specific that got my attention—but simply because I had neglected to take a

6

course in Milton. For reasons which now sound baroque I needed a degree by the end of that summer, and the English department finally agreed, if I would come down from Sacramento every Friday and talk about the cosmology of *Paradise Lost*, to certify me proficient in Milton. I did this. Some Fridays I took the Greyhound bus, other Fridays I caught the Southern Pacific's City of San Francisco on the last leg of its transcontinental trip. I can no longer tell you whether Milton put the sun or the earth at the center of his universe in *Paradise Lost*, the central question of at least one century and a topic about which I wrote 10,000 words that summer, but I can still recall the exact rancidity of the butter in the City of San Francisco's dining car, and the way the tinted windows on the Greyhound bus cast the oil refineries around Carquinez Straits into a grayed and obscurely sinister light. In short my attention was always on the periphery, on what I would see and taste and touch, on the butter, and the Greyhound bus. During those years I was traveling on what I knew to be a very shaky passport, forged papers: I knew that I was no legitimate resident in any world of ideas. I knew I couldn't think. All I knew then was what I couldn't do. All I knew then was what I wasn't, and it took me some years to discover what I was.

7   Which was a writer.

8   By which I mean not a "good" writer or a "bad" writer but simply a writer, a person, whose most absorbed and passionate hours are spent arranging words on pieces of paper. Had my credentials been in order I would never have become a writer. Had I been blessed with even limited access to my own mind there would have been no reason to write. I write entirely to find out what I'm thinking, what I'm looking at, what I see and what it means. What I want and what I fear. Why did the oil refineries around Carquinez Straits seem sinister to me in the summer of 1956? Why have the night lights in the bevatron burned in my mind for twenty years? *What is going on in these pictures in my mind?*

9   When I talk about pictures in my mind I am talking, quite specifically, about images that shimmer around the edges. There used to be an illustration in every elementary psychology book showing a cat drawn by a patient in varying stages of schizophrenia. This cat had a shimmer around it. You could see the molecular structure breaking down at the very edges of the cat: the cat became the background and the background the cat, everything interacting, exchanging ions. People on hallucinogens describe the same perception of objects. I'm not a schizophrenic, nor do I take hallucinogens, but certain images

do shimmer for me. Look hard enough, and you can't miss the shimmer. It's there. You can't think too much about these pictures that shimmer. You just lie low and let them develop. You stay quiet. You don't talk to many people and you keep your nervous system from shorting out and you try to locate the cat in the shimmer, the grammar in the picture.

❧ If I had to pick one essay that describes how I feel about being a writer and about writing, this essay would certainly be a finalist, and it would probably win. Didion gets to the very center of the writing process. This piece is packed with a writer's truth. ❧

Just as I meant "shimmer" literally I mean "grammar" literally. 10 Grammar is a piano I play by ear, since I seem to have been out of school the year the rules were mentioned. All I know about grammar is its infinite power. To shift the structure of a sentence alters the meaning of that sentence, as definitely and inflexibly as the position of a camera alters the meaning of the object photographed. Many people know about camera angles now, but not so many know about sentences. The arrangement of the words matters, and the arrangement you want can be found in the picture in your mind. The picture dictates the arrangement. The picture dictates whether this will be a sentence with or without clauses, a sentence that ends hard or a dying-fall sentence, long or short, active or passive. The picture tells you how to arrange the words and the arrangement of the words tells you, or tells me, what's going on in the picture. *Nota bene*:

It tells you. 11

You don't tell it. 12

Let me show you what I mean by pictures in the mind. I began 13 *Play It as It Lays* just as I have begun each of my novels, with no notion of "character" or "plot" or even "incident." I had only two pictures in my mind, more about which later, and a technical intention, which was to write a novel so elliptical and fast that it would be over before you noticed it, a novel so fast that it would scarcely exist on the page at all. About the pictures the first was of white space. Empty space. This was clearly the picture that dictated the narrative intention of the book—a book in which anything that happened would happen off the page, a "white" book to which the reader would have to bring his or her own bad dreams—and yet this picture told me no "story," suggested no situation. The second picture did. This second picture was of something actually witnessed. A young woman with long hair and a short white halter dress walks through the casino at the Riviera in Las Vegas at one in the morning. She crosses the casino alone and picks up a house telephone. I watch her because I have heard her paged, and recognize her name: she is a minor actress I see around Los Angeles from time to time, in places like Jax and once in a gynecologist's office in the Beverly Hills Clinic, but have never met. I know nothing about her. Who is paging her? Why is she here to be paged? How exactly did she come to this? It was precisely this moment in Las Vegas that made *Play It as It Lays* begin to tell itself to me, but the moment appears in the novel only obliquely, in a chapter which begins:

14   *Maria made a list of things she would never do. She would never:
      walk through the Sands or Caesar's alone after midnight. She would
      never ball at a party, do S-M unless she wanted to, borrow furs from
      Abe Lipsey, deal. She would never carry a Yorkshire in Beverly Hills.*

15   That is the beginning of the chapter and that is also the end of the chapter, which may suggest what I meant by "white space."

16   I recall having a number of pictures in my mind when I began the novel I just finished, *A Book of Common Prayer*. As a matter of fact one of these pictures was of that bevatron I mentioned, although I would be hard put to tell you a story in which nuclear energy figured. Another was a newspaper photograph of a hijacked 707 burning on the desert in the Middle East. Another was the night view from a room in which I once spent a week with paratyphoid, a hotel room on the Colombian coast. My husband and I seemed to be on the Colombian coast representing the United States of America at a film festival (I recall invoking the name "Jack Valenti" a lot, as if its reiteration could make me well), and it was a bad place to have fever, not only because my indisposition offended our hosts but because every night in this hotel the generator failed. The lights went out. The elevator stopped. My husband would go to the event of the evening and make excuses for me and I would stay alone in this hotel room, in the dark. I remember standing at the window trying to call Bogota (the telephone seemed to work on the same principle as the generator) and watching the night wind come up and wondering what I was doing eleven degrees off the equator with a fever of 103. The view from that window definitely figures in *A Book of Common Prayer*, as does the burning 707, and yet none of these pictures told me the story I needed.

17   The picture that did, the picture that shimmered and made

these other images coalesce, was the Panama airport at 6 A.M. I was in this airport only once, on a plane to Bogota that stopped for an hour to refuel, but the way it looked that morning remained superimposed on everything I saw until the day I finished *A Book of Common Prayer*. I lived in that airport for several years. I can still feel the hot air when I step off the plane, can see the heat already rising off the tarmac at 6 A.M. I can feel my skirt damp and wrinkled on my legs. I can feel the asphalt stick to my sandals. I remember the big tail of a Pan American plane floating motionless down at the end of the tarmac. I remember the sound of a slot machine in the waiting room. I could tell you that I remember a particular woman in the airport, an American woman, a *norteamericana*, a thin *norteamericana* about 40 who wore a big square emerald in lieu of a wedding ring, but there was no such woman there.

I put this woman in the airport later. I made this woman up, 18 just as I later made up a country to put the airport in, and a family to run the country. This woman in the airport is neither catching a plane nor meeting one. She is ordering tea in the airport coffee shop. In fact she is not simply "ordering" tea but insisting that the water be boiled, in front of her, for twenty minutes. Why is this woman in this airport? Why is she going nowhere, where has she been? Where did she get that big emerald? What derangement, or disassociation, makes her believe that her will to see the water boiled can possibly prevail?

> *She has been going to one airport or another for four months, one* 19
> *could see it, looking at the visas on her passport. All those airports*
> *where Charlotte Douglas's passport had been stamped would have*
> *looked alike. Sometimes the sign on the tower would say*
> *"Bienvenidos" and sometimes the sign on the tower would say*
> *"Bienvenue," some places were wet and hot and others dry and hot,*
> *but at each of these airports the pastel concrete walls would rust and*
> *stain and the swamp off the runway would be littered with the*
> *fuselages of cannibalized Fairchild F-227's and the water would need*
> *boiling.*

> *"I knew why Charlotte went to the airport even if Victor did not.* 20

> *"I knew about airports."* 21

These lines appear about halfway through *A Book of Common* 22 *Prayer*, but I wrote them during the second week I worked on the book, long before I had any idea where Charlotte Douglas had been or why she went to airports. Until I wrote these lines I had no character called "Victor" in mind: the necessity for mentioning a name, and the name "Victor," occurred to me as I wrote the sentence. *I knew why Charlotte went to the airport* sounded incomplete. *I knew why Charlotte went to the airport even if Victor did not* carried a little more narrative drive. Most important of all, until I wrote these lines I did not know who "I" was, who was telling the story. I had intended until that moment that the "I" be no more than the voice of the author, a 19th-century omniscient narrator. But there it was:

23   *"I knew why Charlotte went to the airport even if Victor did not."*

24   *"I knew about airports."*

25   This "I" was the voice of no author in my house. This "I" was someone who not only knew why Charlotte went to the airport but also knew someone called "Victor." Who was Victor? Who was this narrator? Why was this narrator telling me this story? Let me tell you one thing about why writers write: had I known the answer to any of these questions I would never have needed to write a novel.

Salvador

1   The three-year-old El Salvador International Airport is glassy and white and splendidly isolated, conceived during the waning of the Molina "National Transformation" as convenient less to the capital (San Salvador is forty miles away, until recently a drive of several hours) than to a central hallucination of the Molina and Romero regimes, the projected beach resorts, the Hyatt, the Pacific Paradise, tennis, golf, water-skiing, condos, *Costa del Sol*; the visionary invention of a tourist industry in yet another republic where the leading natural cause of death is gastrointestinal infection. In the general absence of tourists these hotels have since been abandoned, ghost resorts on the empty Pacific beaches, and to land at this airport built to service them is to plunge directly into a state in which no ground is solid, no depth of field reliable, no perception so definite that it might not dissolve into its reverse.

> ❡ Didion moves fast. She gets right into the subject, but notice how quickly she gets to the irony of the natural cause of death, and how she sets up in the last clauses of the paragraph the method by which she is going to view El Salvador and the difficulty she's going to have doing it. In the following paragraph you have the nice phrase

in the first sentence, the revealing detail of how documents are scrutinized, the clever use of specific vehicles. All through this piece she will use specifics, and she will set up specifics, such as "the grimgram." Note also how she uses statistics. ❼

The only logic is that of acquiescence. Immigration is negoti- 2 ated in a thicket of automatic weapons, but by whose authority the weapons are brandished (Army or National Guard or National Police or Customs Police or Treasury Police or one of a continuing prolif- eration of other shadowy and overlapping forces) is a blurred point. Eye contact is avoided. Documents are scrutinized upside down. Once clear of the airport, on the new highway that slices through green hills rendered phosphorescent by the cloud cover of the trop- ical rainy season, one sees mainly underfed cattle and mongrel dogs and armored vehicles, vans and trucks and Cherokee Chiefs fitted with reinforced steel and bulletproof Plexiglas an inch thick. Such vehicles are a fixed feature of local life, and are popularly associated with disappearance and death. There was the Cherokee Chief seen following the Dutch television crew killed in Chalatenango province in March of 1982. There was the red Toyota three-quarter-ton pickup sighted near the van driven by the four American Catholic workers on the night they were killed in 1980. There were, in the late spring and summer of 1982, the three Toyota panel trucks, one yellow, one blue, and one green, none bearing plates, reported present at each of the mass detentions (a "detention" is another fixed feature of local life, and often precedes a "disappearance") in the Amatepec district of San Salvador. These are the details—the models and colors of armored vehicles, the makes and calibers, the particular methods of dismemberment and decapitation used in particular instances—on which the visitor to Salvador learns immediately to concentrate, to the exclusion of past or future concerns, as in a prolonged amnesiac fugue.

Terror is the given of the place. Black-and-white police cars 3 cruise in pairs, each with the barrel of a rifle extruding from an open window. Roadblocks materialize at random, soldiers fanning out from trucks and taking positions, fingers always on triggers, safeties clicking on and off. Aim is taken as if to pass the time. Every morning *El Diario de Hoy* and *La Prensa Grafica* carry cautionary stories. *"Una madre y sus dos hijos fueron asesinados con arma cortante (corvo) por ocho sujetos desconocidos el lunes en la noche"*: A mother and her two sons hacked to death in their beds by eight *desconocidos*, unknown men. The same morning's paper, the unidentified body of a young man, strangled, found on the shoulder of a road. Same morning, different story: the unidentified bodies of three young men, found on another road, their faces partially destroyed by bayonets, one face carved to represent a cross.

4   It is largely from these reports in the newspapers that the United States embassy compiles its body counts, which are transmitted to Washington in a weekly dispatch referred to by embassy people as "the grimgram." These counts are presented in a kind of tortured code that fails to obscure what is taken for granted in El Salvador, that government forces do most of the killing. In a January 15, 1982 memo to Washington, for example, the embassy issued a "guarded" breakdown on its count of 6,909 "reported" political murders between September 16, 1980 and September 15, 1981. Of these 6,909, according to the memo, 922 were "believed committed by security forces," 952 were "believed committed by leftist terrorists," 136 "believed committed by rightist terrorists," and 4,889 "committed by unknown assailants," the famous *desconocidos* favored by those San Salvador newspapers still publishing. (The figures actually add up not to 6,909 but to 6,899, leaving ten in a kind of official limbo.) The memo continued:

5   *The uncertainty involved here can be seen in the fact that*
responsibility cannot be fixed in the majority of cases. We note,
however, that it is generally believed in El Salvador that a large
number of the unexplained killings are carried out by the security
forces, officially or unofficially. The Embassy is aware of dramatic
claims that have been made by one interest group or another in
which the security forces figure as the primary agents of murder here.
El Salvador's tangled web of attack and vengeance, traditional
criminal violence and political mayhem make this an impossible
charge to sustain. In saying this, however, we make no attempt to
lighten the responsibility for the deaths of many hundreds, and
perhaps thousands, which can be attributed to the security forces. . . .

6   The body count kept by what is generally referred to in San Salvador as "the Human Rights Commission" is higher than the embassy's, and documented periodically by a photographer who goes out looking for bodies. These bodies he photographs are often broken into unnatural positions, and the faces to which the bodies are attached (when they are attached) are equally unnatural, some-

times unrecognizable as human faces, obliterated by acid or beaten to a mash of misplaced ears and teeth or slashed ear to ear and invaded by insects. *"Encontrado en Antiguo Cuscatlan el dia 25 de Marzo 1982: camison de dormir celeste,"* the typed caption reads on one photograph: found in Antiguo Cuscatlan March 25 1982 wearing a sky-blue nightshirt. The captions are laconic. Found in Soyapango May 21 1982. Found in Mejicanos June 11 1982. Found at El Playon May 30 1982, white shirt, purple pants, black shoes.

The photograph accompanying that last caption shows a body 7 with no eyes, because the vultures got to it before the photographer did. There is a special kind of practical information that the visitor to El Salvador acquires immediately, the way visitors to other places acquire information about the currency rates, the hours for the museums. In El Salvador one learns that vultures go first for the soft tissue, for the eyes, the exposed genitalia, the open mouth. One learns that an open mouth can be used to make a specific point, can be stuffed with something emblematic; stuffed, say, with a penis, or, if the point has to do with land title, stuffed with some of the dirt in question. One learns that hair deteriorates less rapidly than flesh, and that a skull surrounded by a perfect corona of hair is a not uncommon sight in the body dumps.

❡ When SALVADOR first came out I read large chunks of it, including the paragraphs above and below this comment to my class in advanced nonfiction. Not to argue her politics, but to reveal the vigor and effectiveness of her prose. All through this piece she combines observation, reporting, and documentation. ❡

All forensic photographs induce in the viewer a certain protec- 8 tive numbness, but dissociation is more difficult here. In the first place these are not, technically, "forensic" photographs, since the evidence they document will never be presented in a court of law. In the second place the disfigurement is too routine. The locations are too near, the dates too recent. There is the presence of the relatives of the disappeared: the women who sit every day in this cramped office on the grounds of the archdiocese, waiting to look at the spiral-bound photo albums in which the photographs are kept. These albums have plastic covers bearing soft-focus color photographs of young Americans in dating situations (strolling through autumn foliage on one album, recumbent in a field of daisies on another), and the women, looking for the bodies of their husbands and brothers and sisters and children, pass them from hand to hand without comment or expression.

9   *One of the more shadowy elements of the violent scene here [is] the death squad. Existence of these groups has long been disputed, but not by many Salvadorans. . . .Who constitutes the death squads is yet another difficult question. We do not believe that these squads exist as permanent formations but rather as ad hoc vigilante groups that coalesce according to perceived need. Membership is also uncertain, but in addition to civilians we believe that both on- and off-duty members of the security forces are participants. This was unofficially confirmed by right-wing spokesman Maj. Roberto D/Aubuisson who stated in an interview in early 1981 that security forces members utilize the guise of the death squad when a potentially embarrassing or odious task needs to be performed.*

10   —From the confidential but later declassified January 15, 1982 memo previously cited, drafted for the State Department by the political section at the embassy in San Salvador.

11   The dead and pieces of the dead turn up in El Salvador everywhere, every day, as taken for granted as in a nightmare, or a horror movie. Vultures of course suggest the presence of a body. A knot of children on the street suggests the presence of a body. Bodies turn up in the brush of vacant lots, in the garbage thrown down ravines in the richest districts, in public rest rooms, in bus stations. Some are dropped in Lake Hopango, a few miles east of the city, and wash up near the lakeside cottages and clubs frequented by what remains in San Salvador of the sporting bourgeoisie. Some still turn up at El Playon, the lunar lava field of rotting human flesh visible at one time or another on every television screen in America but characterized in June of 1982 in the *El Salvador News Gazette*, an English-language weekly edited by an American named Mario Rosenthal, as an "uncorroborated story. . . .dredged up from the files of leftist propaganda." Others turn up at Puerta del Diablo, above Parque Balboa, a national *Turicentro* described as recently as the April-July 1982 issue of *Aboard TACA*, the magazine provided passengers on the national airline of El Salvador, as "offering excellent subjects for color photography."

12   I drove up to Puerta del Diablo one morning in June of 1982, past the Casa Presidencial and the camouflaged watch towers and heavy concentrations of troops and arms south of town, on up a narrow road narrowed further by landslides and deep crevices in the

roadbed, a drive so insistently premonitory that after a while I began to hope that I would pass Puerta del Diablo without knowing it, just miss it, write it off, turn around and go back. There was however no way of missing it. Puerta del Diablo is a "view site" in an older and distinctly literary tradition, nature as lesson, an immense cleft rock through which half of El Salvador seems framed, a site so romantic and "mystical," so theatrically sacrificial in aspect, that it might be a cosmic parody of nineteenth-century landscape painting. The place presents itself as pathetic fallacy: the sky "broods," the stones "weep," a constant seepage of water weighting the ferns and moss. The foliage is thick and slick with moisture. The only sound is a steady buzz, I believe of cicadas.

Body dumps are seen in El Salvador as a kind of visitors' must-do, difficult but worth the detour. "Of course you have seen El Playon," an aide to President Alvaro Magana said to me one day, and proceeded to discuss the site geologically, as evidence of the country's geothermal resources. He made no mention of the bodies . I was unsure if he was sounding me out or simply found the geothermal aspect of overriding interest. One difference between El Playon and Puerta del Diablo is that most bodies at El Playon appear to have been killed somewhere else, and then dumped; at Puerta del Diablo the executions are believed to occur in place, at the top, and the bodies thrown over. Sometimes reporters will speak of wanting to spend the night at Puerta del Diablo, in order to document the actual execution, but at the time I was in Salvador no one had. 13

The aftermath, the daylight aspect, is well documented. "Nothing fresh today, I hear," an embassy officer said when I mentioned that I had visited Puerta del Diablo. "Were there any on top?" someone else asked. "There were supposed to have been three on top yesterday." The point about whether or not there had been any on top was that usually it was necessary to go down to see bodies. The way down is hard. Slabs of stone, slippery with moss, are set into the vertiginous cliff, and it is down this cliff that one begins the descent to the bodies, or what is left of the bodies, pecked and maggoty masses of flesh, bone, hair. On some days there have been helicopters circling, tracking those making the descent. Other days there have been militia at the top, in the clearing where the road seems to run out, but on the morning I was there the only people on top were a man and a woman and three small children, who played in the wet grass while the woman started and stopped a Toyota pickup. She appeared to be learning how to drive. She drove forward and then 14 back toward the edge, apparently following the man's signals, over and over again.

15   We did not speak, and it was only later, down the mountain and back in the land of the provisionally living, that it occurred to me that there was a definite question about why a man and a woman might choose a well-known body dump for a driving lesson. This was one of a number of occasions, during the two weeks my husband I spent in El Salvador, on which I came to understand, in a way I had not understood before, the exact mechanism of terror.

16   Whenever I had nothing better to do in San Salvador I would walk up in the leafy stillness of the San Benito and Escalon districts, where the hush at midday is broken only by the occasional crackle of a walkie-talkie, the click of metal moving on a weapon. I recall a day in San Benito when I opened my bag to check an address, and heard the clicking of metal on metal all up and down the street. On the whole no one walks up here, and pools of blossoms lie undisturbed on the sidewalks. Most of the houses in San Benito are more recent than those in Escalon, less idiosyncratic and probably smarter, but the most striking architectural features in both districts are not the houses but their walls, walls built upon walls, walls stripped of the usual copa de oro and bougainvillea, walls that reflect successive generations of violence: the original stone, the additional five or six or ten feet of brick, and finally the barbed wire, sometimes concertina, sometimes electrified, walls with watch towers, gun ports, closed-circuit television cameras, walls now reaching twenty and thirty feet.

17   San Benito and Escalon appear on the embassy security maps as districts of relatively few "incidents," but they remain districts in which a certain oppressive uneasiness prevails. In the first place there are always "incidents"—detentions and deaths and disappearances—in the *barrancas*, the ravines lined with shanties that fall down behind the houses with the walls and the guards and the walkie-talkies; one day in Escalon I was introduced to a woman who kept the lean-to that served as a grocery in a *barranca* just above the Hotel Sheraton. She was sticking prices on bars of Camay and Johnson's baby soap, stopping occasionally to sell a plastic bag or two filled with crushed ice and Coca Cola, and all the while she talked in a low voice about her fear, about her eighteen-year-old son, about the boys who had been taken out and shot on successive nights recently in a neighboring *barranca*.

In the second place there is, in Escalon, the presence of the 18
Sheraton itself, a hotel that has figured rather too prominently in certain local stories involving the disappearance and death of Americans. The Sheraton always seems brighter and more mildly festive than either the Camino Real or the Presidente, with children in the pool and flowers and pretty women in pastel dresses, but there are usually several bulletproofed Cherokee Chiefs in the parking area, and the men drinking in the lobby often carry the little zippered purses that in San Salvador suggest not passports or credit cards but Browning 9 mm. pistols.

It was at the Sheraton that one of the few American *desapare-* 19
cidos, a young free-lance writer named John Sullivan, was last seen, in December of 1980. It was also at the Sheraton, after eleven on the evening of January 3, 1981, that the two American advisers on agrarian reform, Michael Hammer and Mark Pearlman, were killed, along with the Salvadoran director of the Institute of Agrarian Transformation, José Rodolfo Viera. The three were drinking coffee in a dining room off the lobby, and whoever killed them used an Ingram MAC-10, without sound suppressor, and then walked out through the lobby, unapprehended. The Sheraton has even turned up in the investigation into the December 1980 deaths of the four American churchwomen, Sisters Ita Ford and Maura Clarke, the two Maryknoll nuns; Sister Dorothy Kazel, the Ursuline nun; and Jean Donovan, the lay volunteer. In *Justice in El Salvador: A Case Study*, prepared and released in July of 1982 in New York by the Lawyers' Committee for International Human Rights, there appears this note:

> On December 19, 1980, the [Duarte government's] Special 20
> Investigative Commission reported that 'a red Toyota 3/4-ton pickup
> was seen leaving (the crime scene) at about 11:00 P.M. on December
> 2' and that 'a red splotch on the burned van' of the churchwomen
> was being checked to determine whether the paint splotch 'could be
> the result of a collision between that van and the red Toyota pickup.'
> By February 1981, the Maryknoll Sisters' Office of Social Concerns,
> which has been actively monitoring the investigation, received word
> from a source which it considered reliable that the FBI had matched
> the red splotch on the burned van with a red Toyota pickup belonging
> to the Sheraton hotel in San Salvador. . . . Subsequent to the FBI's
> alleged matching of the paint splotch and a Sheraton truck, the State
> Department has claimed, in a communication with the families of the
> churchwomen, that 'the FBI could not determine the source of the
> paint scraping.'

21   There is also mention in this study of a young Salvadoran businessman named Hans Christ (his father was a German who arrived in El Salvador at the end of World War II), a part owner of the Sheraton. Hans Christ lives now in Miami, and that his name should have even come up in the Maryknoll investigation made many people uncomfortable, because it was Hans Christ, along with his brother-in-law, Ricardo Sol Meza, who in April of 1981, was first charged with the murders of Michael Hammer and Mark Pearlman and José Rodolfo Viera at the Sheraton. These charges were later dropped, and were followed by a series of other charges, arrests, releases, expressions of "dismay" and "incredulity" from the American embassy, and even, in the fall of 1982, confessions to the killings from two former National Guard corporals, who testified that Hans Christ had led them through the lobby and pointed out the victims. Hans Christ and Ricardo Sol Meza have said that the dropped case against them was a government frame-up, and that they were only having drinks at the Sheraton the night of the killings, with a National Guard intelligence officer. It was logical for Hans Christ and Ricardo Sol Meza to have drinks at the Sheraton because they both had interests in the hotel, and Ricardo Sol Meza had just opened a roller disco, since closed, off the lobby into which the killers walked that night. The killers were described by witnesses as well dressed, their faces covered. The room from which they walked was at the time I was in San Salvador no longer a restaurant, but the marks left by the bullets were still visible, on the wall facing the door.

22   Whenever I had occasion to visit the Sheraton I was apprehensive, and this apprehension came to color the entire Escalon district for me, even its lower reaches, where there were people and movies and restaurants. I recall being struck by it on the canopied porch of a restaurant near the Mexican embassy, on an evening when rain or sabotage or habit had blacked out the city and I became abruptly aware, in the light cast by a passing car, of two human shadows, silhouettes illuminated by the headlights and then invisible again. One shadow sat behind the smoked glass windows of a Cherokee Chief parked at the curb in front of the restaurant, the other crouched between the pumps at the Esso station next door, carrying a rifle. It seemed to me unencouraging that my husband and I were the only people seated on the porch. In the absence of the headlights the candle on our table provided the only light, and I fought the impulse to blow it out. We continued talking, carefully. Nothing came of this,

but I did not forget the sensation of having been in a single instant demoralized, undone, humiliated by fear, which is what I meant when I said that I came to understand in El Salvador the mechanism of terror.

Discussion

• Compare Didion's "Why I Write" to Orwell's. What statements in each essay give you insights to your own writing and your own writing experience?

• Discuss how what Didion says about writing relates to her own writing.

• Consider how Orwell's counsel about writing relates to the excerpts from Didion's *Salvador*.

• Reverse the situation and consider how Didion's "Why I Write" illuminates or relates to Orwell's "A Hanging."

• Discuss how Didion's essay on writing relates to the work of other writers in the text.

• Compare her political reporting in *Salvador* to "A Hanging" and to the writing of others, such as Baldwin and King, who are concerned with political issues.

• Discuss how the movie and television camera has influenced writers, such as Didion, and how it has influenced the way in which readers read today.

Activities

• Write a brief description of how you write, trying to get inside the experience of writing, as Didion does.

• Cover a political event in your school or community, or visit an area in your neighborhood or across town and report on it, the way Didion has, mixing revealing details of observation with objective documentation.

• Write a review of Didion for a publication of the right and of the left.

• Since Didion is also a novelist, imagine the journal notes she might write herself if she considered using the material in the excerpt in a novel.

• Write a page of Didion's *Salvador* as she might write it for an essay rather than a piece of reportage.

E. B. White

E. B. White was once chosen as the writer most likely to survive from our century. No one should take bets on that, but the fact remains that E. B. White has influenced the way we use language. All nonfiction writers in our time have been students of his, whether they know it or not. His style, his tone, his ability to speak of heavy matters with a light touch has taught us all.

After he became a well-known writer he published *The Elements of Style*, a book which repeated the edicts of his writing teacher, William Strunk, Jr. For years I had a paragraph from Strunk, by way of White, over my desk:

> *Vigorous writing is concise. A sentence should contain no unnecessary words, a paragraph no unnecessary sentences, for the same reason that a drawing should have no unnecessary lines and a machine no unnecessary parts. This requires not that the writer make all his sentences short, or that he avoid all detail and treat his subjects only in outline, but that every word tell.*

There is a whole semester of a writing course in that one paragraph.

In his own additions to that book White expanded from rules to philosophy. He wrote, "Style takes its final shape more from attitudes of mind than from principles of composition, for as an elderly practitioner once remarked, 'Writing is an act of faith, not a trick of grammar.' This moral observation would have no place in a rule book were it not that style *is* the writer, and therefore what a man is, rather than what he knows, will at last determine his style."

Once More to the Lake

1   One summer, along about 1904, my father rented a camp on a lake in Maine and took us all there for the month of August. We all got ringworm from some kittens and had to rub Pond's Extract on our arms and legs night and morning, and my father rolled over in a canoe with all his clothes on; but outside of that the vacation was a success and from then on none of us ever thought there was any place in the world like that lake in Maine. We returned summer after summer—always on August 1st for one month. I have since become a salt-water man, but sometimes in summer there are days when the

restlessness of the tides and the fearful cold of the sea water and the incessant wind which blows across the afternoon and into the evening make me wish for the placidity of a lake in the woods. A few weeks ago this feeling got so strong I bought myself a couple of bass hooks and a spinner and returned to the lake where we used to go, for a week's fishing and to revisit old haunts.

I took along my son, who had never had any fresh water up his nose and who had seen lily pads only from train windows. On the journey over to the lake I began to wonder what it would be like. I wondered how time would have marred this unique, this holy spot— the coves and streams, the hills that the sun set behind, the camps and the paths behind the camps. I was sure that the tarred road would have found it out and I wondered in what other ways it would be desolated. It is strange how much you can remember about places like that once you allow your mind to return into the grooves which lead back. You remember one thing, and that suddenly reminds you of another thing. I guess I remembered clearest of all the early mornings, when the lake was cool and motionless, remembered how the bedroom smelled of the lumber it was made of and of the wet woods whose scent entered through the screen. The partitions in the camp were thin and did not extend clear to the top of the rooms, and as I was always the first up I would dress softly so as not to wake the others, and sneak out into the sweet outdoors and start out in the canoe, keeping close along the shore in the long shadows of the pines. I remembered being very careful never to rub my paddle against the gunwale for fear of disturbing the stillness of the cathedral.

The lake had never been what you would call a wild lake. There were cottages sprinkled around the shores, and it was in farming country although the shores of the lake were quite heavily wooded. Some of the cottages were owned by nearby farmers, and you would live at the shore and eat your meals at the farmhouse. That's what our family did. But although it wasn't wild, it was a fairly large and undisturbed lake and there were places in it which, to a child at least, seemed infinitely remote and primeval.

I was right about the tar: it led to within half a mile of the shore. But when I got back there, with my boy, and we settled into a camp near a farmhouse and into the kind of summertime I had known, I could tell that it was going to be pretty much the same as it had been before—I knew it, lying in bed the first morning, smelling the bedroom, and hearing the boy sneak quietly out and go off along the shore in a boat. I began to sustain the illusion that he was I, and therefore, by simple transposition, that I was my father. This sensation persisted, kept cropping up all the time we were there. It was not an entirely new feeling, but in this setting it grew much stronger. I seemed to be living a dual existence. I would be in the middle of some simple act, I would be picking up a bait box or laying down a table fork, or I would be saying something, and suddenly it would be not I but my father who was saying the words or making the gesture. It gave me a creepy sensation.

> ❡ White, the master of tone, uses the word creepy to take the pressure off the heavy emotions being discussed just before and—as an adult—he uses a child's term, a nice touch. He probably didn't calculate that, just made the move, but the result is neat. His language moves between that of one generation and another as the actions he was describing move. ❡

5   We went fishing the first morning. I felt the same damp moss covering the worms in the bait can, and saw the dragonfly alight on the tip of my rod as it hovered a few inches from the surface of the water. It was the arrival of this fly that convinced me beyond any doubt that everything was as it always had been, that the years were a mirage and there had been no years. The small waves were the same, chucking the rowboat under the chin as we fished at anchor, and the boat was the same boat, the same color green and the ribs broken in the same places, and under the floor-boards the same fresh-water leavings and debris—the dead helgramite, the wisps of moss, the rusty discarded fish-hook, the dried blood from yesterday's catch. We stared silently at the tips of our rods, at the dragon flies that came and went. I lowered the tip of mine into the water, tentatively, pensively dislodging the fly, which darted two feet away, poised, darted two feet back, and came to rest again a little farther up the rod. There had been no years between the ducking of this dragonfly and the other one—the one that was part of memory. I looked at the boy, who was silently watching his fly, and it was my hands that held his rod, my eyes watching. I felt dizzy and didn't know which rod I was at the end of.

6   We caught two bass, hauling them in briskly as though they were mackerel, pulling them over the side of the boat in a business-like manner without any landing net, and stunning them with a blow on the back of the head. When we got back for a swim before lunch,

the lake was exactly where we had left it, the same number of inches from the dock, and there was only the merest suggestion of a breeze. This seemed an utterly enchanted sea, this lake you could leave to its own devices for a few hours and come back to, and find that it had not stirred, this constant and trustworthy body of water. In the shallows, the dark, watersoaked sticks and twigs, smooth and old, were undulating in clusters on the bottom against the clean ribbed sand, and the track of the mussel was plain. A school of minnows swam by, each minnow with its small individual shadow, doubling the attendance, so clear and sharp in the sunlight. Some of the other campers were in swimming, along the shore, one of them with a cake of soap, and the water felt thin and clear and unsubstantial. Over the years there had been this person with the cake of soap, this cultist, and here he was. There had been no years.

Up to the farmhouse to dinner through the teeming, dusty field, the road under our sneakers was only a two-track road. The middle track was missing, the one with the marks of the hooves and the splotches of dried, flaky manure. There had always been three tracks to choose from in choosing which track to walk in; now the choice was narrowed down to two. For a moment I missed terribly the middle alternative. But the way led past the tennis court, and something about the way it lay there in the sun reassured me; the tape had loosened along the backline, the alleys were green with plantains and other weeds, and the net (installed in June and removed in September) sagged in the dry noon, and the whole place steamed with midday heat and hunger and emptiness. There was a choice of pie for dessert, and one was blueberry and one was apple, and the waitresses were the same country girls, there having been no passage of time, only the illusion of it as in a dropped curtain—the waitresses were still fifteen; their hair had been washed, that was the only difference—they had been to the movies and seen the pretty girls with the clean hair.

Summertime, oh summertime, pattern of life indelible, the fadeproof lake, the woods unshatterable, the pasture with the sweetfern and the juniper forever and ever, summer without end; this was the background, and the life along the shore was the design, the cottagers with their innocent and tranquil design, their tiny docks with the flagpole and the American flag floating against the white clouds in the blue sky, the little paths over the roots of the trees leading from camp to camp and the paths leading back to the outhouses and the can of lime for sprinkling, and at the souvenir counters at the store the miniature birch-bark canoes and the postcards that showed things looking a little better than they looked. This was the American family at play, escaping the city heat, wondering whether the new-comers in the camp at the head of the cove were "common" or "nice," wondering whether it was true that the people who drove up for Sunday dinner at the farmhouse were turned away because there wasn't enough chicken.

9   It seemed to me, as I kept remembering all this, that those times and those summers had been infinitely precious and worth saving. There had been jollity and peace and goodness. The arriving (at the beginning of August) had been so big a business in itself, at the rail-way station the farm wagon drawn up, the first smell of the pine-laden air, the first glimpse of the smiling farmer, and the great impor-tance of the trunks and your father's enormous authority in such mat-ters, and the feel of the wagon under you for the long ten-mile haul, and at the top of the last long hill catching the first view of the lake after eleven months of not seeing this cherished body of water. The shouts and cries of the other campers when they saw you, and the trunks to be unpacked, to give up their rich burden. (Arriving was less exciting nowadays, when you sneaked up in your car and parked it under a tree near the camp and took out the bags and in five min-utes it was all over, no fuss, no loud wonderful fuss about trunks.)

10   Peace and goodness and jollity. The only thing that was wrong now, really, was the sound of the place, an unfamiliar nervous sound of the outboard motors. This was the note that jarred, the one thing that would sometimes break the illusion and set the years moving. In those other summertimes all motors were inboard; and when they were at a little distance, the noise they made was a sedative, an ingre-dient of summer sleep. They were one-cylinder and two-cylinder engines, and some were make-and-break and some were jump-spark, but they all made a sleepy sound across the lake. The one-lungers throbbed and fluttered, and the twin-cylinder ones purred and purred, and that was a quiet sound too. But now the campers all had outboards. In the daytime, in the hot mornings, these motors made a petulant, irritable sound; at night, in the still evening when the afterglow lit the water, they whined about one's ears like mos-quitoes. My boy loved our rented outboard, and his great desire was to achieve singlehanded mastery over it, and authority, and he soon learned the trick of choking it a little (but not too much), and the adjustment of the needle valve. Watching him I would remember the things you could do with the old one-cylinder engine with the heavy

flywheel, how you could have it eating out of your hand if you got really close to it spiritually. Motor boats in those days didn't have clutches, and you would make a landing by shutting off the motor at the proper time and coasting in with a dead rudder. But there was a way of reversing them, if you learned the trick, by cutting the switch and putting it on again exactly on the final dying revolution of the flywheel, so that it would kick back against compression and begin reversing. Approaching a dock in a strong following breeze, it was difficult to slow up sufficiently by the ordinary coasting method, and if a boy felt he had complete mastery over his motor, he was tempted to keep it running beyond its time and then reverse it a few feet from the dock. It took a cool nerve, because if you threw the switch a twentieth of a second too soon you would catch the flywheel when it still had speed enough to go up past center, and the boat would leap ahead, charging bull-fashion at the dock.

We had a good week at the camp. The bass were biting well 11 and the sun shone endlessly, day after day. We would be tired at night and lie down in the accumulated heat of the little bedrooms after the long hot day and the breeze would stir almost imperceptibly outside and the smell of the swamp drift in through the rusty screens. Sleep would come easily and in the morning the red squirrel would be on the roof, tapping out his gay routine. I kept remembering everything, lying in bed in the mornings—the small steamboat that had a long rounded stern like the lip of a Ubangi, and how quietly she ran on the moonlight sails, when the older boys played their mandolins and the girls sang and we ate doughnuts dipped in sugar, and how sweet the music was on the water in the shining night, and what it had felt like to think about girls then. After breakfast we would go up to the store and the things were in the same place—the minnows in a bottle, the plugs and spinners disarranged and pawed over by the youngsters from the boys' camp, the fig newtons and the Beeman's gum. Outside, the road was tarred and cars stood in front of the store. Inside, all was just as it had always been, except there was more Coca Cola and not so much Moxie and root beer and birch beer and sarsaparilla. We would walk out with a bottle of pop apiece and sometimes the pop would backfire up our noses and hurt. We explored the streams, quietly, where the turtles slid off the sunny logs and dug their way into the soft bottom; and we lay on the town wharf and fed worms to the tame bass. Everywhere we went I had trouble making out which was I, the one walking at my side, the one walking in my pants.

12   One afternoon while we were there at that lake a thunderstorm came up. It was like the revival of an old melodrama that I had seen long ago with childish awe. The second-act climax of the drama of the electrical disturbance over a lake in America had not changed in any important respect. This was the big scene, still the big scene. The whole thing was so familiar, the first feeling of oppression and heat and a general air around camp of not wanting to go very far away. In midafternoon (it was all the same) a curious darkening of the sky, and a lull in everything that had made life tick; and then the way the boats suddenly swung the other way at their moorings with the coming of a breeze out of the new quarter, and the premonitory rumble. Then the kettle drum, then the snare, then the bass drum and cymbals, then crackling light against the dark, and the gods grinning and licking their chops in the hills. Afterward the calm, the rain steadily rustling in the calm lake, the return of light and hope and spirits, and the campers running out in joy and relief to go swimming in the rain, their bright cries perpetuating the deathless joke about how they were getting simply drenched, and the children screaming with delight at the new sensation of bathing in the rain, and the joke about getting drenched linking the generations in a strong indestructible chain. And the comedian who waded in carrying an umbrella.

> ❦ Pay attention to this last paragraph, for everything in this piece has been leading up to this emotional ending. White does not communicate it in abstractions, although he is dealing with the master abstraction. He speaks in particulars that we can all feel and understand. ❧

13   When the others went swimming my son said he was going in too. He pulled his dripping trunks from the line where they had hung all through the shower, and wrung them out. Languidly, and with no thought of going in, I watched him, his hard little body, skinny and bare, saw him wince slightly as he pulled up around his vitals the small, soggy, icy garment. As he buckled the swollen belt suddenly my groin felt the chill of death.

Discussion

• Discuss the idea that style is the man. Consider what White is and who others in this book are.

- Discuss how Strunk's edict for vigorous writing can be true of writers who communicate with a rich abundance of language. Do they make every word tell?
- Discuss how White's counsel about writing relates to Didion's and Orwell's.
- Consider if White followed Strunk's advice.
- White has said, "When a mosquito bites me—I scratch. When I write something, I guess I'm trying to get rid of the itchiness inside me." What was itching White? How would writing stop the itching?
- Compare White's autobiographical piece about childhood to some of the other autobiographical pieces in the book.
- Consider White's point of view. What are its advantages and disadvantages?

Activities

- Rewrite a page of White from the son's point of view.
- Write a piece about an event that marked your moving into adulthood.
- Go through a paragraph of White and decide what every word tells. Do the same thing to a paragraph by another writer and to a paragraph of your own.
- Go through the White essay and make a note in the margin by every paragraph, telling how each paragraph prepares the reader for the last sentence of the essay.
- Rewrite the first paragraph using an entirely different environment, one that you know. Once more to the vacant lot, the ball field, the barroom, the abandoned farm, the amusement park, the alley.

Jean Shepherd

Jean Shepherd is a member of the second oldest profession: storyteller. We depended on storytellers before we knew that a cave was a good place to stay out of the rain. They explained what we had done and what it meant. They chronicled our adventures, and each had an individual way of seeing the world. Shepherd sees the world with humor. He is a talker who is always creating and recreating the myths of his life, and therefore showing us the humor and the meaning in our own lives. Years ago he was on radio station

WOR in New York, and I used to go to sleep listening to him talk, talk, talk, telling the same stories over and over again. I would go to sleep smiling. I remember first hearing the story that I later read and that is reprinted below. It has, in print, the same wonderful flavor of speech, of a story being told to a bunch of guys hanging out at the gas station. Shepherd has told his stories live to audiences, large and small. He has told them on radio and television, on tape and on record, and he has told them in print. Listen as he tells the story to you.

Hairy Gertz and the Forty-Seven Crappies

1   Life, when you're a Male kid, is what the Grownups are doing. The Adult world seems to be some kind of secret society that has its own passwords, handclasps, and countersigns. The thing is to get in. But there's this invisible, impenetrable wall between you and all the great, unimaginably swinging things that they seem to be involved in. Occasionally mutterings of exotic secrets and incredible pleasures filter through. And so you bang against it, throw rocks at it, try to climb over it, burrow under it; but there it is. Impenetrable. Enigmatic.

2   Girls somehow seem to be already involved, as though from birth they've got the Word. Lolita has no Male counterpart. It does no good to protest and pretend otherwise. The fact is inescapable. A male kid is really a *kid*. A female kid is a *girl*. Some guys give up early in life, surrender completely before the impassable transparent wall, and remain little kids forever. They are called "Fags," or "Homosexuals," if you are in polite society.

3   The rest of us have to claw our way into Life as best we can, never knowing when we'll be Admitted. It happens to each of us in different ways—and once it does, there's no turning back.

4   It happened to me at the age of twelve in Northern Indiana—a remarkably barren terrain resembling in some ways the surface of the moon, encrusted with steel mills, oil refineries, and honky-tonk bars. There was plenty of natural motivation for Total Escape. Some kids got hung up on kite flying, others on pool playing. *I* became the greatest vicarious angler in the history of the Western world.

5   I say vicarious because there just wasn't any actual fishing to be done around where I lived. So I would stand for hours in front of the

goldfish tank at Woolworth's, landing fantails in my mind, after incredible struggles. I read *Field & Stream, Outdoor Life,* and *Sports Afield* the way other kids read *G-8 And His Battle Aces.* I would break out in a cold sweat reading about these guys portaging to Alaska and landing rare salmon; and about guys climbing the High Sierras to do battle with the wily golden trout; and mortal combat with the steel-heads. I'd read about craggy, sinewy sportsmen who discover untouched bass lakes where they have to beat off the pickerel with an oar, and the saber-toothed, raging smallmouths chase them ashore and right up into the woods.

After reading one of these fantasies I would walk around in a 6
daze for hours, feeling the cork pistol grip of my imaginary trusty six-foot, split-bamboo bait-casting rod in my right hand and hearing the high-pitched scream of my Pflueger Supreme reel straining to hold a seventeen-pound Great Northern in check.

❧ We've talked a lot about Orwell's "pane of glass" and the writer
getting out of the way and revealing the subject directly to the
reader. Then E. B. White quietly stood between us and the subject,
yet we were hardly aware of him. You are aware of Jean Shepherd.
He gets between you and the subject. You see the subject through
him as he jumps around pointing everything out to you. Nothing is
really right or wrong in writing; what works, works. And the writer,
reading others, delights in diversity. What doesn't work for one
writer or for one writing task will work for another.❧

I became known around town as "the-kid-who-is-the-nut-on- 7
fishing," even went to the extent of learning how to tie flies, although I'd never been fly casting in my life. I read books on the subject. And in my bedroom while the other kids are making balsa models of Curtiss Robins, I am busy tying Silver Doctors, Royal Coachmen, and Black Gnats. They were terrible. I would try out one in the bathtub to see whether it made a ripple that might frighten off the wily rainbow.

"Glonk!" 8

Down to the bottom like a rock, my floating dry fly would go. 9
Fishing was part of the mysterious and unattainable Adult world. I wanted In.

My Old Man was In, though he was what you might call a once- 10
in-a-while-fisherman-and-beer-party-goer; they are the same thing in the shadow of the blast furnaces. (I knew even then that there are

people who Fish and there are people who Go Fishing; they're two entirely different creatures.) My Old Man did not drive 1500 miles to the Atlantic shore with 3000 pounds of Abercrombie & Fitch fishing tackle to angle for stripers. He was the kind who would Go Fishing maybe once a month during the summer when it was too hot to Go Bowling and all of the guys down at the office would get The Itch. To them, fishing was a way of drinking a lot of beer and yelling. And getting away from the women. To me, it was a sacred thing. To *fish*.

11   He and these guys from the office would get together and go down to one of the lakes a few miles from where we lived—but never to Lake Michigan, which wasn't far away. I don't know why; I guess it was too big and awesome. In any case, nobody ever really thought of fishing in it. At least nobody in my father's mob. They went mostly to a mudhole known as Cedar Lake.

12   I will have to describe to you what a lake in the summer in Northern Indiana is like. To begin with, heat, in Indiana, is something else again. It descends like a 300-pound fat lady onto a picnic bench in the middle of July. It can literally be sliced into chunks and stored away in the basement to use in winter; on cold days you just bring it out and turn it on. Indiana heat is not a meteorological phenomenon—it is a solid element, something you can grab by the handles. Almost every day in the summer the whole town is just shimmering in front of you. You'd look across the street and skinny people would be all fat and wiggly like in the fun-house mirrors at Coney Island. The asphalt in the streets would bubble and hiss like a pot of steaming Ralston.

13   That kind of heat and sun produces mirages. All it takes is good flat country, a nutty sun, and insane heat and, by George, you're looking at Cleveland 200 miles away. I remember many times standing out in center field on an incinerating day in mid-August, the prairie stretching out endlessly in all directions, and way out past the swamp would be this kind of tenuous, shadowy, cloud-like thing shimmering just above the horizon. It would be the Chicago skyline, upside down, just hanging there in the sky. And after a while it would gradually disappear.

14   So, naturally, fishing is different in Indiana. The muddy lakes, about May, when the sun starts beating down on them, would begin to simmer and bubble quietly around the edges. These lakes are not fed by springs or streams. I don't know what feeds them. Maybe seepage. Nothing but weeds and truck axles on the bottom; flat, low, muddy banks, surrounded by cottonwood trees, cattails, smelly

marshes, and old dumps. Archetypal dumps. Dumps gravitate to Indiana lakes like flies to a hog killing. Way down at the end where the water is shallow and soupy are the old cars and the ashes, busted refrigerators, oil drums, old corsets, and God knows what else.

❡ This is NOT E. B. White's Maine lake, but it can be celebrated just the same. ❡

At the other end of the lake is the Roller Rink. There's *always* a   15
Roller Rink. You can hear that old electric organ going, playing "Heartaches," and you can hear the sound of the roller skates:
"Shhhhhh. . .sssshhhhhhhh. . .sssssshhhhhhhhhhhhhhhh. . ."   16
And the fistfights breaking out. The Roller Rink Nut in heat. The   17
Roller Rink Nut was an earlier incarnation of the Drive-In Movie Nut. He was the kind who was very big with stainless steel diners, motels, horror movies, and frozen egg rolls. A close cousin to the Motorcycle Clod, he went ape for chicks with purple eyelids. You know the crowd. Crewcuts, low foreheads, rumbles, hollering, belching, drinking beer, roller skating on one foot, wearing black satin jackets with SOUTH SIDE A. C. lettered in white on the back around a white-winged roller-skated foot. The kind that hangs the stuff in the back windows of their '53 Mercuries; a huge pair of foam-rubber dice, a skull and crossbones, hula-hula dolls, and football players—Pro, of course, with heads that bob up and down. The guys with ball fringe around the windows of their cars, with phony Venetian blinds in the back, and big white rubber mudguards hanging down, with red reflectors. Or they'll take some old heap and line it with plastic imitation mink fur, pad the steering wheel with leopard skin and ostrich feathers until it weighs seventeen pounds and is as fat as a salami. A TV set, a bar, and a folding Castro bed are in the trunk, automatically operated and all lined with tasteful Sears Roebuck ermine. You know the crew—a true American product. We turn them out like Campbell's Pork & Beans.

This is the system of aesthetics that brought the Roller Rink to   18
Cedar Lake, Indiana, when I was a kid.

About 150 yards from the Roller Rink was the Cedar Lake Eve-   19
ning In Paris Dance Hall. Festering and steamy and thronged with yeasty refugees from the Roller Rink. These are the guys who can't skate. But they can do other things. They're down there jostling back and forth in 400-per-cent humidity to the incomparable sounds of an Indiana dancehall band. Twelve non-Union cretinous musi-

cians—Mickey Iseley's Montgomery Ward altos. The lighting is a tasteful combination of naked light bulbs, red and blue crepe paper, and orange cellophane gels.

20   In between the Roller Rink and the Dance Hall are seventeen small shacks known as Beer Halls. And surrounding this tiny oasis of civilization, this bastion of bonhomie, is a gigantic sea of total darkness, absolute pitch-black Stygian darkness, around this tiny island of totally decadent, bucolic American merriment. The roller skates are hissing, the beer bottles are crashing, the chicks are squealing, Mickey's reed men are quavering, and Life is full.

21   And in the middle of the lake, several yards away, are over 17,000 fishermen, in wooden rowboats rented at a buck and a half an hour. It is 2 A.M. The temperature is 175, with humidity to match. And the smell of decayed toads, the dumps at the far end of the lake, and an occasional *soupçon* of Standard Oil, whose refinery is a couple of miles away, is enough to put hair on the back of a mud turtle. Seventeen thousand guys clumped together in the middle fishing for the known sixty-four crappies in that lake.

22   Crappies are a special breed of Midwestern fish, created by God for the express purpose of surviving in waters that would kill a bubonic-plague bacillus. They have never been known to fight, or even faintly struggle. I guess when you're a crappie, you figure it's no use anyway. One thing is as bad as another. They're just down there in the soup. No one quite knows what they eat, if anything, but everybody's fishing for them. At two o'clock in the morning.

23   Each boat contains a minimum of nine guys and fourteen cases of beer. And once in a while, in the darkness, is heard the sound of a guy falling over backward into the slime:

24   SSSSGLUNK!

25   "Oh! Ah! Help, help!" A piteous cry in the darkness. Another voice:

26   "Hey, for God's sake, Charlie's fallen in again! Grab the oar!"

27   And then it slowly dies down. Charlie is hauled out of the goo and is lying on the bottom of the boat, urping up dead lizards and Atlas Prager. Peace reigns again.

28   The water in these lakes is not the water you know about. It is composed of roughly ten per cent waste glop spewed out by Shell, Sinclair, Phillips, and the Grasselli Chemical Corporation; twelve per cent used detergent; thirty-five per cent thick gruel composed of decayed garter snakes, deceased toads, fermenting crappies, and a

strange, unidentifiable liquid that holds it all together. No one is quite sure *what* that is, because everybody is afraid to admit what it really is. They don't want to look at it too closely.

So this melange lays there under the sun, and about August it is 29 slowly simmering like a rich mulligatawny stew. At two in the morning you can hear the water next to the boat in the darkness:

"Gluuummp. . .Bluuuummmp." 30

Big bubbles of some unclassified gas come up from the bottom 31 and burst. The natives, in their superstitious way, believe that it is highly inflammable. They take no chances.

The saddest thing of all is that on these lakes there are usually 32 about nineteen summer cottages to the square foot, each equipped with a large motorboat. The sound of a 40-horsepower Chris-Craft going through a sea of number-ten oil has to be heard to be believed. RRRRRRRAAAAAAAAHHHHHHHHHWWWWWWWWWWR 33 RRRRRRRR!

The prow is sort of parting the stuff, slowly stirring it into a 34 sluggish, viscous wake.

Natives actually *swim* in this water. Of course, it is impossible 35 to swim near the shore, because the shore is one great big sea of mud that goes all the way down to the core of the earth. There are stories of whole towns being swallowed up and stored in the middle of the earth. So the native rows out to the middle of the lake and hurls himself off the back seat of his rowboat.

"GLURP!" 36

It is impossible to sink in this water. The specific gravity and 37 surface tension make the Great Salt Lake seem dangerous for swimming. You don't sink. You just bounce a little and float there. You literally have to hit your head on the surface of these lakes to get under a few inches. Once you do, you come up streaming mosquito eggs and dead toads—an Indiana specialty—and all sorts of fantastic things which are the offshoot of various exotic merriments which occur outside the Roller Rink.

The bottom of the lake is composed of a thick incrustation of 38 old beer cans. The beer cans are at least a thousand feet thick in certain places.

And so 17,000 fishermen gather in one knot, because it is 39 rumored that here is where The Deep Hold is. All Indiana lakes have a Deep Hole, into which, as the myth goes, the fish retire to sulk in the hot weather. Which is always.

❡ Is Shepherd exaggerating—what scholars call using hyperbole? Would you want a storyteller who didn't exaggerate? It's interesting to note that Shepherd paces this the way Angelou paced hers. He takes plenty of time to set the scene. ❡

40   Every month or so an announcement would be made by my Old Man, usually on a Friday night, after work.

41   "I'm getting up early tomorrow morning. I'm going fishing."

42   Getting up early and going fishing with Hairy Gertz and the crowd meant getting out of the house about three o'clock in the afternoon, roughly. Gertz was a key member of the party. He owned the Coleman lamp. It was part of the folklore that if you had a bright lantern in your boat the fish could not resist it. The idea was to hold the lantern out over the water and the fish would have to come over to see what was going on. Of course, when the fish arrived, there would be your irresistible worm, and that would be it.

43   Well, these Coleman lamps may not have drawn fish, but they worked great on mosquitoes. One of the more yeasty experiences in Life is to occupy a tiny rented rowboat with eight other guys, knee-deep in beer cans, with a blinding Coleman lamp hanging out of the boat, at 2 A.M., with the lamp hissing like Fu Manchu about to strike and every mosquito in the Western Hemisphere descending on you in the middle of Cedar Lake.

44   ZZZZZZZZZZZZZZZZZZZZZZTTTTTTTTTTT

45   They *love* Coleman lamps. In the light they shed the mosquitoes swarm like rain. And in the darkness all around there'd be other lights in other boats, and once in a while a face would float above one. Everyone is coated with an inch and a half of something called citronella, reputedly a mosquito repellent but actually a sort of mosquito salad dressing.

46   The water is absolutely flat. There has not been a breath of air since April. It is now August. The surface is one flat sheet of old used oil laying in the darkness, with the sounds of the Roller Rink floating out over it, mingling with the angry drone of the mosquitoes and muffled swearing from the other boats. A fistfight breaks out at the Evening In Paris. The sound of sirens can be heard faintly in the Indiana blackness. It gets louder and then fades away. Tiny orange lights bob over the dance floor.

47   "Raaahhhhhd sails in the sawwwwnnnnsehhhht. . ."

48   It's the drummer who sings. He figures some day Ted Weems will be driving by, and hear him, and. . . .

". . .haaaahhhhwwww brightlyyyy they shinneee. . ."   49

There is nothing like a band vocalist in a rotten, struggling   50
Mickey band. When you've heard him over 2000 yards of soupy, oily
water, filtered through fourteen billion feeding mosquitoes in the
August heat, he is particularly juicy and ripe. He is overloading the
ten-watt Allied Radio Knight amplifier by at least 400 per cent, the
gain turned all the way up, his chrome-plated bullet-shaped crystal
mike on the edge of feedback.

"Raaahhhhhd sails in the sawwwwnnnnsehhht. . ."   51

It is the sound of the American night. And to a twelve-year-old   52
kid it is exciting beyond belief."

Then my Old Man, out of the blue, says to me: 53

"You know, if you're gonna come along, you got to clean the   54
fish."

Gonna come along! My God! I wanted to go fishing more than   55
anything else in the world, and my Old Man wanted to drink beer
more than anything else in the world, and so did Gertz and the gang,
and more than even *that*, they wanted to get away from all the
women. They wanted to get out on the lake and tell dirty stories and
drink beer and get eaten by mosquitoes; just sit out there and sweat
and be Men. They wanted to get away from work, the car payments,
the lawn, the mill, and everything else.

And so here I am, in the dark, in a rowboat with The Men. I am   56
half-blind with sleepiness. I am used to going to bed at nine-thirty or
ten o'clock, and here it is two, three o'clock in the morning. I'm
squatting in the back end of the boat, with 87,000,000 mosquitoes
swarming over me, but I am *fishing!* I am out of my skull with fantastic excitement, hanging onto my pole.

In those days, in Indiana, they fished with gigantic cane poles.   57
They knew not from Spinning. A cane pole is a long bamboo pole
that's maybe twelve or fifteen feet in length; it weighs a ton, and tied
to the end of it is about thirty feet of thick green line, roughly half
the weight of the average clothesline, three big lead sinkers, a couple
of crappie hooks, and a bobber.

One of Sport's most exciting moments is when 7 Indiana fish-   58
ermen in the same boat simultaneously and without consulting one
another decide to pull their lines out of the water and recast. In total
darkness. First the pole, rising like a huge whip:

"Whoooooooooooooop!"   59

Then the lines, whirling overhead: 60

"Wheeeeeeeeooooooooooooo!"   61

62   And then:

63   "OH! FOR CHRISSAKE! WHAT THE HELL?"

64   Clunk! CLONK!

65   Sound of cane poles banging together, and lead weights landing in the boat. And such brilliant swearing as you have never heard. Yelling, hollering, with somebody always getting a hook stuck in the back of his ear. And, of course, all in complete darkness, the Coleman lamp at the other end of the rowboat barely penetrating the darkness in a circle of three or four feet.

66   "Hey, for God's sake, Gertz, will ya tell me when you're gonna pull your pole up!? Oh, Jesus Christ, look at this mess!"

67   There is nothing worse than trying to untangle seven cane poles, 200 feet of soggy green line, just as they are starting to hit in the other boats. Sound carries over water:

68   "Shhhhh! I got a bite!"

69   The fishermen with the tangled lines become frenzied. Fingernails are torn, hooks dig deeper into thumbs, and kids huddle terrified out of range in the darkness.

70   You have been sitting for twenty hours, and nothing. A bobber just barely visible in the dark water is one of the most beautiful sights known to man. It's not doing anything, but there's always the feeling that at any instant it might. It just lays out there in the darkness. A luminous bobber, a beautiful thing, with a long, thin quill and a tiny red-and-white float, with just the suggestion of a line reaching into the black water. These are special bobbers for *very* tiny fish.

71   I have been watching my bobber so hard and so long in the darkness that I am almost hypnotized. I have not had a bite—ever - but the excitement of being there is enough for me, a kind of delirious joy that has nothing to do with sex or any of the more obvious pleasures. To this day, when I hear some guy singing in that special drummer's voice, it comes over me. It's two o'clock in the morning again. I'm a kid. I'm tired. I'm excited. I'm having the time of my life.

72   And at the other end of the lake:

73   "Raaahhhhhd sails in the sawwwwnnnnsehhht. . ."

74   The Roller Rink drones on, and the mosquitoes are humming. The Coleman lamp sputters, and we're all sitting together in our little boat.

75   Not really together, since I am a kid, and they are Men, but at least I'm there. Gertz is stewed to the ears. He is down at the other end. He has this fantastic collection of rotten stories, and early in the evening my Old Man keeps saying:

"There's a kid with us, you know." 76

But by two in the morning all of them have had enough so 77
that it doesn't matter. They're telling stories, and I don't care. I'm
just sitting there, clinging to my cane pole when, by God, I get a
nibble!

I don't believe it. The bobber straightens up, jiggles, dips, and 78
comes to rest in the gloom. I whisper:

"I got a bite!" 79

The storytellers look from their beer cans in the darkness. 80

"What. . .? Hey, whazzat?" 81

"Shhhh! Be quiet!" 82

We sit in silence, everybody watching his bobber through the 83
haze of insects. The drummer is singing in the distance. We hang
suspended for long minutes. Then suddenly all the bobbers dipped
and went under. The crappies are biting!

You never saw anything like it! We are pulling up fish as fast as 84
we can get them off the hooks. Crappies are flying into the boat, one
after the other, and hopping around on the bottom in the darkness,
amid the empty beer cans. Within twenty minutes we have landed
forty-seven fish. We are knee-deep in crappies. The jackpot!

Well, the Old Man just goes wild. They are all yelling and 85
screaming and pulling the fish in—while the other boats around us
are being skunked. The fish have come out of their hole or whatever
it is that they are in at the bottom of the lake, the beer cans and the
old tires, and have decided to eat.

You can hear the rest of the boats pulling up anchors and row- 86
ing over, frantically. They are thumping against us. There's a big,
solid phalanx of wooden boats around us. You could walk from one
boat to the other for miles around. And still they are skunked. We are
catching the fish!

By 3 A.M. they've finally stopped biting, and an hour later we 87
are back on land. I'm falling asleep in the rear seat between Gertz
and Zudock. We're driving home in the dawn, and the men are hollering, drinking, throwing beer cans out on the road, and having a
great time.

We are back at the house, and my father says to me as we are 88
coming out of the garage with Gertz and the rest of them:

"And now Ralph's gonna clean the fish. Let's go in the house 89
and have something to eat. Clean 'em on the back porch, will ya,
kid?"

In the house they go. The lights go on in the kitchen; they sit 90

down and start eating sandwiches and making coffee. And I am out
on the back porch with forty-seven live-flopping crappies.

91   They are well named. Fish that are taken out of muddy, rotten,
lousy, stinking lakes are muddy, rotten, lousy, stinking fish. It is as
simple as that. And they are made out of some kind of hard rubber.

92   I get my Scout knife and go to work. Fifteen minutes and
twenty-one crappies later I am sick over the side of the porch. But I
do not stop. It is part of Fishing.

93   By now, nine neighborhood cats and a raccoon have joined me
on the porch, and we are all working together. The August heat, now
that we are away from the lake, is even hotter. The uproar in the
kitchen is getting louder and louder. There is nothing like a motley
collection of Indiana office workers who have just successfully
defeated Nature and have brought home the kill. Like cave men of
old, they celebrate around the campfire with song and drink. And
belching.

94   I have now finished the last crappie and am wrapping the clean
fish in the editorial page of the *Chicago Tribune*. It has a very tough
paper that doesn't leak. Especially the editorial page.

☞ Now we get to the true meaning of the piece. Watch carefully for
what happens between here and the end and how it happens. The
narrator is being accepted into manhood, and the author in his very
different voice from E. B. White's is just as serious in dealing with
just as important a subject. How can you avoid being excited about
being a writer when you can hear E. B. White and Jean Shepherd
talking about such important matters, each in his own way? ☜

95   The Old Man hollers out:

96   "How you doing? Come in and have a Nehi."

97   I enter the kitchen, blinded by that big yellow light bulb,
weighted down with a load of five-and-a-half-inch crappies, covered
with fish scales and blood, and smelling like the far end of Cedar
Lake. There are worms under my fingernails from baiting hooks all
night, and I am feeling at least nine feet tall. I spread the fish out on
the sink—and old Hairy Gertz says:

98   "My God! Look at those *speckled beauties*!" An expression he
had picked up from *Outdoor Life*.

99   The Old Man hands me a two-pound liverwurst sandwich and
a bottle of Nehi orange. Gertz is now rolling strongly, as are the other

eight file clerks, all smelly, and mosquito-bitten, eyes red-rimmed from the Coleman lamp, covered with worms and with the drippings of at least fifteen beers apiece. Gertz hollers:

"Ya know, lookin' at them fish reminds me of a story." He is 100 about to uncork his cruddiest joke of the night. They all lean forward over the white enamel kitchen table with the chipped edges, over the salami and the beer bottles, the rye bread and the mustard. Gertz digs deep into his vast file of obscenity.

"One time there was this Hungarian bartender, and ya know, 101 he had a cross-eyed daughter and a bowlegged dachshund. And this. . ."

At first I am holding back, since I am a kid. The Old Man says: 102

"Hold it down, Gertz. You'll wake up the wife and she'll raise 103 hell."

He is referring to My Mother. 104

Gertz lowers his voice and they all scrunch their chairs forward 105 amid a great cloud of cigar smoke. There is only one thing to do. I scrunch forward, too, and stick my head into the huddle, right next to the Old Man, into the circle of leering, snickering, fish-smelling faces. Of course, I do not even remotely comprehend the gist of the story. But I know that it is rotten to the core.

Gertz belts out the punch line; the crowd bellows and beats on 106 the table. They begin uncapping more Blatz.

Secretly, suddenly, and for the first time, I realize that I am In. 107 The Eskimo pies and Nehi oranges are all behind me, and a whole new world is stretching out endlessly and wildly in all directions before me. I have gotten The Signal!

Suddenly my mother is in the doorway in her Chinese-red 108 chenille bathrobe. Ten minutes later I am in the sack, and out in the kitchen Gertz is telling another one. The bottles are rattling, and the file clerks are hunched around the fire celebrating their primal victory over The Elements.

Somewhere off in the dark the Monon Louisville Limited wails 109 as it snakes through the Gibson Hump on its way to the outside world. The giant Indiana moths, at least five pounds apiece, are banging against the window screens next to my bed. The cats are fighting in the backyard over crappie heads, and fish scales are itching in my hair as I joyfully, ecstatically slide off into the great world beyond.

Discussion

- Discuss how Jean Shepherd fulfills Strunk's injunction.
- What are some of the distinctive elements of storytelling as demonstrated by Jean Shepherd? How is his work marked by the fact that he has spoken his stories so many times before writing them?
- In what significant ways do White's and Shepherd's essays differ? In what ways are they similar?
- How does Shepherd's essay compare to other autobiographical essays in the book?
- How is the Shepherd piece paced and organized?
- Is the importance of the last pages foreshadowed early in the piece? Where and how?
- What does voice do for Shepherd, White, and others in the book?

Activities

- Taperecord the best storyteller you know and study the tape to see what it may teach you about writing.
- Taperecord yourself telling a story to some friends. Examine the tape to see how the telling is different from your writing.
- Take a subject you've written a draft on and without referring to the text taperecord your telling of it. Compare the tape and the text to see what you can learn from the telling to improve the written text.
- Take a draft you have written and read it into a taperecorder, adding anything that comes to mind or dropping anything out. In other words, work over the text orally to see how speaking can change and improve the text.
- Listen to someone else telling a story and write it down later to see if you can capture the story and the way it was told.
- Write an account of an event that signaled your acceptance into adulthood.

7

A Meaning Made Clear

The most satisfying part of the writing process comes when there is a draft that can be shaped into meaning by the writer's hand. After all the planning, the collecting, the focusing, the ordering, and the drafting, there is at last a text. The writer is no longer dealing with intangibles, but with the reality of language.

The first thing the writer has to do is to stand back and read the entire text at a distance, sometimes even roleplaying a particular reader to discover what has been said, which is never quite the same as what the writer intended to say. The reading writer is usually disappointed, for the text rarely matches the dream that was in the writer's mind, but the writer is often intrigued by the unexpected that appears on the page. The text is not the dream, it is something both less and more than the dream.

It is helpful if the writer can avoid asking if the text is right or wrong, good or bad. More helpful questions are, "What works?" and "What needs work?" The writer has, first of all, to recognize those elements in the text, such as subject, or organization, or voice that are strong or potentially strong in the draft. Once the writer has discovered the strength of the text the writer can go on to discover its weaknesses. Drafts are not so much corrected against some absolute scale as they are improved on their own terms, worked over until the strengths are made stronger and the weaknesses made strong. School too often gives the young writer an idea that a text can be corrected as if there were an absolute right or wrong. But what works and doesn't work in writing is a complicated matter of context. What works changes according to the writer's purpose, the needs of the reader, the demands of the subject matter itself, the traditions of the form, and the interaction of all the elements in the writing—fact against fact, large structure against small structure, line against sentence, word against phrase. A piece of writing is a living organism, growing to fulfill its own needs.

The writer has to see the entire text. Usually it is helpful for me to sit back in a comfortable chair, to read it as fast as a reader will read it, not putting pen to paper, but swooping over the landscape of the text, seeing the bigger accomplishments and larger failures. The writer, of course, is asking at this stage, "Do I have anything to say? Do I have the information with which to say it? Can it be said?"

The Craft of Revision

If the answer is no, then the writer has to revise, and revise means going back through the planning process, making sure that there is a subject, that there is an adequate inventory of information about the subject, that the piece of writing has a focus and a structure that supports that focus. Too often revision is thought of as a separate writing act that occurs after a draft. It does occur at that time, but it is a reseeing and a rewriting that means, for the writer, replanning.

Rewriting is too often seen as punishment. It is not. It is opportunity, a chance to make meaning clear. As Neil Simon says, "Rewriting is when playwriting really gets to be fun. In baseball you only get three swings and you're out. In rewriting, you get almost as many swings as you want and you know, sooner or later, you'll hit the ball." When rewriting, the writer has the chance to use all the elements of craft, and watching that craft at work is like seeing a photograph coming clear in a tray of chemicals.

Many people make the mistake of plunging immediately into editing. If there is no subject, no information, no structure, then it is impossible to do effective line-by-line editing. The writer saves time by scanning the piece first and answering the larger questions of content and form before attempting to clarify the meaning line by line.

The Craft of Editing

When the larger questions are answered, the writer can go to work, reading the piece carefully paragraph by paragraph, sentence by sentence, phrase by phrase, word by word. Now the writer has the delight of doing the fine work, the cutting and adding and reordering which, when the writing is successful, makes the meaning come clear with an invisible skill. The writer, as editor, is continuously trying to remove the writer from the text, finding a way to make the text immediate to the writer. The writer usually does not want to be standing between the subject and the reader pointing out what is important, but revealing the importance to the reader so the reader discovers the significance directly.

All the selections in this chapter are designed to show how meaning can be made clear. A science writer and a scientist write each in their own way on the same subject. Two journalists report on the bombing of Japan. Members of two ethnic communities reveal their Americas. An economist and two historians counsel us on the discipline of time and the discipline of writing. All of these matters are complicated and could be written in a complicated way. But these writers have found how to make the complex clear.

Denise Grady has revealed some of her craft to us, but behind all of these pieces, all of the other pieces in this book, and all of the effective writing you read there are many acts of craft that have been performed and then made invisible. The work has been done and the craftsperson has cleared up afterward, so that what remains appears natural—the shelf looks as if it had always clung to that wall.

Many writers do not know what they do; they just do it, the way a basketball player doesn't think, "I have to shift the ball to my left hand and get my body between the ball and the guard." The guard moves and the experienced player reacts. Here are some pieces of advice and some tricks of the trade that may be helpful as you edit your own text, reacting to your draft in such a way that your meaning is made to come clear:

- *If It Can Be Cut, Cut It.* Everything in a piece of writing should advance the meaning. That does not mean that you should write in a staccato style likeamachinegun, but that everything in the text must contribute to the clarification of meaning. There may be a time to slow the text down, to repeat, to turn a fine phrase, but whatever is done must make the meaning clear.

- *Define* those words, ideas, or pieces of information that are essential to the reader's understanding of the text. But try, whenever possible, to work the definition right into the sentence at the time the reader needs to know it, sometimes using clauses. A definition should rarely be a big chunk of material dumped on the reader before the reader needs to know it, or when it is too late to assist the reader in understanding the text.
- *Be Specific.* The reader needs accurate, concrete information. The reader wants the authority of such specific details, and the reader needs information on which to base the reader's own conclusions. Specific information gives a piece of writing vigor and liveliness. Although it is logical to write in generalities and abstractions when appealing to a large audience, every writer has learned that the larger the audience the more important it is to reveal the subject in specific terms.
- *Document* each point with evidence that will convince the reader of the authority of the text. Readers cannot be expected to take a piece of writing on faith. They need facts, statistics, quotations, description, anecdotes, all sorts of documentation.
- *Write Short* for emphasis. Brevity gives vigor and clarity. The more complicated the subject, the harder to understand, the more important it is to use the shortest words, the shortest sentences, the shortest paragraphs that communicate the meaning without oversimplifying and distorting it.
- *Achieve Brevity by Selection.* Inexperienced writers try to compress everything into tiny pellets of text. Experienced writers achieve brevity by selecting those pieces of evidence, for example, that are necessary to the reader, and then develop them fully.
- *Edit with Your Ear*, reading and rereading aloud so that the final text has the flow and ease of natural speech. The reader should have the illusion of hearing the text, the illusion of an individual writer speaking directly to an individual reader.
- *Write with Verbs and Nouns*, active verbs and proper nouns whenever possible. Lean on verbs and nouns and avoid adverbs and adjectives, especially at important points in the text. Do not try to put words on the page that may surround

a meaning, but try to find those words that precisely express meaning.

- *Respect the Subject-Verb-Object Sentence.* Turn to it when meaning becomes unclear or where an important point has to be made. Beware of sentences that are unnecessarily complex and go in circles of clauses, like a puppy chasing its own tail.
- *Aim for Simplicity.* You want to make the writing look easy. Of course you don't want it so easy that it does not tell the truth of your subject, but you should not write to complicate or to impress; you should write to communicate.
- *Say One Thing* and say it well. There should be a dominant meaning in your piece. Your sentences should carry one bit of information to your reader. Your paragraphs should develop one idea. Of course there are exceptions. There must be variety in writing, but the focus of the writing should be in the development of single pieces of information that add up to one overall meaning.
- *Clarify* what you have to say and you will find that you are following the traditions of language most of the time. When the writing doesn't come clear look to what you have to say and make sure that you know what you want to say. If it still isn't clear, look to the traditions of language to see what principles and rules may help you clarify the text. But, as George Orwell reminded us, never follow a rule that does not help make meaning clear.
- *Write the Truth.* People sometimes feel that writing is a dishonest trade. Certainly there are politicians, public relations spokesmen, and advertising writers who try to use language in a dishonest way. And sometimes they succeed. But the fact that some drivers drive to endanger does not mean we should imitate them. The most effective writing is honest, and the reader recognizes that honesty.

The lessons of a lifetime spent in the pursuit of craft, a lifetime of trying to write with increasing clarity, vigor, accuracy and grace cannot be summed up in a few pages, but the counsel of experienced writers expressed in the list above and practiced in the texts that follow express attitudes as well as skills. The purpose of writing is to learn and to share that learning. The purpose of revising and editing is to make meaning come clear, first to the writer, then to the reader.

Case Study: A Science Writer Writes and Reads

Denise Grady

Many of our best writers were not English majors. (The reverse is also true: many of our worst student writers are English majors.) Denise Grady majored in biology at the State University of New York at Stony Brook and worked as an editor at *Physics Today* before going to the University of New Hampshire, where she received a master's degree in writing and also taught writing. Grady was an assistant editor at the *New England Journal of Medicine*, a senior editor of *Medical Month*, and a staff writer for three years at *Discover*, a science magazine published by Time, Inc. She is the author of more than 50 magazine articles, most of them dealing with science and medicine. The article published here is a health column written for *Newsday*.

Grady does a lot of writing in her head, which is a fine place to work, but she has given us some interesting examples of false starts with her marginal comments saying why she found them false.

FALSE STARTS

Today, more and more couples are finding out that
they cannot have children. According to WHOEVER TK, some
TK% of American couples are infertile, a TK% increase over
the YEAR TK figure. The rise has two probable causes: an
increase in the rates of sexually transmitted diseases,
which can damage the female reproductive system, and

*Wrong focus.
not a
piece about
infertility*

An Australian woman who thought she would never be
able to have children gave birth to quadruplets
last winter, four little boys who were conceived outside
her body when doctors mixed her eggs and her husband's sperm
in laboratory dishes.

*Wrong focus, too
slow—
not about
multiple
births*

Has medical technology solved the problem of infertility?
Clinics specializing in in vitro fertilization—"test-tube
babies"—are springing up across the United States, offering
hope to the NUMBER TK Americans couples who cannot have
children on their own. According to the American Fertility
Society, there are now NUMBER TK hospital based in vitro
programs in TK states. And private clinics are also getting
into the business.

*Just
too
flat.
And it's a
lazy + a
cop-out to
start
with a
question.*

Grady has also provided some early drafts of the paragraphs she reworked the most, with marginal comments showing the problems she experienced.

Early

Draft of paragraph 3, 4

I thought of leaving this paragraph in the lead, but decided that's a tired device

She was, the doctors said, an ideal candidate for in vitro fertili~ation. All that kept her from getting pregnant were blockages in the Fallopian tubes, the ~~passages~~ ~~an egg would normally travel through in order to get from~~ ~~the ovary to the uterus~~ the passages where an egg is normally fettilized, *on its way from* ~~and through~~ ~~which it must pass to get from~~ the ovary to the uterus. ~~the passages leading from ovary at to uterus~~

The in vitro procedure would, ~~in essence~~ bypass the blocked tubes: eggs would be surgically removed from her ovaries, *fertilized with what?* fertilized in a dish outside her body, and, if fertilization occurred, transferred back into her uterus. With luck, one would implant itself there and grow into a ~~normal~~ *redundant* healthy baby.

She and her husband decided to try it. (They had been trying to conceive for several years; surgery could not open her tubes,) surgery had not helped, she was in her mid-thirties, and time was running out. *Just seems to read better* The couple traveled from New York to the Yale University — *This is* Medical Center, in New Haven. The procedure seemed to go well: hormone treatments before surgery made ~~the ovaries~~ *makes* *makes them mature; they don't want them released.* ~~release~~ four eggs, ~~simultaneously, instead of the usual~~ *is usu :)* (one a month), and all four fertilized and were placed into her uterus.

Early draft of paragraph 8 (p. 4 of final version)

Like Linda and Bill, some NUMBER OR % TK American couples are infertile. Their numbers are growing, probably because of the increase in sexually transmitted infections that damage the female xpdmx reproductive organs, and because more women are *postponing pregnancy until* ~~trying to start their families later in life~~, ~~start families in~~ their thirties, when fertility may begin to decline. Many of these couples look to in vitro fertilization clinics for a solution. For some, the procedure works. But most wind up like Linda and Bill.

tighten

But I haven't said how these 2 wound up yet.

What follows are several pages from Grady's last draft before the final version, with the changes she edited into the text and her comments about why she made those *changes*.

Last draft ~~ith final ~~~~.

They may well be the happiest parents in the world--

the couples who, once told they would never have

children, have now become families with the aid of

the ~~pree~~ medical technology known as in vitro

fertilization. ~~Their appearances~~ pictures of them and their babies on television

and in newspapers and magazines have undoubtedly

~~spurred~~- inspired ~~hundreds~~ the thousands of other childless couples who have put

~~to check in~~ their names on waiting lists at ~~the~~ in vitro clinics that are

opening all across ~~the country~~. America.

more definite this way, with "the" -- and there are thousands

a new piece of information

But how many of these couples ~~really~~ understand

what they're getting into--the physical and emotional

stress, and the expense they will have to ~~incur~~ for what amounts

to a small chance of getting pregnant? ~~Aixiaaa~~ One For

New Yorker, ~~aaa has described~~ in vitro fertilization turned out to be

~~as~~ "one of the most emotionally disturbing things

my husband and I have ever been through."

Surgery had failed → ~~could~~ ...~~~
Cut

Doctors had told ~~Linda~~ Linda she was an ideal candidate for
the procedure.
~~in vitro fertilization.~~ All that kept her from having

a baby were ~~blockages in her~~ blocked F-llopian tubes, the two

passages where eggs are normally fertilized on their

way from the ovaries to the uterus. The in vitro ~~procedure~~

would ~~essentially~~ bypass the ~~blocked tubes~~ eggs would

be surgically removed from ~~Linda's~~ Linda's ovaries, mixed with

her husband's sperm in a laboratory dish, and, if

fertilization occurred, transferred back into her

uterus. with luck, one would implant itself ~~itself~~

there and grow into a ~~normal,~~ healthy baby.

She and her husband Bill decided to ~~try~~ it, ~~she~~

was in her mid-thirties, and time was running out.

~~The couple traveled from Manhattan to~~ at the Yale Univer-

sity Medical Center, in New Haven. There, the pro-

cedure seemed to go well. Hormone treatments before

I'm trying to quickly to define & explain procedure.

A little more dramatic this way! somehow?

surgery made ~~Linda's ovaries release four eggs, instead~~ four of Linda's eggs mature simultaneously (one a month is usual)

~~of the usual one at a time,~~ and all four were fertilized

and placed into her uterus.

Then she and Bill waited. Two weeks later, the dream

was over. She was not pregnant. But she thought, she had consoled herself with the first

come close enough to make it worth another try.

"This time," she says, "We decided to ~~go to~~ try the very

best experts in the country, Late last year, she and Bill went to the oldest and most suc-

cessful in vitro fertilization clinic in the U.S., established

in 1980 at the Eastern Virginia Medical School, in Norfolk. Again,

the prospects looked good. Doctors said she ~~had plenty~~

~~of healthy looking ovarian follicles~~ seemed to have

plenty of eggs that could be ~~matured~~ ripened with hormone shots.

Why introduce "follicles," which would simply need defining?

But they operated too late. The eggs, already

matured and released from the ovaries, were lost. ~~Jennie~~ Linda

She recalls,
and Bill were devastated. "The doctors said, 'Please

come back and let us try again. You're such a good

candidate.' They said they were learning that they

There is no professional body that enforces

practice standards at these clinics or keeps track

of how well they are doing, so patients have no ~~sure~~

~~Checking out clinics other than calling to ask~~

way ~~of telling whether or not they are in exper-~~

~~ienced hands.~~ Their success rates. Calls to the

three clinics that opened in the New York area in

early 1983 yielded the following information ⊙

Unfortunately, the only way to get good at in vitro is to practice on patients.

most of which opened in 1983, have been going through

similar periods of trial and error. When ~~they~~ ^novices^ do

achieve a ~~fixat~~ pregnancy, they may not be sure

what ~~they fin~~ they've finally done right.

insert →

~~Success rates vary~~. In the New York area,

three hospitals opened in vitro clinics ~~in~~ early in

1983. At North Shore University Hospital, in Manhasset,

TK patients have tried the treatment; TK got pregnant, TK

Statistics to come

already
miscarried, and TK have given birth. At Manhattan☺s

Columbia Presbyterian ··edical Center, - ----

Finally, at the Mount Sinai Medical Center, also in

Manhattan, -----

but they are difficult to compare, because they depend

and the patient's age.
to some degree on the cause of the infertility. Women

under 40 with blocked tubes have the best chance.o☒x

Here is Grady's final draft of the column.

In Vitro Fertilization: It Doesn't Always Work

They may well be the happiest parents in the world—the couples who, once told they would never have children, have now become families with the aid of the medical technology known as in vitro fertilization. Pictures of them on television and in the newspapers, cuddling their babies, have undoubtedly inspired the thousands of other couples who have put their names on waiting lists at in vitro clinics that are opening all across America.

But how many of these couples understand what they're getting into—the physical and emotional stress, and the expense they will have to incur for what amounts to a small chance of getting pregnant? For one New Yorker, in vitro fertilization turned out to be "one of the most emotionally disturbing things my husband and I have ever been through."

Linda's doctors had told her she was an ideal candidate for the procedure. All that kept her from having a baby were blocked Fallopian tubes—the two passages where eggs are normally fertilized on their way from the ovaries to the uterus. Surgery had failed to open the tubes. But the in vitro technique would bypass them: eggs would be surgically removed from Linda's ovaries, mixed with her husband's sperm in a laboratory dish, and, if fertilization occurred, transferred back into her uterus. With luck, one would implant itself there and grow into a healthy baby.

> ❧Note how neatly Grady works in the scientific exposition, relating the explanation to a single human being. Grady provides definitions at the point the reader needs them and they are woven right into the text. ❧

Linda was in her mid-thirties, and time was running out. She and her husband Bill decided to go for it, at the Yale University Medical Center, in New Haven, which opened its in vitro clinic in the spring of 1982. There, the procedure seemed to go well. Hormone treatments before surgery made four of Linda's eggs mature (one a month is usual), and all four were fertilized and placed into her uterus.

5   Then she and Bill waited. Two weeks later, the dream was over. She was not pregnant. But she consoled herself with the thought that she had come close enough to make it worth another try.

6   "This time," she says, "we decided to try the very best experts in the country." Late last year, she and Bill went to the oldest and most successful in vitro fertilization clinic in the United States, established in 1980 at the Eastern Virginia Medical School, in Norfolk. Again, the prospects looked good. Doctors said she seemed to have plenty of eggs that could be ripened with hormone shots.

7   But they operated too late. The eggs, already matured and released from the ovaries, were lost. Linda and Bill were devastated. She recalls, "The doctors said, 'Please come back and let us try again. You're such a good candidate.' They said they were learning that they couldn't assume all their patients ran on the same timetable, and next time around they'd operate on me sooner." Linda and Bill made an appointment to return to Eastern Virginia a few months later. But she wasn't looking forward to a third round of hormone treatments, general anesthesia, and surgery, and she and Bill weren't sure they could face another disappointment.

8   Like them, some 15 percent of married couples in America are infertile. Their numbers are growing, probably because of the increase in sexually transmitted infections that damage the female reproductive system, and because more women are postponing pregnancy until their thirties, when fertility may begin to decline. Many of these couples are heartbroken, and willing to put up with any hardship for even the smallest chance of having a baby. They see in vitro fertilization as their only hope.

❡ Grady gives us the background to understand the subject in context. ❷

9   How realistic is this hope? For some, the procedure does work: more than 100 in vitro babies have been born in the United States. But most couples are not so lucky. Indeed, the standing joke among gynecologists is that more women get pregnant on the waiting lists than in the clinics. Actually, pregnancy rates range from zero to 20 percent at in vitro clinics, according to a survey of 37 hospital-based clinics published last spring in *Medical Month* magazine. Eastern Virginia is the exception, reporting an overall pregnancy rate of 30 percent, and a rate of 38 percent during the past six months, among women who had three embryos transferred to the uterus. This

appears to be even better than nature, which gives a couple trying to conceive the usual way about a 20 percent chance of success each month.

But these clinic rates are inflated, because they don't include all 10 patients. Rather, the figures are based only on the number of women able to have fertilized eggs transferred into the uterus. Patients at Eastern Virginia are not even counted if, as happened on Linda's second try, eggs cannot be recovered, or if they are recovered but fail to fertilize. Moreover, not every pregnancy survives: miscarriage rates can run as high as 30 percent to 50 percent, two to three times the rate in naturally occurring pregnancies. Many women who have had children by in vitro fertilization have undergone the procedure— including surgery and general anesthesia repeatedly, some as many as seven times. And they are charged about $5,000 for each attempt; insurance coverage varies.

The disappointing statistics reflect the difficulty of the proce- 11 dure. It may sound like a straightforward matter to take an egg from a woman, fertilize it, and put it back. But it's not that simple. While the patient is taking hormones, she has to have daily blood tests and ultrasound exams to monitor the ripening of the eggs, which must be removed during the short period when they're mature but not yet released from the ovaries. Then the eggs are incubated in a nutrient solution for a few hours before being mixed with a measured amount of specially treated sperm from the patient's husband. Forty hours later, if fertilization has occurred and the embryos have begun dividing normally, they're transferred into the woman's uterus.

Things can go wrong at any point—with the hormonal stimu- 12 lation, egg retrieval, fertilization, or implantation. Even if they all go well, the woman can still miscarry. Failures are rarely explainable. Was it timing, temperature, nutrients, or handling? A defective egg or sperm? Or something in the woman's physiology?

❡With the subjects Grady writes about, she must document what she has to say. Note how skillfully—and gracefully—she does that.❡

Each new in vitro clinic has to work the bugs out of its tech- 13 niques. Even Eastern Virginia had its growing pains—namely, a year and a half during which none of its patients got pregnant. The other 35 clinics polled by *Medical Month* magazine, most of which opened in 1983, have been going through similar periods of trial and error. Unfortunately, the only way to get good at in vitro is to practice it—

on patients. When novices do achieve a pregnancy, they may not be sure what they've finally done right. There is no professional body that enforces practice standards at in vitro clinics or keeps track of how well they are doing, so patients have no easy means of checking up on the clinics.

14   In the New York area, four hospitals have in vitro programs: North Shore University Hospital, in Manhasset; Glen Cove Community Hospital; and the Mount Sinai and Columbia Presbyterian medical centers, both in Manhattan. At North Shore, 35 patients have been treated, but the hospital will not reveal how they've fared, because they're already under stress, according to a spokesman, and "we don't want to put them under a microscope." At Glen Cove, about a dozen patients have been treated, and the team is hoping that a recent, promising one will be the first to get pregnant. The Mount Sinai program has treated 42 couples and produced one pregnancy; because of this low success rate, the program stopped temporarily to analyze its problems, and is about to reopen, with an emphasis on new methods of hormone therapy and selection of younger patients. At Columbia, 15 patients had undergone embryo transfer as of last January, and three were pregnant. Many others had begun the program but never made it to the transfer stage, a spokesman says. New figures are not available because of the current hospital strike.

> ❦ Grady has to know her audience and answer its questions. NEWSDAY is published on Long Island, near New York City. The reader asks, "Where can I get help or information near here? How are our local centers doing?" Grady hears her readers' questions and answers them. ❦

15   The one encouraging note is that success rates are climbing, gradually, at most clinics, as medical teams learn more about handling human eggs and sperm and using hormones to prime the body for pregnancy. In fact, Dr. Victor Reyniak, head of the team at Mount Sinai, says it is reasonable for women under the age of 36 to postpone in vitro for a year or two, to take advantage of the better odds that the future will bring.

> ❦ Grady ends on a note of hope, and ties this technical subject back to an individual couple so that the medical facts are related to a person. She also shows, rather than tells, about one alternative: adoption. ❦

For those who can't seem to beat the odds, there may be other 16
solutions. Linda and Bill, for instance, were packing for a return trip
to Eastern Virginia when a phone call from their lawyer changed
their plans. They emptied the suitcases, cancelled the appointment
in Norfolk, and went out to buy clothes for the newborn baby who
was waiting for them to adopt him.

Discussion

• Discuss the problems of the science writer whose job is to communicate complex information that is important to the reader.
• Discuss the ways in which the reader can be given definitions when
needed.
• Discuss how Grady paces the piece, getting the reader interested in
the human problem with a large proportion of information about the effect
on people, and then switches gears to deliver a large proportion of exposition. Consider how this can be applied to other forms of writing.
• Compare Grady's problems and techniques to Freda's, Selzer's, and
other writers in the text.
• This column was written for a newspaper, as was Scanlan's. Are
there any generalizations you can make from these two pieces about newswriting as compared to other forms of nonfiction writing?
• How might this piece be written differently if Grady had done it for
a science magazine? For a book on in vitro fertilization?

Activities

• Write a newspaper column on a subject of importance to readers
on which you are an authority or can become an authority. Submit it to a
campus or local newspaper.
• Choose a complicated subject you know or care about and use Grady's techniques to write about it.
• Choose a subject you and your readers need to know about and list
the places where you can get information about it.
• Go through one of your drafts and see if there are places where the
reader needs a definition woven into the text.
• Go through a draft of your own and list the questions the readers
will ask in the margin. Answer them.

How the Column Was Written

1   Whenever I sit down to write an article or an essay, I force myself to write a sentence or two summarizing what I'm trying to say. If I can't do it, or if I have to keep rethinking my purpose as I write, I know I'm in trouble; I've got some long nights and a lot of false starts ahead of me. When I'm really struggling I feel like the college student who, going over a paper with a writing-teacher friend of mine, blurted, "Why does everything have to have a goddamn *point*?" and burst into tears.

2   The piece included here is a health column I wrote on assignment for the Long Island, New York, newspaper *Newsday*. The choice of subject was mine, and I started out with a pretty clear idea of what was on my mind: "In vitro fertilization requires a lot of time and money, and involves risk and pain, all for a very small chance of success. Some hospitals are a lot better at it than others."

3   I wanted to write the column because research I'd done previously on the topic for a medical magazine convinced me that all the media hype about test tube babies is obscuring the truth about this procedure. I hoped especially to make readers aware of the extent to which in vitro teams are using patients for on-the-job training. This is apparently the only way they can learn the techniques, and I'm not condemning that. What does disturb me is the impression I've gotten, that these patients—who are so desperate for babies that they'll try anything—think the in vitro doctors know exactly what they're doing. I know what it is to want children, and I'm not trying to destroy the hopes of childless couples. But I am trying to destroy false hopes.

4   One issue I often grapple with in reporting on medicine is what to say about medical practices that look bad to me. In researching this subject, for instance, I saw a surgical resident teaching a medical student how to work a trochar—a metal tube with a point attached to one end, which is used by in vitro surgeons to punch through a woman's navel and introduce other instruments into the abdomen. The unconscious patient they were practicing on was a woman about my age. I had talked to her before the operation; she was trusting and optimistic and very eager to have a baby. They poked that thing around inside her like a pair of plumbers. Later, the photographer I was working with described their technique to another surgeon, who said, "Well, you can do it that way nine times out of ten. But the

tenth time you might puncture the patient's gut." Which might kill her, or at least make her very sick.

Is it fair to report this? Only if you're sure it's bad practice. To find out, you've got to watch more operations, talk to more surgeons, give the plumbers a chance to defend themselves. What's the right way to handle a trochar? Have there been mishaps? Do most hospitals let students practice on unconscious patients? Had the patient given permission?

Some people would say it's unfair *not* to report this, because the public has a right to know what goes on in hospitals. But people also have a right not to be scared unnecessarily by sensationalistic reporting. The fact is, most surgery looks shocking. The first time I saw an operation, I was stunned by how crude and violent it seemed, how roughly the body was handled. Anybody who watches surgery—and I mean first-rate surgery—could describe it honestly in terms that would make an audience swear off doctors and hospitals for life. So I would have to do a lot of research to feel confident enough to write a story portraying a particular surgeon as a clod. It's just not enough to know in my gut that he is a clod.

But I can't turn every assignment into an exposé. Investigative reporting takes time, patient editors, lots of room for the story, and lots of money—either the publication's, or mine if I'm working freelance and the fee is the same regardless of how much time I spend reporting.

So sometimes I wind up compromising. I stick to what I *can* say, ever mindful of what I *want* to say, the gut feeling that would influence my choices if I were the patient or if I were speaking privately to a friend. Within my own arbitrary bounds of fairness I let what I want to say help shape the piece—the tone, the selection of material, the topic sentences that set the course for each paragraph. In this case, the job was not difficult, because the failure rates at the clinics tell their own story.

As I reread my drafts, I'm constantly checking to make sure I can back up what I've said, and have been faithful to what I perceive as the spirit of the piece.

So much for the moral tribulations of a medical reporter. I fret just as much over technical matters of writing. Like most writers, I can't really get anywhere until I've come up with a decent lead. I want those first few paragraphs to be interesting, and also to reveal where the piece is going. I've come to despise myself for resorting to the hack medical writer's anecdotal lead of the "Mary woke up one morning with a pain in her toe" variety. I almost gave up and used one for this in vitro piece. Paragraph three was nearly the lead, but it made me cringe every time I reread it. And it took too long to get to the point. So I wrote two opening paragraphs and stuck them in front of the sad story of Linda, and found myself in business.

11   Once I'm satisfied that the lead has put an article on course, the most important things I look for are organization and something that writing textbooks call "coherence." I don't think I got control of these until I began writing articles regularly and seeing editors turn them inside out regularly. Wounded pride and frustration made me determined to put my pieces together so tightly and logically that they would need no rearranging, and editors would find them hard to cut. I accomplished one of these goals: I learned how to organize an article and construct paragraphs well enough so that editors would leave the structure alone. But editors always want to cut, and as my sense of structure became stronger and stronger, I found that the cutting was more and more often left to me. Which is both a reward and a punishment.

12   I find that to organize an article I need a thorough understanding of my material and what I'm trying to do with it. Then I've got to figure out what my main ideas are, how they're related to one another, and the most logical way to order them. I usually do this by drawing up lists or even writing a series of rough topic sentences to be fleshed out into paragraphs. I rarely follow these to the letter; sometimes the ideas change in the writing.

13   Coherence pertains more to the paragraphs themselves. I use the term to mean a smooth, logical flow of ideas that lets the audience read without having to double back, skip ahead, or stop to wonder if the piece is going anywhere. Every sentence has a reason for being where it is, a link to the one before and one after. The transitions from one paragraph to another are strong—and by strong I don't mean heavy-handed, just clearly reasoned.

14   Once I've got a piece put together to my satisfaction, I look at stylistic details like punctuation, word choice, and conciseness, and I labor over spontaneous touches of grace and wit, which I think I manage to achieve about once every three articles. I can't explain every change; some just feel right, and I trust my instincts. I look for places to plug in leftover facts, and I check to see if my explanations and definitions—especially of scientific concepts—make sense. But I have to confess that I've never disciplined myself to ignore these

things while writing, and I do slow myself down by diddling with words and semicolons and phrases all along the way. This is a particularly stupid waste of time, because it hurts much more later to drop a paragraph I've labored over than one I've whipped out.

By the time I'm through with all this reading and rereading, I've 15 practically memorized my article. The drafts are usually black with cross-outs, because I'm so humiliated by my mistakes that I have to obliterate them. Once an article is published, I usually try to avoid reading it again, because I know I'll find things I should have said better.

Lewis Thomas

Dr. Lewis Thomas, President of The Memorial Sloan-Kettering Cancer Center in New York City, is a distinguished scientist whose collections of essays have won national awards and made him a best seller. In this short essay he writes in the same territory as Grady from his own perspective.

On Embryology

A short while ago, in mid-1978, the newest astonishment in 1 medicine, covering all the front pages, was the birth of an English baby nine months after conception in a dish. The older surprise, which should still be fazing us all, is that a solitary sperm and a single egg can fuse and become a human being under any circumstance, and that, however implanted, a mere cluster of the progeny of this fused cell affixed to the uterine wall will grow and differentiate into eight pounds of baby; this has been going on under our eyes for so long a time that we've gotten used to it; hence the outcries of amazement at this really minor technical modification of the general procedure—nothing much, really, beyond relocating the beginning of the process from the fallopian tube to a plastic container and, perhaps worth mentioning, the exclusion of the father from any role likely to add, with any justification, to his vanity.

There is, of course, talk now about extending the technology 2 beyond the act of conception itself, and predictions are being made that the whole process of embryonic development, all nine months of it, will ultimately be conducted in elaborate plastic flasks. When this happens, as perhaps it will someday, it will be another surprise, with more headlines. Everyone will say how marvelously terrifying is the new power of science, and arguments over whether science should be stopped in its tracks will preoccupy senatorial subcommittees, with more headlines. Meanwhile, the sheer incredibility of the process itself, whether it occurs in the uterus or *in* some sort of vitro, will probably be overlooked as much as it is today.

❡ It is instructive to follow how Thomas develops his idea and the way he uses specific images to allow us to see the wonders to which he is calling our attention. ❡

3   For the real amazement, if you want to be amazed, is the process. You start out as a single cell derived from the coupling of a sperm and an egg, this divides into two, then four, then eight, and so on, and at a certain stage there emerges a single cell which will have as all its progeny the human brain. The mere existence of that cell should be one of the great astonishments of the earth. People ought to be walking around all day, all through their waking hours, calling to each other in endless wonderment, talking of nothing except that cell. It is an unbelievable thing, and yet there it is, popping neatly into its place amid the jumbled cells of every one of the several billion human embryos around the planet, just as if it were the easiest thing in the world to do.

4   If you like being surprised, there's the source. One cell is switched on to become the whole trillion-cell, massive apparatus for thinking and imagining and, for that matter, being surprised. All the information needed for learning to read and write, playing the piano, arguing before senatorial subcommittees, walking across a street through traffic, or the marvelous human act of putting out one hand and leaning against a tree, is contained in that first cell. All of grammar, all syntax, all arithmetic, all music.

5   It is not known how the switching on occurs. At the very beginning of an embryo, when it is still nothing more than a cluster of cells, all of this information and much more is latent inside every cell in the cluster. When the stem cell for the brain emerges, it could be that the special quality of brainness is simply switched on. But it could as well be that everything else, every other potential property, is switched off, so that this most specialized of all cells no longer has

its precursors' option of being a thyroid or a liver or whatever, only a brain.

No one has the ghost of an idea how this works, and nothing 6 else in life can ever be so puzzling. If anyone does succeed in explaining it, within my lifetime, I will charter a skywriting airplane, maybe a whole fleet of them, and send them aloft to write one great exclamation point after another, around the whole sky, until all my money runs out.

Discussion

• To me, his piece of writing defines the essay, a form of writing in which the writer thinks about a subject and invites the reader to think as well. Discuss the qualities of an essay and consider how an argument, for example, differs from an essay. Discuss what other pieces in the book might be called essays, and why.

• Compare how the Thomas essay differs from Selzer's, from Grady's, from Freda's.

• Consider how the Thomas piece is similar to Roethke, to Trillin, to White.

• Discuss how Thomas makes complicated matters clear.

• Discuss how important Thomas's voice is in the piece. Identify examples of that voice. Imagine how the piece might have been written by Shepherd or Syfers or King.

Activities

• Write a short essay making readers aware of the wonderment of something in their life, being as specific as Thomas.

• Look at one of your drafts and imagine what Thomas might say about it. See if what he says makes sense and improves the draft.

• In a piece of writing explain why you feel strongly about something in such a way that the reader will feel strongly too.

• Redraft Thomas's piece as the introduction to a proposal for research funding in embryology.

• Use Thomas's words to make a short poem from his piece.

William L. Laurence

I remember how excited I was when I met William L. Laurence of *The New York Times*. I was a young editorial writer, writing pieces on science and the military, and here was the dean of science writers, the journalist who had been chosen to be allowed behind the scenes of the creation of atomic power and its terrible weapons. What do I remember of the meeting? Not much. He seemed a shy man, who was obviously a good observer and a good listener, the sort of ordinary man with whom you'd like to talk, a person who would nod and grunt in delight at your explanations. He was like other journalists I know who are reprinted in this book—Scanlan, McPhee, Zinsser, Grady—the kind of person who would sit beside you on a long plane flight, and after you got off the plane, you realized how much you talked and how much your companion seemed to enjoy your talking. As you read the article below, note how much Laurence has observed and how well he must have listened to deliver the information he had to report to the world.

Atomic Bombing of Nagasaki Told by Flight Member

1   With the Atomic Bomb Mission to Japan, Aug. 9 [1945](Delayed)—We are on our way to bomb the mainland of Japan. Our flying contingent consists of three specially designed B-29 "Superforts," and two of these carry no bombs. But our lead plane is on its way with another atomic bomb, the second in three days, concentrating in its active substance an explosive energy equivalent to 10,000 and, under favorable conditions, 40,000 tons of TNT.

> ❧ This is simply not a great example of a news lead. It backs into the story and is rather clumsy but remember that the dropping of the bomb has been announced. This is the story of the flight to drop the bomb. Laurence was not expected to be a great prose stylist. He was expected to report complex stories with clarity and accuracy. ❧

We have several chosen targets. One of these is the great indus- 2
trial and shipping center of Nagasaki on the western shore of Kyushu,
one of the main islands of the Japanese homeland.

I watched the assembly of this man-made meteor during the 3
past two days, and was among the small group of scientists and Army
and Navy representatives privileged to be present at the ritual of its
loading in the "Superfort" last night, against a background of threatening black skies torn open at intervals by great lightning flashes.

It is a thing of beauty to behold, this "gadget." In its design 4
went millions of man-hours of what is without doubt the most concentrated intellectual effort in history. Never before had so much
brainpower been focused on a single problem.

> ❡ Note the tone of voice which may be offensive now but may have
> been appropriate in wartime. At one moment he is objective and
> then he uses words such as "beauty." Note the description of the
> natural thunder storm. Be aware of the context in which this story
> was written, a war was being fought in which Americans were being
> killed. Now we can question the dropping of the bomb in the
> context of history, a perspective we did not have in 1945. ❡

This atomic bomb is different from the bomb used three days 5
ago with such devastating results on Hiroshima.

I saw the atomic substance before it was placed inside the 6
bomb. By itself it is not at all dangerous to handle. It is only under
certain conditions, produced in the bomb assembly, that it can be
made to yield up its energy, and even then it gives only a small fraction of its total contents—a fraction, however, large enough to produce the greatest explosion on earth.

The briefing at midnight revealed the extreme care and the tre- 7
mendous amount of preparation that had been made to take care of
every detail of the mission, to make certain that the atomic bomb
fully served the purpose for which it was intended. Each target in
turn was shown in detailed maps and in aerial photographs. Every
detail of the course was rehearsed—navigation, altitude, weather,
where to land in emergencies. It came out that the Navy had sub-
marines and rescue craft, known as Dumbos and Superdumbos, stationed at various strategic points in the vicinity of the targets, ready
to rescue the fliers in case they were forced to bail out.

The briefing period ended with a moving prayer by the chap- 8
lain. We then proceeded to the mess hall for the traditional early
morning breakfast before departure on a bombing mission. . . .

In Storm Soon After Take-off

9   We took off at 3:50 this morning and headed northwest on a straight line for the Empire. The night was cloudy and threatening, with only a few stars here and there breaking through the overcast. The weather report had predicted storms ahead part of the way but clear sailing for the final and climactic stages of our odyssey.

10   We were about an hour away from our base when the storm broke. Our great ship took some heavy dips through the abysmal darkness around us but it took these dips much more gracefully than a large commercial airliner, producing a sensation more in the nature of a glide than a "bump," like a great ocean liner riding the waves, except that in this case the air waves were much higher and the rhythmic tempo of the glide much faster.

11   I noticed a strange eerie light coming through the window high above the navigator's cabin and as I peered through the dark all around us I saw a startling phenomenon. The whirling giant propellers had somehow become great luminous disks of blue flame. The same luminous blue flame appeared on the plexiglass windows in the nose of the ship, and on the tips of the giant wings it looked as though we were riding the whirlwind through space on a chariot of blue fire.

12   It was, I surmised, a surcharge of static electricity that had accumulated on the tips of the propellers and on the di-electric material in the plastic windows. One's thoughts dwelt anxiously on the precious cargo in the invisible ship ahead of us. Was there any likelihood of danger that this heavy electric tension in the atmosphere all about us might set it off?

13   I expressed my fears to Captain Bock, who seems nonchalant and imperturbed at the controls. He quickly reassures me.

14   "It is a familiar phenomenon seen often on ships. I have seen it many times on bombing missions. It is known as St. Elmo's Fire."

15   On we went through the night. We soon rode out the storm and our ship was once again sailing on a smooth course straight ahead, on a direct line to the Empire.

16   Our altimeter showed that we were traveling through space at a height of 17,000 feet. The thermometer registered an outside temperature of 33 degrees below zero centigrade; about 30 below Fahrenheit. Inside our pressurized cabin the temperature was that of a comfortable air-conditioned room, and a pressure corresponding to an altitude of 8,000 feet. Captain Bock cautioned me, however, to

keep my oxygen mask handy in case of emergency. This, he explained, might mean either something going wrong with the pressure equipment inside the ship or a hole through the cabin by flak.

The first signs of dawn came shortly after 5 o'clock. Sergeant 17 Curry, who had been listening steadily on his earphones for radio reports, while maintaining a strict radio silence himself, greeted it by rising to his feet and gazing out the window.

"It's good to see the day," he told me. "I get a feeling of claus- 18 trophobia hemmed in in this cabin at night."

He is a typical American youth, looking even younger than his 19 20 years. It takes no mind-reader to read his thoughts.

"It's a long way from Hooperston Ill.," I find myself remarking. 20

"Yep," he replies, as he busies himself decoding a message from 21 outer space.

"Think this atomic bomb will end the war?" he asks hopefully. 22

"There is a very good chance that this one may do the trick," I 23 assure him, "but if not, then the next one or two surely will. Its power is such that no nation can stand up against it very long."

This was not my own view. I had heard it expressed all around 24 a few hours earlier, before we took off. To anyone who had seen this man-made fireball in action, as I had less than a month ago in the desert of New Mexico, this view did not sound overoptimistic.

By 5:50 it was real light outside. We had lost our lead ship, but 25 Lieutenant Godfrey, our navigator, informs me that we had arranged for that contingency. We have an assembly point in the sky above the little island of Hakoshima, southeast of Kyushu, at 9:10. We are to circle there and wait for the rest of our formation.

Our genial bombardier, Lieutenant Levy, comes over to invite 26 me to take his front-row seat in the transparent nose of the ship and I accept eagerly. From that vantage point in space, 17,000 feet above the Pacific, one gets a view of hundreds of miles on all sides, horizontally and vertically. At that height the vast ocean below and the sky above seem to merge into one great sphere.

❡ Do you think "genial" is used ironically? I think not but I may be wrong. I don't think it was read ironically then, but it would be today. ❡

I was on the inside of that firmament, riding above the giant 27 mountains of white cumulous clouds, letting myself be suspended in infinite space. One hears the whirl of the motors behind one, but it soon becomes insignificant against the immensity all around and is before long swallowed by it. There comes a point where space also swallows time and one lives through eternal moments filled with an oppressive loneliness, as though all life had suddenly vanished from the earth and you are the only one left, a lone survivor traveling endlessly through interplanetary space.

28   My mind soon returns to the mission I am on. Somewhere beyond these vast mountains of white clouds ahead of me there lies Japan, the land of our enemy. In about four hours from now one of its cities, making weapons of war for use against us, will be wiped off the map by the greatest weapon ever made by man. In one-tenth of a millionth of a second, a fraction of time immeasurable by any clock, a whirlwind from the skies will pulverize thousands of its buildings and tens of thousands of its inhabitants.

29   Our weather planes ahead of us are on their way to find out where the wind blows. Half an hour before target time we will know what the winds have decided.

30   Does one feel any pity or compassion for the poor devils about to die? Not when one thinks of Pearl Harbor and of the Death March on Bataan.

❧ Here he anticipates a reader's question and answers it in a wartime context. ❧

31   Captain Bock informs me that we are about to start our climb to bombing altitude.

32   He manipulates a few knobs on his control panel to the right of him and I alternately watch the white clouds and ocean below me and the altimeter on the bombardier's panel. We reached our altitude at 9 o'clock. We were then over Japanese waters, close to their mainland. Lieutenant Godfrey motioned to me to look through his radar scope. Before me was the outline of our assembly point. We shall soon meet our lead ship and proceed to the final stage of our journey.

33   We reached Yakoshima at 9:12 and there, about 4,000 feet ahead of us, was The Great Artiste with its precious load. I saw Lieutenant Godfrey and Sergeant Curry strap on their parachutes and I decided to do likewise.

34   We started circling. We saw little towns on the coastline, heedless of our presence. We kept on circling, waiting for the third ship in our formation.

It was 9:56 when we began heading for the coastline. Our 35
weather scouts had sent us code messages, deciphered by Sergeant
Curry, informing us that both the primary target as well as the secondary were clearly visible.

The winds of destiny seemed to favor certain Japanese cities 36
that must remain nameless. We circled about them again and again
and found no opening in the thick umbrella of clouds that covered
them. Destiny chose Nagasaki as the ultimate target.

We had been circling for some time when we noticed black 37
puffs of smoke coming through the white clouds directly at us. There
were fifteen bursts of flak in rapid succession, all too low. Captain
Bock changed his course. There soon followed eight more bursts of
flak, right up to our altitude, but by this time were too far to the left.

We flew southward down the channel and at 11:33 crossed the 38
coastline and headed straight for Nagasaki about 100 miles to the
west. Here again we circled until we found an opening in the clouds.
It was 12:01 and the goal of our mission had arrived.

We heard the prearranged signal on our radio, put on our arc- 39
welder's glasses and watched tensely the maneuverings of the strike
ship about half a mile in front of us.

"There she goes!" someone said. 40

Out of the belly of The Great Artiste what looked like a black 41
object went downward.

Captain Bock swung around to get out of range; but even though 42
we were turning away in the opposite direction, and despite the fact
that it was broad daylight in our cabin, all of us became aware of a
giant flash that broke through the dark barrier of our arc-welder's
lenses and flooded our cabin with intense light.

We removed our glasses after the first flash, but the light still 43
lingered on, a bluish-green light that illuminated the entire sky all
around. A tremendous blast wave struck our ship and made it tremble from nose to tail. This was followed by four more blasts in rapid
succession, each resounding like the boom of cannon fire hitting our
plane from all directions.

❧ It is Laurence's job to report on what was going on in the plane.
Someone else's job to report what was happening on the ground. Do
you agree? ❧

Observers in the tail of our ship saw a giant ball of fire rise as 44
though from the bowels of the earth, belching forth enormous white

smoke rings. Next they saw a giant pillar of purple fire, 10,000 feet high, shooting skyward with enormous speed.

45   By the time our ship had made another turn in the direction of the atomic explosion the pillar of purple fire had reached the level of our altitude. Only about forty-five seconds had passed. Awestruck, we watched it shoot upward like a meteor coming from the earth instead of from outer space, becoming ever more alive as it climbed skyward through the white clouds. It was no longer smoke, or dust, or even a cloud of fire. It was a living thing, a new species of being, born right before our incredulous eyes.

46   At one stage of its evolution, covering millions of years in terms of seconds, the entity assumed the form of a giant square totem pole, with its base about three miles long, tapering off to about a mile at the top. Its bottom was brown, its center was amber, its top white. But it was a living totem pole, carved with many grotesque masks grimacing at the earth.

47   Then, just when it appeared as though the thing has settled down into a state of permanence, there came shooting out of the top a giant mushroom that increased the height of the pillar to a total of 45,000 feet. The mushroom top was even more alive than the pillar, seething and boiling in a white fury of creamy foam, sizzling upward and then descending earthward, a thousand Old Faithful geysers rolled into one.

48   It kept struggling in an elemental fury, like a creature in the act of breaking the bonds that held it down. In a few seconds it had freed itself from its gigantic stem and floated upward with tremendous speed, its momentum carrying into the stratosphere to a height of about 60,000 feet.

49   But no sooner did this happen when another mushroom, smaller in size than the first one, began emerging out of the pillar. It was as though the decapitated monster was growing a new head.

50   As the first mushroom floated off into the blue it changed its shape into a flowerlike form, its giant petal curving downward, creamy white outside, rose-colored inside. It still retained that shape when we last gazed at it from a distance of about 200 miles.

Discussion

- What other evidence is there of the wartime context in which this piece was written and read?

- Take a piece from the morning newspaper and show how it reveals its context. Discuss how it might appear 40 or 50 years later.
- Take an article written in class that is not a news story. Discuss how it reveals context.
- What obligations does the writer have to be aware of context?
- Discuss how the reader's context changes the way the same piece of writing may be read. How is this story read by a pacifist and a soldier, a Japanese and an American, an anti-Bomb demonstrator and a pro-Bomb activist, a veteran and a civilian, a German or a Russian or a citizen of the "Third World," someone 65 years old and someone 19 years old?
- Discuss how Laurence makes complicated information clear.
- Consider how narrative is used in this story. What does it do for the writer and the reader? What are its dangers?

Activities

- Do a similar story by riding an ambulance, a police car, a tug boat, a train, a ferry and reporting on what happened in narrative form. Write it in another form.
- Take a story of your own or of a classmate and mark the spots where the context of the story is revealed.
- Write an explanation of a complicated technical subject for a non-technical reader.
- Take a news story or one of your own pieces of writing and write it in a different context: from the point of view of a different person, a different place, a different time.

John Hersey

When I heard an atomic bomb was dropped on Japan, I was delighted. Of course I didn't know what it was—just another big bomb—but I was in the paratroops in combat in Europe where 90 percent of our division had been killed or wounded. We had seen so much of bullets and bombs and rockets and grenades and shells and flamethrowers we could not be shocked by any other way man could dream up to kill each other. And we were scheduled to go to the Pacific and jump into Tokyo.

Even after we marched in the Victory Parade in New York and were discharged, and read stories such as the one by William Laurence published on page 540, few veterans had any idea that there was anything special about the atomic bomb. I went back to college and one night a group of us met for a regular meeting of a literary club at the home of Professor Carroll Towle, and without much introduction he started reading the entire issue of *The New Yorker* to us. I was appalled at that idea, but within paragraphs, I was caught up in the text of John Hersey's *Hiroshima* which was later published as a book. Hersey is a major journalist and novelist, but I can't imagine anything he could write that would be more important than this article. The editor of the *New Yorker* felt that it was important enough to toss everything else out and devote an entire issue to it. The text proves writers *can* make a difference, and Hersey's report was really the beginning of our education to the meaning of the atomic age, an education that is still going on today. We have just reprinted the first part of the book, which catches that second when our world was forever changed.

A Noiseless Flash

1   At exactly fifteen minutes past eight in the morning, on August 6, 1945, Japanese time, at the moment when the atomic bomb flashed above Hiroshima, Miss Toshiko Sasaki, a clerk in the personnel department of the East Asia Tin Works, had just sat down at her place in the plant office and was turning her head to speak to the girl at the next desk. At that same moment, Dr. Masakazu Fujii was settling down crosslegged to read the Osaka *Asahi* on the porch of his private hospital, overhanging one of the seven deltaic rivers which divide Hiroshima; Mrs. Hatsuyo Nakamura, a tailor's widow, stood by the window of her kitchen, watching a neighbor tearing down his house because it lay in the path of an air-raid-defense fire lane; Father Wilhelm Kleinsorge, a German priest of the Society of Jesus, reclined in his underwear on a cot on the top floor of his order's three-story mission house, reading a Jesuit magazine, *Stimmen der Zeit*; Dr. Terufumi Sasaki, a young member of the surgical staff of the city's large, modern Red Cross Hospital, walked along one of the hospital corridors with a blood specimen for a Wassermann test in his hand; and the Reverend Mr. Kiyoshi Tanimoto, pastor of the Hiroshima Methodist Church, paused at the door of a rich man's house in Koi, the city's western suburb, and prepared to unload a handcart full of things he had evacuated from town in fear of the massive B-29 raid which everyone expected Hiroshima to suffer. A hundred thousand people were killed by the atomic bomb, and these

six were among the survivors. They still wonder why they lived when so many others died. Each of them counts many small items of chance or volition—a step taken in time, a decision to go indoors, catching one streetcar instead of the next—that spared him. And now each knows that in the act of survival he lived a dozen lives and saw more death than he ever thought he would see. At the time, none of them knew anything.

> ❧ Imagine Hersey's challenge. His task was to tell people who were not there, the meaning of a bomb so vast that it seems truly indescribable. He decides to tell the story in terms of individual victims with whom the reader can identify, to show their ordinary lives at the moment the bomb was dropped, what they did, felt, and suffered. Again and again we see writers turning to the specific, the larger the subject to be confronted. ❧

The Reverend Mr. Tanimoto got up at five o'clock that morning. 2 He was alone in the parsonage, because for some time his wife had been commuting with their year-old baby to spend nights with a friend in Ushida, a suburb to the north. Of all the important cities of Japan, only two, Kyoto and Hiroshima, had not been visited in strength by *B-san*, or Mr. B, as the Japanese, with a mixture of respect and unhappy familiarity, called the B-29; and Mr. Tanimoto, like all his neighbors and friends, was almost sick with anxiety. He had heard uncomfortably detailed accounts of mass raids on Kure, Iwakuni, Tokuyama, and other nearby towns; he was sure Hiroshima's turn would come soon. He had slept badly the night before, because there had been several air-raid warnings. Hiroshima had been getting such warnings almost every night for weeks, for at that time the B-29s were using Lake Biwa, northeast of Hiroshima, as a rendezvous point, and no matter what city the Americans planned to hit, the Superfortresses streamed in over the coast near Hiroshima. The frequency of the warnings and the continued abstinence of Mr. B. with respect to Hiroshima had made its citizens jittery; a rumor was going around that the Americans were saving something special for the city.

Mr. Tanimoto is a small man, quick to talk, laugh, and cry. He 3 wears his black hair parted in the middle and rather long; the prominence of the frontal bones just above his eyebrows and the smallness of his mustache, mouth, and chin give him a strange, old-young look, boyish and yet wise, weak and yet fiery. He moves nervously and fast, but with a restraint which suggests that he is a cautious, thoughtful man. He showed, indeed, just those qualities in the uneasy days before the bomb fell. Besides having his wife spend the nights in Ushida, Mr. Tanimoto had been carrying all the portable things from his church, in the close-packed residential district called Nagaragawa, to a house that belonged to a rayon manufacturer in Koi, two miles from the center of town. The rayon man, a Mr. Matsui, had opened his then unoccupied estate to a large number of his friends and acquaintances, so that they might evacuate whatever they wished to a safe distance from the probable target area. Mr. Tanimoto had had no difficulty in moving chairs, hymnals, Bibles, altar gear, and church records by pushcart himself, but the organ console and an upright piano required some aid. A friend of his named Matsuo had, the day before, helped him get the piano out to Koi; in return, he had promised this day to assist Mr. Matsuo in hauling out a daughter's belongings. That is why he had risen so early.

4   Mr. Tanimoto cooked his own breakfast. He felt awfully tired. The effort of moving the piano the day before, a sleepless night, weeks of worry and unbalanced diet, the cares of his parish—all combined to make him feel hardly adequate to the new day's work. There was another thing, too; Mr. Tanimoto had studied theology at Emory College, in Atlanta, Georgia; he had graduated in 1940; he spoke excellent English; he dressed in American clothes; he had corresponded with many American friends right up to the time the war began; and among a people obsessed with a fear of being spied upon—perhaps almost obsessed himself—he found himself growing increasingly uneasy. The police had questioned him several times, and just a few days before, he had heard that an influential acquaintance, a Mr. Tanaka, a retired officer of the Toyo Kisen Kaisha steamship line, an anti-Christian, a man famous in Hiroshima for his showy philanthropies and notorious for his personal tyrannies, had been telling people that Tanimoto should not be trusted. In compensation, to show himself publicly a good Japanese, Mr. Tanimoto had taken on the chairmanship of his local *tonarigumi*, or Neighborhood Association, and to his other duties and concerns this position had added the business of organizing air-raid defense for about twenty families.

❧Remember that at the time of the writing, Japan was our enemy and Hersey, to tell his story, had to make the reader identify with the victims, before they were victims, not as the propaganda stereotyped "Japs" (we had, after all, had our own concentration camps for Japanese-Americans during World War II), but as human beings just like us.❧

Before six o-clock that morning, Mr. Tanimoto started for Mr. 5
Matsuo's house. There he found that their burden was to be a *tansu*,
a large Japanese cabinet, full of clothing and household goods. The
two men set out. The morning was perfectly clear and so warm that
the day promised to be uncomfortable. A few minutes after they
started, the air-raid siren went off—a minute-long blast that warned
of approaching planes but indicated to the people of Hiroshima only
a slight degree of danger, since it sounded every morning at this time,
when an American weather plane came over. The two men pulled
and pushed the handcart through the city streets. Hiroshima was a
fan-shaped city, lying mostly on the six islands formed by the seven
estuarial rivers that branch out from the Ota River; its main commercial and residential districts, covering about four square miles in
the center of the city, contained three-quarters of its population,
which had been reduced by several evacuation programs from a wartime peak of 380,000 to about 245,000. Factories and other residential districts, or suburbs, lay compactly around the edges of the city.
To the south were the docks, an airport, and the island-studded
Inland Sea. A rim of mountains runs around the other three sides of
the delta. Mr. Tanimoto and Mr. Matsuo took their way through the
shopping center, already full of people, and across two of the rivers
to the sloping streets of Koi, and up them to the outskirts and foot-
hills. As they started up a valley away from the tight-ranked houses,
the all-clear sounded. (The Japanese radar operators, detecting only
three planes, supposed that they comprised a reconnaissance.) Pushing the handcart up to the rayon man's house was tiring, and the
men, after they had maneuvered their load into the driveway and to
the front steps, paused to rest awhile. They stood with a wing of the
house between them and the city. Like most homes in this part of
Japan, the house consisted of a wooden frame and wooden walls supporting a heavy tile roof. Its front hall, packed with rolls of bedding
and clothing, looked like a cool cave full of fat cushions. Opposite
the house, to the right of the front door, there was a large, finicky
rock garden. There was no sound of planes. The morning was still;
the place was cool and pleasant.

Then a tremendous flash of light cut across the sky. Mr. Tani- 6
moto has a distinct recollection that it travelled from east to west,
from the city toward the hills. It seemed a sheet of sun. Both he and
Mr. Matsuo reacted in terror—and both had time to react (for they
were 3,500 yards, or two miles, from the center of the explosion).
Mr. Matsuo dashed up the front steps into the house and dived

among the bedrolls and buried himself there. Mr. Tanimoto took four or five steps and threw himself between two big rocks in the garden. He bellied up very hard against one of them. As his face was against the stone, he did not see what happened. He felt a sudden pressure, and then splinters and pieces of board and fragments of tile fell on him. He heard no roar. (Almost no one in Hiroshima recalls hearing any noise of the bomb. But a fisherman in his sampan on the Inland Sea near Tsuzu, the man with whom Mr. Tanimoto's mother-in-law and sister-in-law were living, saw the flash and heard a tremendous explosion; he was nearly twenty miles from Hiroshima, but the thunder was greater than when the B-29s hit Iwakuni, only five miles away.)

7   When he dared, Mr. Tanimoto raised his head and saw that the rayon man's house had collapsed. He thought a bomb had fallen directly on it. Such clouds of dust had risen that there was a sort of twilight around. In panic, not thinking for the moment of Mr. Matsuo under the ruins, he dashed out into the street. He noticed as he ran that the concrete wall of the estate had fallen over—toward the house rather than away from it. In the street, the first thing he saw was a squad of soldiers who had been burrowing into the hillside opposite, making one of the thousands of dugouts in which the Japanese apparently intended to resist invasion, hill by hill, life for life; the soldiers were coming out of the hole, where they should have been safe, and blood was running from their heads, chests, and backs. They were silent and dazed.

8   Under what seemed to be a local dust cloud, the day grew darker and darker.

9   At nearly midnight, the night before the bomb was dropped, an announcer on the city's radio station said that about two hundred B-29s were approaching southern Honshu and advised the population of Hiroshima to evacuate to their designated "safe areas." Mrs. Hatsuyo Nakamura, the tailor's widow, who lived in the section called Nobori-cho and who had long had a habit of doing as she was told, got her three children—a ten-year-old boy, Toshio, an eight-year-old girl, Yaeko, and a five-year-old girl, Myeko—out of bed and dressed them and walked with them to the military area known as the East Parade Ground, on the northeast edge of the city. There she unrolled some mats and the children lay down on them. They slept until about two, when they were awakened by the roar of the planes going over Hiroshima.

As soon as the planes had passed, Mrs. Nakamura started back 10 with her children. They reached home a little after two-thirty and she immediately turned on the radio, which to her distress, was just then broadcasting a fresh warning. When she looked at the children and saw how tired they were, and when she thought of the number of trips they had made in past weeks, all to no purpose, to the East Parade Ground, she decided that in spite of the instructions on the radio, she simply could not face starting out all over again. She put the children in their bedrolls on the floor, lay down herself at three o'clock, and fell asleep at once, so soundly that when planes passed over later, she did not waken to their sound.

The siren jarred her awake at about seven. She arose, dressed 11 quickly, and hurried to the house of Mr. Nakamoto, the head of her Neighborhood Association, and asked him what she should do. He said that she should remain at home unless an urgent warning—a series of intermittent blasts of the siren—was sounded. She returned home, lit the stove in the kitchen, set some rice to cook, and sat down to read that morning's Hiroshima *Chugoku*. To her relief, the all-clear sounded at eight o'clock. She heard the children stirring, so she went and gave each of them a handful of peanuts and told them to stay on their bedrolls, because they were tired from the night's walk. She had hoped that they would go back to sleep, but the man in the house directly to the south began to make a terrible hullabaloo of hammering, wedging, ripping, and splitting. The prefectural government, convinced, as everyone in Hiroshima was, that the city would be attacked soon, had begun to press with threats and warnings for the completion of wide fire lanes, which, it was hoped, might act in conjunction with the rivers to localize any fires started by an incendiary raid; and the neighbor was reluctantly sacrificing his home to the city's safety. Just the day before, the prefecture had ordered all able-bodied girls from the secondary schools to spend a few days helping to clear these lanes, and they started work soon after the all-clear sounded.

Mrs. Nakamura went back to the kitchen, looked at the rice, 12 and began watching the man next door. At first, she was annoyed with him for making so much noise, but then she was moved almost to tears by pity. Her emotion was specifically directed toward her neighbor, tearing down his home, board by board, at a time when there was so much unavoidable destruction, but undoubtedly she also felt a generalized, community pity, to say nothing of self-pity. She had not had an easy time. Her husband, Isawa, had gone into the

Army just after Myeko was born, and she had heard nothing from or of him for a long time, until, on March 5, 1942, she received a seven-word telegram: "Isawa died an honorable death at Singapore." She learned later that he had died on February 15th, the day Singapore fell, and that he had been a corporal. Isawa had been a not particularly prosperous tailor, and his only capital was a Sankoku sewing machine. After his death, when his allotments stopped coming, Mrs. Nakamura got out the machine and began to take in piecework herself, and since then had supported the children, but poorly, by sewing.

13   As Mrs. Nakamura stood watching her neighbor, everything flashed whiter than any white she had ever seen. She did not notice what happened to the man next door; the reflex of a mother set her in motion toward her children. She had taken a single step (the house was 1,350 yards, or three-quarters of a mile, from the center of the explosion) when something picked her up and she seemed to fly into the next room over the raised sleeping platform, pursued by parts of her house.

14   Timbers fell around her as she landed, and a shower of tiles pommelled her; everything became dark, for she was buried. The debris did not cover her deeply. She rose up and freed herself. She heard a child cry, "Mother, help me!," and saw her youngest— Myeko, the five-year-old—buried up to her breast and unable to move. As Mrs. Nakamura started frantically to claw her way toward the baby, she could see or hear nothing of her other children.

15   In the days right before the bombing, Dr. Masakazu Fujii, being prosperous, hedonistic, and at the time not too busy, had been allowing himself the luxury of sleeping until nine or nine-thirty, but fortunately he had to get up early the morning the bomb was dropped to see a house guest off on a train. He rose at six, and half an hour later walked with his friend to the station, not far away, across two of the rivers. He was back home by seven, just as the siren sounded its sustained warning. He ate breakfast and then, because the morning was already hot, undressed down to his underwear and went out on the porch to read the paper. This porch—in fact, the whole building—was curiously constructed. Dr. Fujii was the proprietor of a peculiarly Japanese institution: a private, single-doctor hospital. This building, perched beside and over the water of the Kyo River, and next to the bridge of the same name, contained thirty rooms for thirty patients and their kinfolk—for, according to Japanese custom, when

a person falls sick and goes to a hospital, one or more members of his family go and live there with him, to cook for him, bathe, massage, and read to him, and to offer incessant familial sympathy, without which a Japanese patient would be miserable indeed. Dr. Fujii had no beds—only straw mats—for his patients. He did, however, have all sorts of modern equipment: an X-ray machine, diathermy apparatus, and a fine tiled laboratory. The structure rested two-thirds on the land, one-third on piles over the tidal waters of the Kyo. This overhang, the part of the building where Dr. Fujii lived, was queer-looking, but it was cool in summer and from the porch, which faced away from the center of the city, the prospect of the river, with pleasure boats drifting up and down it, was always refreshing. Dr. Fujii had occasionally had anxious moments when the Ota and its mouth branches rose to flood, but the piling was apparently firm enough and the house had always held.

Dr. Fujii had been relatively idle for about a month because in 16
July, as the number of untouched cities in Japan dwindled and as Hiroshima seemed more and more inevitably a target, he began turning patients away, on the ground that in case of a fire raid he would not be able to evacuate them. Now he had only two patients left—a woman from Yano, injured in the shoulder, and a young man of twenty-five recovering from burns he had suffered when the steel factory near Hiroshima in which he worked had been hit. Dr. Fujii had six nurses to tend his patients. His wife and children were safe; his wife and one son were living outside Osaka, and another son and two daughters were in the country on Kyushu. A niece was living with him, and a maid and a manservant. He had little to do and did not mind, for he had saved some money. At fifty, he was healthy, convivial, and calm, and he was pleased to pass the evenings drinking whiskey with friends, always sensibly and for the sake of conversation. Before the war, he had affected brands imported from Scotland and America; now he was perfectly satisfied with the best Japanese brand, Suntory.

Dr. Fujii sat down cross-legged in his underwear on the spotless 17
matting of the porch, put on his glasses, and started reading the Osaka *Asahi*. He liked to read the Osaka news because his wife was there. He saw the flash. To him—faced away from the center and looking at his paper—it seemed a brilliant yellow. Startled, he began to rise to his feet. In that moment (he was 1,550 yards from the center), the hospital leaned behind his rising and, with a terrible ripping noise, toppled into the river. The Doctor, still in the act of getting to

his feet, was thrown forward and around and over; he was buffeted and gripped; he lost track of everything, because things were so speeded up; he felt the water.

18   Dr. Fujii hardly had time to think that he was dying before he realized that he was alive, squeezed tightly by two long timbers in a V across his chest, like a morsel suspended between two huge chopsticks—held upright, so that he could not move, with his head miraculously above water and his torso and legs in it. The remains of his hospital were all around him in a mad assortment of splintered lumber and materials for the relief of pain. His left shoulder hurt terribly. His glasses were gone.

19   Father Wilhelm Kleinsorge, of the Society of Jesus, was, on the morning of the explosion, in rather frail condition. The Japanese wartime diet had not sustained him, and he felt the strain of being a foreigner in an increasingly xenophobic Japan; even a German, since the defeat of the Fatherland, was unpopular. Father Kleinsorge had, at thirty-eight, the look of a boy growing too fast—thin in the face, with a prominent Adam's apple, a hollow chest, dangling hands, big feet. He walked clumsily, leaning forward a little. He was tired all the time. To make matters worse, he had suffered for two days, along with Father Cieslik, a fellow-priest, from a rather painful and urgent diarrhea, which they blamed on the brans and black ration bread they were obliged to eat. Two other priests then living in the mission compound, which was in the Noboro-cho section—Father Superior LaSalle and Father Schiffer—had happily escaped this affliction.

20   Father Kleinsorge woke up about six the morning the bomb was dropped, and half an hour later—he was a bit tardy because of his sickness—he began to read Mass in the mission chapel, a small Japanese-style wooden building which was without pews, since its worshippers knelt on the usual Japanese matted floor, facing an altar graced with splendid silks, brass, silver, and heavy embroideries. This morning, a Monday, the only worshippers were Mr. Takemoto, a theological student living in the mission house; Mr. Fukai, the secretary of the diocese; Mrs. Murata, the mission's devoutly Christian housekeeper; and his fellow priests. After Mass, while Father Kleinsorge was reading the Prayers of Thanksgiving, the siren sounded. He stopped the service and the missionaries retired across the compound to the bigger building. There, in his room on the ground floor, to the right of the front door, Father Kleinsorge changed into a military uniform which he had acquired when he was teaching at the

Rokko Middle School in Kobe and which he wore during air-raid alerts.

After an alarm, Father Kleinsorge always went out and scanned 21 the sky, and in this instance, when he stepped outside, he was glad to see only the single weather plane that flew over Hiroshima each day about this time. Satisfied that nothing would happen, he went in and breakfasted with the other Fathers on substitute coffee and ration bread, which, under the circumstances, was especially repugnant to him. The Fathers sat and talked awhile, until, at eight, they heard the all-clear. They went then to various parts of the building. Father Schiffer retired to his room to do some writing. Father Cieslik sat in his room in a straight chair with a pillow over his stomach to ease his pain, and read. Father Superior LaSalle stood at the window of his room, thinking. Father Kleinsorge went up to a room on the third floor, took off all his clothes except his underwear, and stretched out on his right side on a cot and began reading his *Stimmen der Zeit*.

After the terrible flash—which, Father Kleinsorge later realized, 22 reminded him of something he had read as a boy about a large meteor colliding with the earth—he had time (since he was 1,400 yards from the center) for one thought: A bomb has fallen directly on us. Then, for a few seconds or minutes, he went out of his mind.

Father Kleinsorge never knew how he got out of the house. The 23 next things he was conscious of were that he was wandering around in the mission's vegetable garden in his underwear, bleeding slightly from small cuts along his left flank; that all the buildings round about had fallen down except the Jesuits' mission house, which had long before been braced and double-braced by a priest named Gropper, who was terrified of earthquakes; that the day had turned dark; and that Murata-*san*, the housekeeper, was nearby, crying over and over, "*Shu Jesusu, awaremi tamai!* Our Lord Jesus, have pity on us!"

On the train on the way into Hiroshima from the country, 24 where he lived with his mother, Dr. Terufumi Sasaki, the Red Cross Hospital surgeon, thought over an unpleasant nightmare he had had the night before. His mother's home was in Mukaihara, thirty miles from the city, and it took him two hours by train and tram to reach the hospital. He had slept uneasily all night and had wakened an hour earlier than usual, and, feeling sluggish and slightly feverish, had debated whether to go to the hospital at all; his sense of duty finally forced him to go, and he had started out on an earlier train than he took most mornings. The dream had particularly frightened him because it was so closely associated, on the surface at least, with a disturbing actuality. He was only twenty-five years old and had just completed his training at the Eastern Medical University, in Tsingtao, China. He was something of an idealist and was much distressed by the inadequacy of medical facilities in the country town where his mother lived. Quite on his own, and without a permit, he had begun visiting a few sick people out there in the evenings, after his eight hours at the hospital and four hours' commuting. He had recently learned that the penalty for practicing without a permit was severe; a fellow-doctor whom he had asked about it had given him a serious scolding. Nevertheless, he had continued to practice. In his dream, he had been at the bedside of a country patient when the police and the doctor he had consulted burst into the room, seized him, dragged him outside, and beat him up cruelly. On the train, he just about decided to give up the work in Mukaihara, since he felt it would be impossible to get a permit, because the authorities would hold that it would conflict with his duties at the Red Cross Hospital.

25   At the terminus, he caught a streetcar at once. (He later calculated that if he had taken his customary train that morning, and if he had had to wait a few minutes for the streetcar, as often happened, he would have been close to the center at the time of the explosion and would surely have perished.) He arrived at the hospital at seven-forty and reported to the chief surgeon. A few minutes later, he went to a room on the first floor and drew blood from the arm of a man in order to perform a Wassermann test. The laboratory containing the incubators for the test was on the third floor. With the blood specimen in his left hand, walking in a kind of distraction he had felt all morning, probably because of the dream and his restless night, he started along the main corridor on his way toward the stairs. He was one step beyond an open window when the light of the bomb was reflected, like a gigantic photographic flash, in the corridor. He ducked down on one knee and said to himself, as only a Japanese would, "Sasaki, *gambare!* Be brave!" Just then (the building was 1,650 yards from the center), the blast ripped through the hospital. The glasses he was wearing flew off his face; the bottle of blood crashed against one wall; his Japanese slippers zipped out from under his feet—but otherwise, thanks to where he stood, he was untouched.

26   Dr. Sasaki shouted the name of the chief surgeon and rushed around to the man's office and found him terribly cut by glass. The hospital was in horrible confusion: heavy partitions and ceilings had

fallen on patients, beds had overturned, windows had blown in and cut people, blood was spattered on the walls and floors, instruments were everywhere, many of the patients were running about screaming, many more lay dead. (A colleague working in the laboratory to which Dr. Sasaki had been walking was dead; Dr. Sasaki's patient, whom he had just left and who a few moments before had been dreadfully afraid of syphillis, was also dead.) Dr. Sasaki found himself the only doctor in the hospital who was unhurt.

Dr. Sasaki, who believed that the enemy had hit only the build- 27
ing he was in, got bandages and began to bind the wounds of those inside the hospital; while outside, all over Hiroshima, maimed and dying citizens turned their unsteady steps toward the Red Cross Hospital to begin an invasion that was to make Dr. Sasaki forget his private nightmare for a long, long time.

Miss Toshiko Sasaki, the East Asia Tin Works clerk, who is not 28
related to Dr. Sasaki, got up at three o'clock in the morning on the day the bomb fell. There was extra housework to do. Her eleven-month-old brother, Akio, had come down the day before with a serious stomach upset; her mother had taken him to the Tamura Pediatric Hospital and was staying there with him. Miss Sasaki, who was about twenty, had to cook breakfast for her father, a brother, a sister, and herself, and—since the hospital, because of the war, was unable to provide food—to prepare a whole day's meals for her mother and the baby, in time for her father, who worked in a factory making rubber earplugs for artillery crews, to take the food by on his way to the plant. When she had finished and had cleaned and put away the cooking things, it was nearly seven. The family lived in Koi, and she had a forty-five minute trip to the tin works, in the section of town called Kannonmachi. She was in charge of the personnel records in the factory. She left Koi at seven, and as soon as she reached the plant, she went with some of the other girls from the personnel department to the factory auditorium. A prominent local Navy man, a former employee, had committed suicide the day before by throwing himself under a train—a death considered honorable enough to warrant a memorial service, which was to be held at the tin works at ten o'clock that morning. In the large hall, Miss Sasaki and the others made suitable preparations for the meeting. This work took about twenty minutes.

Miss Sasaki went back to her office and sat down at her desk. 29
She was quite far from the windows, which were off to her left, and

behind her were a couple of tall bookcases containing all the books of the factory library, which the personnel department had organized. She settled herself at her desk, put some things in a drawer, and shifted papers. She thought that before she began to make entries in her lists of new employees, discharges, and departures for the Army, she would chat for a moment with the girl at her right. Just as she turned her head away from the windows, the room was filled with a blinding light. She was paralyzed by fear, fixed still in her chair for a long moment (the plant was 1,600 yards from the center).

30   Everything fell, and Miss Sasaki lost consciousness. The ceiling dropped suddenly and the wooden floor above collapsed in splinters and the people up there came down and the roof above them gave way; but principally and first of all, the bookcases right behind her swooped forward and the contents threw her down, with her left leg horribly twisted and breaking underneath her. There in the tin factory, in the first moment of the atomic age, a human being was crushed by books.

Discusssion

- Compare the Laurence piece written from the bomber with the Hersey piece which reconstructs the scene on the ground. Compare the piece written *during* the war with the one written after the war.
- It often helps to know something of the time in which a piece is written. This piece is very much a 1946 piece of writing, although it hits the reader with great impact today. What were some of the problems Hersey faced in writing *Hiroshima* when he did?
- This is an example of journalism—history written in a hurry. What are some other examples of journalism in the book? What are the advantages and limitations of journalism?
- What are the advantages and disadvantages of the method of focusing on a few individuals that Hersey has chosen?
- What other ways could Hersey have written his article?
- What techniques has Hersey used to make the people sympathetic?
- Is narrative the best way to tell the story? What other choices did Hersey have?
- How is the exposition—the background material you need to know—woven into the article?

Activities

- Write about an individual, catching that person at an important moment.
- Write a page about the Hiroshima bombing without using Hersey's method: a page from a play, a history book, a news story, an editorial, a sermon, a poem, a short story, a government report (from the Japanese government and the US government).
- Rewrite a page from Hersey as it might be written by someone else in the book.
- Interview the survivors of a fire or the victims of a crime to report on the effect of a story reported in the paper.
- Go to the library to see how the Hiroshima bombing was reported in local newspapers. Compare that coverage to Hersey.

Enrique Hank Lopez

We often make the mistake of only taking those writers seriously who make publishing a career, but each year there are hundreds of writers who publish only a piece or two of writing—an article, a poem, a short story, perhaps a book—then go on to other things. The pieces they publish usually have special authority: they demand to be written. The writers have obvious talent but they do not choose to continue to publish. Such a person is Enrique Hank Lopez whose account of his return to Bachimba continues to be reprinted and reread. You should all take comfort in the fact that you do not have to be a writer to write—and to write with such skill that the reader is forced to think and to care.

Back to Bachimba

I am a *pocho* from Bachimba, a rather small Mexican village in 1
the state of Chihuahua, where my father fought with the army of Pancho Villa. He was, in fact, the only private in Villa's army.

Pocho is ordinarily a derogatory term in Mexico (to define it 2
succinctly, a *pocho* is a Mexican slob who has pretensions of being a gringo sonofabitch), but I use it in a very special sense. To me that word has come to mean "uprooted Mexican," and that's what I have been all my life. Though my entire upbringing and education took

place in the United States, I have never felt completely American; and when I am in Mexico, I sometimes feel like a displaced gringo with a curiously Mexican name—Enrique Preciliano Lopez y Martinez de Sepulveda de Sapien (—de Quien-sabe-quien). One might conclude that I'm either a schizo-cultural Mexican or a cultured schizoid American.

> ⟪Lopez has a particular problem because he has to use a language most readers do not understand. Note how skillfully he defines these terms throughout the piece.⟫

3   In any event, the schizo-ing began a long time ago, when my father and many of Pancho Villa's troops fled across the border to escape the oncoming *federales* who eventually defeated Villa. My mother and I, traveling across the hot desert plains in a buckboard wagon, joined my father in El Paso, Texas, a few days after his hurried departure. With more and more Villistas swarming into El Paso every day, it was quickly apparent that jobs would be exceedingly scarce and insecure; so my parents packed our few belongings and we took the first available bus to Denver. My father had hoped to move to Chicago because the name sounded so Mexican, but my mother's meager savings were hardly enough to buy tickets for Colorado.

4   There we moved into a ghetto of Spanish-speaking residents who chose to call themselves Spanish-Americans and resented the sudden migration of their brethren from Mexico, whom they sneeringly called *surumatos* (slang for "southerners"). These so-called Spanish-Americans claimed direct descent from the original conquistadores of Spain. They also insisted that they had *never* been Mexicans, since their region of New Spain (later annexed to the United States) was never a part of Mexico. But what they claimed most vociferously—and erroneously—was an absence of Indian ancestry. It made no difference that any objective observer could see by merely looking at them the results of considerable fraternization between the conquering Spaniards and the Comanche and Navaho women who crossed their paths. Still, these *manitos*, as they were snidely labeled by the *surumatos*, stubbornly refused to be identified with Mexico, and would actually fight anyone who called them Mexican. So intense was this intergroup rivalry that the bitterest "race riots" I have ever witnessed—and engaged in—were between the look-alike, talk-alike *surumatos* and *manitos* who lived near Denver's

Curtis Park. In retrospect the harsh conflicts between us were all the more silly and self-defeating when one recalls that we were all lumped together as "spiks" and "greasers" by the Anglo-Saxon community.

Predictably enough, we *surumatos* began huddling together in a subneighborhood within the larger ghetto, and it was there that I became painfully aware that my father had been the only private in Pancho Villa's army. Most of my friends were the sons of captains, colonels, majors, and even generals, though a few fathers were admittedly mere sergeants and corporals. My father alone had been a lowly private in that famous Division del Norte. Naturally I developed a most painful complex, which led me to all sorts of compensatory fibs. During one brief spell I fancied my father as a member of the dread *los dorados*, the "golden ones," who were Villa's favorite henchmen. (Later I was to learn that my father's cousin, Martin Lopez, was a genuine and quite notorious *dorado*.) But all my inventions were quickly uninvented by my very own father, who seemed to take a perverse delight in being Pancho's only private.

No doubt my chagrin was accentuated by the fact that Pancho Villa's exploits were a constant topic of conversation in our household. My entire childhood seems to be shadowed by his presence. At our dinner table, almost every night, we would listen to endlessly repeated accounts of this battle, that strategem, or some great act of Robin Hood kindness by *el centauro del norte*. I remember how angry my parents were when they saw Wallace Beery in *Viva Villa!* "Garbage by stupid gringos" they called it. They were particularly offended by the sweaty, unshaven sloppiness of Berry's portrayal. "Pancho Villa was clean and orderly, no matter how much he chased after women. This man's a dirty swine."

As if to deepen our sense of *Villismo*, my parents also taught us "Adelita" and "*Se Ilevaron el canon para Bachimba*" ("They took the cannons to Bachimba"), the two most famous songs of the Mexican revolution. Some twenty years later (during my stint at Harvard Law School), while strolling along the Charles River, I would find myself softly singing "*Se Ilevaron el canon para Bachimba, para Bachimba, para Bachimba*" over and over again. That's all I could remember of that poignant rebel song. Though I had been born there, I had always regarded "Bachimba" as a fictitious, made-up, Lewis Carroll kind of word. So that eight years ago, when I first returned to Mexico, I was literally stunned when I came to a crossroad south of Chihuahua and saw an old road marker: "Bachimba 18 km." Then it really exists—

I shouted inwardly—Bachimba is a real town! Swinging onto the narrow, poorly paved road, I gunned the motor and sped toward the town I'd been singing about since infancy. It turned out to be a quiet, dusty village with a bleak worn-down plaza that was surrounded by nondescript buildings of uncertain vintage.

8   Aside from the songs about Bachimba and Adelita and all the folk tales about Villa's guerrilla fighters, my early years were strongly influenced by our neighborhood celebrations of Mexico's two most important patriotic events: Mexican Independence Day on September 16, and the anniversary of the battle of Puebla on May 5. On those two dates Mexicans all over the world are likely to become extremely chauvinistic. In Denver we would stage annual parades that included three or four floats skimpily decorated with crepe-paper streamers, a small band, several adults in thread-bare battle dress, and hundreds of kids marching in wild disorder. It was during one of these parades—I was ten years old then—that I was seized with acute appendicitis and had to be rushed to a hospital. The doctor subsequently told my mother that I had made a long impassioned speech about the early revolutionist Miguel Hidalgo while the anesthetic was taking hold, and she explained with pardonable pride that it was the speech I was to make at Turner Hall that evening. Mine was one of the twenty-three *discursos* scheduled on the postparade program, a copy of which my mother still retains. My only regret was missing the annual *discurso* of Don Miguel Gomez, my godfather, a deep-throated orator who would always climax his speech by falling to his knees and dramatically kissing the floor, almost weeping as he loudly proclaimed: "*Ay, Mexico! Beso tu tierra, tu mero corazon*" ("Ah, Mexico! I kiss your sacred soil, the very heart of you"). He gave the same oration for seventeen years, word for word and gesture for gesture, and it never failed to bring tears to his eyes. But not once did he return to Chihuahua, even for a brief visit.

9   My personal Mexican-ness eventually produced serious problems for me. Upon entering grade school I learned English rapidly and rather well, always ranking either first or second in my class; yet the hard core of me remained stubbornly Mexican. This chauvinism may have been a reaction to the constant racial prejudice we encountered on all sides. The neighborhood cops were always running us off the streets and calling us "dirty greasers," and most of our teachers frankly regarded us as totally inferior. I still remember the galling disdain of my sixth-grade teacher, whose constant mimicking of our heavily accented speech drove me to a desperate study of *Webster's*

Dictionary in the hope of acquiring a vocabulary larger than hers. Sadly enough, I succeeded only too well, and for the next few years I spoke the most ridiculous high-flown rhetoric in the Denver public schools. One of my favorite words was "indubitably," and it must have driven everyone mad. I finally got rid of my accent by constantly reciting "Peter Piper picked a peck of pickled peppers" with little round pebbles in my mouth. Somewhere I had read about Demosthenes.

❡ Although the writer uses specifics he has to use them to a purpose. See how in the beginning of the paragraph below Lopez begins with a generalization, but makes us understand the meaning of the specifics to follow. In emphasizing specifics we should not ignore the important role a generalization can play. ❡

During this phase of my childhood the cultural tug of war 10 known as "Americanization" almost pulled me apart. There were moments when I would identify completely with the gringo world (what could have been more American than my earnest high-voiced portrayal of George Washington, however ridiculous the cotton wig my mother had fashioned for me?); then quite suddenly I would feel so acutely Mexican that I would stammer over the simplest English phrase. I was so ready to take offense at the slightest slur against Mexicans that I would imagine prejudice where none existed. But on other occasions, in full confidence of my belonging, I would venture forth into social areas that I should have realized were clearly forbidden to little *chicanos* from Curtis Park. The inevitable rebuffs would leave me floundering in self-pity; it was small comfort to know that other minority groups suffered even worse rebuffs than we did.

The only non-Mexican boy on our street was a negro named 11 Leroy Logan, who was probably my closest childhood friend. Leroy was the best athlete, the best whistler, the best liar, the best horseshoe player, the best marble shooter, the best mumblety-pegger, and the best shoplifter in our neighborhood. He was also my "partner," and I thus entitled myself to a fifty-fifty share of all his large triumphs and petty thefts. Because he considered "Mexican" a derogatory word bordering on obscenity, Leroy would pronounce it "Me sican" so as to soften its harshness. But once in a while, when he'd get angry with me, he would call me a "lousy Me sican greasy spik" with the most extraordinarily effective hissing one can imagine. And I'm embarrassed to admit that I would retaliate by calling him "alligator bait." As a matter of fact, just after I had returned from the hospital, he came to visit me, and I thoughtlessly greeted him with a flippant "Hi, alligator ba—" I never finished the phrase because Leroy whacked me on the stomach with a Ping-Pong paddle and rushed out of my house with great, sobbing anger.

12   Weeks later, when we had re-established a rather cool rapport, I tried to make up for my stupid insult by helping him steal cabbages from the vegetable trucks that rumbled through our neighborhood on their way to the produce markets. They would come down Larimer Street in the early dawn, and Leroy and I would sneak up behind them at the 27th Street stop sign, where they were forced to pause for cross traffic. I would be waiting below to catch them with an open gunny sack. Our system was fabulously successful for a while, and we found a ready market for the stolen goods; but one morning, as I started to unfurl my sack, a fairly large cabbage conked me on the head. Screaming with pain, I lunged at Leroy and tried to bite him. He, laughing all the while—it was obviously a funny scene—glided out of my reach, and finally ran into a nearby alley. We never engaged in commercial affairs thereafter.

13   Still and all, I remember him with great affection and a touch of sadness. I say sadness because eventually Leroy was to suffer the misery of being an outsider in an already outside ghetto. As he grew older, it was apparent that he longed to be a Mexican, that he felt terribly dark and alone. "Sometimes," he would tell me, "I feel like my damn skin's too tight, like I'm gonna bust out of it." One cold February night I found him in the coal shed behind Pacheco's store, desperately scraping his forearm with sandpaper, the hurt tears streaming down his face. "I got to get this off, man. I can't stand all this blackness." We stood there quietly staring at the floor for a long, anguished moment, both of us miserable beyond word or gesture. Finally he drew a deep breath, blew his nose loudly, and mumbled half audibly, "Man, you sure lucky to be a Me sican."

14   Not long after this incident Leroy moved out of Denver to live with relatives in Georgia. When I saw him off at the bus station, he grabbed my shoulder and whispered huskily, "You gonna miss me, man. You watch what I tellya." "Indubitably," I said. "Aw, man, cut that stuff. You the most fancy-pants Me sican I know." Those were his last words to me, and they caused a considerable dent in my ego. Not enough, however, to diminish my penchant for fancy language. The dictionary continued to be my comic book well into high school.

15   Speaking of language, I am reminded of a most peculiar circum-

stance: almost every Mexican-American lawyer that I've ever met speaks English with a noticeable Spanish accent, this despite the fact that they have all been born, reared, and educated exclusively in America. Of the forty-eight lawyers I have in mind, only three of us are free of any accent. Needless to say our "cultural drag" has been weighty and persistent. And one must presume that our ethnic hyphens shall be with us for many years to come.

My own Mexican-ness, after years of decline at Harvard University, suddenly burst forth again when I returned to Chihuahua and stumbled on the town of Bachimba. I had long conversations with an uncle I'd never met before, my father's younger brother, Ramon. It was Tio Ramon who chilled my spine with eyewitness stories about Pancho Villa's legendary *dorados*, one of whom was Martin Lopez. "He was your second cousin. The bravest young buck in Villa's army. And he became a *dorado* when he was scarcely seventeen years old because he dared to defy Pancho Villa himself. As your papa may have told you, Villa had a bad habit of burying treasure up in the mountains and also burying the man he took with him to dig the hole for it. Well, one day he chose Martin Lopez to go with him. Deep in the mountains they went, near Parral. And when they got to a suitably lonely place, Pancho Villa told him to dig a hole with pick and shovel. Then, when Martin had dug down to his waist, Villa leveled a gun at the boy. "Say your prayers, *muchacho*. You shall stay here with the gold—forever." But Martin had come prepared. In his large right boot he had a gun, and when he rose from his bent position, he was pointing that gun at Villa. They stood there, both ready to fire, for several seconds, and finally Don Pancho started to laugh in that wonderful way of his. "*Bravo, bravo, muchacho!* You've got more guts than a man. Get out of that hole, boy. I need you for my *dorados*."

Tio Ramon's eyes were wet with pride. "But what is more important, he died with great valor. Two years later, after he had terrorized the *federales* and Pershing's gringo soldiers, he was finally wounded and captured here in Bachimba. It was a bad wound in his leg, finally turning to gangrene. Then one Sunday morning they hauled Martin Lopez and three other prisoners to the plaza. One by one they executed the three lesser prisoners against that wall. I was up on the church tower watching it all. Finally it was your uncle's turn. They dragged him off the buckboard wagon and handed him his crutches. Slowly, painfully, he hobbled to the wall and stood there. Very straight he stood. 'Do you have any last words?' said the captain of the firing squad. With great pride Martin tossed his crutches aside and stood very tall on his one good leg. 'Give me, you yellow bastards, give me a gun—and I'll show you who is the man among . . .' Eight bullets crashed into his chest and face, and I never heard that final word. That was your second cousin. You would have been proud to know him.''

18   As I listened to Tio Ramon's soft nostalgic voice that evening, there in the sputtering light of the kerosene lamp on his back patio, I felt as intensely Mexican as I shall ever feel.

19   But not for long. Within six weeks I was destined to feel *less* Mexican than I had ever felt. The scene of my trauma was the Centro Mexicano de Escritores, where the finest young writers of Mexico met regularly to discuss works in progress and to engage in erudite literary and philosophical discussions. Week after week I sat among them, dumbstruck by my inadequacy in Spanish and my total ignorance of their whole frame of reference. How could I have possibly imagined that I was Mexican? Those conversations were a dense tangle of local and private allusions, and the few threads I could grasp only magnified my ignorance. The novelist Juan Rulfo was then reading the initial drafts of his *Pedro Paramo*, later to be acclaimed the best avant-garde fiction in Mexican literature. Now that I have soaked myself in the *ambiance* of Mexico, Rulfo's novel intrigues me beyond measure; but when he first read it at the Centro, he might just as well have been reading ''Jabberwocky'' in Swahili for all I understood of it. And because all of the other Mexican writers knew and greatly appreciated *Paramo*, I could only assume that I was really ''too gringo'' to comprehend it. For this reason, I, a person with no great talent for reticence, never opened my mouth at the Centro. In fact, I was so shell-shocked by those sessions that I even found it difficult to converse with my housekeeper about such simple matters as dirty laundry or the loose doorknob in the bathroom.

20   Can any of us really go home again? I, for one, am convinced that I have no true home, that I must reconcile myself to a schizo-cultural limbo, with a mere hyphen to provide some slight cohesion between my split selves. This inevitable splitting is a plague and a pleasure. Some mornings as I glide down the Paseo de la Reforma, perhaps the most beautiful boulevard in the world, I am suddenly angered by the *machismo*, or aggressive maleness, of Mexican drivers who crowd and bully their screeching machines through dense traffic. What terrible insecurity, what awful dread of emasculation, produces such assertive bully-boy conduct behind a steering wheel? Whatever the reasons, there is a part of me that can never accept this

much celebrated *machismo*. Nor can I accept the exaggerated nationalism one so frequently encounters in the press, on movie screens, over the radio, in daily conversations—that shrill barrage of slogans proclaiming that "there is only one Mexico."

Recently, when I expressed these views to an old friend, he   21
smiled knowingly: "Let's face it, Hank, you're not really a Mexican—despite that long, comical name of yours. You're an American through and through." But that, of course, is a minority view and almost totally devoid of realism. One could just as well say that Martin Luther King is not a Negro, that he's merely an American. But the plain truth is that neither I nor Martin Luther King can escape the fact that we are a Mexican and a Negro whose roots are so deeply planted in the United States that we have grown those strong little hyphens that make us Mexican-American and Negro-American. This assertion may not please some idealists who would prefer to blind themselves to our obvious ethnic and racial differences, who are unwittingly patronizing when they insist that we are all alike and indistinguishable. But the politicians, undoubtedly the most pragmatic creatures in America, are completely aware that ethnic groups *do* exist and that they seem to huddle together, and sometimes vote together.

When all is said and done, we hyphenated Americans are here   22
to stay, bubbling happily or unhappily in the great nonmelting pot. Much has been gained and will be gained from the multiethnic aspects of the United States, and there is no useful purpose in attempting to wish it away or to homogenize it out of existence. In spite of the race riots in Watts and ethnic unrest elsewhere, there would appear to be a kind of modus vivendi developing on almost every level of American life.

And if there are those of us who may never feel completely at   23
home, we can always make that brief visit to Bachimba.

Discussion

• What problems of clarity face Lopez that are different from ones which faced the writers of the other autobiographical pieces in the book? How does he solve them?

• What is the meaning of this article? What do you think Lopez wanted to say? Do you think he has said it?

- What other ways could Lopez have organized his article to make his meaning clearer?
- What questions did you want Lopez to answer in the piece? Did he answer them? If not, how could he have answered them?
- Are there places where your attention wandered? If so, what could Lopez have done to hold it?

Activities

- Write an article that explores your ethnic background and what it has meant to you.
- Outline the article as Lopez has written it. See how many outlines you can make to organize the article.
- Edit a page of Lopez to improve the text if you can.
- Edit a page of Lopez as it might have been written by the author of another autobiographical piece in the book.
- Write a piece about going back to a place where you used to live.

Maxine Hong Kingston

Maxine Hong Kingston's first book, *Woman Warrior*, became an instant classic when it was published, winning the National Book Critics Award for "The best book of nonfiction published in 1976." Its subtitle was "Memoirs of a Girlhood among Ghosts" and it was a book that combined the experience of being a Chinese-American with the experience of being a woman, and its prose was woven with a wonderful combination of myth and reality. I can remember reading it sitting in a car, parked on a city street waiting for a member of my family; I can see the brick walls, the crowds on the sidewalk, hear the traffic. Somehow, when the writing or reading goes well it stimulates all my senses and I not only remember what I wrote or read but where and how I felt. *Woman Warrior* was that kind of a book.

from *The Woman Warrior*

1   We were working at the laundry when a delivery boy came from the Rexall drugstore around the corner. He had a pale blue box of pills, but nobody was sick. Reading the label we saw that it belonged

to another Chinese family, Crazy Mary's family. "Not ours," said my father. He pointed out the name to the Delivery Ghost, who took the pills back. My mother muttered for an hour, and then her anger boiled over. "That ghost! That dead ghost! How dare he come to the wrong house?" She could not concentrate on her marking and pressing. "A mistake! Huh!" I was getting angry myself. She fumed. She made her press crash and hiss. "Revenge. We've got to avenge this wrong on our future, on our health, and on our lives. Nobody's going to sicken my children and get away with it." We brothers and sisters did not look at one another. She would do something awful, something embarrassing. She'd already been hinting that during the next eclipse we slam pot lids together to scare the frog from swallowing the moon. (The word for "eclipse" is *frog-swallowing-the-moon*.) When we had not banged lids at the last eclipse and the shadow kept receding anyway, she'd said, "The villagers must be banging and clanging very loudly back home in China."

("On the other side of the world, they aren't having an eclipse, 2 Mama. That's just a shadow the earth makes when it comes between the moon and the sun."

"You're always believing what those Ghost Teachers tell you. 3 Look at the size of the jaws!")

"Aha!" she yelled. "You! The biggest." She was pointing at me. 4 "You go to the drugstore."

"What do you want me to buy, Mother?" I said. 5

"But nothing. Don't bring one cent. Go and make them stop 6 the curse."

"I don't want to go. I don't know how to do that. There are no 7 such things as curses. They'll think I'm crazy."

"If you don't go, I'm holding you responsible for bringing a 8 plague on this family."

"What am I supposed to do when I get there?" I said, sullen, 9 trapped. "Do I say, 'Your delivery boy made a wrong delivery'?"

"They know he made a wrong delivery. I want you to make 10 them rectify their crime."

I felt sick already. She'd make me swing stinky censers around 11 the counter, at the druggist, at the customers. Throw dog blood on the druggist. I couldn't stand her plans.

"You get reparation candy," she said. "You say, 'You have 12 tainted my house with sick medicine and must remove the curse with sweetness.' He'll understand."

"He didn't do it on purpose. And no, he won't, Mother. They 13 don't understand stuff like that. I won't be able to say it right. He'll call us beggars."

14   "You just translate." She searched me to make sure I wasn't hiding any money. I was sneaky and bad enough to buy the candy and come back pretending it was a free gift.

15   "Mymotherseztagimmesomecandy," I said to the druggist. Be cute and small. No one hurts the cute and small.

16   "What? Speak up. Speak English," he said, big in his white druggist coat.

17   "Tatatagimme somecandy."

18   The druggist leaned way over the counter and frowned. "Some free candy," I said. "Sample candy."

19   "We don't give sample candy, young lady," he said.

20   "My mother said you have to give us candy. She said that is the way the Chinese do it."

21   "What?"

22   "That is the way the Chinese do it."

23   "Do what?"

24   "Do things." I felt the weight and immensity of things impossible to explain to the druggist.

25   "Can I give you some money?" he asked.

26   "No, we want candy."

27   He reached into a jar and gave me a handful of lollipops. He gave us candy all year round, year after year, every time we went into the drugstore. When different druggists or clerks waited on us, they also gave us candy. They had talked us over. They gave us Halloween candy in December, Christmas candy around Valentine's day, candy hearts at Easter, and Easter eggs at Halloween. "See?" said our mother. "They understand. You kids just aren't very brave." But I knew they did not understand. They thought we were beggars without a home who lived in back of the laundry. They felt sorry for us. I did not eat their candy. I did not go inside the drugstore or walk past it unless my parents forced me to. Whenever we had a prescription filled, the druggist put candy in the medicine bag. This is what Chinese druggists normally do, except they give raisins. My mother thought she taught the Druggist Ghosts a lesson in good manners (which is the same word as "traditions").

☞ Study how Kingston makes you experience these painful moments with her. ☜

My mouth went permanently crooked with effort, turned down 28
on the left side and straight on the right. How strange that the emi-
grant villagers are shouters, hollering face to face. My father asks,
"Why is it I can hear Chinese from blocks away? Is it that I understand the language? Or is it they talk loud?" They turn the radio up
full blast to hear the operas, which do not seem to hurt their ears.
And they yell over the singers that wail over the drums, everybody
talking at once, big arm gestures, spit flying. You can see the disgust
on American faces looking at women like that. It isn't just the loud-
ness. It is the way Chinese sounds, chingchong ugly, to American
ears, not beautiful like Japanese sayonara words with the consonants
and vowels as regular as Italian. We make guttural peasant noise and
have Ton Duc Thang names you can't remember. And the Chinese
can't hear Americans at all; the language is too soft and western
music unhearable. I've watched a Chinese audience laugh, visit, talk-
story, and holler during a piano recital, as if the musician could not
hear them. A Chinese-American, somebody's son, was playing Chopin, which has no punctuation, no cymbals, no gongs. Chinese piano
music is five black keys. Normal Chinese women's voices are strong
and bossy. We American-Chinese girls had to whisper to make ourselves American-feminine. Apparently we whispered even more
softly than the Americans. Once a year the teachers referred my sister
and me to speech therapy, but our voices would straighten out,
unpredictably normal, for the therapists. Some of us gave up, shook
our heads, and said nothing, not one word. Some of us could not
even shake our heads. At times shaking my head no is more self-
assertion than I can manage. Most of us eventually found some voice,
however faltering. . . .

We have so many secrets to hold in. Our sixth-grade teacher, 29
who liked to explain things to children, let us read our files. My
record shows that I flunked kindergarten and in first grade had no
IQ—a zero IQ. I did remember the first-grade teacher calling out
during a test, while students marked X's on a girl or a boy or a dog,
which I covered with black. First grade was when I discovered eye
control; with my seeing I could shrink the teacher down to a height
of one inch, gesticulating and mouthing on the horizon. I lost this
power in sixth grade for lack of practice, the teacher a generous man.
"Look at your family's old addresses and think about how you've
moved," he said. I looked at my parents' aliases and their birthdays,
which variants I knew. But when I saw Father's occupations I

exclaimed, "Hey, he wasn't a farmer, he was a . . ." He had been a gambler. My throat cut off the word—silence in front of the most understanding teacher. There were secrets never to be said in front of the ghosts, immigration secrets whose telling could get us sent back to China.

30   Sometimes I hated the ghosts for not letting us talk; sometimes I hated the secrecy of the Chinese. "Don't tell," said my parents, though we couldn't tell if we wanted to because we didn't know. Are there really secret trials with our own judges and penalties? Are there really flags in Chinatown signaling what stowaways have arrived in San Francisco Bay, their names, and which ships they came on? "Mother, I heard some kids say there are flags like that. Are there? What colors are they? Which buildings do they fly from?"

31   "No. No, there aren't any flags like that. They're just talking-story. You're always believing talk-story."

32   "I won't tell anybody, Mother. I promise. Which building are the flags on? Who flies them? The benevolent associations?"

33   "I don't know. Maybe the San Francisco villagers do that; our villagers don't do that."

34   "What do our villagers do?"

35   They would not tell us children because we had been born among ghosts, were taught by ghosts, and were ourselves ghostlike. They called us a kind of ghost. Ghosts are noisy and full of air; they talk during meals. They talk about anything.

36   "Do we send up signal kites? That would be a good idea, huh? We could fly them from the school balcony." Instead of cheaply stringing dragonflies by the tail, we could fly expensive kites, the sky splendid in Chinese colors, distracting ghost eyes while the new people sneak in. Don't tell. "Never tell."

37   Occasionally the rumor went about that the United States immigration authorities had set up headquarters in the San Francisco or Sacramento Chinatown to urge wetbacks and stowaways, anybody here on fake papers, to come to the city and get their files straightened out. The immigrants discussed whether or not to turn themselves in. "We might as well," somebody would say. "Then we'd have our citizenship for real."

38   "Don't be a fool," somebody else would say. "It's a trap. You go in there saying you want to straighten out your papers, they'll deport you."

39   "No, they won't. They're promising that nobody is going to go

to jail or get deported. They'll give you citizenship as a reward for turning yourself in, for your honesty."

"Don't you believe it. So-and-so trusted them, and he was 40 deported. They deported his children too."

"Where can they send us now? Hong Kong? Taiwan? I've never 41 been to Hong Kong or Taiwan. The Big Six? Where?" We don't belong anywhere since the Revolution. The old China has disappeared while we've been away.

"Don't tell," advised my parents. "Don't go to San Francisco 42 until they leave."

Lie to Americans. Tell them you were born during the San Fran- 43 cisco earthquake. Tell them your birth certificate and your parents were burned up in the fire. Don't report crimes; tell them we have no crimes and no poverty. Give a new name every time you get arrested; the ghosts won't recognize you. Pay the new immigrants twenty-five cents an hour and say we have no unemployment. And, of course, tell them we're against Communism. Ghosts have no memory anyway and poor eyesight. And the Han people won't be pinned down.

Even the good things are unspeakable, so how could I ask about 44 deformities? From the configurations of food my mother set out, we kids had to infer the holidays. She did not whip us up with holiday anticipation or explain. You only remembered that perhaps a year ago you had eaten monk's food, or that there was meat, and it was a meat holiday; or you had eaten moon cakes or long noodles for long life (which is a pun). In front of the whole chicken with its slit throat toward the ceiling, she'd lay out just so many pairs of chopsticks alternating with wine cups, which were not for us because they were a different number from the number in our family, and they were set too close together for us to sit at. To sit at one of those place settings a being would have to be about two inches wide, a tall wisp of an invisibility. Mother would pour Seagram's 7 into the cups and after a while, pour it back into the bottle. Never explaining. How can Chinese keep any traditions at all? They don't even make you pay attention, slipping in a ceremony and clearing the table before the children notice specialness. The adults get mad, evasive, and shut you up if you ask. You get no warning that you shouldn't wear a white ribbon in your hair until they hit you and give you the sideways glare for the rest of the day. They hit you if you wave brooms around or drop chopsticks or drum them. They hit you if you wash your hair on certain days, or tap somebody with a ruler, or step over a brother whether it's during your menses or not. You figure out what you got hit for and don't do it again if you figured correctly. But I think that if you don't figure it out, it's all right. Then you can grow up bothered by "neither ghosts nor deities." "Gods you avoid won't hurt you." I don't see how they kept up a continuous culture for five thousand years. Maybe they didn't; maybe everyone makes it up as they go along. If we had to depend on being told, we'd have no religion, no babies, no menstruation (sex, of course, unspeakable), no death.

Discussion

- Compare the Lopez piece with Kingston. What works in each piece? What needs work? Which probes deeper? How?
- How do Lopez and Kingston reveal a culture that is alien to most readers? What other techniques could be used to do this?
- This is the last autobiographical piece in the book. How does Kingston compare with the other writers? What could they—and you—learn from her? What could she—and you—learn from them?
- List the principal problems of writing autobiography. List a number of ways each problem can be solved.
- Discuss the ways Kingston makes complicated material clear.

Activities

- Write an incident from your childhood that reveals how your family's ideas or standards were different from the neighbors'.
- Interview a foreign student in your school or someone who comes from a culture different from yours. Write a story that reveals that difference.
- Take a draft you have written and write it as it might be written by someone with a different cultural background.
- Rewrite a fragment of the scene in the basement from the other girl's point of view.
- Interview someone in your family or someone else who came to this country from another culture to discover a problem they had adjusting. Write about that problem.

John Kenneth Galbraith

John Kenneth Galbraith, journalist, diplomat, political commentator, and, most of all, economist, is a fine writer whose principal subject has been one which is rarely written about with clarity or style. Yet Galbraith served for years as Paul M. Warburg Professor of Economics and has written many best-selling books on economic subjects. He has proven, again and again, that such complex matters can be written about in a fashion that is both responsible and lively.

Writing, Typing and Economics

Six or seven years ago, when I was spending a couple of terms at Trinity College, Cambridge, I received a proposal of more than usual interest from the University of California. It was that I resign from Harvard and accept a chair there in English. More precisely, it was to be the chair in rhetoric; they assured me that rhetoric was a traditional and not, as one would naturally suppose, a pejorative title. My task would be to hold seminars with the young on what I had learned about writing in general and on technical matters in particular.

I was attracted by the idea. I had spent several decades attempting to teach the young about economics. And the practical consequences were not reassuring. When I entered the field in the early 1930s, it was generally known that the modern economy could suffer a serious depression, and that it could have a serious inflation. In the ensuing forty years my teaching had principally advanced to the point of telling that it was possible to have both at once. This was soon to be associated with the belief of William Simon and Alan Greenspan, the gifts of Richard Nixon and Gerald Ford to our science, that progress in this subject is measured by the speed of the return to the ideas of the eighteenth century. A subject where it can be believed that you go ahead by going back has many problems for a teacher. Things are better now, Mr. Carter's economists do not believe in going back. But they are caught in a delicate balance between their fear of inflation and unemployment and their fear of doing anything about them. It is hard to conclude that economics is a productive intellectual and pedagogical investment.

3   Then I began to consider what I could tell about writing. My experience was certainly ample. I had been inititated by two inspired professors in Canada, O. J. Stevenson and E. C. McLean. They were men who deeply loved their craft and who were willing to spend endless hours with a student, however obscure his talent. I had been an editor of *Fortune*, which in my day meant mostly being a writer. Editor was thought a more distinguished title and justified more pay. Both as an editor proper and as a writer, I had had the close attention of Henry Robinson Luce. Harry Luce is in danger of being remembered for his political judgments, which left much to be desired; he found unblemished merit in John Foster Dulles, Robert A. Taft, and Chiang Kai-shek. But more important, he was an acute businessman and a truly brilliant editor. One proof is that while Time, Inc. publications have become politically more predictable since he departed, they have become infinitely less amusing.

4   Finally, as I reflected, among my qualifications was the amount of my life that I have spent at a typewriter. Nominally I have been a teacher. In practice I have been a writer—as generations of Harvard students have suspected. Faced with the choice of spending time on the unpublished scholarship of a graduate student or the unpublished work of Galbraith, I have rarely hesitated. Superficially, at least, I was well qualified for that California chair.

5   There was, however, a major difficulty. It was that I could tell everything I knew about writing in approximately half an hour. For the rest of the term I would have nothing to say except as I could invite discussion, this being the last resort of the empty academic mind. I could use up a few hours telling how a writer should deal with publishers. This is a field of study in which I especially rejoice. All authors should seek to establish a relationship of warmth, affection, and mutual mistrust with their publishers. This is in the hope that the uncertainty will add, however marginally, to compensation. But instruction on how to deal with publishers and how to bear up under the inevitable defeat would be for a very advanced course. It is not the sort of thing that the average beginning writer at Berkeley would find immediately practical.

6   So I returned to the few things that I could teach. The first lessons would have to do with the all-important issue of inspiration. All writers know that on some golden mornings they are touched by the wand—are on intimate terms with poetry and cosmic truth. I have experienced those moments myself. Their lesson is simple: It's a total illusion. And the danger in the illusion is that you will wait for those

moments. Such is the horror of having to face the typewriter that you will spend all your time waiting. I am persuaded that most writers, like most shoemakers, are about as good one day as the next (a point which Trollope made), hangovers apart. The difference is the result of euphoria, alcohol, or imagination. The meaning is that one had better go to his or her typewriter every morning and stay there regardless of the seeming result. It will be much the same.

All professions have their own ways of justifying laziness. Harvard professors are deeply impressed by the jeweled fragility of their minds. More than the thinnest metal, these are subject terribly to fatigue. More than six hours teaching a week is fatal—and an impairment of academic freedom. So, at any given moment, they are resting their minds in preparation for the next orgiastic act of insight or revelation. Writers, in contrast, do nothing because they are waiting for inspiration. 7

In my own case there are days when the result is so bad that no fewer than five revisions are required. However, when I'm greatly inspired, only four revisions are needed before, as I've often said, I put in that note of spontaneity which even my meanest critics concede. My advice to those eager students in California would be, "Do not wait for the golden moment. It may well be worse." I would also warn against the flocking tendency of writers and its use as a cover for idleness. It helps greatly in the avoidance of work to be in the company of others who are also waiting for the golden moment. The best place to write is by yourself, because writing becomes an escape from the terrible boredom of your own personality. It's the reason that for years I've favored Switzerland, where I look at the telephone and yearn to hear it ring. 8

❧ Galbraith is a master of the conversational tone and, in his case, that voice includes irony. Notice how many times he says one thing and means another. He also employs sarcasm and old-fashioned ridicule. You might consider the advantages and considerable dangers of these techniques. ☙

The question of revision is closely allied with that of inspiration. There may be inspired writers for whom the first draft is just right. But anyone who is not certifiably a Milton had better assume that the first draft is a very primitive thing. The reason is simple: Writing is difficult work. Ralph Paine, who managed *Fortune* in my time, used to say that anyone who said writing was easy was either a bad writer 9 or an unregenerate liar. Thinking, as Voltaire avowed, is also a very tedious thing which men—or women—will do anything to avoid. So all first drafts are deeply flawed by the need to combine composition with thought. Each later draft is less demanding in this regard. Hence the writing can be better. There does come a time when revision is for the sake of change—when one has become so bored with the words that anything that is different looks better. But even then it may be better.

10   For months in 1955-1956, when I was working on *The Affluent Society*, my title was "The Opulent Society." Eventually I could stand it no longer: the word opulent had a nasty, greasy sound. One day, before starting work, I looked up the synonyms in the dictionary. First to meet my eye was the word "affluent." I had only one worry; that was whether I could possibly sell it to the publisher. All publishers wish to have books called *The Crisis in American Democracy*. My title, to my surprise, was acceptable. Mark Twain once said that the difference between the right adjective and the next-best adjective is the difference between lightning and a lightning bug.

11   Next, I would stress a rather old-fashioned idea to those students. It was above all the lesson of Harry Luce. No one who worked for him ever again escaped the feeling that he was there looking over one's shoulder. In his hand was a pencil; down on each page one could expect, any moment, a long swishing wiggle accompanied by the comment: "This can go." Invariably it could. It was written to please the author and not the reader. Or to fill in the space. The gains from brevity are obvious; in most efforts to achieve brevity, it is the worst and dullest that goes. It is the worst and dullest that spoils the rest.

12   I know that brevity is now out of favor. The *New York Review of Books* prides itself on giving its authors as much space as they want and sometimes twice as much as they need. Even those who have read only Joyce must find their thoughts wandering before the end of the fortnightly article. Writing for television, I've learned in the last year or two, is an exercise in relentless condensation. It has left me with the feeling that even brevity can be carried to extremes. But the danger, as I look at some of the newer fashions in writing, is not great.

13   The next of my injunctions, which I would impart with even less hope of success, would concern alcohol. Nothing is so pleasant. Nothing is so important for giving the writer a sense of confidence in himself. And nothing so impairs the product. Again there are

exceptions: I remember a brilliant writer at *Fortune* for whom I was responsible, who could work only with his hat on and after consuming a bottle of Scotch. There were major crises in the years immediately after World War II, when Scotch was difficult to find. But it is, quite literally, very sobering to reflect upon how many good American writers have been destroyed by this solace—by the sauce. Scott Fitzgerald, Sinclair Lewis, Thomas Wolfe, Ernest Hemingway, William Faulkner—the list goes on and on. Hamish Hamilton, once my English publisher, put the question to James Thurber: "Jim, why is it so many of your great writers have ruined themselves with drink?" Thurber thought long and carefully and finally replied: "It's this way, Jamie. They wrote their novels, and they sold very well. They made a lot of money and so they could buy whiskey by the case."

Their reputation was universal. A few years before his death, 14 John Steinbeck, an appreciative but not a compulsive drinker, went to Moscow. It was a triumphal tour; and in a letter that he sent me about his hosts, he said, "I found I enjoyed the Soviet hustlers pretty much. There was a kind of youthful honesty about their illicit intensions that was not without charm. And their lives are difficult under their four-party system [a reference that escapes me]. It takes a fairly deft or very lucky man to make his way upward in the worker's paradise." I later heard that one night, after a particularly effusive celebration, he decided to make his way back to the hotel on foot. On the way he was overcome by fatigue and the hospitality he had received and sat down on a bench in a small park to rest. A policeman, called a militiaman in Moscow, came along and informed John, who was now asleep, and his companion, who spoke Russian, that the benches could not be occupied at that hour. His companion explained, rightly, that John was a very great American writer and that an exception should be made. The militiaman insisted. The companion explained again, insisted more strongly. Presently a transcendental light came over the policeman's face. He looked at Steinbeck asleep on the bench, inspected his condition more closely, recoiled slightly from the fumes, and said, "Oh, oh, Gemingway." Then he took off his cap and tiptoed carefully away.

We are all desperately afraid of sounding like Carry Nation. I 15 must take the risk. Any writer who wants to do his best against a deadline should stick to Coca-Cola. If he doesn't have a deadline, he can risk Seven-Up.

Next, I would want to tell my students of a point strongly 16 pressed, if my memory serves, by Shaw. He once said that as he grew older, he became less and less interested in theory, more and more interested in information. The temptation in writing is just the reverse. Nothing is so hard to come by as a new and interesting fact. Nothing is so easy on the feet as a generalization. I now pick up magazines and leaf through them looking for articles that are rich with facts; I do not care much what they are. Richly evocative and deeply percipient theory I avoid. It leaves me cold unless I am the author of it. My advice to all young writers is to stick to research and reporting with only a minimum of interpretation. And especially this is my advice to all older writers, particularly to columnists. As the feet give out, they seek to have the mind take their place.

17   Reluctantly, but from a long and terrible experience, I would urge my young writers to avoid all attempts at humor. It does greatly lighten one's task. I've often wondered who made it impolite to laugh at one's own jokes; it is one of the major enjoyments of life. And that is the point. Humor is an intensely personal, largely internal thing. What pleases some, including the source, does not please others. One laughs; another says, "Well, I certainly see nothing funny about that." And the second opinion has just as much standing as the first, maybe more. Where humor is concerned, there are no standards—no one can say what is good or bad, although you can be sure that everyone will. Only a very foolish man will use a form of language that is wholly uncertain in its effect. That is the nature of humor.

18   There are other reasons for avoiding humor. In our society the solemn person inspires far more trust than the one who laughs. The politician allows himself one joke at the beginning of his speech. A ritual. Then he changes his expression, affects an aspect of morbid solemnity signaling that, after all, he is a totally serious man. Nothing so undermines a point as its association with a wisecrack—the very word is pejorative.

19   Also, as Art Buchwald has pointed out, we live in an age when it is hard to invent anything that is as funny as everyday life. How could one improve, for example, on the efforts of the great men of television to attribute cosmic significance to the offhand and hilarious way Bert Lance combined professed fiscal conservation with an unparalleled personal commitment to the deficit financing of John Maynard Keynes? And because the real world is so funny, there is almost nothing you can do, short of labeling a joke a joke, to keep people from taking it seriously. A few years ago in *Harper's* I invented the theory that socialism in our time was the result of our dangerous

addiction to team sports. The ethic of the team is all wrong for free enterprise. The code words are cooperation; team spirit; accept leadership, the coach is always right. Authoritarianism is sanctified; the individualist is a poor team player, a menace. All this our vulnerable adolescents learn. I announced the formation of an organization to combat this deadly trend and to promote boxing and track instead. I called it the C.I.A.—Congress for Individualist Athletics. Hundreds wrote in to *Harper's* asking to join. Or demanding that baseball be exempted. A batter is on his own. I presented the letters to the Kennedy Library.

Finally, I would come to a matter of much personal interest, 20 intensely self-serving. It concerns the peculiar pitfalls of the writer who is dealing with presumptively difficult or technical matters. Economics is an example, and within the field of economics the subject of money, with the history of which I have been much concerned, is an especially good case. Any specialist who ventures to write on money with a view to making himself intelligible works under a grave moral hazard. He will be accused of oversimplification. The charge will be made by his fellow professionals, however obtuse or incompetent. They will have a sympathetic hearing from the layman. That is because no layman really expects to understand about money, inflation, or the International Monetary Fund. If he does, he suspects that he is being fooled. One can have respect only for someone who is decently confusing.

In the case of economics there are no important propositions 21 that cannot be stated in plain language. Qualifications and refinements are numerous and of great technical complexity. These are important for separating the good students from the dolts. But in economics the refinements rarely, if ever, modify the essential and practical point. The writer who seeks to be intelligible needs to be right, he must be challenged if his argument leads to the erroneous conclusion and especially if it leads to the wrong action. But he can safely dismiss the charge that he has made the subject too easy. The truth is not difficult.

Complexity and obscurity have professional value—they are 22 the academic equivalents of apprenticeship rules in the building trades. They exclude the outsiders, keep down the competition, preserve the image of a privileged or priestly class. The man who makes things clear is a scab. He is criticized less for his clarity than for his treachery.

23   Additionally, and especially in the social sciences, much unclear writing is based on unclear or incomplete thought. It is possible with safety to be technically obscure about something you haven't thought out. It is impossible to be wholly clear on something you do not understand. Clarity thus exposes flaws in the thought. The person who undertakes to make difficult matters clear is infringing on the sovereign right of numerous economists, sociologists, and political scientists to make bad writing the disguise for sloppy, imprecise, or incomplete thought. One can understand the resulting anger. Adam Smith, John Stuart Mill, John Maynard Keynes were writers of crystalline clarity most of the time. Marx had great moments, as in *The Communist Manifesto*. Economics owes very little, if anything, to the practitioners of scholarly obscurity. If any of my California students should come to me from the learned professions, I would counsel them in all their writing to keep the confidence of their colleagues. This they should do by being always complex, always obscure, invariably a trifle vague.

24   You might say that all this constitutes a meager yield for a lifetime of writing. Or that writing on economics, as someone once said of Kerouac's prose, is not writing but typing. True.

Discusssion

• Consider how Galbraith's advice could be applied to writing in your own major.

• Ask your major advisor or favorite teacher to recommend an excellent writer in your field, read an example of that person's writing, and then report to the class on the qualities of writing demonstrated by that writer. Compare that prose style to Galbraith or other writers in the book.

• Use library reference sources to see if there are any articles by that writer on the writer's craft.

• Ask the expert in your discipline if there are writing guides or texts on writing, for example, as a literary critic, a computer scientist, a physicist, a historian, a business executive, a sports information specialist, a nurse, a soldier, a government official. You will find most professions have their own writing guides and texts.

• Read something by Galbraith and discuss how he followed—or failed to follow—his own advice.

Activities

- Take a paper you have written in your major or on the job and revise it with Galbraith's counsel—and perhaps some of the counsel from this book—in mind. If you don't have a major, write an assignment you might receive in the career you'd like to enter: a legal brief, a physical therapy case history, a sales letter, a piece of movie criticism, a science laboratory report, a political speech, a letter applying for a job, whatever might help you after graduation.
- Interview a writer in the career in which you're interested—the law, engineering, medical technician, sales, whatever—to see what advice they have and write a report for the class on what they said.
- Make out a personal list of rules, principles, or pieces of advice about writing from Galbraith—and others in this book—that will help you solve your own writing problems in the future. Stick it in your notebook.
- Take a page from a textbook in another course and edit it, imagining that you are Galbraith.

Jacques Barzun and Henry F. Graff

There are some quotations by writers and one piece of writing that I paste in my calendar book each year to comfort and stimulate me. Not all of this advice comes from poets, fiction writers, or people who belong in English Departments. There are fine science writers such as Denise Grady and Lewis Thomas, economists such as John Kenneth Galbraith, and the historians whose work we are reprinting here. The article which follows comes from an excellent book on scholarly—especially historical—research, *The Modern Researcher*, which is now in its third edition. If you want to discover the adventure of academic research, read that book. And if you want to be a productive writer, pay attention to the down-to-earth advice from productive scholars in the following piece.

Afterword: A Discipline for Work

You have now reached the end of a long course of advice, 1 exhortation, and instruction. It may seem to you that you have been told too many things to be able to apply all of them at once to your research and writing; you have been made self-conscious about unsuspected traps, and this has damped your carefree mood. Or again, you may think that you have been told some useful things, but not the ones that you needed for your project in hand. If either of these impressions is yours at the moment, your reading has not been in vain. You have been shaken out of your normal ways and made to reflect on your powers and responsibilities. The only alarming symptom at this point would be the feeling that now you know all there is to know and can apply it forthwith.

2   Such a belief would be dangerous for two reasons: first, because this book has given you but the principles of research and writing, with some illustrations; which means that you still have to make the transfer and adaptation of the rules and suggestions to your work and your needs; and second, because no new knowledge can ever be grasped and made use of in one sweep of the mind. Time is needed to assimilate it by the formation of new habits. Time is also needed to go back to one or another topic in order to refresh your memory about what was actually said. In a word, now that you have finished reading or studying this book, you should begin to use it as a mentor at your elbow and as a work of reference on your desk.

3   This suggestion brings up a matter we have not yet discussed, one that is generally taken for granted, though perhaps without warrant—the matter of when and how to work. Some hints were given in Chapter 2 about the division of tasks in research, and we may repeat it here: you should keep your clearest stretches of time for the uninterrupted study of your main sources. Verifying dates, hunting down references, and, generally, all broken-field running should be reserved for occasions when you have a shorter time at your disposal or when you are feeling less alert or energetic than usual. Your best mind should go to what takes thought.

4   The same principle applies to writing, with variations and additions. Faced with the need to write, most people (including practiced writers) experience a strong and strange impulse to put off beginning. They would do anything rather than confront that blank sheet of paper. They start inventing pretexts for doing something else: they need to look up another source, they have not sufficiently mulled over the organization of the paper, they want to steep themselves in their notes once more. Or—what is really cowardly—there is some shopping that cannot wait, or again, the typewriter keys need a thorough cleaning. Let it be said once for all: *there is no cure for this desire to escape.* It will recur as long as you live. But there are palliatives, and some of them are good enough to turn the struggle virtually into a game.

The palliative principle is that a regular force must be used to   5
overcome a recurrent inertia: if you can arrange to write regularly,
never missing your date with yourself, no matter whether you are in
the mood or not, you have won half the battle. You do not have to
be pleased with what you do, nor expect a set amount to be done by
the end of the session, but *some* writing you must do on the morning
or afternoon or evening that is kept sacred for the purpose. The writer's problem is the inverse of the reformed drunkard's. The latter
must *never* touch a drop; the former must *always* do his stint. Skip
but one writing period and you need the strength of Samson to get
started again.

It goes without saying that these writing periods must be close   6
enough together to create a rhythm of work, and that they must be
chosen with an eye to the greatest convenience in your present mode
of life. For example, if you possibly can, set aside one free morning
or day for writing. The longer the free period, the better. A time with
no fixed obligation at the end is preferable to one that will draw your
eye to the clock halfway through, and so on. Similarly with the place.
Do not try to write at home if you can hear your roommate's hi-fi
tapes or the domestic symphony of kitchen and nursery noises; con-
versely, do not attempt to write in an office where the phone and
your associates will interrupt every ten minutes.

> ℊ Over my desk is the motto attributed to Pliny and Horace,
> advocated by those productive writers Trollope and Updike: nulla
> dies sine linea—never a day without a line. It is THE rule for
> writing. Write something, anything, keep the writing muscles limber
> and then if writing comes you'll be like Flannery O'Connor, ready
> for it. 𝕍

In making your arrangements, consider that a likely cause of the   7
distaste for beginning is that writing is for all of us an act of self-
exposure. Writing requires that we create some order in our thoughts
and project it outside, where everybody can see it. The instinct of
self-protection, of shyness, combines with the sense of our mental
confusion or uncertainty to make us postpone the trial of strength.
Hence the desirability of being alone and uninterrupted. In silence
our thoughts can settle into their proper shapes; they will be exclusively the thoughts bearing on our topic, and as soon as a few of them
are down on paper they will draw out the rest. The momentum will
increase until, after a time, the bulk of work done will set up a desire

to keep adding to it. The hour or day set aside for writing will be waited for, and the work will truly be *in progress*.

8   Since the problem is best seen as one of inertia and momentum, other rules of thumb suggest themselves as corollaries:

9   1. Do not wait until you have gathered all your material before starting to write. Nothing adds to inertia like a mass of notes, the earliest of which recede in the mists of foregone time. On the contrary, begin drafting your ideas as soon as some portion of the topic appears to hang together in your mind.

❨Amen❩

10   2. Do not be afraid of writing down something that you think may have to be changed. Paper is not granite, and in a first draft you are not carving eternal words in stone. Rather, you are creating substance to be molded and remolded in successive drafts.

> ❨Amen and Amen. One of those quotations I keep in my calendar is from the poet William Stafford: "I can imagine a person beginning to feel that he's not able to write up to that standard he imagines the world has set for him. But to me that's surrealistic. The only standard I can rationally have is the standard I'm meeting right now . . . you should be more willing to forgive yourself. It really doesn't make any difference if you are good or bad today. The assessment of the product is something that happens after you've done it."❩

11   3. Do not hesitate to write up in any order those sections of your total work that seem to have grown ripe in your mind. There is a moment in any stretch of research when all the details come together in natural cohesion, despite small gaps and doubts. Learn to recognize that moment and seize it by composing in harmony with your inward feeling of unity. Never mind whether the portions that come out are consecutive.

12   4. Once you start writing, keep going. Resist the temptation to get up and verify a fact. Leave it blank. The same holds true for the word or phrase that refuses to come to mind. It will arise much more easily on revision, and the economy in time *and momentum* is incalculable.

❨Amen. Amen. Amen.❩

5. When you get stuck in the middle of a stretch of writing, 13 reread your last two or three pages and see if continuity of thought will not propel you past dead center. Many writers begin the day's work by reading over the previous day's accumulation. But there are other ways of beginning, such as writing one or two letters, transcribing or expanding a few notes, making an entry in a diary, and the like. The common feature of such a wind-up or running start is that the chosen act is one of *writing* and that it is brief—a *few* notes or lines before tackling the main task.

6. Since the right openings for chapters or sections are difficult, 14 special attention must be paid to them. As you collect your materials, be on the watch for ideas or facts or even words that would make a good beginning. Remember that in any extended work you begin many times, not only at each new chapter, but often at each subsection. Supposing that writing a twenty-page chapter takes you three sessions, you may find it helpful to break off in the middle of, and not at, a subdivision. In this way you take up the story in midstream, instead of having to begin the day *and* the section together. Some writers make a point of breaking off the day's work just before they completely run down and while they still see ideas ahead. They scribble two or three final words to call these up at once on resuming work.

> ❢I try to stop in midsentence as did such writers as Faulkner and Hemingway. It helps to pick up the sentence and finish it. Then you are back in the *writing.* ❥

7. It will often happen that the opening paragraph of the whole 15 piece (or of any of its parts) will on rereading seem quite alien to what follows. This calls for a pair of scissors. What has happened is that the first paragraph was simply the warming up, and the true beginning was set down in the second. From this common experience you should infer that a slow sluggish start on Saturday morning is no reason for discouragement. You are priming the pump, choking the car, and the splutter is of no consequence.

8. A writer should as soon as possible become aware of his 16 peculiarities and preferences regarding the mechanics of composing. He should know whether he likes the pen or the typewriter, what size and color paper he prefers, which physical arrangement of his notes and books pleases him best, even what kind of clothes and

which posture he likes to assume for work. In all these matters he is entitled to complete self-indulgence provided he remains faithful to his choices. This is consistent with our underlying principle: indulge yourself so that you will have no excuse for putting off the task; and stick to your choice, so that the very presence of your favorite implements will confirm the habits of the good workman.

> ❡ Writers, including this one, are addicted to word processors because they are such helpful tools. ❧

17   When the first draft is done the back of the job is broken. It is then a pleasure—or it should be one—to carve, cut, add, and polish until what you say corresponds reasonably well to what you know. The span of time and other conditions of revising are less rigorous than those of first drafting. If your manuscript has passed into typed form, you can use a spare half-hour to proofread it and mark the rough spots with little x's or wavy lines in the margin. You can be thinking about substitutions and additions until the next free hour when you can Revise with a big R, as against typographical revising with a small one—respectively the big operations described in Chapters 2, 12, and 13, and the lesser mentioned in Chapter 16.

18   Ideally, a report should be in progress in its entirety long before it is finished. The earlier parts will be well advanced while the last ones are still in the rough, the research for them not yet finished. Research will in fact continue to the end, which is, in the case of a book, indexing in page proof. But the revision at one time of different parts in different stages of perfecting is an excellent way of seeing one's construction as a whole and in detail. Each critical observation supplies hints to be carried out in other parts, and this evens out the advantages of experience gathered on the way. Follow this suggestion and your work will not seem like so many, better done in proportion as it approaches the end.

19   But it is a little premature to speak here of the end. Despite what was said at the outset of this section about having completed a sizable course with us, the reader is only at the beginning of real work. Whatever his enterprise—short report or extended monograph—let him take his courage in both hands and, by the application of his best mind, bring order and meaning out of the welter of facts. With the best will in the world, his work will not be free from error—so much it is safe to predict. But that part of it which is sound, clear, readily grasped and remembered will be a contribution, no matter

how limited its scope, to that order among ideas which we call knowledge. For as Francis Bacon wisely observed in his *New Method*, "truth will sooner come out from error than from confusion."

Discussion

• Relate what Barzun and Graff say about using time to what Drucker recommends.

• Compare Barzun and Graff's advice on writing to counsel given by others in the book such as Orwell, Didion, Strunk, White, and others.

• Discuss Barzun and Graff's counsel on writing in terms of your own writing experience. Also discuss it in terms of the writing demanded in this course and other courses.

• Discuss how their counsel relates to writing you have to do and will have to do outside of school.

Activities

• Write a memo to yourself about writing that you may use to solve writing problems you may face in the future.

• Edit Barzun and Graff to fit a particular kind of writing you have to do in school or outside of school.

• Show Barzun and Graff to a professional writer or someone who writes in the field you are studying to see what fits and may not fit a particular kind of writing.

• Try one of the techniques Barzun and Graff suggest on a writing project you have underway. If you don't have one underway, go back and recall such a project and decide how their counsel could help you.

• Work with your class to produce a brief guide to writing that distills the most important advice from Barzun and Graff—and all the other writers in this text—so that you will have a checklist that can be copied and kept by every member of the class to be used on future writing assignments in school and after graduation.

8

Watch Out: After School May Come Reading and Writing

For some of you, especially some of you who do not think it possible, coming to the end of this book will mean the beginning of a lifetime of writing and reading. You will be lucky if that is the case, for in writing you will hear your own voice and you will be able to make your voice heard. You will be able to join and influence communities of engineers, poetry lovers, businessmen, voters, football fans, educators, soldiers, environmentalists, speaking of your concerns to those who can affect the world in which you are interested.

As writers, you will learn by writing, finding out what you know when it appears on your page, reading, rewriting, and rereading as your meanings come clear. You will think by writing and therefore change and grow in your understanding and appreciation of your world. Writing increases awareness and the more you write, the more you see and feel. At times this is painful and you may wish for a numbing oblivion, but in the long run you will see those about you paralyzed by boredom and you will be grateful that you will never be bored, that there are always people to watch, questions to ask, places to observe, processes to follow, all sorts of material for the writing you have yet to do.

As a reading writer, you will learn from others, living their lives, hearing their counsel, enjoying their individual and diverse voices. In addition, you will be able to go behind the scenes, reading with a special understanding of the problems faced and solved by the writer. You will have a particular appreciation of the text that flows toward meaning with a simple, unaffected and appropriate grace, for you will know something of the invisible craft that made that text come clear. You will become a member of the community of writers, living and dead, in your language and others, who have labored at your craft.

If you wish to know more about what writers say about their own books, their reading of other books, and the process with which they write, there is an abundance of material available. Interviews with writers have become an entire genre of its own. Each month, it seems, new collections of interviews with writers are published. The basic collection is the series of six *Paris Review* interviews published by Viking Penguin. Everyone seriously interested in writing should have those books on the shelf. There are many collections of articles by writers. One of the best is *The Writer on Her Work*, edited by Janet Sternberg and published by Norton in 1980. There are also collections of interviews by single writers.

In addition to interviews, there are the published journals of writers, their letters, the prefaces and commentary they have written on their own work and on the work of others, their autobiographies and biographies, the reproductions of their own manuscripts with the crossings out and insertions that reveal the creative process in action.

The writers' own works, of course, are most important, but the evidence of why and how they wrote puts the writing itself in context. Even more is your own writing. And from this interaction of reading and writing you will stay alive intellectually and artistically, enjoying the perpetual youth of the artist who always discovers the world anew.

Others of you will not write but only read. I hope that this text has helped you see something of what goes into the creation of an effective text, that you will read with increased skill and enjoyment because of what you have seen, while reading this book, happen on your page and on the pages of other writers in your class and in this text.

Reading is a way of escaping the lifetime imprisonment in your present world. By reading, you can live other lives, see with other eyes, visit other places, consider new and old information, new and old ideas. Reading is a private activity that allows us to change and grow in our own way, escaping the loneliness of our lives, reaching out to other people across the barriers of time or place.

Be comforted in the fact that you will never be able to read all the books you should read. Read for fun and escape, read for stimulation and comfort, read for information, read for belief and disbelief, for confirmation and for challenge, read for all the hundreds of reasons you will need to read in school and beyond.

When you discover an author who speaks to you, see what else that person has written and read those books. When you discover a genre you enjoy—science fiction or history, poetry or books on how to suceed in business, autobiography, or novels—see what else has been written in that form and read some of it. When you find a subject that interests you—big business or little business, psychology or theology, sports or science—read other works on the same subject. Follow your own interests and then, through reading, reach out, exploring the subjects that interest you.

It's all there in paperback or hardcover, bookstore or library, in magazine or newspaper, waiting to catch your eye—and your mind.

And watch out. As you live and as you read there will probably come a time—especially if you don't believe such a time could come for you—when you will be invited to write or commanded to write or when you will simply have the itch to write. Then write. When you are in terminal middle age or beyond you may not be able to dance as you once intended to dance or twist and turn toward the goal line as you once believed you could, but it is never too late to write—and all that reading you have done is stored away, waiting to be called upon as your words move across your page.

(continued from copyright page)

Joan Didion, "Why I Write" reprinted by permission of Wallace & Sheil Agency, Inc. Copyright © 1976 by Joan Didion. First appeared in *New York Times Book Review*. From *Salvador*. Copyright © 1983 by Joan Didion. Reprinted by permission of Simon & Schuster, Inc.

Ken Dryden, from *The Game*. Copyright © 1983 by Ken Dryden.

Ralph Ellison, from *Shadow and Act*. Copyright © 1964 by Ralph Ellison. Reprinted by permission of Random House, Inc.

John Kenneth Galbraith, from *Annals of an Abiding Liberal* by John Kenneth Galbraith. Copyright © 1979 by John Kenneth Galbraith. Reprinted by permission of Houghton Mifflin Company.

William Gibson, excerpted from "Sunset I Saw By" from *A Mass for the Dead*. Copyright © 1968 Tamarack Productions Ltd. and George S. Klein and Leo Garel as Trustees under three (3) separate Deeds of Trust. Used with the permission of Atheneum Publishers.

John Hersey, from *Hiroshima*. Copyright © 1946 and renewed 1974 by John Hersey. Reprinted by permission of Alfred A. Knopf, Inc. Originally appeared in *The New Yorker*.

Martin Luther King Jr., "I Have a Dream" reprinted by permission of Joan Daves. Copyright © 1963 by Martin Luther King, Jr.

Maxine Hong Kingston, from *The Woman Warrier: Memoirs of a Girlhood among Ghosts*. Copyright © 1975, 1976 by Maxine Hong Kingston. Reprinted by permission of Alfred A. Knopf, Inc.

William L. Laurence, "Atomic Bombing of Nagasaki Told by Flight Member," *The New York Times,* September 9, 1945. Copyright © 1945 by The New York Times Company. Reprinted by permission.

Enrique Hank Lopez, from *Horizon* (Winter 1967). Copyright © 1967 American Heritage Publishing Company, Inc. Reprinted by permission.

Joseph Mitchell, from *Up in the Old Hotel*. Reprinted by permission of Harold Ober Associates. Copyright © 1959 by Joseph Mitchell.

John McPhee, excerpts from *Oranges*. Copyright © 1966, 1967 by John McPhee. Reprinted by permission of Farrar, Straus and Giroux, Inc. This material first appeared in *The New Yorker*.

William Least Heat Moon, from *Blue Highways*. Copyright © 1982 by William Least Heat Moon. By permission of Little, Brown and Company in association with the Atlantic Monthly Press.

Toni Morrison, from *The Bluest Eye*. Copyright © 1970 by Toni Morrison. Reprinted by permission of Holt, Rinehart and Winston, Publishers.

Flannery O'Connor, from *A Good Man Is Hard to Find*. Copyright © 1955, by Flannery O'Connor. Reviewed 1983 by Regina O'Connor. Reprinted by permission of Harcourt Brace Jovanovich, Inc. From *Mystery and Manners* by Flannery O'Connor. Copyright © 1969 by the estate of Mary Flannery O'Connor. Reprinted by permission of Farrar, Straus and Giroux, Inc.

George Orwell, from *Shooting an Elephant and Other Essays*. Copyright © 1950 by Sonia Brownell Orwell; renewed 1978 by Sonia Pitt-Rivers. From *Such, Such*

Were the Joys. Copyright © 1953 by Sonia Brownell Orwell; renewed 1981 by Mrs. George K. Perutz, Mrs. Miriam Gross, Dr. Michael Dickson, Executors of the Estate of Sonia Brownell Orwell. Reprinted by permission of Harcourt Brace Jovanovich, Inc. and the estate of the late Sonia Brownell Orwell and Secker and Warburg Ltd.

Theodore Roethke, "My Papa's Waltz" copyright 1942 by Hearst Magazines, Inc. "Frau Bauman, Frau Schmidt, and Frau Schwartze", copyright 1952 by Theodore Roethke originally in *The New Yorker.* "The Waking" and "Elegy for Jane," copyright 1948 and 1950 by Theodore Roethke. "Cuttings" and "Cuttings (later)," copyright 1948 by Theodore Roethke. Excerpt from "Words for the Wind," copyright © 1955 by Theodore Roethke. All from *The Collected Poems of Theodore Roethke* and reprinted by permission of Doubleday and Company, Inc.

Richard Selzer. "Letters to a Young Surgeon III," from *Letters to a Young Doctor.* Copyright © 1982 by David Goldman and Janet Selzer, Trustees. Reprinted by permission of Simon & Schuster, Inc.

Jean Shepherd, "Hairy Gertz and the Forty-Seven Crappies" from *In God We Trust— All Others Pay Cash.* Copyright © 1966 by Jean Shepherd. Reprinted by permission of Doubleday & Company, Inc.

Charles Simic, "Stone" from the work *Dismantling the Silence,* copyright © 1971. Used by permission of the publisher, George Braziller, Inc., New York.

James Stevenson, "Cinematographer." Reprinted by permission; copyright © 1978 The New Yorker Magazine, Inc.

Judy Syfers, "I Want a Wife," originally in *Ms.* Magazine. Copyright © 1971 by Judy Syfers. Reprinted by permission.

Lewis Thomas, from *The Medusa and the Snail.* Copyright © 1979 by Lewis Thomas. Reprinted by permission of Viking Penguin, Inc.

Alice Trillin, "Of Dragon and Peas" in the *New England Journal of Medicine.* Vol. 304; pp. 699–701; 1981. Copyright 1984 Massachusetts Medical Society. Reprinted by permission of the *New England Journal of Medicine.*

Barbara W. Tuchman, from *A Distant Mirror: The Calamitous 14th Century.* Copyright © 1978 by Barbara W. Tuchman. Reprinted by permission of Alfred A. Knopf, Inc.

John Updike, from *Five Boyhoods* (Doubleday) edited by Martin Levin. Copyright © 1962 by Martin Levin. Reprinted by permission of Martin Levin.

E. B. White, from *Essays of E. B. White.* Copyright © 1941 by E. B. White. Reprinted by permission of Harper & Row, Publishers, Inc.

Thomas Whiteside, from "Tomatoes." Reprinted by permission; copyright © 1977 by The New Yorker Magazine, Inc.

William Carlos Williams, "The Red Wheelbarrow" from *Collected Earlier Poems.* Copyright 1938 by New Directions Publishing Corporation. Reprinted by permission of New Directions Publishing Corporation.

William K. Zinsser, excerpt from a letter to Donald M. Murray. "Shanghai" from *Willie and Dwike: An American Profile,* copyright © 1984 by William K. Zinsser. Reprinted by permission of the author.

Writing Problems Solved

Reference Index to Rhetorical Techniques Demonstrated within the Selections

The selections in this book show you how master writers have solved the writing problems you face on your own pages. The writers in this book demonstrate solutions to many writing problems in every selection and also offer advice to beginning writers. Here are a few references for you to use when trying to solve problems in your own drafts. You should add references of your own as you study the selections and observe experienced writers solving the problems you face in writing. You should also add other writing problems you identify in your work and add references to how writers in this collection solved your particular writing problems. This book should be a reference which you can use during all your school years, and afterwards.

To the Student

We would appreciate your evaluation of **Read To Write**. Your suggestions will be very helpful to us when we plan the next edition. Please return this questionnaire to the English Editor, College Department, Holt, Rinehart and Winston, 383 Madison Avenue, New York, N.Y. 10017

School _____ Course Title _____

Instructor _____

	Keep	Drop	Didn't Read
Christopher Scanlan, **The Young Who Died Delivered Us**	___	___	___
Robert Caro, **The Sad Irons**	___	___	___
Joseph Mitchell, **Up in the Old Hotel**	___	___	___
William Least Heat Moon, **Nameless**	___	___	___
John McPhee, **Oranges**	___	___	___
Thomas Whiteside, **Tomatoes**	___	___	___
Amiri Baraka, **School**	___	___	___
Ken Dryden, **The Game**	___	___	___
Gary Lindberg, **Naming**	___	___	___
Ralph Ellison, **Hidden Name and Complex Fate**	___	___	___
James Baldwin, **Notes of a Native Son**	___	___	___
William Gibson, **Sunset I Saw By**	___	___	___
Judy Syfers, **I Want A Wife**	___	___	___
Martin Luther King Jr., **I Have a Dream**	___	___	___
Barbara Tuchman, **"This Is the End of the World": The Black Death**	___	___	___
Alice Trillin, **Of Dragons and Garden Peas**	___	___	___
Joseph Freda, **Canoe Paddling and the Craft of Communicating Concepts**	___	___	___
Richard Selzer, **Letters to a Young Surgeon III**	___	___	___
William Zinsser, **Shanghai**	___	___	___
James Stevenson, **Cinematographer**	___	___	___
Flannery O'Connor, **Writing Short Stories**	___	___	___
Good Country People	___	___	___
Toni Morrison, **The Bluest Eye**	___	___	___
Raymond Carver, **The Bath**	___	___	___
A Small, Good Thing	___	___	___
Mekeel McBride, **Red Letters**	___	___	___
Theodore Roethke, **My Papas's Waltz**	___	___	___
Elegy for Jane	___	___	___
Frau Bauman, Frau Schmidt, and Frau Schwartze	___	___	___
Cuttings, Cuttings, (Later)	___	___	___
The Waking	___	___	___

Maya Angelou, **Graduation** ⎯⎯ ⎯⎯ ⎯⎯
John Updike, **Schools** ⎯⎯ ⎯⎯ ⎯⎯
   Three Boys ⎯⎯ ⎯⎯ ⎯⎯
George Orwell, **Why I Write** ⎯⎯ ⎯⎯ ⎯⎯
   A Hanging ⎯⎯ ⎯⎯ ⎯⎯
Joan Didion, **Why I Write** ⎯⎯ ⎯⎯ ⎯⎯
   Salvador ⎯⎯ ⎯⎯ ⎯⎯
E. B. White, **Once More to the Lake** ⎯⎯ ⎯⎯ ⎯⎯
Jean Shepherd, **Hairy Gertz and the Forty-Seven**
   Crappies ⎯⎯ ⎯⎯ ⎯⎯
Denise Grady, **In Vitro Fertilization: It Doesn't**
   Always Work ⎯⎯ ⎯⎯ ⎯⎯
Lewis Thomas, **On Embryology** ⎯⎯ ⎯⎯ ⎯⎯
William Laurence, **Atomic Bombing of Nagasaki**
   Told by Flight Member ⎯⎯ ⎯⎯ ⎯⎯
John Hersey, **A Noiseless Flash** ⎯⎯ ⎯⎯ ⎯⎯
Enrique Hank Lopez, **Back to Bachimba** ⎯⎯ ⎯⎯ ⎯⎯
Maxine Hong Kingston, **from The Woman**
   Warrior ⎯⎯ ⎯⎯ ⎯⎯
John Kenneth Galbraith, **Writing, Typing, and**
   Economics ⎯⎯ ⎯⎯ ⎯⎯

2. Please indicate which of the chapters prepared you to appreciate and discuss the selections

	Helpful	Not Helpful
1. Reading as a Reader	⎯⎯	⎯⎯
2. Reading as a Writer	⎯⎯	⎯⎯
3. Information Collected	⎯⎯	⎯⎯
4. A Focus Found	⎯⎯	⎯⎯
5. An Order Designed	⎯⎯	⎯⎯
6. A Draft That Flows	⎯⎯	⎯⎯
7. A Meaning Made Clear	⎯⎯	⎯⎯
8. Watch Out: After School May Come Reading and Writing	⎯⎯	⎯⎯

3. Please list any authors not included whose work you would have liked to see in the book. ⎯⎯⎯⎯⎯⎯⎯⎯⎯⎯⎯⎯⎯⎯⎯⎯⎯⎯⎯

⎯⎯⎯⎯⎯⎯⎯⎯⎯⎯⎯⎯⎯⎯⎯⎯⎯⎯⎯⎯⎯⎯⎯⎯⎯⎯⎯

⎯⎯⎯⎯⎯⎯⎯⎯⎯⎯⎯⎯⎯⎯⎯⎯⎯⎯⎯⎯⎯⎯⎯⎯⎯⎯⎯

4. Were the Questions for Discussion and Writing generally helpful?

Yes ⎯⎯ No ⎯⎯

5. How could the questions be improved? ⎯⎯⎯⎯⎯⎯⎯⎯⎯⎯

⎯⎯⎯⎯⎯⎯⎯⎯⎯⎯⎯⎯⎯⎯⎯⎯⎯⎯⎯⎯⎯⎯⎯⎯⎯⎯⎯

6. Would you encourage your professor to assign this book next year?
   Yes _____ No _____

7. Will you keep this book? Yes _____ No _____

8. Please add any comments or suggestions to help us improve this book. _____
   _____